Afrikaans– English
English– Afrikaans
Dictionary

Afrikaans–
English
English–
Afrikaans
Dictionary

GEDDES & GROSSET

Published 2018 by Geddes & Grosset,
an imprint of The Gresham Publishing Company Ltd,
Academy Park, Building 4000, Gower Street, Glasgow,
G51 1PR, Scotland, UK

First published 2014
Reprinted 2015, 2018

Editorial Consultant: Alet Kruger
for Alet Kruger Multilingual Language Services (Pty) Ltd
www.multilanguage.co.za

ISBN: 978-1-84205-800-8

Printed and bound in the E.U.

Foreword

Afrikaans is an official language of South Africa that is spoken by around 6 million people as their first language.

If Afrikaans is not your first language, as a student or as a visitor to South Africa, and you are trying to learn Afrikaans vocabulary, this simple and practical Afrikaans–English dictionary will give you the right word whenever you need it.

Its comprehensive content provides a wide range of useful and frequently used Afrikaans vocabulary, including a large selection of up-to-date words. With an accessible and easy-to-use layout that includes parts of speech to aid understanding and correct usage, this dictionary makes it simpler than ever to use Afrikaans effectively and with confidence.

Abbreviations

adj	adjective	*npl*	plural noun
adv	adverb	*pers pron*	personal pronoun
conj	conjunction	*poss pron*	possessive pronoun
indef pron	indefinite pronoun	*prep*	preposition
inter pron	interrogative pronoun	*pron*	pronoun
interj	interjection	*rel pron*	relative pronoun
n	noun	*vb*	verb

Afrikaans–English Dictionary

Afrikaans–English

A

A: van A–Z *adv* from beginning to end

A-bom *n* atom(ic) bomb; nuclear bomb

aaklig *adj, adv* horrible; dull; nasty

aal *n* eel

aalmoes *n* alms; charity

aalwee (*or* **aalwyn**) *n* aloe

aalwyn *see* **aalwee**

aambeeld *n* anvil

aambeie *npl* piles; haemorrhoids

aamborstig *adj* asthmatic; hoarse

aan *prep* to; at; on; near; in; by; *adv* in; upon; onwards

aanbestee *vb* to invite tenders

aanbetref *vb* to be concerned about someone or something

aanbeveel *vb* to recommend

aanbevelenswaardig *adj* commendable

aanbeveling *n* recommendation; introduction; reference

aanbid *vb* to worship; to adore

aanbied *vb* to offer; to present; to volunteer

aanbind *vb* to tie; to fasten

aanblaas *vb* to blow; stir up; to fan; to foment

aanblik *n* sight; view; glance; look; *vb* to glance

aanbly *vb* to continue; to remain

aanbod *n* offer; proposal; supply

aanbots *vb* collide with; hit against

aanbou *n* annex; construction; erection; building; *vb* to build on to; to add (by building)

aanbrand *vb* to burn; to get burnt

aanbreek *vb* to dawn; to break; to close in; **by die — van die dag** *adv* at daybreak

aanbring *vb* to bring; to install; to construct; to make improvements)

aand *n* evening; night

aandag *n* attention; **— gee aan** *vb* to pay attention to

aandag(s)gebrekhiperaktiwiteit-sindroom *n* attention deficit hyperactivity syndrome (ADHD)

aandag(s)gebreksindroom *n* attention deficit disorder (ADD)

aandagtig *adj* attentive

aandblad *n* evening paper

aandeel *n* share; portion; part

aandeelhouer *n* shareholder

aandenking *n* memory; remembrance; keepsake; souvenir

aandete *n* supper

aandien *vb* to announce someone

aandik *vb* to thicken; to emphasize; to underline

aandoen *vb* to cause; to affect; to touch

aandoening *n* emotion; a touch of

aandoenlik *adj* touching; affecting; moving

aandra *vb* to bring; to carry; to inform against; **nuus —** *vb* to tell tales

aandraai *vb* to turn on; to tighten

aandrang *n* pressure; urge; instigation

aandrif *n* impetus; impulse

aandring *vb* to urge; to insist upon

aandruis *vb* to clash

aandruk *vb* to hug; to press against; to hurry along

aandryf (*or* **aandrywe**) *vb* to float along; to urge; to drive on

aandrywe *see* **aandryf**

aandsitting *n* night session

aandskool *n* night school

aandster *n* evening star

aandui *vb* to indicate; to describe; to denote

aandurf *vb* to dare

aaneengeslote *adv* together; consecutively

aangaan *vb* to concern; to make (an agreement); to call (at a house; on a person); to begin; to proceed; to continue

aangaande *prep* about; concerning; on the subject of

aangaap *vb* to stare at; to gaze at

aangebore *adj* hereditary; congenital; innate

aangedaan *adj* moved; affected

aangee *n* pass (in football); *vb* to hand; to pass on; to notify; to report

aangeklaagde *n* accused; defendant

aangeleerd *adj* acquired

aangenaam *adj* pleasant; agreeable; **aangename kennis** pleased to meet you

aangenome *adj* accepted; adopted; taken on; *conj* assuming that

aangesien *conj* whereas; since

aangesig *n* face; countenance

aangeteken *adj* registered; noted

aangetroude *adj* by marriage

aangewese *adj* obvious; correct; **die — persoon** *n* the right person

aangrensend *adj* adjacent; adjoining

aangroei *vb* to grow; to increase

aangryp *vb* to seize; to take; to catch hold of

aangrypend *adj* touching; gripping

aanhaak *vb* to hook on; to hitch on

aanhaal *vb* to bring along; to carry; to tighten; to cite

aanhalingstekens *npl* inverted commas; quotation marks

aanhang *n* adherents; faction; followers; *vb* to adhere to; to follow

aanhanger *n* adherent; supporter; follower

aanhangsel *n* appendage; addendum; appendix (book)

aanhê *vb* to have on; to wear

aanhef *n* preamble; beginning; *vb* to begin; to commence

aanheg *vb* to fasten; to affix; to attach

aanhelp *vb* to help along; to assist

aanhits *vb* to instigate; to incite

aanhoor *vb* to listen to

aanhou *vb* to continue; to persevere; to insist; to detain (goods); to arrest (a criminal)

aanhoudend *adj* continual; incessant

aanjaag *vb* to hurry on; to drive along; **vrees —** *vb* to frighten

aankla *vb* to accuse; to charge with

aanklaagster *n* female accuser; female plaintiff; female prosecutor

aanklaer *n* accuser; plaintiff; prosecutor

aanklag *n* accusation; charge

aankleef (*or* **aanklewe**) *vb* to stick to

aanklop *vb* to knock at the door

aanknoop *vb* to establish (a friendship); to begin (a conversation)

aankom *vb* to come along at; to arrive; to be born; to improve

aankomeling *n* newcomer; beginner

aankomend *adj* coming; next; prospective

aankondig *vb* to announce; to notify; to advertise; to post (on internet)

aankondiging *n* announcement; advertisement

aankoop *vb* to purchase; to buy

aankry *vb* to get into; to put on (one's clothes)

aankweek *vb* to cultivate; to grow; to raise; to foster

aankyk *vb* to look at

aanland *vb* to land; to arrive

aanlas *vb* to join; to add to

aanlê *vb* to aim; to take aim; to apply (a bandage); to build; to install

aanleer *vb* to learn; to acquire

aanleg *n* talent; aptitude; design; plan

aanleiding *n* cause; reason; **na — van** *prep* with reference to; as a result of

aanlok *vb* to attract; to entice; to charm; to lure

aanloklik *adj* alluring; tempting; inviting

aanloop *vb* to run along; to walk along; to call in passing

aanloopplank *n* springboard

aanlyn *adv* online (internet)

aanmaak *vb* to prepare; to mix

aanmaan *vb* to warn; to urge

aanmaning *n* warning; notice; reminder

aanmatig *vb* to presume; to pretend; to assume

aanmatigend *adj* arrogant; haughty

aanmekaar *adv* together; consecutively

aanmeld *vb* to announce; to report; to notify

aanmeldbaar *adj* notifiable

aanmeldbare siekte *n* notifiable disease

aanmerking *n* observation; remark; criticism; **'n — maak op** *vb* to make a remark

aanmerklik *adj* considerable

aanmoedig *vb* to encourage; to give support

aanneem *vb* to accept; to receive; to adopt; to assume; to embrace; to admit; to confirm (as a member); to pass (a bill)

aanneemlik *adj* acceptable; credible

aannemer *n* contractor; builder; undertaker

aanneming *n* acceptance; adoption; confirmation (of church members)

aanpak *vb* to seize; to take hold of; to attack

aanpas *vb* to fit; to try on; to adapt oneself; to adjust

aanpassing *n* adjustment

aanpeiltoestel *n* homing device

aanpiekel *vb* to struggle along; to drag

aanplakbiljet *n* bill; poster

aanplant *vb* to plant; to grow

aanpor *vb* to jab; to prompt

aanpresenteer *vb* to offer

aanprys *vb* to (re)commend; sing the praises of

aanraai *vb* to advise; to recommend

aanraak *vb* to touch

aanrand *vb* to attack; to assault

aanreik *vb* to hand on; to pass

aanreken *vb* to blame someone for something; to lay a charge on someone

aanrig *vb* to cause; to commit; to do

aanroep *vb* to invoke; to call; to hail

aanroer *vb* to touch; to mention; to touch on; to hurry; to go quickly

aanruk *vb* to march; to advance on

aanry *vb* to drive on; to convey; to transport

aansê *vb* to announce; to inform

aansien *n* appearance; respect; esteem; *vb* to look at; to consider

aansienlik *adj* handsome; considerable; distiguished

aansit *vb* to sit at (a table); to add; join; to incite; to instigate

aanskaf *vb* to get; to provide; to buy

aanskou *vb* to behold; to contemplate; to look at

aanskoulik *adj* clear; graphic; visible

aanskroef *vb* to screw on

aanskryf (*or* **aanskrywe**) *vb* to write on; to summon; to demand payment

aanslaan *vb* to touch; to strike (a note);

to present (arms); to switch on; to start a car

aanslag *n* stroke; attempt; assessment (tax)

aansleep *vb* to drag along; to lug along

aansluit *vb* to connect; to link; to enrol; to join

aansluiting *n* junction; joining; connection; linking up

aansmeer *vb* to smear; to put on; to palm off; to fob off; to foist off

aansoek *n* application; request; proposal

aanspoel *vb* to wash up on the shore; to drift ashore

aanspoor *vb* to encourage; to urge on

aanspraak *n* speech; claim; title; right

aanspreek *vb* to accost; to address; to speak to

aanspreeklik *adj* responsible for; liable to

aanstaan *vb* to suit; to please

aanstaande *n* intended; fiancé; fiancée; *adj* next; forthcoming

aanstaar *vb* to stare at; to gaze at

aanstalte(s) *n* preparation(s)

aanstap *vb* to walk on; to step out

aansteek *vb* to pin on; to put on; to light; to infect

aansteeklik *adj* infectious

aansteking *n* kindling; infection; lighting

aanstel *vb* to appoint; to pretend; to behave; to put on airs

aanstellerig *adj* affected

aanstellerigheid *n* affectation; airs; conceitedness

aanstelling *n* appointment

aansterk *vb* to recover; get better

aanstig *vb* to instigate

aanstip *vb* to jot down; to touch on

aanstons *adv* presently; directly

aanstook *vb* to incite; to kindle

aanstoot *n* offence

aanstootlikheid *n* sleaze

aanstryk *vb* to walk along on

aanstuur *vb* to pass on; to send on; to forward; to steer to; to aim at

aansuiwer *vb* to settle; to pay off; to adjust

aansukkel *vb* to struggle along

aansyn *n* existence; life
aantal *n* number
aantas *vb* to attack; to affect
aanteel *vb* to breed; to increase
aanteken *vb* to note; to record; to register; to score (a try)
aantekening *n* note; record
aantekeningboek *n* notebook; scribbler
aantog *n* approach; advance
aantoon *vb* to show; to demonstrate
aantref *vb* to meet with; to come across
aantrek *vb* to pull; to attract; to dress; to brace
aantrekkingskrag *n* gravitation; gravity
aantreklik *adj* attractive; stylish; sensitive
aanvaar *vb* to set out for; to accept (a position); to face (the consequences)
aanval *n* attack; *vb* to attack; to charge
aanvallig *adj* amiable; sweet; charming
aanvang *n* beginning; start; *vb* to begin; to commence; to start
aanvanklik *adj* elementary; initial; original; commencing
aanvanklik *adv* at first
aanverwant *adj* related; allied; kindred
aanvoeg *vb* to add; to join
aanvoeging *n* addition
aanvoer *vb* to bring; to convey; to supply; to raise (objections); to command
aanvoerder *n* leader; commander
aanvra *vb* to apply for; to request
aanvraag *n* request; application; demand
aanvul *vb* to replenish; to complete; to make good
aanvuur to inspire; to incite
aanwakker *vb* to encourage; to animate; to rouse
aanwas *vb* to increase; to grow
aanwen *vb* to fall into the habit of; to become accustomed to; to reclaim
aanwend *vb* to employ; to apply; to take the trouble to
aanwensel *n* habit
aanwerf *vb* to recruit; to enlist; to enroll
aanwerk *vb* to sew on; to work more quickly
aanwesig *adj* present; available

aanwesigheid *n* presence
aanwins *n* gain; acquisition; asset
aanwys *vb* to show; to indicate; to point out
aanwysend *adj* demonstrative (pronoun)
aap *n* monkey; ape
aar *n* ear (corn); vein (blood vessel); lode; seam
aarbei *n* strawberry
aarbeikonfyt *n* strawberry jam
aard *n* nature; disposition; kind; sort; *vb* to get on well
aardbaan *n* orbit of the earth
aardbewing *n* earthquake
aardbewingsleer *n* seismology
aardbewoner *n* mortal; human being
aardbol *n* globe; the earth's surface
aarde *n* earth; ground; soil
aardig *adj* nice; agreeable; disagreeable; strange
aardkunde *n* geology
aardryk *n* the earth
aardrykskunde *n* geography
aardskok *n* shock (earthquake)
aardskudding *n* earth tremor
aardvark (*or* **erdvark**) *n* anteater
aardverwarming *n* global warming
aarsel *vb* to hesitate; to waver
aartappel (*or* **ertappel**) *n* potato
aartappelmoer (*or* **ertappelmoer**) *n* seed potato
aartappelskil *n* potato skin; potato peel
aartsbiskop *n* archbishop
aartsvader *n* patriarch
aas[1] *n* ace (playing cards)
aas[2] *n* bait; carrion; prey; *vb* to feed on; to prey on
aasvoël *n* vulture
ab *n* abbot
abbaskip *n* aircraft carrier
abdis *n* abbess
abdy *n* abbey; monastery
abnormaal *adj* abnormal
abseil *vb* to abseil
absolusie *n* absolution
absoluut *adv* absolutely
abstrak *adj* abstract; abstracted
absurd *n* absurd; nonsensical
abuis *n* mistake; error; **per —** by mistake

adder *n* adder; viper
addisioneel *adj* additional
adel *n* nobility
adelaar *n* eagle
adellik *adj* noble; titled
adem *n* breath; *vb* to breathe
ademloos *adj* breathless
adieu! *sentence substitute* goodbye!
adjektief *n* adjective
adjudant *n* adjutant; aide-de-camp
adjunk *n* deputy; assistant
administrasie *n* administration
administrateur *n* administrator; trustee
administreer *vb* to administrate
admiraal *n* admiral
adolessent *n* adolescent; *adj* adolescent
adres *n* address
adresseer *vb* to address; to direct
adverteer *vb* to advertise; to post (internet)
adverteerprogram *n* infomercial
advertensie *n* advertisement
advertensieballon *n* advertisement balloon
advies *n* advice
adviseer *vb* to advise
adviseur *n* adviser
advokaat *n* advocate; barrister; lawyer
aërobiese *adj* aerobic
aërobiese oefeninge *n* aerobics
aërosolblik *n* aerosol (can)
af *prep* off; down; **— en toe** *adv* now and then; off and on
afbeelding *n* portrayal; depiction; portrait
afbetaal *vb* to pay off; to settle
afbetaling *n* payment; settlement
afbly *vb* to keep off; to leave alone
afborsel *vb* to brush off
afbrand *vb* to burn down
afbreek *vb* to break off; to snap; to interrupt; to demolish
afbreuk *n* damage; injury
afbring *vb* to bring down; to lead off; to reduce
afbrokkel *vb* to crumble away
afdaal *vb* to descend; to come down
afdak *n* shed; sloping roof
afdam *vb* to dam up

afdank *vb* to dismiss; to discharge; to discard
afdek *vb* to clear (table)
afdeling *n* division; portion; section; detachment; compartment; floor
afding *vb* to haggle; to beat down the price
afdoen *vb* to complete; to finish; to detract from
afdoende *adj* decisive; conclusive
afdra *vb* to wear out (clothes, etc.); to carry down
afdraand *n* decline; slope; *adv* descending; downhill
afdroog *vb* to wipe dry; to dry
afdruk *n* copy; reproduction; *vb* to print; to reproduce
afdryf (*or* **afdrywe**) *vb* to drift away; to blow over
afdwaal *vb* to wander; to stray
afdwing *vb* to extort; to command (respect)
affêre *n* affair; business
affront *n* affront
affronteer *vb* to insult; to affront
afgaan *vb* to descend; to go off; to stray
afgee *vb* to hand over; to deliver; to surrender; to give off
afgeleë *adj* distant; remote
afgeleef *adj* worn out; decrepit
afgelope *adj* finished; ended
afgemat *adj* exhausted; tired
afgemete *adj* dignified; stately; formal
afgesaag *adj* stale; trite; hackneyed
afgesant ambassador; messenger
afgesien van *prep* apart from
afgeskeidene *n* dissenter; nonconformist
afgesonder *adj* lonely; isolated
afgestorwe *adj* deceased; dead
afgetrokke *adj* abstract; absent-minded
afgevaardigde *n* deputy; delegate
afgly *vb* to slide down; to slip off
afgod *n* idol
afgodediens (*or* **afgodery**) *n* idolatry
afgooi *vb* to throw down; to throw off
afgrond *n* precipice; abyss; gulf
afgryslik *adj* horrible; dreadful
afguns *n* envy; jealousy
afhaal *vb* to fetch; to call for; to meet
afhandel *vb* to settle; to conclude

afhang *vb* to hang down; droop; to depend on

afhanklik *adj* dependent

afhanklikheid *n* dependence

afhou *vb* to keep off

afjak *n* affront; insult; *vb* to insult; to snub

afkap *vb* to cut off; to cut down; to chop off

afkappingsteken *n* apostrophe

afkeer *n* aversion; dislike; *vb* to avert; to ward off

afkeur *vb* to condemn; to reject; to disapprove

afkeurig van *adj* averse to

afklim *vb* to dismount; to alight; to climb down

afklop *vb* to flick away; to dust; to peg out; to die

afkoel *vb* to cool down; to chill; to calm down

afkom *vb* to come down; to get off; to get rid of

afkoms *n* descent; birth; origin

afkondig *vb* to declare; to proclaim; to publish (banns)

afkondiging *n* declaration; proclamation

afkook *vb* to decoct; to boil off

afkort *vb* to shorten; to abbreviate

afkorting *n* abbreviation

aflaai *vb* to unload; to discharge; to download (internet)

aflaat[1] *n* indulgence

aflaat[2] *vb* to let off; to desist

afleer *vb* to unlearn; to cure of

aflees *vb* to read; to call out

aflê *vb* to lay down; to pay (visit); to cover (distance); to take (oath)

aflei *vb* to lead away; to divert; to deduce; to derive

afleiding *n* derivation; diversion

aflewer *vb* to deliver

aflewering *n* delivery; instalment

afloer *vb* to spy; to watch

afloop *n* termination; end; issue; result; *vb* to end; to terminate; to flow down; to run down; to wear out; to conclude

aflos *vb* to redeem (loan); to relieve; to take turns

afluister *vb* to overhear

afmaak *vb* to finish off; to kill; to make up (a quarrel); to run down

afmat *vb* to exhaust; to tire

afmeet *vb* to measure off

afmeting *n* measurement; dimension

afneem *vb* to take away; to take down; to clear (table); to decrease; to diminish; to fall; to sink; to take (photograph)

afnemer *n* photographer

afpak *vb* unload; unpack

afpers *vb* to extort (money)

afpluk *vb* to pick (off); to gather (flowers)

afraai *vb* to dissuade

afransel *vb* to flog; to thrash

afreis *n* departure

afreken *vb* to settle one's account

afrig *vb* to train; to coach

Afrikaan *n* African; person from Africa

Afrikaan-Amerikaan *n* African-American

Afrikaans *n, adj* Afrikaans

Afrikaner *n* Afrikaner; Boer; South African

Afrikane *npl* Africans

afrokkel *vb* to entice away from; to wheedle out of

afrol *vb* to roll down; to unroll; to unwind

afrond *vb* to round off

afroom *vb* to skim

afruk *vb* to tear off

afsaag *vb* to saw off

afsê *vb* to countermand; (*informal*) to sack; (*informal*) to dump

afset *n* sale; turnover

afsetter *n* starter (sport); swindler; cheat

afsien *vb* to waive (a right); to relinquish; to abandon; to give up

afsit *vb* to start (a race); to dismiss; to rope off; to amputate (a limb); to dethrone (a king)

afskaaf (*or* **afskawe**) *vb* to plane; to smooth; to graze; to chafe (skin)

afskaf *vb* to abolish; to repeal; to give up (luxuries)

afskaffer *n* abstainer; teetotaller

afskaling *n* downsizing

afskawe *see* **afskaaf**

afskeep *vb* to fob off; to neglect
afskei *vb* to separate; to extract
afskeid *n* leave-taking; departure
afskiet *vb* to fire; to discharge (gun)
afskil *vb* to peel; to skin
afskilder *vb* to depict; to describe
afskilfer *vb* to peel off
afskink *vb* to pour off; to decant
afskort *vb* to partition off
afskorting *n* partition
afskraap *vb* to scrape off
afskraapsel *n* scrapings
afskrif *n* copy; duplicate
afskrikmiddel *n* deterrent
afskrik *vb* to frighten; to scare; to dishearten; to discourage
afskryf (*or* **afskrywe**) *vb* to copy; to write off; to cancel
afsku *n* aversion; horror
afskud *vb* to shake off
afskuim *vb* to skim; to remove scum
afskutting *n* partition; fence
afskuwelik *adj* horrible; hideous; vile
afslaan *vb* to beat off; to decline; to refuse; to repel
afslaer *n* auctioneer
afslag *n* discount; reduction
afsloof (*or* **afslowe**) *vb* to slave away at; to toil
afslooffabriek *n* sweatshop
afslowe *see* **afsloof**
afsluit *vb* to lock; to shut; to turn off; to fence off; to close; to balance (books)
afsluiting *n* closure
afslyt *vb* to wear out; to wear down; to waste
afsmeek *vb* to beg; to beseech; to implore
afsmyt *vb* to hurl; to fling away
afsnou *vb* to snub; to snarl at; to snap at
afsny *vb* to cut; to cut short; to prune; to dock (horse's tail)
afsoen *vb* to kiss away
afsonder *vb* to isolate; to separate
afsonderlik *adj* separate; special
afsondering *n* separation; isolation; privacy
afspieël *vb* to reflect
afspoel *vb* to rinse; to wash
afspraak *n* agreement; appointment; arrangement

afspraakverkragting *n* date rape
afspreek *vb* to agree upon; to arrange
afspring *vb* to jump off; to leap down
afstaan *vb* to cede; to yield; to surrender
afstam *vb* to be descended from; to be derived from
afstammeling *n* descendant
afstand *n* distance; range; interval
afstanddoening *n* abdication; renunciation
afsteek *vb* to cut; to deliver (a speech); to mark out; **— by** *vb* to contrast with
afstem *vb* to reject
afstempel *vb* to stamp
afsterf (*or* **afsterwe**) *vb* to die; to lose touch with
afstof *vb* to dust; to beat
afstoot *vb* to throw down; to repel; to push off; to shove off
afstort *vb* to tumble down; to fling down
afstyg *vb* to dismount; to alight
afsweer *vb* to abjure
aftap *vb* to draw off; to tap; to drain
afteken *vb* to draw; to sketch; to mark
aftel *vb* to count off; to subtract
aftog *n* retreat
aftrede *n* retirement
aftree *vb* to resign; to retire
aftrek *vb* to deduct; to subtract; to divert; to withdraw
aftrekking *n* subtraction; deduction
aftreksel *n* extract; decoction; infusion; tincture
aftuig *vb* to unharness (a horse); to unrig (a ship)
afvaardig *vb* to delegate; to deputize
afval *n* refuse; offal; waste; *vb* to fall off; to fall down; to lose weight; to secede
afvalhoop *n* scrapheap
afvallige *n* deserter; renegade; apostate
afvee *vb* to wipe off; to dust
afveelappie *n* wet wipe
afvryf (*or* **afvrywe**) *vb* to rub off; to polish
afwag *vb* to wait for; to bide (one's time)
afwas *vb* to wash; to wash up
afwater *vb* to drain; to pour off
afwatering *n* drainage
afweeg *vb* to weigh

afweer *vb* to prevent; to ward off

afwei *vb* to graze; to browse

afwen *vb* to unlearn; to break (habit)

afwend *vb* to avert; to turn aside; to parry; to divert

afwerp *vb* to throw off; to shed

afwesig *adj* absent

afwissel *vb* to alternate; to change; to vary

afwisselend *adj* alternate

afwyk *vb* to deviate; to diverge; to differ; to disagree

afwys *vb* to refuse admittance; to reject; to decline (invitation)

ag[1] *n* care; *vb* to esteem; to respect; to value; **— slaan op** *vb* to pay attention to

ag[2] *interj* oh!

ag[3] *see* **agt**

ag nee! *interj* oh no!

agbaar *adj* honourable; venerable

agent *n* agent; policeman

agentskap *n* agency

aggregaat *n* aggregate (soil and sand particles)

aggressive *adj* aggressief

ag(t)hoek *n* octagon

AGHS *see* **aandag(s)gebrekhiperaktiwiteitsindroom**

agie *n* an inquisitive person; a 'nosey parker'

AGS *see* **aandag(s)gebreksindroom**

ag(t)ste *adj, n* eighth

agt(e) *n, determiner* eight

agteloos (*or* **agterlosig**) *adj* careless; negligent

agtenswaardig *adj* respectable; honourable

agter *prep* behind; at the back of; *adv* at the back; behind; slow

agteraan *adv* at the back; behind; in the rear

agteraf *adv* backward; secretly; out of the way

agterbaks *adj* sly; underhand; secret

agterbly *vb* to lag behind; to remain behind; to straggle

agterbuurt *n* slum; backstreet

agterdek *n* poop deck

agterdeur *n* back door

agterdog *n* suspicion

agtereen *adv* consecutively; one after the other; in order

agtereenvolgens *adv* consecutively; successively

agterent *n* back part; rear

agterhaal *vb* to overtake; to hunt down

agterhoede *n* rearguard

agterhou *vb* to keep back; to keep behind; to withhold

agterhoudend *adj* reserved; close; secret

agterkant *n* back; backside

agterkleinkind *n* great-grandchild

agterkom *vb* to find out; to discover

agterlik *adj* backward

agte(r)losig *adj* careless; negligent

agtermekaar *adj* spick and span; in order; up-to-date; neat

agtermiddag *n* afternoon

agterna *adv* after; behind; later; afterwards

agternaam *n* surname

agteroor *adv* backwards; on one's back

agterpoot *n* hind leg

agterryer *n* attendant

agterskip *n* stern; poop

agterstaan *vb* to be neglected; to be behind others

agterstallig *adj* outstanding (payment); in arrears

agterstel *vb* to place behind; to handicap; to put at a disadvantage

agterstevoor *adj, adv* back to front; wrong way round; upside down

agteruit *adv* back; backwards

agteruitgang *n* fall; decline; decay; deterioration

agtervoegsel *n* affix; suffix

agtervolg *vb* to pursue; to persecute

agthoek (*or* **aghoek**) *n* octagon

agtien *n, determiner* eighteen

agtiende *adj, n* eighteenth

agting *n* regard; esteem

agste *adj, n* eighth

ag(t)uur *n* eight o'clock

agurkie *n* gherkin

ai *interj* ah!; oh!; ouch!

akademie *n* academy

akkedis *n* lizard

akker *n* field; acre; acorn

akkerboom *n* oak tree

akkertjie *n* flowerbed
akklamasie *n* acclamation; acclaim
akkomodasie *n* accommodation
akkoord *n* chord; agreement
akkordeer *vb* to agree; to get on with
akkuraat *adj* accurate
akoestiek *n* acoustics
akriel *adj* acrylic (fibre)
aksent *n* accent
aksie *n* action; agitation; **regstellende — ** *n* affirmative action
aksioma (*or* **aksioom**) *n* axiom
aksyns *adj* excise (duty)
akte *n* deed; diploma; act
akteur *n* actor; player
aktief *adj* active
aktrise *n* actress
aktueel *adj* actual; topical
akuut *adj* acute
akwa-aërobiese oefeninge *n* aquarobics
akwarel *n* aquarelle; watercolour (painting)
al[1] *adv* already; yet
al[2] *conj* even though; even if; though; although
al[3] *adj* every; all; each
alarm *n* alarm; uproar
albei *pron; conj* both
albino *n* albino
album *n* album; scrapbook
alchemie *n* alchemy
aldag *adv* every day; daily
aldeur *adv* all the time; all along
alfabet *n* alphabet
algar *pron* all; everybody
algebra *n* algebra
algemeen *adj* general; universal; *adv* generally; commonly; unanimously; **met — mene stemme** *adv* unanimously
algemene praktisyn *n* general practitioner; doctor
alhier *adv* here; at this spot; locally
alhoewel *conj* (al)though
alias *n* alias
alikreukel (*or* **alikruikel**) *n* periwinkle
aljimmers *adv* always; ever
alkohol *n* alcohol
alkoholis *n* alcoholic
alkoof *n* alcove
alledaags *adj* common; ordinary; stale; trivial

alleen *adj* alone; single; lonely; only
alleenhandel *n* monopoly
alleenheerser *n* autocrat; absolute
alleenspraak *n* soliloquy
allengs *adv* gradually
allerbeste *adj* very best
allerhande *pron* all and sundry
allerisikopolis *n* all-risks policy
allerlaas *adj* very last; the very latest
allerlei *adj* miscellaneous; all kinds of
alles *pron* everything; all
allesbehalwe *adv* anything but; not at all
alleswinkel *n* hypermarket; supermarket
alliansie *n* alliance
allokeer *vb* to allocate
allooi *n* alloy; standard; quality
almag *n* omnipotence
almagtig *adj* all powerful; almighty
almal *pron* all; everybody
almanak *n* almanac; calendar
almiskie *conj* even although; nevertheless
almelewe *adv* all the while; all the time; always
alom *adv* everywhere
alomteenwoordig *adj* present everywhere
alreeds *adv* already
alsiende *adj* all-seeing
alsydig *adj* all-round; universal
altar *n* altar
altans *adv* at least; anyhow
alte *adv* too; also
altemit *adv* perhaps; possibly
alternatief *n* alternative; *adj* alternative
alternatiewe *adj* alternative (lifestyle, comedy)
altesame *adv* altogether
altyd *adv* always; for ever
alvorens *conj* before; until
al weer *adv* again; once more
alwetend *adj* all-knowing
amalgamasie *n* amalgamation
amandel *n* almond
amateur *n* amateur
ambag *n* trade; business; profession
ambagskool *n* trade school
ambassade *n* embassy
ambassadeur *n* ambassador

ambisie *n* ambition
ambisieus *adj* ambitious
ambulans *n* ambulance
Amerasiër *n* Amerasian
Amerasies *adj* Amerasian
Amerikaanse *n* American English
Amerikaanse Nasionale Lugvaarten Ruimteadministrasie *n* National Aeronautics and Space Administration (NASA)
Amerindiaan *n* Amerind; Amerindian; American Indian (linguistics)
amfetamine (*or* **amfetamien**) *n* amphetamine
ametis *n* amethyst
ammoniak *n* ammonia
ammunisie *n* ammunition
amnestie *n* amnesty; pardon
amp *n* office; post; employment
amper (*or* **ampertjies**) *adv* nearly; almost
ampgenoot *n* colleague; fellow worker
amptenaar *n* official; officer; civil servant
amusant *adj* amusing
amuseer *vb* to amuse
analfabeet *n* illiterate person
analise *n* analysis
analiseer *vb* to analyse
anargie *n* anarchy
ander *determiner* other; another; **onder —e** *adv* among other things
anderland *adv* abroad; in another country
anders *adv* or else; otherwise; differently
andersdenkend *adj* dissenting; holding a different opinion
andersins *adv* otherwise
andersom *adv* the other way round
anekdote *n* anecdote
angel *n* bee sting
angelier *n* carnation
angs *n* anxiety; fear; terror; agony
angstig *adj* anxious; uneasy
angsvallig *adj* scrupulous; precise
angswekkend *adj* alarming
aniem *n* anime
animeer *vb* to animate
animasie *n* animation
anker *n* anchor; *vb* to anchor; to drop anchor

ankerplaas (*or* **ankerplek**) *n* anchorage
annale *npl* annals
annekseer *vb* to annex; to take
annuïteit *n* annuity
anoniem *adj* anonymous
anoreksie *n* anorexia
anoreksielyer (*or* anorektikus) *n* anorectic (*or* anorexic) person
anoreksies *adj* anorexic (*or* anorectic)
anorganies *adj* inorganic
antenne *n* aerial; antenna
anti *prefix* anti; against
antibioties *adj* relating to antibiotics
antibiotikum *n* antibiotic
antiek *adj* antique
antiekwinkel *n* antique shop
antigeen *n* antigen
antiloop *n* antelope
antipsigoties *n* antipsychotic (drug)
antiretrovirale behandeling *n* antiretroviral treatment (ART)
antisepties *adj* antiseptic
antisipeer *vb* to anticipate
antiviraal *adj* antiviral
antropologie *n* anthropology
antwoord *n* answer; reply; *vb* to answer; to reply
anys *n* anise
apart *adj* separate; *adv* apart; separately
apartheid *n* the official government policy of racial segregation in SA that ended with the multiracial; democratic elections of 1994
apologie *n* apology
apostel *n* apostle
apostroof *n* apostrophe (')
apparaat *n* apparatus
appel *n* apple
appèl *n* appeal
appelliefie *n* Cape gooseberry
appeleer *vb* to appeal
appelkoos *n* apricot
appendisitis *n* appendicitis
applikant *n* applicant
applikasie *n* application
approudisseer *vb* to applaud; to clap
applous *n* applause
appelwyn *n* cider
April *n* April
apteek *n* pharmacy; chemist's shop

apteker *n* chemist; pharmacist
aptyt *n* appetite
ARB *see* **antiretrovirale behandeling**
arbei *vb* to work; to labour
arbeid *n* work; labour; toil
arbeider *n* worker; labourer; workman
arbeidsaam *adj* industrious; laborious
arbeidsterapie *n* occupational therapy
arbitrasie *n* arbitration
arend *n* eagle
argief *n* archive
argipel *n* archipelago
argitek *n* architect
argivaris *n* archivist
arglistig *adj* cunning; crafty
argwaan *n* suspicion; mistrust
aria *n* air; tune; aria
aristokraat *n* aristocrat
ark *n* ark
arm[1] *n* arm
arm[2] *adj* poor; needy; indigent
armband *n* bracelet
armoede *n* poverty; want
armsalig *adj* pitiful; miserable; poor
armstoel *n* easy chair; armchair
aroma *n* smell (usually pleasant); aroma; fragrance; scent
arres *n* arrest; custody
arresteer *vb* to arrest
arrogant *adj* arrogant; presumptuous
artikel *n* article; clause; commodity
arties *n* artist
artillerie *n* artillery
arts *n* physician; doctor
as[1] *n* ash
as[2] *n* axle; axis
as[3] *adv; conj; prep* as; like; such as; when; as if
asbak *n* ashtray
asbes *n* asbestos
asem *n* breath; *vb* to breathe
asemhaling *n* the act of breathing; respiration

asemloos *adj* breathless
asfalt *n* asphalt; bitumen
ashoop *n* rubbish dump; scrapheap
asma *n* asthma
asmaties *adj* asthmatic
asof *conj* as if
asook *adv* as well as; and also
aspaai *n* 'I spy' (the game)
aspersie *n* asparagus
aspirien *n* aspirin
asseblief *adv* please
assegaai *n* assegai; spear
assessor *n* assessor
assisteer *vb* to help; to assist
assistent *n* assistant; helper
assuransie *n* insurance; assurance
astrant *adj* cheeky; impudent
astrologie *n* astrology
astronomie *n* astronomy
astronomies *adj* astronomic(al)
astronout *n* astronaut
asuur *n, adj* azure; sky blue
asvaal *adj* deathly pale; ashen
asyn *n* vinegar
ateïs *n* atheist
ateljee *n* studio; workshop
atjar *n* chutney; achar
atlas *n* atlas
atleet *n* athlete
atleties *adj* athletic
atmosfeer *n* atmosphere
atomies *adj* atomic
atoom *n* atom
atoombom *n* atom(ic) bomb; nuclear bomb
attent *adj* attentive; considerate
attestasie *n* attestation; certification
attraksie *n* attraction
Augustus *n* August
avatar *n* avatar (computing)
avontuur *n* adventure
avonturier *n* adventurer

B

baadjie *n* jacket; coat
baai[1] *n* bay
baai[2] *vb* to bathe
baaierd *n* muddle; chaos
baal *n* bale
baan *n* path; road; way; orbit; (traffic) lane; (tennis) court; *vb* to level; to clear
baanbreker *n* pioneer
baantjie *n* job; employment; berth
baar[1] *n* bier (for corpse); stretcher
baar[2] *n* wave (in sea)
baar[3] *vb* to bear; to create; to give birth to
baar[4] *adj* unskilled; untrained
baard *n* beard
baarmoeder *n* womb; uterus
baas *n* master; boss; top dog
baasspeel *vb* to bully; to order someone around
baat[1] *n* profit; benefit; **— vind by** *vb* to benefit from
baat[2] *vb* to avail; to be of use
baatsugtig *adj* selfish
baba (*or* **babatjie**) *n* baby
babagolf *n* baby boom
babatjie *see* **baba**
babbel *vb* to chatter; to babble
babbelkous *n* chatterbox
babelas *n* hangover
Bach-blommeraat *n* Bach flower remedy
bad *n* bath
badkamer *n* bathroom
bagasie *n* baggage; luggage
bagasiebakvendusie *n* car boot sale; boot sale
baie *adj* much; many; *adv* very
bajonet *n* bayonet
bak[1] *n* basin; bowl; trough; snake's hood
bak[2] *vb* to bake; to roast
bakboord *n* port side (left side) of a vessel
baken *n* beacon; buoy
bakermat cradle
bakker *n* baker
bakkie[1] small dish
bakkie[2] *n* a pick-up truck

baklei *vb* to fight
bakoond *n* oven
bakpoeier *n* baking powder
baksteen *n* brick
bakterie *n* bacterium
bal[1] *n* ball (tennis, etc.)
bal[2] *n* ball; dance; **gemaskerde —** *n* fancy dress ball
balans *n* balance
balanseer *vb* to balance
baldadig *adj* mischievous; naughty; rowdy
balein *n* whalebone
balhorig *adj* cross; headstrong
balie *n* tub; bar
baljaar *vb* to romp; to frolic; to play
balju *n* bailiff; sheriff
balk *n* beam; rafter; staff; stave (music)
balkon *n* balcony; (train) platform
ballade *n* ballad
ballas *n* ballast
ballet *n* ballet
balling *n* exile; outcast
ballingskap *n* exile
ballon *n* balloon
balsamiese asyn *see* **balsemasyn**
balsem *n* balm; balsam; *vb* to embalm
balsemasyn (*or* **balsamiese asyn**) *n* balsamic vinegar
balsturig *adj* obstinate; unruly
bamboes *n* bamboo
ban *n* excommunication; banishment; *vb* to banish; to expel
banaal *adj* banal; common; vulgar
banana *n* banana
band *n* ribbon; tape; band; chain; cord; tie
bandelier *n* soldier's shoulder belt; bandoleer
bandeloos *adj* undisciplined; lawless
bandiet *n* convict
bang *adj* afraid; timid; frightened
bangbroek *n* coward
banier *n* banner
bank[1] *n* bench; seat; desk; pew
bank[2] *n* bank (for depositing money); *vb* to bank; to deposit

bank[3] *n* bank (snow, river)
banket *n* feast; banquet; confectionery
bankier *n* banker
banknoot *n* banknote
bankrot *adj* bankrupt; — **speel** *vb* to be insolvent
bankrotskap *n* bankruptcy
banneling *n* exile; outcast
barak *n* barracks
barbaar *n* barbarian; savage
barbaars *adj* barbarian; barbarous
barbier *n* barber
barbituraat *n* barbiturate
bariton baritone
barmhartig *adj* compassionate; merciful
barnsteen *n* amber
barometer *n* barometer
baron *n* baron
barones *n* baroness
barrikade *n* barricade
bars[1] *vb* to burst; to crack; to split
bars[2] *adj* rough; harsh; gruff
bas[1] *n* bass (singing)
bas[2] *n* (tree) bark; rind
basaar *n* bazaar
basiel *n* basil (herb)
basil *n* bacillus
basis *n* base; basis
basta! *interj* stop! enough!
baster *n* bastard; half-breed; mongrel
basuin *n* trombone; trumpet
bataljon *n* battalion
bate *n* asset; credit
battery *n* battery
beaam *vb* to assent to; to approve of
beampte *n* official; employee
beangs *adj* afraid; uneasy
beantwoord *vb* to answer; to reply; to return (love)
bearbei *vb* to work; to cultivate (ground); to treat (material)
beboet *vb* to fine
bebou *vb* to till; to cultivate
bed *n* bed
bedaar *vb* to calm (down); to soothe; to abate
bedaard *adj* calm; composed
bedag *adj* mindful of; prepared for
bedags *adv* in daytime; during the day
bedagsaam *adj* thoughtful; considerate

bedank *vb* to thank; to refuse; to dismiss; to resign
beddegoed *n* bedding; bed linen
bedding *n* riverbed; layer
beddinkie *n* flowerbed
bede *n* prayer; petition
bedees *adj* timid; shy
bedek *vb* to cover; to conceal
bedektelik *adv* secretly
bedel *vb* to beg
bedelaar *n* beggar
bedenking *n* consideration; objection
bedenklik *adj* critical; precarious; serious
bederf *n* corruption; decay; *vb* to corrupt; to spoil; to ruin; to turn bad
bedevaart *n* pilgrimage
bedien *vb* to serve; to attend; to administer
bediende *n* servant; waiter; attendant
bediener *n* server (computing)
bediening *n* service; attendance; ministration
bedink *vb* to consider; to reflect; to recollect; to invent; to contrive
bedlêend *adj* bedridden; confined to bed
bedoel *vb* to mean; to intend
bedoeling *n* meaning; intention
bedompig *adj* damp; close; stuffy
bedorwe *adj* bad; spoiled; corrupt
bedra *vb* to amount to; to come to
bedrag *n* amount
bedreig *vb* to threaten; to menace
bedremmeld *adj* perplexed; confused
bedrewe *adj* skilled; well-versed
bedrieër *n* impostor; deceiver
bedrieg *vb* to deceive; to cheat; to trick; to defraud
bedrieglik *adj* itchy
bedroë *adj* deceived
bedroef *vb* to grieve; *adj* sad; sorrowful
bedrog *n* deceit; deception
bedruk *adj* oppressed; dejected
bedryf *n* deed; business; act; *vb* to run (a business)
bedrywig *adj* active; busy
bedug *adj* apprehensive; afraid
beduie *vb* to signify; to mean; to explain; to point out
beduidend *adj* considerable

beduiweld *adj* mad; crazy; daft
bedwang *n* control; restraint
bedwelm *vb* to stun; to drug; to intoxicate
bedwelmend *adj* intoxicating
bedwelmer *n* stun gun
bedwing *vb* to restrain; to check; to control
beëdig *vb* to swear; to put on oath
beëdigde *adj* sworn
beef (*or* **bewe**) *vb* to shiver; to tremble; to shake
beeld *n* image; statue; figure; picture; metaphor
beelddiens *n* idolatry
beeldhouer *n* sculptor
beeldpoetser *n* spin doctor
beeldradio *n* television
beeldsaai (*or* **beeldsend**) *vb* to televise
beeldskoon *adj* very beautiful
beeldspraak *n* figurative language
beeltenis *n* image; portrait
been *n* leg; bone
beer *n* bear; boar
beërf (*or* **beërwe**) *vb* to inherit
bees *n* beast; brute; animal; ox; cow
beesagtig *adj* savage; brutal; bestial; *adv* brutally; savagely
beeste *n* cattle
beesvleis *n* beef
beet[1] *n* beet; beetroot
beet[2] *n* bite; grip
beethê *vb* to have hold of
beetneem *vb* to take hold of; to cheat
befaamd *adj* notorious; famous
begaaf *adj* gifted; talented
begaan *vb* to commit (crime); to make (mistake)
begeef *vb* to forsake; to resort to; to proceed to
begeer *vb* to desire; to wish for; to covet
begeerlik *adj* desirable
begeerte *n* desire; wish
begelei *vb* to accompany; to escort
begeleide lees *n* guided reading
begiftig *vb* to endow
begin *n* beginning; commencement; start; *vb* to begin; to commence; to start
beginsel *n* principle; beginning

beginselloos *adj* unprincipled
begraaf (*or* **begrawe**) *vb* to bury
begraafplaas *n* cemetery; graveyard
begrafnis *n* funeral; burial
begrawe *see* **begraaf**
begrens *vb* to limit; to bound
begrip *n* idea; notion; understanding; (*informal*) savvy
begroet *vb* to welcome; to greet
begroot *vb* to estimate; to budget
begroting *n* budget; estimate
begryp *vb* to understand; to comprehend; to grasp
begryplik *adj* clear; understandable; conceivable
begunstig *vb* to favour; to protect
behaag (*or* **behae**) *vb* to please
behaal *vb* to gain; to attain
behae *n* delight; pleasure
behalwe *prep* except; save for; besides
behandel *vb* to treat; to handle; to deal with; to attend
behandelende dokter *n* attending physician
behandeling *n* treatment; — **ondergaan** *vb* to undergo treatment
behang *vb* to paper; to cover; to adorn
behanger *n* paperhanger
behangsel *n* wallpaper
behartig *vb* to manage; to look after; to take care of
beheer *n* control; management; *vb* to manage; to administer
beheerder *n* manager
beheers *vb* to control; to manage; govern; rule
behels *vb* to contain; to comprise
behendig *adj* skilful; dexterous
behep *prep* subject to; liable to
behoed *vb* to protect; to guard
behoedsaam *adj* cautious; careful
behoef *vb* to require; to need; to want
behoefte *n* need; want
behoeftig *adj* poor; needy; destitute
behoewe: ten — van *prep* on behalf of; in aid of
behoort *vb* to belong; to ought to
behoorlik *adj* proper; becoming; *adv* properly; decently
behou *vb* to keep; to save; to retain
behoud *n* preservation; retention

behoue *adj* safe; unhurt

behulp *n* help; aid; **met — van** *prep* with the help of

behulpsaam *adj* useful; helpful

bekend maak *vb* to out; to reveal as a homosexual

beide *determiner* both; **een van —** *n* either one

beïnvloed *vb* to influence

beitel *n* chisel; *vb* to chisel

bejaard *adj* aged; elderly

bejaardesorg *n* care of the aged

bejammer *vb* to bewail; to deplore

bejeën *vb* to treat; to act towards

bek *n* mouth; bill; beak; snout

bekaamd *adj* ashamed

bekaf *adj* downhearted; crestfallen

bekeer *vb* to convert

beken *vb* to acknowledge (a debt); to confess (a sin)

bekend *adj* known; well-known

bekende *n* acquaintance

bekendmaking *n* announcement; notice

bekendstel *vb* to launch

bekendstellingstoer *n* roadshow

bekentenis *n* avowal; confession

beker *n* cup; mug; jug

bekken *n* basin; font; pelvis (anatomy)

bekla *vb* to pity; to lament

beklaagde *n* accused; defendant

beklad *vb* to blot; to stain; to slander

beklaenswaardig *adj* pitiful; lamentable

beklag *n* complaint

beklee(d) *vb* to cover; to invest; to hold (office); to upholster

beklem *vb* to oppress; to stress

beklemd *adj* oppressed

beklemtoon *vb* to accent

beklim *vb* to climb; to ascend

beklink *vb* to settle; to arrange

beklonke *adj* settled

beknop *adj* concise; abridged

beknor *vb* to chide; to scold

bekom *vb* to recover; to obtain

bekommer *vb* to worry; to be troubled over

bekommerd *adj* worried; anxious; uneasy

bekoms *n* satiety

bekoor *vb* to charm; to enchant

bekoorlik *adj* charming; fascinating

bekostig *vb* to defray; to pay; to afford

bekragtig *vb* to confirm; to sanction

bekreun *vb* to worry; to mind; to be troubled

bekrompe *adj* narrow-minded; confined; limited

bekroon *vb* to crown; to award (prize)

bekruiper *n* stalker

bekwaam *vb* to qualify; to train; *adj* able; capable; fit

bekyk *vb* to look at; to examine

bel *n* bell; *vb* to ring (bell); to telephone

belaai *vb* to load; to burden

belaglik *adj* ridiculous

beland *vb* to land

belang *n* importance; interest; concern

belangeloos *adj* disinterested

belanghebbend *adj* interested

belanghebbers *npl* stakeholders

belangrik *adj* important

belangstel *vb* to take an interest in

belas *vb* to burden; to charge; to tax

belasbaar *adj* taxable; dutiable

belaster *vb* to slander

belasting *n* tax; taxation; duty; rates

belastingklaringsvorm *n* tax clearance form

belê *n* to invest (money); to convene (meeting)

beledig *vb* to offend; to insult

belediging *n* offence; insult

beleef[1] (*or* **belewe**) *vb* to experience; to go through

beleef[2] *adj* polite; courteous

beleefdheid *n* courtesy; politeness

beleër *vb* to besiege

beleëring (*or* **beleg**) *n* siege

beleid *n* policy; **met — te werk gaan** *vb* to act with discretion

beleg *see* **beleëring**

belemmer *vb* to hinder; to impede; to obstruct

belese *adj* well-read

belet *vb* to hinder; to prevent; to forbid

beletsel *n* obstacle; hindrance

belewe *see* **beleef**[1]

belhamel *n* ringleader

beliggaam *vb* to embody

belofte *n* promise

beloning *n* reward; recompense
beloof (*or* **belowe**) *vb* to promise
beloon *vb* to reward; to recompense
beloop *n* course; way
belowe *see* **beloof**
bely *vb* to confess
belydenis *n* confession
bemagtig *vb* to empower
beman *vb* to man; to garrison
bemantel *vb* to cloak; to disguise
bemerk *vb* to observe; to notice; to perceive
bemiddel *vb* to mediate
bemiddeld *adj* wealthy; well-to-do
bemin *vb* to love
bemind *adj* loved; beloved
beminde *n* lover; sweetheart; betrothed
beminlik *adj* lovable; amiable
bemoedig *vb* to encourage; to animate
bemoei *vb* to meddle; to interfere
bemoeilik *vb* to hinder; to obstruct
bemoeisiek *adj* meddlesome
bemoeisug *n* meddlesomeness
bemors *vb* to dirty; to soil
benadeel *vb* to injure; to harm; to wrong
benader *vb* to estimate; to approximate
benaderde bedrag *n* ball park
benadoring *n* approximation
benaming *n* name; title
benard *adj* distressed; hard (times)
bende *n* troop; band; gang
benede *prep* below; beneath; under; *adv* downstairs; downwards
beneem *vb* to take away; to deprive
benepe *adj* cramped; narrow
benerig *adj* bony
benewens *adv* together with; besides
benodig *adj* wanted; required; necessary
benodigdhede *npl* requirements; accessories
benoem *vb* to nominate; to appoint
benoeming *n* appointment; nomination
benoud *adj* oppressive; sultry; suffocating; afraid
benul *n* notion
beny *vb* to envy; to be jealous of
beoefen *vb* to practise (profession); to study

beoog *vb* to aim at
beoordeel *vb* to judge; to review
bepaal *vb* to fix; to define; to determine; to limit
bepaald *adj* fixed; specified; decided; *adv* positively; decidedly; unmistakably
bepalend *adj* defining; qualifying
bepaling *n* limitation; definition; regulation
beperk *vb* to limit; to confine; *adj* limited
beperking *n* restriction
beperkingskode *n* restriction password or code (iPhone, etc.)
beperkte verlof *n* capped leave
beplant *vb* to plant
bepleit *vb* to plead
bepraat *vb* to discuss
beproef *vb* to try; to test; to attempt
beproewing *n* condition of great distress; affliction; trial
beraadslaag *vb* to consult; to debate; to deliberate
beraam *vb* to contrive; to plan; to estimate
bêre (*or* **berg**) *vb* to save; to store; to conceal; to salvage
beredderaar *n* administrator (estate, inheritance, etc.)
beredo *adj* mounted
beredeneer *vb* to discuss; to reason; to argue
berei *vb* to prepare
bereid *adj* willing; ready; prepared
bereik *vb* to reach; to attain; to achieve
bereis *vb* to travel over; to travel through
bereken *vb* to calculate; to charge
berg[1] *n* mountain; mount
berg[2] *see* **bêre**
bergaf *adj, adv* downhill
bergketting *n* mountain range
bergop *adj, adv* uphill
berig *n* advice; news; notice; account; return; intelligence; *vb* to notify; to inform; to report
beriggewer *n* reporter (news); informant
berispe *vb* to reprove; to rebuke
berk(eboom) *n* birch (tree)

beroem *vb* to boast; to brag
beroemd *adj* famous; noted
beroep *n* profession; trade; business; call; *vb* to call; to appeal
beroer *vb* to stir; to rouse up; to inflame
beroerd *adj* miserable
beroerte *n* stroke; apoplectic fit; apoplexy
berokken *vb* to cause
beroof (*or* **berowe**) *vb* to rob; to deprive
berou *n* repentance; remorse; *vb* to repent; to regret
berowe *see* **beroof**
berug *adj* notorious
berus *vb* to resign oneself; to be in the hands of
berustend *adj* submissive; agreeing without protest
berym *vb* to rhyme; to put into rhyming verse
bes *adv* very well; *adj* utmost
besadig *adj* composed; calm; deliberate
beseer *vb* to hurt; to injure
besef *n* notion; idea; sense; *vb* to be conscious of; to realize
besem *n* broom
besending *n* consignment
beset *vb* to occupy (a place); to engage; *adj* occupied; engaged
besiel *vb* to enliven; to encourage; inspire
besien *vb* to inspect; to look at
besig *adj* busy; occupied; engaged
besigheid *n* business; occupation
besigtig *vb* to view; to examine
besin *vb* to reflect; to consider
besing *vb* to sing the praises of
besink *vb* to settle down; to subside
besinksel *n* sediment; residue
besit *n* possession; asset; *vb* to possess; to have
besitlik *adj* possessive
besitting *n* possession; property
beskaaf *adj* civilized; polite
beskaam *vb* to shame; to put to shame
beskadig *vb* to damage; to injure
beskadu *vb* to shade
beskawing *n* civilization
beskeidenheid *n* modesty; discretion
beskeie *adj* discreet; modest

beskerm *vb* to protect; to defend; to guard
beskermeling *n* protégé
beskermengel *n* guardian angel
beskermheer *n* patron; sponsor
beskiet *vb* to fire upon; to shell
beskik *vb* to arrange; to manage; to dispose of
beskikbaar *adj* available
beskikking *n* disposal
beskimmel *vb* to grow mouldy
beskimp *vb* to insult; to mock
beskinder *vb* to slander; to blacken (name)
beskonke *adj* intoxicated; drunk
beskot *n* partition
beskou *vb* to consider; to contemplate; to regard
beskroomd *adj* timid; shy
beskryf (*or* **beskrywe**) *vb* to describe; to depict
beskuit *n* rusk
beskuldig *vb* to accuse; to charge with
beskuldigde *n* defendant; accused
beskuldiger *n* accuser; plaintiff
beskuldiging *n* charge; accusation
beskut *vb* to protect; to shelter
beslaan *vb* to cover (area); to shoe (a horse)
beslag *n* seizure (goods); clasps; fittings; furniture; **— lê op** *vb* to seize goods; to confiscate property
besleg *vb* to settle; to decide
beslis *vb* to decide; *adj* decisive; final; conclusive; *adv* decidedly; positively
beslommering *n* care; bother; trouble
beslote *adj* private; closed to others; determined
besluit *n* resolution; decision; *vb* to decide; to resolve; to conclude
besluiteloos *adj* irresolute; undecided
besmeer *vb* to soil; to besmirch
besmet *vb* to infect; to contaminate; to pollute
besmetlik *adj* contagious; infectious
besnoei *vb* to prune; to trim; to curtail; to retrench
besnydenis *n* circumcision
besoedel *vb* to defile; to pollute
besoek *n* visit; short call; *vb* to visit; to call on

besoeker *n* visitor; guest
besoeking *n* visitation; affliction
besoek weer *vb* to revisit
besoldiging *n* pay; salary
besonder *adj* special; particular; peculiar; *adv* specially; particularly; peculiarly
besonders *adj* extraordinary; special
besope *adj* drunk; intoxicated
besorg *vb* to deliver; to procure; *adj* anxious; solicitous; concerned about
bespaar *vb* to save; to economize
bespeel *vb* to play (instrument)
bespeur *vb* to perceive; to observe; to notice
bespied *vb* to spy on; to watch
bespiegeling *n* speculation; contemplation
bespoedig *vb* to accelerate
bespot *vb* to mock; to ridicule, to sneer at
bespotlik *adj* ridiculous
bespreek *vb* to talk over; to discuss; to book (a seat)
bespring *vb* to spring upon
besproei *vb* to water; to irrigate
bessie *n* berry
bessiesap *n* berry juice
bestaan *n* existence; livelihood; *vb* to exist; to live on
bestaan uit *vb* to consist of
bestaanbaar *adj* possible; reasonable
bestanddeel *n* part; ingredient
bestaansbeveiliging *n* social security
beste *n* best; *adj* best; first class
bestee *vb* to spend
besteel *vb* to rob
bestek *n* space; plan; design
bestel *vb* to order; to deliver
bestelling *n* order; delivery; appointment
bestem *vb* to apportion; to fix; *adj* intended; fixed
bestemming *n* destination; destiny
bestendig *vb* to make permanent; to confirm; *adj* sure; steady
bestorm *vb* to storm; to attack
bestorming *n* attack
bestorwe *adj* deadly pale; — **boedel** *n* deceased estate
bestraal *vb* to beam on; to shine on

bestraat *vb* to pave
bestraf *vb* to rebuke; to censure; to punish
bestraffing (*or* **bestrawwing**) *n* rebuke; punishment
bestrating *n* pavement
bestrawwing *see* **bestraffing**
bestry *vb* to contest; to dispute; to defray (expenses)
bestryk *vb* to spread over
bestudeer *vb* to study
bestuur *n* government; management; direction; *vb* to manage; to rule; to govern; to steer (vessel)
bestuurder *n* manager; director
bestyg *vb* to mount; to climb
besuinig *vb* to economize; to reduce expenses
beswaar¹ *n* objection; scruple; grievance
beswaar² *vb* to burden; *adj* uneasy; troubled; burdened
beswaarlik *adj* hard; difficult; *adv* with difficulty
beswaarskrif *n* petition
besweer *vb* to conjure; to beseech
besweet *adj* perspiring
beswil *adj* best
beswyk *vb* to die; to succumb
beswym *vb* to faint; to swoon
beswyming *n* swoon; fainting fit
betaal *vb* to pay
betaam *vb* to become; to suit
betaamlik *adj* becoming; proper; seemly
betakel *vb* to dirty; to grab
betaling *n* payment
betas *vb* to touch; to feel
beteken *vb* to signify; to mean
betekenis *n* meaning; sense; importance
beter *adj* better
beterskap *n* recovery; improvement
beteuel *vb* to bridle; to restrain
beteuterd *adj* embarrassed; confused
betig *vb* to accuse; to impute
beton *n* concrete
betoog *n* demonstration; argument; *vb* to demonstrate; to prove
betoon *vb* to show
betower *vb* to bewitch; to enchant; to fascinate

betrag *vb* to consider; to practise; to perform; to stare at

betrap *vb* to detect; to catch

betree *vb* to tread on

betref *vb* to concern; to regard; to relate

betreffende *prep* concerning; regarding; about

betrek *vb* to move into; to cloud over; to involve; to cheat

betrekking *n* relation; situation; **met — tot** *prep* with reference to

betreklik *adj* relative; *adv* relatively

betreur *vb* to express great sorrow; to regret; to deplore

betrokke *adj* cloudy; overcast; gloomy; **— wees by** to be concerned with; to be involved in

betroubaar *adj* reliable

betuig *vb* to declare; to testify

betuiging *n* declaration

betwis *vb* to contest; to dispute

betwyfel *vb* to doubt; to question

betyds *adv* in good time

beuk(eboom) *n* beech (tree)

beul *n* executioner

beur *vb* to lift; to struggle

beurs *n* purse; stock exchange; scholarship

beurt *n* turn

beurtelings *adv* in turn; alternately; one after the other

beusel *vb* to trifle

beuselagtig *adj* trifling; petty

bevaar *n* to navigate

bevaarbaar *adj* navigable

beval[1] *vb* to please

beval[2] *vb* to give birth to

bevallig *adj* charming; graceful

bevalling *n* confinement; childbirth

bevange *adj* overcome

bevat *vb* to contain; to comprise

beveel *vb* to order; to command

beveilig *vb* to protect; to safeguard

bevel *vb* order; command

bevelskrif *n* mandate; warrant

bevestig *vb* to confirm; to affirm; to fasten

bevind *vb* to find; to experience

bevlek *vb* to stain; to pollute

bevlieg *vb* to fly at; to attack

bevoeg *adj* competent; qualified; authorized

bevogtig *vb* to moisten; to wet

bevolk *n* people

bevolking *n* population

bevoordeel *vb* to favour; to benefit

bevooroordeel(d) *adj* prejudiced; biased

bevoorreg *n* privilege

bevorder *vb* to promote; to advance

bevorderlik *adj* beneficial; conducive

bevrag *vb* to load

bevredig *vb* to satisfy; to indulge; to gratify

bevredigend *adj* satisfying; gratifying

bevreem(d) *vb* to surprise; to wonder; **dit — my** it surprises me

bevrees *adj* afraid of

bevriend *adj* friendly; intimate

bevries *vb* to freeze; to congeal

bevrug *vb* to make pregnant; to cause to conceive; *adj* pregnant

bevry *vb* to free; to deliver from; to rescue

bevuil *adj* soiled; dirty

bewaak *vb* to watch; to guard

bewaar *vb* to keep; to maintain; to preserve; to save

bewaarheid *vb* to corroborate; to bear out; to prove true

bewaarkissie *n* safe deposit box

bewaarplaas (*or* **bewaarplek**) *n* storeroom; storehouse

bewaker *n* caretaker; guardian

bewandel *vb* to walk on

bewapen *vb* to arm

bewaring *n* safekeeping; custody

bewater *vb* to irrigate

bewe *see* **beef**

beweeg *vb* to move; to persuade

beween *vb* to feel great sorrow; to express great sorrow

beweer *vb* to assert; to contend

beweging *n* motion; movement

bewerasie (*or* **bibberasie**) *n* shivering; the shakes

bewerig *adj* shaky

bewering *n* assertion; contention

bewerk *vb* to work; to effect; to manage; to till (the ground)

bewerkstellig *vb* to cause; to bring about

bewind n government; administration
bewoë adj moved; affected
bewolk adj overcast; cloudy
bewonder vb to admire
bewonderaar n admirer
bewondering n admiration
bewoner n inhabitant; resident; occupant; lodger
bewoon vb to inhabit; to live in; to occupy; to reside
bewoording n expression; wording
bewus adj conscious; aware
bewussyn n consciousness
bewusteloos adj unconscious
bewys n proof; evidence; sign; token; vb to prove; to show; to demonstrate
bewysgrond n argument
bewysstuk n document; exhibit
beywer vb to try to do something
bibberasie see **bewerasie**
bibliografie n bibliography
bibliotekaris n librarian
bid vb to pray
bidstond (or **biduur**) n prayer meeting
bied¹ vb to offer
bied² (or **bie**) vb to bid
biefstuk n beefsteak
bieg vb to confess; n confession
bier n beer
bierbrouery n brewery
biesie n rush; reed
bietjie n little bit; moment; adj a few; a little; some; adv rather; somewhat; slightly; **alle —s help** every little helps
bigamie n bigamy
biggel vb to trickle
biljart n billiards; vb to play billiards
biljartstok n billiard cue
biljet n bill; note; ticket
billik vb to approve of; adj just; fair; reasonable
biltong n strips of meat (salted and dried)
bind(e) vb to bind; to fasten; to tie
bindsel n bandage
binne prep in; inside; adv inside; within
binnegaan vb to go in; to enter
binnegoed n intestines; entrails
binne-in adv inside; within

binnekant adv inside
binnekom vb to enter; to come in
binnekort adv shortly; soon
binnekring n inner circle
binneland adv interior; inland
binnenshuis adv indoors
binnensmonds adv under one's breath
binneste adj innermost
binneplaas n courtyard
binnewerk n indoor work
biodiesel n biodiesel
biodiversiteit n biodiversity
bio-etiek n bioethics
biografie n biography
biologie n biology
biometries adj biometric (scanner)
biosensor n biosensor
bioskoop n cinema; bioscope
bisdom n diocese; bishopric
biskop n bishop
biskoplik adj episcopal
bitsig adj sharp; harsh
bitter adj bitter; grievous
blaadjie n sheet (paper)
blaai vb to turn over pages
blaam n blame; taint
blaar¹ n blister
blaar² n leaf (plant)
blaas¹ n bladder
blaas² n bubble
blaas³ vb to blow; to puff; to breathe
blaasbalk n bellows
blad n leaf (book); newspaper; sheet (paper); shoulder blade; leaf (tree)
bladsak n satchel; schoolbag
bladsy n page
bladwyser n bookmark
blaf vb to bark; n bark
blakend adj ardent; glowing; perfect (health)
blaker n candlestick
blameer vb to blame
blanke n white person
blanko adj blank
blas adj dark (complexion); sallow (complexion)
blatjang n chutney; sauce
bleek adj pale; pallid; faint
bleeksiel n (informal) dweeb; geek; nerd
bleeksug n anaemia
bleik vb to bleach

blêr *vb* to bleat
blêrboks *n* beatbox (music)
blêrkas *n* jukebox
bles *n* horse with a blaze; bald head
bleshoender *n* waterfowl
blik[1] *n* tin; *adj* tinned
blik[2] *n* look; glance
bliksem *n* lightning; scoundrel; *vb* to strike with lightning; to flash
bliksemafleier *n* lightning conductor
bliksemsnel *adv* quick as lightning
blimp *n* blimp; nonrigid airship
blind *adj* blind; *adv* blindly
blinddoek *n* blindfold; *vb* to blindfold; to hoodwink
blindederm *n* appendix
blindedermontsteking *n* appendicitis
blindelings *adv* blindly
blindemol *n* blind man's buff
blinding *n* blind; shutter
blindheid *n* blindness
blink *vb* to shine; to glitter; *adj* shiny; glistening; bright
blink idee *n* brainwave
blits *n* lightning; flash
bloed *n* blood
bloedbad *n* massacre; bloodbath
bloeddorstig *adj* bloodthirsty
bloeddruk *n* blood pressure
bloederig *adj* bloody
bloedgeld *n* blood money
bloedhond *n* bloodhound
bloeding *n* haemorrhage; bleeding
bloedjong (*or* **bloedjonk**) *adj* very young
bloedoortapping *n* blood transfusion
bloedrooi *adj* blood-red
bloedsuier *n* leech; bloodsucker; someone who preys on others
bloedtransfusie *n* blood transfusion
bloedverwant *n* (blood) relation; relative
bloedvint *n* boil
bloedwors *n* blood sausage; black pudding
bloei[1] *vb* to bloom; to flower; to flourish; *n* bloom; blossom
bloei[2] *vb* to bleed; to haemorrhage
bloeisel *n* blossom
bloekom *n* eucalyptus; blue gum (tree)
bloekomolie *n* eucalyptus oil

bloemis *n* florist
bloes(e) *n* blouse
blok[1] *n* log; block
blok[2] *vb* to plod; to cram; to swot
blokbespreking *n* block booking
blokbom *n* blockbuster (movie)
blokkade *n* roadblock; blockade
blokkeer *vb* to blockade
blokkiesraaisel *n* crossword puzzle
blom *n* flower; blossom; *vb* to flower; bloom
blombedding *n* flowerbed
blomkelk *n* calyx
blomkool *n* cauliflower
blomkweker *n* florist; nurseryman
blomkwekery *n* nursery
blompot *n* flowerpot
blond *adj* fair; blond
bloos *vb* to blush; to go pink
bloot *adj* naked; bare; mere; *adv* only; merely
bloots *adj* unsaddled; *adv* bareback; without a saddle
blootshoof *adj* bareheaded
blootstel *vb* to expose to; to subject to
blootstelling *n* exposure; subjection
blootsvoet *adj, adv* barefooted; barefoot
blos *n* blush; bloom
blou *n, adj* blue
blousel *adj, n* indigo blue
blousuur *n* prussic acid
bluf *vb* to boast; to brag; *n* boasting; bragging
blus *vb* to extinguish; to put out (fire); to quell (riot)
bly[1] *vb* to remain; to stay; to continue; to live
bly[2] *adj* glad; joyful; pleased
blydskap *n* joy; gladness
blyk *n* token; sign; mark; *vb* to appear; to be evident; to be obvious
blykbaar *adj* apparent; clear; evident; obvious; *adv* apparently; clearly; obviously
blykens *adj* according to
blymoedig *adj* joyful; cheerful
blyspel *n* comedy
bo *prep* above; over; *adv* upstairs; at the top; *adj* upper
bobaadjie *n* coat; jacket

bobaas *n* champion; top dog
bobbejaan *n* baboon
bobbejaanspinnekop *n* baboon spider; tarantula
bobotie *n* curried mincemeat
bod *n* offer; bid
bode *n* messenger
bodem *n* bottom; soil; territory
bodeur *adv* through the top
boedel *n* estate; inheritance; property
boeg *n* bow; prow (ship)
boeglam *adj* fatigued; tired out
boei *vb* to chain; to fetter; to handcuff; to captivate; to fascinate; *n* handcuff
boeiend *adj* interesting; fascinating
boek *n* book; *vb* to enter; to book
boekbinder *n* bookbinder
boekdrukker *n* printer
boekhandel *n* book trade
boekhandelaar *n* bookseller
boekhouer *n* book-keeper
boekrak *n* bookcase; bookshelf
boeksak *n* schoolbag
boekwurm *n* bookworm
boel *n* large quantity; lots
boelie *n* bully
boent *n* upper half; top end
boemelaar *n* vagrant; tramp
boepens *n* paunch
boer *n* farmer; jack (playing cards); knave (playing cards); *vb* to farm; to stay
boer(e)beskuit *n* rusk
boeredisko *n* informal dance
boerplaas *n* farm
boereverneuker *n* conman; cheat
boesel *n* bushel
boesem *n* bosom; breast
boesemvriend *n* bosom friend; close friend
Boesman *n* Bushman
boet[1] *n* brother
boet[2] *vb* to atone for; to make amends for
boete *n* fine; penalty
boetebossie *n* burweed
boetvaardig *adj* penitent
bof *n* den; tee (golf); base (baseball)
bofbal *n* baseball
bog[1] *n* bend; bay
bog[2] *n* trash; bad stuff; fool

boggel *n* hump; hunch
bohaai *n* hubbub; fuss
bok[1] *n* goat; antelope; trestle
bok[2] *n* blunder
bokant *n* upper side; top side; *prep* above
bokbaard *n* goatee beard
bokhaar *n* mohair
bokkem *see* **bokkom**
bokker *n* rascal; rogue
bokkie[1] *n* buggy
bokkie[2] *n* little goat
bokkom (*or* **bokkem**) *n* kippered herring
bokmelk *n* goat's milk
bokooi *n* she-goat
bokram *n* he-goat; billy goat
boks *vb* to box
bokseil *n* tarpaulin
bokser *n* boxer
bokspring *vb* to caper
bol *n* ball; globe; bulb; crown (of hat); *adj* convex
bolip *n* upper lip
bolletjie *n* bun; roll
bolmakiesie *n* somersault
bol(punt)pen *n* ballpoint pen
bolwerk *n* bulwark; earthwork
bom *n* bomb; shell; *vb* to bomb; to shell
bombasties *adj* bombastic
bonatuurlik *adj* supernatural
bond *n* alliance; confederation; league
bondel *n* bundle
bondgenoot *n* ally
bondig *adj* concise; terse
bons *n* bump; bang; thud; *vb* to bounce; to beat
bont[1] *n* fur
bont[2] *adj* spotted; mixed; motley; — **en blou** *adj* black and blue
bonus *n* bonus
boodskap *n* message; errand; alert (SMS)
boog *n* bow; curve; arch
boogskiet *n* archery
booglamp *n* arc lamp
boom[1] *n* tree; beam; bar
boom[2] *n* bottom
boomsingertjie *n* cicada
boomskraap *adj* empty; finished
boomskraapsel *n* dregs

boomstam *n* tree trunk
boon (*or* **boontjie**) *n* bean
boonop *adv* in addition; besides
boonste *adj* upper
boontjie *see* **boon**
boontjieso(e)p *n* bean soup
boontoe *adv* up; upwards
bo-op *adv* at the top
boor *n* drill; auger; gimlet; *vb* to drill; to bore; to pierce
boord[1] *n* orchard
boord[2] *n* border; edge; **aan —** *adv* on board (ship)
boordjie *n* collar
boorgat *n* borehole
boorsuur *n* boracic acid
boortjie *n* drill; gimlet
boos *adj* wicked; evil; angry
boosaardig *adj* malicious
booswig *n* villain; criminal
boot *n* boat
bord *n* plate; board
bordeel *n* brothel
bordpapier *n* cardboard
borduur *vb* to embroider
borg *n* surety; bail; pledge
borgstaan *vb* to become surety; to guarantee
borgtog *n* bail; guarantee
borrel *n* bubble; tot; tipple
borrie *n* turmeric
bors *n* breast; chest; bosom
borsbeeld *n* bust
borsbeen *n* breastbone; sternum
borsel *n* brush; *vb* to brush
borshemp *n* dress shirt
borslap *n* bib; feeder
borsspeld *n* brooch
borsrok *n* vest; singlet; corset
borsvliesontsteking *n* pleurisy
borswering *n* parapet
bos[1] *n* bunch; tuft
bos[2] *n* forest; shrub
bosduif *n* wood pigeon
bose *n* devil
bosluis *n* tick
bossie *n* shrub; copse
bossiestee *n* bush tea
bostaande *adj* above mentioned
boswagter *n* game ranger
bot[1] *vb* to bud; to sprout

bot[2] *adj* blunt; dull
botanie *n* botany
botheid *n* dullness
botoks *n* botox
bots *vb* to collide; to clash
botstil *adj* motionless; quite still
bottel *n* bottle; flask; *vb* to bottle
botter *n* butter
botterblom *n* buttercup
botvier *vb* to give rein to
botweg *adv* straight out; point-blank
bou *vb* to build; to erect
boud *n* leg; buttock; rump
bouer *n* builder
boukuns *n* architecture
boul *vb* to bowl
bouler *n* bowler (cricket)
boustof *n* material (building)
bout *n* bolt; peg; pin
boutiek *adj* boutique (hotel)
bouval *n* ruin
bouvallig *adj* dilapidated
bouvereniging *n* building society
bowendien *adv* moreover; besides
bra *adv* really; very
braaf *adj* good; honest
braai *vb* to roast; to fry in a pan; to grill; to broil (over fire)
braaivleis *n* roast meat; barbecue
braak[1] *vb* to vomit
braak[2] *adj* fallow; **— lê** *vb* to lie fallow
braakland *n* fallow land; undeveloped land that has potential
braakmiddel *n* something that causes vomiting; emetic
braam *n* bramble; blackberry
brak[1] *n* mongrel (dog)
brak[2] *adj* brackish
brakkie *n* small dog
brand *n* fire; mildew; inflammation; *vb* to burn; to scald; to roast (coffee); to brand (cattle)
brandend *adj, adv* ablaze
brandalarm *n* fire alarm
brandarm *adj* very poor
brandbaar *adj* combustible
brandblusser *n* fire extinguisher
brander *n* large wave
brandewyn *n* brandy
brandhout *n* firewood
branding *n* surf; breakers

brandkas *n* safe
brandmaer *adj* skinny
brandmerk *n* brand; stain; stigma
brandnetel *n* stinging nettle
brandplek *n* burn
brandpunt *n* focus
brandslang *n* fire hose
brandslaner *n* firefighter
brandspiritus *n* methylated spirits
brandspuit *n* fire hydrant
brandstapel *n* stake; pile
brandstigting *n* arson
brandstof *n* fuel
brandtrap *n* fire escape
brandwag *n* guard; sentry
brandweer *n* fire brigade
brandweerman *n* firefighter
brandweerwa *n* fire engine
brandwond *n* burn
bredie *n* stew
breëband *n* broadband
breed *adj* broad; wide
breedsprakig *adj* voluble; long-winded
breedte *n* breadth; latitude
breedvoerig *adj* full; detailed
breek *vb* to break; to destroy
breekgoed *n* crockery
breeknuus *n* breaking news
brei[1] *vb* to knit
brei[2] *vb* to cure (skins); to coach
breigoed *n* knitting; knitted things
brein *n* brain; intellect
breinaald *n* knitting needle
breinknoop *n* brain teaser
breiwerk *n* knitting
brekfis *n* breakfast
bres: in die — tree *vb* to defend
breuk *n* breach; rupture; fracture; hernia (bodily); fraction
brief *n* letter; **begeleidende —** *n* covering letter
briefkaart *n* postcard
briefwisseling *n* correspondence
briek *n* brake; **die —e aandraai** *vb* to apply the brakes
bries[1] *n* breeze
bries[2] *vb* to roar; to snort
briesend *adj* roaring; foaming
briewebesteller *n* postman
briewebus *n* letter box; pillar box
briewesak *n* mailbag; postbag

brigade *n* brigade
bril *n* spectacles
brilhuisie *n* spectacle case
briljant *n* cut diamond; *adj* brilliant
brilmaker *n* optician
bring *vb* to bring; to take
Brittanje *n* Britain
broeder *n* brother
broederlik *adj* brotherly; fraternal
broei *vb* to brood; to hatch; to ponder
broeikas *n* hothouse
broeimasjien *n* incubator
broeis *adj* broody
broeisel *n* hatch; brood
broek *n* trousers; (pair of) pants
broekiekouse *n* pantihose; tights
broer *n* brother
broerskind *n* nephew; niece
brokstuk *n* piece; bit; morsel
brom *vb* to growl; to mutter; to grumble
brommer *n* bluebottle
brompot *n* grumbler
bron *n* well; spring; source
brongitis *n* bronchitis
brons *n* bronze
bronstig *adj* on heat; ruttish
bronstyd *n* rutting season
brood *n* bread; loaf
broodmes *n* bread knife
broodnodig *adj* indispensable
broodrolletjie *n* bread roll; bun
broodwinner *n* breadwinner
bros *adj* crisp; brittle; fragile
brou *vb* to brew; to prepare
brug[1] *n* bridge (card game)
brug[2] *n* bridge; parallel bars
bruid *n* bride
bruidegom *n* bridegroom
bruidskat *n* dowry
bruidskoek *n* wedding cake
bruidsmeisie *n* bridesmaid
bruikbaar *adj* useful; serviceable
bruikhuur *n* leasing; lease
bruikleen *n* loan for use; lease
bruilof *n* wedding
bruin *n, adj* brown; bay
bruinvis *n* porpoise
bruis *vb* to foam; to froth
bruismelk *n* milkshake
bruiswyn *n* sparkling wine
brul *vb* to roar; to bellow

brulpadda *n* bullfrog
brunet *adj* brunette
brutaal *adj* impudent; cheeky
bruto *adj* gross; total; — **gewig** *n* gross weight
buffel *n* buffalo; (*informal*) rude person
buffelagtig *adj* rude; churlish
buffet *n* sideboard; bar
buffetete *n* buffet meal
bui *n* shower (rain); mood; humour; whim
buideldier *n* marsupial animal
buierig *adj* whimsical; showery
buig *vb* to bend; to bow; to stoop
buigbaar *adj* bendable; agile (computing)
buigsaam *adj* flexible; pliable
buik *n* belly; stomach; abdomen
buikspreker *n* ventriloquist
buikvlies *n* peritoneum
buikvol *adj* fed up
buil *n* boil; swelling
builepes *n* bubonic plague
buis *n* tube; pipe; duct
buit *n* booty; plunder; prize; *vb* to rob; to plunder
buite *adv* outside; outdoors
buitegebou *n* outbuilding; outhouse
buitekant *adj*, *adv* outside
buiteland *n* foreign country
buitelands *adv* abroad
buitelug *n* open air
buiten *prep* except; without; besides
buitendien *conj* besides; moreover
buitengewoon *adj* extraordinary; peculiar
buitenshuis *adv* out of doors
buitensporig *adj* extravagant; excessive
buitenste *n* exterior; *adj* outermost; exterior
buitepasiënt *n* outpatient
buite seisoen *n* silly season
buitestaander *n* outsider
buitewêreld *n* outer world; outside world
buitmaak *vb* to rob; to seize
buk *vb* to stoop; to bend; to submit
buks *n* small rifle; little person
bul[1] *n* (papal) bull
bul[2] *n* bull; steer
bulder *vb* to roar; to rage; to thunder; to boom (gun)

bulimia *n* bulimia
bulk *vb* to low (cattle); to bellow (cattle)
bullebak *n* surly person; bully
bulletin *n* notice; bulletin
bulletinbord *n* bulletin board
bulsak *n* mattress; feather bed
bult *n* hillock; rising land; hunch
bundel *n* volume; bundle; collection
burg[1] *n* castle; stronghold
burg[2] *n* castrated boar; hog
burgemeester *n* mayor
burger *n* citizen; civilian; burgher
burgerklere *n* civilian clothes
burgeroorlog *n* civil war
burgerreg *n* civil rights; citizenship
burggraaf *n* viscount
buro *n* office; desk; bureau
burokrasie *n* bureaucracy; red tape
bus[1] *n* box; bush (of a wheel)
bus[2] *n* bus
busdiens *n* bus service
busdrywer *n* bus driver
buskaartjie *n* bus ticket
buskruit *n* gunpowder
buurman *n* neighbour
buurt *n* neighbourhood; area; quarter
by[1] *n* bee
by[2] *prep* by; at; near; with; on; to
bybehore *n* accessories
Bybel *n* Bible
bybly *vb* to keep pace with
bybring *vb* to afford; to teach; to instil; to bring forward
bydam *vb* to accost; to buttonhole; to detain in conversation
byderhand *adj* handy; *adv* close by; at hand; on hand
bydra *vb* to contribute
bydrae *n* contribution
byeen *adv* together
byeenkoms *n* meeting; gathering
byekorf *n* beehive
bygaande *adj* enclosed; accompanying
bygeloof *n* superstition
byhou *vb* to keep pace with
bykom *vb* to reach; get at; to recover; to revive; to come up with
bykomend *adj* additional
byl *n* axe; hatchet
bylae *n* appendix
bymekaar *adv* together

byna *adv* almost; nearly
bynaam *n* nickname
bysaak *n* secondary matter
bysiende *adj* short-sighted
bystaan *vb* to help; to assist
bystand *n* assistance; help
bystandmodus *n* standby (mode)
bystandselfmoord *n* assisted suicide
byster *adj, adv* astray
byt *n* bite; *vb* to bite; to snap at
bytel *vb* to add
byval *n* approval; applause

byverdienste *n* sideline; extra earnings
byvoeg *vb* to add; to join
byvoegdiens *n* add-on service
byvoeglik *adj* adjectival; —**e naam-woord** *n* adjective
byvoegsel *n* supplement; appendix
byvoorbeeld *n* for example (e.g.)
bywoner *n* tenant farmer; squatter
bywoon *vb* to attend; to witness; to be present at
bywoord *n* adverb
bywoordelik *adj* adverbial

C

Calvinis *n* Calvinist
CFK *see* **chlorofluoorkoolstof**
chaos *n* chaos; complete disorder; chaos (physics)
chaoties *adj* chaotic
chauvinis *n* chauvinist
chemie *n* chemistry
chemies *adj* chemical
chemiese afskilfering *n* chemical peel
chiropraktisyn *n* chiropractor
chirurg (*or* **sjirurg**) *n* surgeon
chloor *n* chlorine
chlorofluoorkoolstof *n* chlorofluoro-

carbon (CFC)
chloroform *n* chloroform
cholera *n* cholera
ciabatta *n* ciabatta
crêche *n* crêche
Christelik *adj* Christian
Christen *n* Christian
Christendom *n* Christianity
Christus *n* Christ
chronies (*or* **kronies**) *adj* chronic; —**e siekte** *n* chronic illness
chronologies (*or* **kronologies**) *adj* chronological; in order of time

D

daad *n* deed; act; action; **op die —** at once

daagliks *adj* daily

daal *vb* to descend; to fall

daar *adv* there; then; *conj* as; since; because; **—deur** *conj* thereby

daarbo *adv* up there

daarbuite *adv* outside

daarby *prep* in addition; besides

daardie *pron* that; that one

daarheen *adv* there; thither

daarin *adv* therein; in that

daarlaat *vb* not to touch upon a subject

daarmee *adv* therewith; with that

daarna *adv* afterwards

daarnatoe *adv* there; thither

daarom *conj* therefore

daaromtrent *adv* thereabout(s)

daaronder *prep* underneath; *adv* down there

daaroor *adv* about that

daarop *adv* on that; thereupon

daarso *adv* there

daarsonder *adv* without that

daarstel *vb* to bring about; to make

daarteenoor *adj* opposite

daartussen *adv* between that; in between

daaruit *adv* thence; out of that

daarvan *adv* of that; thereof

dadel *n* date

dadelik *adv* immediately; at once

dader *n* perpetrator; doer

dag *n* day; **—!** *sentence substitute* good day! goodbye!

dagblad *n* daily paper

dagboek *n* journal; diary

dagbreek *n* dawn; daybreak

dagga *n* wild hemp; marijuana

dagha *see* **messelkalk**

dagploeg *n* day shift

dagtaak *n* daily task

dagvaar *vb* to summon; to subpoena

dagvaarding *n* summons; subpoena

dahlia *n* dahlia

dak *n* roof

daklig *n* skylight

dakloos *adj* roofless; homeless

dakpan *n* tile

daktuin *n* roof garden

dal *n* valley; dale; glen

dalk *adv* perhaps; maybe

dalkies *adv* before long; presently; perhaps

dam^1 *n* dam; reservoir

dam^2 *vb* to dam (up); to crowd together

dam^3 *vb* to play draughts

damas *n* damask

dambord *n* draughtboard; draughts (game)

dame *n* lady

damp *n* steam; smoke; fume

dampkring *n* atmosphere

damwal *n* dam wall

damspel *n* game of draughts

dan *adv* then; at that time; *conj* after that; with that

danig *adj* full of vitality; lavish; *adv* over-friendly

dank *n* thanks; **—ie!** *sentence substitute* thank you!

dankbaar *adj* thankful; grateful

dans *n* dance; ball; *vb* to dance

danser *n* dancer

dansparty *n* informal dance

dansskoene *n* (dancing) pumps

dapper *adj* brave

darem *conj* in spite of that; nevertheless; all the same; after all

dartel *adj* playful; frisky

das *n* (neck)tie; bow tie

dassie *n* (rock) rabbit

dat *conj* that; in order that

dateer *vb* to date; to mark with a date

datum *n* date

dawer *vb* to rumble; to roar; to thunder

de *definite article* the; **—s** of the

dê! *interj* so there!

debat *n* debate; discussion

debatteer *vb* to debate; to discuss

debet *n* debit

debiet *n* sale; market

debiteer *n* to debit

debiteur *n* debtor

deeg *n* dough
deeglik *adj* sound; solid; *adv* thoroughly; solidly
deel *n* part; portion; share; volume; *vb* to divide; to participate
deelbaar *adj* divisible
deelgenoot *n* partner
deelneem *vb* to take part in; to participate in
deelneming *n* pity; sympathy
deeloproep *n* share call; conference call
deels *adv* partly
deeltal *n* dividend
deelwoord *n* participle
deemoed *n* humility; meekness
deemoedig *adj* humble; meek
deer *vb* to hurt; to harm
deerlik *adj* pitiful; miserable; *adv* badly; profoundly
deernis *n* sympathy; compassion
defek *n* defect; hitch; *adj* damaged; faulty; defective; punctured (tyre)
defensief *adj* defensive
definieer *vb* to define
definisie *n* definition
deftig *adj* stately; grand; fashionable; stylish; (*informal*) posh
degenereer *vb* to degenerate
dein *vb* to swell; to surge; to heave
deining *n* swell (sea); heave
deins *vb* to shrink back from; to recoil from
dek *n* cover; deck (ship); *vb* to cover; to deck; to thatch
deken *n* blanket; quilt
dekgras *n* thatch
dekker *n* thatcher
deklamasie *n* declamation; recitation
deklameer *vb* to declaim; to recite
deklarasie *n* declaration
dekmantel *n* cloak; excuse
dekoreer *vb* to decorate
deksel *n* cover; lid
dekstoel *n* deckchair
delegasie *n* delegation
delegeer *vb* to delegate
deler *n* divider; divisor
delf (*or* **delwe**) *vb* to dig; to mine
delfstof *n* mineral
delwe *see* **delf**
delwer *n* miner; digger

demokraat *n* democrat
demokrasie *n* democracy
demokraties *adj* democratic
demonstrasie *n* demonstration
demonstreer *vb* to demonstrate
demp *vb* to fill up with earth; to extinguish (fire); to put out (fire); to dim (light)
den *n* fir (tree)
denkbaar *adj* imaginable
denkbeeld *n* idea; notion
denkbeeldig *adj* imaginary
denke *n* thought; thinking
denklik *adj* possible; probable
denkprikkel *n* brain teaser
denkwyse *n* opinion
dennebol *n* pine cone; fir cone
denneboom *n* pine tree; fir tree
dennehout *n* pine wood; fir wood
dennenaald *n* pine needle; fir needle
deoksiribonukleïensuur *n* deoxyribonucleic acid (DNA)
departement *n* department; office
deponeer *vb* to deposit
deposito *n* deposit
depressie *n* depression
deputasie *n* deputation
derde *adj*, *n* third
derdepartydekking *n* third party cover (insurance)
derderangs *adj* third-rate; mediocre
dergelik *adj* such; like; similar
derhalwe *adv* therefore; consequently
derm *n* intestine
dertien *n, determiner* thirteen
dertiende *adj, n* thirteenth
dertig *n, determiner* thirty
dertigste *adj, n* thirtieth
Desember *n* December
desgelyks *adv* likewise
desimaal *n* decimal place; *adj* decimal
deskundig *adj* expert
deskundige *n* expert
desnoods *adv* if need be
despoot *n* tyrant; despot
dessert *n* dessert
destyds *adv* at that time; then
detoksifikasie *n* detox
deug *n* virtue; good quality; *vb* to be good for; to be useful; to be fit for purpose

deugdelik *adj* valid; reliable; genuine

deugniet *n* rascal; good-for-nothing

deugsaam *adj* virtuous

deuntjie *n* air; tune; ditty

deur[1] *n* door; gate

deur[2] *prep* through; by; **— en deur** *adv* thoroughly

deurboor *vb* to pierce

deurbring *vb* to waste; to squander (money); to spend

deurbringer *n* spendthrift

deurdat *conj* because; as

deurdring *vb* to penetrate; to permeate

deurdryf *vb* to persist; to push through

deurgaans *adv* commonly; usually

deurgang *n* corridor; passage

deurgestoke kaart *n* put-up job; pre-arranged matter

deurgrond *vb* to see through; to fathom

deurhaal *vb* to scratch out; to delete

deurknop *n* door knob

deurkom *vb* to come through; to pass; to survive

deurkruis *vb* to cross

deurkyk *vb* to skim; to look over

deurlaat *vb* to let through

deurlê *vb* to get bedsores

deurloop[1] *n* arcade

deurloop[2] *vb* to move on; to wear out (shoes); to examine with care

deurlopend *adj* continuous

deurmaak *vb* to go through

deurmekaar *adj* mixed; muddled; insane

deurnat *adj* wet through

deurreis *vb* to journey through

deursien *vb* to see through; to sum up

deursig *n* insight; keen perception

deursigtig *adj* transparent; obvious

deursigtigheid *n* glasnost

deursit *vb* to sit through; to carry through

deurskynend *adj* transparent; translucent; see-through (top)

deurslag *n* boggy ground; decisive factor; carbon copy

deurslaggewend *adj* clear; conclusive (proof)

deurslagpapier *n* carbon paper

deursnee *n* diameter; average; section; **in —** *adv* on average

deursnuffel *vb* to rummage; to ransack

deurstaan *vb* to endure; to pull through (illness); to weather (a storm)

deursteek *vb* to pierce

deurtastend *adj* energetic; thorough; decisive

deurtog *n* passage; right of way

deurtrap *adj* sly; crafty

deurtrek[1] *vb* to pass through; to pull through

deurtrek[2] *vb* to soak with

deurtrokke *adj* saturated with; soaked

deurwagter *n* doorkeeper; porter; janitor

devalueer *vb* to depreciate

diadeem *n* diadem; crown

diagnose *n* diagnosis

diaken *n* deacon

dialek *n* dialect

dialoog *n* dialogue

diamant *n* diamond

diarree *n* diarrhoea

die *definite article* the

dié *determiner* this (these); that (those)

dieet *n* diet

dief *n* thief; burglar

diefagtig *adj* thievish

diefalarm *n* burglar alarm

diefstal *n* robbery; theft

diegene *determiner* those

dien *vb* to serve; to attend

dienaar *n* servant; valet

dienlik *adj* suitable; useful

dienooreenkomstig *adv* accordingly

diens[1] *n* service; duty

diens[2] *n* to service (car)

diensbode *n* domestic servant

diensjaar *n* year of service; financial year

dienskneg *n* manservant

dienstyd *n* term of office

diensvaardig *adj* obliging

dienswillig *adj* obedient

diep *adj* deep; profound

diepsinnig *adj* profound; mysterious

diepte *n* depth

dier *n* animal; brute

dierbaar *adj* dear; precious; loved

dierekliniek *n* veterinary clinic

diereriem *n* zodiac

diereryk *n* animal kingdom

dieretuin *n* zoological garden; zoo
dierkunde *n* zoology
dierlik *adj* brutal; bestial; *adv* like an animal
dieselfde *n* the same
dig[1] *vb* to write poetry
dig[2] *adj* close; dense; compact; near
digby *adv* close by; nearby
digestie *n* digestion
digitaal *adj* digital
digitale oudiouitsending *n* digital audio broadcasting (DAB)
digkuns *n* poetry
digmaat *n* metre; verse
digter *n* poet
digterlik *adj* poetic
dik *adj* thick; fat; stout
dikkop *n* obstinate person; stupid person
diktaat *n* dictation
diktator *n* dictator
diktatuur *n* dictatorship
dikte *n* thickness
diktee *n* dictation
dikteer *vb* to dictate
dikwels *adv* often; frequently
dilemma *n* dilemma
dimensie *n* dimension
diminutief *adj* diminutive
dinamies *adj* dynamic
dinamiet *n* dynamite
dinastie *n* dynasty
dinee *n* dinner
dineer *vb* to dine
ding[1] *n* thing; object; matter
ding[2] *vb* to aspire after; to try for; compete for
dink *vb* to think; to reflect; to consider; to imagine
dinkskrum *n* brainstorm
Dinsdag *n* Tuesday
dip *n* dip; *vb* to dip
diploma *n* diploma; certificate
diplomaat *n* diplomat
diplomaties *adj* diplomatic
direk *adj* prompt; direct; *adv* promptly; at once
direksie *n* direction; management; board of directors
direkteur *n* director; manager
dirigeer *vb* to conduct (orchestra)

dirigent *n* conductor
dis[1] *n* table
dis[2] *contraction* (dit is) it is
diskoers *n* conversation; discourse
diskonto *n* discount
diskresie *n* discretion; judgment
diskussie *n* discussion
diskwalifikasie *n* disqualification
disleksie *n* dyslexia
dispuut *n* dispute; controversy
disselboom *n* beam; shaft
dissertasie *n* dissertation
dissipline *n* discipline
dissiplinêr *adj* disciplinary
dissonant *n* discord
distansie *n* distance
distilleer *vb* to distil
distribusie *n* distribution
distrik *n* district
dit *pron* it; this
dividend *n* dividend
divisie *n* division
DNS *see* deoksiribonukleïensuur
DNS profilering *n* DNA profiling
dobbel *vb* to play dice; to gamble
dobbelsteen *n* die1; cube
dobber *n* float; buoy; *vb* to float; to bob up and down
dodelik *adj* deadly; fatal
dodetol *n* death toll
doeane *n* custom house
doedelsak *n* bagpipe
doek *n* cloth; nappy (baby)
doel *n* aim; purpose; object; goal
doelgemaak *adj* custom made
doelloos *adj* aimless
doellyn *n* goal line
doelmatig *adj* suitable; appropriate
doelpaal *n* goal post
doelskop *n* goal kick
doeltreffend *adj* efficient; effective
doelwitte *npl* goalposts
doen *vb* to do; to make
doenlik *adj* feasible; practicable
doepa *n* charm; talisman; love potion
dof *adj* dull; faint; dim; numb
dog *conj* yet; but; still; however
dogma *n* dogma
dogmaties *adj* dogmatic
dogter *n* daughter; girl
dok *n* dock

dokter *n* doctor; physician; *vb* to nurse; to treat

doktersbenadering *n* bedside manner

dokterstakt *n* bedside manner

doktor *n* doctor (literature, etc.)

doktorsgraad *n* doctor's degree

dokument *n* document

dol *adj* mad; furious; crazy

dolf (*or* **dolwe**) *vb* to dig a trench

dolfyn *n* dolphin

dolhuis *n* bedlam; madhouse; lunatic asylum

dolk *n* dagger

dolleeg *adj* quite empty

dolwe *see* **dolf**

dom[1] *n* dome; cathedral

dom[2] *adj* stupid; dull; dense

domastrant *adj* impudent; cheeky

domein *n* domain; territory

domheid *n* dullness

dominee *n* minister; clergyman

domineer *vb* to dominate; to domineer

domkrag *n* car jack

domp *vb* to dim

dompel *vb* to plunge; to immerse

dompelskoot *n* slam dunk (basketball)

donateur *n* donor; contributor

donder *n* thunder; *vb* to thunder; to boom

donderbui *n* thunderstorm

Donderdag *n* Thursday

donderslag *n* thunderclap

donga *n* donga; gully

dongel *n* dongle (computing)

donker *n* darkness; dark; *adj* dark; dusky; deep

donkerblou *n* dark blue

donkie *n* donkey

dons *n* down; fluff

donserig *adj* downy; fluffy

dood *n* death; demise; *adj* dead; deceased; extinct

doodarm *adj* very poor; stony-broke

dood(s)berig *n* obituary; death notice

doodblaas *vb* to extinguish

doodeenvoudig *adj* quite simple

doodgaan *vb* to die

doodgebore *adj* stillborn

doodgerus *adj* quite at ease; suspecting nothing

doodgewoon *adj* very simple

dood(s)kis *n* coffin

doodmaak *vb* to kill

doodmoeg *adj* tired out; dead beat

doods *adj* deathlike; desolate

doodsangs *n* mortal fear

doodsbleek *adj* deathly pale

doodshoof *n* skull

doodsiek *adj* dangerously ill

doodskleed *n* shroud

doodstill *adj* very quiet; silent as death

doodstraf *n* capital punishment

doodstryd *n* agony

doodswyg *vb* to ignore

doodvonnis *n* death sentence

doof[1] *adj* deaf

doof[2] *vb* to put out; to extinguish

doofstom *adj* deaf and dumb

dooi[1] *vb* to thaw

dooi[2] *adj* dead; deceased

dooie *n* the dead; the deceased

dooier *n* yolk of an egg

dooierig *adj* dead; lifeless; listless; slow

dool *vb* to wander; to roam

doolhof *n* labyrinth; maze

doop *n* christening; baptism; *vb* to baptize; to christen

doopnaam *n* Christian name

doopseel *n* baptismal certificate

doopvont *n* baptismal font

doos *n* box; case

dop *n* shell; husk; pod; drink; *vb* to shell; to pod; to husk; to fail (exam)

dopertjie *n* green pea

dophou *vb* to keep an eye on; to watch

doppie *n* percussion cap; shell; tot (drink)

dor *adj* dry; withered; barren

doring *n* thorn; prickle

doringboom *n* mimosa; thorn tree; acacia

doringdraad *n* barbed wire

dorp *n* village; town

dorpenaar *n* villager

dors[1] *n* thirst; — **wees** *vb* to be thirsty

dors[2] *vb* to thresh (ripe corn)

dorsmasjien *n* threshing machine

dorstig *adj* thirsty

doseer[1] *vb* to teach; to lecture

doseer[2] *vb* to dose (animals)

dosent *n* teacher; lecturer

dosis *n* dose

dosyn *n* dozen
dotjie *n* dot; point
dou *n* dew
douvoordag *adv* before daybreak
douwurm *n* ringworm
dra *vb* to carry; to bear; to wear; to suffer; to endure
draad *n* thread; fibre; wire
draadloos *n* wireless
draadknipper *n* wire-cutters
draadloosstasie *n* broadcasting station
draagbaar[1] *n* bier; stretcher
draagbaar[2] *adj* portable; wearable
draaglik *adj* bearable; tolerable
draagrak *n* carrier (on a car)
draai *n* turn; twist; bend; spin; *vb* to turn; to wind; to revolve; to spin; to trifle; to loiter
draaibank *n* lathe
draaihek *n* turnstile
draaikolk *n* whirlpool
draaiorrel *n* barrel organ
draaitafel *n* turntable
draak *n* dragon
draal *vb* to delay; to linger
draer *n* carrier; pallbearer
draf *vb* to trot; to jog
drafbroekie *n* running shorts
drafsport *n* jogging
drag *n* load; burden; dress; costume
drama *n* drama; play
dramakoningin *n* drama queen
dramatiseer *vb* to dramatize
drang *n* urgency; pressure
drank *n* strong drink; beverage; liquor
dranksugtige *n* alcoholic
drankvergryping *n* binge drinking
drapeer *vb* to drape
drasties *adj* drastic
drawwer *n* jogger
dreef: op — kom *vb* to get into one's stride
dreig *vb* to threaten; to menace
dreigement *n* menace; threat
dreineer *vb* to drain
drek *n* filth; muck; dung; dirt
drempel *n fig* threshold
drenkeling *n* drowning person; drowned person
drentel *vb* to loiter; to saunter

dresseer *vb* to train; to break in (horse)
dreun *vb* to rumble; to roar; to boom
drie *n, determiner* three
driedubbel *adj* treble; triple
driehoek *n* triangle
driehoekig *adj* triangular
driehoeksmeting *n* trigonometry
driekuns *n* hat-trick
driemaal *adv* thrice; three times
driemaandeliks *adv* quarterly
drie-uur *n, adj* three o'clock
drievoet *n* trivet; tripod
drievoudig *adj* triple; treble
drif[1] *n* anger; passion
drif[2] *n* ford
drifkop *n* spitfire; hothead
driftig *adj* passionate; hasty
dril *vb* to drill; to train; to exercise
dring *vb* to press; to urge; to crowd; to push
dringend *adj* urgent; pressing
drink *vb* to drink; to tipple
drinkbaar *adj* drinkable
drinkbeker *n* goblet; cup
droë *vb* to dry; to become dry; *n* dry land
droef *adj* sad; dejected
droef(e)nis *n* sorrow; grief
droefgeestig *adj* gloomy; sad
droefheid *n* sadness; grief
droesem *n* dregs; lees
droewig *adj* sad; gloomy
drom *n* drum; container; *vb* to throng; to flock
dromedaris *n* dromedary
dromer *n* dreamer
drommel *n* devil; wretch
dronk *adj* drunk; intoxicated
dronkaard *n* drunk; drunkard
dronkbestuur *n* drunk driving
dronklap *n* drunkard
droog *vb* to dry; to make dry; *adj* dry; arid; parched
drooglê *vb* to drain
droogmaak *vb* to dry
droogte *n* drought
droom *n* dream; *vb* to dream
droombeeld *n* illusion; vision
droomgesig *n* vision
drop *n* liquorice
dros *vb* to run away; to desert

droster *n* deserter; runaway

druif *n* grape

druip *vb* to drip; to trickle; to fail (exam)

druipnat *adj* soaked; wet through

druis *vb* to swirl; to roar

druiwekonfyt *n* grape jam

druiwestok *n* vine

druk *n* pressure; distress; print; edition; *vb* to press; to print; to push; *adj* busy; lively

drukfout *n* printer's error; misprint; erratum

drukgroep *n* pressure group

drukker *n* printer

drukkery *n* printing works

drukpers *n* printing press

drukkuns *n* the art of printing; typography

drukskrif *n* type; print

drukte *n* work; bustle; stir; fuss

drukwerk *n* printing; printed matter

drumpel *n* threshold; doorstep

drup *vb* to drop; to trickle

druppel *n* drop; *vb* to drip; to drop

dryf (*or* **drywe**) *vb* to float; to swim; to impel; to drive

dryfbaan *n* driving range

dryfsand *n* quicksand

dryfstok *n* driver (golf)

dryfveer *n* motive

dryfys *n* drift ice; ice floe

drywe *see* **dryf**

drywer *n* (train) driver; fanatic

DTP *n* desktop publishing; DTP

dubbel *adv* double; twice

dubbelganger *n* double; doppelganger

dubbelhartig *adj* two-faced; hypocritical

dubbelpad *n* dual carriageway

dubbelpunt *n* colon (:)

dubbelsinnig *adj* ambiguous

duel *n* duel

duet *n* duet

dug *vb* to fear; to dread

dugtig *adj* sound; strong; thorough

duidelik *adj* clear; plain; distinct; legible

duif *n* pigeon; dove

duik[1] *n* dent; cavity; *vb* to dent

duik[2] *vb* to dive; to plunge

duikboot *n* submarine

duiker *n* diver; duiker (antelope)

duiklong *n* aqualung

duim *n* thumb; inch

duimgooi *vb* to hitchhike

duimspyker *n* drawing pin

duimstok *n* foot rule

duin *n* sand dune

duisel *vb* to reel; to become giddy

duiselig *adj* giddy; dizzy

duiseligheid *n* giddiness; dizziness

duisend *n* thousand

duisendpoot *n* millipede; centipede

duister *n* darkness; dark; obscurity; *adj* dark; gloomy; obscure

duisternis *n* darkness

duit *n* farthing; **geen — werd nie** *adj* not worth anything; worthless

duiwel *n* devil

duld *vb* to bear; to endure; to tolerate

dun *adj* thin; slight; sparse

dunk *n* opinion

dupe *n* dupe; victim

duplikaat *n* duplicate

duplo *n* double; **in —** *adv* in duplicate

durf *n* pluck; daring; courage; *vb* to dare; to risk; to venture

dus *conj* so; therefore; thus

duskant *adv* on this side of

dusver: tot — *adv* up to the present; so far

dutjie *n* nap; snooze

duur[1] *n* duration; length; *vb* to last; to continue

duur[2] *adj* dear; expensive

duursaam *adj* durable; lasting

duurte *n* dearness; expensiveness

duvet *n* duvet

dwaal *vb* to roam; to wander; to err

dwaalbegrip *n* error; wrong idea

dwaalleer *n* fallacy; heresy

dwaallig *n* will-o'-the-wisp

dwaalspoor *n* wrong way

dwaas *n* fool; *adj* foolish; silly

dwaasheid *n* folly; stupidity

dwaling *n* error; mistake

dwangarbeid *n* hard labour

dwangbuis *n* straitjacket

dwarrel *vb* to whirl

dwarrelwind (*or* **warrelwind**) *n* whirlwind

dwars *adj* cross; across; contrary

dwarsdeur *adv* right through; straight across

dwarsdrywe *vb* to oppose; to obstruct; to thwart

dwarslêer *n* sleeper (railway)

dwarsoor *adv* athwart; across; right over

dwarsstraat *n* crossroad(s)

dwarstrek *vb* to squabble

dweep *vb* to be fanatical about; to rave about

dweepsiek *adj* fanatical

dweepsug *n* fanaticism

dwelm *n* drug

dwelmafhanklikheid *n* drug addiction

dwelmmiddel *n* drug

dwelmslaaf *n* drug addict

dwelmverslawing *n* drug addiction

dweper *n* fanatic; zealot

dwerg *n* dwarf; pygmy

dwing *vb* to force; to compel; to constrain

dwingeland *n* tyrant

dy[1] *n* thigh

dy[2] *vb* to do well; to prosper

dyk *n* embankment; dam; dyke

dynserig *adj* hazy; misty

E

e-besigheid *n* e-business
e-boek *n* e-book
e-handel *n* e-commerce
e-leser *n* e-reader
E-nommer *n* E-number
e-pos *n* email
eb *n* ebb; ebb tide
ebbehout *n* ebony
edel *adj* noble; generous; precious
Edelagbare *title* Your Worship/Honour
edelgesteente *n* gem; precious stone
edelman *n* nobleman; peer
edelmoedig *adj* generous
edik *n* edict
eed *n* oath; **'n — aflê** *vb* to take an oath
eedafneming *n* administration of an oath
eedbreuk *n* perjury
eekhorinkie *n* squirrel
eelt *n* callus
eeltagtig *adj* horny like a callus
een *n, determiner* one; *pron* someone; one
eend *n* duck
eendag *adv* one day
eenders *adj* similar; the same
eendrag *n* concord; union; unity
eendragtig *adj* united; harmonious
eendvoël *n* wild duck
eenheid *n* unity; unit; unanimity
eenhoring *n* unicorn
eenkeer *adv* once
eenlettergrepig *adj* monosyllabic
eenlopend *adj* single; unmarried
eenmaal *adv* once; one day
eenparig *adj* unanimous
eenrigtingstraat *n* one-way street
eens *adv* once; of one accord
eensaam *adj* solitary; lonely
eensellig *adj* unicellular
eenselwig *adj* reserved; solitary
eensgesind *adj* unanimous
eensklaps *adv* suddenly; all of a sudden
eenspoorstelsel *n* monorail system
eenstemmig *adj* unanimous
eensydig *adj* one-sided; partial

eentonig *adj* monotonous
eentonigheid *n* monotony
eenuur *n, adj* one o'clock
eenvormig *adj* uniform
eenvoud *n* simplicity
eenvoudig *adj* simple; plain
eer[1] *n* honour; reputation; homage; *vb* to honour; to respect
eer[2] *conj* before
eer[3] *adv* sooner; rather
eerbaar *adj* honest; honourable; respectable
eerbetoon (*or* **eerbewys**) *n* homage
eerbied *n* respect; regard
eerbiedig *adj* respectful; reverent; *vb* to respect; to revere
eerder *adv* sooner; before
eergierig *adj* ambitious
eergister *n* the day before yesterday
eerlik *adj* honest; fair; *adv* honestly; fairly
eerlikheid *n* honesty
eerloos *adj* infamous
eers *adv* firstly; primarily; formerly; at first
eersdaags *adv* one of these days
eersgeboortereg *n* birthright
eersgeborene *adj* first-born
eersgenoemde *n* the first mentioned; the former
eerskomende *adj* next; following
eerste *adj* first; prime (minister)
eerstehulp *n* first aid
eersteklas *adj* first class
eerstens *adv* firstly; in the first place
eersug *n* ambition
eersugtig *adj* ambitious
eertyds *adv* formerly
eerwaarde *adj* reverend
eerwaardig *adj* time-honoured; venerable
eet *vb* to eat
eetafwyking *n* eating disorder
eetbaar *adj* edible; eatable
eetkamer *n* dining room
eetlepel *n* tablespoon
eetlus *n* appetite

eetmaal *n* meal
eetstaking *n* hunger strike
eetversteuring *n* eating disorder
eetware *n* food; victuals
eeu *n* century; age
eeufees *n* centenary
effe *adj* even; level; smooth; flat
effek *n* effect; result
effekte *npl* stocks; shares; bonds; property
effektebeurs *n* stock exchange
effektehandelaar *n* stockbroker
effektief *adj* effective; real
effen *vb* to make even; to level
effenheid *n* evenness; smoothness
effens *adv* slightly; just a little
eg[1] *adj* legitimate; authentic; real
eg[2] *n* wedlock; marriage
eg[3] *vb to* harrow
egalig *adj* smooth; uniform
egbreker *n* adulterer
egbreuk *n* adultery
eggenoot *n* husband; spouse
eggenote *n* wife; spouse
eggo *n* echo
ego *n* ego; self
egoïs *n* egotist
egskeiding *n* divorce
egtelik *adj* conjugal; matrimonial
egter *conj* however; yet
egtheid *n* genuineness; authenticity
egverbintenis *n* marriage
eie *adj* own; natural; peculiar; innate; familiar
eiebaat *n* selfishness; egoism
eiegeregtig *adj* self-righteous
eien *vb* to recognize; to appropriate
eienaam *n* proper name
eienaar *n* owner; proprietor
eienaardig *adj* peculiar
eienares *n* owner; proprietress
eiendom *n* estate; property; possessions
eienskap *n* quality; nature; property
eier *n* egg
eierdop *n* eggshell
eierkelkie *n* egg cup
eierklitser *n* eggbeater
eierkokertjie *n* egg timer; hourglass
eierstok *n* ovary
eiervrug *n* brinjal; eggplant
eiesinnig *adj* wilful; headstrong

eievuur *n* friendly fire
eiewys *adj* conceited; cocky
eikeboom *n* oak (tree)
eiland *n* island; isle
eina *adj* poor; weak; painful; *adv* poorly; painfully; *interj* ow! oh!
einddoel *n* aim; goal
einde *n* end; termination
eindelik *adj* final; last; *adv* finally; at last
eindeloos *adj* endless
eindig *vb* to come to an end; to finish; to stop
eindpaal *n* goal; limit; endgame
eindpunt *n* end; terminus
einste *adj* same
eintlik *adj* real; proper; *adv* really; truly
eis *n* demand; claim; *vb* to demand; to claim
eiser *n* claimant; plaintiff
ek *pers pron* I
eklips *n* eclipse
ekologie *n* ecology
ekonomie *n* economy
ekonomies *adj* economical
eksamen *n* examination
eksaminator *n* examiner
eksamineer *vb* to examine
eksekuteur *n* executor
eksemplaar *n* copy; sample
eksentriek *adj* eccentric; odd
eksepsie *n* exception
ekserp *n* extract; excerpt
eksklusief *adj* exclusive; *adv* exclusively
ekskursie *n* outing
ekskuseer *vb* to excuse; to pardon
ekskuus *n* apology; excuse; **—!** *interj* pardon me! sorry!
ekspatriasie *n* expatriation
ekspatrieer *vb* to expatriate
ekspedisie *n* expedition
eksperiment *n* experiment
ekspert *n* expert
ekspliseer *vb* to make clear; to explain
eksploitasie *n* exploitation
eksploiteer *vb* to exploit
eksponent *n* exponent
eksport *n* exportation
eksporteer *vb* to export (computing)
ekspres *adv* expressly; on purpose
eksprestrein *n* express train
ekstase *n* ecstasy

ekstern *adj* external
ekstra *adj* extra; additional; *adv* specially
ekstrak *n* extract
ekstra suiwer *adj* extra virgin (oil)
ekwator *n* equator
ekwiteit *n* equity
ekwivalent *adj* equivalent
eland *n* eland
elasties *adj* elastic
elastisiteit *n* elasticity
elders *adv* elsewhere
elegant *adj* elegant; stylish
eleksie *n* election
elektries *adj* electric; electrical; *adv* electrically
elektrifikasie *n* electrification
elektrifiseer *vb* to electrify
elektrisiën *n* electrician
elektrisiteit *n* electricity
elektronies *adj* electronic
elementêr *adj* elementary; simple
elf[1] *n* elf; fairy
elf[2] *n, determiner* eleven
elfde *adj, n* eleventh
elfuur *n, adj* eleven o'clock
elikser *n* elixir
elimineer *vb* to eliminate
elk *pron* every; each
elkeen *pron* everyone; everybody
ellende *n* misery
ellendig *adj* miserable; wretched
ellipties *adj* elliptical; oval
elmboog *n* elbow
els[1] *n* alder (tree)
els[2] *n* awl
emalje *n* enamel
embleem *n* emblem
emblematies *adj* emblematic
embrio *n* embryo
emigrant *n* emigrant
emigrasie *n* emigration
emigreer *vb* to emigrate
emmer *n* pail; bucket
emosikoon *n* emoticon
empatie-engel *n* agony aunt
en *conj* and
end *n* end; close; conclusion
endjie *n* bit; piece; short distance
endosseer *vb* to endorse
enduit *adv* right to the end

ene *pron* one; *adj* a certain
enemale: **ten —** *adv* entirely; completely
energie *n* energy
eng *adj* narrow; tight
engel *n* angel
engelagtig *adj* angelic
Engelse sout (*or* **Epsom-sout**) *n* Epsom salts
Engelssprekend *adj* English-speaking
enghartig *adj* narrow-minded
engte *n* narrowness; strait; pass
enig *adj* only; sole; any; unique
enigeen *pron* anyone
enigheid *n* loneliness; **in my —** *adv* by myself
enigiets *pron* anything
enigsins *adv* slightly; somewhat
enigste *adj* only; sole
enjin *n* engine
enkel[1] *n* ankle
enkel[2] *adj* single; *adv* only; solely; merely
enkelbed *n* single bed
enorm *adj* enormous; (*informal*) ginormous
ensiklopedie *n* encyclopedia
ent[1] *n* graft; vaccination; inoculation; *vb* to graft; vaccinate; to inoculate
ent[2] *n* end; length; piece; way
enterovirus *n* enterovirus
entjie *n* bit; piece; short distance
entoesiasties *adj* enthusiastic
entrée *n* entry; entrance
entstof *n* serum; vaccine
envelop *n* envelope
epidemie *n* epidemic
epikuris *n* epicure
epilepsie *n* epilepsy
epilepties *adj* epileptic
episode *n* episode
Epsom-sout *see* **Engelse sout**
erbarming *n* pity; compassion
erbarmlik *adj* pitiful; miserable
erd *n* earth; clay
erdepot *n* earthenware pot
erdewerk *n* pottery; crockery; earthenware
erdvark *see* **aardvark**
erdwurm *n* earthworm
ere *n* honour

erediens *n* public worship
eregraad *n* honorary degree
erelid *n* honorary member
êrens *adv* somewhere
ereplek *n* place of honour
erewag *n* guard of honour
erf[1] *n* plot; stand; premises
erf[2] (*or* **erwe**) *vb* to inherit
erfenis *n* inheritance; heritage
erfgenaam *n* heir
erflik *adj* hereditary
erfporsie *n* share of inheritance
erfreg *n* law of succession; hereditary law
erfstuk *n* heirloom
erg *adj* ill; bad; *adv* very badly; extremely; *vb* to annoy; to be vexed
erger *vb* to annoy; to be vexed
erger *adj* worse
ergerlik *adj* offensive; annoying
ergernis *n* offence; annoyance
erken *vb* to acknowledge; to admit; to own up
erkentlik *adj* grateful; thankful
erns *n* earnestness; seriousness
ernstig *adj* serious; grave
ertappel *see* **aartappel**
ertappelmoer *see* **aartappelmoer**
ertjie *n* pea
ertjiedop *n* pea pod
erts *n* ore
ervaar *vb* to experience
ervare *adj* experienced; skilled
ervaring *n* experience
erwe *see* **erf**[2]
es[1] *n* fireplace
es[2] *n* ash (tree)
es[3] *n* sharp turn
esel[1] *n* ass; donkey; mule; dunce
esel[2] *n* easel
eskader *n* squadron (navy, airforce)
eskort *n* guard; escort
essensieel *adj* essential
esteties *adj* aesthetic(al)
ete *n* food; meal

etenstyd *n* meal time; dinner time
eter[1] *n* eater
eter[2] *n* ether
etiek *n* ethics
eties *adj* ethical
etiket[1] *n* etiquette
etiket[2] *n* label
etimologie *n* etymology
etmaaldiens *n* twenty-four-hour service
etlike *adj* several
etnies *adj* ethnic
etniese suiwering *n* ethnic cleansing
ets *n* etching; *vb* to etch
etter *n* pus; *vb* to suppurate
EU *see* **Europese Unie**
euro *n* euro
Europese Unie *n* European Union (EU)
euroskeptikus *n* eurosceptic
eurosone *n* eurozone
euwel *n* evil; fault
evangelie *n* gospel
evangelies *adj* evangelic(al)
evangelis *n* evangelist
evolusie *n* evolution
ewe *adj* equal; even; *adv* equally; quite; just as
ewebeeld *n* likeness; image; the very picture
eweknie *n* match; equal
ewemens *n* fellow man
ewenaar[1] *n* equator
ewenaar[2] *vb* to equal; to be a match for
ewenaaste *n* fellow man; neighbour
eweneens *adv* similarly
eweredig *adj* proportionate; commensurate
ewe(n)wel *conj* however; yet
eweveel *adv* just as much
ewewig *n* equilibrium; balance
ewewydig *adj* parallel
ewig *adj* eternal; everlasting
ewigheid *n* eternity

F

faal *vb* to fail
faam *n* fame; reputation
fabel *n* fable; fiction
fabelleer *n* mythology
fabriek *n* factory; works
fabrieksmerk *n* trademark
fabrieksprys *n* cost price
fabriekswerker *n* factory worker
fabrikaat *n* make; brand; fabric
fabrikant *n* manufacturer; maker
fabrikasie *n* manufacture
fabriseer *vb* to manufacture
fakkel *n* torch; flare
faks *n* fax; *vb* to fax
faktor *n* factor
faktuur *n* invoice; bill
fakultatief *adj* optional
fakulteit *n* faculty
familie *n* family; relations
familiekring *n* family circle
familiêr *adj* familiar; intimate
fanatiek *adj* fanatic(al)
fanatikus *n* fanatic
fantaseer *vb* to fancy; to imagine
fantasie *n* phantasy; imagination
fantasties *adj* fantastic
farmaseuties *adj* pharmaceutical
fase *n* phase
faset *n* facet
fataal *adj* fatal
fatalis *n* fatalist
fataliteit *n* fatality
fatsoen *n* cut; shape; fashion; workmanship; manners
fatsoenlik *adj* respectable; decent
Februarie *n* February
federasie *n* federation
fee *n* fairy
feeks *n* vixen; shrew
fees *n* feast; festival; treat
feesdag *n* feast day
feesmaal *n* banquet
feestelik *adj* festive
feesvier *vb* to celebrate; to feast
feil *n* fault; mistake; *vb* to make a mistake; to err
feilbaar *adj* fallible

feilloos *adj* faultless
feit *n* fact
feitlik *adv* really; truly; as a matter of fact; virtually
fel *adj* fierce; violent; sharp
felisiteer *vb* to congratulate
feniks *n* phoenix
ferm *adj* firm; resolute
ferweel *n* velvet; corduroy; cords (trousers)
festiwiteit *n* festivity
fiasko *n* fiasco; failure
fier *adj* proud; high-spirited
fiets *n* bicycle; bike; *vb* to cycle
fietsryer *n* cyclist; biker
figuratief *adj* figurative
figuur *n* figure; form; shape
figuurlik *adj* figurative; *adv* figuratively
fiks *adj* quick; energetic; healthy
fikseer *vb* to stare
fiksie *n* fiction
fiktief *adj* fictitious; imaginary
filantroop *n* philanthropist
filantropie *n* philanthropy
filantropies *adj* philanthropic
filatelie *n* philately
fillet *n* fillet (meat, fish)
film *n* film; *vb* to film
film noir *n* film noir
filmster *n* film star
filologie *n* philology
filosofeer *vb* to philosophize
filosofie *n* philosophy
filosoof *n* philosopher
filter *n* filter; percolator
filtreer *vb* to filter; to percolate
finaal *adj* final; total
finale *n* finale; final
Financial Times-effektebeursindeks *n* Financial Times Stock Exchange Index (FTSE)
finansieel *adj* financial; monetary
finansier *n* financier; *vb* to finance
finansiewese *n* finance
firma *n* firm
firmablad *n* house magazine
firmamotor *n* company car**

fisant *n* pheasant
fisiek *n* physique; *adj* physical
fisika *n* physics
fisiologie *n* physiology
fisioterapie *n* physiotherapy
fisionomie *n* physiognomy
fiskaal *n* fiscal; bailiff; shrike; butcher-bird
fladder *vb* to flutter; to flap
flambou *n* torch
flamink *n* flamingo
flank *n* flank; side
flap *n* flap; bishopbird; widowbird; iris (flower); *vb* to flap
flapteks *n* blurb (book)
flard *n* rag
flater *n* blunder; mistake
flegmaties *adj* phlegmatic
fleksie *n* inflection
flenelet *n* flannelette
flennie *n* flannel
flensie *n* thin pancake
flenter[1] *n* rag; tatter; **aan —s** *adv* in rags; in tatters; in pieces
flenter[2] *vb* to stroll; to wander about
flerrie *n* flirt
fles *n* bottle; flask
flets *adj* faded; pale
fleur *n* bloom; prime
fliek *n* cinema; bioscope
flikflooi *vb* to flatte; to coax
flikker *vb* to glitter; to sparkle; to flicker; to twinkle
flikkers *n* playful skips and leaps
flink *adj* robust; spirited; energetic; lively; *adv* energetically; soundly; vigorously
flits *n* flash; *vb* to flash
flitslig *n* flashlight; torch
floers *n* crepe
flonker *vb* to sparkle
flonkering *n* sparkling; twinkling
flora *n* flora
floreer *vb* to flourish; to prosper
florerend *adj* flourishing; prosperous
floryn *n* florin
flou *adj* faint; weak; dim; silly
flouhartig *adj* faint-hearted
flouiteit *n* silly joke; foolish talk
flous *vb* to take in; to cheat
floute *n* faint; fainting fit

fluister *vb* to whisper
fluisterend *adv* in a whisper; under one's breath
fluistering *n* whisper; whispering
fluit *n* flute; whistle; *vb* to whistle; to play the flute
fluitspeler *n* flute player; flautist
fluks *adj* capable; hardworking; quick; *adv* lively; quickly
fluoresseerlamp *n* fluorescent lamp
flus *adv* a moment ago; just now (past)
flussies *adv* directly; in a moment; just now (future)
fluweel *n* velvet
foefies *npl* bells and whistles
foeilelik *adj* hideous; ugly
foelie *n* (tin)foil
foeter *vb* to beat; to thrash; to bother; to trouble
foei tog! (*or* **foeitog!**) *interj* shame!
fok! *interj* (*vulgar*) fuck!
fokus *n* focus
folio *n* folio
folter *vb* to torture
fondament *n* foundation; bottom
fonds *n* fund; funds
fonetiek *n* phonetics
fontein *n* fountain; spring
fooi *n* tip; gratuity; *vb* to tip
foon *n* phone
fop *vb* to hoax; to cheat; to trick
foppos *n* spoof mail
fopprys *n* booby prize
fopspeen *n* baby's dummy
fopwebwerf *n* spoof website
forel *n* trout
formaat *n* size; shape
formaliteit *n* formality; matter of form
formeel *adj* formal
formeer *vb* to form; to shape
formule *n* formula
formuleer *vb* to formulate
fors *adj* robust; violent
forseer *vb* to force; to compel
fort *n* fort; fortress
fortuin *n* luck; fortune; wealth
fosfaat *n* phosphate
fosfor *n* phosphorus
fossiel *n* fossil
foto *n* photo(graph)
fotoalbum *n* photograph album

fotogenies *adj* photogenic
fotograaf *n* photographer
fotografeer *vb* to take a photograph
fotostateer *vb* to photocopy
fout *n* fault; mistake; error
foutief *adj* incorrect; faulty
fraai *adj* pretty; handsome; nice
fraiing *n* fringe
framboos *n* raspberry
frank *adj* frank; free
frankeer *vb* to prepay postage; to frank; to stamp
frase *n* phrase
fratse *npl* tricks; pranks
fregat *n* frigate
Freudiaanse *adj* Freudian
frikkadel *n* minced meatball; patty; rissole
frikkadelbroodjie *n* hamburger
fris *adj* fresh; strong; well; stout
friseer *vb* to frizz; to curl
frok *n* vest

fromage frais *n* fromage frais
frommel *vb* to crumple; to crease; to rumple
frons *n* frown; scowl; *vb* to frown; to scowl
frontlinie *n* front line
fuif *n* celebration; spree; *vb* to party; to have a good time
fundi *n* (*informal*) boffin
fungeer *vb* to act as; to officiate
funksie *n* function; capacity
fuoreseerverf *n* fluorescent paint
fusie *n* fusion
fut *n* spirit; mettle; verve
futiel *adj* futile; frivolous
futiliteit *n* futility
fyn *adj* fine; thin; delicate; nice; devout
fyngevoelig *adj* sensitive; delicate
fynkam *n* fine comb; *vb* to search thoroughly
fynproewer *n* connoisseur; gourmet
fyt *n* whitlow

G

G-kol *n* G-spot
gaaf *adj* sound; perfect; good; undamaged; nice
gaan *vb* to go; to move; to walk
gaap *n* yawn; yawning; *vb* to gape; to yawn
gaar *adj* done; sufficiently cooked
gaas *n* gauze; netting
gade *n* spouse
gadeslaan *vb* to watch
gaffel *n* pitchfork
gal *n* gall; bile; spleen
galagtig *adj* bilious
galant *adj* polite; courteous
galanterie *n* courtesy; gallantry
galei *n* galley
galery *n* gallery
galg *n* gallows
galjoen *n* galleon (ship)
gallerig *adj* bilious
galm *n* peal; boom; *vb* to peal; to sound
galop *n* gallop; *vb* to gallop
galopdraf *n* canter
galsteen *n* gallstone
galsterig *adj* rancid; strong
galvanies *adj* galvanic
galvaniseer *vb* to galvanize
gang *n* gait; walk; way; alley; passage
gangbaar *adj* current; passable
gangmaker *n* pacemaker
gans[1] *n* goose
gans[2] *adj* whole; entire; *adv* wholly; entirely; **— en gaar nie** *adv* not at all; by no means
gapend *adj* gaping
garage *n* garage
garandeer *vb* to guarantee
garansie *n* guarantee; security
garde *n* guard;bodyguard
gare (*or* **garing**) *n* thread; yarn; cotton
garingklip *n* asbestos
garnaal *n* shrimp
garneer *vb* to trim; garnish
garnisoen *n* garrison
gars *n* barley
gas[1] *n* gas
gas[2] *n* guest; visitor
gasel *n* gazelle

gasfabriek *n* gasworks
gasheer *n* host
gasie *n* pay; wages
gaslig *n* gaslight
gasmaal *n* feast; banquet
gasmasker *n* gas mask; respirator
gasspreker *n* guest speaker
gasvrou *n* hostess
gasvry *adj* hospitable
gat[1] *n* hole; aperture; gap
gat[2] *n* anus
Gautrein-snelspooraansluitpunt *n* Gautrain Rapid Rail Link
gawe *n* gift; bounty; talent
gawerig *adj* good; nice
gayikoon *n* gay icon
geaardheid *n* disposition; nature
geanimeer *adj* animated
gearm *adv* arm-in-arm
gebaar *n* gesture
gebabbel *n* babble; talk; gossip
gebak *n* pastry; cake; *adj* baked
gebal *adj* clenched
gebarespel *n* pantomime
gebaretaal *n* sign language
gebed *n* prayer
gebedel *n* begging
gebeente *npl* bones
gebergte *n* mountain range
gebeur *vb* to happen; to occur
gebeurlik *adj* possible
gebeurtenis *n* event; occurrence
gebied[1] *n* territory; department; jurisdiction; sphere
gebied[2] *vb* to command; to order
gebiedend *adj* commanding; compelling
gebieder *n* ruler; master
gebiedsoorlog *n* turf war (gangs)
gebit *n* set of teeth; bit (harness)
geblaf *n* bark; barking
geblêr *n* bleat; bleating
gebod *n* commandment; precept; decree; banns (marriage)
gebonde *adj* bound
geboorte *n* birth
geboortebeperking *n* birth control
geboortebewys *n* birth certificate

geboortedag *n* birthday
geboortegrond *n* native soil
geboorteland *n* native land
geboortereg *n* birthright
gebore *adj* born
gebou *n* building
gebraai *adj* broiled; grilled; roasted
gebrabbel *n* gibberish
gebrand *adj* burnt
gebreek *adj* broken
gebrek *n* want; fault; defect; lack
gebrekkig *adj* defective; faulty
gebreklik *adj* disabled; infirm
gebroke *adj* broken
gebruik *n* use; habit; custom; practice;
  adj used; second-hand; *vb* to use; to
  employ
gebruiklik *adj* usual; customary
gebrul *adj* roaring; howling
gebukkend *adj* stooping; crouching
gebulder *n* rumble; rumbling; boom;
  booming
gedaagde *n* defendant; respondent
gedaan *adj* done; finished
gedaante *n* shape; form; figure
gedaanteverwisseling *n* transformation; metamorphosis
gedagte *n* thought; opinion; idea
gedagteloos *adj* thoughtless
gedagtenis *n* memory; remembrance;
  keepsake; memento
gedagtig *adj* mindful of
gedeelte *n* part; portion; share
gedeeltelik *adj* partial; *adv* partially;
  partly
gedelegeerde *n* delegate
gedenk *vb* to remember
gedenkdag *n* anniversary
gedenkpenning *n* commemorative
  medal
gedenkplaat *n* plaque
gedenkskrif *n* memoir
gedenkteken *n* monument; memorial
gedenkwaardig *adj* memorable
gedienstig *adj* serviceable; officious
gediertes *npl* animals; insects; creatures; vermin
gedig *n* poem
geding *n* lawsuit; quarrel
gedoe *n* bustle; noise; fuss
gedoente *n* fuss; noise; ado

gedoog *vb* to permit; to tolerate
gedra *vb* to behave; to act
gedrag *n* behaviour; demeanour; conduct
gedrang *n* crowd; crush, squash
gedrog *n* monster
gedruis *n* rumbling; noise
gedug *adj* formidable; severe; strong
geduld *n* patience; forbearance
geduldig *adj* patient
gedurende *prep* during
gedurig *adj* constant; continual; *adv*
  constantly; continually
gedwee *adj* docile; submissive; meek
gedwonge *adj* forced; compulsory
gedy *vb* to prosper; to thrive
gee *vb* to give; to produce; to deal (playing cards)
geel *n, adj* yellow
geelbruin *n* tawny
geelkoper *n* brass
geelslang *n* cobra
geelsug *n* jaundice
geelvink *n* yellow weaverbird
geen (*or* **g'n**) *determiner* no; none; not
  one; — **Deurgang** No Thoroughfare
geeneen *pron* no one; not one
geensins *adv* not at all; by no means
gees *n* spirit; ghost; wit; mind; vein
geesdodend *adj* monotonous; dull
geesdrif *n* enthusiasm
geesdriftig *adj* enthusiastic
geeskrag *n* energy; strength of mind
geestelik *adj* spiritual; intellectual
geestelike *n* clergyman; minister
geesteskind *n* brainchild
geesteswêreld *n* spirit world
geestig *adj* witty; smart
geestigheid *n* wit; humour
geesvermoëns *n* mental faculties; intellectual power
geesvervoering *n* ecstasy; trance
geesverwant *n* kindred spirit
gegewens *n* data; information
gegiggel *n* giggling
gegoed *adj* well-to-do; wealthy
gegoedheid *n* wealth; affluence
gegoogel *vb* to Google
gegote *n* cast iron
gegradueerde *n* graduate
gegrond *adj* well-founded; sound; legitimate

gehalte *n* standard; quality; grade
gehard *adj* hardened
geheel *n* whole; entirety; *adj* complete; entire; *adv* completely; entirely; **— en al** altogether; quite
geheelonthouer *n* teetotaller
geheg aan *adj* fond of; attached to
gehegtheid *n* fondness; devotion
geheim *n* mystery; secret; *adj* secret; private; hidden
geheimhouding *n* secrecy; concealment
geheimsinnig *adj* mysterious
geheue *n* memory; remembrance
geheuestafie *n* dongle (computing)
gehoor *n* hearing; audience
gehoorsaam *vb* to obey
gehoorsaam *adj* obedient; *vb* to obey; to be obedient
gehoorsaamheid *n* obedience
gehoorsaal *n* auditorium
gehoorafstand *n* hearing distance; earshot
gehug *n* small village; hamlet
gehuud *adj* married
geil *adj* fertile; luxuriant; showing profuse growth
geïllustreer *adj* illustrated
geitjie *n* lizard; gecko
gejaag *n* hurry; racing; *adj* hurried
gejuig *n* rejoicing; cheering
gek *n* fool; madman; lunatic; *adj* foolish; mad; silly; *vb* to joke; jest; **— na** *adj* fond of
gekekkel *n* cackling
gekerm *n* moaning; groaning; lamenting
gekheid *n* nonsense; folly
gekibbel *n* bickering; quarrelling
gekielie *n* tickle; tickling
geklee *adj* dressed
geklets *n* twaddle; rubbish
gekleurd *adj* coloured
geknoei *n* bungling; plotting
gekompliseer *adj* complicated
gekrenk *adj* hurt; offended
gekriewel *n* tickling; itching
gekskeer *vb* to joke; to jest
gekunsteld *adj* affected; formal
gelaat *n* face; countenance
gelaatskleur *n* complexion
gelaatstrek *n* feature
gelag[1] *n* laughter

gelag[2] *n* score; bill
gelang: na — van *adj* according to; in proportion to
gelas[1] *vb* to order; to instruct
gelas[2] *adj* joined; welded
gelate *adj* resigned
gelatien *n* gelatine
geld[1] *n* money; cash
geld[2] *vb* to apply; to prevail; to concern; to regard
geldbelegging *n* investment
geldboete *adj* fine
geldelik *adj* monetary; pecuniary; financial
geldgierig *adj* covetous; avaricious
geldig *adj* valid; binding
geldkas *n* safe (valuables)
geldmagnaat *n* tycoon
geldskieter *n* moneylender
geldstuk *n* coin
geldtrommel *n* cash box
gelede *adv* since; past; ago
geleë *adj* situated; convenient
geleed *adj* articulate; articulated
geleentheid *n* opportunity; occasion
geleer *adj* learned; scholarly
geleerde *n* scholar
geleibrief *n* waybill; permit
geleide *n* escort; guard
geleidelik *adj* gradual; *adv* gradually
gelief *adj* beloved; dear
geliefde *n* sweetheart; beloved
geliefkoosde *n* favourite
geliewe *adv* please
geliniëer(d) *adj* ruled (paper)
gelofte *n* vow; promise
geloof *n* belief; faith; creed; religion; *vb* to believe; to trust; to think; to suppose
geloofbaar *adj* believable; credible
geloofbaarheid *n* credibility
geloofsbelydenis *n* creed; credo; formal statement of beliefs
geloofsbriewe *n* credentials
geloofwaardig *adj* trustworthy; reliable
geloofwaardigheid *n* reliability; credibility
gelowig *adj* faithful; believing
geluid *n* sound; noise
geluk *n* joy; happiness; (good) luck; prosperity; *vb* to succeed; to prosper

gelukkig *adj* happy; fortunate; lucky
geluksalig *adj* blessed
geluksaligheid *n* bliss; blessedness
gelukskind *n* fortune's favourite
gelukslag *n* piece of good luck; fluke
geluksoeker *n* adventurer
gelukwens *vb* to wish good luck; to communicate pleasure or praise
gelukwensing *n* congratulations
gelyk *adj* even; equal; similar; *adv* equally; similarly
gelykbenig *adj* isosceles (triangle)
gelyke *n* equal; the like; peer; match
gelykenis *n* likeness; resemblance; parable
gelykheid *n* equality; similarity
gelykluidend *adj* exact; homologous
gelykmaak *vb* to equalize; to level; to raze to the ground
gelykmatig *adj* regular; uniform
gelyksoortig *adj* similar; homogeneous
gelykstelling *n* equalization
gelyksydig *adj* equilateral (triangle)
gelyktydig *adj* simultaneous; *adv* simultaneously
gelykvloeiend *adj* regular
gelykvloers *adj* on the ground floor; on the same floor; plain; homely
gelykvormig *adj* uniform; regular
gemaak *adj* ready-made; affected
gemaaktheid *n* affectation
gemaal *n* consort; spouse
gemaalde vleis *n* mince; minced meat
gemak *n* ease; comfort; leisure
gemaklik *adj* easy; comfortable
gemalin *n* spouse; consort
gemanier *adj* well-mannered
gemasker *adj* masked
gematig *adj* moderate; temperate
gematigdheid *n* moderation; temperateness
gemeen *adj* common; ordinary; vulgar
gemeenplaas *adj* commonplace
gemeensaam *adj* familiar
gemeenskap *n* community
gemeenskaplik *adj* common; joint
gemeente *n* parish; congregation
gemeng *adj* mixed
gemeubileer *adj* furnished
gemiddeld *adj* average; mean; medium
gemiddelde *n* mean; average

gemis *n* want; neediness; destitution; lack
gemmer *n* ginger
gemoed *n* heart; mind; feelings
gemoedelik *adj* kind-hearted; good-natured
gemoedsaandoening *n* emotion; excitement
gemoedstemming *n* frame of mind; mood
gemoedstoestand *n* state of mind; disposition
gemoedstryd *n* mental struggle
gemoeid *adj* concerned
gemors *n* mess; bungling
gemorspos *n* spam (emails)
gemsbok *n* gemsbok antelope
genaakbaar *adj* accessible; approachable
genaamd *adj* named; called
genade *n* mercy; grace; clemency
genadebrood *n* charity
genadeslag *n* knockout blow; death blow
genadig *adj* gracious; merciful
genant *n* namesake
geneë *adj* inclined; disposed
geneentheid *n* inclination; disposition; attachment
genees *vb* to cure; to heal; to recover
geneesheer *n* physician; doctor
geneeskrag *n* healing power
geneeskragtig *adj* medicinal
geneeskruid *n* drug
geneeskunde *n* medical science
geneeskundig *adj* medical
geneesmiddel *n* medicine; remedy
geneig *adj* inclined; prone to
geneigdheid *n* inclination; propensity
generaal *n* general
generasie *n* generation
generasiegaping *n* generation gap
genesing *n* recovery; cure; closure
geniaal *adj* gifted; brilliant
genialiteit *n* genius; giftedness
genie *n* genius
geniepsig *adj* underhand; false; bullying
geniet *vb* to enjoy
genoeë *n* pleasure; delight; satisfaction
genoeg *adj* enough; sufficient; *adv* enough
genoeglik *adj* agreeable; pleasant

genoegsaam *adj* sufficient
genoem *adj* named; called; above mentioned
genootskap *n* society; company
genot *n* enjoyment; pleasure
genre *n* kind; genre
geoefen(d) *adj* trained; drilled; well-versed
geografie *n* geography
geologie *n* geology
geometrie *n* geometry
geoorloof *adj* allowed; lawful
gepaard *adv* in pairs
gepantser *adj* armoured
gepas *adj* becoming; proper; fit
gepeins *n* meditation; reflection
gepeupel *n* mob; rabble
gepeuter *adj* fumbling; fiddling; worrying
gepraat *n* talk; talking
geprikkel *adj* irritated
geraak[1] *vb* to attain; to get
geraak[2] *adj* offended
geraamte *n* skeleton; outline
geraas *n* din; noise
geraasbestryding *n* noise abatement
geredelik *adv* readily
gereed *adj* ready; done; prepared; — **maak** *vb* to prepare; to get ready
gereedskap *n* tools; instruments; utensils; gear (as in hiking)
gereeld *adj* regular; orderly; fixed; consecutive
gereformeer *adj* reformed
gereg[1] *n* dish; course
gereg[2] *n* court of justice; tribunal
geregsaal *n* law court
geregsbode *n* messenger of the court
geregshof *n* court of justice
geregtig *adj* entitled; authorized
geregtigheid *n* justice
gerek *adj* tedious; long-winded; stretched
gerf *n* sheaf
gerief *n* comfort; convenience; *vb* to accommodate; to oblige
gerieflik *adj* comfortable; convenient
geriffel *adj* fluted; corrugated
gerimpel *adj* wrinkled
gering *adj* small; slight; inferior
geringskat *vb* to slight; to disparage; to undervalue
geritsel *n* rustle; rustling

geroep *n* calling; shouting; cries
geroggel *n* gurgling; rattling; death rattle
gerug *n* report; rumour
geruime *adj* considerable
geruis *n* rustling; murmur(ing); babbling
geruit *adj* checked (material); checkered
gerus *adj* safe; quiet; *adv* safely
gerusstel *vb* to quiet; to soothe
gesaaide *n* crop
gesaaides *npl* crops
gesag *n* authority; power
gesaghebber *n* commander
gesagvoerder *n* commander
gesamentlik *adj* complete; united; joint; *adv* together; jointly; collectively
gesang *n* hymn; song
gesanik *n* bother(ation); nagging
gesant *n* ambassador; envoy; minister
geseën *adj* blessed; fortunate
gesegde *n* expression; saying; predicate
geseglik *adj* docile; obedient
gésel *n* lash; whip; *vb* to flog; to whip
gesèl *n* companion
gesellig *adj* pleasant; sociable; snug; cosy
geselligheid *n* conviviality; cosiness
gesels *vb* to chat; to talk
geselskamer *n* chatroom
geselskap *n* company; society; party
geselslyn *n* chatline
geset *adj* corpulent; stout
gesien *adj* esteemed
gesig *n* sight; view; face; vision
gesiggie *n* smiley
gesigsbedrog *n* optical illusion
gesigseinder *n* horizon
gesigskundige *n* optician
gesigspunt *n* aspect; point of view
gesin *n* immediate family; nuclear family; household
gesind *adj* disposed; inclined
gesindheid *n* disposition; opinion; conviction
gesinskrediet *n* family credit
geskakeer *adj* chequered
geskater *n* loud laughter
geskatte bedrag *n* ball park
geskeide *adj* divorced; separated
geskenk *n* gift; present
geskied *vb* to happen; to occur
geskiedenis *n* history; story; affair
geskik *adj* fit; suitable; proper; capable

geskil *n* dispute; quarrel
geskilpunt *n* matter at issue
geskool *adj* trained; skilled
geskree(u) *n* screaming; screams; cries; crying; shouting
geskrif *n* writing; document
geskut *n* artillery; guns
geslag *n* gender; sex; generation; kind; race; family
geslagkunde *n* genealogy
geslag(s)boom *n* family tree; pedigree
geslagsdele *n* genitals
geslagsgaping *n* gender gap
geslagsorgane *n* genitals
geslag(s)register *n* genealogical table
geslagte *adj* slaughtered; butchered
geslepe *adj* cunning; sly
geslote *adj* closed; shut
gesmeek *n* entreaty; coaxing; supplication
gesmoord *adj* suppressed
gesond *adj* healthy; well; sound; wholesome; **—e verstand** *n* common sense
gesondheid *n* health
gesondheidsleer *n* hygiene
gesout *adj* salted; pickled; cured
gespanne *adj* strained; stretched
gespe *n* buckle; clasp
gespier *adj* muscular
gespikkel *adj* speckled; spotted
gesplete lip *n* harelip
gespoor *adj* spurred
gespot *n* mockery
gesprek *n* conversation; talking
gespuis *n* rabble; riffraff; scum
gestadig *adj* regular; steady; constant
gestalte *n* figure; stature
gesteente *n* stone; boulder
gestel *n* constitution; system
gesteldheid *n* condition; nature; character
gestem *adj* disposed; tuned
gesternte *n* stars; constellation
gestewel *adj* booted
gestig *n* institution; establishment
gestoelte *n* seat; chair
gestrand *adj* stranded
gestrem(d) *adj* challenged (physically, etc.)
gesuis *n* buzzing; tinkling; singing (in the ears)

gesukkel *n* botheration; trouble
geswel *n* swelling; tumour; growth
geswets *n* bragging; swearing
geswolle *adj* bombastic; stilted; swollen (river)
geswore *adj* sworn
getal *n* number
getalm *n* loitering; delay
getob *n* worry; bother; toiling
getroos *vb* to submit; to endure; to bear
getroue *adj* faithful; true; reliable
getroud *adj* married
getuie *n* witness
getuienis *n* evidence; testimony
getuig *vb* to testify; to give evidence; to bear witness
getuigskrif *n* testimonial; reference
gety *n* tide
getygolf *n* tidal wave
geur *n* fragrance; scent; odour; *vb* to smell
geurig *adj* fragrant
geut *n* gutter; drain; sewer
gevaar *n* danger; peril; risk; hazard
gevaarlik *adj* dangerous; perilous; risky; hazardous
geval[1] *n* case; instance; matter
geval[2] *vb* to like; to suit
gevange *adj* imprisoned; captive; caught
gevangene *n* prisoner
gevangeneming *n* arrest; capture
gevangenis *n* prison; goal
gevange(n)skap *n* imprisonment; captivity
gevat *adj* clever; smart; seized
geveg *n* fight; battle
geveins *adj* false; pretended; hypocritical
geveinsde *n* hypocrite
gevestig *adj* established; fixed
gevlek *adj* spotted; speckled
gevloek *n* swearing; cursing
gevoel *n* feeling; sentiment; *vb* to feel; to understand
gevoelens *npl* feelings; sentiments
gevoelig *adj* tender; sensitive
gevoelloos *adj* callous; insensible
gevoerde *adj* lined (clothes); fed (animals)
gevolg *n* consequence; result; followers
gevolglik *adv* consequently
gevolgtrekking *n* conclusion
gevolmagtigde *n* proxy
gevorder *adj* advanced

gewaag *adj* risky; hazardous
gewaande *adj* feigned; pretended
gewaarmerkte *adj* hallmarked; certified
gewaarwording *n* feeling; sensation; perception
gewag *n* mention; — **maak van** *vb* to make mention of
gewapen *adj* armed
gewapende beton *n* reinforced concrete
gewas *n* growth; harvest; crop
geween *n* weeping; wailing
geweer *n* gun; rifle; weapon
geweermaker *n* gunsmith
gewel *n* front; gable
geweld *n* force; violence
gewelddadig *adj* violent
geweldig *adj* violent; powerful; enormous
gewelf *n* dome; vault
gewens *adj* desirable; desired
gewer *n* donor
gewerskaf *n* bustle
gewerwelde *adj* vertebrate (animals)
gewese *adj* late; retired; former; ex
geweste *n* region; area
gewete *n* conscience
gewete(n)loos *adj* unscrupulous
gewetenswroeging *n* remorse
gewettig *adj* legitimate; entitled
gewig *n* weight; importance; **soortlike** — *n* specific gravity
gewigtig *adj* very important; weighty
gewild *adj* desired; popular
gewillig *adj* willing; ready
gewin *n* profit; gain
gewis *adj* sure; certain; *adv* certainly; surely
gewoel *n* crowd; bustle
gewoon *adj* common; ordinary; usual
gewoond: — **aan** *adj* accustomed to; used to
gewoonlik *adv* usually; generally
gewoonte *n* habit; custom
gewrig *n* joint; wrist
gewyde *adj* consecrated; sacred
ghi *n* ghee
ghitaar (*or* **kitaar**) *n* guitar
gholf *n* golf
gholfbaan *n* golf course; golf links
gholfstok *n* golf club
ghong *n* gong
ghries *n* grease

gids *n* guide; directory
gidshond *n* guide dog
gier *n* fancy; whim; yell; scream; *vb* to scream
gierig *adj* miserly; stingy; greedy
gierigaard *n* miser
gierigheid *n* avarice; miserliness; greed
giet *vb* to pour (liquids); to cast (iron)
gieter *n* watering can
gietery *n* foundry
gietyster *n* cast iron
gif *n* poison; venom
gifstof *n* toxin
giftig *adj* poisonous
gigagreep *n* gigabyte
giggel *vb* to giggle; to snigger
gil *n* scream; yell; *vb* to scream; to shriek; to yell
gilde *n* guild
gimnas *n* gymnast
gimnasium *n* gymnasium
gimnastiek *n* gymnastics
ginekoloog *n* gynaecologist; obstetrician; (*informal*) ob-gyn
gips *n* gypsum; plaster of Paris
giraf *see* **kameelperd**
gis[1] *n* yeast; *vb* to rise; to ferment
gis[2] *n* guess; conjecture; *vb* to guess; to conjecture
gissing *n* conjecture; guess; estimation
gister *n* yesterday
gisteraand *n* last night
gisting *n* fermentation
git *n* jet (jewellery)
gits! *interj* oh dear!
gitswart *n, adj* jet-black
glasoog *n* glass eye; artificial eye
glasplafon *n* glass ceiling (work)
glad *adj* smooth; slippery; sleek; *adv* altogether; smoothly; quite
glans *n* gloss; lustre; brilliancy; *vb* to gleam; to polish
glansryk *adj* radiant; brilliant
glas *n* glass; tumbler
glasblaser *n* glassblower
glasuur *n* glaze (pottery); enamel (teeth); icing (cakes); *vb* to glaze; to ice
gletser *n* glacier
gleuf *n* groove; slit
glibberig *adj* slippery
glimdrag *n* safety clothing

glimlag *n* smile; *vb* to smile
glimverf *n* fluorescent paint
glimwurm *n* glow-worm
glinster *vb* to twinkle; to glitter; to sparkle
glip *vb* to slip
glipperig *adj* slippery
glisemiese indeks *n* glyc(a)emic index
glisemiese lading *n* glyc(a)emic load
gliserien *n* glycerine
glo[1] *vb* to believe; to trust; to think; to suppose
glo[2] *adv* evidently; seemingly
globaal *adj* rough; general; *adv* roughly; generally
globale *adj* global
globaleposisioneringstelsel *n* global positioning system (GPS)
gloed *n* glow; flame; ardour
gloei *vb* to glow; to be red-hot
gloeiend *adj* glowing; red-hot
gloeilamp *n* light bulb
glorie *n* fame; glory; delight
glos *n* note; comment
glos(sarium) *n* gloss(ary)
gluur *vb* to peep; to spy; to peer
gly *vb* to slide; to slip
glyskaal *n* sliding scale
g'n *adj, pron* none; not one; *adv* no; not; never
gnu (*or* **wildebees**) *n* wildebees; gnu
God *n* God; **— sy dank!** *interj* thank God!
god *n* god; idol
goddelik *adj* divine
goddeloos *adj* godless; wicked
godedrank *n* nectar
godeleer *n* mythology
godgeleerdheid *n* theology
godheid *n* divinity; deity
godin *n* goddess
godloënaar *n* atheist
godsakker *n* graveyard; cemetery
godsalig *adj* pious; godly
godsdiens *n* religion; divine worship
godsdiensoefening *n* divine service
godsdienstig *adj* religious; devout
godslastering *n* blasphemy
godspraak *n* prophecy
godsvrug *n* devotion; piety
godvresend *adj* God-fearing; pious

goed[1] *n* good; goodness; *adj* good; good-natured; kind; right; *adv* well; correctly; properly
goed[2] *n* goods; property; stuff
goedaardig *adj* good-natured
goederetrein *n* goods train
goedgelowig *adj* trusting; credulous; gullible
goedgunstig *adj* kind
goedhartig *adj* kind-hearted
goedheid *n* goodness; kindness
goedig *adj* good-natured; kind
goedjies *npl* things; goods
goedkeur *vb* to approve; to confirm; to pass
goedkoop *adj* cheap
goedmaak *vb* to make amends for; to make up for
goedskiks *adv* willingly
goedsmoeds *adv* cheerfully; deliberately
goedvind *vb* to approve of
goeiedag! *sentence substitute* good day! goodbye!
goeiemiddag! *sentence substitute* good afternoon!
goeiemôre! *sentence substitute* good morning!
goeienaand! *sentence substitute* good evening!
goeienag! *sentence substitute* good night!
goël *vb* to juggle; to conjure
goëlaar *n* juggler; conjuror; magician
goëlery *n* juggling; conjuring
goeters *npl* things; small fry
goewernante *n* governess
goewerneur *n* governor
gogga *n* insect; vermin
golf[1] *n* wave; billow; *vb* to wave; to undulate
golf[2] *n* gulf; bay
golfbreker *n* breakwater
golwend *adj* wavy; rolling; surging
gom *n* gum; glue
gomboom *n* gum tree
gomlastiek *n* rubber; elastic
gons *vb* to buzz; to hum
Google *n* Google
gooi *vb* to throw; to fling
goor *adj* nasty
gord *n* band; belt; girdle; *vb* to gird; to put on a belt

gordel n belt; girdle; zone; — **vas!** interj buckle up!
gordyn n curtain; blind
gorilla n gorilla
gorrel n throat; larynx; vb to gargle
gort n groats; barley
goties adj goth (music, culture)
gou adj quick; rapid; swift; adv quickly; soon; swiftly
goud n gold
goudblad n gold leaf; gold foil
gouderts n gold ore
goudief n sneak thief; pickpocket
goudmyn n gold mine
goudrif n gold reef
goudsmid n goldsmith
goue adj golden
gou-gou adv quickly
gousblom n marigold
GPS see **globaleposisioneringstelsel**
graad n degree; rank; grade
graaf[1] n count; earl
graaf[2] n spade
graag adv gladly; eagerly
graagte n eagerness; **met —** adv with pleasure
graan n grain; corn
graanskuur n granary
graat n fishbone
gradedag n graduation day
gradeplegtigheid n graduation ceremony
gradering n graduation
gradueer vb to graduate
graf n grave; sepulchre
grafiek n graph
grafies adj graphic
grafkelder n vault; crypt
grafskrif n epitaph
grafsteen n tombstone
grag n canal; ditch; moat
gram n gram
grammatika n grammar
grammatikale adj grammatical
granaat n grenade; shell; pomegranate; garnet
granaatsteen n garnet
graniet n granite
grap n jest; joke; (informal) gag; fun
grapmaker n joker; wag
grappenderwys adj amusing; funny

gras n grass
grasetend adj herbivorous
grashalm n blade of grass
grasie n grace; pardon
grasieus adj graceful; gracious
grasland n grassland
grasperk n lawn; green
grasvlakte n grassy plain; prairie
gratifikasie n gratuity; tip
gratis adj gratis; free
gratis openbare vervoer n zero-fare public transport
graveer vb to engrave
graveerder n engraver
graveur n engraver
gravin n countess
gravure n engraving
grawe vb to dig; to burrow; to excavate
grawer n digger
greep n grasp; clutch
greinhout n white pinewood
greintjie n grain; scrap
grenadella n granadilla; passion fruit
grendel n bolt; bar
grens[1] n border; boundary; limit; vb to border on; to adjoin
grens[2] vb to cry; to weep; to howl
grensbalie n crybaby
grensbewoner n borderer
grenshou n boundary (cricket)
grensloos adj boundless; unlimited; unbounded
grenssetel n marginal seat (politics)
gretig adj eager; greedy
grief n sorrow; grievance; vb to grieve; to hurt
griep n influenza; flu
grieselig adj creepy; nasty
griesmeel n semolina
griffier n registrar; recorder
gril[1] n whim; fancy
gril[2] n shudder; shiver; vb to shudder; to shiver
grillerig adj creepy
grimeer n make-up
grimmig adj angry; furious
grinnik vb to sneer; to grin
grint n gravel; grit
grip n furrow; ditch
groef n groove
groei n growth; vb to grow; to increase

groeikrag *n* vitality; vigour
groen *n* green; greenery *adj* green; fresh; unripe
groenblywend *adj* evergreen
groenboontjies *n* green beans
groente *npl* vegetables; greens
groentjie *n* freshman; fresher; novice
groep *n* group; cluster
groepkontraktering *n* crowd sourcing
groepeer *vb* to group; to classify
groet *n* greeting; *vb* to salute; to greet; to shake hands
groete (*or* **groetnis**) *n* regards; greetings
grof *adj* coarse; rude
grofbrood (*or* **growwebrood**) *n* coarse brown bread
grom *vb* to grumble
grond *n* ground; earth; soil; bottom; foundation; reason; —**-tot-lug missiel** *n* ground-to-air missile; *vb* to base; to ground; to found
grondbeginsel *n* principle
grondbelasting *n* land tax
grondbesitter *n* proprietor; landowner
grondboontjie *n* peanut
grondeienaar *n* proprietor; landowner
grondgebied *n* territory
grondig *adj* thorough; sound
grondlêer *n* founder
grondopvulling *n* landfill
grondslag *n* foundation; basis; first layer (paint)
grondstof *n* element; raw material
grondtoon *n* keynote
grondverf *n* first coat (paint)
grondves *vb* to found
grondwet *n* constitution
groot *adj* great; large; tall; full-grown; important
grootbek *n* boaster
grootboek *n* ledger
groothandel *n* wholesale trade
grootheid *n* greatness; largeness; magnitude
grootjie *n* great-grandparent
grootliks *adv* greatly; to a great extent
grootmaak *vb* to rear; to bring up

grootmens *n* adult; grown-up
grootmoeder *n* grandmother
grootmoedig *adj* magnanimous
grootouers *n* grandparents
grootpad *n* main road
grootpraat *vb* to brag; to boast
groots *adj* grand; proud
grootskaals *adv* on a large scale
grootskeeps *adj* princely; grand; *adv* on a large scale
grootspraak *n* boasting; bragging; bravado
grootte *n* bigness; extent; greatness; magnitude
grootvader *n* grandfather
grootwordfliek *n* coming-of-age movie
gros *n* gross; mass; greater part
grot *n* cave; grotto
grotendeels *adv* chiefly; largely; mainly
grou[1] *n, adj* grey
grou[2] *n* growl; snarl
growwebrood *see* **grofbrood**
gruis *n* gravel; grit
grungemusiek *n* grunge (music)
gruwel *n* horror; abomination; crime
gruweldaad *n* atrocity; crime
gruwelik *adj* atrocious; mischievous; naughty
gryns *n* grimace; grin; sneer; *vb* to grin; to sneer
gryp *vb* to catch; to clutch; to seize; to snatch
grypdief *n* pickpocket; sneak thief
grys *n, adj* grey
grysaard *n* old man; greybeard
guerillaoorlog *n* guerrilla warfare
gul *adj* liberal; cordial; generous
gulp *n* fly (trousers)
gulsig *adj* gluttonous; greedy
gun *vb* to grant; to allow
guns *n* favour; kindness; support
gunsteling *adj* favourite
gunstig *adj* favourable
gunter *adv* yonder; over there
gure weer *n* foul weather
guur *adj* bleak; raw; cold
gyselaar *n* hostage

H

haagdoring *n* hawthorn
haai[1] *n* shark
haai![2] *interj* hi!
haak *n* hook; clasp; *vb* to hook
haakplek *n* difficulty; obstruction
haaks *adj* square; right-angled
haakspeld *n* safety pin
haal *n* pull; dash; stroke; stride; *vb* to fetch; to get; to pull; to draw; to catch
haal-en-betaal *n* cash-and-carry
haan *n* cock; rooster; cock (gun); hammer (gun)
haar[1] *n* hair
haar[2] *adj* right
haar[3] *poss pron* her
haarborsel *n* hairbrush
haard *n* fireplace; fireside; hearth
haarfyn *adj* very fine; as fine as hair; minute
haarkam *n* (hair)comb
haarklowery *n* hairsplitting; quibbling
haarnaald *n* hairpin
haarom *adv* clockwise; to the right
haarsny *n* haircut
haarsnyer *n* hairdresser; barber
haarwasmiddel *n* shampoo
haarwurm *n* threadworm
haas[1] *n* hare
haas[2] *n* haste; hurry; speed; *vb* to hurry; to make haste
haas[3] *adv* almost; nearly
haastig *adj* quick; hurried; hasty
haat *n* hatred; hate; *vb* to hate; to detest
haatdraend *adj* resentful; vindictive
haatlik *adj* hateful; malicious; detestable
hael *n* hail; shot (guns)
haelbui *n* hailstorm; shower of hail
haelgeweer *n* shotgun
haelkorrel *n* hailstone; small pellet of shot
haelstorm *n* hailstorm
haglik *adj* critical; risky; awful
hak[1] *n* heel; hock
hak[2] *vb* to chop; to cut; to mince
haker *n* hooker (rugby)
hakie *n* bracket; small hook
hakkel *vb* to stammer; to stutter

half *prefix* half; semi
halfedel *adj* semiprecious
halfdonker *n, adj* semi-darkness; twilight
halfdood *adj* half-dead
halfedel *adj* semiprecious
halfedelstene *npl* semiprecious stones
halfhartig *adj* half-hearted; diffident
halfklaar *adj* half-done
halfmaan *n* half-moon; crescent
halfpad *adj, adv* halfway
halfrond *n* hemisphere
halfslyt *adj* second-hand; partly worn
halfvol *adj* half-full
halfwas *adj* half-grown
halfweg *adj, adv* halfway
halm *n* blade; stalk
hals *n* neck
halsband *n* collar; necklace
hals-oor-kop *adv* head over heels; completely
halsstarrig *adj* headstrong; obstinate
halt! *interj* halt! stop!
halter *n* halter
halveer *vb* to halve; to bisect
ham *n* ham
hamburger *n* hamburger
hamer *n* hammer
hamerkop *n* head of a hammer; hammerhead (bird, shark)
hand *n* hand
handboeie *n* handcuffs
handboek *n* manual; handbook; textbook
handdoek *n* towel
handdruk *n* handshake
handearbeid *n* manual labour
handel *n* trade; commerce; business; *vb* to act; to deal; to trade; to carry on a business
handelaar *n* trader; merchant; dealer
handelbaar *adj* manageable; docile
handeling *n* action; act; transaction; handling
handelsaak *n* business; commercial concern
handelsbank *n* commercial bank

handelsmerk *n* trade mark
handelsonderneming *n* commercial venture
handelsreg *n* commercial law
handelwyse *n* method; course of action
handeviervoet *adv* on all fours
handewerk *n* handiwork; handwork
handgeklap *n* applause
handgemeen: — **raak** *vb* to exchange blows
handhaaf *vb* to maintain; to uphold; to assert (oneself)
handig *adj* handy; clever
handlanger *n* assistant; handyman
handleiding *n* textbook; manual
handperd *n* led horse
handsak *n* handbag
handskoen *n* glove
handskrif *n* manuscript; handwriting
handtekening *n* signature
handvatsel *n* handle; hilt
handvol *n* handful
handwerk *n* trade; handwork; needlework
handwerkman *n* artisan
hanebalk *n* rafter
hanepoot *n* a variety of muscat grape
hang *n* slope; *vb* to hang; to suspend
hangbrug *n* suspension bridge
hangkas *n* wardrobe
hangmat *n* hammock
hangslot *n* padlock
hans *adv* cheekily
hansdier *n* hand-fed animal; orphan animal
hanskalf *n* hand-fed calf; orphan calf
hanslam *n* pet lamb; orphan lamb
hanswors *n* clown; buffoon
hanteer *vb* to handle; to manage; to operate
hap *n* bite; morsel; *vb* to bite; to snap
haper *vb* to ail; to be impeded; to falter
hard *adj* hard; tough; loud; stern; quick; difficult
hardepad *n* main road; hard labour
harder *n* herring
hardhandig *adj* rough; rude
hardhoofdig *adj* stubborn; headstrong
hardhorig *adj* hard of hearing
hardkoppig *adj* obstinate; stubborn

hardloop *vb* to run; to race; to hurry
hardlywig *adj* constipated
hardnekkig *adj* obstinate
hardop *adv; adj* aloud
hardvogtig *adj* hard; unfeeling
harem *n* harem
harig *adj* hairy
haring *n* herring
hark *n* rake; *vb* to rake
harlekyn *n* buffoon
harmonie *n* harmony
harmonika *n* accordion; harmonica
harmonium *n* harmonium; reed organ
harnas *n* armour
harp *n* harp
harpoen *n* harpoon
harpuis *n* resin
harsings *n* brain
harsingskudding *n* concussion
harsingvliesontsteking *n* meningitis
harspan *n* skull; head
hart *n* heart
hartaanval *n* heart attack
hartbees *n* hartebeest (antelope)
hartbeeshuisie *n* wattle and daub hut
hartbrekend *adj* heartbreaking; heart-rending
hartebreker *n* lady's man
harteloos *adj* heartless
hartens *npl* hearts (playing cards)
hartewens *n* dearest wish
hartjie *n* darling (little heart)
hartklop *n* heartbeat
hartkwaal *n* heart disease
hartlam *n* darling; sweetheart
hartlik *adj* sincere; cordial
hartomleiding *n* heart bypass
hartoorplanting *n* heart transplant
hartroerend *adj* touching; pathetic; heart-rending
hartseer *n* grief; sorrow; *adj* heartsore; sad
hartseerhoekie *n* agony column
hartstog *n* passion
hartstogtelik *adj* passionate
hartversaking *n* heart failure; cardiac arrest
hartverskeurend *adj* heart-rending
hartvormig *adj* heart-shaped
harwar *n* squabble; bickering
hasie *n* baby rabbit

hawe[1] *n* goods; property; fortune
hawe[2] *n* harbour; port
hawehoof *n* pier; jetty
hawer *n* oats
hawergerf *n* oat sheaf
hè![1] *interj* ah!
hê[2] *vb* to have; to possess
hebsug *n* greed
hebsugtig *adj* greedy
hede *n* the present; this day; *adv* today; at present
hedendaags *adj* modern; present-day; *adv* nowadays; at present
heel[1] *vb* to heal; to cure
heel[2] *adj* whole; sound; *adv* very; quite
heelal *n* universe
heeldag *adv* all day; the whole day; frequently
heelhuids *adj* unscathed
heelkunde *n* the art of healing
heeltyds *adj, adv* full-time
heeltemal *adv* altogether; quite
heelwat *pron* a good many; a lot
heen *adv* away; towards
heen-en-weertjie *n* a moment; a return journey
heengaan *vb* to depart; to go away
heenkome *n* refuge; escape
heenreis *n* outward journey; forward journey
Heer[1] *n* the Lord; God
heer[2] *n* gentleman; lord
herlaai *vb* reboot a computer
heerlik *adj* delightful; delicious: grand; glorious
heers *vb* to rule; to govern; to be in vogue; to prevail
heerskappy *n* dominion; authority; power
heerssug *n* ambition; lust for power
hees *adj* hoarse; husky
heet[1] *vb* to call; to name; to be called after
heet[2] *adj* hot; burning
heethoofdig *adj* hot-headed
hef *n* handle; hilt
hef *vb* to raise; to levy
hefboom *n* lever
heffing *n* levy; surtax
heftig *adj* violent; vehement
heg *vb* to attach; to fasten; *adj* firm; strong

hegpleister *n* sticking plaster
hegtenis *n* custody; detention; **in — neem** *vb* to take into custody
heiblom *n* heather
heide *n* heath; moor
heiden *adj* pagan
heil *n* welfare; good; benefit
heildronk *n* toast
heilig *vb* to consecrate; to sanctify; *adj* holy; sacred
heiligdom *n* sanctuary
heilige *n* saint
heiligheid *n* holiness; sanctity
heiligskennis *n* sacrilege
heiligverklaring *n* canonization
heilsaam *adj* beneficial; salutary; wholesome
heimlik *adj* secret; clandestine
heimwee *n* homesickness
heinde en ver *adv* far and wide
heining *n* fence; hedge
hek *n* gate; railing; bar; boom
hekel[1] *n* dislike; aversion
hekel[2] *vb* to criticize; to heckle
hekel[3] *vb* to crochet
hekeldig *n* satire
hekelpen *n* crochet hook
hekelwerk *n* crocheting
hekgeld *n* gate money; admission
heks *n* witch; vixen
heksejag *n* witch-hunt;
heksewerk *n* witchcraft; difficult job
hekstormer *n* gate-crasher
hektaar *n* hectare
hel[1] *n* hell
hel[2] *vb* to lean; slant; slope
held *n* hero
heldedaad *n* heroic deed
heldemoed *n* heroism
helder *adj* clear; bright; lucid; serene; **— oordag** *adv* in broad daylight
helderheid *n* brightness
heldersiende *n* clairvoyant
heldhaftig *adj* heroic; brave
heldin *n* heroine
heler *n* healer
helfte *n* half
helikopter *n* helicopter
heliblad *n* helipad
hellend *adj* sloping; inclined
helling *vb* slope; incline

helm *n* helm
helmet *n* helmet
help *vb* to help; to assist; to aid
hemel *n* heaven; sky; canopy
hemeling *n* angel; celestial being
hemelliggaam *n* celestial body
hemels *adj* heavenly; celestial
hemelsblou *n, adj* sky blue; azure
hemelswil: om —! *interj* for goodness' sake!
hemeltergend *adj* shameful; atrocious
hemisfeer *n* hemisphere
hemp *n* shirt
hempsmou *n* shirtsleeve
hen *n* hen
hengelaar *n* angler
hengelgerei *n* fishing tackle
hennep *n* hemp
heraldies *adj* heraldic
herberg *n* inn; public house; pub; tavern; hotel; *vb* to shelter; to accommodate
herbergsaam *adj* hospitable
herbore *adj* reborn
herbou *n* rebuilding; reconstruction; *vb* to rebuild; to build again
herdenk *vb* to commemorate
herder *n* shepherd
herderin *n* shepherdess
herderlik *adj* pastoral
herdruk *n* reprint; new edition; *vb* to reprint
herenig *vb* to reunite
hereniging *n* reunion
herfs *n* autumn
herfsagtig *adj* autumnal
herhaal *vb* to repeat; to say again
herhaaldelik *adv* repeatedly
herhaling *n* repetition
herinner *vb* to remember; to recollect
herinnering *n* remembrance; reminiscence; souvenir; keepsake
herken *vb* to recognize
herkies *vb* to re-elect
herkoms *n* origin; descent; source; extraction; derivation
herkou *vb* to chew the cud; to ruminate
herleef *vb* to revive
herlei *vb* to reduce
herleide webwerf *n* diverted website (computing)

herlewing *n* revival
hermafrodiet *n* hermaphrodite
hermelyn *n* ermine
hermeties *adj* airtight
hernuwe *vb* to renew; to renovate
hernuwing *n* renewal; renovation
heropen *vb* to reopen
herout *n* herald
herower *vb* to reconquer
herrie *n* confusion; noise
herroep *vb* to recall; to repeal; to revoke; to retract
herrysenis *n* resurrection
hersenskim *n* fancy; hallucination
hersien *vb* to revise; to reconsider
hersiene *adj* revised
hersiening *n* revision; review
herskape *adj* transformed; reborn
herskep *vb* to recreate; to regenerate; to transform
herskepsessie *n* makeover session
herstel *n* recovery; redress; repair; *vb* to mend; to repair; to recover
hertog *n* duke
hertogdom *n* duchy
hertogin *n* duchess
hertrou *vb* to remarry; to marry again
hervat *vb* to resume; to begin again
hervorm *vb* to reform; to remodel
hervorming *n* reform; reformation
herwin *vb* to regain; to retrieve; to recycle
het *vb* have; has
heuglik *adj* memorable; joyful
heugenis *n* remembrance; memory
heul *vb* to connive; to collude
heuning *n* honey
heuningvoël *n* honey-bird
heup *n* hip; haunch
heupjig *n* sciatica
heupvervanging *n* hip replacement
heuwel *n* hill
heuwelagtig *adj* hilly
hewig *adj* severe; terrible; fierce
hiaat *n* gap; hiatus
hiasint *n* hyacinth
hidroulies *adj* hydraulic
hiëna *n* hyena
hier *adv* here
hierbo *adv* up here
hierby *adv* herewith; enclosed; attached

hierdie *pron* this; these
hierheen *adv* hither; this way
hierlangs *adv* along here; this way
hiermee *adv* herewith
hierna *adv* after this; hereafter; according to this
hiernaas *adv* next to this; next door
hiernamaals *adv* hereafter
hiernatoe *adv* hither; this way
hierom *adv* for this reason
hieronder *adv* under here
hieroor *adv* for this reason; about this
hierso *adv* here
hierteen *adv* against this
hiertoe *adv* thus far; for this purpose
hiervan *adv* of this; about this
higiëne *n* hygiene
hik *n* hiccup; *vb* to hiccup
himne *n* hymn
hinder *n* hindrance; obstacle; *vb* to hinder; to annoy; to impede; to disturb; to trouble
hinderlaag *n* ambush
hinderlik *adj* troublesome; inconvenient; annoying
hindernis *n* obstacle
hinderpaal *n* hindrance; obstacle
hings *n* stallion; studhorse
hingsel *n* handle; hinge
hink *vb* to be uncertain; to limp
hinnik *vb* to neigh
hiperkrities *adj* hypercritical
hipermark *n* hypermarket
hipertensie *n* hypertension
hip-hop-musiek *n* hip-hop (music, culture)
hipnose *n* hypnosis
hipnoties *n* hypnotic
hipnotiseer *vb* to hypnotize
hipnotisme *n* hypnotism
hipokondries *adj* hypochondriac(al)
hipotese *n* hypothesis
histerektomie *n* hysterectomy
histerie *n* hysterics
histeries *adj* hysterical
historie *n* history; story
histories *adj* historical; historic
historikus *n* historian
hitte *n* heat
hittegolf *n* heatwave
hittesteek *n* heatstroke

hobbel *vb* to rock; to seesaw; to jolt
hobbelagtig *adj* bumpy; uneven
hobbelperd *n* rocking horse
hoe *adv* how; what
hoë bloeddruk *n* high blood pressure
hoed *n* hat; bonnet
hoedanig *adv* how
hoedanigheid *n* quality; capacity
hoede *n* protection; care; guard
hoededoos *n* hatbox
hoederak *n* hall stand
hoedespeld *n* hatpin
hoef[1] *n* hoof
hoef[2] *vb* to need
hoefsmid *n* farrier
hoefyster *n* horseshoe
hoek *n* corner; angle; hook
hoeka: van — se tyd af *adv* from time immemorial; of old
hoekig *adj* angular; jagged
hoekom *adv* why; how; for what reason
hoeksteen *n* cornerstone; foundation stone
hoektand *n* eyetooth; canine
hoe lank *adv* how long
hoender *n* hen; chicken
hoenderhok *n* hencoop; henhouse
hoenderkop *adj* drunk
hoendervleis *n* chicken (meat); gooseflesh; goosebumps; **— kry** *vb* to get gooseflesh
hoepel *n* hoop
hoepelbeen *adj* bandy-legged
hoëpriester *n* high priest
hoer *n* whore
hoër *adj* upper
hoera! *interj* hurrah!
hoerê! *interj* hooray!
hoes *n* cough; *vb* to cough
hoesbui *n* coughing fit
hoërskool *n* high school; secondary school
hoeveel *adv* how much; how many
hoeveelheid *n* amount; quantity
hoewe *n* smallholding; plot
hoewel *conj* although; though
hof *n* court; garden; yard; **die — maak** *vb* to court
hofdame *n* maid of honour
hofdigter *n* poet laureate
hoflik *adj* polite; courteous

hofnar *n* court jester
hofsaak *n* court case
hok *n* shed; kennel; pen; sty; coop
hokkie[1] *n* small shed; cubicle; pigeon-hole
hokkie[2] *n* hockey (game)
hol[1] *n* cave; den; hold
hol[2] *vb* to run; to rush; to bolt
hol[3] *adj* hollow; empty; concave
holte *n* hollow; cavity; socket (eye); pit (stomach)
hom *pers pron* him; it
homeopaat *n* homeopath
homeopatie *n* homeopathy
homeopaties *adj* homeopathic
hommel *n* bumblebee
homofobie *n* homophobia
homogeen *adj* same; similar; homogeneous
homoseksueel *n, adj* homosexual
hond *n* dog
hondeherberg *n* kennel
honderd *n* hundred
honderdjarig *adj* centenary; centennial
honderdste *adj, n* hundredth
hondeweer *n* horrible weather
hondjie *n* small dog; puppy
honds *adj* rude; churlish
hondsdolheid *n* rabies; hydrophobia
honger *n* hunger; appetite
hongerig *adj* hungry
hongersnood *n* famine
honneurs *n* honours
honorarium *n* honorarium; fee; royalty
hoof *n* head; brains; leader; chief; heading; *adj* principal; main; important
hoofartikel *n* leader (newspaper); leading article
hoofbestuurder *n* chief executive
hoofkwartier *n* headquarters
hoofletter *n* capital letter
hoofonderwyser *n* principal
hoofpyn *n* headache
hoofsin *n* principal sentence
hoofstad *n* capital
hoofstuk *n* chapter
hoofvak *n* main subject
hoog *adj* high; lofty; tall; high-pitched
hoogag *vb* to esteem highly; to respect

hoogagting *n* esteem; respect
hooggebore *adj* high-born
hooggeregshof *n* supreme court
hooghartig *adj* proud; haughty
Hoogheid *title* Highness
hoogleraar *n* professor
hoogmoed *n* pride
hoogmoedig *adj* proud; haughty
hoognodig *adj* highly necessary
hoogs *adv* highly; exceedingly
hoogskat *vb* to esteem highly
hoogstens *adv* at best; at most
hoogte *n* height; hill; altitude; pitch (voice)
hoogverraad *n* high treason
hoogvlakte *n* plateau; tableland
hoogwater *n* high water; high tide
hooi *n* hay
hooikoors *n* hay fever
hooimied *n* haystack
hoon *n* derision; scorn; *vb* to scorn; to jeer; to deride
hoop[1] *n* hope; *vb* to hope
hoop[2] *n* heap; pile; crowd
hoopvol *adj* hopeful; promising
hoor *vb* to hear; to listen; to learn
hoorbaar *adj* audible
hop *n* hop (plant)
hopeloos *adj* hopeless
horing[1] *n* horn (animal)
horing[2] *n* bugle; car horn
horingvlies *n* cornea
horison *n* horizon
horisontaal *adj* horizontal; flat; level
horlosie *n* watch; clock
horrelpyp *n* hornpipe
hortjie *n* blind; shutter
hospitaal *n* hospital
hotel *n* hotel
hotklou *n* left-handed person; southpaw (boxing)
hou[1] *n* blow; stroke; cut
hou[2] *vb* to hold; to keep; to contain; to take for; — **van** *vb* to like; to be fond of
houding *n* conduct; attitude; deportment
houer *n* container
houerskip *n* container ship
hout *n* wood; timber
houterig *adj* wooden; clumsy

houthakker *n* woodcutter
houthandel *n* timber trade
houtskool *n* charcoal
houtsnywerk *n* woodcarving
houtwerf *n* timber yard
houtwerk *n* woodwork
hovaardig *adj* proud; haughty
huid *n* skin; hide
huidige *adj* present; modern
huidsiekte *n* skin disease
huiduitslag *n* rash
huigel *vb* to pretend; to dissemble; to feign
huigelaar *n* hypocrite
huigelary *n* hypocrisy
huil *vb* to howl; to cry; to weep
huis *n* house; home; dwelling; family; household
huisapteek *n* home medicine cupboard
huisarts *n* general practitioner
huisbaas *n* landlord
huisbesoek *n* home visit
huisbraak *n* housebreaking; burglary
huisbybel *n* family bible
huisdier *n* domestic animal
huisgenoot *n* housemate; inmate
huisgenote *npl* members of a household; family
huisgesin *n* family; household
huishoudelik *adj* domestic
huishouding *n* household
huishoudkunde *n* home economics; domestic science
huishulp *n* domestic (servant)
huishuur *n* rent (house, etc.)
huislik *adj* homely; domestic
huismiddel *n* home remedy
huismoeder *n* matron; housemother
huisraad *n* furniture
huissleutel *n* front-door key
huisves *vb* to house; to take in
huisvesting *n* accommodation; housing
huisvriend *n* family friend
huisvrou *n* housewife
huiswaarts *adv* homeward
huiswerk *n* homework
huiwer *vb* to tremble; to shiver; to shudder; to fear
huiwerig *adj* shivery; cold; afraid

hulle (*or* **hul**) *pers pron* they; them; poss prontheir
hulde *n* homage
huldeblyk *n* mark of esteem
huldig *vb* to honour; to do homage
hulp *n* help; aid; assistance
hulpbehoewend *adj* indigent; needy
hulpbron *n* resource
hulpeloos *adj* helpless; destitute
hulponderwyser *n* assistant teacher
hulpprediker *n* curate
hulpvaardig *adj* helpful; willing to help
hulpwerkwoord *n* auxiliary (verb)
humeur *n* mood
humeurig *adj* moody; sulky
humor *n* wit; humour
humoris *n* humorist
hunker *vb* to hanker after; to long for
huppel *vb* to skip; to hop
hups *adj* lively; polite
hurke *npl* haunches; **op die — sit** *vb* to squat (down)
hut *n* hut; cabin; cottage
huur *n* wages; rent; hire; lease; service; *vb* to hire; to rent; to employ
huurder *n* tenant; lessee
huurgeld *n* rent money; rental
huurkontrak *n* lease
huurprys *n* rent
huwelik *n* marriage; wedding; matrimony; wedlock
huweliksberader *n* marriage counsellor
huweliksbevestiging *n* marriage ceremony
huweliksgebooie *npl* banns
huwelikslewe *n* married life
huweliksonthaal *n* wedding reception
huweliksreis *n* honeymoon
huweliksvoorwaardekontrak *n* antenuptial (*or* prenuptial) agreement; (*informal*) prenup
HVK *see* **huweliksvoorwaardekontrak**
hy *pers pron* he; it
hyg *vb* to pant; to gasp for breath
hys *vb* to hoist
hysbak *n* skip
hyser *n* lift; elevator
hyskraan *n* crane

I

ideaal *n* ideal
idealis *n* idealist
idee *n* idea; notion
ideëkaart *n* Mind Map
identies *adj* identical
identifiseer *vb* to identify
identiteit *n* identity
idiomaties *adj* idiomatic
idioom *n* idiom
idioot *n* idiot; imbecile
ieder *pron* every; each
iedereen *pron* everyone; everybody
iemand *pron* someone; somebody
iesegrimmig *adj* surly; churlish
iets *pron* something; anything; **— anders** *pron* something else
iewers *adv* somewhere
ignoreer *vb* to ignore
ikoon *n* icon (computing)
illuminasie *n* illumination
illusie *n* illusion
illustreer *vb* to illustrate
imitasie *n* imitation
immer *adv* alwaysvb
immers *conj* yet; but; though
immigrant *n* immigrant
immigrasie *n* immigration
immoreel *adj* immoral
imperatief *adj* imperative
imperfek *adj* imperfect
imperialisme *n* imperialism
impi *n* impi; Zulu regiment
imponeer *vb* to impose; to impress
importeer *vb* to import (computing)
impressie *n* impression
improvisasie *n* improvisation
in[1] *prep* in; into; within
in[2] *vb* to collect (debts); to gather
inagneming *n* observance
inasem *vb* to inhale; to breathe
inbaar *adj* collectible
inbegrip *n* inclusion; **met — van** *prep* including
inbeslagneming *n* seizure; attachment; embargo
inbind *vb* to bind (books)
inbly *vb* to stay indoors

inboek *vb* to enter; to indenture
inboesem *vb* to inspire
inbors *n* character; nature
inbraak *n* housebreaking; burglary
inbreek *vb* to burgle; to break into
inbreuk *n* infringement; violation; **maak — op** *vb* to infringe upon
inburger *vb* to acclimatize
incognito *adv; adj* incognito
indeel *vb* to group; to classify
indeks *n* index
inderdaad *adv; conj; interj* indeed; really
inderhaas *adv* in a hurry; hurriedly
indertyd *adv* at the time; formerly
indien[1] *vb* to hand in; to lodge; to tender
indien[2] *conj* if; in case
indiensnemer *n* employer
indiensneming *n* employment
indiensopleiding *n* in-service training
indigestie *n* indigestion
indirek *adj* indirect
individu *n* individual
indommel *vb* to drop off; to doze off
indompel *vb* to dip in; to steep in; to immerse
indoop *vb* to dip into
indraai *vb* to turn into (road)
indring *vb* to break into; to intrude; to penetrate
indringer *n* intruder
indrink *vb* to absorb; to drink in
indruk *n* impression; *vb* to impress; to push in; to jump the queue
indrukker *n* queue jumper
indrukwekkend *adj* impressive
industrie *n* industry
industrieel *adj* industrial
ineen *adv* together
ineenkrimping *n* contraction
ineens *adv* at once; suddenly
ineensmelting *n* merging; fusion; amalgamation
ineenstorting *n* meltdown
inent *vb* to inoculate; to vaccinate
infanterie *n* infantry

infeksie *n* infection
inflammasie *n* inflammation
influensa *n* influenza
informasie *n* information
infosupersnelweg *n* information superhighway
ingaan *vb* to enter; to go in
ingang *n* entrance; doorway
ingebore *adj* innate; inborn
ingedagte *adj* absent-minded; preoccupied
ingee *vb* to give in; to administer; to stop; to surrender
ingelê *adj* inlaid; pickled; preserved; canned
ingenieur *n* engineer
ingenome *adj* pleased
ingenomenheid *n* satisfaction
ingerig *adj* arranged; prepared; organized
ingesetene *n* inhabitant; resident
ingesluit *adj* enclosed; inclusive
ingetoë *adj* modest; reserved
ingevolge *prep* according to; in respect of; in terms of
ingewande *npl* intestines; bowels
ingewandskoors *n* enteric fever; typhoid fever
ingewandsvirus *n* enterovirus
ingewikkel(d) *adj* intricate; complicated
ingewing *n* inspiration; brainwave
ingewortel(d) *adj* inveterate; deeprooted
ingewyde *adj* adept
ingryp *vb* to intervene
ingrypend *adj* important; far-reaching; drastic
inhaak *vb* to hook in; to take someone's arm
inhaal *vb* to overtake; to catch up; to make up for
inhalig *adj* grasping; greedy
inham *n* inlet; bay
inhegtenisneming *n* arrest
inhou *vb* to restrain; to contain
inhoud *n* contents; capacity
inhoudsmaat *n* cubic measure; measure of capacity
inisiatief *n* initiative
inisieer *vb* to initiate

ink *n* ink
inkalwe *vb* to cave in
inkamp *vb* to enclose; to fence in
inkeep *vb* to nick; to notch; to indent (paragraph)
inkeer *n* repentance
inkennig *adj* shy; timid
inklaar *vb* to clear (customs); to check in
inklee *vb* to express in words
inklim *vb* to climb into; to rebuke
inkluis *adj* included
inklusief *adj* inclusive
inklusiwiteit *n* inclusivity
inkom *vb* to come in; to enter
inkomste *n* income; earnings; revenue
inkomstebelasting *n* income tax
inkomstesteun *n* income support
inkonsekwent *adj* inconsistent
inkoop *n* purchase; *vb* to buy; to purchase; to buy into
inkopie *n* purchase; **—s doen** *vb* to go shopping
inkoopprys *n* cost price
inkorporeer *vb* to incorporate
inkort *vb* to shorten; to curtail
inkrimp *vb* to shrink; to contract
inkrimping *n* retrenchment; contraction
inkring *n* in-crowd
inkruip *vb* to creep into; to crawl into
inkry *vb* to get in; to get (food) down
inkvis *n* cuttlefish; squid
inkvlek *n* inkblot; ink stain
inkwartier *vb* to billet; to quarter
inlaat *n* intake; *vb* to let in; to admit
inlas *vb* to insert
inlê *vb* to lay in; to can; to preserve; to invest; to deposit; to inlay with
inlei *vb* to introduce; to preface
inleiding *n* introduction; preface
inleidingsartikel *n* leader; leading article
inleier *n* initiator; opener (of a debate)
inlewer *vb* to deliver; to hand in; to submit
inlig *vb* to inform
inligting *n* information
inligtingadvertensie *n* infomercial
inligtingstoer *n* roadshow
inloer *vb* to peep in; to pry into

inloop *n* catchment (area); *vb* to enter; to call in; to drop in; to overtake
inlyf *vb* to incorporate; to annex
inmaak *vb* to can; to preserve
inmeng *vb* to meddle; to interfere
inneem *vb* to bring in; to take in (clothes); to load (cargo, etc.); to capture; to conquer; to charm; to take (medicine)
innemend *adj* charming; captivating
inneming *n* taking; capture (of a town)
innerlik *adj* inner; internal
innig *adj* cordial; earnest; sincere
In(n)uïet *n*, *adj* In(n)uit
inpak *vb* to pack; to wrap up
inpas *vb* to fit in
inpekel *vb* to salt; to cure
inpeper *vb* to pepper
inperk *vb* to ban; to restrict
inperking *n* restriction
inplant *vb* to implant
inplanting *n* implant
inprent *vb* to imprint; to impress
inrig *vb* to manage; to arrange
inrigting *n* institution; arrangement
inroep *vb* to call in; to invoke
inruil *vb* to exchange; barter
inruim *vb* to make room
inry *vb* to ride in; to drive in
insamel *vb* to gather in; to collect
insake *prep* regarding; re
inseën *vb* to induct; to consecrate
inseep *vb* to soap; to lather
insek *n* insect
insekdoder *n* insecticide; pesticide
insektekunde *n* entomology
insender *n* contributor
insending *n* contribution
insgelyks *adv* likewise; in a similar way
insien *vb* to glance over; to look into; to understand
insig *n* view; opinion; insight
insink *vb* to subside; to relapse; to sink in
insinking *n* subsidence; relapse; slump; decline
insinuasie *n* insinuation
insinueer *vb* to insinuate
inskakel *vb* to switch on; to engage
inskeep *vb* to embark; to board (ship; plane)

inskep *vb* to ladle into; to dish up
inskiklik *adj* complying; obliging
inskiklikheid *n* compliance
inskink *vb* to pour out; to pour in
inskryf *vb* to inscribe; to enrol; to tender (for)
inslaan *vb* to drive in; to turn down (road); to smash; to strike (lightning)
inslaap *vb* to doze off; to fall asleep
insleepdiens *n* breakdown service
insluimer *vb* to doze off; to fall asleep
insluip *vb* to steal into
insluit *vb* to enclose; to include; to shut in; to contain
insluk *vb* to swallow
insmeer *vb* to grease; to rub in
insny *vb* to cut into; to engrave
insolvensie *n* insolvency
insolvent *adj* insolvent; bankrupt
insonderheid *adv* especially
insout *vb* to salt
inspan *vb* to exert; to inspan
inspanning *n* exertion; strain
inspeksie *n* inspection
inspekteer *vb* to inspect
inspekteur *n* inspector
inspirasie *n* inspiration
inspraak *n* participation; joint consultation
inspuit *vb* to inject
inspuiting *n* injection; (*informal*) jab
instaan *vb* to guarantee; to warrant; to stand surety
instandhouding *n* maintenance; upkeep
instansie *n* instance; place; body
instap *vb* to step in; to get in
insteek *vb* to put in(to); to thread
instel *vb* to institute; to establish; to set (text)
instellings *npl* settings
instem *vb* to agree; to concur
instemmer *n* tuner
instink *n* instinct
instinkmatig *adj* instinctive; *adv* instinctively
instituut *n* institute
instorm *vb* to rush in(to)
instort *vb* to collapse; to relapse
instorting *n* collapse; breakdown
instruksie *n* instruction
instrukteur *n* instructor

instrument *n* instrument; tool; implement

instudeer *vb* to study; to practise; to rehearse

insweer *vb* to take an oath; to swear

inswelg *vb* to devour; to swallow

insypel *vb* to infiltrate

inteendeel *adv* on the contrary

integrasie *n* integration

integriteit *n* integrity

inteken *vb* to subscribe to

intekenaar *n* subscriber

intellek *n* intellect

intelligent *adj* intelligent

intens *adj* intense

intensie *n* intention

intensief *adj* intensive

interessant *adj* interesting

interieur *n* interior

intermediêr *n* intermediate

intern *adj* internal; —e eksamen *n* internal exam

internasionaal *adj* international

interneer *vb* to intern

internering *n* internment

internetluisteropname *n* podcast

internis *n* physician

internskap *n* internship

interplanetêr *adj* interplanetary

interpretasie *n* interpretation

interpunksie *n* punctuation

interrogeer *vb* to interrogate

intiem *adj* intimate

intimiteit *n* intimacy

intog *n* entrance; entry

intoom *vb* to curb; to restrain; to pull up; to rein in

intranet *n* intranet (computing)

intree *vb* to enter; to go in

intreegeld *n* admission fee; entrance fee

intreepreek *n* induction sermon

intrek *n* home; residence; lodgings; *vb* to go in; to move in; to repeal (act); to cancel (leave); to inhale

intrige *n* intrigue; plot

intussen *adv* meanwhile

inval *n* inroad; raid; invasion; idea; thought; *vb* to occur; to collapse; to invade

invalide *n* invalid; sick person

inventaris *n* inventory

invleg *vb* to plait in; to intertwine; to intersperse

invlieg *vb* to fly in; to reprimand; to rebuke

invloed *n* influence

invloedryk *adj* influential

invoer *n* import; importation; *vb* to import

invoerder *n* importer

invoerreg *n* import duty

invorder *vb* to demand (payment); to collect (taxes); to recover (debts)

invorderbaar *adj* leviable; collectable; recoverable

invou *vb* to fold in

invreet *vb* to corrode

invryf *vb* to rub in

invul *vb* to fill up (in); 'n vorm — *vb* to complete a form

inwendig *adj* internal; inner; interior

inwerk *vb* to act on; to work on; to influence

inwerking *n* influence; action

inwikkel *vb* to cover up; to wrap up

inwillig *vb* to comply with; to agree to; to concede

inwin *vb* to obtain (information); to make (enquiries)

inwoner *n* inhabitant; occupier; resident

inwoon *vb* to live in; to lodge; to board

inwy *vb* to open; to initiate; to consecrate; to inaugurate

inwyding *n* ordination; dedication; inauguration; opening

ipekonders *npl* imaginary ailments; hypochondria

iris *n* iris (eye)

ironie *n* irony

ironies *adj* ironical; sarcastic

irriteer *vb* to irritate

isolasie *n* isolation

isoleer *vb* to insulate

isoleerband *n* insulation tape

isolering *n* insulation

ivoor *n* ivory

J

ja *sentence substitute* yes; yea
jaag *vb* to chase; to pursue
jaagstrik *n* speed trap
jaar *n* year
jaarboek *n* annual; yearbook
jaarboeke *npl* annals
jaarfees *n* anniversary
jaargang *n* volume (of a periodical)
jaargeld *n* annuity
jaargety *n* season
jaarliks *adv* annually; yearly
jaart *n* yard
jaartal *n* date
jaartelling *n* era
jaarvergadering *n* annual general meeting (AGM)
jaarverslag *n* annual report
jabroer *n* yes man
jag[1] *n* hunt; hunting; chase; *vb* to hunt; shoot; chase
jag[2] *n* yacht
jaghond *n* hunting dog; pointer; setter
jagspinnekop *n* hunting spider
jagter *n* hunter
jakkals *n* jackal; sly person
jakkalsdraai *n* excuse; pretext
jakkalsstreek *n* cunning; shrewdness
jakker *vb* to hurry; to career along
jakob-regop *n* zinnia
jaloers *adj* jealous; envious
jaloesie *n* jealousy; envy
jammer *n* pity; misery; *vb* to lament; to wail; **ek is —** I am sorry
jammerhartig *adj* compassionate; softhearted
jammerklag *n* lamentation
jammerlik *adj* miserable; pitiable
jammerte *n* sorrow; pity
janfiskaal *n* butcher bird; fiscal shrike
janfrederik *n* Cape robin
jannas *n* jeans
Januarie *n* January
japonika *n* japonica
jappie *n* yuppie
jas *n* coat; overcoat
jasmyn *n* jasmine
jaspis *n* jasper

jawoord *n* consent; permission
jeans *n* jeans
jeens *prep* towards; to
jekker *n* jacket; anorak
jellie *n* jelly
jenewer *n* gin
jeug *n* youth
jeugdig *adj* young; youthful; adolescent
jeugdige *n* juvenile; youth; adolescent
jeugherberg *n* youth hostel
jeuk *n* itch; *vb* to itch
jeukte *n* itching
jig *n* gout
jil *vb* to joke; to jest; to tease
jobsgeduld *n* patience of Job
jodium *n* iodine
joernaal *n* journal
joernalis *n* journalist
joernaliste *n* paparazzi
joggie *n* caddie (golf)
jogurt *n* yoghurt
jok *vb* to tell a fib; to lie
jokkie *n* jockey
jong *n* young of animals; *vb* to bring forth young; *adj* young
jongeling *n* youth; young man; adolescent
jongkêrel *n* young man; bachelor
jongmeisie *n* young girl; adolescent
jongspan *n* young people
jonk *n* junk (boat)
jonkheid *n* youth
jooloptog *n* rag procession
jota *n* iota
jou *pers pron* you; *poss pron* your
joune (*or* **joue**) *poss pron* yours; **dis —** it's yours
jubel *vb* to rejoice; to cheer
jubileum *n* jubilee
juffrou *n* young lady; Miss; Madam; female teacher
juig *vb* to rejoice
juis *adj* correct; exact; *adv* correctly; exactly
juistement *adv* exactly; precisely
juistheid *n* correctness; precision; exactitude

juk *n* yoke
jukbeen *n* cheekbone
Julie *n* July
jul *pers pron* you; *poss pron* your
Jungiaans *adj* Jungian
Junie *n* June
junior *n, adj* junior

juridies *adj* judicial
jurie *n* jury
juris *n* lawyer; barrister; juror
justisie *n* justice
juweel *n* jewel; gem
juwelier *n* jeweller
jy *pers pron* you

K

kaai *n* quay; wharf
kaaiman *n* cayman; alligator
kaak[1] *n* jaw
kaak[2] *n* pillory; **aan die — stel** *vb* to expose to public contempt
kaal *adj* bare; naked; bald; shabby
kaalbas *n* nudist
kaalgrond *n* arable land
kaalhol *vb* to streak
kaalholler *n* streaker
kaalkop *n* bald head; *adj* bald
kaalnaeler *n* streaker
kaalperske *n* nectarine
kaalvoet *adj* barefoot
kaap[1] *n* cape; headland
kaap[2] *vb* to steal; to hijack; to practise piracy
kaart *n* card; map; chart; ticket
kaartjie *n* ticket; card
kaartjiesmasjien *n* ticket vending machine
kaartmannetjie *n* jack-in-the-box
kaartspeel *vb* to play cards
kaartveemasjien *n* card-swipe machine
kaas *n* cheese
kaasburger *n* cheeseburger
kaasstremsel *n* rennet
kaatser *n* reflector
kabaal *n* noise; commotion
kabaret *n* cabaret
kabbel *vb* to babble; to ripple
kabel *n* cable; hawser
kabelgram *n* cable; cablegram
kabeljou *n* cod (fish)
kabinet *n* cabinet; case; ministry; cabinet
kadet *n* cadet
kadriel *n* quadrille
kaduks *adj* dilapidated; decrepit; in poor health
kaf *n* chaff; nonsense; **praat —** *vb* to talk nonsense
kafee *n* café
kafeïenvry *adj* decaffeinated; (*informal*) decaf
kafeteria *n* cafeteria

kaffeïene *n* caffeine
kafloop *vb* to beat; to overcome
kafoefelry *n* (*informal*) snog
kafpraatjies *n* nonsense; trash
kaggel *n* fireplace
kajuit *n* cabin
kajuitpersoneel *n* cabin staff
kak *vb to* pass faeces; (*vulgar*)to shit
kakao *n* cocoa
kakebeen *n* jawbone; jaw
kaketoe *n* cockatoo
kakie *adj* khaki (colour)
kakiebos *n* blackjack (plant)
kakkerlak *n* cockroach
kaktus *n* cactus
kalander *n* weevil
kalant *n* rogue; scoundrel
kalbas *n* gourd; calabash
kalender *n* calendar; almanac
kalf *n* calf; *vb* to calve
kalfsvleis *n* veal
kalium *n* potassium; potash
kalief *n* caliph
kalifaat *n* caliphate
kalk *n* lime; *vb* to whitewash
kalkbank *n* limestone rock
kalkoen *n* turkey
kalkoond *n* lime kiln
kalm *adj* calm; cool; quiet; collected; composed
kalmeer *vb* to calm; to soothe
kalmeermiddel *n* sedative; tranquillizer
kalorie *n* calorie
kalwerliefde *n* calf love; puppy love
kam *n* comb; crest; cog (of a wheel); *vb* to comb; to card (wool)
kameel *n* camel
kameeldoring(boom) *n* mimosa (tree)
kameelperd *n* giraffe
kamer *n* room; chamber
kamera *n* camera
kameraad *n* comrade; companion
kameraadskap *n* comradeship; companionship
kamerjas *n* dressing gown
kamermusiek *n* chamber music
kamille *n* camomile

kamma (or **kammakastig** or **kamma-lielies**) adv quasi; as if; adj would-be; pseudo; pretended

kamp n camp; encampment; vb to camp; encamp

kampanje n campaign

kampeer vb to camp; encamp

kampioen n champion

kampus n campus

kan[1] n jug; can

kan[2] vb to be able

kanaal n channel; canal

kanapee[1] n couch; sofa

kanapee[2] n canapé

kanarie n canary

kandelaar n candlestick

kandidaat n candidate; applicant

kaneel n cinnamon

kanfer n camphor

kanferfoelie n honeysuckle

kangaroe n kangaroo

kanker n cancer; (figurative) canker

kannibal n cannibal

kanniedood n diehard

kano n canoe

kanon[1] n cannon; gun

kanon[2] n canon

kanoniek adj canonical

kanoniseer vb to canonize

kanonkoeël n cannonball

kanonnier n gunner

kans n chance; opportunity; hazard; risk

kansel n pulpit

kant[1] n side; edge; brink; margin; **van — maak** vb to kill; **— en klaar** adv quite ready

kant[2] n lace

kantate n cantata

kantel vb to tilt; to capsize

kantien n canteen; bar; pub; tin can

kantoor n office

kantwerk n lace work

kap[1] n bonnet (car); hatch

kap[2] n cut; chop; vb to fell; to chop; to cut (hair)

kapabel adj able; capable

kapel[1] n chapel

kapel[2] n cobra

kapelaan n chaplain

kapitaal n capital; principal

kapitalis n capitalist

kapittel[1] n chapter

kapittel[2] vb to lecture

kapituleer vb to capitulate

kapok n kapok; silk cotton; snow

kapokhoender n bantam (domestic fowl)

kapot adj broken; dilapidated; exhausted

kapper n hairdresser

kappie n sunbonnet

kapsel n hairstyle

kapstok n hall stand; hat stand

kaptein n captain; chief

kar n cart; motorcar

karaat n carat

karakter n character

karakteristiek n characteristic; adj characteristic

karakterloos adj characterless; without principles

karaktertrek n trait; characteristic

karavaan n caravan

karbied n carbide

karbol adj carbolic

karbolsuur n carbolic acid

kardinaal n cardinal; adj chief; cardinal

kardiograaf n cardiograph

kardiogram n cardiogram

karikatuur n caricature

karig adj meagre; slender

karkatjie n stye (on the eye)

karmosyn n, adj crimson

karnallie n rascal; rogue

karnuffel vb to hug; cuddle; to use roughly; to manhandle

karperd n carthorse

karring n milk churn; vb to churn

karringmelk n buttermilk

karton n cardboard; pasteboard; carton

karweier n carrier; haulier

kas[1] n wardrobe; cupboard; bookcase; box; case; chest

kas[2] n cashbox; coffer; vb to deposit; to bank

kasboek n cash-book

kaserne n barracks

kaskenade n prank; trick; fuss; uproar

kasregister n till; cash register

kassier n cashier; banker

kastaiing n chestnut

kasteel *n* castle
kasterolie *n* castor oil
kastrol *n* saucepan; casserole
kasty *vb* to punish; to chastise
kastyding *n* punishment; chastisement;
kat *n* cat
katalogus *n* catalogue
katar *n* catarrh
katarsis *n* catharsis
katedraal *n* cathedral
kategorie *n* category
katel *n* bedstead
katelknaap *n* toy boy
katjiepiering *n* gardenia
katkisasie *n* catechism class
katoen *n* cotton; calico
katoeter *n* gadget
katoog *n* cat's eye (on roads)
katrol *n* pulley
kats *n* cat-o'-nine-tails
katswink *adj* unconscious; senseless
kattekwaad *n* mischief
kavallerie *n* cavalry
kaviaar *n* caviar(e)
keel *n* throat
keël *n* cone; skittle; icicle
keelgat *n* gullet
keelholte *n* pharynx
keelpyn *n* sore throat
keelseer *n* sore throat
keëlvormig *adj* conical
keep *n* notch
keer *n* change; turn; time; *vb* to turn; to
    stop; to prevent
keerkring *n* tropic (line of latitude)
keerpunt *n* turning point; crisis
keerweer *n* cul-de-sac
kef *vb* to yelp; to bark
kegelvormig *adj* conical
keil *n* top hat; wedge
keiser *n* emperor
keiserin *n* empress
keiserryk *n* empire
keisersnee *n* Caesarian operation
kekkel *vb* to cackle; to gossip
kekkelbek *n* gossip; chatterbox
kelder *n* cellar
kelim *n* kelim; Turkish carpet
kelk *n* chalice; cup; calyx
kelkie *n* wineglass
kelner *n* waiter; steward

ken[1] *n* chin
ken[2] *vb* to know; to recognize; to be ac-
    quainted with
kenbaar *adj* discernible; recognizable;
    manifest
kenmerk *n* characteristic feature; dis-
    tinguishing mark; *vb* to mark; to
    characterize
kenmerkend *adj* characteristic; distinc-
    tive
kenner *n* expert; connoisseur; (*infor-
    mal*) boffin
kennis *n* knowledge; skill; acquaint-
    ance; consciousness
kennisgewing *n* notice; announcement
kenskets *vb* to describe
kenteken *n* characteristic; distinctive
    mark; badge
kentering *n* turn; change
keps *n* cap
kêrel *n* (*informal*) bloke; (*informal*) guy;
    (*informal*) fellow
kerf *n* incision; notch; *vb* to notch; to
    carve; to cut
kerk *n* church; chapel; congregation
kerkbank *n* church pew
kerkhervorming *n* reformation
kerkhof *n* churchyard; cemetery
kerker *n* dungeon
kerktoring *n* church steeple; tower
kerm *vb* to groan; to moan; to lament
kermis *n* fair; fête
kermisbed *n* shakedown
kern *n* kernel; stone; core; nucleus; gist
kernaangedrewe *adj* nuclear powered
kernafval *n* atomic waste
kernagtig *adj* pithy; terse
kernas *n* nuclear fallout
kernbom *n* atom(ic) bomb; nuclear
    bomb
kernkrag *n* nuclear power
kernoorlog *n* nuclear war
kernwapens *npl* nuclear weapons
kerrie *n* curry
kers *n* candle
Kersaand *n* Christmas Eve
kersboom *n* Christmas tree
Kersdag *n* Christmas Day
Kersfees *n* Christmas
kersie *n* cherry
Kerslied *n* Christmas carol

Kerspastei *n* mince pie
Kersvader *n* Father Christmas; Santa Claus
ketel *n* kettle; boiler
ketter *n* heretic
kettery *n* heresy
ketting *n* chain
kettingbrug *n* suspension bridge
kettingreaksie *n* chain reaction
keur *n* choice; selection; *vb* to test; to examine
keurig *adj* fine; exquisite
keuring *n* choice; selection; pick; alternative
keurraad *n* selection board
keus(e) *n* choice; selection
kewer *n* beetle
KGV *see* **kweekhuisgasvrystelling**
kiaathout *n* teak wood
kibbel *vb* to quarrel; to wrangle
kiekie *n* snapshot
kiel *n* keel (of a ship)
kielie *vb* to tickle
kielierig *adj* ticklish
kiem *n* seed; germ; embryo; *vb* to germinate
kierie *n* walking stick
kies[1] *n* cheek
kies[2] *vb* to choose; to pick; to elect; to select
kies[3] *adj* dainty; delicate
kieskaart *n* menu (computing)
kiesafdeling *n* constituency; electoral division
kiesbaar *adj* eligible
kiesdistrik *n* constituency
kieser *n* voter; elector
kieserslys *n* electoral register; voters' roll
kieskeurig *adj* particular; fastidious
kiestand *n* molar
kiets *adj* quits; equal; even
kieu *n* gill
kiewiet *n* peewit; lapwing
kilogram *n* kilogram
kilometer *n* kilometre
kim[1] *n* horizon; rim
kim[2] *n* mould
kind *n* child; baby
kinderagtig *adj* childish; silly
kinderarts *n* paediatrician

kinderhawe *n* children's home
kinderjare *n* childhood
kinderlik *adj* childlike; innocent
kindermolestering *n* child abuse
kindertuin *n* nursery school; kindergarten
kinderwaentjie *n* pram
kindkeerder *n* child restraint
kinds *adj* childish; senile
kindveilige prop *n* childproof cap
kinesiologie *n* kinesiology
kinien *n* quinine
kink *n* knot; kink; twist; *vb* to turn; to twist
kinkhoes *n* whooping cough
kiosk *n* kiosk
kir *vb* to coo
kis *n* chest; box; case; trunk; coffin
kisklere *npl* best clothes; (*informal*) Sunday best
kitaar *n* guitar
kits *n* moment; instant
kitsbank *n* automatic teller machine (ATM)
kitskoffie *n* instant coffee
kla *vb* to complain; to lament
klaaglied *n* dirge
klaar *adj* ready; finished; done; clear; bright; evident; obvious
klaarblyklik *adj* apparent; obvious
klaarkry *vb* to finish
klaarmaak *vb* to get ready; to prepare; to finish
Klaasvakie *n* the Sandman; Wee Willie Winkie
klad *n* stain; blot
kladpapier *n* blotting paper
kla *vb* to complain; to lament
klaer *n* complainant; plaintiff
klagte *n* complaint
klam *adj* damp; moist
klamp *n* clamp; *vb* to clamp
klandisie *n* customers; clientele
klank *n* sound; tone
klankdemper *n* silencer (car)
klant *n* customer
klap *n* slap; clap; rattle; flap; *vb* to smack; to clap; to crack (a whip); to strike
klapper[1] *n* cracker; explosive sound
klapper[2] *n* coconut

klapper[3] *vb* to chatter (teeth)
klapperdop *n* coconut shell; (*informal*) numbskull
klarinet *n* clarinet
klas *n* class; grade
klaskamer *n* classroom
klasonderwyser *n* class teacher
klassiek *adj* classic(al)
klassifikasie *n* classification
klassifiseer *vb* to classify
klavier *n* piano
klavierbegeleiding *n* piano accompaniment
klawer *n* clover; shamrock
klawerbord *n* keyboard
klawers *npl* clubs (playing cards)
kleding *n* clothes; clothing
kledingstuk *n* garment
kleedkamer *n* dressing room; cloakroom
kleef *vb* to cling; to stick
klei *n* clay
klein *adj* small; little; minute
kleindogter *n* granddaughter
kleiner *adj* minor
kleingeestig *adj* narrow-minded
kleingeld *n* change; small cash
kleingoed *n* children; (*informal*) kids
kleinhandel *n* retail trade
kleinhandelprys *n* retail price
kleinhuisie *n* toilet; loo
kleinigheid *n* small thing; trifle
kleinkind *n* grandchild
kleinkry *vb* to conquer; to subdue
kleinmaak *vb* to get change (money); to break up
kleinood *n* jewel; gem
kleinserig *adj* sensitive; delicate
kleinseun *n* grandson
kleinsielig *adj* narrow-minded
kleinspan *n* youngsters; little ones
kleintongetjie *n* uvula
kleinvee *n* sheep; goats
klem *n* stress; accent; lockjaw; *vb* to clasp; to clench; to jam
klemtoon *n* accent; emphasis
klep *n* flap; valve
klerasie *n* clothes; clothing
klere *n* clothes; clothing
klereborsel *n* clothes brush
kleredrag *n* fashion; mode of dress

klerekas *n* wardrobe
kleremaker *n* tailor
klerk *n* clerk
klerklik *n* clerical
klets *vb* to talk; to chatter
kletter *vb* to clatter; to clash; to clang
kleur *n* colour; complexion; *vb* to colour; to stain; to blush
kleurblind *adj* colour-blind; making no distinction on grounds of race
kleurgekodeer *adj* colour-coded
kleuter *n* toddler
kleuterskool *n* nursery school
klewe *vb* to cling; to stick
klewerig *adj* sticky
kliek *n* clique; set
kliënt *n* customer; client
klier *n* gland
klik *n* click (with the tongue); *vb* to click; to tell tales
klim *vb* to climb; to ascend
klimaat *n* climate
klimaks *n* climax
klimop *n* creeper; ivy
klimplant *n* rambler (botanical)
klimtol *n* yo-yo
kliniek *n* clinic
klinies *n* clinical
klink[1] *vb* to rivet; to clinch
klink[2] *vb* to sound; to ring
klinker *n* vowel
klinknael *n* rivet
klip *n* rock; stone; pebble
klipdassie *n* dassie; rock rabbit
kliphard *adj, adv* very hard
klipsalmander *n* salamander
klits[1] *vb* to beat (eggs); to whip (cream)
klits[2] *n* burdock
kloek *vb* to cluck
klok *n* clock; bell
klokreël *n* curfew
klokslag *n* striking of a clock; *adv* sharp; exactly
klomp[1] *n* number; crowd; lot; lump
klomp[2] *n* clog; wooden shoe
klont *n* lump of sugar; clod of earth; blood clot
klonter *vb* to clot; to curdle
kloof *n* chasm; ravine; cleft; *vb* to cleave; to split
klooster *n* monastery; convent; abbey

kloosterskool *n* convent school

klop *n* knock; beat; tap; rap; *vb* to tap; to knock; to throb; to beat

klos *n* bobbin; spool; coil (electricity)

klots *vb* to beat; to splash

klou *n* claw; paw

klousule *n* clause

klouter *vb* to climb; to clamber; to scramble

klowe (*or* **kloof**) *vb* to cleave; to split

klub *n* club

klug *n* farce; joke; scream

kluif *vb* to gnaw

kluis *n* vault; strongroom

kluisenaar *n* hermit; recluse

kluister *n* fetter; chain; shackle; *vb* to fetter; to chain; to shackle

kluit *n* clod; lump

kluitjie *n* dumpling; lie

kluitklaplys *n* bucket list

knaag *vb* to gnaw

knaagdier *n* rodent

knaap *n* boy; lad

knabbel *n* to nibble

knak *n* injury; crack; *vb* to crack; to snap

knal *n* loud noise; crack; clap; *vb* to clap; to crash

knaldop *n* detonator

knap[1] *adj* clever; able; handsome; *adv* ably

knap[2] *adj* tight; close-fitting

knaphandig *adj* dexterous; skilful

knapsak *n* knapsack

kneg *n* manservant; valet

knel *n* pinch; scrape; difficulty; *vb* to pinch; to squeeze tightly; to jam

knelpunt *n* bottleneck; problem area

kners *vb* to grate; to grind (teeth)

knetter *vb* to crackle

kneukel *n* knuckle

kneus *n* bruise; *vb* to bruise; to hurt; to squash

knewel *n* (*informal*) whopper; stunner

knibbel *vb* to haggle

knie[1] *n* knee

knie[2] *vb* to knead; to mould

kniebroek *n* knickers; smalls

kniediep *adj* knee-deep

kniel *vb* to kneel

knies *vb* to grumble; to fret; to sulk

knieserig *adj* fretful

knieskyf *n* knee-cap; patella

knik *n* nod; rut (in a road); *vb* to nod

knip *n* bolt; clasp; clip; wink; *vb* to cut; to snip; to clip; to wink; to blink

knippie *n* pinch (of salt)

knipspeld *n* safety pin

knobbel *n* bump; knob; swelling

knoei *vb* to bungle; to botch

knoes *n* knot (in wood)

knoffel *n* garlic

knol *n* old crock; tuber

knoop *n* button; bow; knot; curse; swearword; *vb* to knot; to tie; to swear

knoopsgat *n* buttonhole

knop *n* bud; knob; head; door handle; pommel (saddle)

knopkierie *n* club; stick; knobkerrie

knor *n* grunt; growl; *vb* to grumble; to growl

knortjor *n* go-cart

knorrig *adj* grumpy; peevish

knou *n* bite; injury; *vb* to hurt; to injure

knyp *n* pinch; *vb* to pinch; to squeeze

knyptang *n* pincers; pliers

koalisie *n* coalition

koddig *adj* comic; droll; funny

kode *n* code

kodeer *vb* to code

koedoe *n* kudu

koeël *n* bullet; pellet; ball

koeëlvaste bulletproof vest

koeëlvry *adj* bulletproof

koei *n* cow

koejawel *n* guava

koek *n* cake

koekbakker *n* confectioner

koekoek *n* cuckoo

koekpan *n* baking pan

koeksoda *n* sodium bicarbonate

koel *adj* cold; cool; fresh

koelbloedig *adj* cold-blooded

koeldrank *n* cool drink; soft drink

koelkas *n* refrigerator

koelsak *n* cool bag

koelte *n* light breeze; shade

koeltrok *n* refrigerator truck

koepel *n* dome; cupola

koeplet *n* couplet; stanza; verse

koepon *n* coupon

koerant *n* newspaper

koers *n* course; direction; currency; rate
koes *vb* to duck down; to dodge
koester *vb* to cherish; to pamper
koets[1] *n* coach; carriage
koets[2] *vb* to duck down; to dodge
koevert *n* envelope
koevoet *n* crowbar
koffer *n* trunk; box; chest
koffie *n* coffee
koffiehuis *n* coffee house
koffiekan *n* coffee pot
koggel *vb* to mimic; to mock
kok *n* cook
kokaïen *n* cocaine
koket *adj* coquettish
kokketiel *n* cockatiel
kokkewiet *n* bush shrike
kokosboom *n* coconut tree
kokosneut *n* coconut
kol *n* spot; bull's eye; blaze (horse)
kolhou *n* hole in one
koliek *n* colic
koljander *n* coriander
kolk *n* abyss; whirlpool
kollageen *n* collagen
kollega *n* colleague
kollege *n* college
kollekte *n* collection (church, street)
kollekteer *vb* to collect
kollig *n* spotlight
kolofonblad *n* imprint page (book)
kolom *n* column
kolonel *n* colonel
koloniaal *adj* colonial
kolonie *n* colony; settlement
koloniseer *vb* to colonize
koloriet *n* colouring; shade; hue
kolossaal *adj* huge; colossal; (*informal*) ginormous
kolostomie *n* colostomy
kolskoot *n* bull's eye
kolwer *n* batsman; batter
kom[1] *vb* to come; to arrive
kom[2] *n* basin; bowl; dale
kombers *n* blanket
kombinasie *n* combination
kombineer *vb* to combine
kombuis *n* kitchen
kombuisgoed *n* kitchenalia
komediant *n* comedian
komedie *n* comedy; farce

komeet *n* comet
komies *adj* comic(al); droll
komitee *n* committee
komkommer *n* cucumber
komma *n* comma
kommandant *n* commandant; commander
kommandeer *vb* to command; to commandeer
kommando *n* commando
kommapunt *n* semicolon (;)
kommentaar *n* commentary
kommer *n* trouble; anxiety; distress
kommersieel *adj* commercial
kommetjie *n* mug; cup
kommissariaat *n* commissariat
kommissaris *n* commissioner
kommissie *n* commission
kommunikasie *n* communication
kommunis *n* communist
kompakskyf *n* compact disk (CD)
kompakskyfspeler *n* CD player
kompanjie *n* company (business)
kompartement *n* compartment
kompas *n* compass
kompensasie *n* compensation
kompenseer *n* to compensate
kompeteer *vb* to compete
kompetisie *n* competition
kompleet *adj* complete; *adv* just; exactly
kompleks *adj* complex
komplementêr *adj* complementary
kompliment *n* compliment
komplot *n* plot; intrigue
komponeer *vb* to compose
komponis *n* composer
kompos *n* compost
komposisie *n* composition; setting
kompromis *n* compromise
kompromitteer *vb* to compromise
koms *n* arrival; coming
kondensasie *n* condensation
kondenseer *vb* to condense
kondisie *n* condition; state
kondoom *n* condom
konfederasie *n* confederation
konfereer *vb* to consult; to confer
konferensie *n* conference
konferensieganger *n* conference delegate

konfessie *n* confession
konfidensieel *adj* confidential
konfiskasie *n* confiscation
konfiskeer *vb* to confiscate; to seize
konflik *n* conflict
konfrontasie *n* confrontation
konfyt *n* jam; preserve
kongestie *n* congestion
koning *n* king
koningin *n* queen
koningskap *n* royalty
koninklik *adj* royal; regal
koninklikes *n* royalty (books, songs, etc.)
koninkryk *n* kingdom
konjunksie *n* conjunction
konka *n* empty (petrol) tin; drum; brazier
konkel *vb* to intrigue; to plot; botch
konklusie *n* conclusion
konkurreer *vb* to compete
konkurrensie *n* competition; rivalry
konkurrent *n* competitor; rival
konneksie *n* connection
konnekteer *vb* to connect
konsensie *n* conscience
konsensieus *adj* conscientious
konsensus *adj* concensus; agreement
konsentrasie *n* concentration
konsep *n* draft; concept
konsepsie *n* conception
konsepwetgewing *n* draft legislation
konsert *n* concert
konsertina *n* concertina
konservatorium *n* conservatoire; conservatory
konserwatief *adj* conservative
konsessie *n* concession
konsiderasie *n* consideration
konskripsie *n* conscription
konsonant *n* consonant
konstabel *n* constable
konstellasie *n* constellation
konsternasie *n* consternation; alarm
konstitusie *n* constitution
konstruksie *n* construction; structure
konsul *n* consul
konsulaat *n* consulate
konsultasie *n* consultation
konsulteer *vb* to consult
konsumpsie *n* consumption

kontak *n* contact; touch
kontaklens *n* contact lens
kontant *n* cash; ready money; — by aflewering** *n* cash on delivery
kontant terug *n* cashback
kontantvloei *n* cash flow
kontinent *n* continent
kontinuïteit *n* continuity
kontoer *n* contour
kontrak *n* contract
kontrakteur *n* contractor
kontras *n* contrast
kontrei *n* region; area; district
kontribusie *n* contribution
kontrole *n* control; check
kontroleer *vb* to control; check
konveks *adj* convex
konvensie *n* convention
konvensioneel *adj* conventional
konvooi *n* convoy
konyn *n* rabbit
kooi *n* bed; cage
kooigoed *n* bedding
kook *vb* to boil; to cook
kookboek *n* cookery book
kookkuns *n* cookery
kookwater *n* boiling water
kool[1] *n* cabbage
kool[2] *n* coal
koolstof *n* carbon
koolstofbelasting *n* carbon tax
koolstofspoor (*or* **koolstofvoetspoor**) *n* carbon footprint
koop *n* bargain; purchase; *vb* to buy; to purchase
koopbrief *n* deed of sale
koop-en-loop *n* cash-and-carry
koöperasie *n* cooperation
koophandel *n* trade; commerce
koopkrag *n* buying power
koopman *n* merchant; dealer
koopwaar *n* merchandise; commercial goods
koor *n* choir; chorus
koord *n* cord; string; rope
koördinasie *n* coordination
koors *n* fever
koorsagtig *adj* feverish; frenzied
koorsang *n* choral song; choral singing
koorsblaar *n* fever blister
koorsboom *n* fever tree

koorspen(netjie) *n* clinical thermometer

koorsig *adj* feverish

kop[1] *n* cob; ear (mealie)

kop[2] *n* head; brains

koper[1] *n* buyer

koper[2] *n* copper

koperdraad *n* copper wire

kopie[1] *n* copy

kopie[2] *n* bargain

kopieer *vb* to copy

kopiereg *n* copyright

kopkool *n* cabbage

koppel *vb* to couple; to connect; to hyphenate; to interface (computing)

koppelteken *n* hyphen (-)

koppenent *n* head (of a bed)

koppie *n* cup; small hill

koppig *adj* headstrong; obstinate

kopseer *n* headache

kopsku *adj* shy; timid; evasive

kopstuk *n* head; heading; leader

koraal[1] *n* coral

koraal[2] *n* chorale

koraalrif *n* coral reef

kordaat *adj* bold; brave

kordon *n* cordon

korent *n* currant

korf *n* beehive

korhaan *n* bustard

koring *n* wheat; corn; grain

koringboer *n* grain farmer

koringskuur *n* granary

koronêre trombose *n* coronary thrombosis

korporaal *n* corporal

korporasie *n* corporation

korps *n* corps

korrek *adj* correct; right

korreksie *n* correction

korrel *n* grain; sight (of gun); bead

korrespondeer *vb* to correspond

korrespondensie *n* correspondence

korrespondent *n* correspondent

korrigeer *vb* to correct

korrosie *n* corrosion

korrup *adj* corrupt

korrupsie *n* corruption

kors *n* crust; scab

korset *n* corset; foundation garment

korsie *n* crust (bread)

korswel *n* joke; jest; *vb* to jest; to joke

kort *vb* shorten; *adj* short; brief; *adv* shortly; briefly

kortaf *adj* abrupt; blunt

kortasem *adj* short of breath

korting *n* discount

kortkom *vb* to run short

kortliks *adv* in short; briefly

kortom *adv* in short

kortpad *n* short cut

kortsigtig *adj* near-sighted; short-sighted

kortsluiting *n* short circuit

kortstondig *adj* short; short-lived

kortverhaal *n* short story

kos[1] *n* food; board; **— en blyplek** *n* board and lodging

kos[2] *vb* to cost

kosbaar *adj* precious; dear; expensive

kosganger *n* boarder

koshuis *n* boarding house

kosjer *adj* kosher

kosmeties *adj* cosmetic; superficial

kosmopoliet *n* cosmopolitan

kosmopolities *adj* cosmopolitan

kosskool *n* boarding school

koste *npl* expenses; costs

kostelik *adj* precious; beautiful; excellent

kosteloos *adj* free; gratis

koster *n* churchwarden; beadle; sexton

kostuum *n* costume

kosyn *n* window frame; windowsill

kotelet *n* cutlet

kothuis *n* cottage

kou[1] *n* cold; chill; **vat —e** *vb* to catch a cold; to catch a chill

kou[2] *n* cage

kou[3] *vb* to chew; to gnaw; to masticate

koud *adj* cold; chilly

koudlei *vb* to cool (a horse)

koudvuur *n* gangrene

koue *n* cold; chill

kouekoors *n* the shivers; shivering fit

koue oorlog *n* cold war

kougom *n* chewing gum; bubble gum

koukus *n* caucus

kous *n* stocking; sock

koutjie[1] *n* cud (cow)

koutjie[2] *n* cage

kraag *n* collar

kraai *n* crow; *vb* to crow
kraak *n* crack; flaw; *vb* to crack; to creak
kraakbeen *n* cartilage
kraal[1] *n* pen; kraal; fold; tribal village
kraal[2] *n* bead
kraam[1] *n* labour; childbirth
kraam[2] *n* booth; stall
kraamvrou *n* woman in labour
kraan *n* tap; stopcock; crane
kraanvoël *n* crane
krabbel *vb* to scratch; to scrawl
kraffie *n* water bottle; decanter
krag *n* strength; force; power
kragdadig *adj* energetic; effective; powerful
kragmas *n* pylon
kragsentrale *n* power station
kragteloos *adj* powerless; weak
kragtens *prep* by virtue of; on account of; in terms of
kragtig *adj* powerful; strong; able-bodied
kram *n* clamp; staple; *vb* to clamp; to staple
kramdrukker *n* stapler
krammer *n* stapler
krammetjie *n* staple
kramp *n* cramp; spasm; convulsion
krampagtig *adj* convulsive; spasmodic
kranig *adj* clever; smart; bold
kranksinnig *adj* mad; insane; lunatic
kranksinnige *n* lunatic
krans[1] *n* wreath
krans[2] *n* sheer rock face; krans; cliff
krap[1] *n* crab
krap[2] *n* scratch; *vb* to scratch
kras[1] *adj* strong; drastic
kras[2] *vb* to screech
krat *n* crate
krater *n* crater
krediet *n* credit
kredietkaart *n* credit card
kredietnota *n* credit note
krediteer *vb* to credit
krediteur *n* creditor
kreef *n* lobster; crayfish
kreet *vb* scream; cry
krematorium *n* crematorium
kremetart *n* cream of tartar
kremetartboom *n* baobab tree
krenk *vb* to hurt; to injure; to offend

kreukel *n* crease; fold; *vb* to crease; to fold
kreukel *vb* to crease; to rumple
kreukeltraag *adj* crease resistant
kreun *n* groan; moan; *vb* to groan; to moan
kreupel *adj* lame; crippled; limping
krewel *n* prawn
kriek *n* cricket (insect)
krieket *n* cricket (sport)
krieketbal *n* cricket ball
krieketkolf *n* cricket bat
krieseltjie *n* small bit; particle
kriewel *vb* to tickle; to itch; to wriggle
kriewelrig *adj* ticklish
krimineel *adj* criminal
krimp *vb* to shrink
krimpvry *adj* unshrinkable
kring *n* circle; orb; sphere
kringloop *n* cycle; circuit
krink *vb* to swing round
krioel *vb* to swarm; to teem with
krip *n* manger; crib
krisis *n* crisis
kristal *n* crystal; cut glass
kristalliseer *vb* to crystallize
kriterium *n* criterion; benchmark
kritiek *n* criticism; critique
krities *adj* critical
kritikus *n* critic
kritiseer *vb* to criticize
kroeg *n* public house; bar
kroep *n* croup
krokodil *n* crocodile
krom *adj* crooked; bent; curved
kroniek *n* chronicle
kronies *see* **chronies**
kroning *n* coronation
kronkel *vb* to twist; to coil; to wind; to meander
kronologies *see* **chronologies**
kroon[1] *n* crown; *vb* to crown
kroon[2] *n* chandelier
kroonjuwele *npl* crown jewels
kroonprins *n* crown prince
kroos *n* offspring; descendants
kroostrooster *n* babysitter
krop *n* crop; gizzard
kropslaai *n* lettuce
krot *n* hovel; shanty
krotbuurt *n* slum

kruid *n* herb
kruidenier *n* grocer
kruie *n* spice
kruier *n* porter
kruik *n* pitcher; jar
kruin *n* top; crown; summit
kruip *vb* to creep; to crawl; to stalk
kruis *n* cross; small of the back; affliction; sharp (music); *vb* to cross; to cruise; to intersect
kruisband *n* braces
kruisbeeld *n* crucifix
kruisement *n* mint
kruiser *n* cruiser
kruisig *vb* to crucify
kruising *n* crossbreeding; crossing; intersection
kruispad *n* crossroad
kruistog *n* crusade
kruisverhoor *n* cross-examination
kruisvra *vb* to cross-examine
kruit *n* gunpowder
kruiwa *n* wheelbarrow
kruk *n* crutch; crank
krul *n* curl (hair); shaving (wood); *vb* to curl (hair); to wave (hair)
krummel *n* crumb
kruppel *adj* crippled; limping; lame
kry *vb* to get; to obtain; to procure
kryg *n* fight; war
krygsdiens *n* military service
krygsgevangene *n* prisoner of war
krygshaftig *adj* warlike
krygslis *n* strategem
krygsmag *n* army
krygsman *n* warrior; soldier
krygsraad *n* court martial
krygstog *n* military campaign
krygswet *n* martial law
kryt[1] *n* ring (boxing); arena
kryt[2] *n* chalk; crayon
kuber *prefix* cyber; to do with computers
kuberagtervolging *n* cyberstalking
kuberkraker *n* hacker
kuberruimte *n* cyberspace
kuberteistering *n* cyberbullying; cyberharassment
kubiek *adj* cubic
kubus *n* cube
kudde *n* herd; flock

kuier *n* outing; visit; *vb* to visit; to call on
kuiergas *n* guest; visitor
kuif *n* crest; tuft
kuiken *n* young chicken
kuil *n* pit; hole; pool; dam; bunker (golf)
kuip *n* tub; coop; pit (motor racing)
kuis *adj* chaste; pure
kuit *n* calf (leg)
kul *vb* to cheat; to swindle
kularties *n* magician
kultureel *adj* cultural
kultuur *n* culture; civilization
kunde *n* knowledge; learning
kundig *adj* competent; skilful
kundige *n* (*informal*) boffin
kundigheid *n* skill; expertise
kundigheidsverlies *n* brain drain
kuns *n* art; skill; knack
kunsgalery *n* art gallery
kunsgebit *n* dentures; false teeth
kunsmatig *adj* artificial
kunsskilder *n* artist; painter
kunsstuk *n* work of art; masterpiece
kunstenaar *n* artist
kunstig *adj* clever; ingenious
kunswerk *n* work of art
kurator *n* curator; custodian
kuriositeit *n* curiosity; curio; relic
kurk *n* cork
kurktrekker *n* corkscrew
kurper *n* tilapia
kurrikulum *n* curriculum
kursief *n* italics; in italics
kursus *n* course
kus[1] *n* shore; coast
kus[2] *n* kiss; *vb* to kiss
kussing *n* cushion; pillow
kussingsloop *n* pillowcase; pillowslip
kussingtuig *n* hovercraft
kwaad *n* evil; mischief; wrong; *adj* angry; bad; evil
kwaadaardig *adj* malignant; malicious
kwaaddenkend *adj* suspicious
kwaaddoener *n* criminal;
kwaadwillig *adj* malevolent
kwaai *adj* vicious; hot-tempered
kwaaivriende *npl* bad friends
kwaak *vb* to croak; to quack
kwaal *n* disease; ailment; complaint
kwadraat *n, adj* square

kwagga *n* quagga; zebra
kwalifikasie *n* qualification
kwalifiseer *vb* to qualify
kwalik *adv* hardly; scarcely
kwaliteit *n* quality
kwansel *vb* to haggle; to bargain
kwantiteit *n* quantity
kwarantyn *n* quarantine
kwart *n* quart; quarter
kwartaal *n* quarter; term
kwartel *n* quail
kwartet *n* quartet
kwartier *n* quarter (of an hour, of a moon)
kwartiere *npl* quarters (military)
kwarts *n* quartz
kwas[1] *n* brush; tassel; knot (in wood)
kwas[2] *n* squash
kweek[1] *n* couch grass
kweek[2] *vb* to cultivate; to train
kweekhuis *n* hothouse; greenhouse
kweekpêrel *n* cultured pearl
kweekskool *n* seminary; training school
kweekhuisgas *n* greenhouse gas (GHG)
kweekhuisgasvrystelling *n* greenhouse gas emissions (GGE)
kwekeling *n* cadet; trainee

kwekery *n* nursery
kwel *vb* to tease; to torment; to worry; to trouble; to vex
kwelgees *n* tease; tormentor
kwelling *n* anxiety; trouble
kweper *n* quince
kwes *vb* to injure; to wound; to hurt; to offend
kwesbaar *adj* vulnerable
kwessie *n* matter; question; point
kwiksand *n* quicksand
kwiksilwer *n* mercury
kwikstertjie *n* wagtail
kwistig *adj* lavish; wasteful
kwitansie *n* receipt
kworum *n* quorum
kwosiënt *n* quotient
kwota *n* quota
kwotasie *n* quotation; estimate
kwoteer *vb* to quote; to estimate
kwyl *vb* to slaver; to dribble saliva from the mouth
kwyn *vb* to pine; to languish; to fade
kyf *vb* to quarrel
kyfagtig *adj* quarrelsome
kyk *n* look; *vb* to look; to see; to view
kyker *n* looker-on; spectator; viewer (TV); eye; pupil; telescope
kykgat *n* peephole

L

laaf *see* **lawe**
laafnis *n* refreshment; relief
laag[1] *n* layer; stratum; coating
laag[2] *adj* low; mean; base
laaghartig *adj* vile; base
laagheid *n* meanness; vulgarity
laagte *n* dale; valley
laai[1] *n* till; drawer
laai[2] *n* trick; dodge
laai op *vb* to upload (computing)
laaikas *n* chest of drawers
laak *vb* to blame
laakbaar *adj* blameworthy; reprehensible
laan *n* avenue; lane
laas *adj* last; recent; *adv* lastly; recently
laasgenoemde *n* the latter
laaslede *adj* last
laaste *n* last one; *adj, adv* last, latest
laat[1] *vb* to let; to permit; to grant leave; to allow; — **jouself geld** *vb* to assert oneself
laat[2] *adj, adv* late
labirint *n* labyrinth
laboratorium *n* laboratory
lading *n* cargo; shipment
laer[1] *n* camp; lager
laer[2] *adj* lower; inferior
laerskool *n* primary school
laeveld *n* low country; low veld
laevet *adj* low-fat; (*informal*) skinny
laf *adj* insipid; cowardly; silly
lafaard *n* coward
lafenis *n* refreshment; relief
lafhartig *adj* cowardly
lag *n* laughter; laugh; *vb* to laugh
laggas *n* laughing gas
lak[1] *n* sealing-wax; lacquer; *vb* to seal; lacquer
lak[2] *vb* to tackle
lakei *n* footman; lackey
laken *n* cloth; bedsheet
laks *adj* lax; indolent
lakseermiddel *n* laxative
laksman *n* hangman; butcher bird; fiscal shrike
lam[1] *n* lamb; *vb* to lamb

lam[2] *adj* lame; paralysed
lambada *n* lambada (dance, music)
lamheid *n* paralysis; tiredness
lamp *n* lamp
lampkap *n* lamp shade
lampolie *n* paraffin oil
lamsak *n* shirker; lazybones
land *n* country; land; field; *vb* to land; to disembark
landbou *n* agriculture
landboukundig *adj* agricultural
landdros *n* magistrate
landelik *adj* rustic; rural
landengte *n* isthmus
landgenoot *n* compatriot; fellow countryman
landingstrook *n* airstrip; landing strip
landkaart *n* map
landmyn *n* landmine
landskap *n* landscape
landstaal *n* the language of a country; native language; vernacular
landstreek *n* region; district
landswyd *adj* nationwide
lanfer *n* crepe
lang (*or* **lank**) *adj* long; tall; high
langdradig *adj* long-winded; wordy; tedious
langdurig *adj* long; longstanding
langs *prep* along; next to; beside
langsaam *adj* slow; *adv* slowly
langsamerhand *adv* gradually
langslewende *n* survivor
langwerpig *adj* oblong
laning *n* hedge; avenue
lank *see* **lang**
lankal *adv* long ago
lankmoedig *adj* patient; long-suffering
lankmoedigheid *n* patience; longsufferance
lans *n* spear; lance
lanseer *vb* to launch; to start
lanseerblad *n* launch pad
lansering *n* lift-off
lantern *n* lantern
lap *n* cloth; patch; rag; *vb* to mend; to patch

lappop *n* rag doll
larwe *n* larva
las[1] *n* seam; joint; *vb* to join; to weld
las[2] *n* load; burden; freight; order; charge; nuisance; trouble
laser *n* laser
laserskyf *n* compact disk (CD)
laserskyfspeler *n* CD player
laslorrie *n* articulated lorry
laspos *n* nuisance
lastig *adj* annoying; difficult
lat *n* latch; stick; cane
latei *n* lintel
later *adv* later; afterwards
Latyn *n, adj* Latin
laveer *vb* to tack (sailing)
lavental *n* lavender
lawa *n* lava
lawaai *n* noise; hubbub
lawe (*or* **laaf**) *vb* to refresh
lawine *n* avalanche
lê *vb* to put; to place; to lie; to lay
ledemaat *n* limb
ledig *vb* to empty; *adj* vacant; idle; without employment
ledigheid *n* emptiness; idleness
leed *n* pain; sorrow; grief
leedwese *n* regret; sorrow
leef (*or* **lewe**) *vb* to live; to exist
leefstyl *n* lifestyle
leeftog *n* sustenance
leeftyd *n* lifetime; time of life; age
leeg *adj* empty; void
leek *n* layman; novice
leemte *n* defect; gap
leen *vb* to lend; to borrow
leer[1] *n* ladder
leer[2] *n* leather
leer[3] *n* doctrine; apprenticeship; *vb* to learn; to study; to teach
leër *n* army; *vb* to encamp
lêer *n* layer (hen); railway sleeper; file (papers)
leerboek *n* textbook; manual
leerder *n* learner
leergang *n* syllabus
leergierig *adj* studious
leerjare *n* apprenticeship
leerling *n* pupil; scholar; learner
leerlooier *n* tanner
leerlooiery *n* tannery

lêeroordragprotokol *n* file transfer protocol (FTP)
leerplan *n* curriculum
leersaam *adj* informative; instructive
leerstoel *n* (university) chair
leerstuk *n* dogma; doctrine
leervak *n* subject (school)
leerwerk[1] *n* studies
leerwerk[2] *n* leather work
lees[1] *n* last (shoes); figure; waist
lees[2] *vb* to read
leesbaar *adj* legible; readable
leesboek *n* reader; reading book
leesgebrek *n* dyslexia
leesteken *n* punctuation mark
leeu *n* lion
leeubekkie *n* snapdragon
leeuwyfie *n* lioness
legendaries *adj* legendary
legende *n* legend
legioen *n* legion
legkaart *n* jigsaw puzzle
lei[1] *n* slate
lei[2] *vb* to lead; to guide; to conduct
leidak *n* slate roof
leiding *n* lead; guidance; direction
leidraad *n* clue; lead; guideline
leidster *n* female leader; guiding star
leier *n* leader; guide
leierskap *n* leadership
leiriem *n* leash; lead
leisel *n* rein
lek[1] *n* leak; leakage; puncture; *vb* to leak
lek[2] *vb* to lick; to lap
lekker *adj* nice; dainty; sweet; delicious; well; tipsy
lekkergoed *n* sweets; confectionery
lekkerlyf *adj* tipsy
lekkers *npl* sweets
leksikon *n* dictionary; lexicon
lektor *n* lecturer
lektuur *n* reading matter; literature
lelie *n* lily
lelik *adj* ugly; unsightly; bad; nasty; *adv* badly; nastily
lem *n* blade (knife)
lemmetjie *n* lime (fruit)
lemoen *n* orange (fruit)
lemoensap *n* orange juice
lende *n* loin; **die —ne omgord** *vb* to gird one's loins

lendelam *adj* shaky; rickety
lendepyn *n* lumbago
lengte *n* length; longitude
lenig[1] *vb* to relieve; to alleviate (pain)
lenig[2] *adj* supple; lithe
lening *n* loan
lens *n* lens
lensie *n* lentil
lensiesop *n* lentil soup
lente *n* spring
lepel *n* spoon; ladle
leraar *n* minister (religion)
lering *n* instruction; teaching
les[1] *n* lesson
les[2] *vb* to satisfy one's thirst
leser *n* scanner
lesing *n* lecture; reading
lessenaar *n* desk
lessenaarpublikasie *n* desktop publishing (DTP)
let op *vb* to mind; to heed
letsel *n* damage; hurt; injury
letter *n* letter
letterdief *n* plagiarist
lettere *n* literature
lettergreep *n* syllable
letterkunde *n* literature
letterlik *adj* literal; *adv* literally
letternaam *n* acronym
letterskilder *n* signwriter
leuen *n* lie; falsehood
leuenaar *n* liar
leuenagtig *adj* lying; false; untrue
leuentaal *n* falsehood; untruth
leun *vb* to lean on; to lean against
leuning *n* back (chair); rail; support
leuningstoel *n* armchair
leuse *n* motto; slogan
lewe *n* life; *vb* to live; to exist
lewendig *adj* living; alive; lively
lewensbeskrywing *n* biography
lewensgroot *adj* life-size
lewenslang *adj* lifelong
lewensloop *n* lifetime; course of life; career
lewenslus *n* energy
lewensmaat *n* life partner
lewensmiddele *n* foodstuffs; provisions
lewensvatbaar *adj* viable; capable of life

lewensversekering *n* life insurance
lewenswyse *n* lifestyle; conduct; manner of life
lewer[1] *n* liver
lewer[2] *vb* to supply; to deliver
leweransier *n* supplier
lewerik *n* skylark
lewertraan *n* cod-liver oil
lewerwors *n* liver sausage
liberaal *n* liberal; broadminded
lid *n* member
liddoring *n* corn
lidland *n* member state
lidmaat *n* member (church)
lidwoord *n* article
lied *n* song; hymn
liederlik *adj* filthy; dirty; debauched
liedjie *n* song; tune
lief *adj* beloved; dear; sweet; *adv* sweetly; nicely
liefdadig *adj* charitable
liefdadigheid *n* charity
liefde *n* love; affection
liefdeloos *adj* loveless; unfeeling
liefdesverhaal *n* love story
liefhê *vb* to love
liefhebbend *adj* loving; affectionate
liefhebbery *n* hobby; favourite pursuit
liefie *n* dear; darling
liefkoos *vb* to caress; to fondle
lieflik *adj* charming; lovely
liefling *n* darling; favourite; pet
liefs *adv* rather; preferably
liefste *n* darling; sweetheart; *adj* dearest; beloved
lieftallig *adj* sweet; amiable
lieg *vb* to lie; to tell lies
lier *n* lyre
lies *n* groin
liter *n* litre
liewer(s) *adv* rather
lig[1] *n* light; *adj* light; clear; bright; — **word** *vb* to become light, to dawn
lig[2] *vb* to lift; to pick up; to raise
lig[3] *adj* easy; mild; slight
ligblou *n*, *adj* pale blue
liggaam *n* body
liggaamlik *adj* bodily; physical; corporal
liggaamsbou *n* build; stature
liggaamsdeel *n* part of the body; limb

liggaamsmassaindeks *n* body mass index (BMI)
liggaamsoefening *n* physical exercise
liggaamstraf *n* corporal punishment
liggaamstaal *n* body language
liggelowig *adj* credulous
liggeraak *adj* touchy; oversensitive
liggewend *adj* luminous
ligging *n* situation; site; position
lighartig *adj* light-hearted
lighoofdig *adj* dizzy; light-headed
ligkrans *n* halo; corona
ligsinnig *adj* frivolous; flippant
ligstraal *n* ray of light
ligtelaaie: in — *adj, adv* ablaze; burning fiercely; in flames
ligvaardig *adj* reckless; rash
likeur *n* liqueur
likied *adj* liquid
likkewaan *n* iguana
likwidasie *n* liquidation
likwideer *vb* to liquidate
limiet *n* limit
limonade *n* lemonade
lindeboom *n* linden tree
linguis *n* linguist
liniaal *n* ruler (measuring)
linieer *vb* to rule (lines)
linker *adj* left; near (foreleg, etc.)
linkerkant *n* left side
links *adj* left-handed; *adv* on the left
linne *n* linen
linoleum *n* linoleum
lint *n* ribbon; tape
lintwurm *n* tapeworm
lip *n* lip
lipstiffie *n* lipstick
liriek *n* lyric poetry
lis[1] *n* noose; loop
lis[2] *n* trick; ruse
lisensie *n* licence
lispel *vb* to murmur; to lisp
lissie *n* loop; bow
listig *adj* cunning; artful; sly
lit *n* joint; **uit —** *adv* out of joint
liter *n* litre
literaries *adj* literary
literatuur *n* literature
literêr *adj* literary
litteken *n* scar
liturgie *n* liturgy

lobotomie *n* lobotomy
loei *vb* to low; to roar
loer *vb* to spy; to watch; to peep; to peer; to lie in wait for
loerkamera *n* surveillance camera
loesing *n* thrashing
lof[1] *n* praise; eulogy; **met — slaag** *vb* to pass with honours
lof[2] *n* foliage; leaves
loflik *adj* praiseworthy; laudable
lofrede *n* eulogy
lofsang *n* hymn; ode
lofwaardig *adj* praiseworthy
logaritme *n* logarithm
logboek *n* logbook
logies *adj* logical
logika *n* logic
lojaal *adj* loyal
lojaliteit *n* loyalty
lojaliteitskaart *n* loyalty card
lok[1] *n* lock (hair); curl (hair)
lok[2] *vb* to decoy; to entice
lokaal[1] *n* hall; room
lokaal[2] *adj* local
lokaas *n* bait; lure; decoy
lokasie *n* location
loket *n* ticket-office window; box office
lokfilm *n* trailer (movie)
lokomotief *n* locomotive; engine
lokteks *n* teaser (marketing)
lokval *n* ambush; trap
lokvoël *n* decoy
lol *vb* to bother; to nag
lomerig *adj* weary; sleepy
lomp *adj* awkward; clumsy
long *n* lung
longontsteking *n* pneumonia
longtering *n* consumption; pulmonary tuberculosis
lons *vb* to train on a long rope; to lunge (horse)
lont *n* fuse; **— ruik** *vb* to smell a rat
lood *n* lead; plumb line
loodgieter *n* plumber
loodreg *adj* vertical; perpendicular
loods[1] *n* shed
loods[2] *n* pilot
loods[3] *n* launch; *vb* to launch (book, scheme, etc.)
loof *vb* to praise; to extol
looi *vb* to tan; to beat

looiery *n* tannery
loom *adj* heavy; slow; drowsy
loon *n* wages; salary; reward; *vb* to reward; to pay
loongeskil *n* wage dispute
loontrekker *n* wage earner
loonverhoging *n* wage increase
loop *n* walking; walk; gait; barrel (gun); course (river); *vb* to walk; to run; to go; to flow
loopbaan *n* career; course
loopgeselser *n* walkie-talkie
loopgraaf *n* trench
loopplank *n* gangway (ship)
loot[1] *n* shoot (plant); offspring
loot[2] *vb* to draw lots; to raffle
lootjie *n* lottery ticket
LOP *see* **lêeroordragprotokol**
lopend *adj* current; present
lopende rekening *n* current account
loper[1] *n* runner; stair carpet; walker
loper[2] *n* buckshot
lopie *n* a little stream; run (cricket)
lorrie *n* lorry
los *vb* to loosen; to release; to let go; *adj* loose; extra; odd; spare; free; *adv* loosely
losbandig *adj* dissipated; dissolute
losbars *vb* to burst out; to break loose; to explode; to let fly
losbol *n* playboy
losbreek *vb* to break loose; to break away
loseer *vb* to lodge; to board
loseerder *n* lodger
losgeld *n* ransom
losgord *vb* to unbuckle
loshand *adj* hands-free
losies *n* board; lodging
losknoop *vb* to untie
loskom *vb* to get loose; to get free
loskoop *vb* to ransom; to redeem
loskop *n* (*informal*) bimbo
loslaat *vb* to release; to let go
losloop *vb* to be at large; to run free
losmaak *vb* to loosen; to undo; to untie
losprys *n* ransom
losryg *vb* to unlace; to undo
losskroewe *vb* to unscrew
lossny *vb* to cut loose
lostorring *vb* to unsew; to unpick

lostrek *vb* to pull loose
lot[1] *n* fate; destiny; crowd; multitude
lot[2] *n* lot (auction sale); lot; destiny; fortune
lotery *n* lottery; raffle
loting *n* drawing of lots; draw
lotgeval *n* adventure
lou *adj* tepid; lukewarm
louere *n* laurels
lourier *n* laurel; bay (tree)
louter *vb* to purify; to refine; *adj* pure; simple; mere; *adv* purely; simply; merely
loutering *n* catharsis
lower *n* foliage
lug *n* air; sky; smell; *vb* to air; to ventilate
lugballon *n* hot-air balloon
lugblik *n* aerial view
lugbombardement *n* air raid
lugbus *n* monorail
lugdig *adj* airtight
luggat *n* air hole; air pocket
lughartig *adj* light-hearted
lughawe *n* airport
lugledig *adj* airless; with no air
lugmag *n* air force
lugmyle *npl* air miles
lugpos *n* airmail
lugpyp *n* windpipe
lugredery *n* airline
lugreis *n* air travel
lugskip *n* airship
lugspieëling *n* mirage; fata morgana
lugstreek *n* climate; zone
lugtig *adj* airy; light; light-hearted; *adv* lightly
lugtyd *n* airtime
lugvaart *n* aviation; aeronautics
lugverfrisser *n* air freshener
lugversorging *n* air conditioning
lui[1] *vb* to sound; to ring; to toll
lui[2] *adj* lazy; idle; inert
luiaard *n* lazybones; slacker
luid *adj* loud; *adv* loudly
luidroeper *n* loud-hailer
luidrugtig *adj* noisy; clamorous; boisterous
luidspreker *n* loudspeaker
luier[1] *n* nappy; swaddling-cloth
luier[2] *vb* to idle (motor engine); to be lazy

luik *n* shutter; manhole; hatch; trapdoor
luikrug *n* hatchback (car)
luilekkerland *n* fool's paradise
luim *n* whim; mood; humour
luimig *adj* comic; humorous
luiperd *n* leopard
luis *n* louse
luislang *n* python; boa constrictor
luister[1] *n* lustre; splendour; glory
luister[2] *vb* to listen; to hear; to obey
luisteraar *n* radio listener
luisterryk *adj* brilliant; splendid
luistervink *n* eavesdropper
luistervlooi *n* electronic bug
luit *n* lute
luitenant *n* lieutenant
luitoon *n* ringtone
lukraak *adv* at random; haphazardly
lukwart *n* loquat
lus[1] *n* desire; appetite; inclination; *vb* to like; to desire; to feel like
lus[2] *n* loop (out of the loop, in the loop)
lusern *n* lucerne
lusteloos *adj* dull; listless
lustig *adj* cheerful; merry
luukse *n* luxury
ly *vb* to suffer; to endure; to tolerate
lydelik *adj* passive; submissive
lyding *n* suffering; distress

lydsaamheid *n* meekness; patience
lyer *n* sufferer; patient
lyf *n* body
lyfband *n* belt; waistband
lyfdubbel *n* body double (movies)
lyfstraf *n* corporal punishment
lyftaal *n* body language
lyfwag *n* bodyguard
lyk[1] *n* corpse; dead body
lyk[2] *vb* to resemble; to seem; to look
lyksbesorger *n* undertaker
lyksdiens *n* funeral service
lykshuis *n* mortuary; morgue
lykskleed *n* shroud
lykskouing *n* autopsy; postmortem
lykstoet *n* funeral procession
lyksverbranding *n* cremation
lykswa *n* hearse
lym *n* glue; *vb* to glue
Lymesiekte *n* Lyme disease
lyn *n* rope; line; string; cord
lynolie *n* linseed oil
lynregter *n* linesman; line judge
lynsaad *n* linseed
lynstaan *n* rugby line-out
lys *n* list; schedule; catalogue; picture frame; picture rail
lywig *adj* thick; bulky; fat

M

ma *n* ma; mama; mother; mummy
maag *n* stomach; belly
maagd *n* virgin; maiden
maagkoors *n* gastric fever
maagkwaal *n* stomach complaint
maagpyn *n* stomach ache
maai *vb* to mow; to reap
maaier[1] *n* mower; reaper
maaier[2] *n* maggot
maak *n* make; making; *vb* to make; to manufacture; to produce; to do
maal[1] *n* time
maal[2] *n* meal
maal[3] *vb* to grind; to mince; to circle round and round
maalstroom *n* whirlpool
maaltand *n* molar (tooth)
maaltyd *n* meal
maalvleis *n* mince; minced meat
maan *n* moon
maand *n* month
Maandag *n* Monday
maandblad *n* monthly magazine
maandeliks *adj, adv* monthly
maandstonde *n* menstruation; periods
maanhaar *n* mane
maanlanding *n* moon landing
maanlig *n* moonlight
maansverduistering *n* eclipse of the moon
maar *conj* but; and yet; nevertheless; *adv* yet; only; just
maarskalk *n* marshall
Maart *n* March
maas *n* (a)maas; sour milk
maaskaas *n* cottage cheese
maat[1] *n* mate; friend; comrade
maat[2] *n* measure (music); size; dimension
maatreël *n* measure; step; **—s tref** to take steps; to take measures
maatskaplik *adj* social
maatskaplike beveiliging *n* social security
maatskaplike werker *n* social worker
maatskappy *n* society; company; partnership
maatstaf *n* standard; rule; criterion; benchmark
macaroni *n* macaroni; **— en kaas** *n* macaroni cheese
madeliefie *n* daisy
maer *adj* thin; lean; meagre; scanty
mag[1] *n* power; might; authority
mag[2] *vb* may
magasyn *n* warehouse; store
magasynmeester *n* storeman
magistraat *n* magistrate
magnaat *n* magnate
magneet *n* magnet
magnesium *n* magnesium
magneties *adj* magnetic
magnetisme *n* magnetism
magteloos *adj* powerless
magtig *vb* to authorize; to empower; *adj* powerful; mighty; empowered
magtiging *n* authorization; warrant
mahoniehout *n* mahogany
majesteit *n* majesty; splendour
majestueus *adj* majestic
majoor *n* major
mak *adj* tame; gentle; docile
makeer *vb* to ail; to lack; to matter
makelaar *n* broker
maker *n* maker; creator
maklik *adj* easy
makou *n* muscovy duck
makriel *n* mackerel
makrolletjie *n* almond cake; macaroon
makrostraler *n* jumbo jet
maksimum *n* maximum
mal *adj* foolish; silly; mad; insane; **— oor** *adj* fond of
malaria *n* malaria
malheid *n* madness; nonsense; foolishness
malhuis *n* lunatic asylum
malkop *n* madcap; tomboy
mallemeule *n* merry-go-round
malligheid *n* silliness; nonsense
mals *adj* juicy; tender; soft; lush
maltrap *n* madcap; tomboy
malva *n* geranium
mama *n* mam(m)a; mother
mamba *n* mamba (snake)

mampoer *n* home-distilled brandy
man *n* man; husband
mandaat *n* mandate
mandjie *n* basket; hamper
mandolien *n* mandolin
maneuver *n* manoeuvre
manewales *npl* antics
mangaan *n* manganese
mangat *n* manhole
mangel *n* tonsil
mango *n* mango
manhaftig *adj* manly; brave
maniak *n* maniac
manie *n* mania
manier *n* manner; way; fashion
manierlik *adj* polite; courteous
manifes *n* manifesto
manikuur *n* manicure
mank *adj* lame; limping
manlik *adj* masculine; male; manly
manmoedig *adj* brave; courageous
manna *n* manna
mannekrag *n* manpower; labour force
mannekyn *n* mannequin
mannetjie *n* male; little man
mansjet *n* cuff
mansjetknoop *n* cufflink
manskap *n* man; crew; soldier
manslag *n* manslaughter; homicide
mantel *n* cloak; cape; mantle; casing
manteldraaier *n* turncoat
manuskrip *n* manuscript
marginale setel *n* marginal seat (politics)
marginaliseer *vb* to marginalize
marineblou *n, adj* navy blue
marionet *n* puppet
mark *n* market
markeer *vb* mark
markeetent *n* marquee
markies *n* marquis
markiesin *n* marchioness
marknavorsing *n* market research
markplein *n* market square
markprys *n* market price
marmelade *n* marmalade
marmer *n* marble
marmotjie *n* marmot
mars *n* march
marsjeer *vb* to march
martel *vb* to torture; to torment

martelaar *n* martyr
martelaarskap *n* martyrdom
mas *n* mast; pole
masels *n* measles; **Duitse —** *n* German measles
masjien *n* machine; engine
masjinis *n* engine driver
masker *n* mask; disguise
maskerbal *n* fancy-dress ball
massa *n* mass; crowd; lump; bulk
massamedia *n* mass media
massaproduksie *n* mass production
massaversending *n* bulk posting
masseer *vb* to massage
massief *adj* massive
mastig! *interj* my word!
masurka *n* mazurka
maswerk *n* sailor's knot
mat¹ *n* mat; doormat
mat² *adj* lacklustre; dull; tired; exhausted
mate *n* measure; **tot 'n —** *adv* to an extent
materiaal *n* material
materialisties *adj* materialistic
matesis *n* mathematics
matig *vb* to curb; to restrain; to moderate; *adj* sober; restrained; moderate
matigheid *n* moderation; restraint
matras *n* mattress
matriek *n* matric
matrikulasie *n* matriculation
matrikuleer *vb* to matriculate
matrone *n* matron
matroos *n* sailor
medalje *n* medal
medaljon *n* medallion; locket
mededeel *vb* to communicate; to inform
mededeelsaam *adj* communicative; charitable
mededeling *n* communication
mededingend *adj* rival
mededinger *n* rival; competitor
mededoë *n* compassion; pity
medeeienaar *n* joint owner
medegevangene *n* fellow prisoner
medegevoel *n* sympathy
medeklinker *n* consonant
medelye *n* pity; compassion
medemens *n* fellow man

medepligtige *n* accomplice
medewerking *n* cooperation; collaboration
medewete *n* knowledge
media *n* media
mediaan *n* median
mediasentrum *n* media centre
medies *adj* medical
mediese ondersoek *n* medical examination
medikasie *n* medication
medikus *n* physician; medical practitioner; doctor
medisyne *n* medicine
medium *n* medium; means
meebring *vb* to bring along; to bring with; to cause (illness); to involve (danger)
meedeel *vb* to communicate; to inform
meedeelsaam *adj* communicative; charitable
meedeling *n* communication
meeding *vb* to compete; to rival
meedoë *n* compassion; pity
meedoënloos *adj* pitiless
meegaande *adj* tolerant; attached
meegevoel *n* sympathy
meel *n* meal; flour
meelblom *n* flour
meeldraad *n* stamen
meeloper *n* sympathizer; collaborator
meeluister *vb* to listen together; to monitor; to tap (telephone)
meeluisterapparaat *n* bugging device
meen *vb* to mean; to intend; to suppose
meeneem *vb* to take with
meenthuis *n* townhouse
meer[1] *n* lake
meer[2] *vb* to moor; to tie up
meer[3] *adj* more
meerdere *n* superior (person)
meerderheid *n* majority
meerkat *n* meercat
meermin *n* mermaid
meermaal *adv* frequently; often; more than once
meervoud *n* plural
meervoudig *adj* plural
mees *adj* most; *adv* mostly
mees(t)al *adv* mostly; generally; as a rule

meester *n* teacher; master; template
meesteres *n* mistress
meesterlik *adv* excellent; masterly
meesterstuk *n* masterpiece
meet *vb* to measure; to gauge; to compare
meetband *n* tape measure
meetkunde *n* geometry
meetstok *n* measuring rod
meeu *n* seagull; gull
meeval *vb* to cause surprise; to succeed beyond expectation
meewarig *adj* sympathetic
meewerk *vb* to cooperate; to collaborate
meewerking *n* cooperation
meewete *n* knowledge
meganies *adj* mechanical
Mei *n* May
meineed *n* perjury
meisie *n* girl
meisieskool *n* girls' school
mejuffrou *n* Miss
mekaar *pron* each other; one another
melaatse *n* leper
melaatsheid *n* leprosy
melancholies *adj* depressed; sad
meld *vb* to mention; to inform; to report
melding *n* mention
melk *n* milk; *vb* to milk
melkery *n* dairy
melksuiker *n* lactose
melksuur *n* lactic acid
melktand *n* milk tooth
melktert *n* milk tart
Melkweg *n* Milky Way
melodie *n* melody
melodieus *adj* melodious
memoriseer *vb* to memorize
meneer *title* Mr; Sir
meng *vb* to mix; to blend; to mingle
mengsel *n* mixture
menig(e) *determiner* many; several
menigeen *determiner* many; several; many a one
menigmaal *adv* often
menigte *n* crowd
mening *n* opinion; belief; view
meningverskil *n* difference of opinion
mens *n* human being; man; woman; person; **'n —** *pron* one; they; people

mensdom *n* mankind; humanity
mensebronne *npl* human resources
mensehandel *n* human trafficking
mensehater *n* misanthrope
menseras *n* human race
menseregte *n* human rights
menseverhoudinge *n* human relations
mensevriend *n* humanitarian; philan-
　thropist
mensheid *n* humankind; humanity
mensliewend *adj* philanthropic
menslik *adj* human
menstruasie *n* menstruation
mensvreter *n* cannibal
menu *n* menu; bill of fare
mentaliteit *n* mentality
menuet *n* minuet
merendeel *n* majority
merendeels *adv* mostly
meridiaan *n* meridian
merino *n* merino (sheep)
merk *n* mark; sign; brand; token; scar;
　vb to mark; to notice; to perceive
merkbaar *adj* perceptible; noticeable
merkteken *n* mark; sign; token
merkwaardig *adj* remarkable; notewor-
　thy
merrie *n* mare
mes *n* knife
messel *vb* to lay bricks; to build
messelaar *n* mason; bricklayer
messelkalk (*or* **messelklei**) *n* mortar
met *prep* with; by; at; in
metaal *n* metal
metaalagtig *adj* metallic
metaalverklikker *n* metal detector
metafisies *adj* metaphysical
metafoor *n* metaphor
meteen *adv* at the same time
meteens *adv* all at once; suddenly
meteoor *n* meteor
meter *n* meter; gauge; metre
metgesel *n* escort; companion
meting *n* measuring
metode *n* method; mode
metodiek *n* method
metodies *adj* methodical
metries *adj* metric; metrical
metrum *n* metre
mettertyd *adv* gradually; in the course
　of time

meubels *n* furniture
meubelmaker *n* cabinet-maker; joiner
meubileer *vb* to furnish
meul(e) *n* mill
meulenaar *n* miller
mevrou *title* Mrs; madam
miaau *vb* to miaow; to mew
middae *adv* in the afternoon
middag *n* noon; midday
middagdutjie *n* afternoon nap; siesta
middagete *n* dinner
midde *n* midst; middle
middel[1] *n* waist; middle; centre
middel[2] *n* means; instrument; medium;
　remedy
middelaar *n* mediator
middelbaar *adj* secondary; average;
　moderate; middle
middeldeur *adj* in two; in half
Middeleeue *n* Middle Ages
middeleeus *adj* medieval
middelerwyl *adv* meanwhile
middeljarig *adj* middle-aged
middellyn *n* diameter; equator
middelmatig *adj* fair; middling; medio-
　cre; medium
middelpunt *n* centre
middelpuntvliedend *adj* centrifugal
middelste *adj* middle; central
middelvinger *n* middle finger
middeweg *n* middle course
middernag *n* midnight
midstroom *n* midstream
mied *n* pile; heap; stack
mielie *n* mealie; maize
mieliekop *n* mealie cob
mieliemeel *n* mealie meal
mieliepap *n* mealie porridge
mier *n* ant
miershoop *n* ant hill
miet *n* mite (insect)
migraine *n* migraine
mik[1] *n* fork (branch)
mik[2] *vb* to aim (at)
mika *n* mica
mikpunt *n* aim; target; objective
mikrofilm *n* microfilm
mikrofoon *n* microphone
mikrogolf *n* microwave
mikrogolfbaar *adj* microwaveable
mikrorekenaar *n* microcomputer

mikrobe *n* microbe
mikroskoop *n* microscope
mikroskyfie *n* microchip
mikrotuig *n* microlight (aircraft)
mild *adj* liberal; generous
milddadig *adj* liberal; charitable
militant *adj* militant
militêr *n* military man; *adj* military
miljard *n* billion
miljoen *n* million
miljoener *n* millionaire
milligram *n* milligram
millimeter *n* millimetre
milt *n* spleen
mimiek *n* mimicry
min[1] *n* love; *vb* to love
min[2] *adj* little; few; less; *prep; adj* minus
minag *vb* to despise; to slight
minagting *n* disdain; contempt
minder *adj* less; inferior; minor
mindere *n* inferior (person)
minderheid *n* minority; inferiority
minderjarig *adj* under age; minor
minderjarige *n* minor
minderwaardig *adj* inferior
mineraal *n* mineral; *adj* mineral
mineur *n* minor (music); *adj* minor
minimeer *vb* to minimize
minimum *n* minimum
miniromp *n* miniskirt
minister *n* minister
ministerie *n* ministry; cabinet
ministerieel *adj* ministerial
minnaar *n* lover
minnares *n* mistress
minnebrief *n* love letter
minnelied *n* love song
minsaam *adj* kind; affable
minste *adj* least; smallest
minstens *adv* at least; not less than
minuut *n* minute (time)
mirre *n* myrrh
mirt *n* myrtle
mis[1] *n* mass
mis[2] *n* manure; dung
mis[3] *n* fog; mist
mis[4] *vb* to miss; to fail; to lack; to lose; *adj, adv* wrong; amiss
misbaar *adj* expendable; dispensable
misbruik *n* abuse; misuse
misdaad *n* crime; misdeed

misdadig *n* criminal
misdadiger *n* criminal
misdryf *n* offence; crime
miserabel *adj* miserable
misgis *vb* to be mistaken
misgreep *n* mistake; blunder
misgun *vb* to begrudge; to envy
mishaag *vb* to displease
mishandel *vb* to ill-treat; to ill-use
mishê *vb* to be mistaken
mishoring *n* siren; foghorn
miskien *adv* perhaps; possibly
miskraam *n* miscarriage; abortion
miskruier *n* dung beetle
misleidend *adj* deceptive; misleading
mislik *adj* sick; nauseous; squeamish; disgusting
misluk *vb* to fail; to miscarry
mislukking *n* failure; miscarriage
mismaak *vb* to deform; to disfigure
mismaak *adj* deformed
mismoedig *adj* dejected; gloomy
misnewel *n* fog
misnoeë *n* displeasure; discontent
misnoeg *adj* displeased; disgruntled
misplaas *adj* misplaced; misdirected
misreken *vb* to be mistaken
missiel *n* missile
misslaan *vb* to miss
misstap *n* false step
misstof *n* manure; fertilizer
misterie *n* mystery
misterieus *adj* mysterious
mistiek *adj* mystic(al)
mistig *adj* foggy; misty
misverstand *n* misunderstanding; error
mite *n* myth
mitologie *n* mythology
mits *conj* provided that
mobiel *adj* mobile; movable
mobilisasie *n* mobilization
mobiliseer *vb* to mobilize
modder *n* mud; mire
modderig *adj* muddy
modderskerm *n* fender; mudguard
mode *n* fashion; vogue
model *n* model; pattern
modelleer *vb* to model; to shape
modern *adj* modern; fashionable
modernisme *n* modernism

modiste *n* milliner; dressmaker
moed *n* courage; nerve; morale
moedeloos *adj* disheartened; dejected
moeder *n* mother
moederskap *n* motherhood; maternity
moedertaal *n* mother tongue
moedervlek *n* birthmark
moedig *adj* courageous; brave
moedswillig *adj* petulant; wilful; *adv* wilfully
moeg *adj* tired; weary
moeilik *adj* difficult; hard
moeilikheid *n* difficulty; trouble
moeisaam *adj* tiring; tiresome
moeite *n* difficulty; trouble; **die — doon** *vb* to take the trouble
moeitevol *adj* troublesome; difficult
moenie! *contraction* don't (do not)
moer *n* nut (with bolt)
moeras *n* marsh; swamp
moerbei *n* mulberry
moes *n* pulp
moesie *n* mole; beauty spot
moet *n* dent; mark; scar
moet *vb* to have to; to be obliged to
mof *n* socket
moffie *n* mitten; (*informal*) gay person, homosexual
moker *vb* to strike; to beat
mol[1] *n* mole (animal)
mol[2] *n* flat (music)
molekule *n* molecule
moles *n* harm; row; rumpus
molesteer *vb* to molest
mollig *adj* plump; chubby
molshoop *n* molehill
molvel *n* moleskin
moltrein *n* underground (train system); tube; metro
moltreinstasie *n* underground station; tube station; metro station
mombakkies *n* mask
moment *n* moment
momenteel *adj* momentary; *adv* momentarily
mompel *vb* to mutter; to grumble
monarg *n* monarch
monargie *n* monarchy
mond *n* mouth
mondeling *adj* oral; verbal
mondering *n* uniform; equipment

mondfluitjie *n* mouth-organ
mondig *adj* major; of age
mondjievol *n* small mouthful; tiny amount
mondstuk *n* mouthpiece
monitor *n* monitor
monnik *n* monk; friar
monoloog *n* monologue; soliloquy
monopolie *n* monopoly
monster[1] *n* monster; brute
monster[2] *n* sample; *vb* to compare; to muster
monsterneming *n* sampling
monsteragtig *adj* monstrous
monteer *vb* to mount; to assemble; to fit out
monteur *n* fitter
monument *n* monument
mooi *adj* pretty; fine; handsome; nice
mooimaaksessie *n* makeover session
mooipraat *vb* to flatter; to talk nicely about
moondheid *n* state; power
moontlik *adj* possible
moor *vb* to ill treat; to murder
moord *n* murder
moorddadig *adj* murderous; cruel
moordenaar *n* murderer
moraal *n* moral
moraliteit *n* morality
moratorium *n* moratorium
môre (*or* **more**) *n, adv* morning; tomorrow
moreaand *n, adv* tomorrow evening
môre! (*or* **more!**) *sentence substitute* good morning!
moreel *adj* moral; *n* morale
môreoggend *n, adv* tomorrow morning
morfien *n* morphine; morphia
mors *vb* to mess; to waste
morsdood *adj* stone-dead
morsig *adj* dirty; filthy
mortier *n* mortar
mos[1] *n* moss
mos[2] *adv* indeed; though
mosaïek *n* mosaic
mosie *n* motion; vote
moskee *n* mosque
mossel *n* mussel
mossie *n* sparrow

mosterd *n* mustard
mot *n* moth
motel *n* motel
motief *n* motive
motiveer *vb* to give reasons for; to motivate
motor *n* car; motorcar; engine
motorbom *n* car bomb
motorfiets *n* motorbike
motorhawe *n* garage (business)
motorhuis *n* garage (home)
motorkap *n* bonnet (car)
motorkaping *n* car hijacking; carjacking
motorskuiling *n* carport
motreën *n* drizzle
mou *n* sleeve
mout *n* malt
mp3-speler *n* MP3 player
muf *adj* stuffy; musty
muggie *n* midge; gnat
muil[1] *n* mule
muil[2] *n* mouth
muilband *n* muzzle
muilbandbevel *n* gagging order
muis *n* mouse; ball of thumb
muishond *n* skunk; polecat; mongoose
muistand *n* milk tooth
muisval *n* mousetrap
muit *vb* to mutiny; to revolt
muitery *n* mutiny
multikultureel *adj* multicultural
multimedia *n* multimedia
mummie *n* mummy (Egyptian)
munisipaliteit *n* municipality

munt *n* coin; mint; *vb* to coin
muntoutomaat *n* vending machine
muntstuk *n* coin
murasie *n* ruins
murg *n* marrow
murgbeen *n* marrowbone
murmel *vb* to murmur; to babble
murmureer *vb* to grumble
mus *n* cap; tea cosy
muse *n* muse
museum *n* museum
musiek *n* music
musikaal *adj* musical
musikant *n* member of a band
musiekkorps *n* band
musikus *n* musician
muskaatneut *n* nutmeg
muskadel *n* muscadel
muskeljaatkat *n* genet (wild cat)
muskiet *n* mosquito
muskus *n* musk
muur *n* wall
muurkas *n* built-in cupboard
muurpapier *n* wallpaper
my *pers pron* me; *poss pron* my
myl *n* mile
mymer *vb* to ponder; to muse
myn *n* mine; *vb* to mine
mynbou *n* mining (industry)
myne *poss pron* mine
myner *n* miner
mynlamp *n* safety lamp
mynwerker *n* miner
myter *n* mitre

N

'n *indefinite article* a; an
'n **trap** *n* flight of stairs
na[1] *prep* after; towards; to; according to; at
na[2] *adv* near; close
naaf *n* nave; hub
naafdop *n* hubcap
naai *vb* to sew
naaigare *n* sewing cotton; thread
naaikissie *n* workbox; sewing box
naaimasjien *n* sewing machine
naaister *n* seamstress
naaiwerk *n* sewing; needlework
naak *adj* naked; nude; bare; **die —te waarheid** *n* the naked truth
naaktheid *n* nakedness; nudity
naald *n* needle; obelisk
naaldekoker *n* needle case; dragonfly
naaldekussing *n* pincushion
naaldwerk *n* needlework; needlecraft
naam *n* name; **— gee** *vb* to name
naambord *n* signboard; nameplate
naamgenoot *n* namesake
naamlik *adv* namely; viz.; to wit
naamloos *adj* nameless; anonymous
naamplaatjie *n* name tag
naamtekening *n* signature
naamval *n* case
naamwoord *n* nomenclature; **selfstandige — ** *n* noun
naand! *sentence substitute* good evening!
naaper *n* (*informal*) wannabe
naar *adj* sick; giddy; sad; dreary; terrible
naarheid *n* unpleasantness; giddiness
naarstig *adj* diligent
naas *prep* next to; beside
naasaan *prep* next to; next door to
naasagter *n, adj* last but one
naasbestaande *n* next of kin
naasgrootste *n, adj* second biggest
naaste *n* neighbour; fellow man; *adj, adv* nearest
naaste(n)by *adv* approximately; more or less
naasvoor *n, adj* front but one
naaswenner *n* runner-up

naaswit *n, adj* off-white
naat *n* seam; suture; joint
naatlos *adj* seamless
nabetragting *n* reflection; meditation
naboots *vb* to imitate; to mimic; to copy
naburig *adj* neighbouring
naby *adj* near; nearby; *adv* close by; nearby; *prep* near; close to
nabygeleë *adj* adjacent; neighbouring
nabyheid *n* vicinity; proximity
nadat *conj* after; when
nadeel *n* loss; downside; disadvantage; injury
nadelig *adj* injurious; disadvantageous
nadenkend *adj* meditative; pensive
nader *vb* to approach; to come nearer; *adv, adj* nearer
naderende *adj* approaching; oncoming
naderhand *adv* afterwards
nadink *vb* to reflect; to consider
nadoods *adj* posthumous; after death; *adv* after death; posthumously
nadoodse ondersoek *n* autopsy; post-mortem
nadruk *n* emphasis; stress
nadruklik *adj* emphatic; *adv* emphatically
nael[1] *n* nail; rivet; *vb* to nail
nael[2] *n* navel
nael[3] *vb* to spring; to sprint; to race
naelkouer *n* cliffhanger (movie, TV drama, etc.)
naelloper *n* sprinter
naelstring *n* umbilical cord
naeltjie *n* hyacinth
naeltjies *npl* cloves
naeltjieolie *n* oil of cloves
nag *n* night; **—!** *sentence substitute* good night!
nagaan *vb* to follow with the eye; to run over with the eye; to trace; to check
nagaap *n* bushbaby
nageboorte *n* placenta; afterbirth
nagedagtenis *n* remembrance
nagemaak *adj* counterfeit; forged; false; artificial
nagenoeg *adv* almost; nearly
nagereg *n* dessert

nageslag *n* posterity; offspring; future generations

nagmerrie *n* nightmare

nagskof *n* night shift

nagtegaal *n* nightingale

nagtelik *adj* nightly; nocturnal

nagwag *n* night watchman

naïef *adj* naive; simple

naïwiteit *n* simplicity; naivety

najaag *vb* to run after; to chase

najaar *n* autumn

nakend *adj* naked; nude; bare

naklank *n* echo

naklink *vb* to resound; to re-echo

nakom *vb* to fulfil; to keep; to obey

nakomeling *n* descendant

nakomelingskap *n* posterity; progeny; offspring

nakoming *n* adherent

nakyk *vb* to examine; to revise; to correct

nalaat *vb* to bequeath; to leave; to neglect; to omit

nalatenskap *n* inheritance

nalatig *adj* negligent; neglectful

nalatigheid *n* negligence; carelessness

naleef *vb* to observe; to comply with

nalees *vb* to read over; to peruse

naloop *vb* to follow; to run after

namaak *vb* to imitate; to copy

namaaksel *n* imitation; counterfeit

namens *prep* for; in the name of

namiddag *n* afternoon

nanotegnologie *n* nanotechnology

naoorlogse baba (*or* **naoorlogse kind**) *n* baby-boomer

napartytjie *n* afterparty

napraat *vb* to repeat; to mimic

nar *n* fool; jester

narede *n* epilogue

nareken *vb* to calculate; to verify; to check

narigheid *n* unpleasantness; giddiness; squeamishness

narkose *n* narcosis; anaesthesia; anaesthetic

narkotiseur *n* anaesthetist

narsing *n* narcissus

naartjie *n* mandarin orange; nartjie

Nasa *see* **Amerikaanse Nasionale Lugvaarten Ruimteadministrasie**

nasaal *adj* nasal

nasaat *n* descendant

nasê *vb* to repeat

nasie *n* nation

nasien *vb* to mark; to correct; to revise; to examine; to check

nasionaal *adj* national

nasionale pad national road

nasionalisme *n* nationalism

nasionaliseer *vb* to nationalize

nasionaliteit *n* nationality

naskrif *n* postscript

naslaan *vb* to look up; to consult

naslaanwerk *n* reference work; reference book

nasleep[1] *n* result; consequence

nasleep[2] *vb* to drag behind

nasmaak *n* aftertaste

nat *adj* wet; moist

natheid *n* dampness; wetness

natrium *n* sodium

natterig *adj* damp; wettish

natterigheid *n* dampness; rain

naturalisasie *n* naturalization

naturaliseer *vb* to naturalize

natuur *n* nature; temper; temperament

natuurbewaring *n* nature conservation

natuurbronne *n* natural resources

natuurkunde *n* physics

natuurlik *adj* natural; *adv* naturally; of course

natuurwetenskap *n* natural science

naverwant *adj* closely related

NAVO *see* **Noord-Atlantiese Verdragsorganisasie**

navolg *vb* to follow; to imitate

navors *vb* to investigate; to research

navraag *n* enquiry; query

naweek *n* weekend

nawel *n* navel

nawerking *n* aftereffect

naywer *n* jealousy; envy

né *question tag* is it not; isn't it

nederig *adj* humble; meek

nedersetting *n* settlement; colony

nee *sentence substitute* no

neef *n* cousin (male); nephew

neem *vb* to take; to accept

neer *adv* down; downwards; below

neerdaal *vb* to descend; to come down

neerkom *vb* to come down to

neerlaag *n* defeat

neerlê *vb* to lay down; to abdicate; to resign

neersien *vb* to look down upon

neersit *vb* tp put down; to place

neerslaan *vb* to knock down; to strike; to fall down

neerslagtig *adj* depressed; dejected

neet *n* nit; egg of a louse

negatief *adj* negative

nege *n, determiner* nine

negeer *vb* to ignore

negende *adj, n* ninth

negentien *n, determiner* nineteen

negentiende *adj, n* nineteenth

negentig *n, determiner* ninety

negentigste *adj, n* ninetieth

nege-uur *n, adj* nine o'clock

negevoud *adj* ninefold

negosie *n* goods; trade

negosieware *n* merchandise

neig *vb* to incline

neiging *n* inclination; tendency

nek *n* neck; mountain pass

nektar *n* nectar

nektarien *n* nectarine

nêrens *adv* nowhere

nerf *n* grain (leather, etc.); outer skin

nering *n* trade; occupation

nes[1] *n* nest

nes[2] *adv* just like; just as

neseier *n* nest-egg

nesskop *vb* to build a nest

net[1] *n* net

net[2] *adj* neat; exact; clean; pretty

net[3] *adv* only; just

neteldoek *n* muslin

netelig *adj* thorny; difficult

netheid *n* neatness; tidiness

netjies *adj* neat; nice

netnou *adv* just now; directly

netto *n* net (profits)

netwerk *n* network (computing)

netvlies *n* retina

neuk *vb* to hit; to bother

neul *vb* to bother; to pester; to annoy

neuralgie *n* neuralgia

neurie *vb* to hum; to croon

neus *n* nose

neusgat *n* nostril

neut *n* nutmeg; nut

neutkraker *n* nutcracker(s)

neutraal *adj* neutral

neutraliseer *vb* to neutralize

neutraliteit *n* neutrality

newel *n* fog; mist; haze

newens *prep* next to; beside

neweproduk *n* by-product

nie *prefix* not; non

niefiksie *n* nonfiction

niegestremd *adj* able; normal

niemand *n* nobody; no one

nier *n* kidney

nierassig *adj* nonracial

nies *n* sneeze; *vb* to sneeze

niet *n* nothing; nothingness

nieteenstaande *prep* notwithstanding; in spite of

nietemin *conj* nevertheless

nietig *adj* insignificant; almost meaningless

nig(gie) *n* female cousin; niece

nikkel *n* nickel

nikotien *n* nicotine

niks *n* nothing

niksnuts *n* good-for-nothing

nimf *n* nymph

nimmer *adv* never

nippel *n* nipple

nis *n* niche

nismark *n* niche market

nitraat *n* nitrate

noagkar *n* vintage car

nodeloos *adj* unnecessary

nodig *adj* necessary

noem *vb* to call; to name; to mention

noemenswaardig *adj* important; worth mentioning

noemer *n* denominator

nog[1] *adv* yet; again; still; also

nog[2]: **nog . . . nog** neither . . . nor

nogal *adv* rather; quite; fairly

nogmaals *adv* again; once more

nogtans *conj* however; yet; nevertheless

nomade *n* nomad

nomadies *adj* nomadic

nominaal *adj* nominal

nominasie *n* nomination

nomineer *vb* to nominate

nommer *n* number; size; copy (newspaper); *vb* to number

nommerplaat *n* numberplate

non *n* nun
nonneklooster *n* convent
nonsens (*or* **nonsies**) *n* nonsense
nood *n* need; distress; danger
noodberig *n* emergency message
nooddeur *n* fire escape; emergency door
nooddruftig *adj* needy; indigent
noodhulp *n* first aid
noodklok *n* alarm bell
noodleuen *n* white lie
noodlot *n* fate
noodlottig *adj* fatal; ill-fated
noodlydend *adj* destitute; indigent
noodmaatreël *n* emergency measure
noodoproep *n* emergency call
noodsaak *n* necessity; *vb* to oblige; to compel; to force
noodsaaklik *adj* necessary; imperative
noodsaaklikheid *n* necessity
noodsein *n* distress signal
noodskag *n* emergency shaft (mining)
noodtoestand *n* state of emergency
noodweer *n* self-defence
noodwiel *n* spare wheel
nooi[1] *n* girl; young lady; sweetheart
nooi[2] *vb* to invite
nooiensvan *n* maiden name
nooit! *interj* never!
noop *vb* to compel; to induce
noord *n* north; *adj, adv* north
Noord-Atlantiese Verdrags-organisasie *n* North Atlantic Treaty Organisation (NATO)
noorde *n* north; the north
noordekant *n* north side
noordelik *adj* northern; northerly
noorderhalfrond *n* northern hemisphere
noorderlig *n* aurora borealis; northern lights
noordewind *n* north wind
noordoos *adj, adv* north-east
noordooste *n* north-east; the north-east
noordwes *adj, adv* north-west
noordweste *n* north-west; the north-west
noot *n* note (music)
norm *n* standard; rule; benchmark
normaal *adj* normal; able; standard

nors *adj* cross; surly; peevish
nosie *n* notion; idea
notebalk *n* staff; staves (music)
noteer *vb* to note; to make a note of; to quote
notering *n* quotation; **— op die beurs** *n* stock exchange listing
notisie *n* note; notice
notule *n* minutes
notuleer *vb* to record; to minute
nou[1] *adj* narrow; tight; strict
nou[2] *adv* now
nougeset *adj* scrupulous; conscientious
noukeurig *adj* exact; accurate
nouliks *adv* scarcely; hardly
nou-nou *adv* just now; in a moment
noute *n* narrowness; narrow pass
noutevrees *n* claustrophobia
novelle *n* short novel
November *n* November
nudis *n* nudist
nudisme *n* nudism
nugter *adj* sober; clear-headed; **— weet!** *interj* goodness knows!
nuk *n* whim; caprice
nukkerig *adj* moody; whimsical
nul *n* nil; naught; zero
numeries *adj* numerical
nut *n* use; benefit; profit
nutsman *n* handyman
nutteloos *adj* useless; fruitless
nuttig[1] *vb* to partake (food, etc.)
nuttig[2] *adj* useful; profitable
nuus *n* news; tidings
nuusberig *n* news item
nuusblad *n* newspaper
nuuskierig *adj* curious; inquisitive
nuuskierigheid *n* curiosity; inquisitive-ness
nuusuitsending *n* news broadcast
nuut *adj* new; recent
Nuwejaar *n* New Year
Nuwejaarsvoorneme *n* New Year's resolution
nuweling *n* novice; beginner
nuwerwets *adj* modern; new
nuwigheid *n* novelty
nyd *n* envy; grudge
nydig *adj* envious; angry; cross
nyweraar *n* manufacturer; industrialist
nywerheid *n* industry

O

o! *interj* oh!
oase *n* oasis
objeksie *n* objection
objekteer *vb* to object
obligasie *n* bond; debenture
observasie *n* observation
observatorium *n* observatory
observeer *vb* to observe
obsessie *n* obsession
obstinaat *adj* obstinate
obstruksie *n* obstruction
ode *n* ode
oefen *vb* to practise; to exercise; to train; to coach
oefenboek *n* exercise book
oefening *n* exercise; practice; training
oefenskoen *ns* cross-trainer
oënskynlik *adj* apparent; ostensible; *adv* apparently; seemingly
oerknal *n* big bang
oermens *n* primitive man
oeroud *adj* primeval
oerwoud *n* native forest; jungle
oes[1] *n* harvest; crop; *vb* to harvest; to reap
oes[2] *adj* out of sorts; off-colour
oester *n* oyster
oestyd *n* harvest time
oewer *n* riverbank
of *conj* or; if; whether; either
offensief *adj* offensive; aggressive
offer *n* sacrifice; offering; *vb* to offer; to sacrifice
offerande *n* sacrifice; offering
offisieel *adj* official; *adv* officially
offisier *n* officer
ofskoon *conj* although; though
oggend *n* morning
oggendete *n* breakfast
ogiesdraad *n* wire netting
oker *n* ochre
okkasie *n* occasion
okkerneut *n* walnut
okkupasie *n* occupation
okkupeer *vb* to occupy
oksel *n* armpit
oksideer *vb* to oxidize

oktaaf *n* octave
Oktober *n* October
oktrooi *n* charter; patent
okulasie *n* inoculation
okuleer *vb* to inoculate
oleander *n* oleander
olie *n* oil; *vb* to oil
olieboortoring *n* oil rig
oliekan *n* oilcan
olienhout *n* wild olive
oliepypleiding *n* oil pipeline
olieverfskildery *n* oil painting
olifant *n* elephant
olifantstand *n* elephant tusk; ivory
oligargie *n* oligarchy
olik *adj* bad; unwell; out of sorts
olimpiade *n* olympiad (maths, etc.)
olm *n* elm (tree)
olyf *n* olive
olyfolie *n* olive oil
om *adv* up; out; round; over; *prep* at; about; for; to; in order to; on
omblaai *vb* to turn over (pages of a book)
omboor *n* to hem; to edge
ombuig *vb* to bend; to turn (up, down, back)
omdat *conj* because; since; as
omdraai *vb* to turn round; to turn back; to reverse a car
omelet *n* omelette
omgaan *vb* to mix with; to go round with; to associate with
omgang *n* social intercourse; sexual intercourse; association
omgee *vb* to care
omgekeerd *adj* reversed
omgewe *vb* to surround
omgewing *n* environment; surroundings; vicinity
omgewings *adj* ambient
omgewingsake *n* environmental affairs
omgewingsleer *n* ecology; environmental studies
omgewingsvriendelike tegnologie *n* green technology

omgooi *vb* to upset; to throw down

omhaal *n* commotion; fuss; to-do

omheen *adv* round; around

omhein *vb* to fence in; to enclose

omheining *n* fence; enclosure

omhels *vb* to embrace

omhelsing *n* embrace

omkantel *vb* to topple over; to fall over; to tip over

omkeer *n* change; reversal; *vb* to turn round; to turn out; to reverse; to turn upside down

omkom *vb* to die; to perish; to come round

omkoop *vb* to bribe; to corrupt

omkoopgeld *n* bribe

omkopery *n* bribery; corruption

omkrap *vb* to upset; to throw into confusion; to disarrange

omkyk *vb* to look round; to look back; to see to; to attend to

omlaag *adv* below; down

omleiding *n* bypass (heart surgery)

omliggend *adj* surrounding; neighbouring

omloop *n* circulation

omlope *n* ringworm

omlyn *vb* to outline

ommuur *vb* to wall in

ompad *n* round-about-way; detour

ompraat *vb* to persuade; to dissuade

omring *vb* to surround; to encircle

omringend *adj* ambient

omroer *vb* to stir

omruil *vb* to exchange; to swop

omruk *vb* to pull down

omry *vb* to drive down; to drive round; to ride round; to knock down; to run over

omsendbrief *n* circular

omset *n* turnover; sale; **jaarlikse —** *n* annual turnover; annual sales

omsien *vb* to look round; to look back

omsigtig *adj* cautious; circumspect

omsigtigheid *n* care; prudence; caution

omsingel *vb* to surround; to encircle; to enclose

omsit *vb* to to put round; to sit round; to turn round suddenly

omskep[1] *vb* to change; to convert

omskep[2] *vb* to transform; to recreate

omskrywe *vb* to describe; to define

omskrywing *n* description; definition

omslaan *vb* to topple over; to turn over

omslag[1] *n* cover; jacket (book); cuff

omslag[2] *n* fuss; commotion

omslagteks *n* blurb

omslagtig *adj* long-winded; wordy

omsluit *vb* to circle

omsoom *vb* to hem

omspit *vb* to dig up

omspoel *vb* to rinse; to wash

omspring *vb* to jump around

omstander *n* bystander; spectator

omstandigheid *n* circumstance

omstap *vb* to step round; to walk round

omstrede *adj* controversial; contentious

omstreeks *adv* about; in the neighbourhood of

omstreke *npl* vicinity; neighbourhood

omswerwend *adj* rambling

omswerwer *n* rambler

omtrek *n* circumference; outline; neighbourhood; *vb* to circle

omtrent *adv* about; almost; nearly; *prep* about; with regard to

omval *vb* to topple over; to fall down

omvang *n* extent; size; circumference

omvangryk *adj* extensive; bulky

omvat *vb* to embrace; to include

omvattende versekering *n* comprehensive insurance

omver *adv* over; upside down

omvergooi *vb* to upset; knock over

omwenteling *n* revolution; rotation

omwoel *vb* to dig up; to stir; to scatter

onaandoenlik *adj* impassive; unemotional

onaangenaam *adj* unpleasant; disagreeable

onaangeroer *adj* untouched; intact

onaanneemlik *adj* unacceptable

onaansienlik *adj* plain; unattractive; insignificant

onaardig *adj* unpleasant; nasty; rude

onafgebroke *adj* uninterrupted; continuous

onafhanklik *adj* independent

onafsienbaar *adj* immeasurable

onafskei(d)baar *adj* inseparable

onafskeidelik *adj* inseparable

onbaatsugtig *adj* disinterested; unselfish

onbarmhartig *adj* merciless

onbeantwoord *adj* unanswered; unrequited

onbedagsaam *adj* thoughtless; rash; incautious

onbedorwe *adj* unspoiled; innocent

onbedrewe *adj* inexperienced; unskilled

onbeduidend *adj* insignificant

onbegaanbaar *adj* impassable

onbegonne *adj* impossible

onbegrens *adj* unlimited; endless

onbegryplik *adj* inconceivable; incomprehensible

onbehaaglik *adj* unpleasant; uncomfortable; uneasy

onbeholpe *adj* awkward; clumsy; helpless

onbehoorlik *adj* improper; indecent

onbehoue *adj* rough; rude

onbekeerd *adj* unconverted

onbekend *adj* unknown; unfamiliar

onbekende *n* stranger

onbekendheid *n* strangeness; ignorance

onbekommerd *adj* careless; unconcerned

onbekook *adj* rash; thoughtless

onbekwaam *adj* unfit; incapable

onbelangrik *adj* unimportant

onbelas *adj* unencumbered

onbeleef *adj* impolite; rude

onbeleefdheid *n* rudeness; impoliteness

onbelemmer *adj* unhindered; unimpeded

onbemiddeld *adj* poor; not wealthy;

onbepaald *adj* indefinite; unlimited

onbeperk *adj* unlimited

onbeproef *adj* untried; untested

onbereikbaar *adj* inaccessible; unattainable

onberekenbaar *adj* incalculable

onberispelik *adj* faultless; impeccable; blameless

onbeset *adj* unoccupied; vacant (post, university chair)

onbeskaaf(d) *adj* rude; uncivilized

onbeskaamd *adj* impudent; impertinent; insolent

onbeskaamdheid *n* impudence; impertinence

onbeskadig *adj* undamaged; unharmed

onbeskeie *adj* immodest; forward; indiscreet

onbeskerm(d) *adj* unprotected; undefended

onbeskof *adj* insolent; rude; impudent

onbeskoftheid *n* insolence; rudeness

onbeskroom(d) *adj* fearless; bold

onbeskryflik *adj* indescribable; untold

onbeslis *adj* undecided; uncertain; pending

onbesoedel(d) *adj* spotless; unpolluted

onbesonne *adj* thoughtless

onbesorg *adj* unconcerned; cheerful

onbesproke *adj* irreproachable

onbestaanbaar *adj* impossible

onbestelbaar *adj* undeliverable

onbestemd *adj* vague; indefinite

onbestendig *adj* unsettled; unstable; changeable

onbestrede *adj* unopposed; undisputed

onbetaal(d) *adj* unpaid

onbetaamlik *adj* indecent; improper

onbetaamlikheid *n* indecency; unseemliness;

onbetroubaar *adj* unreliable; untrustworthy

onbetwis *adj* undisputed

onbetwisbaar *adj* indisputable

onbevaarbaar *adj* unnavigable

onbevange *adj* impartial; unbiased

onbevatlik *adj* incomprehensible; stupid

onbevlekte *adj* unblemished

onbevoeg *adj* unqualified; incompetent

onbevolk *adj* unpopulated

onbevooroordeeld *adj* unbiased; unprejudiced

onbevredig *adj* unfulfilled; unsatisfied

onbevredigend *adj* unsatisfactory

onbevrees *adj* fearless; unafraid; undaunted

onbewaak *adj* unguarded

onbeweegbaar *adj* immovable

onbeweeglik *adj* immovable; motionless

onbewimpeld *adj* undisguised; frank

onbewoë *adj* unmoved

onbewolk *adj* cloudless

onbewoon(d) *adj* unoccupied; empty; uninhabited

onbewus *adj* unconscious; unaware; *adv* unwittingly; unconsciously

onbillik *adj* unjust; unfair; unreasonable

onblusbaar *adj* unquenchable

onbrandbaar *adj* incombustible; fireproof

onbreekbaar *adj* unbreakable

onbruik *n* disuse

onbruikbaar *adj* useless; naughty; unemployable

onbuigbaar *adj* inflexible; rigid; unbendable

onchristelik *adj* unchristian

ondank *n* ingratitude

ondankbaar *adj* ungrateful

ondankbaarheid *n* ingratitude

ondanks *prep* in spite of; notwithstanding

ondeelbaar *adj* indivisible

ondenkbaar *adj* inconceivable; unimaginable

onder *prep* under; among; below; during

onderaan *adv* at the bottom

onderaards *adj* subterranean; underground

onderafdeling *n* subdivision

onderarm *n* forearm

onderbaadjie *n* waistcoat

onderbeklemtoning *n* understatement

onderbewussyn *n* subconsciousness

onderbreek *vb* to interrupt

onderbroek *n* underpants (pair of)

onderdaan *n* subject (of a country)

onderdak *n* shelter; home

onderdanig *adj* humble; obedient

onderdeel *n* subdivision; spare part

onderdeur[1] *prep* under

onderdeur[2] *n* lower half of door

onderdruk[1] *vb* to press; to hold down

onderdruk[2] *vb* to oppress; to suppress; to quell

onderdrukking *n* oppression; suppression

onderduims *adj* underhand; cunning

onderent *n* bottom; lower end

ondergaan[1] *vb* to suffer; to undergo; **behandeling —** *vb* to undergo treatment; to receive treatment

ondergaan[2] *vb* to go under; to set (sun); to be ruined; to be destroyed; to die

ondergang *n* downfall; destruction; setting (sun)

ondergeskik *adj* subordinate; inferior

ondergeskikte *n* subordinate; underling

ondergetekende *n* (the) undersigned

ondergoed *n* underwear

ondergronds *adj* underground; below ground level

ondergrondse spoorweg *n* underground railway; tube; metro

onderhandel *vb* to negotiate

onderhandelaar *n* negotiator

onderhandeling *n* negotiation

onderhands *adj* underhand; secret; private

onderhawig *adj* this; present; in question

onderhemp *n* vest

onderhewig *adj* subject to; liable

onderhoof *n* vice-principal

onderhorig *adj* dependent; subordinate

onderhou[1] *vb* to maintain; to keep; to support

onderhou[2] *vb* to hold down; to hold under

onderhoud[1] *n* maintenance; upkeep; support

onderhoud[2] *n* interview

onderhoudend *adj* entertaining; amusing

onderhuur *n* subtenancy

onderhuurder *n* subtenant

onderkakebeen *n* lower jaw

onderkant *n* bottom; lower side

onderken *n* double chin

onderklere *n* underwear

onderkomitee *n* subcommittee

onderkoning *n* viceroy

onderkruip *vb* to undercut; to undersell; to swindle

onderlaag *n* bottom layer; substratum

onderlangs *prep* along the foot of; *adv* lower down; along the bottom part

onderlê *vb* to inform (as in the principles which inform modern teaching)

onderlip *n* bottom lip

onderling *adj* mutual

onderlyf *n* lower part of the body

onderlyfie *n* camisole
ondermaans *adj* earthly; mundane
ondermyn *vb* to undermine; to weaken
onderneem *vb* to undertake; to attempt
ondernemend *adj* enterprising
onderneming *n* undertaking; enterprise; venture
onderoffisier *n* noncommissioned officer
onderpand *n* pledge; guarantee
onderpresteerder *n* underachiever
onderrig *n* tuition; instruction; *vb* to instruct; to teach; to educate
ondersees *adj* undersea(s); submarine; *adv* below the surface of the sea
onderskat *vb* to underestimate; to undervalue
onderskei *vb* to distinguish; to discern
onderskeid *n* difference; distinction
onderskeidelik *adv* respectively
onderskeiding *n* distinction
onderskeie *adj* different; various; respective
onderskep *vb* to intercept
onderskrif *n* signature; caption; inscription
onderskrywe *vb* to endorse; to sign; to confirm
ondersoek *n* examination; investigation; inquiry; research; probe; *vb* to investigate; to inquire; to examine
onderspit *n* defeat; **die — delf** *vb* to come off worst; to come off second best
onderstaande *adj* following; undermentioned
onderste *n* bottom; *adj* lowest; bottom
onderstebo *adj* topsy-turvy; upside down; confused
onderstel[1] *n* undercarriage; chassis
onderstel[2] *vb* to suppose; to presume
onderstelling *n* supposition
ondersteun *vb* to support; to assist; to sponsor
ondersteuning *n* adherent
onderstreep *vb* to underline
onderteken *vb* to sign
ondertekening *n* signature
ondertitel *n* subheading; subtitle
ondertoe *adv* to the bottom; downwards; lower down
ondertussen *adv* meanwhile; in the meantime

ondervind *vb* to experience
ondervinding *n* experience
ondervoed *adj* underfed; malnourished
ondervoeding *n* malnutrition; underfeeding
ondervoorsitter *n* vice-chairman
ondervra *vb* to cross-examine; to question; to interrogate
ondervraging *n* interrogation
onderweg *adv* on the way; in transit
onderwerp[1] *n* topic; theme; subject; point; text
onderwerp[2] *vb* to subdue; to subject
onderwerping *n* submission; subjection
onderworpe *adj* submissive; resigned; **— aan goedkeuring** *adj* subject to approval
onderwyl *adv* meanwhile; while
onderwys *n* education; tuition; **— vir volwassenes** *n* adult education; **hoër —** *n* higher education (university); *vb* to teach; to educate
onderwyser *n* teacher
onderwyseres *n* female teacher
ondeund *adj* naughty; mischievous
ondeurdag *adj* thoughtless; rash
ondeurdringbaar *adj* impenetrable
ondeurgrondbaar *adj* unfathomable
ondeurgrondelik *adj* inscrutable
ondeurskynend *adj* opaque
ondienlik *adj* useless; unserviceable
ondier *n* monster; brute
ondig *adj* not watertight; leaky
ondraaglik *adj* unbearable; intolerable
ondrinkbaar *adj* undrinkable
onduidelik *adj* indistinct; illegible; not clear
onduldbaar *adj* unbearable; intolerable
onedel *adj* ignoble; base; **—e metale** *npl* base metals
oneer *n* dishonour; disgrace
oneerbiedig *adj* irreverent; disrespectful
oneerlik *adj* dishonest; unfair; fraudulent
oneerlikheid *n* dishonesty
oneetbaar *adj* inedible; uneatable
oneg *adj* fake; false
oneindig *adj* endless; infinite
onenig *adj* discordant; divided

onenigheid *n* discord; disagreement
onervare *adj* inexperienced
onewe *adj* unequal; uneven
onewe getal *n* odd number
oneweredig *adj* disproportional
onfatsoenlik *adj* improper; indecent; rude
onfeilbaar *adj* infallible
ongasvry *adj* inhospitable
ongeag *adj* unnoticed; irrespective of; regardless of; *adv* regardless; *prep* in spite of; notwithstanding
ongebleik *adj* unbleached
ongebonde *adj* unfettered; free
ongebruik *adj* unused
ongedaan *adj* undone
ongedeerd *adj* unhurt; uninjured; unscathed
ongedierte *npl* vermin; wild animals
ongedoop *adj* unbaptized; unchristened
ongeduld *n* impatience
ongeduldig *adj* impatient
ongedurig *adj* restless; fidgety
ongedwonge *adj* unrestrained; spontaneous; unforced
ongeërg *adj* calm; unruffled; imperturbable
ongeëwenaard *adj* unequalled; unparalleled
ongegrond *adj* false; unfounded
ongehinder *adj* unhindered; undisturbed
ongehoor(d) *adj* unheard of; unprecedented
ongehoorsaam *adj* disobedient
ongehoorsaamheid *n* disobedience
ongekend *adj* unknown; unparalleled
ongekeur *adj* not selected; unseeded (sport)
ongekunsteld *adj* natural; simple; unaffected
ongeldig *adj* invalid; null and void
ongeleë *adj* inconvenient; unseasonable
ongeleer(d) *adj* uneducated; illiterate
ongeletter(d) *adj* illiterate
ongelooflik *adj* incredible; unbelievable
ongelowig *adj* sceptical; incredulous
ongeluk *n* accident; misfortune; **per —** *adv* by accident; by mistake
ongelukkig *adj* unfortunate; unlucky;

unhappy; unsuccesful; *adv* sadly; unfortunately
ongelyk *adj* unequal; uneven; irregular; **—e wegspring** *n* false start
ongemak *n* discomfort; hardship; inconvenience
ongemaklik *adj* uncomfortable; difficult
ongemanierd *adj* rude; ill-mannered
ongemeen *adj* uncommon; unusual
ongemerk *adj* unperceived; unobserved
ongemeubileer(d) *adj* unfurnished
ongemoei *adj* undisturbed
ongenaakbaar *adj* inaccessible; unapproachable
ongenadig *adj* unmerciful; cruel
ongeneë *adj* unwilling; disinclined
ongeneeslik *adj* incurable
ongeneig *adj* disinclined
ongenoeë *n* displeasure
ongenooi *adj* unwelcome; uninvited
ongeoefen *adj* unpractised; untrained; inexperienced
ongeoorloof *adj* unlawful; forbidden; illicit
ongepas *adj* improper; unseemly
ongepoets *adj* ill-mannered; rude
ongereeld *adj* irregular; disorderly
ongerekend *adj* careless; casual
ongerep *adj* untouched; pure
ongerief *n* discomfort; inconvenience
ongerieflik *adj* inconvenient; uncomfortable
ongerus *adj* uneasy; anxious
ongesellig *adj* unsociable
ongeskik *adj* unfit; unsuitable
ongeskonde *adj* unhurt; uninjured; intact
ongeskool *adj* untrained; unskilled; **— de arbeid** *n* unskilled labour
ongesond *adj* unhealthy; unwholesome
ongesteld *adj* unwell; indisposed
ongestraf *adj* unpunished
ongeteken(d) *adj* unsigned; anonymous
ongetroud *adj* unmarried; single
ongetwyfeld *adv* undoubtedly
ongeval *n* accident; mishap
ongeveer *adv* roughly; about
ongeveins *adj* sincere; unfeigned
ongevoelig *adj* insensible; insensitive
ongevraag *adj* uncalled for

ongewapen *adj* unarmed
ongewend *adj* unaccustomed
ongewens *adj* undesirable
ongewerwel(d) *adj* invertebrate (animals)
ongewillig *adj* unwilling
ongewoon *adj* unusual; uncommon
ongrondwetlik *adj* unconstitutional
onguns *n* disfavour; disgrace
ongunstig *adj* unfavourable; adverse
onguur *adj* coarse; rough
onhandelbaar *adj* unmanageable; difficult
onhandig *adj* clumsy; awkward
onheil *n* calamity; disaster
onheilspellend *adj* ominous
onherbergsaam *adj* inhospitable; barren
onherkenbaar *adj* unrecognizable
onherroeplik *adj* irrevocable
onherstelbaar *adj* beyond repair; irreparable
onheuglik *adj* immemorial
onhoorbaar *adj* inaudible
onhoudbaar *adj* untenable
oniks *n* onyx
onjuis *adj* incorrect; erroneous
onkant *adj* offside (sport)
onkenbaar *adj* unrecognizable
onklaar *adj* out of order; defective; *adv* out of order
onkoste *npl* costs; expenses
onkreukbaar *adj* blameless; unimpeachable
onkruid *n* weed
onkruiddoder *n* weedkiller
onkuis *adj* indecent; immoral
onkunde *n* ignorance
onkundig *adj* ignorant
onkwesbaar *adj* invulnerable
onlangs *adv* lately; recently
onleesbaar *adj* illegible; unreadable
onlesbaar *adj* unquenchable
onlogies *adj* illogical
onlus *n* dislike; listlessness
onluste *n* disturbance; trouble; riot
onluspolisie *n* riot police
onmag *n* inability; impotence
onmanlik *adj* unmanly
onmatig *adj* excessive; immoderate
onmeetlik *adj* immeasurable; immense

onmens *n* brute; monster
onmenslik *adj* cruel; inhuman
onmerkbaar *adj* unnoticeable; imperceptible
onmiddellik *adj* immediate; *adv* immediately; directly
onmisbaar *adj* indispensable; essential
onmoontlik *adj* impossible
onnadenkend *adj* thoughtless; inconsiderate
onnatuurlik *adj* unnatural
onnodig *adj* unnecessary
onnoemlik *adj* countless
onnosel *adj* innocent; silly; stupid
onnoukeurig *adj* inexact; inaccurate
onnut *adj* useless
onomatopee *n* onomatopoeia
onnutsig *adj* naughty; mischievous
onomwonde *adj* plain; frank; *adv* plainly; frankly
onontbeerlik *adj* indispensable
onontwikkeld *adj* undeveloped; illiterate
onooglik *adj* unsightly; unattractive
onoorganklik *adj* intransitive
onoorkoomlik *adj* insurmountable
onoortrefbaar *adj* insurpassable
onoorwinlik *adj* invincible; unconquerable
onopgelos *adj* unsolved; undissolved
onopgemerk *adj* unnoticed
onopgevoed *adj* uneducated; rude
onophoudelik *adj* incessant; continuous
onoplettend *adj* inattentive
onoplosbaar *adj* insoluble; unsolvable
onopreg *adj* insincere
onordelik *adj* disorderly
onpaar *adj* odd; unmatched
onpartydig *adj* impartial; fair; unbiased
onpersoonlik *adj* impersonal
onplesierig *adj* unpleasant
onprakties *adj* unpractical
onraad *n* trouble; danger
onredelik *adj* unreasonable; unfair
onreëlmatig *adj* irregular
onreg *n* wrong; injustice
onregmatig *adj* unlawful; illegal
onregverdig *adj* unjust; unfair
onregverdigheid *n* injustice
onrein *adj* impure; unclean

onroerend *adj* immovable
onrus *n* unrest; anxiety; disturbance; restlessness
onrusbarend *adj* alarming
onrustig *adj* restless; uneasy; anxious
onryp *adj* unripe; immature
ons[1] *n* ounce
ons[2] *pers pron* we; us; *poss pron* our
onsamehangend *adj* disconnected; rambling; incoherent
onsedelik *adj* immoral
onsedelikheid *n* immorality
onseker *adj* uncertain; unsafe
onsekerheid *n* uncertainty; doubt
onselfsugtig *adj* unselfish
onsigbaar *adj* invisible
onsin *n* nonsense
onsindelik *adj* dirty; unclean
onsinnig *adj* absurd; foolish
onskadelik *adj* harmless
onskatbaar *adj* invaluable; immeasurable
onskei(d)baar *adj* inseparable
onskuld *n* innocence
onskuldig *adj* innocent; harmless
onsmaaklik *adj* unsavoury; unpleasant
onstandvastig *adj* fickle; inconstant
onsterflik *adj* immortal
onstuimig *adj* turbulent; wild; stormy; boisterous
onsydig *adj* neuter; neutral; impartial
ontaard *vb* to degenerate; to deteriorate
ontaarding *n* degeneracy; degeneration
ontbering *n* hardship
ontbied *vb* to summon; to send for
ontbind *vb* to undo; to untie; to dissolve; to decompose; to disband
ontbinding *n* decomposition; dissolution; deprivation
ontblok *vb* unblock (account)
ontbloot *vb* to strip; to deprive; to lay bare; *adj* uncovered; deprived; devoid
ontbrand *vb* to catch fire; to burst into flames; to ignite
ontbreek *vb* to lack; to be wanting
ontbyt *n* breakfast
ontdek *vb* to discover; to find out
ontdekking *n* discovery; revelation
ontdooi *vb* to thaw
ontduik *vb* to shirk; to avoid; to dodge
onteenseglik *adj* unquestionable

ontelbaar *adj* countless; innumerable
ontembaar *adj* untam(e)able
onterf *vb* to disinherit
ontevrede *adj* discontented; dissatisfied
ontferm *vb* to commiserate; to take pity on
ontferming *n* pity; commiseration
ontgaan *vb* to evade; to escape
ontgin *vb* to cultivate (land); to clear (forest); to work (a mine)
ontglip *vb* to slip from; to escape
ontgroen *vb* to initiate
ontgroening *n* initiation; induction
onthaal *n* reception; treat; *vb* to entertain; to treat
onthef *vb* to exempt; to exonerate
ontheilig *vb* to desecrate
onthoof *vb* to behead; to decapitate
onthou *vb* to remember; to recall; to bear in mind; to abstain from
onthouer *n* abstainer; teetotaller
onthul *vb* to unveil; to reveal
ontken *vb* to deny
ontkennend *adj* negative; *adv* negatively
ontkenning *n* denial
ontketen *vb* to unchain
ontkiem *vb* to germinate
ontklee *vb* to undress; to strip
ontknoop *vb* to unbutton; to undo; to unravel
ontknoping *n* unravelling
ontkom *vb* to escape
ontkoming *n* escape
ontlas *vb* to unburden; to relieve
ontlasting *n* relief; discharge; motion; stool; faeces
ontleding *n* analysis; dissection
ontledingstaat *n* spreadsheet
ontleed *vb* to dissect; to analyse; to parse
ontleen *vb* to borrow from
ontlont *vb* to defuse (crisis)
ontluik *vb* to open; to expand; to bud
ontluikend *adj* opening; budding (author); dawning
ontman *vb* to castrate
ontmasker *vb* to unmask; to expose
ontmoedig *vb* to discourage; to dishearten
ontmoediging *n* discouragement
ontmoet *vb* to meet; to encounter

ontmoeting *n* meeting; encounter

ontneem *vb* to take away; to deprive of

ontnugter *vb* to disillusion; to make sober

ontnugtering *n* disillusion; disillusionment

ontoeganklik *adj* inaccessible; unapproachable

ontoereikend *adj* inadequate; insufficient

ontperk *vb* to unban

ontplof *vb* to explode

ontplofbaar *n* explosive

ontploffing *n* explosion; blast

ontploffingstof *n* explosive

ontplooi *vb* to unfold; to unfurl; to deploy (troops)

ontrek *n* vicinity; neighbourhood

ontroer *vb* to affect; to touch; to move

ontroering *n* emotion

ontroof *vb* to rob of

ontroosbaar *adj* inconsolable; disconsolate

ontrou *n* infidelity; disloyalty; *adj* disloyal; unfaithful

ontruim *vb* to vacate; to evacuate; to clear

ontsag *n* awe; respect

ontsaglik *adj* awful; terrible; tremendous; *adv* awfully; terribly

ontsenu *vb* to unnerve; to refute

ontsettend *adj* apalled; aghast; shocked

ontsetting *n* fright; terror; consternation; relief

ontsien *vb* to respect; to fear; to spare (feelings)

ontsier *vb* to disfigure; to deface

ontskeep *vb* to disembark

ontslaan *vb* to dismiss; to fire; to sack

ontslag *n* acquittal; discharge; release; resignation

ontslag gee *vb* to dismiss; to fire

ontslagneem *vb* to resign

ontslape *adj* deceased

ontslapene *n* the deceased; the departed

ontsluier *vb* to unveil; to reveal; to disclose

ontsluit *vb* to open; to unlock

ontsmet *vb* to disinfect

ontsmettingsmiddel *n* disinfectant

ontsnap *vb* to escape

ontsnapping *n* escape; gaolbreak; jailbreak

ontspan *vb* to relax; to unbend

ontspanning *n* recreation; relaxation

ontspanningsgeriewe *n* recreational facilities

ontspoor *vb* to derail

ontsporing *n* derailment

ontspruit *vb* to sprout; to shoot forth; to arise; to result

ontstaan *vb* to begin; to arise; to originate

ontsteek *vb* to light; to kindle; to inflame

ontsteking *n* kindling; inflammation

ontstel *vb* to frighten; to startle; to disconcert

ontstel(d) *adj* upset; alarmed

ontstoke *adj* inflamed

ontsyfer *vb* to decipher; to make out

onttrek *vb* to withdraw; to withhold

onttroon *vb* to dethrone

ontug *n* prostitution; fornication; immorality

ontuis *adj* ill at ease

ontvang *vb* to receive; to conceive; to welcome

ontvangenis *n* conception

ontvanger *n* receiver; tax collector; — **van inkomste** *n* receiver of revenue

ontvangs *n* reception; receipt; takings; returns

ontvangsdame *n* receptionist

ontvanklik *adj* receptive; susceptible

ontveins *vb* to disguise; to conceal

ontvlam *vb* to catch fire; to burst into flames; to inflame

ontvlug *vb* to flee; to escape

ontvlugting *n* escape; flight

ontvoer *vb* to abduct; to kidnap

ontvoerder *n* kidnapper

ontvreem *vb* to steal; to embezzle

ontwaak *vb* to wake up; to awake

ontwaar *vb* to perceive

ontwaking *adj* awakening

ontwapen *vb* to disarm; to pacify

ontwapening *n* disarmament

ontwar *vb* to unravel; to disentangle

ontwater *vb* to dehydrate

ontwerp *n* draft; sketch; design; project; *vb* to project; to draft; to plan

ontwerpers *adj* designer (designer clothes, etc.)
ontwikkel *vb* to develop; to evolve
ontwikkelaar *n* developer
ontwikkeld *adj* developed; educated
ontwikkeling *n* development; evolution
ontwil *n* sake; **om my —** *adv* for my sake
ontwrig *vb* to dislocate; to disrupt
ontwyk *vb* to avoid; to shun; to evade; to escape
ontwykend *adj* evasive
ontydig *adj* untimely; premature
onuitbluslik *adj* inextinguishable
onuitputlik *adj* inexhaustible
onuitspreeklik *adj* unspeakable (joy); unutterable (sorrow)
onuitstaanbaar *adj* intolerable; unbearable
onuitvoerbaar *adj* impracticable
onuitwisbaar *adj* indelible
onvanpas *adj* inconvenient; unsuitable
onvas *adj* unstable; unsteady; shaky
onvatbaar *adj* impervious to; deaf to; immune to
onveilig *adj* unsafe
onveranderd *adj* unchanged; unaltered
onveranderlik *adj* unchangeable; constant
onverantwoordelik *adj* irresponsible; inexcusable
onverbiddelik *adj* relentless; inexorable
onverdeel(d) *adj* undivided; unanimous
onverderflik *adj* imperishable
onverdien(d) *adj* undeserved; unearned
onverdraagbaar *adj* unbearable
onverdraagsaam *adj* intolerant
onverflou(d) *adj* unflagging; unabated
onverganklik *adj* imperishable; everlasting
onvergeeflik *adj* unpardonable
onvergeetlik *adj* unforgettable; memorable
onvergelyklik *adj* incomparable; matchless; peerless
onvergenoeg *adj* discontented; dissatisfied
onverhoeds *adv* unexpectedly; suddenly
onverklaarbaar *adj* inexplicable; unaccountable

onverkort *adj* unabridged
onvermengd *adj* unmixed; unblended
onverminder(d) *adj* undiminished
onvermoë *n* impotence; inability
onvermoeid *adj* untiring
onvermoënd *adj* incapable; unable; impecunious
onvermydelik *adj* unavoidable; inevitable
onverpoos *adj* uninterrupted; unceasing
onverrigtersake *adv* unsuccessfully
onversadig *adj* unsatisfied
onversadiglik *adj* insatiable
onversetlik *adj* stubborn; obstinate
onversigtig *adj* imprudent; careless
onverskillig *adj* indifferent; rash; reckless
onverskrokke *adj* intrepid; bold; undaunted
onversoenlik *adj* irreconcilable
onversorg *adj* uncared for; unprovided for; slovenly
onverstaanbaar *adj* incomprehensible; inaudible
onverstandig *adj* unwise; foolish
onverteerbaar *adj* indigestible
onvervals *adj* unadulterated; pure
onvervreembaar *adj* inalienable
onverwag *adj* unexpected
onverwags *adv* unexpectedly; suddenly; unawares
onverwoesbaar *adj* indestructible
onverwyld *adv* immediately; at once
onvoldaan *adj* unsettled; unpaid; dissatisfied
onvoldoende *adj* inadequate; insufficient
onvolkome *adj* imperfect; incomplete
onvolledig *adj* incomplete
onvolmaak *adj* imperfect; faulty
onvoltooi *adj* imperfect; incomplete; unfinished
onvoorbereid *adj* unprepared
onvoordelig *adj* unprofitable
onvoorsien *adj* unexpected; sudden
onvoorsiens *adv* suddenly
onvoorwaardelik *adj* unconditional
onvrede *n* discord; strife; feud; dispute
onvriendelik *adj* unfriendly; unkind
onvrugbaar *adj* barren; sterile; infertile

onwaar *adj* untrue; false
onwaardeerbaar *adj* invaluable; priceless
onwaardig *adj* unworthy
onwaarheid *n* falsehood; untruth
onwaarskynlik *adj* improbable
onwankelbaar *adj* firm; steadfast
onweer *n* bad weather; storm; thunderstorm
onweerlegbaar *adj* irrefutable
onweerstaanbaar *adj* irresistible
onwelluidend *adj* discordant; inharmonious
onwelwillend *adj* unkind; unsympathetic
onwenslik *adj* undesirable
onwetend *adj* ignorant
onwettig *adj* illegal; unlawful; naughty
onwillekeurig *adj* involuntary; instinctive; *adv* involuntarily
onwillig *adj* unwilling; reluctant
onwilligheid *n* unwillingness; reluctance
onwrikbaar *adj* unshakable; steadfast; firm
onwys *adj* unwise; foolish
oog *n* eye; fountain; source
oogarts *n* eye specialist; ophthalmologist
oogappel *n* eyeball; darling
ooggetuie *n* eyewitness
ooghaar *n* eyelash
oogknip *n* wink
oogkundige *n* optometrist
ooglid *n* eyelid
ooglopend *adj* obvious; salient
oogluikend *adv* stealthily
oogmerk *n* object; aim; intention
oogopslag *n* glance
oogwimper *n* eyelash
oogwink *n* wink
ooi *n* ewe
ooievaar *n* stork
ooit *adv* ever; at any time
ook *adv* also; too; likewise
oom *n* uncle
oomblik *n* moment; instant
oombliklik *adj* instantaneous; immediate; direct; instant; *adv* immediately; directly; instantly
oond *n* oven; stove; furnace
oop *adj* open; free; candid; vacant

oopgaan *vb* to open; to disclose; to expand
oopmaak *vb* to open
ooppadtolinvordering *n* open-road tolling
oopstel *vb* to throw open
oopval *vb* to fall open; to become vacant
oor[1] *n* ear
oor[2] *prep* over; past; across; via; beyond; opposite; because of; on account of; about; *adv* over; past; left; *conj* because
oorbekend *adj* well-known; notorious
oorbeklemtoning *n* overstatement
oorbel *n* earring
oorbluf *vb* to bluff; to frighten; to bully; to fluster
oorblyfsel *n* remainder; remnant
oorbodig *adj* superfluous; redundant; excessive
oorboord *adv* overboard
oorbring *vb* to transport; to transfer; to carry forward; to take; to deliver
oorbrug *n* viaduct; *vb* to bridge
oord *n* place; region
oordaad *n* excess; extravagance
oordadig *adj* excessive; superfluous
oordag *adv* in the daytime; by day
oordeel *n* judgment; verdict; opinion; *vb* to judge
oordeelkundig *adj* judicious; discerning
oordeelsdag *n* doomsday
oordenking *n* reflection; meditation; epilogue
oordraa *vb* to transfer
oordrag *n* transfer
oordraagbaar *adj* transferable
oordrewe *adj* exaggerated; overdone
oordrywe *vb* to overdo; to exaggerate
ooreenkom *vb* to agree
ooreenkoms *n* resemblance; conformity; agreement; contract
ooreenkomstig *adj* corresponding; similar
ooreenstem *vb* to agree; to concur
ooreenstemming *n* agreement; concord; harmony
ooreet *vb* to overeat
oor-en-oor *adv* again and again; repeatedly

oorerf *vb* to inherit
oorerflik *adj* hereditary
oorgaan *vb* to go over; to cross over; to clear up; to blow over
oorgang *n* transition; change
oorgawe *n* surrender; transfer; handing over
oorgee *vb* to surrender; to cede; to hand over
oorgenoeg more than enough
oorgerus *adj* overconfident
oorgooilap *n* throw (interior decorating)
oorgrootmoeder *n* great-grandmother
oorgrootouers *npl* great-grandparents
oorgrootvader *n* great-grandfather
oorhaal *vb* to persuade; to induce
oorhaas *vb* to hurry
oorhand *n* upper hand; mastery
oorhandig *vb* to hand over; to deliver; to present
oorhandiging *n* delivery; presentation
oorheen *prep* across; over
oorheers *vb* to rule; to dominate
oorheersing *n* domination
oorhel *vb* to slant; to incline
oorhoeks *adj* diagonal; *adv* diagonally
oorhoofse lyn *n* overhead line
oorjas *n* overcoat
oorkant *n* other side; opposite side
oorklank *vb* to dub
oorkom *vb* to happen to; to befall
oorkoms *n* visit; arrival
oorkonde *n* deed; document
oorkook *vb* to boil over
oorkrabbetjie *n* earring
oorkruiper *n* earwig (insect)
oorkruis *adv* crosswise; across
oorkyk *vb* to look over; to go over; to read over; to go through; to correct
oorlaai *vb* to overload; to overburden; to overcharge
oorlaat *vb* to entrust; to leave (to others)
oorlams *adj* clever; cunning; crafty
oorlas *n* trouble; nuisance
oorlede *adj* deceased; the late
oorledene *n* the deceased; the departed
oorlees *vb* to peruse; to read through
oorleg *n* deliberation; consideration; counsel; *vb* to deliberate; to think over; to consider
oorlel *n* earlobe

oorlewe *vb* to survive; to outlive
oorlewer *vb* to deliver; to surrender; to hand down
oorlewering *n* tradition
oorlewing *n* survival
oorlewingskundige *n* survivalist
oorlog *n* war; — **voer** *vb* to wage war
oorlogskip *n* man-of-war (ship)
oorlogsugtig *adj* warlike
oorlogverklaring *n* declaration of war
oorloop *n* overflow; *vb* to overflow; to defect; to desert
oorloper *n* deserter
oorlosie *n* watch
oormaak *vb* to do over again; to re-make; to transfer
oormaaksessie *n* makeover session
oormaat *n* excess
oormeester *vb* to overwhelm; to overpower
oormoed *n* rashness
oormoedig *adj* rash; reckless; arrogant
oormôre *n* the day after tomorrow
oornag *vb* to stay overnight
oorname *n* takeover
oorneem *vb* to take over; to take from
oorpak *adj, adv* overall
oorpeins *vb* to meditate; to consider
oorpeinsing *n* meditation
oorplaas *vb* to remove; to transfer
oorplant *vb* to transplant
oorplasing *n* removal; transfer
oorprikkel *vb* to overstimulate
oorproduksie *n* overproduction
oorprop *n* earplug
oorpyn *n* earache
oorreed *vb* to persuade
oorring *n* earring
oorrompel *vb* to take by surprise; to overwhelm
oorryp *adj* overripe
oorsaak *n* reason; cause
oorslaanjaar *n* gap year
oorsê *vb* to say again; to repeat
oorsee *adv* overseas
oorsese handel *n* foreign trade
oorsien *vb* to oversee; to overlook; to excuse
oorsig *n* view; survey; summary
oorsit *vb* to translate; to put over; to move up (pupils)

oorskadu *vb* to overshadow; to out-shine

oorskat *vb* to overestimate

oorskiet *n* remains; remainder; rest; *vb* to remain; to be left over

oorskot *n* remainder; residue; remains; surplus; **stoflike —** *n* mortal remains

oorskotwaarde *n* scrap value

oorskry *vb* to exceed; to surpass

oorskryf *vb* to rewrite; to copy out; to transcribe

oorslaan *vb* to omit; to pass; to miss out

oorspanning *n* over-exertion; over-work

oorsprong *n* origin; source; root

oorspronklik *adj* original; primary; *adv* originally

oorspronklikheid *n* originality

oorstaan *vb* to stand over

oorstap *vb* to step over; to pass over

oorsteek *vb* to cross a street

oorstelp *vb* to overwhelm

oorstroom *vb* to overflow; to inundate

oorstuur *vb* to send over

oortel *vb* to count again; to recount

oortog *n* passage; crossing

oortollig *adj* superfluous; redundant; surplus

oortreder *n* trespasser; offender

oortref *vb* to surpass; to excel

oortreffend *adj* superlative

oortrek *vb* to overdraw

oortrekking *vb* bank overdraft

oortuig *vb* to convince

oortuigend *adj* convincing

oortuiging *n* conviction

oortyd *n* overtime

oorvaart *n* passage; crossing

oorverdowend *adj* deafening

oorvloed *n* abundance; plenty

oorvloedig *adj* abundant; plentiful

oorvra *vb* to overcharge

oorweeg *vb* to consider; to deliberate

oorweg *n* level crossing; crossroads

oorweging *n* consideration; delibera-tion

oorweldig *vb* to overpower; to overwhelm

oorwerk *n* overtime; overwork

oorwin *vb* to conquer; to surmount

oorwinnaar *n* conquerer; victor

oorwinning *n* victory; triumph

oorwinter *vb* to hibernate

oorwoë *adj* considered; contemplated; **— mening** *n* considered opinion

oorwurm *n* earwig (insect)

oos *adj, adv* east

ooste *n* east; the east; the orient

oostekant *n* east side

oostelike *adj* eastern; easterly; oriental

oostergrens *n* eastern border; eastern frontier

oostewind *n* east wind

ooswaarts *adj* eastward

ootmoed *n* humility

ootmoedig *adj* humble

op *adj* finished; *adv* up; on; *prep* on; upon; at; in

op peil *adv* on form; in good shape

opaal *n* opal

opbel *vb* to phone; to ring up

opberg *vb* to store; to stock up on; to stockpile

opbeur *vb* to cheer up

opblaas *vb* to blow up; to inflate

opborrel *vb* to bubble up

opbou *vb* to build up

opbouend *adj* constructive; edifying

opbrander *n* scolding; reprimand

opbreek *vb* to break up

opbring *vb* to bring up; to serve up (meal); to rear (a child); to vomit

opbrings *n* output; yield; crop; pro-ceeds; produce

opdaag *vb* to arrive; to turn up

opdam *vb* to dam up; to block up

opdat *conj* in order that; that

opdien *vb* to serve up; to dish up

opdoen *vb* to get; to gain; to obtain; to overhaul; to recondition

opdomkrag *vb* to jack up (car)

opdons *vb* to do carelessly; to knock about

opdra *vb* to carry up; to wear out (clothes); to entrust; to dedicate

opdraand *n* rise; slope; rising ground; *adj* uphill; ascending; sloping up-wards; *adv* uphill

opdrag *n* instruction; order; brief; com-mission; terms of reference

opdrifsel *n* driftwood; debris

opdring *vb* to push on

opdringerig *adj* intrusive; obtrusive

opdroë *vb* to dry up

opdruk *vb* to urge on; to hurry; to drive

ope *adj* open; free; candid; vacant

opedag *n* open day

opeen *adv* altogether

opeenhoop *vb* to accumulate; to pile up

opeens *adv* suddenly

opeenvolgend *adj* consecutive

opeet *vb* to eat up; to finish

opeis *vb* to demand; to claim

openbaar *vb* to make public; to disclose; to reveal; *adj* public

openbare betrekkings *n* public relations

openbare-privaat vennootskap *n* public-private partnership

openhartig *adj* frank; candid

openheid *n* glasnost

opening *n* opening; gap

openlik *adv* publicly; openly

opera *n* opera

operasie *n* operation; 'n — ondergaan *vb* to undergo an operation

operateur *n* operator

opereer *vb* to operate on

opfris *vb* to refresh; to revive

opgaaf *n* task; assignment; brief; statement; income tax return; schedule

opgaan *vb* to go up; to rise

opgaar *vb* to collect; to store up

opgang *n* rise; ascent; growth; success; fame

opgeblaas *adj* blown up; inflated

opgee *vb* to give up; to hand over; state (reasons, opinions, etc.); to specify (details); to quit (smoking)

opgemaak *adj* made up; used up; instigated

opgeruimd *adj* cheerful; bright

opgeskote *adj* grown-up; adolescent

opgetoë *adj* delighted; elated

opgewasse *adj* equal to

opgewek *adj* bright; cheerful; lively

opgewonde *adj* excited; thrilled

opgewondenheid *n* excitement; agitation

opgooi *vb* to throw up; to vomit

opgrawe *vb* to dig up; to exhume; to excavate

opgroei *vb* to grow up

ophaal *vb* to draw up; to pull up; to hoist

(flag); to weigh (anchor); to shrug (shoulder)

ophande *adj, adv* nearby; *adv* close by

ophang *vb* to hang; to suspend

ophark *vb* to rake

ophef *n* fuss; *vb* to waive; to abolish; to repeal; to lift up; to raise

ophelder *vb* to clear up; to explain; to elucidate

ophits *vb* to stir up; to instigate; to incite

ophoop *vb* to pile up; to heap up; to accumulate

ophou *vb* to keep up; to support; keep on; to uphold; to cease; to stop; to detain

opinie *n* opinion

opiniepeiling *n* opinion poll

opium *n* opium

opkikker *vb* to cheer up; (*informal*) to up the ante

opklaar *vb* to clear up; to brighten

opklim *vb* to climb; to ascend; to mount (horse)

opklouter *vb* to climb up; to scramble up

opknap *vb* to tidy up; to renovate; to revamp

opknapmiddel *n* tonic

opknappertjie *n* pick-me-up

opkom *vb* to rise; to come up; to occur; to crop up

opkommandeer *vb* to commandeer; to requisition

opkoms *n* rise; rising (of the sun); beginning

opkrop *vb* to conceal; to restrain; to hide; to bottle up (anger)

oplaag *n* edition; impression (book); circulation (periodical)

oplaai *vb* to give a lift; to load up

oplaas *adv* at last; finally

oplap *vb* to patch up; to mend

oplê *vb* to put on; to apply; to impose; to inflict

opleef *vb* to revive

oplei *vb* to educate; to train; to instruct

opleideling *n* trainee

opleier *n* trainer

opleiding *n* education; training

opleidingskursus *n* training course

oplet *vb* to pay attention; to take notice; to observe; to heed

oplettend *adj* attentive
oplewe *vb* to revive
oplewer *vb* to bring in; to yield; to deliver
oplewing *n* revival
oplig *vb* to lift up; to raise
oploop *vb* to accumulate; to accrue
oplopend *adj* short-tempered; irascible
oplos *vb* to dissolve; to solve; to work out
oplossing *n* solution; explanation
opmaak *vb* to spend; to use up; to make (bed); to draw up (report)
opmeet *vb* to survey; to measure
opmerk *vb* to notice; to observe; to remark
opmerking *n* remark; observation
opmerklik *adj* remarkable
opmeter *n* surveyor
opmeting *n* survey
opnaaisel *n* tuck
opname *n* admission; survey
opneem *vb* to take up; to pick up; to film; to borrow (money); to include; to digest
opnoem *vb* to name; to mention; to enumerate
opnuut *adv* again; once more
opoffer *vb* to sacrifice
opoffering *n* sacrifice
oponthoud *n* delay; stoppage; breakdown
oppas *vb* to look after; to take care of; to be careful; to take care; **pas op!** *interj* be careful! look out!
oppassend *adj* steady; diligent
oppasser *n* caretaker; attendant; carer
opper *vb* to suggest; to propose; to raise; to broach; *adj* upper; supreme
opperhoof *n* chief; chieftain
opperhuid *n* epidermis; cuticle
oppermag *n* supremacy; supreme power
oppermagtig *adj* supreme
opperste *adj* highest; uppermost
oppervlakkig *adj* superficial
oppervlak *n* surface
oppervlakte *n* area
opplak *vb* to stick on; to mount
opponeer *vb* to oppose
opponent *n* opponent
opposisie *n* opposition
opposisiekant *n* the opposition

opraak *vb* to run short; to give out
opraap *vb* to pick up; to take up
opreg *adj* sincere; genuine; true
oprig *vb* to erect; to found; to establish
oprit *n* on-ramp
oproep *n* summons; phone call; *vb* to call up; to commandeer
oproer *n* revolt; insurrection; riot
oproerig *adj* rebellious; riotous
oproermaker *n* agitator; rebel; insurgent
oprol *vb* to roll up
oprui *vb* to incite; to instigate
opruim *vb* to clear away; to tidy
oprylaan *n* driveway
opsaal *vb* to saddle
opsê *vb* to recite; to say; to give notice; to dismiss
opsetlik *adj* premeditated; deliberate; *adv* deliberately; on purpose
opsie *n* option
opsien *vb* to look up to
opsiener *n* overseer; supervisor; invigilator; commissioner
opsienbarend *adj* sensational
opsiesleutel *n* toggle key (computing)
opsietoets *n* toggle key (computing)
opsig[1] *n* supervision
opsig[2] *n* respect; **ten —te van** *prep* in respect of; with regard to
opsigtelik *adj* showy; gaudy
opsigter *n* overseer; supervisor; caretaker
opsit *vb* to sit up; to stay up; to wait up; to dish up
opskep *vb* to dish up; to serve up
opskik *n* finery; trappings
opskop *vb* to kick up (fuss)
opskort *vb* to adjourn; to postpone; to delay (sentence, judgment)
opskrif *n* heading; inscription; title
opskrik *vb* to start; to startle
opskrywe *vb* to write down; to list; to note; to score
opskudding *n* commotion; bustle; fuss; sensation; agitation
opslaan *vb* to raise; to put up; to lift up (eyes); to set up; to pitch (a tent)
opslaanhuis *n* prefabricated house
opslag *n* rise; increase; ricochet; bounce; herbage; young grass
opsluit[1] *vb* to lock up; to confine

opsluit[2] *adv* absolutely

opsluk *vb* to swallow up

opsny *vb* to cut up

opsoek *vb* to look up (word); to look for; to look (someone) up; to visit

opsom *vb* to summarize; to sum up

opsomming *n* summary

opspaar *vb* to save up

opspoor *vb* to trace; to track

opspraak *n* talk; scandal; stir

opspring *vb* to bounce

opstaan *vb* to stand up; to rise; to get up; to revolt

opstal *n* buildings; premises (farm)

opstand *n* rebellion; revolt; insurrection

opstandig *adj* insurgent; rebellious; revolutionary

opstanding *n* resurrection

opstapel *vb* to pile up; to accumulate

opsteek *vb* to raise; to put up; to light; to kindle; to incite

opstel *n* composition; essay; paper; *vb* to plan; to draft; to compose

opstelling *n* setup (computing)

opstook *vb* to incite; to instigate; to stir up; to agitate

opstoker *n* instigator; inciter

opstop *vb* to stuff; to fill up

opstopper[1] *n* stuffer; taxidermist

opstopper[2] *n* slap; smack

opstyg *vb* to rise; to ascend

opstyging *n* ascent; rising; liftoff

opsuig *vb* to absorb

opsweep *vb* to whip up; to incite

opswel *vb* to swell up; to inflate

opteken *vb* to write down; to note down; to record

optel *vb* to add; to count; to pick up; to lift; to raise

optelling *n* addition

opties *adj* optic(al)

optimis *n* optimist

optimisme *n* optimism

optog *n* procession

optree *vb* to appear; to take action

optrek *vb* to draw up; to erect; to lift; to rise

optuig *vb* to harness

opvallend *adj* striking; conspicuous

opvang *vb* to catch up; to intercept; to catch water

opvanggebied *n* catchment area

opvat *vb* to take up; to understand

opvatting *n* idea; opinion; view

opveil *vb* to sell by auction

opvlieënd *adj* quick-tempered; hot-tempered

opvoed *vb* to educate; to rear; to bring up

opvoeder *n* educator

opvoeding *n* training; education

opvoedkunde *n* pedagogy

opvoedkundig *adj* pedagogic; educational

opvoedkundige vermaak *n* edutainment

opvoer *vb* to perform; to lead up to

opvoering *n* performance (theatre)

opvolg *vb* to follow; to succeed

opvolgaanval *n* hot pursuit

opvolger *n* successor

opvou *vb* to fold up

opvra *vb* to call in; to demand back; to withdraw

opvraging *n* withdrawal (money)

opvreet *vb* to devour (animal)

opvrolik *vb* to cheer up

opvrywe *vb* to polish

opvul *vb* to fill up; to stuff

opwaarts *adv* upward; on high

opwag *vb* to wait for

opweeg *vb* to counterbalance

opwek *vb* to waken up; to stimulate; to rouse; to generate

opwekkend *adj* rousing; stimulating

opwekking *n* awakening; stimulation

opwel *vb* to bubble up; to gush; to rise

opwen *vb* to wind up; to excite

orakel *n* oracle

oral(s) *adv* everywhere

orang-oetang *n* orang-outang

oranje *n, adj* orange (colour)

orde *n* order; arrangement

ordelik *adj* orderly

orden *vb* to arrange; to put in order

ordentlik *adj* decent; reasonable

order *n* order; command; *vb* to order; to command

ordinêr *adj* common; ordinary

ordonnans *adj* orderly

orent *adj* erect; upright

orgaan *n* organ

organiseer *vb* to organize
organisme *n* organism
orgidee *n* orchid
oriëntering orientation; induction
orig *adj* superfluous; meddlesome
origens *adv* for the rest; besides
origineel *adj* original
orkaan *n* hurricane
orkes *n* orchestra; band
orkesleier *n* bandleader
orkesmeester *n* conductor; bandmaster
ornament *n* ornament
orrel *n* organ
orrelis *n* organist
ortodoks *adj* orthodox
ortodontist *n* orthodontist
ortopedies *adj* orthopaedic
ortopeed *n* orthopaedist
os *n* ox
oseaan *n* ocean
osoon *n* ozone
osoonvriendelik *adj* ozone friendly
osoonlaag *n* ozone layer
ossewa *n* ox-wagon
osvel *n* oxhide
otjie *n* young pig; grunter (fish)
OTM *see* **outomatiese tellermasjien**
otter *n* otter
ou *n* guy; fellow; chap; boyfriend
ouboet *n* eldest brother
oud *adj* old; aged; ancient; vintage
oudag *n* old age
ouderdom *n* age; old age
ouderdomsgaping *n* generation gap
oudergewoonte *adv* as usual
ouderling *n* elder (person)
ouderwets *adj* old-fashioned; forward; precocious
oudgediende *n* veteran; exserviceman
oudheid *n* antiquity
oudheidkunde *n* archaeology
oudheidkundig *adj* archaeological; antiquarian
oudheidkundige *n* archaeologist

oudiënsie *n* audience
ouditeur *n* auditor
oudiovisueel *adj* audiovisual; **—visuele hulpmiddels** *npl* audiovisual aids
oudit *n* audit; *vb* to audit
ouditeer *vb* to audit; to check
ouditeur *n* auditor
oudleerling *n* ex-pupil (of a school)
oudste *adj* eldest; oldest
ouer *n* parent; *adj* elder
ouerlik *adj* parental
ouetehuis *n* old age home
Oujaarsdagaand *n* New Year's Eve
oujongkêrel *n* (old) bachelor
oujongnooi *n* spinster; old maid
oukêrel *n* old man
Oukersaand *n* Christmas Eve
ouland *n* fallow land
oulaas: vir — *adv* for the last time
oulik *adj* precocious; tricky; nice; smart; cute
ouma *n* grandmother
oumagrootjie *n* great-grandmother
oupa *n* grandfather
oupagrootjie *n* great-grandfather
outentiek *adj* authentic
outeur *n* author
outeursreg *n* copyright
outobiografie *n* autobiography
outografeer *vb* to autograph
outokraties *adj* autocratic
outomaties *adj* automatic
outomatiese tellermasjien *n* automatic teller machine (ATM)
outonomie *n* autonomy; self-government
outoriteit *n* authority
outyds *adj* old-fashioned
ouverture *n* overture
ovaal *adj* oval
ovasie *n* ovation
owerheid *n* authority
owerheidsektor *n* public sector
owerspel *n* adultery
owerste *n* chief; head

P

pa *n* pa; dad
paadjie *n* footpath; track
paai *vb* to appease; to coax
paaiboelie *n* bogeyman; bugbear
paaiement *n* instalment
paal *n* pole; post; stake
paaltjie *n* stump (cricket)
paap *n* pope
paar *n* pair; couple; a few; *vb* to match; to pair off; to mate
Paasfees *n* Easter; Passover
Paasmaandag *n* Easter Monday
pad *n* road; path; way
padblokkade *n* roadblock
padda *n* toad; frog
paddastoel *n* toadstool; mushroom
padkos *n* food (for a journey)
padlangs *adv* straight on
padskraper *n* grader
padteken *n* road sign
padvark *n* roadhog
padverlegging *n* road deviation; road diversion
padwaardig *adj* roadworthy
padwoede *n* road rage
pag *n* lease; rent; *vb* to lease; to hire out; to rent
page *n* page(boy)
pagina *n* page
pagineer *vb* to page; to paginate
pagter *n* lessee; tenant
pajama *n* pyjamas
pak *n* suit; parcel; bundle; thrashing; *vb* to pack up; to seize; to grasp
pakhuis *n* warehouse; store
pakkamer *n* storeroom
pakkasie *n* luggage
pakkend *adj* arresting; gripping
pakket *n* parcel; packet; package
pakketakkoord *n* package deal
pakketpos *n* parcel post
pakkie *n* parcel; small packet
pakstapper *n* backpacker
pakstuk *n* gasket (car)
pal *adj* fixed; immovable; firm
paleis *n* palace
paleontologie *n* palaeontology

palet *n* palette
paling *n* eel
paljas *n* charm; magic spell; *vb* to bewitch
palm[1] *n* palm (hand)
palm[2] *n* palm tree; palm branch
palmblad *n* palm leaf
palmboom *n* palm tree
palmolie *n* palm oil
palmiet *n* bulrush
pamflet *n* pamphlet
pampelmoes *n* bluefish; pomelo
pampelmoesie *n* Cape gooseberry; physalis
pamperlang *vb* to cajole; to wheedle; to coax
pampoen *n* pumpkin
pampoenkoekie *n* pumpkin fritter
pampoentjies *n* mumps
pan *n* pan (cooking); tile (roof); small lake
pand *n* pledge; pawn; *vb* to pawn; to pledge
pandak *n* tiled roof
pandjiesbaas *n* pawnbroker
pandjieswinkel *n* pawnshop
paneel *n* panel
paneelkassie *n* cubbyhole
paneelklopper *n* panel beater
paneelwa *n* panel van
paniek *n* panic
paniekbevange *adj* panicky; panic-stricken
paniekerig *adj* panicky; panic-stricken
pannekoek *n* pancake
panorama *n* panorama
pant *n* coat-tail
panteïsme *n* pantheism
panter *n* panther
pantoffel *n* slipper
pantser *n* armour; mail; armour plate (ships)
pantserhemp *n* coat of mail
pantserskip *adj* iron-clad
pantsertrein *n* armoured train
pap[1] *n* porridge; poultice; *vb* to poultice
pap[2] *adj* soft; weak; deflated; **— band** *n* deflated tyre

papaja *n* papaw
papawer *n* poppy
papbroek *n* (*informal*) softy; coward
papegaai *n* parrot
papie *n* pupa; chrysalis
papier *n* paper
papiere *npl* papers; certificates; documents
papierfabriek *n* paper mill
papkuil *n* bulrush
papnat *adj* soaking wet
paraat *adj* ready; prepared
parabool *n* parabola
parade *n* parade; review
paradoks *n* paradox
paradoksaal *adj* paradoxical
paradys *n* paradise
parafeer *vb* to initial
paraffien *n* paraffin oil
paragraaf *n* paragraph
parallel *adj* parallel
paramedies *adj* paramedical
paramedikus *n* paramedic
parapleeg *n* paraplegic
parasiet *n* parasite; sponger
parentese *n* parenthesis
parfuum *n* perfume
pari *n* par; **onder** — *adj* below par
paria *n* outcast; pariah
park *n* park
parkade *n* parkade
parkeer *vb* to park
parkeer-en-ry *n* park and ride
parkeermeter *n* parking meter
parkeerplek *n* parking place; parking space
parlement *n* parliament
parlementêr *adj* parliamentary
parmantig *adj* cheeky; impertinent; impudent
parodie *n* parody; travesty
parool *n* parole
part *n* part; portion; share
partikel *n* particle
partikulier *adj* private; special
partituur *n* score (music)
party[1] *n* party; faction
party[2] *adj* some; a few
partydig *adj* partial; prejudiced; biased
partykeer *adv* sometimes
partymaal *adv* sometimes

pas[1] *n* pace; step; gait; pass; permit; pass (mountain); passage
pas[2] *vb* to suit; to fit; to try on
pas[3] *adv* scarcely; only just; hardly
pasaangeër *n* pacemaker
Pase *n* Easter
pasiënt *n* patient
pasklaar *adj* ready-made
paslik *adj* fitting; proper; suitable
pas op! *interj* be careful! look out!
paspoort *n* passport
passaatwind *n* trade wind
passasie *n* passage
passasier *n* passenger
passasierswa *n* passenger rail car (*or* railway carriage)
passeer *vb* to pass; to go past; to overtake
passend *adj* suitable; proper
passer *n* compasses (pair of)
passer en draaier *n* fitter and turner
passie *n* passion; craze
passief *adj* passive
pasta[1] *n* paste
pasta[2] *n* pasta
pastei *n* pastry; pie
pastoor *n* priest; pastor
pastorie *n* parsonage; rectory
patat *n* sweet potato
patent *n* patent
patenteer *vb* to patent; to register
pateties *adj* pathetic
patogeen *n* pathogen
patriarg *n* patriarch
patriotisme *n* patriotism
patrolleer *vb* to patrol
patrollie *n* patrol
patroon[1] *n* pattern; model; template; patron; employer
patroon[2] *n* cartridge
patrys *n* partridge
patryspoort *n* porthole
paviljoen (*or* pawiljoen) *n* pavilion
pedaal *n* pedal
pedagogiek *n* pedagogy; pedagogics; theory of education
pedagoog *n* pedagogue
pedanties *adj* pedantic; priggish; conceited
pedikuur *n* pedicure
pedofiel *n* paedophile; child molester

peer *n* pear
peerboom *n* pear tree
peet *n* sponsor; godparent
peetkind *n* godchild
peetouers *npl* godparents
peil *n* watermark; mark; gauge; level; *vb* to measure; to fathom; to sound
peilloos *adj* unfathomable
peins *vb* to meditate
peinsend *adj* meditative; pensive
peits *vb* to whip
pekel *n* brine; pickle; *vb* to salt; to pickle
pelgrim *n* pilgrim
pelgrimsreis *n* pilgrimage
pelikaan *n* pelican
peloton *n* squad; platoon
pels *n* fur; skin
pelser *n* pilchard
pelsjas *n* fur coat
pen *n* pen; nib; quill
pendel *vb* to commute
pendelaar *n* commuter
pendeldiens *n* shuttle service
pendeltuig *n* space shuttle
pendule *n* pendulum
pennelekker *n* clerk; penpusher
penning *n* penny; medal
penningmeester *n* treasurer
penorent *adj* erect; upright
penregop *adj* straight up; perpendicular
pens *n* belly; stomach; paunch
penseel *n* brush (artist)
pensioen *n* pension
pensioenaris *n* pensioner
pensioenfonds *n* pension funds
pensioentrekker *n* pensioner
pensklavier *n* accordion
pentameter *n* pentameter
peper *n* pepper
peperduur *adj* exorbitant; highly priced
peperment *n* peppermint
peperwortel *n* horseradish
per *prep* via; by; per
perd *n* horse
perdeby *n* wasp
perdekrag *n* horsepower
perdevlieg *n* horsefly; cleg
perderuiter *n* horseman; equestrian
perdesport *n* showjumping; horseriding

perde(wed)renne *n* horse racing; turf racing
perdgerus *adj* suspecting nothing
pêrel *n* pearl
perestroika *n* perestroika
perfek *adj* perfect
perfeksie *n* perfection
perforeer *vb* to perforate
periodiek *adj* periodic(al); *adv* from time to time; periodically
perfek *adj* perfect
periskoop *n* periscope
perk *n* limit; boundary; flowerbed; lawn
perkament *n* parchment
perlemoen (*or* **perlemoer**) *n* mother-of-pearl
permanent *adj* permanent; lasting
permissie *n* permission
permissiwiteit *n* permissiveness
permit *n* pass; permit
permitteer *vb* to allow; to permit
pers[1] *n* printing press; *vb* to press; to squeeze
pers[2] *n, adj* purple
perseel *n* lot; plot; premises
persent *adv* per cent
persentasie *n* percentage
persepsie *n* perception
perske *n* peach
perskekonfyt *n* peach jam
perskesnaps *n* peach brandy
personeel *n* personnel; staff
persoon *n* person; individual
persoonlik *adj* personal
persoonlikheid *n* personality
perspektief *n* perspective
persvryheid *n* freedom of the press
pertinent *adj* pertinent; relevant
pervers *adj* perverse
pes *n* pest; plague
pessimis *n* pessimist
pessimisme *n* pessimism
pessimisties *adj* pessimistic
pestilensie *n* pestilence
petisie *n* petition
petisioneer *vb* to petition; to request
petrol *n* petrol
petrolpomp *n* petrol pump
petroltenk *n* petrol tank
peul[1] *n* husk; shell
peul[2] *n* cushion; bolster

peul³ *vb* to protrude; to swell

peusel *vb* to nibble; to pick at (one's food)

peuselhappie *n* snack

peuselkroeg *n* snackbar

peuter¹ *vb* to fiddle; to potter; to fuss; to worry; to tamper; **— aan** *vb* to tamper with

peuter² *n* toddler; tot

peuterskool *n* nursery school; playschool

peutervry *adj* foolproof; tamper-proof

pianis *n* pianist

piek *n* peak

piekel *vb* to drag along; to carry with difficulty

piekfyn *adj* spick and span; immaculate; fine; grand

piekniek *n* picnic

pienk *adj, n* pink

piep *vb* to squeak; to chirp; to peep

pieperig *adj* squeaky; weak; sickly

pier *n* pier; jetty

piering *n* saucer

piesang *n* banana

piesangskil *n* banana skin; banana peel

piet-my-vrou *n* red-chested cuckoo; piet-my-vrou

pigmee *n* pygmy

pik¹ *n* peck; pickaxe; *vb* to peck; to carp at; to nag; to pick on

pik² *n* pitch

pikant *adj* piquant; pungent; spicy

pikdonker *adj* pitch-dark; extremely dark; completely dark

pikkewyn *n* penguin

pikswart *n, adj* pitch-black; jet-black

pil *n* pill

pilaar *n* pillar; column

Pilates *n* Pilates

piment *n* allspice

pimpel en pers *adj* black and blue

pinkie *n* little finger

pint *n* pint

pion *n* pawn (chess)

pionier *n* pioneer

piramide (*or* **piramied**) *n* pyramid

pis *n* urine; *vb* to urinate

pistool *n* pistol

pit *n* pip; stone; kernel; wick (candle; lamp)

pla *vb* to tease; to vex; to torment; to worry; to annoy

plaag *n* plague; pest; nuisance

plaagbeheer *n* pest control

plaagdoder *n* pesticide

plaak *n* plaque (teeth)

plaas *n* place; farm; *vb* to place; to put; to locate

plaaskiosk *n* farm stall

plaaslik *adj* local

plaasvervangend *adj* acting

plaasvervanger *n* substitute; deputy

plaat *n* plate; slab; sheet; plateau; stretch

plafon *n* ceiling

plagiaat *n* plagiarism

plak¹ *n* slab; ferule; **— sjokolade** *n* slab of chocolate

plak² *vb* to paste; to glue; to paper (wall); to squat

plakboek *n* scrapbook

plakkaat *n* poster; placard

plakker *n* paper-hanger; squatter

plakkery *n* squatting

plakkies *n* slip-slops

plakpapier *n* wallpaper

plan *n* project; plan; scheme; intention

planeet *n* planet

plank *n* plank; board

plankekoors *n* stage fright

plankvloer *n* wooden floor

plant *n* plant; *vb* to plant; to transplant; to tackle; to bring down

plantasie *n* plantation

plantegroei *n* vegetation

plantetend *adj* herbivorous

plantkunde *n* botany

plantkundig *adj* botanical

plantkundige *n* botanist

plas *n* puddle; pond; pool; *vb* to splash; to paddle

plasmaskerm *n* plasma screen

plaspoel *n* paddling pool

plastiek *n* plastic

plasties *adj* plastic

plastiese chirurgie *n* plastic surgery; cosmetic surgery

plat *adj* flat; level; low

plataanboom *n* plane tree

platdruk *vb* to flatten; to crush

platejoggie *n* disc jockey

platform *n* platform
plato *n* plateau
platonies *adj* platonic
platorand *n* escarpment
platriem *n* strap
platsak *adj* hard up; broke
platskiet *vb* to shoot down
platteland *n* country; rural districts
platweg *adv* plainly; downright
plavei *vb* to pave
plaveisel *n* pavement
pleeg *vb* to commit; to perpetrate
pleegkind *n* foster child
pleegouers *npl* foster parents
plegtig *adj* solemn; grave; stately
plegtigheid *n* ceremony; solemnity
pleidooi *n* plea; argument; defence
plein *n* square
pleister[1] *n* plaster; *vb* to plaster
pleister[2] *n* poultice
pleit *n* plea; *vb* to plead; to intercede
plek *n* place; spot; room; space; position
pleks *prep* instead of
plesier *n* pleasure; fun; enjoyment
plesierig *adj* pleasant; happy; cheerful
plig *n* duty
pligsgevoel *n* sense of duty
ploeg *n* plough; shift (work); *vb* to plough
ploegvoor *n* furrow
plof *n* thud; bump
plofbaar *adj* explosive (situation)
plofstof *n* explosive
plons *n* splash; *vb* to splash
plooi *n* fold; crease; pleat; tuck; *vb* to fold; to crease; to pleat
plooibaar *adj* pliable; flexible
plotseling *adj* sudden; abrupt; unexpected; *adv* suddenly; all at once
pluim *n* plume; feather
pluimbal *n* badminton; shuttlecock
pluimpie *n* compliment
pluimvee *n* poultry
pluis *adj* in order; reliable
pluk *vb* to pluck; to pick; to gather; to fleece
plunder *vb* to loot; to plunder; to ransack
plus *prep; adj, adv* plus
plusminus *adv* about; more or less
podiatrie *n* podiatry

poedel *n* poodle
poedelnaak (*or* **poedelnakend**) *adj* stark-naked
poeding *n* pudding
poëet *n* poet
poeier *n* powder; *vb* to powder
poel *n* puddle; pool
poësie *n* poetry
poëties *adj* poetic(al)
poets[1] *n* trick; prank; **'n — bak** *vb* to play a trick on
poets[2] *vb* to polish; to rub
pofadder *n* puff adder
pofbroek *n* plus fours
poffertjie *n* fritter
poging *n* endeavour; effort
pokkies *n* smallpox
pol *n* clod; sod; tuft of grass
polemies *adj* polemic; controversial
polisie *n* police
polisiehond *n* police dog
polisiekantoor *n* police station; charge office
polisieman *n* constable; policeman
poligamie *n* polygamy
polis *n* insurance policy
politegnies *adj* polytechnic(al)
politiek *n* politics; policy; *adj* politic; political
polities korrek *n* political correctness (PC)
politikus *n* politician
polka *n* polka
pols *n* pulse; *vb* to feel the pulse; to sound
polshorlosie (*or* **polsoorlosie**) *n* wristwatch
pomelo *n* pomelo; grapefruit
pomp *n* pump; *vb* to pump
pond *n* pound (weight); pound (money); sovereign
pondok *n* hut; hovel; shanty
ponie *n* pony
poniekoerant *n* tabloid (newspaper)
pont *n* ferry; ferryboat; pontoon
poog *vb* to try; to attempt
pool *n* pole; **negatiewe —** *n* cathode; **positiewe —** *n* anode
poolstreek *n* polar region
poort *n* gate(way); doorway; pass (mountain); port (computing)

poos *n* while; pause; time
poot *n* paw; leg; foot
pootjie[1] *n* small paw (animal)
pootjie[2] *vb* to trip (someone)
pootuit *adj* run-down; exhausted
pop *n* doll; puppet
populariteit *n* popularity
populêr *adj* popular
populier *n* poplar (tree)
por *n* jab; stab; poke; *vb* to jab; to poke; to urge
poreus *adj* porous
porie *n* pore
pornografies *adj* pornographic
porselein *n* china; porcelain
porsie *n* portion; share
portaal *n* porch; lobby
portefeulje *n* portfolio; wallet
portier *n* porter
portret *n* photo(graph); portrait
portuur *n* equal; match
portwyn *n* port wine
pos[1] *n* post; post office; *vb* to post
pos[2] *n* job; post; position; billet
pos[3] *n* entry; *vb* to enter
posbeskrywing *n* job description
posbesteller *n* postman
posbus *n* post-office box; letterbox
poseer *vb* to pose
posgeld *n* postage
posgids *n* postal guide
posisie *n* position
positief *adj* positive; sure
positiewe *npl* wits; senses
positiewe pool *n* anode
poskaart *n* postcard
poskantoor *n* post office
poslotery *n* lottery; sweepstake
poslys *n* mailing list
posmeester *n* postmaster
posmerk *n* postmark
posorder *n* postal order
posseël *n* postage stamp
post-modernisme *n* post-modernism
postuur *n* posture; figure
posvry *adj* post-free
pot *n* pot; jar; stake; pool; game (tennis)
potdoek *n* dishcloth
potdoof *adj* stone-deaf
potensiaal *n* potential
potensieel *adj* potential

potgooi *n* podcast
potjie *n* hip socket
potjiekos *n* stew cooked in a cast-iron pot; potjiekos
potlepel *n* **ladle**
potsierlik *adj* funny; odd; ridiculous
pottebakker *n* potter; ceramist
pou *n* peacock
pous *n* pope
pousdom *n* papacy
pouse *n* interval; pause; break
pouslik *adj* papal
power *adj* poor; miserable
praal *n* splendour; pomp; *vb* to brag; to boast; to parade
praalgraf *n* mausoleum; tomb
praalkoets *n* state coach
praat *vb* to talk; to speak; to chat
prag *n* splendour; magnificence
pragtig *adj* beautiful; splendid; magnificent
pragwerk *n* thing of beauty
prakseer *vb* to think; to consider; to plan
prakties *adj* practical; *adv* practically; virtually
praktiseer *vb* to practise
praktisyn *n* practitioner; **algemene —** *n* general practitioner; doctor
praktyk *n* practice
pratende kop *n* talking head
predikant *n* minister; clergyman
predikasie *n* sermon
prediker *n* preacher
preek *n* sermon; *vb* to preach
preekstoel *n* pulpit
prefek *n* prefect
prehistories *adj* prehistoric(al)
prei *n* leek
preliminêr *adj* preliminary
premie *n* premium; bounty; bonus
premier *n* premier; prime minister
premis *n* premiss; premise
prent *n* picture; print; illustration
prenteboek *n* picture book
prentverhaal *n* comic strip
presedent *n* precedent
presensie *n* presence; attendance
presensielys *n* attendance roll; attendance register
present *n* present; gift

presentabel *adj* presentable
presentasie *n* presentation
presenteer *vb* to offer; to present
preservasie *n* preservation
preserveer *vb* to preserve
president *n* president
presies *adj* exact; precise; punctual; *adv* exactly; precisely; punctually
prestasie *n* achievement; performance
presteer *vb* to achieve; to perform
presteerder *n* achiever
pret *n* fun; pleasure; amusement
pretbederwer *n* killjoy; spoilsport
pretdraf *n* jogging
pretloop *n* fun run
preuts *adj* prudish; coy; prim and proper
prewel *vb* to mumble; to mutter
prieel *n* arbour; summerhouse; pergola
priester *n* priest
priesteres *n* priestess
prik *n* prick; stab; puncture; *vb* to prick
prikkel *n* spur; stimulant; stimulus; *vb* to prick; to irritate; to excite; to stimulate
prikkelbaar *adj* irritable
prikkelteks *n* blurb
prima *adj* best; first-rate
primêr *adj* primary
primêre onderwys *n* primary education
primitief *adj* primitive
prins *n* prince
prinses *n* princess
prinsipe (*or* **prinsiep**) *n* principle
prinsipaal *n* principal; head teacher
prioriteit *n* priority
prisma *n* prism
prisonier *n* prisoner
privaat[1] *n* lavatory
privaat[2] *adj* private
privaatsektor *n* private sector
privaatskool *n* private school
privatiseer *vb* to privatize
privatisering *n* privatization
proaktief *adj* proactive
probeer *vb* to try; to attempt
probleem *n* problem; puzzle
produk *n* product; produce
produksie *n* production; output
produktief *adj* productive
produktiwiteit *n* productivity
produsent *n* producer
proe *vb* to taste; to sample

proef *n* experiment; proof; trial; test; specimen; sample
proefbeampte *n* probation officer
proefbuisbaba *n* test-tube baby
proefmonster *n* specimen
proefneming *n* experiment
proefondervindelik *adj* experimental
proefskrif *n* thesis; doctorate
proeftyd *n* apprenticeship; probation
proes *vb* to snort; to sneeze aloud
profeet *n* prophet
profesie *n* prophecy
professie *n* profession
professioneel *adj* professional
professor *n* professor
profeteer *vb* to prophesy
profetes *n* prophetess
profiel *n* profile; side view of face
profilering *n* profiling
profiteer *vb* to profit by; to take advantage of
profyt *n* profit; gain
program *n* program; programme
programmatuur *n* software (computing)
programmeerder *n* programmer (computing)
progressief *adj* progressive
projek *n* project
projeksie *n* projection
projekteer *vb* to project
projektiel *n* projectile
pro-keuse *adj* pro-choice (pressure group)
proklamasie *n* proclamation
proklameer *vb* to proclaim
prokureur *n* attorney; solicitor
pro-lewe *adj* pro-life (pressure group)
proloog *n* prologue
promosie *n* promotion; product launch; graduation
promotor *n* promoter; presenter
promoveer *vb* to graduate; to take one's degree
pronk *vb* to show off; to display
pronk-ertjie *n* sweet pea
pront *adj* prompt; punctual; regular; *adv* promptly; punctually; regularly
prooi *n* prey
prop *n* plug; stopper; cork; gag
propaganda *n* propaganda

proporsie *n* proportion
proporsioneel *adj* proportional
propvol *adj* packed; crammed
prosa *n* prose
prosaïes *adj* prosaic; *adv* prosaically
prosedure *n* proceeding; procedure
proses *n* process
prosessie *n* procession
prospekteer *vb* to prospect
prospekteerder *n* prospector
prospektus *n* prospectus
prostituut *n* prostitute
proteïen(e) *n* protein
protes *n* protest
protesoptog *n* public demonstration
protesteer *vb* to protest; to object
protokol *n* protocol
prototipe *n* prototype
provinsiaal *adj* provincial
provinsie *n* province
pruik *n* wig
pruim[1] *n* plum; prune
pruim[2] *vb* to chew (tobacco)
pruimedant *n* prune
pruisiesblou *n, adj* prussian blue
pruisiessuur *n* prussic acid
prul *n* trash; rubbish; trifle
prulkos *n* junk food
pryk *vb* to look good; to shine; to show off
prys[1] *n* price; value; *vb* to price
prys[2] *n* prize; award
prys[3] *n* praise; *vb* to praise
prysbeheer *n* price control
prysenswaardig *adj* praiseworthy
prysgee *vb* to give up; to abandon
prysgeld *n* prize money
pryslys *n* price list; catalogue
prysopgawe *n* quotation; estimate
prysuitdeling *n* prize-giving; awards ceremony
psalm *n* psalm
pseudoniem *n* pseudonym
psige *n* psyche; mind
psigiater *n* psychiatrist
psigologie *n* psychology
psigoloog *n* psychologist

psigose *n* psychosis
puberteit *n* puberty
publiek *n* the public; *adj* public
publikasie *n* publication
publiseer *vb* to publish; to make public; to post (on internet)
publisiteit *n* publicity
puik *adj* excellent; choice; splendid
puimsteen *n* pumice (stone)
puin *n* ruins; debris
puisie *n* pimple; swelling
punktuasie *n* punctuation
punt[1] *n* point; top; tip
punt[2] *n* full stop; full point; dot
puntenerig *adj* touchy; easily offended; fussy
puntetelling *n* score
pupil *n* pupil (eye)
purgeer *vb* to purge
purgeermiddel *n* purgative; laxative
purper *n, adj* purple
purperwinde *n* morning glory (plant)
put *n* well; pit; cesspool; cesspit; *vb* to draw (water)
puur *adj* pure; absolute
pure onsin sheer nonsense
pyl *n* arrow; dart; *vb* to dart; to go straight
pylkoker *n* quiver
pylstert *n* pintail (duck); stingray
pyltjie *n* darts (game)
pylvak *n* home straight; home stretch
pyn *n* ache; pain; *vb* to ache; to hurt; to smart
pynappel *n* pineapple
pyndoder *n* painkiller
pynig *vb* to torture; to torment
pyniging *n* torture; torment
pynlik *adj* painful; distressing; sad
pynloos *adj* painless
pynstillend *adj* soothing
pynstiller *n* analgesic; painkiller
pyp *n* pipe (tobacco, water, gas); tube; leg (trouser); flue (chimney)
pypkan *n* feeding bottle; *vb* to cheat; to fool
pypleiding *n* pipeline

Q

quidproquo *n* quid pro quo; a reciprocal exchange

R

raad[1] *n* advice; counsel
raad[2] *n* council; board
raadgewend *adj* advisory; consulting
raadgewing *n* advice; counsel
raadskamer *n* council chamber; board-room
raadpleeg *vb* to consult; to take counsel with
raadsaal *n* council chamber
raadsaam *adj* advisable; expedient
raadslid *n* councillor
raaf *n* raven
raai *vb* to guess; to advise
raairaam *n* guestimate
raaisel *n* riddle; enigma; puzzle
raaiselagtig *adj* puzzling; incomprehensible
raaiskoot *n* guess
raak *vb* to hit; to touch; to concern; *adj* effective; telling (blow; smile); *adv* effectively
raam[1] *n* window; frame
raam[2] *vb* to estimate; to calculate
raap[1] *n* turnip; swede
raap[2] *vb* to gather; to pick up
raapolie *n* rapeseed oil
raar *adj* funny; strange; odd
raas *vb* to rage; to make a noise; to make a row
raasparty *n* rave
raat *n* traditional remedy; means; advice
rabarber *n* rhubarb
rabat *n* allowance; rebate; discount
rabbedoe *n* tomboy
rabbi (*or* **rabbyn**) *n* rabbi
radar *n* radar
radeloos *adj* desperate
radiator *n* radiator
radikaal *adj* radical
radio *n* radio; wireless; broadcasting
radioaktief *adj* radioactive
radioloog *n* radiologist
radio-omroeper *n* announcer
radius *n* radius
radys *n* radish
raffinadery *n* refinery (oil, sugar, etc.)
raffineer *vb* to refine (oil, sugar, etc.)

rak *n* rack; shelf; web
rakleeftyd *n* shelf life
raket *n* racket
rakker *n* rascal; rogue
ram *n* ram
raming *n* estimate; calculation
rammel *vb* to rattle; to clatter; to batter; to chink (money)
ramp *n* calamity; disaster
ramparty *n* stag party
rampokker *n* gangster; gunman; racketeer
rampsalig *adj* wretched; miserable
rampspoedig *adj* calamitous; disastrous
rand[1] *n* rand
rand[2] *n* brim; edge; verge; border; ledge; ridge
randsteen *n* kerb; kerbstone
rang *n* rank; class; degree; grade; **die laer —s** *n* the rank and file
rangeer *vb* to shunt
rangskik *vb* to classify; to arrange
rangtelwoord *n* ordinal (number)
rank[1] *n* shoot; sprout; tendril; *vb* to sprout; to trail; to twine; to shoot (tendrils); to reach high (rugby)
rank[2] *adj* slender; thin
ranonkel *n* ranunculus
rant *n* hill; ridge; reef
rantsoen *n* ration; allowance
rapport *n* report; statement
rapporteur *n* reporter
raps *n* whack; blow; flick; cut; *vb* to hit; to strike; to flick
rapsodie *n* rhapsody
rariteit *n* curiosity; curio; rarity
ras *n* race; breed
raseg *adj* thoroughbred; pure bred
rasieleier *n* cheerleader
rasend *adj* raving; furious; mad
raserny *n* madness; fury
rasioneel *adj* rational
rasper *vb* to rasp; to grate; *n* rasp; grater
rassehaat *n* racism
rassehater *n* racist

rassisties *adj* racist
rassisme *n* racism
rat *n* gear; cog (wheel)
ratbraak *vb* to mutilate
ratel[1] *n* rattle; *vb* to rattle; to clatter
ratel[2] *n* honey badger
ratelslang *n* rattlesnake
ratkas *n* gearbox
rats *adj* quick; swift; nimble
ravyn *n* gorge; ravine; kloof; donga
reageer *vb* to react
reaksie *n* reaction
realiseer *vb* to realize
realiteits-TV *n* reality TV
realisties *adj* realistic
rebel *n* rebel
rebelleer *vb* to rebel
rebellie *n* rebellion; revolt
red *vb* to save; to rescue
redaksie *n* editorial staff
redakteur *n* editor
reddeloos *adj* hopeless; irretrievable
redder *n* rescuer
redding *n* rescue
reddingsboei *n* life buoy
reddingsboot *n* lifeboat
reddingsvlot *n* life raft
rede *n* reason; cause; ground; motive;
  sense; speech; oration
rededeel *n* part of speech
redelik *adj* reasonable; fair; tolerable
redeloos *adj* irrational
redenaar *n* speaker; orator
redeneer *vb* to argue; to reason
redenering *n* argument; reasoning
reder *n* shipowner
redery *n* shipping firm; transport firm;
  airline
redetwis *n* dispute
redevoering *n* speech; public speaking
redigeer *vb* to edit (newspaper)
reduksie *n* reduction
reduseer *vb* to reduce
reebok *n* rhebok
reeds *adv* already
reeks *n* series; row; sequence
reeksnommer *n* serial number
reeksmoordenaar *n* serial killer
reël[1] *adj* real; genuine
reël[2] *n* rule; line; custom; *vb* to regulate;
  to arrange; to settle

reëling *n* arrangement; regulation; adjustment
reëlmatig *adj* regular; orderly
reën *n* rain; *vb* to rain
reënbak *n* cistern; tank
reënboog *n* rainbow
reënbui *n* shower (rain)
reënerig *adj* rainy
reënjas *n* mackintosh
reëntyd *n* rainy season
reënwater *n* rainwater
referaat *n* lecture; paper; treatise
refereer *vb* to refer; to report
referendum *n* referendum
referensie *n* reference
referent *n* reporter; informer; lecturer;
  referee (testimonial)
refrein *n* refrain; chorus
reg *n* right; law; claim; title; justice; *adj*
  straight; right; true; just; correct; *adv*
  rightly; straight
regaf *adv* straight down
regbank *n* court of justice; tribunal;
  bench
regeer *vb* to rule; to govern; to reign
regeerder *n* ruler
regenerasie *n* regeneration
regent *n* regent
regering *n* government; reign; rule;
  governance
regeringloos *adj* anarchic(al)
reghoek *n* rectangle
reghoekig *adj* rectangular
regie *n* stage management
regiment *n* regiment
regisseur *n* stage manager
register *n* register; index; record
registrasie *n* registration
registrateur *n* registrar
registreer *vb* to register
reglement *n* rules; regulations; bye-laws
regmaak *vb* to put right; to pay; to repair; to spay
regmakertjie *n* pick-me-up
regmatig *adj* lawful; rightful; fair
regop *adj* erect; upright; perpendicular;
  straight up
regs *adj* right-handed; right; *adv* to the
  right
regsaak *n* lawsuit

regsadvies *n* legal advice
regs afhou *vb* to turn right
regsgeleerde *n* lawyer; jurist
regsgeleerdheid *n* jurisprudence
regsgeneeskunde *n* forensic medicine
regsinnig *adj* orthodox
regskapenheid *n* integrity
regspleging *n* administration of justice
regspraktyk *n* legal practice
regspunt *n* point of law; legal point
regstreeks *adj* straight; direct; *adv* directly; straight
regstel *vb* to rectify; to amend; to right
regstellende aksie *n* affirmative action
regstelling *n* correction
regswetenskap *n* jurisprudence; law
regte¹ *n* rights; law
regte² *adv* really; very; truly
regter¹ *n* judge; justice
regter² *adj* right
regterhand *n* right hand
regterkant *n* right side
regtig (*or* **rêrig**) *adj* real; true; *adv* really; truly
reguit *adj* straight; honest; outspoken; candid
regulasie *n* regulation
reguleer *vb* to regulate
regverdig *vb* to justify; *adj* just; fair
regverdigheid *n* justice
rehabilitasie *n* rehabilitation; discharge
rehabiliteer *vb* to rehabilitate; to discharge
reier *n* heron
reik *vb* to reach; to extend to; to stretch
reiki *n* reiki
reikhalsend *adv* longingly
rein *adj* pure; clean; chaste
reinheid *n* purity; chastity
reinig *vb* to cleanse; to purify; to clean
reiniging *n* purification; cleansing cleaning
reïnkarnasie *n* reincarnation
reis *n* journey (land); voyage (sea); trip; *vb* to travel
reisagentskap *n* travel agency
reisdeken *n* rug (travelling)
reisgeld *n* fare
re(i)sies *n* races
re(i)siesbaan *n* racecourse
re(i)siesperd *n* racehorse

reisiger *n* traveller; tourist
reiskoste *n* travelling expenses
reisplan *n* itinerary
rek *n* elasticity; *vb* to stretch; to extend; to protract
rekbaar *adj* elastic
reken *vb* to count; to calculate; to compute; to reckon; — **op** *vb* to depend upon
rekenaar *n* computer; calculator; reckoner
rekenaarfoendie *n* (*informal*) techie
rekenaargesteunde *adj* computer-aided; computer-assisted
rekenaarwetenskap *n* computer science
rekenaarvirus *n* computer virus
rekenariseer *vb* to computerize
rekene *n* arithmetic
rekening *n* bill; account; statement
rekeningkunde *n* accountancy; accounting
rekeningkundige *n* accountant
rekenkunde *n* arithmetic
rekenmeester *n* accountant
rekenskap *n* account
rekker *n* stretcher; elastic; catapult; garter
reklame *n* advertising
reklameagentskap *n* advertising agency; advertising firm
rekonsiliasie *n* reconciliation
rekonstrueer *vb* to reconstruct
rekonstruksie *n* reconstruction
rekord *n* record
rekruut *n* recruit
rekspring *n* bungy jumping
rekspringer *n* bungy jumper
rektor *n* rector
rekwisisie *n* requisition
relaas *n* story; statement
relatiwiteit *n* relativity
relatiwiteitsteorie theory of relativity
relegeer *vb* to relegate
reliëf *n* relief
reling *n* railing
rem *n* brake; skid; drag; *vb* to brake; to apply the brakes
remedieer *vb* to remedy
remediërend *adj* remedial
rempedaal *n* brake pedal

remskoen *n* brake; brake shoe
ren *n* to run; to race
renbaan *n* racecourse
rendier *n* reindeer
renegaat *n* renegade
renjaer *n* racing driver
renmotor *n* racing car
renoster *n* rhinoceros
renperd *n* racehorse
renstel *n* dragster
rensteljaer *n* drag racer
rente *n* interest; annuity
rentekoers *n* rate of interest
renteloos *adj* interest free; bearing no interest
reorganiseer *vb* to reorganize
reparasie *n* repair
repatrieer *n* to repatriate
repeteer *vb* to repeat; to rehearse
repetisie *n* repetition; rehearsal
reproduksie *n* reproduction
reptiel *n* reptile
republiek *n* republic
reputasie *n* reputation
rêrig *see* **regtig**
res *n* rest; remainder
resenseer *vb* to review; to criticize
resensent *n* reviewer; critic
resensie *n* review; criticism
resep *n* recipe; prescription
resepsie *n* reception
reserveer *vb* to reserve
reservering *n* reservation
reservis *n* reservist
reserwe *n* reserve
reses *n* recess
resessie *n* reservation
residensie *n* residency; residence
resitasie *n* recitation
resiteer *vb* to recite
resolusie *n* resolution
resoluut *adj* resolute; determined
respek *n* respect; esteem; regard
respektabel *adj* respectable; presentable
restant *n* remainder
restaurant *see* **restourant**
restitueer *vb* to restitute; to restore
restitusie *n* restitution; restoration
restorasie *n* restoration
restourant (*or* **restaurant**) *n* restaurant

resultaat *n* result; outcome
retireer *vb* to retreat
retoer *n* return
retoerkaartjie *n* return ticket
retoereis *n* return journey
retories *adj* rhetorical
retrovirus *n* retrovirus
reuk *see* **ruik**
reukorgaan *n* olfactory organ
reuksout *n* smelling salts
reukwater *n* perfume; scent
reukweerder *n* deodarant
reun *n* male dog
reünie *n* reunion
reunperd *n* gelding
reus *n* giant
reusagtig *adj* gigantic; colossal; huge; (*informal*) ginormous
reusekrag *n* herculean strength; strength of a giant
reuseskrede *n* giant stride
reusetaak *n* herculean task; huge task
revisie *n* revision
revolusie (*or* **rewolusie**) *n* revolution; *adj* revolutionary
revolusionêr (*or* **rewolusionêr**) *n* revolutionary
rewolwer *n* revolver
rib *n* rib
ribbebeen *n* rib
ribbekas *n* thorax
ridder *n* knight; chevalier
ridderlik *adj* chivalrous; brave
ridderskap *n* knighthood
ridderspoor *n* larkspur
riem[1] *n* oar
riem[2] *n* strap; thong; belt
riem[3] *n* ream (paper)
riemspring *vb* to skip
riemtelegram *n* rumour
riet *n* reed; thatch; cane
rietblits *n* cane spirits
rietdak *n* thatch roof
rietskraal *adj* very thin; thin as a rake
rif *n* reef
riffel *n* wrinkle; ripple; corrugation; *vb* to wrinkle; to corrugate
rig *vb* to aim; to direct; to address
riglyn *n* guideline
rigsnoer *n* rule; guide; example
rigter *n* judge

rigting *n* direction; trend
riksja *n* rickshaw
ril *vb* to shudder; to shiver
riller *n* thriller (book, film)
rillerig *adj* shivery; creepy
rilling *n* shudder; shiver; chill
rimpel *n* wrinkle; fold; crease; ripple; *vb* to wrinkle; to ripple
ring *n* ring; circle; pool (people)
ringvinger *n* ring finger
rinkhals *n* ring-necked spitting cobra; rinkhals
rinkink *vb* to jingle; to rattle; to romp; to play boisterously
rioel *see* **riool**
rioleer *vb* to drain
riolering *n* sewerage; drainage
riool (*or* **rioel**) *n* sewer; drain
risiko *n* risk
riskant *adj* risky; hazardous
rissie *n* chilli; cayenne pepper
ritjie *n* ride; drive; spin
ritme *n* rhythm
ritmies *adj* rhythmic(al)
rits *n* string; series; zip; zip fastener
ritsel *vb* to rustle
ritseling *n* rustling; rustle
ritssluiter *n* zip fastener
rittel *vb* to shake; to shiver; to tremble
rituaal *n* ritual
ritueel (*or* **rituele**) *n* ritual; *adj* ritual
rivier *n* river
rob *n* seal
robot *n* outomaat; robot (traffic light)
robyn *n* ruby
rock *n* rock (music)
roede *n* rod; birch
roei *vb* to row
roeibootjie *n* rowing boat
roeier *n* rower
roeispaan *n* oar
roeiwedstryd *n* boat race; regatta
roekeloos *adj* reckless; rash
roem *n* fame; renown; praise; glory; *vb* to praise
roemryk *adj* famous; renowned
roep *vb* to call; to cry; to scream; to shout; **— en ry** *vb* to hail and ride
roeping *n* calling; vocation
roer[1] *n* rifle; gun
roer[2] *n* rudder; helm

roer[3] *vb* to stir; to move; to touch
roereiers *npl* scrambled eggs
roerend *adj* touching; moving; movable; **—e goedere** *npl* movables
roerloos *adj* motionless
roes[1] *n* rust; blight; *vb* to rust
roes[2] *n* intoxication; infatuation; ecstasy
roesvlek *n* rust stain
roesvry *adj* rustproof; stainless
roet *n* soot
roete *n* route; road
roetine *n* routine; *adj* routine
roetine-ondersoek *n* check-up (medical)
roetinetaak *n* chore(s)
rofie *n* scab
rofstoei *n* all-in wrestling; *vb* to wrestle (professionally)
rofstoeier *n* all-in wrestler
rog *n* rye
roggel *n* phlegm; sputum; *vb* to expectorate; to cough up (phlegm, sputum)
rojaal *adj* royal; generous; lavish
rok *n* dress
roker *n* smoker
rol *n* roll; list; roller; part; role; *vb* to roll; to bowl
rolbaan *n* runway
rolbal *n* bowl (ball); bowls; bowling
rolbalk *n* scroll bar (computing)
rolbesetting *n* cast (play)
rolgang *n* (automated) people mover
roller *n* roller
rolletjie *n* roll; reel (cotton); castor (wheel)
rol op (*or* **af**) *vb* to scroll (computing)
rolprent *n* film; movie
rolprentster *n* film star
rolsaag *n* circular saw
rolskaats *npl* roller skates
rolstoel *n* wheelchair
roltrap *n* escalator
rolverdeling *n* cast
rolvertolking *n* role play
roman[1] *n* novel
roman[2] *n* red roman (fish)
romanse *n* romance
romanskrywer *n* novelist
romanties *adj* romantic
rommel[1] *n* rubbish; junk; litter

rommel² *vb* to rumble
rommelpos *n* spam (computing)
rommelstrooier *n* litterbug
rommelverkoping *n* jumble sale
romp *n* trunk; torso; hull (ship); fuselage; skirt
rompslomp *n* red tape
rond *adj* round; circular
rondawel *n* round hut; rondavel
rondborstig *adj* candid; frank
rondborstigheid *n* candour; frankness
ronddraai *vb* to rotate; to turn round
ronde *n* round; tour
rondgaan *vb* to go about; to circle
rondgaande hof *n* circuit court
rondgee *vb* to pass round
rondkyk *vb* to look about
rondleiding *n* conducted tour
rondloop *vb* to stroll; to loaf
rondloperhond *n* stray dog
rondom *adv* round about; all round; *prep* around
rondomtalie *adv* round about; in a circle; *n* round robin (sport)
rondreis *n* circuit; tour
rondreis *vb* to travel about; to tour
rondskrywe *n* circular letter
rondstrooi *vb* to scatter; to strew about
rondswerf (*or* **rondswerwe**) *vb* to roam; to wander about; to ramble
rondtas *vb* to grope about
rondte *n* circle; circumference; lap
rondtrek *vb* to move about; to journey about; to pull about
ronduit *adv* frankly; openly
rondvaar *vb* to cruise
rondvaart *n* cruise
roof¹ *n* plunder; booty; robbery; (*or* **rowe**) *vb* to plunder; to rob
roof² *n* scab; crust
roofdier *n* beast of prey
roofvoël *n* bird of prey
rooi *n, adj* red
rooibekkie *n* common waxbill
rooibok *n* impala
rooiborsie *n* robin redbreast
rooibostee *n* redbush tea; rooibos tea
rooikat *n* caracal wild cat
rooinek *n* Englishman (nickname)
rook *n* smoke; *vb* to smoke

rookskerm *n* smokescreen
rookklikker *n* smoke detector
room *n* cream
roomvla *n* custard
roomys *n* ice cream
roos¹ *n* rose
roos² *n* eczema
rooskleurig *n* rose-coloured
roosmaryn *n* rosemary
rooster *n* gridiron; grate; timetable; roster; schedule; *vb* to roast; to grill
roosterbrood *n* toast
roostervlug *n* scheduled flight
roostuin *n* rose garden
rosekrans *n* rosary
roset *n* rosette
roskam *n* currycomb; *vb* to currycomb; to rebuke; to criticize severely
rosyn(tjie) *n* raisin
rot¹ *n* rat
rot² *adj* rotten
rotasie *n* rotation
roteer *vb* to rotate
rots *n* rock; cliff
rotsagtig *adj* rocky
rotstuin *n* rockery
rottang *n* cane; rattan
rottekruid *n* rat poison; ratsbane; arsenic oxide
rou¹ *n* mourning; sorrow; *vb* to mourn
rou² *adj* raw; hoarse (cry)
roubrief *n* death notice
roudig *n* elegy
roukoets *n* hearse
rowe *see* **roof¹**
rower *n* robber; pirate
rowerbende *n* gang of robbers
ru *adj* rough; rude; coarse
rubber *n* rubber
rubriek *n* rubric; heading; column (newspaper)
rug¹ *n* back
rug² *n* ridge; hill
rugby *n* rugby
rugbyspeler *n* rugby player
rugbywedstryd *n* rugby match
ruggraat *n* spine; backbone
rugleuning *n* chair back; back rest
rugpyn *n* backache
rugsak *n* rucksack

rugsteun *n* support; *vb* to back up; to support

rugstring *n* spinal cord

ruheid *n* coarseness; rudeness

ruig *adj* bushy; dense

ruigte *n* undergrowth; jungle

ruik (*or* **reuk**) *n* smell; scent; odour; *vb* to smell; to scent; **lont —** *vb* to smell a rat

ruiker *n* bouquet; nosegay; posy

ruikertjie *n* buttonhole (flower)

ruil *vb* to exchange; to swop; to barter

ruim *n* hold (ship); *vb* to make room; to clear; *adj* wide; spacious; ample; abundant; *adv* abundantly; amply

ruimte *n* space; room; scope

ruimteman *n* spaceman; astronaut

ruimtereisiger *n* space traveller

ruimterommel *n* space debris

ruimtetuig *n* spacecraft

ruimtevaarder *n* astronaut

ruimtevaart *n* space travel

ruïne *npl* ruins

ruis *vb* to rustle; to murmur

ruit *n* (window)pane

ruitens *npl* diamonds (playing cards)

ruiter *n* rider; horseman; equestrian

ruitery *n* cavalry

ruitkoevert *n* window envelope

ruitveër *n* windscreen wiper

ruk *n* pull; jerk; tug; *vb* to tug; to pull; to jerk

rukkie *n* while

rukwind *n* squall; gust

rum *n* rum

rumatiek *n* rheumatism

rumaties *adj* rheumatic

rumoer *n* noise; uproar; clamour; *vb* to make a noise

runnik *vb* to neigh

rus *n* rest; quiet; repose; safety catch; rest (music) *vb* to rest; to repose; to lie down

rusie *n* quarrel; dispute; brawl; **— maak** *vb* to brawl

rusiesoeker *n* bully; troublemaker;

ruskamp *n* rest camp

ruspe(r) *n* caterpillar

rusteloos *adj* restless

rustend *n* retired

rustiek *adj* rustic; rural

rustig *adj* quiet; calm; still; restful

rustyd *n* holiday; interval; half-time

ry[1] *n* row; series; line

ry[2] *vb* to ride; to drive

ryk[1] *n* empire; kingdom; realm

ryk[2] *adj* rich; wealthy

rykdom *n* riches; wealth

ryloper *n* hitchhiker

rym *n* rhyme; *vb* to rhyme; to tally; to agree

ryp[1] *n* frost

ryp[2] *adj* ripe; mature; **— word** *vb* to ripen; to mature

rypad *n* bridle path; bridleway

ryperd *n* saddle horse; riding horse; mount

ryplank *n* scooter; surfboard

rys[1] *n* rice

rys[2] *vb* to rise; to ferment

ryskool *n* riding school

rysmier *n* white ant; termite

rystoel *n* rocking chair; wheelchair

rytuig *n* carriage; vehicle; coach

rytuigmaker *n* coach-builder

S

saad *n* seed; sperm; offspring
saadeter *n* seedeater (bird)
saag *n* saw; *vb* to saw; to cut
saagmeul(e) *n* sawmill
saagsel *n* sawdust
saai[1] *vb* to sow; to scatter
saai[2] *adj* dull; dreary; tedious
saailand *n* cultivated land
saak *n* thing; case; matter; business; concern; action; (court) case
saaklik *adj* business-like; precise; to the point
saal[1] *n* hall
saal[2] *n* saddle
saalkleedjie *n* saddlecloth
saalknop *n* pommel
saam *adv* together; jointly
saambring *vb* to bring; to bring together; to bring along
saamdruk *vb* to compress; to squeeze together
saamgaan *vb* to go together; to accompany; to agree
saamgesteld *adj* compound; complex
saamhoort *vb* to belong together
saamhorigheid *n* solidarity; unity
saamkom *vb* to come together; to assemble; to meet
saamleef (*or* **saamlewe**) *vb* to live together; to cohabit
saamsmelt *vb* to merge; to amalgamate
saamspan *vb* to plot together; to conspire
saamstel *vb* to put together; to compile; to compose
saamstem *vb* to agree; to concur
saamsweer *vb* to conspire; to plot
saamtrek *n* rally; gathering
saamvat *vb* to include; to summarize; to take with
saamvloei *vb* to flow together
saamvoeg *vb* to unite; to join
saamwerk *vb* to cooperate; to join hands
saans *adv* in the evening; at night
sabel[1] *n* sword; sabre
sabel[2] *n* sable antelope

sabotasie *n* sabotage
saboteer *vb* to sabotage
saboteur *n* saboteur
sadisme *n* sadism
safari *n* safari; hunting trip
saffier *n* sapphire
saffraan *n* saffron
sag *adj* gentle; soft; mild; tender; smooth
sage *n* legend; myth; fairy tale
saggeaard *adj* gentle; meek
saggies *adv* gently; softly; quietly
sago *n* sago
sagsinnig *adj* gentle; mild
sagtebal *n* softball (sport)
sagteware *n* software (computing); soft goods
sagtheid *n* gentleness; softness
sak[1] *n* bag; sack; pocket; pouch
sak[2] *vb* to sink; to subside; to fail (exam)
sakdoek *n* hanky; handkerchief
sake: ter — *adj* relevant; to the point
sakekennis *n* business knowledge
sakkeroller *n* pickpocket
sakelui *n* businessmen
sakelys *n* agenda
sakevernuf *n* expertise; know-how
sakgeld *n* pocket money
sakmes *n* pocketknife
sakrament *n* sacrament
sakrekenaar *n* calculator
saksofoon *see* **saxofoon**
sal *vb* will; shall
salaris *n* salary; pay
salarisskaal *n* salary scale
saldo *n* balance (bank account)
salf *n* ointment; balm
salie *n* sage; salvia
salig *adj* blessed; blissful
salm *n* salmon
salot *n* shallot
salpeter *n* saltpetre
salpetersuur *n* nitric acid
salueer *vb* to salute
saluut *n* salute
salvo *n* salvo; volley
sambok *n* sjambok

sambreel *n* umbrella
samekoms *n* meeting; assembly
samelewing *n* society; community
sameloop *n* concourse; confluence; junction
sameroeper *n* convener
samesmelting *n* fusion; union; amalgamation
samespraak *n* dialogue
samespreking *n* interview; conference; discussion
samestelling *n* composition; construction; compilation
samestemming *n* agreement; harmony; concordance
sameweerder *n* conspirator
sameswering *n* plot; conspiracy
samevatting *n* summary
samevloeiing *n* confluence; junction
samevoeging *n* union; joining together; bond
samewerking *n* cooperation; collaboration
sampioen *n* mushroom
sanatorium *n* sanatorium
sand *n* sand
sandaal *n* sandal
sandbank *n* shoal; sandbank; sandbar
sandelhout *n* sandalwood
sanderig *adj* sandy
sandhoop *n* heap of sand; dump (mine)
sandkorrel *n* grain of sand
sandlopertjie *n* hourglass
sandpad *n* sandy path
sandsuiker *n* crystallized sugar
sandwoestyn *n* desert
sang *n* singing; song; tune
sanger *n* singer; vocalist
sangeres *n* female singer; female vocalist
sangerig *adj* melodious; tuneful
sangvereniging *n* choral society
sangvoël *n* songbird
sanik *vb* to bother; to worry
sanitêr *adj* sanitary
sanksie *n* approval; sanction
sap *n* juice; sap
sappig *adj* juicy; succulent
sardientjie *n* sardine
sarkasme *n* sarcasm
sarkasties *n* sarcastic
sarkofaag *n* sarcophagus

sarsie *n* volley
sat *adj* full up; satiated
satanies *adj* satanic(al); diabolical
satelliet *n* satellite
satellietfoto *n* satellite photo
Saterdag *n* Saturday
satire *n* satire
satiries *n* satirical
satyn *n* satin
saxofoon (*or* **saksofoon**) *n* saxophone
s-draai *n* hairpin bend
sê *vb* to say; to tell; to speak; to remark;
   om iemand af te — *vb* to break up with someone; (*informal*) to dump someone
sebra *n* zebra
sebraoorgang *n* zebra crossing
sede *n* habit; custom; morals; manners
sedeleer *n* ethics
sedelik *adj* moral; ethical
sedeloos *adj* immoral
seder *n* cedar
sedert *prep* since
sedig *adj* demure; modest; coy
see *n* sea; ocean
seebene *n* sea legs
seebreker *n* breakwater
see-engte *n* strait
seegras *n* seaweed
seehawe *n* seaport; harbour
seehond *n* seal
seekat *n* cuttlefish
seekoei *n* hippopotamus
seekreef *n* lobster
seekus *n* seashore; coast
seel *n* certificate
seël *n* seal; stamp; *vb* to seal
seëlbelasting *n* stamp duty
seeleeu *n* seal; sea lion
seëllak *n* sealing wax
seëlreg *n* stamp duty
seëlring *n* signet ring
seemag *n* naval force; navy
seeman *n* sailor
seemeeu *n* seagull
seemsleer *n* chamois leather; shammy
seemyl *n* nautical mile
seën *n* blessing; benediction; *vb* to bless
seënwens *n* blessing; good wishes
seep *n* soap
seepbakkie *n* soap dish
seepbossie *n* soap bush

seepklip *n* soapstone
seepsoda *n* caustic soda
seepsop *n* soapsuds
seer *n* sore; wound; *adj* sore; painful
seereg *n* maritime law
seereis *n* voyage; sea trip
seerower *n* pirate
seesiek *adj* seasick
seeskilpad *n* sea turtle
seeskulp *n* seashell
seeslag *n* naval battle
seespieël *n* sea level
seester *n* starfish
seestrand *n* beach; seashore
seestrooming *n* ocean current
seevaarder *n* navigator
seevaart *n* navigation
seevaartkundig *adj* nautical
seevark *n* porpoise
seeversekering *n* marine insurance
seëvier *vb* to triumph; to conquer
seevlak *n* sea level
seewier *n* seaweed
sege *n* victory; triumph
seggenskap *n* say; authority
seggingskrag *n* expressiveness
segregasie *n* segregation
segsman *n* spokesman
seldissol *see* **suidissel**
seil *n* sail; tarpaulin; canvas; *vb* to sail
seilboot *n* sailing boat
seildoek *n* sailcloth; canvas
seilgare *n* string; twine
seiljag *n* yacht (sailing)
seilplankry *n* windsurfing
seilskoen *n* tackie
seilskip *n* sailing vessel
sein *n* signal; *vb* to signal; to telegraph
seinfakkel *n* flare
seis *n* scythe
seismograaf *n* seismograph
seisoen *n* season
seisoenaal *adj* seasonal
seisoenkaartjie *n* season ticket
sekel *n* sickle
seker *adj* sure; certain; positive; *adv* certainly; surely
sekerheid *n* surety; certainty
sekering *n* fuse (electricity)
sekerlik *adv* certainly; decidedly
sekondant *n* seconder; second

sekonde *n, adj* second
sekondeer *vb* to second; to support
sekondwyster *n* second hand (watch, etc.)
sekretaris *n* secretary
sekretarisvoël *n* secretary bird
seks *n* sex; sexuality
sekskat *n* (*informal*) bimbo
seksie *n* section
sekstant *n* sextant
sekstrek *n* sex appeal
seksueel *adj* sexual
sekte *n* sect
sektor *n* sector
sekulêr *adj* secular
sekuriteit *n* security
sekuriteitswag *n* security guard
sekuur *adj* secure; precise
sekwestrasie *n* sequestration
sekwestreer *vb* to seize; to sequestrate
sel *n* cell
selde *adv* seldom; rarely
seldsaam *adj* rare; scarce
seleksie *n* selection
selery *n* celery
self *n* self
selfbediening *n* self-service
selfdienwinkel *n* self-service shop; supermarket
selfbedwang *n* restraint
selfbeheersing *n* self-control
selfbehoud *n* self-preservation
selfbestuur *n* self-government; home rule
selfbewus *adj* self-conscious
selfde *adj* same; identical
selfgeldendheid *n* assertiveness
selfgenoegsaam *adj* self-sufficient
selfhandhawing *n* assertiveness
selfmoord *n* suicide
selfondersoek *n* self-examination; introspection
selfoon *n* cell (phone); mobile (phone)
selfrespek *n* self-respect; self-esteem
selfs *adv* even
selfsorgeenheid *n* self-catering (holiday) unit
selfstandig *adj* independent; unaided; **—e naamwoord** *n* noun; substantive (grammar)
selfstandigheid *n* independence

selfsugtig *adj* selfish; egotistic
selfverdediging *n* self-defence
selfvertroue *n* self-confidence
selibaat *n* celibacy
sellulose *n* cellulose
selonsroos *n* oleander
semels *n* bran
sement *n* cement
semester *n* semester
semifinaal *n* semifinal
seminarie *n* seminary
senaat *n* senate
senator *n* senator
send *vb* to send; to forward
sendbrief *n* letter; epistle
sendeling *n* missionary
sender *n* sender; transmitter
sending *n* consignment; mission
sening *n* sinew; tendon
senior *adj* senior; **— burger** *n* senior citizen
sensasie *n* sensation
sensor *n* censor
sensueel *adj* sensual
sensureer *vb* to censure
sensus *n* census
sent *n* cent
sentiment *n* sentiment
sentimenteel *adj* sentimental
sentimeter *n* centimetre
sentraal *adj* central
sentralisasie *n* centralization
sentrum *n* centre
senuaanval (*or* **senuwee-aanval**) *n* nervous attack
senulyer *n* neurotic
senupyn (*or* **senuweepyn**) *n* neuralgia
senusiekte *n* neurosis
senustelsel (*or* **senuweestelsel**) *n* nervous system
senuwee *n* nerve
senuwee-aanval *see* **senuaanval**
senuweeagtig *adj* nervous
senuweepyn *see* **senupyn**
senuweestelsel *see* **senustelsel**
sepie *n* soap opera
September *n* September
septer *n* sceptre
serebraal *adj* cerebral
serebraalverlamming *n* cerebral palsy
seremonie *n* ceremony

seremoniemeester *n* master of ceremonies
serenade *n* serenade
serie *n* series; issue
seringboom *n* lilac tree
serp *n* muffler; scarf; sash
sersant *n* sergeant
sertifikaat *n* certificate
sertifiseer *vb* to certify
serum *n* serum
servet *n* serviette; napkin
ses *n, determiner* six
sesde *n, adj* sixth
seshoekig *adj* hexagonal
seskantig *adj* six-sided
sesmaandeliks *adj, adv* half-yearly
sessie *n* cession; sitting
sestien *n, determiner* sixteen
sestiende *n, adj* sixteenth
sestig *n, determiner n* sixty
sestigste *n, adj* sixtieth
sesuur *n, adj* six o'clock
set *n* move; stroke; trick; putt; *vb* to putt; to set up (printing)
setel *n* seat; residence (government); chair
setlaar *n* settler
setperk *n* green (golf)
setter *n* compositor; putter
seun *n* son; boy
seunskool *n* boys' school
sewe *n, determiner* seven
sewende *n, adj* seventh
sewentien *n, determiner* seventeen
sewentiende *n, adj* seventeenth
sewentig *n, determiner* seventy
sewentigste *n, adj* seventieth
sewe-uur *n, adj* seven o'clock
sfeer *n* sphere
sfinks *n* sphinx
Shakesperiaans *adj* Shakespearian
sidder *vb* to shudder; to tremble
sies! *interj* for shame!
siek *adj* ill; sick; diseased
sieke *n* invalid; patient
siekeboeg *n* sickbay
siekefonds *n* sick fund
sieklik *adj* sickly; ailing
siekte *n* illness; disease; **aansteeklike — ** *n* infectious disease; **besmetlike — ** *n* contagious disease
siel *n* soul; spirit; mind

sielkunde *n* psychology
sielkundig *adj* psychological
sielkundige *n* psychologist
sielloos *adj* soulless; lifeless
sielsiek *adj* mentally deranged; psychopathic
sielsieke *n* mental patient; psychopath
sielsiekehospitaal *n* mental hospital
sielsrus *n* peace of mind
sien *vb* to see; to look; to observe
siener *n* seer; prophet
sienswyse *n* opinion; view
sieraad *n* ornament; trinket
sierlap *n* throw (cover)
sierlik *adj* ornamental; elegant; neat
sierwa *n* parade float
sies tog! (*or* **siestog!**) *interj* shame!
sif *n* sieve; *vb* to sift
sifdraad *n* wire netting; gauze
sig *n* sight; visibility
sigaar *n* cigar
sigaret *n* cigarette
sigbaar *adj* visible
sigbaarheid *adj* visible
sigeuner *n* gipsy
sigsag *n* zigzag
sikadee *n* cycad
sikloon *n* cyclone
siklus *n* cycle
silhoeët *n* silhouette
silinder *n* cylinder
sillabe *n* syllable
sillabus *n* syllabus
silo *n* grain silo
silwer *adj, n* silver
silwerbruilof *n* silver wedding
silwerdoek *n* the silver screen (movies)
silwersmid *n* silversmith
silwergoed *n* silverware
simbaal *n* cymbal
simbolies *adj* symbolic(al)
simbool *n* symbol
simfonie *n* symphony
simmetries *adj* symmetrical
simpatie *n* sympathy
simpatiek *adj* sympathetic
simpatiseer *vb* sympathize
simpel *adj* simple; mere; silly
simptoom *n* symptom
simuleer *vb* to copy; to simulate; to pretend

sin[1] *n* sense; desire; mind; meaning
sin[2] *n* sentence
sinagoge *n* synagogue
sindelik *adj* clean; neat; tidy; house-trained (pets)
sindikaat *n* syndicate; ring; pool (people)
sindroom *n* syndrome
sinds *prep* since
sing *vb* to sing; to warble
singel *n* crescent; moat
sinies *adj* cynical
sinikus *n* cynic
sinjaal *n* signal
sink[1] *n* zinc; corrugated iron; galvanized iron
sink[2] *vb* to sink
sinkgat *n* sinkhole
sinkings *n* neuralgia; rheumatic pains
sinkingskoors *n* rheumatic fever
sinkopeer *vb* to syncopate
sinkplaat *n* sheet of zinc; sheet of corrugated iron
sinksalf *n* zinc ointment
sinlik *adj* sensual; carnal
sinloos *adj* senseless; meaningless; absurd
sinnebeeld *n* emblem; symbol
sinneloos *adj* insane; mad; senseless
sinnigheid *n* liking; inclination
sinode *n* synod
sinoniem *n* synonym; *adj* synonymous
sinopties *adj* synoptic
sinsbedrog *n* hallucination; illusion
sinsbou *n* syntax
sint *n* saint
sintaksis *n* syntax
sinteties *adj* synthetic
sintuig *n* sense organ
sinvol *adj* meaningful
sipres *n* cypress
sirene *n* siren
sirkel *n* circle
sirkelgang *n* circuit
sirkelsaag *n* circular saw
sirkoon *n* zircon
sirkulasie *n* circulation
sirkuleer *vb* to circulate
sirkulêre *n* circular
sirkumfleks *n* circumflex (ˆ)
sirkus *n* circus

sirokko *n* sirocco (wind)
sis[1] *n* chintz
sis[2] *vb* to hiss
sisteem *n* system; method
sistematies *adj* systematic
sit[1] *vb* to sit
sit[2] *vb* to set; to place; to put
sitbank *n* seat; bench
siteer *vb* to quote
siter *n* zither
sitgordel *n* seat belt
sitkamer *n* lounge; sitting room
sitkom *n* sitcom
sitplek *n* seat; place
sitplek gordel *n* seat belt
sitrus *n* citrus
sitting *n* session; meeting; sitting
situasie *n* situation
siviel *adj* civil
sjaal *n* shawl
sjabloon *n* template
sjampanje *n* champagne
sjampoe *n* shampoo
sjarmant *adj* charming
sjebien (*or* **sjebeen**) *n* shebeen
sjef *n* chief; chef
sjerrie *n* cherry
sjiek *adj* chic; smart
sjimpansee *n* chimpanzee
sjirurg *see* **chirurg**
sjokolade *n* chocolate
sjokoladevraat *n* chocoholic
skaad *vb* to damage; to injure; to harm
skaaf (*or* **skawe**) *n* plane (tool); *vb* to plane; to scrape; to chafe
skaafbank *n* carpenter's bench
skaafplek *n* abrasion
skaafsels *npl* shavings (wood, grated cheese, etc.)
skaak[1] *n* chess; check
skaak[2] *vb* to carry off; to kidnap; to elope
skaakbord *n* chessboard
skaakmat *n* checkmate
skaaktoernooi *n* chess tournament
skaakspel *n* game of chess
skaakstukke *n* chessmen
skaal *n* scale; balance
skaam *vb* to be ashamed; *adj* ashamed; shy; timid; bashful
skaap *n* sheep

skaapboer *n* sheep farmer
skaapboud *n* leg of mutton
skaapplaas *n* sheep farm
skaapsteker *n* skaapsteker (snake)
skaapvel *n* sheepskin
skaapvleis *n* mutton
skaapwagter *n* shepherd
skaars *adj* scarce; *adv* scarcely; hardly
skaarste *n* scarcity; want
skaats *n* skate; *vb* to skate
skaatsbaan *n* skating rink; ice rink
skaatsbord *n* skateboard
skaatsplank *n* skateboard
skade *n* damage; loss; injury
skadelik *adj* harmful
skadeloos *adj* harmless
skadevergoeding *n* compensation; damages
skadubeeld *n* silhouette
skaduryk *adj* shady; shadowy
skadusy *n* dark side; unpleasant side
skaduwee *n* shade; shadow
skaduweekant *n* shady side
skaduweepersoneel *n* skeleton staff
skag *n* shaft
skakel *n* link; shackle; *vb* to dial (telephone); to (tele)phone; to link; to connect; to switch on; to switch off
skakelaar *n* switch
skakelbord *n* switchboard
skakelhuis *n* semidetached house
skaker[1] *n* chess player
skaker[2] *n* seducer; kidnapper
skakering *n* shade; nuance
skandaal *n* scandal; disgrace
skandalig *adj* scandalous; disgraceful; outrageous
skande *n* disgrace; shame
skandeer *vb* to scan
skandelik *adj* disgraceful; outrageous
skandering *n* scan; scansion
skandvlek *n* disgrace; stigma
skare *n* crowd; mob
skarlaken *n, adj* scarlet
skarlakenkoors *n* scarlet fever; scarlatina
skarnier *n* hinge
skat *n* treasure; (*informal*) darling; dearest; *vb* to estimate; to value; to esteem
skater *vb* to laugh loudly
skaterlag *n* loud laughter

skatkis *n* exchequer; treasury

skatpligtig *n* tributary

skatryk *adj* very rich

skattejag *n* treasure hunt

skatting *n* tax; estimation; estimate

skavot *n* scaffold

skawe *see* **skaaf**

skedel *n* skull; cranium

skeef *adj* crooked; awry; slanting

skeefkyk *vb* to look awry; to be surprised

skeel[1] *vb* to differ; to lack; to ail; to matter; to care

skeel[2] *n* squinting

skeelhoofpyn *n* migraine

skeen *n* shin

skeepsbemanning *n* crew

skeepsbou *n* shipbuilding

skeepskaptein *n* skipper; ship's captain

skeepslading *n* cargo; load

skeepsredery *n* shipping line

skeepsreg *n* maritime law

skeepsruim *n* ship's hold

skeepswerf *n* dockyard

skeepvaart *n* navigation

skeer *vb* to shave; to shear; to trim

skeerboot *n* hydrofoil

skeerjel *n* shaving gel

skeerkwas *n* shaving brush

skeermes *n* razor

skeerriem *n* strop

skeerseep *n* shaving soap

skei *vb* to separate; to part; to divorce

skeiding *n* parting; separation; divorce

skeidsmuur *n* partition; dividing wall

skeidsregter *n* arbitrator; umpire; referee

skeikunde *n* chemistry

skeikundig *adj* chemical

skeikundige *n* chemist

skel *vb* to abuse; to scold

skel(d)naam *n* nickname

skel(d)woord *n* invective; abusive language

skelet *n* skeleton

skelm *n* rogue; rascal; crook

skelvis *n* haddock

skema *n* scheme; sketch; outline

skemer *n* twilight; dusk; *vb* to glimmer; to grow darker

skemerkelkie *n* sundowner; cocktail

skemerparty *n* cocktail party

skend *vb* to violate; to damage; to desecrate; to maim

skending *n* violation; mutilation

skenk *vb* to give; to present

skenker *n* donor

skenking *n* endowment; donation; grant

skep[1] *vb* to create

skep[2] *n* scoop; spoonful; spadeful; *vb* to scoop; to dig out

skepper[1] *n* creator

skepper[2] *n* scooper

skeppie *n* spoonful; helping

skepping *n* creation

skeprat *n* paddle wheel

skepsel *n* creature; human being

skepskop *n* drop kick (rugby)

skepties *adj* sceptical

skêr *n* scissors (pair of); shears (pair of)

skerf *n* piece; bit; morsel

skerm[1] *n* protection; screen; curtain (theatre)

skerm[2] *vb* to fence; to spar

skermbeskermer *n* screensaver

skermdrag *n* protective clothing

skermkuns *n* fencing (art of)

skermmaat *n* sparring partner

skermskut *n* screensaver

skermutseling *n* skirmish; brush

skerp *adj* sharp; keen; acute; severe

skerpioen *n* scorpion

skerpmaak *n* to sharpen; to whet

skerpsinnig *adj* intelligent; sharp-witted; discerning

skerpskutter *n* sharpshooter; sniper

skerts *n* joke; jest; fun

skets *n* sketch; draft

skets *vb* to sketch; to draw roughly

sketsboek *n* sketchbook

skeur *n* tear; rip; crack; fissure; *vb* to tear; to rip

skeurbuik *n* scurvy

skeuring *n* division; schism; split

skeurpapier *n* wastepaper

skewebek *n* wry face; grimace

skielik *adj* quick; sudden; prompt; *adv* quickly; suddenly; promptly

skiereiland *n* peninsula

skiet *vb* to shoot; to fire; to dart; to blast

skietbaan *n* rifle range

skietgat *n* loophole

skietgeveg *n* shootout
skietstaking *n* ceasefire
skietstilstand *n* ceasefire
skif *vb* to curdle; to divide
skik[1] *n* pleasure; delight; high spirits; liking
skik[2] *vb* to arrange; to adjust; to order; to settle
skikking *n* arrangement; agreement
skiklik *adj* tolerable; reasonable; fair
skiktyd *n* flexitime; staggered hours
skil *n* peel; skin; shell; rind; *vb* to peel; to pare; to skin
skild *n* shield
skilder *n* painter; artist; *vb* to paint
skilderagtig *adj* picturesque
skilderstuk *n* painting; picture
skildery *n* painting; picture
skildklier *n* thyroid gland
skildknaap *n* shield bearer
skildvel *n* rawhide shield
skildwag *n* sentry
skilfer *n* dandruff; scale
skilpad *n* tortoise
skim *n* shadow; ghost
skimp *n* jeer; gibe; mockery *vb* to scoff; to scorn
skinder *vb* to gossip; to slander
skinderbek *n* gossip (person); slanderer
skinderpraatjies *n* gossip; slander
skink *vb* to pour in
skinkbord *n* tray; salver
skinkjuffrou *n* barmaid
skinkjuffie *n* barmaid
skip *n* ship; vessel; boat
skipbreuk *n* shipwreck
skipper *n* captain; skipper
skisofrenie *n* schizophrenia
skitter *vb* to glitter; to sparkle
skitterend *adj* brilliant; glittering
skobbejak *n* rogue; scoundrel
skoen *n* shoe; boot; footwear
skoenlapper *n* butterfly
skoenmaker *n* cobbler; shoemaker
skoenveter *n* shoe lace
skoenwaks *n* shoe/boot polish
skof[1] *n* part of a journey; stage; shift
skof[2] *n* shoulder (cattle); withers (horse)
skoffel *n* hoe; *vb* to hoe; to dance
skok *n* shock; fright; *vb* to shock; to frighten

skokdemper *n* shock absorber
skokkend *adj* shocking
skolier *n* pupil; scholar
skolierpatrollie *n* scholar patrol
skommel *n* swing; *vb* to swing; to rock; to shake; to fluctuate
skommeldrankie *n* smoothie
skon *n* scone
skool[1] *n* school; *vb* to train; to school
skool[2] *n* shoal; *vb* to collect together; to flock together
skoolboek *n* schoolbook
skoolgebou *n* school building
skoolgeld *n* school fees
skoolhoof *n* school principal
skoolhou *vb* to teach
skoolkind *n* pupil; schoolchild
skoolraad *n* school board
skoon *adj* clean; pure; beautiful; fine
skoondogter *n* daughter-in-law
skoonheid *n* beauty
skoonheidskundige *n* beautician
skoonmaak *vb* to clean
skoonmaker *n* cleaner
skoonmoeder *n* mother-in-law
skoonouers *npl* parents-in-law
skoonseun *n* son-in-law
skoonsuster *n* sister-in-law
skoonvader *n* father-in-law
skoonveld *n* fairway (golf); *adv* out of sight; gone
skoorsoeker *n* troublemaker
skoorsteen *n* chimney; chimney stack; funnel
skoorsteenmantel *n* mantelpiece
skoorsteenveër *n* chimney sweep
skoorvoetend *adv* reluctantly
skoot[1] *n* lap; bosom; fold
skoot[2] *n* shot; report; turn; time
skoothondjie *n* lapdog
skootrekenaar *n* laptop
skop[1] *n* trowel; spade; scoop
skop[2] *n* kick; recoil; *vb* to kick; to recoil
skopgraaf *n* shovel
skoppelmaai *n* swing
skoppens *npl* spades (playing cards)
skor *adj* hoarse; husky
skorriemorrie *n* rabble; riffraff
skors *vb* to suspend (school, membership)

skorsie *n* squash (vegetable)
skorsing *n* suspension
skort *vb* to hinder; to postpone; to ail; to lack
skottel *n* dish; basin
skottelgoed *n* crockery; dishes
skotvry *adj* scot-free
skou *n* show; exhibition
skouburg *n* theatre; cinema
skouer *n* shoulder
skouhuis *n* show house
skouput *n* manhole
skouspel *n* spectacle; sight; scene
skouspelagtig *adj* spectacular
skouspring *n* showjumping
skraag *n* support; prop
skraaginspuiting *n* booster injection
skraal *adj* thin; meagre
skraap *n* scratch; *vb* to scrape; to scratch
skrander *adj* intelligent; clever
skrap *vb* to scratch out; to strike off; to erase
skrapnel *n* shrapnel
skraps *adj* scarce; *adv* scarcely; barely; narrowly
skrede *n* pace; step; stride
skree(u) *n* scream; shout; cry; yell; *vb* to scream; to shout; to cry; to yell
skree(u)balie *n* crybaby
skree(u)ery *n* shouting; crying
skree(u)lelik *adj* very ugly
skree(u)snaaks *adj* very funny; hilarious
skrefie *n* slit; small opening
skrif *n* handwriting
skrifgeleerde *n* scribe
skrifte *n* exercise book
skriftelik *adj* written
skrik *n* fright; scare; start; terror; *vb* to start; to be frightened; to be scared
skrikbeeld *n* scarecrow; bogeyman
skrikkeljaar *n* leap year
skrikkerig *adj* shy; easily frightened; nervous; skittish (horse)
skrikmaak *vb* to frighten; to startle
skrikwekkend *adj* terrifying; alarming
skril *adj* shrill; glaring
skroef (*or* **skroewe**) *n* screw; propeller; *vb* to screw
skroefsleutel *n* shifting spanner; adjustable spanner

skroei *vb* to burn; to scorch; to singe; to cauterize
skroewe *see* **skroef**
skroewedraaier *n* screwdriver
skroom *vb* to hesitate; to fear; to dread
skroomvallig *adj* timid; timorous; shy
skrop *vb* to scrub; to scratch (hens); to work (doing odd jobs)
skropborsel *n* scrubbing brush
skrum *n* scrum; *vb* to scrum
skryf (*or* **skrywe**) *vb* to write
skryfbehoeftes *n* stationery
skryfblok *n* writing pad
skryfboek *n* exercise book; writing pad
skryfgoed *n* stationery
skryfpapier *n* notepaper
skryftafel *n* desk; writing table
skrynwerk *n* cabinet making; joinery
skrynwerker *n* cabinet maker; joiner
skrywe *see* **skryf**
skrywer *n* author; writer
sku *vb* to shun; *adj* shy; timid; afraid
skubbe *n* scales (fish)
skud *vb* to shake; to jolt; to shuffle (playing cards)
skugter *adj* shy; timid
skuif (*or* **skuiwe**) *n* bolt; slide; move; *vb* to push; to shove; to move; to slide
skuifdeur *n* sliding door
skuifel *vb* to shuffle
skuifkelder *n* air-raid shelter
skuifleer *n* extension ladder
skuifraam *n* sash window
skuiftrompet *n* trombone
skuil *vb* to hide; to take shelter
skuilnaam *n* pseudonym
skuilplek *n* hiding place; shelter; retreat
skuim *n* scum; foam; froth; *vb* to foam; to froth
skuins *adj* slanting; sloping; oblique
skuinste *n* incline; slope
skuit *n* boat
skuiwe *see* **skuif**
skuld *n* debt; fault; guilt; *vb* to owe; — **bewys** *vb* to convict
skuldeiser *n* creditor
skuldenaar *n* debtor
skuldig *adj* guilty; — **vind** *vb* to convict
skuldige *n* guilty person; culprit
skulp *n* shell
skurf *adj* scabby; rough; chapped

skurfte *n* scab; itch; roughness
skurk *n* rascal; rogue; thug
skut[1] *n* protection; guard; pad (cricket); *vb* to protect
skut[2] *n* pound (animals); *vb* to impound
skuur[1] *n* barn; shed
skuur[2] *vb* to scour; to polish; to rub
skuurpapier *n* sandpaper; emery paper
skyf *n* slice; disc; quarter; target
skyfie *n* slice
skyfletsel *n* slipped disc
skyfskiet *vb* to shoot at a target
skyn *n* light; shine; appearance; pretence; *vb* to shine; to appear; to seem
skynbaar *adv* apparently; evidently
skynheilig *adj* hypocritical
skynheilige *n* hypocrite
skynheiligheid *n* hypocrisy
skynsel *n* glow; light; shine
skynwerklikeheid *n* virtual reality
slaaf (*or* **slawe**) *n* slave
slaafs *adj* slavish; servile
slaag *vb* to succeed; to pass
slaai *n* salad; lettuce
slaan *vb* to beat; to hit; to strike
slaap[1] *n* sleep; *vb* to sleep
slaap[2] *n* temple
slaapdrank *n* narcotic
slaapkamer *n* bedroom
slaapkop *n* sleepyhead
slaapklere *n* pyjamas
slaaploos *see* **slapeloos**
slaaploosheid *see* **slapeloosheid**
slaapsaal *n* dormitory
slaapsak *n* sleeping bag
slaapliedjie *n* lullaby
slaapsiekte *n* sleeping sickness
slaaptyd *n* bedtime
slaapwandelaar *n* sleepwalker
slag[1] *n* blow; knock; stroke; battle; loss; slap; bang; beat; clap (thunder)
slag[2] *vb* to slaughter; to kill
slagaar *n* artery
slaggat *n* pothole
slaghuis *n* butchery
slagoffer *n* victim
slagorkes *n* percussion band
slagplaas *n* abattoir
slagreën *n* downpour; heavy rain
slagspreuk *n* slogan; motto
slagtand *n* tusk; fang

slagter *n* butcher
slagting *n* slaughter; massacre
slagvee *n* slaughter animals
slagveld *n* battlefield
slak *n* snail; slug; slag (dross)
slakkepos *n* (*informal*) snail mail
slang *n* snake
slank *adj* slender; slim;
slap *adj* loose; slack; weak; dull; lacklustre
slapeloos (*or* **slaaploos**) *adj* sleepless
slapeloosheid (*or* **slaaploosheid**) *n* sleeplessness; insomnia
slaperig *adj* sleepy
slapgat *adj* spineless
slapverkeer *n* off-peak traffic
slawehandel *n* slave trade
slawerny *n* slavery
slee *n* sledge; sleigh
sleep *n* train; retinue; *vb* to drag; to tow
sleepboot *n* tug
sleepdraer *n* train bearer
sleepren *n* drag racing
sleeptou *n* towrope
sleepvoetend *adj* shuffling
sleg *adj* bad; evil; wrong; inferior; ill; *adv* badly; poorly
slegs *adv* only; but; merely
slegte spysvertering *n* indigestion; dyspepsia
slenter[1] *n* trick; ploy; bluff
slenter[2] *vb* to saunter
slentering *n* saunter; stroll
sleur *n* habit; rut; routine; *vb* to drag; to loiter
sleutel *n* key; clef (music); register; wrench; spanner
sleutelbeen *n* collarbone
sleutelgat *n* keyhole
slim *adj* sly; crafty; clever; smart; intelligent
slimfoon *n* smart phone
slimkaart *n* smart card
slimpraatjies *n* small talk; claptrap
slinger *n* pendulum; sling; handle; *vb* to swing; to sway; to oscillate; to reel; to pitch
slinks *adj* cunning; treacherous
sloep *n* sloop
sloer *vb* to loiter; to linger; to dawdle
sloop[1] *n* pillowcase

sloop[2] *vb* to demolish

sloot *n* ditch; trench

slordig *adj* untidy; dowdy; careless

slot[1] *n* lock; clasp

slot[2] *n* conclusion; end

slot[3] *n* castle

slotmaker *n* locksmith

slotsom *n* summary; result

slu *adj* cunning; sly; wily

sluier *n* veil; mask

sluimer *vb* to slumber; to doze

sluip *vb* to stalk; to move stealthily; to steal along; to sneak

sluipjagter *n* stalker

sluipmoord *n* assassination

sluipmoordenaar *n* assassin

sluis *n* sluice; lock

sluit *vb* to close; to shut; to lock; to conclude

sluitdatum *n* closing date

sluitkas *n* locker

sluk *n* draught; gulp; *vb* to swallow; to gulp

slukderm *n* gullet; oesophagus

slukkie *n* mouthful; draught

slurp[1] *n* trunk (elephant)

slurp[2] *vb* to sip; to lap; to slurp; to guzzle

slyk *n* dirt; mire; mud

slym *n* slime; mucus; phlegm

slymerig *adj* slimy; mucous

slymvlies *n* mucous membrane

slyp *vb* to sharpen; to whet; to grind; to cut (diamonds)

slypsteen *n* grindstone; whetstone

slyt *vb* to wear out; to pass (one's time); to spend (one's time)

slytasie *n* wear and tear; wastage

smaad *vb* to reproach; to scorn; to deride

smaadheid *n* scorn; derision

smaak *n* taste; flavour; relish; liking; *vb* to taste; to savour

smaaklik *adj* tasty; palatable

smaakloos *adj* insipid; tasteless

smaakvol *adj* elegant; tasteful

smadelik *adj* derisive; scornful

smag *vb* to long for; to pine for

smagtend *adj* languishing; longing

smak *n* thud; crash; smack (lips)

smal *adj* thin; narrow

smalend *adj* sneering

smarag *n* emerald

smaraggroen *adj, n* emerald green

smart *n* pain; grief; sorrow

smartlik *adj* painful

smee *vb* to forge; to weld; to devise

smeebaàr *adj* malleable

smeek *vb* to beg; to beseech; to implore

smeekskrif *n* petition

smeer *vb* to grease; to smear; to oil; to lubricate; to butter

smeergoed *n* ointment; liniment

smeerveldtog *n* smear campaign

smeeyster *n* wrought iron

smelt *vb* to melt; to dissolve; to fuse

smerig *adj* greasy; dirty; squalid

smet *n* stain; spot; blemish

smetloos *adj* stainless; spotless

smeul *vb* to smoulder

smid *n* smith; blacksmith

smiddags *adv* in the afternoon; at midday; at noon

smidswinkel *n* smithy

smokkel *n* smuggling; *vb* to smuggle

smokkelaar *n* smuggler

smokkelary *n* smuggling

smokkelkroeg *n* shebeen

smoor *vb* to smother; to stifle; to suffocate

smoordronk *adj* dead drunk

smoorverlief *adj* head over heels in love

smoorlik *adv* deeply; excessively

smorens (*or* **smôrens**) *adv* in the morning

SMS-stuur *vb* to send short text messages via SMS

smul *vb* to feast

smulparty *n* feast; banquet

smyt *vb* to throw; to fling

snaaks *adj* funny; strange; droll

snaar *n* string; cord

snags *adv* during the night

snak *vb* to long for; to gasp

snap *vb* to catch; to understand

snaphaan *n* flintlock

snapsie *n* drop; dram

snater *n* mouth

snater *vb* to chatter; to jabber

snawel *n* bill; beak

sneeu *n* snow; *vb* to snow

sneeubui *n* snowstorm; snow shower

sneeuklokkie *n* snowdrop
sneeuvlokkie *n* snowflake
sneeuwit *n, adj* snow-white
snel *vb* to hurry; to run; *adj* swift; quick; rapid
sneldiens *n* express service
snelheid *n* speed; velocity
sneller *n* trigger; sprinter
snelperk *n* speed limit
snelrat *n* overdrive
snelskrif *n* shorthand
snelstrik *n* speed trap
sneltrein *n* express train; fast train
snelvuur *n* rapid fire
snelweg *n* expressway
snerpend *adj* smarting; piercing
snesie *n* tissue
sneuwel *vb* to perish; to fall (in battle)
snik *n* gasp; sob; *vb* to sob; to gasp; to sniffle
snipper *n* snippet; scrap; shred
snippermandjie *n* wastepaper basket
snit *n* cut; style; fashion
snob *n* snob
snobisme *n* snobbery
snoei *vb* to clip; to prune
snoeiskêr *n* garden shears; pruning shears
snoek *n* snoek (marine fish)
snoep *vb* to eat on the sly; to withhold; *adj* greedy; gluttonous; tightfisted
snoeperye *npl* snacks
snoephoekie *n* snack bar
snoepwinkel *n* tuck shop
snoer *n* string; cord; *vb* to string; to tie; to silence; to close
snoer pêrels *n* string of pearls
snoet *n* snout; muzzle
snood *adj* base; evil; heinous
snor *n* moustache
snorbaard *n* moustache; whiskers
snork *n* snoring; snort (horse); *vb* to snore; to snort
snot *n* mucus; snot
snou *vb* to snarl
snuffel *vb* to sniff; to smell; to search; to investigate
snuif (*or* **snuiwe**) *n* snuff; *vb* to snort; to sniff; to take snuff
snuifdos *n* snuffbox
snuistery *n* (k)nick-(k)nack; trinket

snuit *n* snout; nose; *vb* to blow one's nose
snuiter *n* youngster; kid
snuiwe *see* **snuif**
sny *n* slice; cut; gash; *vb* to cut; to castrate; to geld (horse); to operate
snyboontjie *n* French bean; green bean
snydokter *n* surgeon
snyer *n* tailor; cutter
snykunde *n* surgery
snypunt *n* point of intersection
snytand *n* incisor
snywerk *n* carving
so *adv* thus; so; like this
sober *adj* sober; temperate
soberheid *n* sobriety
soda *n* soda
sodanig *adv* such
sodat *adv* so that; in order that
sodawater *n* soda water
sodoende *adv* thus; in that manner
sodra *adv* as soon as
soebat *vb* to beg; to implore; to plead
soek *vb* to seek; to look for; to search
soekenjin *n* search engine (internet)
soeklig *n* searchlight
soen *n* kiss; *vb* to kiss
soepel *adj* supple; pliant; flexible; agile (computing)
soet *adj* sweet; good; pleasant
soetigheid *n* sweetness; sweets
soetjies (*or* **suutjies**) *adv* gently; unnoticed; noiselessly
soetlief *n* sweetheart
soetlemoen *n* orange
soetmelk *n* sweet milk; fresh milk
soetolie *n* salad oil
soetriet *n* sugar cane
soetsappig *n* goody-goody
soetwater *n* fresh water
soewenier *n* souvenir; keepsake
soewerein *adj* sovereign; supreme
sofa *n* sofa
sofis *n* sophist
sofisme *n* sophism
sog *n* sow; female pig
sogenaamd *adj* so-called; *adv* ostensibly
soggens *adv* in the morning
soheentoe *adv* thither; that way
sojaboontjie *n* soya bean
sokker *n* soccer; football

sokkie *n* sock
sokkiejol *n* informal dance
solank *conj* so long as; meanwhile
soldaat *n* soldier
soldeer *vb* to solder
soldeerbout *n* soldering iron
solder *n* loft; garret
solderkamer(tjie) *n* attic
soldy *n* soldier's pay
solidariteit *n* solidarity
solied *adj* trustworthy; steady; solid
solis *n* soloist
solo *n* solo
som *n* sum; amount; problem
somber *adj* gloomy; sad; sombre
somer *n* summer
somerhuis *n* arbour; summerhouse
somervakansie *n* summer holidays
sommeer *vb* to summon
sommer *adv* just; at a glance; for no
reason
sommerso *adv* in a way
sommige *pron* some
soms *adv* sometimes; perhaps; possibly
somtyds *adv* sometimes
son *n* sun
sonate *n* sonata
sonbesie *n* cicada
sonbrandolie *n* suntan lotion
sonbruin *n* suntan; tan; *vb* to tan
sondaar *n* sinner
Sondag *n* Sunday
Sondagskool *n* Sunday school
sondares *n* sinner
sonde *n* sin; evil; shame
sondebok *n* scapegoat
sonder *prep* without
sonderling *adj* odd; peculiar; eccentric
sondig *vb* to sin; to commit a sin; *adj*
sinful
sondvloed *n* deluge; great flood
sone *n* zone
songebrand *adj* sunburnt
sonkrag *n* solar power
sonlig *n* sunlight
sonneblom *n* sunflower
sonnet *n* sonnet
sonnewyster *n* sundial
sonnig *adj* sunny
sononder *n* sunset; *adv* at sunset
sonop *n* sunrise; *adv* at sunrise

sonskerm *n* awning; sunshade; sunscreen (lotion)
sonskyn *n* sunshine
sonsondergang *n* sunset
sonsopgang *n* sunrise
sonsteek *n* sunstroke
sonstraal *n* sunbeam
sonsverduistering *n* eclipse of the
sun; solar eclipse
sonverhitting *n* solar heating
sonvlek *n* sunspot
sonwyser *n* sundial
soog *vb* to suckle; to nurse
soogdier *n* mammal
sooi *n* sod; turf
sooibrand *n* heartburn
sooimerk *n* divot (golf)
sool *n* sole
soölogie *n* zoology
soom *n* hem; seam; edge; border; *vb* to
hem; to border
soontoe *adv* thither; that way
soort *n* sort; kind; type
soortgelyk *adj* similar
soortlik *adj* specific
soos *prep* as; like
sop *n* soup; broth
sopie *n* dram; drink; tot
sopraan *n* soprano
sorg *vb* to care for; to take care
sorg *n* care; charge; trouble
sorgeenheid *n* intensive care unit
sorgeloos *adj* careless
sorgsaam *adj* careful
sorgsentrum *n* frail care unit
sorgvuldig *adj* careful; thorough
sorgwekkend *adj* alarming
sorteer *vb* to sort; to assort; to select
sortering *n* selection; assortment
sosatie *n* skewer of curried meat pieces;
sosatie
soseer *adv* so much; to such an extent
sosiaal *adj* social
sosiale vlinder *n* social climber; socialite
sosiale netwerking *n* social networ'k-
ing
sosialis *n* socialist
sosialisme *n* socialism
sot *n* fool; *adj* foolish
sotterny *n* nonsense; foolishness

souffleur *n* prompter
sous *n* sauce; gravy
souskom *n* gravy boat
soustrein *n* gravy train
sout *n* salt; *vb* to salt; to cure; to initiate; *adj* briny; salty
soutpan *n* saltpan
soutsuur *n* hydrochloric acid
soutvleis *n* salted meat
soveel *adv* so much; so many; **vir die —ste maal** *adv* for the hundredth time
sover *adv* so far
sowaar *adv* really; truly
sowat *adv* about
sowel *conj* as well; and
spaan *n* ladle; scoop; skimmer
spaander *n* chip; shaving; splinter; *vb* to run away
spaanderbord *n* chipboard
spaanderhout *n* chipboard
spaar *vb* to save; to economize; to spare
spaarbank *n* savings bank
spaarrekening *n* savings account
spaarsaam *adj* thrifty; economical
spaarsaamheid *n* thrift
spalk *n* splint; *vb* to splint; to set (broken bone, etc.)
span *n* span; team; *vb* to brace; to stretch
spanbroek *n* tights
spandabel *n* spendthrift
spandeer *vb* to spend
spandoek *n* large banner; large streamer
spangees *n* team spirit
spannend *adj* tight; exciting
spanning *n* tension; stress; suspense
spansaag *n* frame saw; span saw
spanspek *n* muskmelon; cantaloupe melon;
spar *n* rafter; spar
spartel *vb* to sprawl; to gambol
spasie *n* space
spasieer *vb* to space (words)
spasiëring *n* spacing
spat *vb* to splash; to spatter; to spurt; to spout
spatsel *n* splash; spatter
speek *n* spoke
speeksel *n* spittle; saliva

speel *vb* to play; to trifle with; to act
speeldoos *n* musical box
speelgoed *n* toys
speelmaat *n* playmate
speelplek *n* playground
speeltyd *n* playtime; recess; interval
speelvak *n* season; run (theatre)
speels *adj* playful
speen *n* teat; nipple; *vb* to wean
speenvark *n* sucking pig
spei *vb* to neuter (female animals); to spay
spek *n* bacon; pork
spektakel *n* row; noise; scene
spekulant *n* speculator
spekuleer *vb* to speculate
spekulasie *n* speculation
spel[1] *n* play; game; performance
spel[2] *vb* to spell
spelbreker *n* killjoy; spoilsport
speld *n* pin
speld(e) *vb* to pin
speldekussing *n* pincushion
speler *n* player; actor
speletjie *n* play; game; fun
spelfout *n* spelling mistake
speling *n* play; range; scope
spelling *n* spelling; orthography
spelonk *n* cave; cavern
speltoetser *n* spellchecker (computing)
spens *n* pantry; larder
sperstreep *n* barrier line (solid white)
spertyd *n* deadline
spesery *n* spice
spesiaal *adj* special
spesialis *n* specialist
spesifiek *adj* specific
spesifikasie *n* specification
spesifiseer *vb* to specify
spesialiteit *n* speciality
speur *vb* to trace; to track; to spy on
speurder *n* detective
speurhond *n* bloodhound; police dog
spieël *n* mirror; *vb* to mirror
spieëlglas *n* plate glass
spieëltafel *n* dressing table
spier *n* muscle
spierbouer *n* bodybuilder
spierkrag *n* brute force; muscular force
spierwit *n, adj* snow-white
spies *n* spear; lance

spieshengel *n* spearfishing
spikkel *n* speck; spot
spiksplinternuut *adj* brand new
spil[1] *n* pivot; axis; spindle
spil[2] *vb* to waste; to spill
spin *vb* to spin; to purr
spinasie *n* spinach
spinnekop *n* spider
spinnerak *n* cobweb
spioen *n* spy; *vb* to spy
spioenasie *n* espionage
spioeneer *vb* to spy; to pry
spiraal *n* spiral
spiritis *n* spiritualist
spiritisme *n* spiritualism
spiritualieë *n* spirit(s); alcohol
spiritualisme *n* spiritualism
spiritus *n* spirit(s); alcohol
spit[1] *n* spadeful; *vb* to dig
spit[2] *n* spit (roasting)
spit[3] *n* lumbago
spitgraaf *n* digging spade
spits *n* point; peak; top; tip; spire; pinnacle; *vb* to point; *adj* pointed; sharp
spitsberaad *n* summit (talks)
spitstyd *n* peak period
spitsuur *n* peak hour; rush hour
spitsverkeer *n* peak traffic
spitsvondig *adj* quick-witted; subtle
spleet *n* split; chink; crevice; fissure
splinter *n* splinter; sliver
splinternuut *adj* brand new
splintervry *adj* shatterproof
split *n* slit; vent
splits *vb* to split; to divide; to splice
splyt *vb* to cleave; to split
spoed *n* speed; haste; *vb* to speed; to hasten
spoedhobbel *n* speed hump
spoedig *adj* speedy; quick; express; *adv* soon; quickly; speedily
spoedwaggel *n* speed wobble
spoedwal *n* speed bump
spoeg (*or* **spuug**) *n* spittle; saliva; *vb* to spit
spoel[1] *n* spool; shuttle
spoel[2] *vb* to rinse; to wash; to flow
spoelbak *n* washtub; cistern
spog *vb* to boast; to show off
spons *n* sponge; *vb* to sponge
sponsrubber *n* foam rubber

spontaan *adj* spontaneous
spook *n* ghost; apparition; phantom; *vb* to haunt; to be very active; to struggle; to fight
spookasem *n* candyfloss
spookhuis *n* haunted house
spookstorie *n* ghost story
spoor[1] *n* track; footprint; trail; scent; rail; railway; *vb* to align (wheels)
spoor[2] *n* spur; *vb* to spur
spoorboek *n* railway timetable
spoorbrug *n* railway bridge
spoorloos *adv* completely
spoorslag *n* incentive; urge
spoorlyn *n* railway line
spoorsnyer *n* tracker
spoorweg *n* railroad; railway
sporadies *adj* sporadic(al)
sport[1] *n* rung; step
sport[2] *n* sport
sportklub *n* sports club
sportmanskap *n* sportsmanship
spot *n* derision; mockery; scorn; *vb* to mock; to deride; to jeer
spotkoop *adj* dirt-cheap
spotlag *n* jeering laugh; mocking smile
spotprent *n* caricature; cartoon
spotprys *n* very low price
spraak *n* speech; language
spraakgebrek *n* speech impediment
spraakgebruik *n* usage, idiom
spraakloos *adj* speechless
spraaksaam *adj* talkative; loquacious; chatty
sprake *n* rumour; talk
sprakeloos *adj* speechless; dumb
spreek *vb* to speak; to talk; to converse
spreekbuis *n* spokesman; spokeswoman; spokesperson
spreekkamer *n* consulting room
spreektaal *n* spoken language
spreektrant *n* manner of speaking
spreekwoord *n* proverb; saying
spreeu *n* starling
sprei[1] *n* quilt; bedspread
sprei[2] *vb* to spread out; to scatter
spreiblad *n* spreadsheet
spreilig *n* floodlight
spreker *n* speaker
spreuk *n* maxim; proverb
spring *n* jump; leap; *vb* to jump; to leap

springbok *n* springbok
springkasteel *n* jumping castle
springlewendig *adj* sprightly
springmat *n* trampoline
springmielies *n* popcorn
springplank *n* springboard
springteuel *n* martingale
springtou *n* skipping rope
sprinkaan *n* grasshopper; locust
sprinkel *vb* to sprinkle
sprinkelbesproeling *n* sprinkler (ir-
    rigation)
sproei *vb* to spray; to water; to irrigate
sproeier *n* sprinkler; jet (water)
sproet *n* freckle
sprokie *n* fairy tale; fairy story
sprong *n* jump; leap; bound; hop
spruit *n* shoot; offshoot; offspring;
    brook; stream
spuit *n* syringe; squirt; *vb* to inject; to
    spout; to spray; to squirt
spuitkan *n* spray can; aerosol can
spuitstof *n* vaccine
spuitverf *n* spray paint
spul *n* affair; case; lot
spulletjie *n* affair; business
spuug *see* **spoeg**
spyker *n* nail; tack
spys(e) *n* food; victuals
spysenier *n* caterer; *vb* to cater
spyskaart *n* menu; bill of fare
spysvertering *n* digestion
spyt *n* regret; sorrow; *vb* to regret; to be
    sorry
staaf[1] (*or* **stawe**) *n* bar; stave; rod; ingot
staaf[2] (*or* **stawe**) *vb* to confirm; to sub-
    stantiate; to prove
staafgoud *n* gold bar; bullion
staak *vb* to cease work; to strike; to dis-
    continue; to stall (car)
staakwag *n* picket
staal *n* steel
staaltjie *n* sample
staan *vb* to stand; to fit; to suit
staande *adj* standing; upright
staander *n* standard
staanspoor *n* start; beginning
staar *vb* to stare; to gaze
staat[1] *n* condition
staat[2] *n* statement; return
staat[3] *n* state

staatkunde *n* politics; statesmanship
staatmaker *n* mainstay; stalwart; reli-
    able person
staatsbegroting *n* budget
staatsaanklaer *n* public prosecutor
staatsamptenaar *n* civil servant
staatsburger *n* citizen
staatsdiens *n* civil service
staatsgreep *n* coup d'état
staatsie *n* pomp; state
staatskoerant *n* government gazette
staatsleer *n* political science
stabiel *adj* solid; stable
stabiliteit *n* stability
stad *n* town; city
stadhuis *n* town hall; city hall; munici-
    pal complex
stadig *adj* slow
stadion *n* stadium
stadium *n* stage; phase
stadsaal *n* town hall; city hall
stadshuis *n* town house
stadsklerk *n* town clerk
stadskouburg *n* civic theatre
stadsraad *n* town council; municipality
stadswapen *n* town coat of arms
staf *n* staff; mace; baton; crozier
staker *n* striker
staking *n* strike; cessation
stal *n* stable; stall; *vb* to stable
stalletjie *n* booth; stand; stall
stam *n* stem; trunk; tribe; clan; *vb* to
    stem from; to descend from
stamboek *n* studbook
stamboom *n* family tree; genealogical
    tree; pedigree
stamel *vb* to stammer; to hesitate
stamgeveg *n* faction fight
stamoorlog *n* tribal war
stamp *n* stamp; knock; bump; *vb* to
    stamp; to pound; to bump; to ram
stamper *n* pestle
stampmotor *n* stock car
stampvol *adj* chock full; packed
stamwoord *n* root word; stem
stand *n* position; standing; rank; stance
standaard *n* standard; norm
standbeeld *n* statue
standerd *n* standard (school class)
standhou *vb* to hold one's own; to
    maintain; to last

standplaas *n* stand; station; post; residence; erf (plot of land)

standpunt *n* point of view; standpoint

standvastig *adj* steadfast; firm; constant

stang *n* bar; bit (bridle)

stank *n* stink; stench; bad smell

stansa *n* stanza

stap *n* step; pace; stride; *vb* to step; to stride; to walk; to hike

stapel *n* pile; heap; stack; *vb* to heap up; to pile; to stack; *adj* staple

stapelgek *adj* raving mad

stapelvoedsel *n* staple food

stapper *n* walker; hike

staptoer *n* hiking trip

stasie *n* station

stasioneer *vb* to station; to place; to locate

staties *adj* static

statig *adj* stately; majestic

statistiek *n* statistics

statuur *n* stature; size; build

statuut *n* statute

steak *n* steak

stede *n* place; **in — van** *prep* instead of

stedelik *adj* municipal; urban

stedeling *n* city dweller; townsman

steeds[1] *adj* urban

steeds[2] *adv* always; constantly

steeg *n* lane; alley

steek *n* prick; stitch; bite; sting; stab; *vb* to sting; to prick; to stab; to jab

steekproef *n* random sample; spot check

steeks *adj* obstinate

steekspel *n* medieval tournament

steel[1] *n* handle; stalk; stem

steel[2] *vb* to steal

steelsgewys *adv* stealthily; furtively

steen *n* brick; stone; bar (soap)

steenagtig *adj* stony; rocky

steengroef *n* quarry

steenhouer *n* stonemason

steenkool *n* coal

steg *vb* to take cuttings

steggie (*or* **stiggie**) *n* slip; cutting

steier[1] *n* scaffold; scaffolding

steier[2] *vb* to stagger; to prance; to rear

steil *adj* steep; precipitous; sheer

steilte *n* gradient; rise; steepness

stel[1] *n* set (tennis); service (dinner); suite (rooms)

stel[2] *vb* to draw up; to fix; to put; to place; to set; to compose

stellasie *n* stand; scaffolding

stellig *adj* definite; firm; certain; sure

stelling *n* doctrine; thesis; theorem

stelsel *n* system

stelselinbreker *n* hacker

stelselmatig *adj* systematical

stelt(e) *n* stilt

steltloper *n* stilt walker

stem *n* voice; vote; *vb* to tune; to vote

stemband *n* vocal chord

stembriefie *n* ballot paper

stembus *n* ballot box

stembuiging *n* intonation; modulation

stemgeregtigde *n* registered voter

stemmer *n* tuner; voter

stemmig *adj* quiet; sedate

stemming *n* election; polling; mood; frame of mind; vein

stemopname *n* voice recording

stemopnemer *n* returning officer; polling officer; scrutineer; flight recorder

stempel *n* stamp; seal; postmark; die; *vb* to stamp; to hallmark

stemreg *n* franchise

stemvurk *n* tuning fork

stenograaf *n* stenographer

stenografie *n* stenography; shorthand

steppe *n* steppe

ster *n* star

stereotipe *n* stereotype

stereofonies *adj* stereophonic

sterf (*or* **sterwe**) *vb* to die; to flatline (heart)

sterfbed *n* deathbed

sterfgeval *n* death; demise

sterfling (*or* **sterweling**) *adj* mortal

sterfte *n* mortality

steriel *adj* sterile; barren

sterilisasie *n* sterilization

steriliseer *vb* to sterilize

sterk *vb* to strengthen; to encourage; *adj* strong; powerful; numerous

sterkte *n* strength; fortress; stronghold; **—!** *interj* good luck!

sterrebeeld *n* constellation

sterrekunde *n* astronomy

sterretjie *n* little star; asterisk

sterrewag *n* observatory
sterrewiggelaar *n* astrologer
sterrewiggelary *n* astrology
stert *n* tail; rear
sterwe *see* **sterf**
sterweling *see* **sterfling**
sterwend *adj* dying
steun[1] *n* support; help; aid; *vb* to support; to aid; to rely on
steun[2] *vb* to groan; to moan
steunpilaar *n* pillar of support
steurnis (*or* **stoornis**) *n* disturbance; nuisance
stewel *n* boot
stewig *adj* firm; strong; solid; thorough
stiebeuel *n* stirrup
stief *prefix* step
stiefbroer *n* stepbrother
stiefmoeder *n* stepmother
stiegriem *n* stirrup leather
stier *n* bull; steer
stig *vb* to found; to establish; to edify
stiggie *see* **steggie**
stigma *n* stigma
stigmatiseer *vb* to stigmatize
stigtelik *adj* edifying
stigting *n* institution; foundation
stik[1] *vb* to choke; to suffocate
stik[2] *vb* to stitch
stiksienig *adj* short-sighted
stikstof *n* nitrogen
stil *vb* to calm; to soothe; to satisfy; *adj* quiet; calm; peaceful
stilbly *vb* to keep quiet
stilet *n* stiletto
stilhou *vb* to come to a stop; to pull up
stilis *n* stylist
stilletjies *adv* quietly; silently; secretly; on the sly
stilmaak *vb* to quiet; to calm; to soothe
stilstaan *vb* to stand still; to stop
stilstand *n* cessation; truce; rest
stilte *n* quiet; silence; calmness
stimuleer *vb* to stimulate
stingel *n* stalk; stem
stink *vb* to stink
stip[1] *n* spot; dot; speck
stip[2] *adj* strict; precise; punctual; exact; *adv* strictly; exactly; precisely
stippel *n* dot; spot; speck

stippellyn *n* dotted line
stiptelik *adv* punctually; promptly
stiptheid *n* preciseness; precision; punctuality
stipuleer *vb* to stipulate
stoei *vb* to romp; to wrestle
stoeier *n* wrestler
stoel *n* chair; seat; stool
stoelgang *n* stool; motion (bowel)
stoep *n* stoep; patio
stoer *adj* sturdy; powerful
stoet[1] *n* procession; retinue; train
stoet[2] *n* stud
stoetery *n* stud farm
stoets *adj* obtuse; blunt
stof[1] *n* stuff; fabric; matter; theme
stof[2] *n* dust; powder
stofbril *n* goggles
stofdoek *n* duster
stoffeer *vb* to furnish; upholster
stoffer *n* duster
stoffering *n* upholstery
stofgoud *n* gold dust
stoflik *adj* material; mortal
stofreën *n* drizzling rain; drizzle; *vb* to drizzle
stofsuier *n* vacuum cleaner
stoïsyns *adj* stoic(al)
stok *n* stick; cane
stokdoof *adj* stone-deaf
stoker *n* stoker; fireman; distiller
stokkie *n* little stick
stokkielekker *n* lollipop
stokkiesdraai *vb* to play truant
stokkiesdraaier *n* truant
stokoud *adj* very old
stokperdjie *n* hobby
stokroos *n* hollyhock
stoksielalleen *adj* all alone
stokstyf *adj* stiff as a poker
stokvis *n* hake
stol *vb* to coagulate; to congeal
stom *adj* dumb; mute; stupid
stommeling *n* fool
stommiteit *n* blunder; stupidity
stomp *n* stump; stub; *adj* blunt; stumpy; dull; dense; obtuse
stompie *n* cigarette end; cigarette stub
stonde[1] *n* time
stonde[2] *n* menstruation
stoof *n* stove; oven

stook *vb* to stoke; to burn; to heat; to distil; to incite

stookketel *n* still

stoom *n* steam; *vb* to steam

stoomboot *n* steamer; steamship

stoomketel *n* boiler

stoommasjien *n* steam engine

stoomskip *n* steamship

stoor *n* storeroom; *vb* to disturb; to trouble; to be in the way of; to interrupt; to store away

stoornis *see* **steurnis**

stoot *n* stab; push; thrust; poke; *vb* to poke; to butt; to push; to hit; to thrust

stootkant *n* false hem

stootskraper *n* bulldozer

stop¹ *vb* to stop; to halt

stop² *vb* to mend; to darn

stophorlosie (*or* **stopoorlosie**) *n* stopwatch

stoppel *n* stubble (field)

stoppelbaard *n* stubble (beard)

stoppelland *n* field of stubble

stoppelrig *adj* stubbly

stopsel *n* tooth filling

stopverf *n* putty

storie *n* story; tale

storm *n* gale; storm; tumult; *vb* to storm; to attack; to rush

stormagtig *adj* stormy; tempestuous

stormram *n* battering ram

stormwind *n* gale; hurricane

stort *vb* to pour; to spill; to take a shower; **trane —** *vb* to shed tears

stortbad *n* shower (bath)

stortbak *n* dumpster

stortreën *n* downpour; heavy shower

stotter *vb* to stutter; to stammer

stout *adj* bold; brave; naughty

stoutmoedig *adj* brave; undaunted

stowe *vb* to stew; to braise; to simmer

stowevleis *n* stew; stewed meat

stowwerig *adj* dusty

straal *n* ray; beam; radius; jet; *vb* to radiate; to beam

straaldraal *n* jet lag

straalvegter *n* jet fighter

straalvliegtuig *n* jet plane

straat *n* street; strait; *vb* to pave

straatboewery *n* hooliganism

straatroof *vb* to mug

straatrower *n* mugger

straattaal *n* street jargon

straatvlinder *n* streetwalker (prostitute)

straatvrou *n* prostitute

straf¹ *n* punishment; penalty; *vb* to punish

straf² *adj* severe; sharp; rigid; stern

strafbaar *adj* punishable

strafbare manslag *n* culpable homicide; manslaughter

straf(fe)loos *adv* with impunity

strafreg *n* criminal law

strafskop *n* penalty kick; free kick

strak *adj* stiff; tight; taut; set; tense

strakkies *adv* presently; just now; by and by

straler *n* jet engine; jetliner; jet plane

stralerjakker *n* jet-setter

stralerkliek *n* jet set

stram *adj* stiff; hard; rigid

strand *n* beach; shore; seaside; *vb* to run ashore; to be stranded

strandjut *n* strandwolf; brown hyena; beachcomber

strandmeer *n* lagoon

strandwag *n* lifeguard

strategie *n* strategy

streef (*or* **strewe**) *vb* to strive; to endeavour

streek *n* district; region; stroke; tract; trick

streekspraak *n* dialect

streel *vb* to caress; to stroke; to flatter

streep *n* stroke; dash; streak; stripe; line

strek *vb* to stretch; to extend; to reach

strekking *n* tendency; tenor; drift

strelend *adj* flattering; pleasant

strem *vb* to obstruct; to hinder; to curdle

streng *adj* strict; severe; stringent

strengheid *n* severity; strictness

strepieskode *n* bar code

stres *n* anxiety; tension; stress

strewe *see* **streef**

strik¹ *n* bow; knot; *vb* to tie; to make a knot

strik² *n* snare; trap

strik³ *adj* strict; precise

strikdas *n* bow tie

strikvraag *n* trick question; puzzling question; poser

string *n* string; skein; trace; strand

stroef *adj* rough; rugged; harsh; gruff

strofe *n* stanza; verse; strophe

strokiesprent *n* comic strip

strokiesverhaal *n* comic strip

stroming *n* stream; current; tendency; drift

strompel *vb* to stumble along

stronk *n* cob (mealie); stalk

stronsium *n* strontium

strooi[1] *n* straw

strooi[2] *vb* to scatter; to distribute

strooibiljet *n* handbill; handout

strooidak *n* thatched roof

strooihoed *n* straw hat

strooijonker *n* best man

strooimeisie *n* bridesmaid; flower girl

strook *n* strip; band; flounce; *vb* to agree

stroom *n* stream; current; *vb* to flow; to stream

stroomaf *adv* downstream

stroomop *adv* upstream

stroop[1] *n* syrup; treacle; molasses

stroop[2] *n* love (tennis)

stroop[3] *vb* to plunder; to pillage; to rustle (cattle)

strooptog *n* raid; invasion

strop *n* strap; halter; rope; strop (razor)

stroper *n* poacher; combine; combine harvester

strot *n* throat

strottehoof *n* larynx

struik *n* shrub; bush

struikel *vb* to stumble; to trip

struikelblok *n* obstacle; stumbling block

struikgewas *n* shrubs; undergrowth

struikrower *n* highwayman

stry *vb* to dispute; to contradict; to quarrel; to argue

stryd *n* fight; struggle; conflict; strife

stry(d)er *n* warrior; fighter

strydig *adj* contrary; inconsistent

strydleuse *n* slogan; motto

strydlustig *adj* quarrelsome; pugnacious

strydvaardig *adj* ready for battle; in fighting trim

stryk[1] *n* stroke; pace; *vb* to walk; stride

stryk[2] *vb* to iron; to smooth; to stroke; **langes —** *vb* to brush

strykorkes *n* string orchestra

strykplank *n* ironing board

strykstok *n* violin bow; fiddlestick

stu *vb* to push; to propel; to stow

studam *n* weir

studeer *vb* to study

studeerkamer *n* study

student *n* student

studenteraad *n* students' council

studie *n* study

studiebeurs *n* bursary; scholarship

stug *adj* stubborn; surly

stuif (*or* **stuiwe**) *vb* to raise dust; to drizzle

stuifmeel *n* pollen

stuifsand *n* drift sand

stuipe *npl* convulsions

stuiptrekking *n* convulsion

stuit *vb* to check; to stop; to annoy

stuitend *adj* offensive; revolting

stuitig *adj* objectionable

stuitjie *n* coccyx

stuiwe *see* **stuif**

stuk *n* piece; fragment; document; play

stukkend *adj* broken; torn

stukrag *n* driving force

stuksgewys *adv* bit by bit; piecemeal

stukwerk *n* piecework

stut *n* support; prop; *vb* to support; to prop

stuur *n* helm; rudder; steering gear; *vb* to steer; to drive; to send; to direct

stuurboord *n, adj* starboard

stuurman *n* chief mate; helmsman; pilot

stuuroutomaat *n* automatic pilot

stuurs *adj* unfriendly; cool; gruff; surly

stuurwiel *n* steering wheel

stuwadoor *n* stevedore; docker

styf (*or* **stywe**) *vb* to starch; to stiffen; to strengthen; *adj* stiff; rigid; tight; tense; formal;

styg *vb* to ascend; to climb; to rise

stygbaan *n* runway

styging *n* rise; increase

styl[1] *n* style; manner

styl[2] *n* doorpost; doorjamb; bedpost

stysel *n* starch

stywe *see* **styf**

subjektief *adj, n* subjective

subjunktief *adj, n* subjunctive

subkomitee *n* subcommittee

subsidie *n* subsidy; grant
subsidieer *vb* to subsidize
subskripsie *n* subscription
substantief *n, adj* substantive
substituut *n* substitute
subtiel *adj* subtle
subtropies *adj* subtropical
suf *vb* to dote; *adj* dull; stupid; dense
sug *n* sigh; desire; *vb* to sigh; to moan
suggereer *vb* to suggest
suggestie *n* suggestion
suid *adj, adv* south
Suid-Afrika *n* South Africa
suide *n* south; the south
suidekant *n* south side
suidelik *adj* southern; southerly
suiderhalfrond *n* southern hemisphere
suidissel (*or* **seidissel**) *n* milk thistle
suidkus *n* south coast
suidoos *adj, adv* south-east
suidoos(te) *n* south-east; the south-east
suidoostewind *n* south-easter; south-east wind
suidwes *adj, adv* south-west
suidwes(te) *n* south-west; the south-west
suidwestelik *adj* south-western; south-westerly
suier *n* sucker; offshoot; piston
suig *vb* to suck; to suckle
suiker *n* sugar; *vb* to sugar; to sweeten
suikerbos *n* protea; sugar bush
suikerriet *n* sugar cane
suikersiekte *n* diabetes
suil *n* column; pillar; obelisk
suinig *adj* economical; thrifty; sparing
suip *vb* to guzzle; to swill; to booze
suiplap *n* drunkard; boozer
suis *vb* to buzz; to rustle; to sigh (wind)
suising *n* buzzing; rustling
suiwel *n* dairy products
suiwer *vb* to purify; to refine; to purge; *adj* pure; clear; clean; true
sukade *n* candied peel
sukkel *vb* to plod on; to progress slowly; to languish
sukkelaar *n* drudge; bungler
sukses *n* success
suksesvol *adj* successful
sulfaat *n* sulphate

sulfer *n* sulphur
sulke *adj, pron* such
sult *n* brawn; pickled meat
sultan *n* sultan
summier *adv* summarily; without formality
superkiem *n* superbug
superlatief *n, adj* superlative
supermark *n* supermarket
supersonies *adj* supersonic
suring *n* sorrel
surplus *n* excess; surplus
surrogaatmoeder *n* surrogate mother
sus *vb* to hush; to soothe; to pacify
sushi *n* sushi
suspisie *n* suspicion; hunch
sussie *n* little sister
suster *n* sister
susterlik *adj* sisterly
susterskind *n* nephew; niece
suur *n* acid; *adj* sour; acid; tart
suurdeeg *n* yeast
suurlemoen *n* lemon
suurlemoensap *n* lemon juice
suurmelk *n* sour milk
suurreën *n* acid rain
suurstof *n* oxygen
suurvy *n* sour fig
suutjies *see* **soetjies**
swaai *n* swing; *vb* to swing; to wave
swaan *n* swan
swaap *n* fool; idiot; clot
swaar *adj* heavy; weighty; difficult
swaard *n* sword
swaardlelie (*or* **swaardblom**) *n* gladiolus
swaarlywig *adj* obese; corpulent
swaarmoedig *adj* depressed; melancholic; gloomy
swaarte *n* weight; heaviness
swaartekrag *n* gravity; gravitation
swaartepunt *n* centre of gravity
swaarweer *n* thunderstorm; storm
swa(w)el[1] *n* brimstone; sulphur
swa(w)el[2] (*or* **swa[w]el[tjie]**) *n* swallow
swa(w)elsuur *n* sulphuric acid
swaer *n* brother-in-law
swak *n* weakness; debility; *adj* weak; feeble; delicate
swakheid *n* weakness; debility
swakkeling *n* weakling

swaksinnig *adj* mentally handicapped
swakte *n* frailty; weakness
swam *n* fungus
swanesang *n* swan song
swanger *adj* pregnant
swangerskap *n* pregnancy
swarigheid *n* obstacle; difficulty
swart *n, adj* black
swartgallig *adj* gloomy; depressed
swartstroop *n* treacle; molasses
sweef (*or* **swewe**) *vb* to hover; to soar; to float; to glide
sweefarties *n* trapeze artist
sweefstok *n* trapeze
sweeftuig *n* glider
sweem *n* semblance; trace
sweep *n* whip
sweer[1] *n* ulcer; sore; abscess; *vb* to fester; to ulcerate
sweer[2] *vb* to swear; to vow; to take an oath
sweet *n* perspiration; *vb* to perspire; to sweat
sweetdruppel *n* drop of perspiration
sweetpak *n* tracksuit
sweis *vb* to weld
swel *vb* to swell; to expand
swem *vb* to swim
swembad *n* swimming bath; swimming pool
swemmer *n* swimmer
swempak *n* swimming costume
swendel *n* fraud; swindling; *vb* to swindle
swendelaar *n* swindler

swendelary *n* spoofing (computing)
swerf (*or* **swerwe**) *vb* to wander; to rove; to roam; to ramble
swerftog *n* odyssey; wanderings; travels
swerm *n* swarm; flock; *vb* to swarm
swernoot *n* rogue; rascal
swerwe *see* **swerf**
swewe *see* **sweef**
swier *n* elegance; gracefulness; swagger; *vb* to loaf; to knock about
swierbol *n* playboy; rake
swig *vb* to yield; to give way
swik *vb* to stumble
swoeg *vb* to toil; to drudge
swoel *adj* sultry; close
swyg *vb* to be silent; to keep quiet
swyn *n* swine; pig; hog
swynehok *n* pigsty
sy[1] *n* side
sy[2] *n* silk
sy[3] *pers pron* she
sy[4] *poss pron* his
sybok *n* angora goat
sydelings *adj* sidelong; — **kyk** *vb* to glance
sydeur *n* side door; side entrance
syfer[1] *n* figure; number; bogey (golf); par (golf)
syfer[2] *vb* to ooze
syg *vb* to strain; to filter
syne *poss pron* his
sypaadjie *n* pavement
sypel *vb* to seep; to drain
sysie *n* seedeater; siskin
sywurm *n* silkworm

T

T-aansluiting *n* T-junction
taai *adj* tough; wiry; sticky; tenacious
taaipitperske *n* clingstone peach
taak *n* task; work; duty
taal *n* language; speech
taalkunde *n* grammar; linguistics
taalkundig *adj* grammatical; linguistic
taalkundige *n* linguist
taalskat *n* vocabulary
taamlik *adj* fair; tolerable; *adv* rather; fairly; tolerably
tabak *n* tobacco
tabaksak *n* tobacco pouch
tabberd *n* dress
tabel *n* table; index
tablet[1] *n* tablet; lozenge
tablet[2] *n* tablet (computing)
tabletrekenaar *n* tablet (computing)
taboe *n* taboo
tafsy *n* taffeta
tafel *n* table
tafelgeld *n* service charge
tafelheer *n* master of ceremonies
tafellaken *n* tablecloth
tafeltennis *n* table tennis
tafereel *n* picture; scene
tagtig *n, determiner* eighty
tagtigste *n, adj* eightieth
tak *n* branch; bough
tak(t) *n* tact
takel *n* tackle
takkantoor *n* branch office
tak(t)loos *adj* tactless
tak(t)vol *adj* tactful
taks *vb* to estimate; to rate; to share
taksasie *n* valuation; appraisal
taksateur *n* valuator; appraiser
takseer *vb* to appraise; to value; to tax
takt *n* tact
taktiek *n* tactic
tal *n* number
talent *n* talent; ability; gift
talentvol *adj* talented; gifted
talisman *n* talisman
talk *n* talc
talkpoeier *n* talcum powder
talm *vb* to dawdle; to linger

talryk *adj* numerous
tam *adj* tired; exhausted
tamaai *adj* huge; giant
tamaryn *n* tamarind
tamatie *n* tomato
tamboer *n* drummer; drum
tameletjie *n* toffee
tand *n* tooth; cog; prong
tandarts *n* dentist
tandeborsel *n* toothbrush
tandepasta *n* toothpaste
tandevlos *n* dental floss
tandpyn *n* toothache
tandrat *n* cogwheel; gearwheel
tandvleis *n* gum
tandvulling *n* filling (tooth)
tang *n* (pair of) tongs; forceps; pliers
tangens *n* tangent
tango *n* tango
tannie *n* auntie
tans *adv* at present; now; presently
tante *n* aunt
tap *n* tap (barrel); spigot; bung; *vb* to draw; to tap
tapisserie *n* tapestry
tapper *n* barman
tappery *n* canteen; beer hall; pub
taptoe *n* military tattoo; last post
tapyt *n* carpet
tarentaal *n* guinea fowl
tarief *n* tariff; rate; scale
tarra *n* tare
tart *vb* to taunt; to defy; to challenge
tarting *n* provocation
tas[1] *n* bag; pouch; wallet
tas[2] *vb* to feel; to grope
tasbaar *adj* tangible; palpable
taster *n* scanner
tatoeëer *vb* to tattoo
tatta *n* goodbye
tattatjek *n* golden handshake
taxi *n* taxi
taxistaanplek *n* taxi stand
te *adv* too; *prep* at; to; on
teater *n* theatre
tee *n* tea
teë *adv* against

teëgif *see* teengif
teëhanger *n* counterpart; contrast; opposite number
teëhou *see* teenhou
teëkanting *see* teenkanting
teëkom *see* teenkom
teekoppie *n* teacup
teël *n* tile; *vb* to tile
teel *vb* to breed; to rear; to raise; to cultivate
teelepel *n* teaspoon
teëloop *see* teenloop
teelt *n* cultivation; culture; breeding
teem *vb* to whine; to drawl
teëmiddel *see* teenmiddel
teemus *n* tea cosy
teen *prep* against; versus; to; towards; for
teenaanvaal *n* counterattack
teenbevel *n* counterorder
teendeel *adj* contrary; opposite
teengif (*or* teëgif) *n* antidote
teenhou (*or* teëhou) *vb* to check; to prevent; to impede
teenkanting (*or* teëkanting) *n* opposition
teenkom (*or* teëkom) *vb* to meet
teenhanger (*or* teëhanger) *n* counterpart; contrast
teeninsurgensie *n* counterinsurgence
teenkanting (*or* teëkanting) *n* opposition
teenkom (*or* teëkom) *vb* to meet
teenloop (*or* teëloop) *vb* to fail; to be unsuccessful; to go wrong
teenmiddel (*or* teëmiddel) *n* antidote; remedy
teennatuurlik *adj* unnatural
teenoffensief (*or* teë-offensief) *n* counteroffensive
teenoor *prep* opposite; compared with
teenoorgestel *adj* contrary; opposite
teenparty (*or* teëparty) *n* opponent; adversary
teenpraat (*or* teëpraat) *vb* to contradict; to gainsay
teenproduktief (*or* teëproduktief) *adj* counterproductive
teenreaksie (*or* teëreaksie) *n* backlash
teensin (*or* teësin) *n* aversion

teenslag (*or* teëslag) *n* reverse
teenspoed (*or* teëspoed) *n* ill-luck; adversity; breakdown
teenspoedwa (*or* teëspoedwa) *n* breakdown van
teenspraak (*or* teëspraak) *n* contradiction
teenspreek (*or* teëspreek) *vb* to contradict; to gainsay
teenstaan (*or* teëstaan) *vb* to resist; to withstand
teenstand (*or* teëstand) *n* opposition; resistance
teenstander (*or* teëstander) *n* adversary; opponent
teenstelling (*or* teëstelling) *n* contrast; antithesis
teenstem (*or* teëstem) *vb* to vote against
teenstrydig *adj* contradictory; conflicting
teenvirusprogram *n* antivirus software
teenvoorstel (*or* teëvoorstel) *n* counterproposal
teenwerk (*or* teëwerk) *vb* to oppose; to thwart
teenwerp (*or* teëwerp) *vb* to object; to refute
teenwerping (*or* teëwerping) *n* objection
teenwind (*or* teëwind) *n* headwind
teenwoordig *adv* at present; nowadays
teenwoordigheid *n* presence
teë-offensief *see* teenoffensief
teëparty *see* teenparty
teëpraat *see* teenpraat
teëproduktief *see* teenproduktief
teer[1] *n* tar; grease; *vb* to tar; to grease
teer[2] *vb* to consume; to live on; to sponge off
teer[3] *adj* tender; delicate; slender
teëreaksie *see* teenreaksie
teerhartig *adj* tender-hearted
teerpad *n* tarred road
teeservies *n* tea service
teesiffie *n* tea strainer
teësin *see* teensin
teëslag *see* teenslag
teëspoed *see* teenspoed
teëspoedwa *see* teenspoedwa

teëspraak *see* **teenspraak**

teëspreek *see* **teenspreek**

teëstaan *see* **teenstaan**

teëstand *see* **teenstand**

teëstander *see* **teenstander**

teëstelling *see* **teenstelling**

teëstem *see* **teenstem**

teëvoorstel *see* **teenvoorstel**

teëwerk *see* **teenwerk**

teëwerp *see* **teenwerp**

teëwerping *see* **teenwerping**

teëwind *see* **teenwind**

tegelyk *adv* at the same time

tegemoetkom *vb* to meet halfway; to compensate

tegniek *n* technical skill; technique

tegnies *adj* technical

tegnikus *n* technician

tegno *prefix* techno; relating to technology

tegnologie *n* technology

tegnomusiek *n* techno (music)

tehuis *n* hostel; home

teiken *n* target

teikenskiet *n* target shooting

teister *vb* to harm; to devastate

teken *n* sign; mark; symptom; token; evidence; *vb* to mark; to sign; to draw; to sketch; to subscribe

tekenaar *n* draughtsman

tekening *n* drawing; plan

tekkie[1] *n* (*informal*) techie

tekkie[2] *n* (pair of) tackies; trainers

tekort *n* deficit; shortage

tekortkoming *n* shortcoming; fault

teks *n* text; context; *vb* to text (SMS)

tekstiel *n* textile

tekstielgoedere *n* soft goods

tekstielnywerheid *n* textile industry

teksverwerker *n* word processor

tel *n* count; *vb* to count; to number

telbord *n* scoreboard

telebemarking *n* telemarketing

telefoneer *vb* to telephone

telefonis *n* telephone operator

telefoon *n* telephone

telefoongids *n* telephone directory

telefoonnommer *n* telephone number

telefoonoproep *n* telephone call

telegraaf *n* telegraph

telegrafeer *vb* to wire; to telegraph

telegram *n* telegram; wire

telekommunikasie *n* telecommunication

telekonferensie *n* share call; conference call

teleks *n* telex; *vb* to telex

teleskoop *n* telescope

teleurgestel *adj* disappointed

teleurstel *vb* to disappoint; to baffle

televisie *n* television

telkens *adv* often; repeatedly; every time

teller *n* bank teller; counter; scorer

telling *n* counting; census; score

telraam *n* abacus

telwoord *n* numeral

tem *vb* to tame; to break in (horse)

tema *n* theme; subject

tembaar *adj* tam(e)able

tempel *n* temple

temper *vb* to restrain; to modify; to soften

temperament *n* temperament; temper

temperamenteel *adj* temperamental

temperatuur *n* temperature

templaat *n* template

tempo *n* tempo; pace

temptasie *n* temptation

ten *prep* at; per; in

tendens *n* tendency

tender *n* tender; offer; *vb* to tender

tenk *n* tank

tennis *n* tennis

tennisbaan *n* tennis court

tennisbal *n* tennis ball

tennisspeler *n* tennis player

tenoor *n* tenor (voice)

tensy *conj* unless

tent *n* tent; hood

tentoonstel *vb* to show; to exhibit

tentoonstelling *n* show; exhibition

teologie *n* theology

teoloog *n* theologian

teoreties *adj* theoretical

teorie *n* theory

tepel *n* nipple; teat

ter *prep* to; to the; at; — **wille van** for the sake of

terapie *n* therapy

terapeut *n* therapist

terdeë *adv* well; thoroughly

tereg *adv* rightly; justly

tereghelp *vb* to set right; to help out of a difficulty

teregstel *vb* to execute

teregstelling *n* execution

teregwys *vb* to admonish; to reprove; to reprimand

teregwysing *n* reproof; admonition

terg *vb* to tease; to annoy; to torment

terggees *n* tease; tormentor

tering *n* consumption; tuberculosis

terloops *adj* casual; incidental; *adv* incidentally; by the way

term *n* term; phrase

termiet *n* termite

terminaal *adj* terminal

terminologie *n* terminology

terminus *n* terminus; terminal

termometer *n* thermometer

termyn *n* term; period; time

terpentyn *n* turpentine

terras *n* terrace

terrein *n* ground; building site; area

terriër *n* terrier

terreur *n* terrorism

terroris *n* terrorist

terrorisme *n* terrorism

tersiêr *adj* tertiary

tersiêre onderwys *n* tertiary education

tert *n* tart; cake

terug *adv* back; backwards

terugblik *n* retrospect; retrospection; *vb* to look back on

terugbring *vb* to return; to bring back

terugdeins *vb* to shrink back from

terugdryf (*or* **terugdrywe**) *vb* to drive back; to repel

terugeis *vb* to reclaim; to demand back

terugflits *n* flashback

teruggaan *vb* to go back; to retrace

teruggawe *n* restitution; giving back

teruggee *vb* to return; to give back

terughoudend *adj* reserved; close

terugkaats *vb* to reflect; to rebound; to echo

terugkeer *n* return; *vb* to return

terugkom *vb* to return; to come back

terugkoms *n* return

terugplof *vb* to backfire

terugreis *n* return journey

terugskiet *vb* to shoot back; to return fire

terugskrik *vb* to shrink from; to recoil

terugslag *n* recoil; setback; reverse

terugtog *n* retreat

terugtrek *vb* to retreat; to withdraw; to retract

terugvoer(ing) *n* feedback

terwyl *conj* while; whereas

tesis *n* thesis; doctorate

tesourie *n* treasury

tesourier *n* treasurer

testament *n* will; testament

testateur *n* testator

teuel *n* bridle; rein

teuelloos *adj* unbridled

teuelriem *n* rein

tevergeefs *adj* futile; useless

tevore *adv* before; previously

tevrede *adj* satisfied; content; pleased

tevredenheid *n* contentment; satisfaction

teweegbring *vb* to bring about; to cause

tewens *adv* besides; too; at the same time

tiemie *n* thyme

tien *n, determiner* ten

tiende *n, adj* tenth

tiendelig *adj* decimal

tiener *n* teenager

tienderjarige *n* teenager

tienkamp *n* decathlon

tienkegelbaan *n* tenpin bowling alley

tiental *n* decade

tienuur *n, adj* ten o'clock

tienvoud *adj, adv* tenfold

tier[1] *n* tiger

tier[2] *vb* to thrive; to flourish; to rage

tierboskat *n* serval

tierlantyntjie *n* scroll; flourish; trifle; (k)nick-(k)nack

tiermelk *n* strong drink

tierwyfie *n* tigress

tiet *n* teat; nipple

tifoon *n* typhoon

tifus *n* typhus; typhoid fever

tik *n* touch; pat; tap; *vb* to touch; to tap; to rap; to type

tikmasjien *n* typewriter

tikskrif *n* typing; typewriting

timmer *vb* to construct; to build

timmerhout *n* timber

timmerman *n* carpenter

tin *n* tin; pewter
tingerig *adj* delicate; slender; fragile
tinktinkie *n* Cape wren
tinktuur *n* tincture
tintel *vb* to sparkle; to twinkle
tinteling *n* twinkling; sparkling
tip *n* tip; point
tipe *n* type; character; specimen
tipies *adj* typical
tipograaf *n* typographer
tipografie *n* typography
tipografiese *adj* typographical
tiramisu *n* tiramisu
tiran *n* tyrant
titel *n* title
titelblad *n* title page
titelrol *n* title role
tittel *n* dot; speck
tjaila *vb* to knock off (work)
tjalie *n* shawl
tjank *vb* to yelp; to howl; to whine
tjankbalie *n* crybaby
tjap *n* stamp; postmark; *vb* to stamp; to mark
tjek *n* cheque
tjekboek *n* cheque book
tjellis *n* cellist
tjello *n* cello
tjiekorie *n* chicory
tjilp *vb* to chirp; to twitter
tjoepstil *adj* very quiet; absolutely still
tjokvol *adj* brimful; chockfull
tjom *n* chum
tjop-tjop *adv* in no time; in a jiffy
toe[1] *adj* shut; closed; dumb; stupid
toe[2] *prep* to; towards
toe[3] *conj* when; as; while
toe[4] *adv* then; in those days; at that time
toe![5] *interj* do!; please!
toebehore *n* accessories; belongings; fittings
toebind *vb* to tie up; to fasten
toebring *vb* to give; to inflict
toebroodjie *n* sandwich
toedraai *vb* to wrap up
toedraaipapier *n* wrapping paper
toegaan *vb* to close; to shut
toegang *n* admission; access; entrance
toegangsbewys *n* admission ticket
toegangsprys *n* entrance fee
toeganklik *adj* accessible

toegee *vb* to yield; to admit
toegeeteken *n* yield sign
toegeeflik *adj* indulgent; lenient
toegeneë *adj* affectionate
toegepas *adj* applied
toegepaste wiskunde *n* applied mathematics
toegespe *vb* to buckle
toegewend *adj* lenient; indulgent
toegewese buslaan *n* dedicated bus lane
toegewing *n* concession
toegif *n* addition; extra; bonus
toejuig *vb* to cheer; to applaud; to approve
toejuiging *n* applause; cheering
toeka *adj* very remote; **van — se dae af** *adv* from time immemorial
toekamotor *n* vintage car
toeken *vb* to grant; to award
toekenning *n* award; prize; grant
toekomend *adj* future; next
toekoms *n* future; **in die —** *adv* in future
toekomstig *adj* future
toekring-TV *n* closed-circuit television; CCTV
toelaag *n* gratification; subsidy; bonus; allowance; grant
toelaat *vb* to permit; to admit; to allow
toelating *n* admission; admittance; permission
toelig *vb* to explain; to explain; to elucidate
toeligting *n* explanation; illustration
toeloop *n* crowd; throng
toeluister *vb* to listen
toemaak *vb* to shut; to close
toenader *vb* to approach; to try to reconcile
toenadering *n* reconciliation; rapprochement
toeneem *vb* to increase; to progress
toenmalig *adj* then; contemporary
toentertyd *adv* then; at the time
toepas *vb* to apply to; to put into practice
toepaslik *adj* appropriate; suitable
toepassing *n* application
toer *n* tour; walk; excursion; trick; *vb* to travel; to tour
toereikend *adj* sufficient; adequate

toerekenbaar *adj* responsible; accountable

toeris *n* tourist

toerisme *n* tourism

toerismebedryf *n* tourist industry; tourism

toeristebedryf *n* tourist industry; tourism

toernooi *n* tournament

toerus *vb* to fit out; to equip

toerusting *n* outfit; equipment

toesig *n* supervision; care; — **hou** *vb* to supervise

toesighouer *n* invigilator; supervisor

toeskouer *n* spectator; onlooker

toeskryf (*or* **toeskrywe**) *vb* to attribute; to ascribe

toesluit *vb* to lock up

toespeling *n* allusion; insinuation

toespraak *n* speech; address

toespreek *vb* to address; to accost

toestaan *vb* to permit; to allow

toestand *n* state; condition; circumstance(s)

toestel *n* apparatus; appliance; device

toestem *vb* to consent; to approve; to grant

toestemmend *adj* affirmative

toestemming *n* consent; permission

toet *vb* to toot; to blow

toeter *n* horn; hooter; *vb* to hoot

toetrek *vb* to close; to cover; to cheat; to become overcast

toets *n* test; trial; key (music); *vb* to test; to sound

toetsrit *n* trial run

toetssaak *n* test case

toetssteen *n* touchstone

toetsvlug *n* test flight

toetswedstryd *n* test match

toeval[1] *n* accident; chance; coincidence

toeval[2] *n* fainting fit; seizure; epileptic fit

toeval[3] *vb* to befall; to happen; to cave in

toeval[4] *vb* to accrue; to come into the possession of

toevallig *adj* accidental; casual; random *adv* accidentally; by chance

toevertrou *vb* to entrust; to confide

toevloed *n* crowd; throng; influx

toevlug *n* refuge; help

toevlug(soord) *n* asylum; refuge; sanctuary

toevoegsel *n* appendix; supplement

toevoer *n* supply; *vb* to supply

toewens *vb* to wish

toewy *vb* to dedicate; to consecrate

toewys *vb* to assign; to allocate; to award

toffie *n* toffee

toffie-appel *n* toffee apple

tog[1] *n* expedition; journey; march; draught; current of air

tog[2] *adv* yet; nevertheless; still

toga *n* gown; robe; toga

togsnelheid *n* cruising speed

toiings *n* tatters; rags

toilet *n* toilet

tokkel *vb* to strum

tol[1] *n* top; *vb* to spin; to turn

tol[2] *n* toll; turnpike; customs duty (import, etc.)

toldans *n* breakdancing

toldeurgang *n* toll pass

toldroër *n* spin-dryer

toleransie *n* toleration

tolereer *vb* to tolerate

tolhek *n* tollgate

tolk *n* interpreter; *vb* to interpret

tolking *n* interpreting

tollenaar *n* publican

tolletjie *n* bobbin; reel

tolvry *adj* duty free; toll free

ton *n* cask; tub; ton

toneel *n* stage; theatre; scene

toneelgeselskap *n* theatrical company

toneelinkleding *n* decor

toneelskrywer *n* dramatist; playwright

toneelspeelster *n* actress

toneelspel *n* acting

toneelspeler *n* actor

toneelstuk *n* play

tong *n* tongue

tongknoper *n* tongue twister

tongval *n* dialect; accent

tongvis *n* sole (fish)

tonnel *n* tunnel; *vb* to tunnel

tonnemaat *n* tonnage

tonsilektomie *n* tonsillectomy

tonsilitis *n* tonsillitis

tonsuur *n* tonsure

tooi *n* ornament; finery; *vb* to decorate; to adorn

tooisel *n* ornament; trimming

toom *n* bridle; rein

toomloos *adj* unbridled; unrestrained
toon[1] *n* toe
toon[2] *n* tone; sound
toon[3] *vb* to show; to indicate; to demonstrate
toonbaar *adj* presentable
toonbank *n* counter
toonbeeld *n* model; example
toonder *n* bearer; holder
toonkas *n* display case; display cabinet
toonkuns *n* music
toonladder *n* scale; gamut; entire range
toonloos *adj* unaccented; toneless
toonset *vb* to put to music; to compose
toor *vb* to conjure; to practise witchcraft
toordokter *n* witch doctor
toorgoed *n* charm; talisman
toorkuns *n* magic; sorcery; witchcraft
toorkunstenaar *n* magician
toorlantern *n* magic lantern
toorn *n* anger; wrath; passion
toornaar *see* **towenaar**
toornig *n* angry; wrathful
toorts *n* torch
toorwoord (*or* **towerwoord**) *n* magic word; spell
top[1] *n* top; peak; point; summit; fingertip
top[2] *vb* to top; to lop; to trim
topaas *n* topaz
toppunt *n* summit; peak; climax; zenith
topswaar *adj* top-heavy
tor *n* beetle
toring *n* tower; steeple; spire
torinkie *n* turret
tornado *n* tornado; whirlwind
torpedo *n* torpedo
torpedeer *vb* to torpedo
torring *vb* to tear; to rip up; to unpick (stitch)
tortelduif *n* turtle dove
tot *conj; prep* to; till; until; as far as
totaal *n* total; whole sum; *adv* altogether; totally
totdat *conj* until; till
totsiens *sentence substitution* goodbye;
totstandbrenging *n* accomplishment; achievement
tou[1] *n* rope; string; cord
tou[2] *n* queue; *vb* to queue up; to straggle
touspring *vb* to skip
toustaan *vb* to form a queue

toutrek *n* tug-of-war
towenaar (*or* **toornaar**) *n* sorcerer; magician; wizard
tower *vb* to enchant; to charm
towerheks *n* witch
towerwoord *see* **toorwoord**
traag *adj* slow; lazy; dull
traak *n* concern; **dit — my nie** I do not care
traan[1] *n* tear
traan[2] *n* blubber; fish oil
tradisie *n* tradition
tradisioneel *adj* traditional
trag *vb* to try; to attempt; to strive; to endeavour
tragedie *n* tragedy
tragies *adj* tragic
trajek *n* trajectory; stretch
traksie *n* traction
traktaat *n* treaty
traktaatjie *n* tract
trakteer *vb* to treat; to entertain
tralie *n* bar; lattice; trellis
trampolien *n* trampoline
trane *npl* tears
transaksie *n* transaction; deal
transie (*or* **trassie**) *n* hermaphrodite
transitief *adj* transitive
transport *n* transport; traffic; transfer
transportakto *n* title deed; deed of transfer
transportpad *n* main road
trant *n* style; manner; taste
trap[1] *n* stair; staircase; step; degree; pedal
trap[2] *vb* to trample; to kick; to go away; to clear off; to press (grapes)
trapesium *n* trapezium
trapleer *n* stepladder
trapmeul *n* treadmill
trapsoetjies (*or* **trapsuutjies**) *n* chameleon
trassie *see* **transie**
trauma (*or* **trouma**) *n* trauma
tred *n* pace; tread
tree *n* step; stride; pace; *vb* to go; to step; to stride; to tread
tref *vb* to hit; to strike; to come across; to meet
trefbal *n* dodgeball
treffend *adj* touching; striking
trefferboek *n* bestseller (book, CD, etc.)

tregter *n* funnel
treil *vb* to tow
treiler *n* trawler; trailer
trein *n* train; retinue; following
treindrywer *n* train driver
treinspoor *n* railway line; railway track
treiter *vb* to tease; to vex
trek *n* pull; draught; desire; liking; appetite; trait; expression; *vb* to draw; to pull; to drag; to drift; to journey; to remove; to emigrate; to travel; to swipe (card)
trekarbeid *n* migrant labour
trekker *n* puller; corkscrew; forceps; tractor
trekklavier *n* accordion
treksluiter *n* zip fastener
trekstang *n* towbar
trekvoël *n* bird of passage
trem *n* tram; tramcar
trembus *n* trolleybus
treur *vb* to mourn; to grieve for
treurig *adj* sad; mournful; gloomy; tearful
treurspel *n* tragedy
treurwilg (*or* **treurwilgerboom**) *n* weeping willow
triangel *n* triangle (music)
triestig *adj* dreary; gloomy
trigonometrie *n* trigonometry
tril *vb* to quaver; to vibrate; to tremble
trilling *n* vibration; tremor
trio *n* trio
triomf *n* triumph; victory
triomfeer *vb* to triumph over
trippel *vb* to trip along
troebel *adj* muddy
troef *n* trump (playing cards)
troef *vb* to play trump; to trump
troep *n* troop; group; band; gang; party
troepe *n* troops; forces
troepdraer *n* troop carrier
troepmag *n* military force
troetel *vb* to caress; to pet; to pamper
troeteldier *n* pet; pet animal
troeteldieretuin *n* petting zoo
troeteldierwinkel *n* pet shop
trofee *n* trophy
troffel *n* trowel
trog *n* trough; manger
Trojaanse perd *n* Trojan horse (computer virus)
trok *n* truck

trollie *n* trolley
trommel *n* drum; trunk; canister; eardrum; *vb* to drum; to beat the drum
trommeldik *adj* satiated; full up
tromp *n* barrel (gun); trunk (elephant); trumpet
trompet *n* trumpet
trompetblaser *n* trumpeter
trompop *adj* point-blank; sudden; close
trompoppie *n* drum majorette
tronk *n* prison; jail; gaol
tronkbewaarder *n* prison warder
tronkstraf *n* imprisonment
tronkvoël *n* gaolbird; prisoner
troon *n* throne; *vb* to reign
troonopvolger *n* heir to the throne
troos *n* consolation; comfort; *vb* to comfort; to console
troos-oom *n* agony uncle
troosprys *n* consolation prize; booby prize
troosrubrriek *n* agony column
troostante *n* agony aunt
trop *n* troop (monkeys); flock (sheep, birds); drove (livestock); pride (lions)
trope *n* tropics
tropies *adj* tropical
tros *n* bunch; cluster; *vb* to cluster
trots[1] *n* pride; haughtiness; *adj* proud; haughty
trots[2] *prep* in spite of
trotseer *vb* to defy; to dare; to face
trou[1] *n* fidelity; loyalty; *adj* faithful; loyal; true
trou[2] *n* marriage; *vb* to marry; to wed
troudag *n* wedding day
troue *n* wedding
troueloos *adj* false; perfidious
trouens *conj* besides; however
troudag *n* wedding day
trouma *see* **trauma**
trouring *n* wedding ring
trubeeld *n* replay (TV)
trui *n* sweater; jersey
trukaatser *n* reflector
truprojektor *n* overhead projector
trurat *n* reverse gear
truspieël *n* rearview mirror
trust *n* trust
trustee *n* trustee
truuk *n* trick; gimmick

tsaar *n* tsar; czar
tuberkulose *n* tuberculosis
tug *n* discipline
tugtig *vb* to chastise; to punish
tuig *n* harness; tack; rigging; tackle
tuimel *vb* to tumble
tuimeldroër *n* tumble drier
tuin *n* garden
tuinbeplanner *n* landscape gardener
tuinbou *n* horticulture
tuinier *n* gardener
tuinslang *n* garden hose; hosepipe
tuis *adv* home; at home
tuisblad *n* home page (computing)
tuisinkope *n* home shopping
tuisplek *n* home; accommodation
tuiswerk *n* homework
tuiste *n* home
tuit[1] *n* spout;nozzle
tuit[2] *vb* to tingle
tulband *n* turban
tulle *n* tulle
tulp *n* tulip
tumor *n* tumour
turf *n* turf; peat
turkoois *adj, n* turquoise
turksvy *n* prickly pear
tussen *prep* between; among
tussenbei kom *vb* to mediate
tussendeks *n* steerage; between decks
tussendeur *adv* in between
tussenganger *n* go-between; mediator
tussenkoms *n* intervention; mediation
tussenmuur *n* partition; dividing wall
tussenpersoon *n* middleman; intermediary; mediator
tussenpoos *n* interval; pause
tussenruimte *n* interstice; space
tussenstedelike bus *n* intercity bus
tussentyd *n* interim; interval
tussenverkiesing *n* by-election
tussenwerpsel *n* interjection
tuur *vb* to stare; to peer at; to pore over
TV-slaaf *n* couch potato
twaalf *n, determiner* twelve
twaalfde *n, adj* twelfth
twaalfuur *n, adj* midday; noon; twelve
   o'clock
twee *n, determiner* two
tweede *n, adj* second

tweedehands *adj* second-hand
tweedens *adv* secondly; in the second
   place
tweederangs *adj* second-rate
tweedrag *n* discord
tweegeveg *n* duel
tweeklank *n* diphthong
tweeledig *adj* binary; ambiguous
tweeling *n* twin
tweeloop *adj* double-barrelled
tweemaal *adv* twice
tweeromper *n* catamaran
tweeslagtig *adj* bisexual; amphibious
tweespalk (*or* **tweespalt**) *n* discord
tweesprong *n* fork; crossroad
tweestryd *n* indecision
tweetalig *adj* bilingual
twee-uur *n, adj* two o'clock
twintig *n, adj* twenty
twintigste *n, adj* twentieth
twis *n* quarrel; strife; row; brawl; *vb* to
   quarrel; to dispute; to brawl
twisappel *n* apple of discord; bone of
   contention
twisgierig *adj* quarrelsome
twissiek *adj* contentious
twyfel *n* doubt
twyfelaar *n* sceptic; doubter
twyfelagtig *adj* doubtful; dubious
twyfelmoedig *adj* undecided; wavering
tyd *n* time; period; season; tense; **op —**
   adv on schedule
tydbom *n* time bomb
tydelik *adj* temporary
tydens *prep* during
tydgenoot *adj* contemporary
tydig *adj* timely; seasonable
tyding *n* tidings; news; intelligence
tydlank *adv* for a time
tydperk *n* time; period
tydrekening *n* chronology; era
tydren *n* rally
tydrowend *adj* time-consuming
tydsaam *adv* slow; leisurely
tydskrif *n* periodical
tydsorde *n* chronological order
tydtafel *n* timetable
tydvak *n* period
tydverdryf *n* hobby

U

u *pers pron* you; *poss pron* your
ui *n* onion
uier *n* udder
uil *n* owl
uilagtig *n* stupid
uit *prep* from; out; of; among; by; on; in; *adv* off; out; over; up
uit(er) *vb* to utter; to express
uitasem *adj, adv* out of breath
uitbagger *vb* to dredge
uitbak *vb* to bake; to unmask; to expose; to discredit
uitbars *vb* to burst out; to explode; to erupt
uitbarsting *n* explosion; eruption
uitbeeld *vb* to draw; to delineate; to sketch
uitbetaal *vb* to pay out
uitblaas *vb* to extinguish; to blow out
uitbleik *vb* to bleach; to fade
uitblink *vb* to excel; to surpass
uitbly *vb* to stay away
uitbreek *vb* to break out; to erupt; to burst out
uitbrei *vb* to spread; to extend; to enlarge
uitbreiding *n* extension; spread
uitbring *vb* to reveal; to bring out; to disclose
uitbroei *vb* to hatch
uitbuit *vb* to exploit; to take advantage of
uitbundig *adj* excessive; exceeding
uitdaag *vb* to challenge; to defy
uitdeel *vb* to distribute; to hand out
uitdelg *vb* to blot out; to exterminate
uitdeling *n* distribution
uitdiep *vb* to deepen; to excavate
uitdink *vb* to devise; to invent
uitdop *vb* to shell (peas)
uitdos *vb* to dress up; to deck out
uitdraai *vb* to turn aside; to evade
uitdrink *vb* to empty; to drain
uitdroog *vb* to dry up; to desiccate
uitdruk *vb* to express; to squeeze out
uitdrukking *n* expression
uitdruklik *adj* emphatic; explicit; express; expressive; *adv* emphatically; explicitly
uitdun *vb* to thin out; to cull
uitdy *vb* to expand; to swell
uiteen *adv* apart; asunder
uiteengaan *vb* to break up; to separate; to disperse
uiteenloop *vb* to diverge; to differ
uiteenlopend *adj* divergent; different
uiteensetting *n* explanation
uiteensit *vb* to explain
uiteinde *n* end; extremity; death
uiteindelik *vb* finally; at last
uiter *see* uit
uiteraard *adv* naturally
uiterlik *n* exterior; outward appearance; *adj* outward; external; *adv* outwardly; externally
uitermate *adv* excessively; exceedingly
uiters *adv* very; exceedingly; utterly
uiterste *n* death; extremity; *adj* extreme; last; utmost
uitfaseer *vb* to phase out
uitflap *vb* to blurt out
uitgaan *vb* to go out; to end in
uitgang *n* outlet; exit; ending
uitgangreisgeld *n* exit fare
uitgawe *n* expenditure; expense; cost; issue; edition
uitgeblus *adj* extinct
uitgebrei *adj* extensive; vast
uitgee *vb* to spend; to distribute; to issue; to publish
uitgehonger *adj* famished; starving
uitgelate *adj* exuberant; boisterous
uitgelese *adj* select; choice; picked
uitgemaak *adj* settled; established
uitgeslape *adj* cunning; knowing
uitgesonder *prep* save for; except; excluding
uitgesterf *adj* extinct
uitgestrek *adj* extensive; vast
uitgeweke *adj* expatriate
uitgewekene *n* expatriate; refugee; (*informal*) expat
uitgewer *n* publisher
uitgewerk *adj* elaborate; extinct
uitgly *vb* to slip; to skid

uitgrawing *n* excavation; exhumation; cutting; dugout
uithaal *vb* to pull out; to take out; to draw out; to root out
uithaler *adj* smart; showy; first-rate
uithangbord *n* sign; signboard
uitheems *adj* foreign; exotic
uithoek *n* out-of-the-way place; outlying district
uithol *vb* to hollow out; to excavate
uithonger *vb* to starve; to be famished
uithou *vb* to endure; to bear; to stand
uithouvermoë *n* endurance
uiting *n* saying; expression; utterance
uitjou *vb* to hiss at; to boo; to hoot
uitkalf (*or* **uitkalwe**) *vb* to hollow out; to wash out; to erode
uitkamp *vb* to camp out
uitkeer *vb* to pay out; to pay back
uitken *vb* to recognize; to identify
uitkies *vb* to select; to choose; to pick out
uitklaar *vb* to clear up; to clarify
uitklee *vb* to strip; to undress
uitklop *vb* to beat out; to dust; to beat; to defeat
uitknip *vb* to cut out
uitknipsel *n* cutting; clipping
uitkoggel *vb* to mock; to deride
uitkom *vb* to appear; to come out; to turn out; to come true; to work out
uitkoms(te) *n* outcome; result; relief
uitkontrakteer *vb* to outsource
uitkoop *vb* to buy off; to buy out
uitkyk *n* lookout; view; *vb* to look out
uitkyker *n* lookout (person)
uitlaat *n* outlet; car exhaust; *vb* to let out; to express; to omit; to skip
uitlaatpyp *n* exhaust pipe
uitlag *vb* to laugh out loud
uitlander *n* alien; foreigner
uitlating *n* omission; remark
uitleen *vb* to lend out; to loan
uitleg *vb* to explain; to expound; *n* explanation; layout; plan
uitlek *vb* to leak out; to trickle out; to transpire
uitlewer *vb* to deliver; to hand over; to surrender; to extradite
uitlewering *n* surrender; delivery
uitlok *vb* to entice; to tempt; to elicit; to evoke; to court (disaster)

uitloof *vb* to offer; to award
uitloop *n* overflow; outlet; *vb* to walk out; to run out; to bud; to end in
uitmaak *vb* to constitute; to form; to decide; to settle; to break off; to cancel; to denounce
uitmoor *vb* to massacre
uitmunt *vb* to excel; to surpass
uitmuntend *adj* excellent
uitnemend *adj* excellent
uitnemendheid *n* excellence
uitnodiging *n* invitation
uitnooi *vb* to invite
uitoefen *vb* to exercise; to practise; to exert
uitoorlê *vb* to get the better of; to outwit; to outmanoeuvre
uitpers *vb* to squeeze out; to press out
uitpeul *vb* to bulge out; to protrude
uitplak *vb* to paper (a wall)
uitpluis *vb* to sift; to investigate
uitplunder *vb* to loot; to plunder
uitput *vb* to exhaust; to deplete
uitputting *n* exhaustion
uitraak *vb* to get out; to end
uitrafel *vb* to fray; to unravel
uitredding *n* rescue; deliverance; escape
uitreik *vb* to issue; to distribute; to hand out
uitreis *n* outward journey
uitrek *vb* to stretch out; to crane (one's neck); to prolong
uitreken *vb* to calculate; to work out
uitrig *vb* to do; to carry out
uitroei *vb* to exterminate; to uproot; to eradicate
uitroep *n* cry; exclamation; *vb* to shout; to cry out; to call out; to exclaim
uitruil *vb* to exchange
uitrus[1] *vb* to repose; to rest
uitrus[2] *vb* to fit out; to equip
uitrusting *n* outfit; equipment
uitsaai *vb* to broadcast; to air
uitsaaistasie *n* broadcasting station; radio station
uitsaaiwese *n* broadcasting
uitsak *vb* to bulge out; to fall; to lag behind
uitsakker *n* dropout
uitset *n* trousseau; output; yield

uitsetting *n* enlargement; expansion; expulsion

uitsien *vb* to look out; to look forward to; to long for

uitsig *n* view; prospect

uitsit *vb* to expel; to evict; to expand; to dilate; to invest

uitskakel *vb* to switch off; to disconnect (electricity); to eliminate

uitskater *vb* to laugh out loud; to burst into laughter

uitskei[1] *vb* to stop; to cease

uitskei[2] *vb* to excrete

uitskeur *vb* to tear out

uitskietstoel *n* ejection seat

uitskink *vb* to pour out

uitskopskakelaar *n* trip switch

uitskot *n* rabble; riffraff; refuse; trash

uitskryf (*or* **uitskrywe**) *vb* to write out; to copy out; to issue

uitskud *vb* to shake out; to clean out; to clear out

uitslag[1] *n* eruption; rash

uitslag[2] *n* result; issue

uitsluit *vb* to exclude

uitsluitend *adj* exclusive; sole; *adv* exclusively; solely

uitsluitlik *adv* exclusively; solely

uitsmyt *vb* to chuck out; to eject

uitsmyter *n* bouncer

uitsny *vb* to cut out; to excise

uitsoek *vb* to select; to choose

uitsonder *vb* to make an exception; to exempt

uitsondering *n* exception; exemption

uitspan *vb* to unharness; to outspan

uitspanning *n* recreation; outspan

uitspansel *n* heavens; sky

uitspoel *vb* to wash out; to rinse

uitspraak *n* pronunciation; sentence; verdict; judgment

uitspreek *vb* to express; to say; to utter

uitsprei *vb* to unfold; to spread out

uitspruit *vb* to bud; to shoot up

uitspruitsel *n* shoot; bud; sprout

uitstaan *vb* to bear; to endure; to withstand; to be outstanding

uitstaande *adj* outstanding; prominent; projecting

uitstal *vb* to display; to exhibit

uitstalkas *n* showcase

uitstalling *n* display; exhibit

uitstalsentrum *n* exhibition centre

uitstap *vb* to get out; to alight

uitstappie *n* outing; trip; excursion

uitsteek *vb* to stretch forth; to protrude; to project; to excel

uitstekend *adj* excellent

uitstel *n* delay; postponement; respite; *vb* to postpone; to put off

uitsterf (*or* **uitsterwe**) *vb* to die out; to become extinct

uitstoot *vb* to expel; to push out

uitstort *vb* to pour out; to spill out; to unburden (oneself)

uitstraling *n* radiation; emission

uitstraal *vb* to beam forth; to emit rays; to emanate; to radiate

uitstrek *vb* to extend; to reach out

uitstrooi *vb* to scatter; to sow; to circulate; to spread abroad

uitstryk *vb* to iron out

uitsuig *vb* to suck out; to drain; to extort

uittart *vb* to defy; to provoke

uitteer *vb* to pine away

uitteken *vb* to delineate; to draw

uittog *n* exodus; departure

uittree *vb* to retire

uittrek *vb* to pull out; to extract; to undress

uittreksel *n* extract; excerpt

uitvaagsel *n* dregs; riffraff; scum

uitvaardig *vb* to enact; to issue; to proclaim

uitval *n* sortie; clash; outburst; *vb* to fall out

uitvee *vb* to erase; to sweep out

uitverkiesing *n* predestination

uitverkoop *n* sale; clearance sale; *vb* to sell out of

uitverkore *vb* to elect; to select

uitverkorene *n* favourite

uitvind *vb* to invent; to find out

uitvinding *n* invention

uitvindsel *n* invention; device

uitvis *vb* to fish out; to ferret out

uitvissing *n* phishing (internet fraud)

uitvloei *vb* to flow out

uitvloeisel *n* result; outcome

uitvlug *n* pretext; excuse

uitvoer *n* export; *vb* to export; to

execute; to perform; to export (computing)

uitvoerbaar *adj* feasible; practicable

uitvoerig *adj* ample; detailed; full; copious; lengthy

uitvoering *n* performance; execution

uitvors *vb* to investigate; to ferret out

uitvra *vb* to ask out; to invite; to question; to examine

uitvreet *vb* to eat away; to corrode

uitwaarts *adj* outward

uitwasem *vb* to exhale; to evaporate; to give off

uitweg *n* outlet; way out; escape

uitwei *vb* to digress

uitwendig *adj* external; outward

uitwerk *vb* to work out; to develop

uitwerking *n* effect; impact; result

uitwerpsel *n* excrement

uitwis *vb* to blot out; to efface; to wipe out

uitwissel *vb* to exchange

uitwyk *vb* to dodge; to turn aside; to go into exile; to emigrate; to expatriate

uitwyking *n* expatriation

uitwys *vb* to show; to point out; to prove

ultimatum *n* ultimatum

ultra *adv* extremely; excessively

ultramodern *adj* (*informal*) edgy

unie *n* union

uniek *adj* unique

uniform *n* uniform; *adj* unvaried in form; uniform

universeel *adj* universal; general

universiteit *n* university

uraan *n* uranium

urelank *adv* for hours

urn *n* urn

utopies *adj* utopian

uur *n* hour

uurwerk *n* clock; timepiece; clockwork

uurwyser *n* hour hand

uwe *poss pron* yours

V

vaag *adj* vague
vaak *adj* sleepy; *adv* often
vaal *adj* pale; sallow; tawny; faded
vaandel *n* standard; flag; banner
vaar *vb* to sail; to navigate
vaardig *adj* clever; skilled; dexterous
vaardigheid *n* dexterity; skill
vaart *n* cruise; voyage; passage; speed
vaartbelyn *adj* streamlined
vaartuig *n* vessel; ship
vaarwel *n* farewell; goodbye
vaas *n* vase; flowerpot
vaatjie *n* barrel; tub; vat; cask
vabond *n* rogue; tramp
vadem *n* fathom
vader *n* father
vaderland *n* fatherland
vaderlandsliefde *n* patriotism
vaderlander *n* patriot
vaderlik *adj* paternal; fatherly
vaderloos *adj* fatherless
vadermoord *n* parricide
vaderskap *n* paternity; fatherhood
vadoek *n* dishcloth
vag *n* fleece
vagevuur *n* purgatory
vak(kie) *n* subject; vocation; trade; pigeonhole; compartment
vakansie *n* holiday; vacation
vakansieganger *n* holidaymaker
vakant *adj* vacant; empty
vakature *n* vacancy
vakbond *n* trade union
vakleerling *n* apprentice
vakman *n* expert; specialist; artisan
vakmanskap *n* workmanship
vakonderwys *n* technical education; vocational education
vakpraatjies *n* shoptalk
vaksien *n* vaccine
vaksinasie *n* vaccination
vaksineer *vb* to vaccinate
val[1] *n* trap
val[2] *n* fall; downfall; gradient; valance; *vb* to fall; to drop; to succumb
valbyl *n* guillotine
valhek *n* boom; portcullis

valhelm *n* crash helmet
valk *n* hawk; falcon
vallei *n* valley; dale
vallend *adj* falling
vallende siekte *n* epilepsy
valluik *n* trapdoor
vals *adj* false; treacherous; artificial; forged
valskerm *n* parachute
valskermspringer *n* parachutist
valstrik *n* trap; snare; pitfall
valuasie *n* valuation
valuta *n* foreign currency
valutabeheer *n* exchange control
vampier *n* vampire
van[1] *n* surname; family name
van[2] *prep* of; from; by; with; for
vanaand *n, adv* this evening; tonight
vanaf *prep* from
vandaan *adv* whence; from
vandaar *conj* hence; therefore
vandag *n, adv* today
vandalisme *n* vandalism
vandat *conj* since
vandeesmaand *n, adv* this month
vandeesweek *n, adv* this week
vaneffe *adv* a moment ago; just now
vang *vb* to catch; to seize; to trap
vangdam *n* catchment dam
vanielje *n* vanilla
vanjaar *n, adv* this year
vanlyn *adv* offline (computing)
vanmelewe *adv* formerly; in the olden days
vanmiddag *n, adv* this afternoon
vanmôre *n, adv* this morning
vannag *n, adv* last night; tonight
vanself *adv* by itself; of its own accord
vanselfsprekend *adj* obvious; self-evident
van stapel stuur *vb* to launch
vanwaar *adv* whence
vanweë *prep* on account of; because of
variasie *n* variation
variëer *vb* to vary; to change
variëteit *n* variety
varing *n* fern**

vark *n* pig; hog; swine
varkhok *n* pigsty
varksog *n* sow
varkspek *n* bacon
varkvet *n* lard
varkvleis *n* pork
vars *adj* fresh; young; new-laid (eggs)
vars nuus *n* breaking news
vas[1] *vb* to fast
vas[2] *adj* fixed; firm; sure; certain; steady; stationary; permanent; *adv* firmly; soundly
vasberade *adj* firm; determined; resolute
vasbeslote *adj* determined
vasbind *vb* to tie; to fasten
vasbrand *vb* to run dry; to get into difficulty
vasdraai *vb* to tighten (nut; screw); to screw down)
vasektomie *n* vasectomy
vasgespe *vb* to buckle up
vasgoed *n* landed property
vashou *vb* to hold; to hold fast; to hang onto; to detain
vashoudend *adj* tenacious
vaskeer *vb* to corner
vasklou *vb* to cling to
vaslê *vb* to steal; to pinch; to stall
vasmaak *vb* to fasten; to tie
vaspen *vb* to control; to peg
vasplak *vb* to glue together; to stick together
vassit *vb* to stick fast; to stall; to fasten
vasspeld *vb* to pin together; to pin up
vasspyker *vb* to nail down
vasstamp *vb* to ram down
vassteek *vb* to fasten; to pin; to stop suddenly; to get stuck
vasstel *vb* to fix; to determine; to establish; to ascertain
vasteland *n* continent
vastheid *n* firmness; solidity; certainty
vastigheid *n* firmness; stability; certainty
vastrap *vb* to stand firm; to persevere
vastrapplek *n* stepping stone; footing
vastrek *vb* to pull tight; to swindle
vasvra *vb* to corner; to quiz
vasvrawedstryd *n* quiz
vaswerk *vb* to sew on; to stitch

vat[1] *n* cask; barrel; tub; vat
vat[2] *n* hold; grip; *vb* to take; to grip; to seize; to catch; to grasp; to understand
vatbaar *adj* susceptible to; capable of
vee[1] *n* livestock (cattle; sheep)
vee[2] *vb* to sweep; to wipe
veearts *n* veterinary surgeon
veeboerdery *n* stock farm
veekraal *n* stockyard
veel[1] *vb* to bear; to stand; to endure
veel[2] *adj* many; frequent; *adv* much; often; frequently
veelal *adv* mostly; often
veelbelowend *adj* very promising
veelbetekenend *adj* significant
veeleer *adv* rather; sooner
veeleisend *adj* exacting
veelheid *n* multitude; a large number; abundance
veelhoek *n* polygon
veelkeusig *n* multiple choice; —e vrae *npl* multiple choice questions
veelkleurig *adj* multicoloured; variegated
veelmeer *adv* sooner; rather
veelomvattend *adj* comprehensive; extensive
veelrassig *adj* multiracial
veels geluk! *sentence substitute* hearty congratulations!
veelseggend *adj* significant; expressive
veelsoortig *adj* various; manifold
veelsydig *adj* many-sided; all-round; versatile
veelvolkig *adj* multinational; multiracial
veelvoud *n* multiple
veelvraat *n* glutton
veelvuldig *adj* frequent; manifold
veelwywer *n* polygamist
veelwywery *n* polygamy
veemark *n* livestock market
veeplaas *n* cattle farm
veer[1] *n* ferry (boat)
veer[2] *n* spring (watch)
veer[3] *n* feather; *vb* to feather
veergewig *adj* featherweight
veerkombers *n* eiderdown; down quilt
veerkrag *n* springiness; elasticity
veerpyltjie *n* dart(s) (game)

veertien *n, determiner* fourteen
veertiendaags *adv* fortnightly
veertiende *n, adj* fourteenth
veertig *n, determiner* forty
veertigste *n, adj* fortieth
veeveiling *n* cattle auction
veeteelt *n* stockbreeding
veewagter *n* shepherd
veg *vb* to fight
veganis *n* vegan
vegetariër *n* vegetarian
veglustig *adj* pugnacious; quarrelsome
vegter *n* fighter; combatant
vegtuig *n* combat vehicle
vegvliegtuig *n* fighter plane
veil *vb* to sell by auction; to put up for sale
veilig *adj* safe; secure
veilige hawe *n* safe haven
veilige seks *n* safe sex
veiligheid *n* safety; security
veiligheidsglas *n* safety glass
veiligheidsgordel *n* safety belt
veiligheidspolisie *n* security police
veiligheidswag *n* security guard
veiling *n* public sale; auction
veins *vb* to simulate; to feign; to pretend
vel[1] *n* skin; hide; sheet (of paper)
vel[2] *vb* to fell (tree); to pass sentence
Velcro *n* Velcro
veld *n* field; plain; veldt
veldbed *n* camp bed
veldblom *n* wild flower
veldfiets *n* scrambler motorbike
veldheer *n* general
veldmaarskalk *n* field marshal
veldparty *n* picnic
veldprediker *n* army chaplain
veldrenne *n* scrambling; off-road racing (cars, motorbikes)
veldskool *n* veld school
veldslag *n* battle
veldtog *n* campaign
veldvoertuig *n* all-terrain vehicle (ATV)
velerlei *adj* various; sundry
velskoen *n* homemade leather shoe
vendusie *n* auction; sale
vendusieafslaer *n* auctioneer
vennoot *n* partner
vennootskap *n* partnership

venster *n* window
vensterbank *n* windowsill
vensterglas *n* windowpane
vensterkoevert *n* window envelope
vensterkykery *n* window shopping
vensterluik *n* shutter
vensterruit *n* windowpane
vent[1] *n* (*informal*) guy; bloke
vent[2] *vb* to hawk; to peddle
venter *n* hawker; pedlar; vendor
ventilasie *n* ventilation
ventileer *vb* to ventilate
venyn *n* venom; poison
venynig *adj* vicious; venomous
ver *adj* far; remote; distant
veraangenaam *vb* to make pleasant
veraf *adj, adv* far away; far off
verafgood *vb* to idolize
verafsku *vb* to detest; to abhor
verag *vb* to despise; to scorn
veragtelik *adj* despicable; contemptible
veragting *n* contempt; scorn
veral *adv* especially; chiefly
verander *vb* to alter; to change
verandering *n* alteration; change
veranderlik *adj* changeable; fickle
verantwoord *vb* to justify; to account for
verantwoordelik *adj* responsible; answerable; accountable
verarm *vb* to impoverish
veras *vb* to cremate
verassing *n* cremation
verassureer *vb* to insure
verbaal *adj* verbal
verbaas *vb* to astonish; to surprise; *adj* astonished; amazed
verban *vb* to banish; to exile
verband[1] *n* bandage; sling
verband[2] *n* mortgage; bond
verband[3] *n* connection; context
verbandgewer *n* mortgagee
verbandhouer *n* mortgager
verbasend *adj* astonishing; surprising
verbasing *n* astonishment; amazement
verbeel *vb* to imagine; to represent; to fancy
verbeelding *n* imagination; fancy
verberg *vb* to hide; to conceal
verbeter *vb* to improve; to correct; to mend

verbetering *n* correction; improvement
verbeur *vb* to lose; to forfeit
verbeurd *adj* forfeited; confiscated; —
verklaar *vb* to confiscate
verbied *vb* to forbid; to prohibit
verbind *vb* to join; to connect; to commit; to bandage; to dress (a wound)
verbinding *n* connection; union; bandaging; junction
verbintenis *n* union; alliance; promise; contract; agreement
verbleek *vb* to turn pale; to fade; *adj* pale; faded
verblind *vb* to dazzle; to blind; to delude
verbluf *adj* nonplussed; dumbfounded
verbly *vb* to gladden; to delight
verblydend *adj* joyful; cheerful
verblyf *n* residence; abode
verblyfkoste *n* living expenses
verbod *n* prohibition; ban; embargo
verbode *adj* prohibited; forbidden; —
toegang no thoroughfare
verbond *n* covenant; treaty; league
verborge *adj* hidden; secret; concealed
verbou *vb* to cultivate; to grow; to rebuild
verbouereerd *adj* embarrassed; confused; flabbergasted
verbrand *vb* to burn; to cremate
verbranding *n* burning; cremation; combustion
verbreek *vb* to break; to burst; to violate
verbrei *vb* to disseminate; to spread abroad
verbroeder *vb* to fraternize
verbrokkel *vb* to crumble
verbrou *vb* to spoil; to make a mess of
verbruik *n* consumption; *vb* to use up; to consume
verbruiker *n* consumer
verbrysel *vb* to shatter; to smash; to crush
verbuiging *n* declension
verby *prep* past; beyond
verbygaan *vb* to pass; to go by; to pass away
verbygaand *adj* passing; transitory
verbyganger *n* passer-by
verbypad *n* bypass

verbyry-skietery *n* drive-by shooting
verbyster *vb* to bewilder; to perplex
verdaag *vb* to adjourn; to postpone
verdag *adj* suspicious; suspected
verdaging *n* adjournment
verdagmaking *n* insinuation
verdamp *vb* to evaporate
verdamping *n* evaporation
verdedig *vb* to defend; to plead for
verdediging *n* defence; plea
verdedigingsmag *n* defence force
verdeel *vb* to divide; to distribute
verdeeld *adj* divided
verdeeldheid *n* discord; dissension; strife
verdelg *vb* to destroy; to exterminate
verdelging *n* destruction; extermination
verdeling *n* division; distribution
verdenking *n* suspicion; mistrust
verder *adv* further; later; farther; besides
verderf *n* decay; ruin; destruction; *vb* to ruin; to corrupt; to destroy
verderflik *adj* dangerous; pernicious
verdien *vb* to earn; to deserve
verdienste *n* wages; merit
verdieping *n* storey; floor
verdig *adj* fictitious
verdigsel *n* invention; fiction
verdink *vb* to suspect; to distrust
verdiskonteer *vb* to discount
verdoem *vb* to reject; to damn; to curse; to slam
verdoemenis *n* doom; damnation
verdof *vb* to dim; to tarnish; to become faint
verdoof (*or* **verdowe**) *vb* to dull; to deaden; to stun
verdor *vb* to wither; to dry up
verdorwe *adj* perverted; corrupt; depraved
verdowe *see* **verdof**
verdowing *n* stupor; numbness
verdowingsmiddel *n* anaesthetic; narcotic
verdra *vb* to bear; to endure; to suffer
verdraagsaam *adj* forbearing; tolerant; patient
verdraai *vb* to twist; to distort
verdrag *n* treaty; pact

verdriet *n* grief; sorrow; trouble
verdrietig *adj* sad; sorrowful
verdring *vb* to jostle; to push aside
verdrink *vb* to drown; to be drowned
verdroog *vb* to dry up; to become dry
verdruk *vb* to oppress
verdryf (*or* **verdrywe**) *vb* to drive away; to expel; to banish; to while away
verdubbel *vb* to double
verduidelik *vb* to clarify; to explain
verduideliking *adj* explanation; rundown
verduister *vb* to darken; to eclipse; to embezzle
verduistering *n* eclipse
verdun *vb* to dilute; to thin
verduur *vb* to endure; to bear
verdwaal *vb* to stray; to wander; to get lost
verdwyn *vb* to disappear; to vanish
verdwyning *n* disappearance; vanishing
veredel *vb* to refine; to improve; to elevate
veredeling *n* improvement; elevation
vereelt *adj* callous; hardened
vereenselwig *vb* to identify
vereenvoudig *vb* to simplify
vereenvoudiging *n* simplification
vereer *vb* to honour; to adore; to respect; to revere
vereerder *n* worshipper; admirer
vereffen *vb* to settle; to adjust; to pay
vereis *vb* to require; to demand; *adj* requisite
vereiste *n* requirement; requisite
verengels *vb* to anglicize
verenig *vb* to unite; to reconcile; to merge; to join
Verenigde Nasies *n* United Nations (UN)
vereniging *n* union; society; association
vererg *vb* to grow angry; to become annoyed
verergde *adj* angry
vererger *vb* to aggravate; to become worse; to make worse
verering *n* worship; veneration
verewig *vb* to immortalize
verf (*or* **verwe**) *n* paint; dye; *vb* to paint; to dye (clothes); to stain

verfilm *vb* to film
verflenter *adj* torn; tattered
verflou *vb* to become faint; to abate
verfoei *vb* to detest
verfoeilik *adj* detestable
verfoes *vb* to spoil
verfris *vb* to refresh
verfrissend *adj* refreshing
verfrissing *n* refreshment
verfrommel *vb* to crumple; to crush
verfyn *vb* to refine
verg *vb* to demand; to require
vergaan *vb* to perish; to decay; to be shipwrecked; to founder
vergader *vb* to meet; to gather
vergadering *n* meeting; assembly; gathering
vergaderingplek *n* meeting place; venue
vergange *adj* last; past; *adv* lately
verganklik *adj* transient; fleeting
vergas[1] *vb* to treat; to regale
vergas[2] *vb* to vaporize
vergasser *n* carburettor
verg *vb* to demand; to require
vergeef *vb* to forgive; to pardon
vergeeflik *adj* pardonable; excusable
vergeefs *adj* fruitless; futile; unsuccessful; *adv* in vain
vergeet *vb* to forget; to omit
vergeetagtig *adj* forgetful
vergeld *vb* to reward; to repay; to requite
vergelding *n* reward; retaliation; retribution
vergelyk *n* comparison; agreement; compromise; *vb* to compare; — **met** *vb* to compare with; to compare to
vergelykend *adj* comparative
vergelyking *n* comparison; equation
vergemaklik *vb* to facilitate
vergenoeg *adj* contented; satisfied
vergesel *vb* to accompany; to attend
vergesig (*or* **vêrgesig**) *n* view
vergetelheid *n* oblivion
vergewe[1] *vb* to forgive; to pardon
vergewe[2] *vb* to poison
vergewing *n* pardon; forgiveness
vergiet *n* colander; strainer
vergif *n* poison; venom
vergifnis *n* forgiveness; pardon

vergiftig *vb* to poison
vergiftiging *n* poisoning
vergis *vb* to mistake; to be mistaken
vergissing *n* mistake; error
verglaassel *n* enamel; glaze
vergoed *vb* to compensate; to defray; to indemnify; to reimburse
vergoeding *n* compensation; indemnification; amends
vergroot *vb* to enlarge; to magnify; to increase
vergrootglas *n* magnifying glass
vergroting *n* enlargement; increase
vergruis *vb* to crush; pulverize; smash to bits
vergryp *n* offence; crime; misdemeanour; *vb* to commit an offence
verguld *vb* to gild
verguldsel *n* gilt; gilding
vergun *vb* to permit; to grant; to allow
vergunning *n* permission; leave; licence
verhaal[1] *n* story; narrative; *vb* to relate; to tell; to narrate
verhaal[2] *n* redress; remedy; *vb* to recover (debt)
verhaar *vb* to lose hair; to moult; to shed hair
verhaas *vb* to hasten; to precipitate
verhandel *vb* to discuss; to barter; to negotiate
verhandeling *n* treatise; essay; dissertation
verhard *vb* to harden
verhaspel *vb* to spoil; to botch
verhef *vb* to raise; to lift up; to elevate
verheffend *adj* elevating; ennobling
verhelp *vb* to remedy; to put in order
verhemelte *n* palate; roof of the mouth
verheug *vb* to delight; to gladden
verhewe *adj* exalted; lofty; grand
verhinder *vb* to hinder; to prevent
verhit *vb* to heat; *adj* heated; hot; flushed
verhoed *vb* to prevent; to ward off
verhoging *n* increase; promotion
verhonger *vb* to starve
verhoog *n* platform; *vb* to raise; to elevate; to promote
verhoor *n* trial; hearing; examination; *vb* to hear; to examine; to interrogate
verhouding *n* ratio; proportion; affair (love)

verhuis *vb* to move out of
verhuising *n* removal; migration
verhuiswa *n* removal van
verhuur *vb* to let; to hire
verhuurder *n* landlord; lessor
verjaar *vb* to celebrate one's birthday
verjaar(s)dag *n* birthday
verjaar(s)daggeskenk *n* birthday present
verjaar(s)dagpartytjie *n* birthday party
verjaring *n* superannuation
verjong *vb* to rejuvenate; make young again
verjonging(s)kuur *n* face-lift
verkalk *vb* to calcify; *adj* calcified
verkas *vb* to shift; to decamp
verkeer *n* traffic; communication; *vb* to keep company with
verkeerbeheer *n* traffic control
verkeerd *adj* wrong; bad
verkeersboete *n* traffic fine
verkeersknoop *n* traffic jam; gridlock
verkeerslig *n* traffic light; robot
verkeersteken *n* traffic sign
verken *vb* to reconnoitre; to spy; to scout
verkenner *n* scout
verkies *vb* to elect; to choose
verkiesbaar *adj* eligible
verkiesing *n* election; choice
verkieslik *adj* preferable
verkla *vb* to accuse; to charge with
verklaar *vb* to declare; to explain; **oorlog —** *vb* to declare war
verklap *vb* to let out; to blab; to give (a person) away; to betray
verklaring *n* explanation; statement; declaration; **— van voorneme** *n* declaration of intent
verklee *vb* to change clothes; to disguise
verkleef *adj* attached to; devoted to
verklein *vb* to reduce; to make smaller; to lessen; to diminish
verkleineer *vb* to disparage; to run down; to belittle
verkleining *n* downsizing
verkleinwoord *n* diminutive
verkleur *vb* to fade; to change colour; to lose colour; to discolour

verkleurmannetjie *n* chameleon
verklik *vb* to disclose; to give away
verklikker *n* detector (metal, smoke)
verkluim *vb* to grow numb with cold
verknoei *vb* to bungle; to spoil; to make a mess of
verknogtheid *n* attachment; devotion
verknorsing *n* quandary; difficulty; predicament; fix
verkoel *vb* to cool down; to refrigerate
verkoeler *n* radiator
verkondig *vb* to proclaim; to announce
verkoop *n* sale; *vb* to sell
verkoop(s)belasting *n* sales tax
verkoop(s)bestuurder *n* sales manager
verkoop(s)prys *n* selling price
verkoper *n* seller; vendor; sales person; something that sells
verkoping *n* auction; sale
verkort *vb* to shorten; to abridge; *adj* abridged
verkorting *n* shortening; abridg(e)ment; *abbreviation*
verkoue *n* cold; chill; **'n — kry** *vb* to catch a cold; **het — ** *vb* to have a cold
verkrag *vb* to infringe; to violate; to rape
verkragting *n* violation; rape
verkramp *adj* unenlightened; ultraconservative
verkreukel *vb* to crease; to crush
verkrop *adj* pent up
verkrummel *vb* to crumble
verkry *vb* to acquire; to obtain
verkrygbaar *adj* obtainable
verkwik *vb* to refresh
verkwikkend *adj* refreshing; comforting
verkwis *vb* to squander; to waste
verkwisting *n* waste; extravagance
verkyker *n* telescope; binoculars
verlaag *vb* to lower; to debase; to reduce
verlaat *vb* to leave; to abandon
verlaging *n* lowering; reduction; degradation
verlak *vb* to lacquer; to varnish
verlam *vb* to paralyse; to cripple
verlamming *n* paralysis
verlang *vb* to desire; to long for
verlange *n* desire; wish; longing

verlate *adj* lonely; abandoned
verlê *vb* to shift; to move; to divert (road); to mislay
verlede *n* the past; *adj* last; past
verleë *adj* shy; timid; perplexed; embarrassed
verleen *vb* to grant; to give
verleentheid *n* embarrassment; confusion; trouble
verleer *vb* to unlearn; to forget
verlegging *n* shifting; deviation; detour
verlei *vb* to tempt; to seduce; to mislead
verleidelik *adj* alluring; enticing; tempting
verleiding *n* seduction; temptation
verleng *vb* to lengthen; to prolong
verlep *vb* to wither; to fade
verlief *adj* in love; fond of; sweet on; amorous; **— neem** to put up with; **— raak op** *vb* to fall in love with
verliefde *n* person in love
verlies *n* loss; bereavement; defeat
verlig[1] *vb* to lighten; to relieve
verlig[2] *vb* to light; to illuminate; to enlighten
verligte *adj* lit up; enlightened
verligting[1] *n* lightening; relief; alleviation
verligting[2] *n* lighting; illumination; enlightenment
verloën *vb* to deny; to disavow
verlof *n* leave; permission; furlough
verlok *vb* to tempt; to entice
verloof *vb* to get engaged; to be betrothed
verloofde *n* fiancé; fiancée; betrothed
verloop *n* course; progress; *vb* to pass; to elapse; to go out (tide)
verloor *vb* to lose
verlore *adj* lost
verlore bagasie *n* lost baggage
verlos *vb* to deliver; to release; to liberate; to save
verloskunde *n* obstetrics; midwifery
verloskundige *n* gynaecologist; midwife
verlowing *n* engagement; betrothal
vermaak *n* pleasure; delight; enjoyment; amusement; *vb* to enjoy; to amuse
vermaaklik *adj* enjoyable; pleasant; amusing; entertaining

vermaan *vb* to warn; to admonish

vermaard *adj* famous; renowned; celebrated

vermaardheid *n* fame; renown

vermaer *vb* to grow thin; to lose flesh; to become emaciated

vermaerd *adj* emaciated

vermaning *n* warning; telling off

vermeende *adj* supposed; reputed

vermeerder *vb* to increase; to enlarge

vermeerdering *n* increase; augmentation; enlargement

vermeld *vb* to mention; to record

vermeng *vb* to mix; to blend

vermenger *n* blender

vermenigvuldig *vb* to multiply

vermenigvuldiging *n* multiplication

vermetel *adj* bold; daring; audacious

vermicelli *n* vermicelli

vermiljoen *n, adj* vermilion

verminder *vb* to decrease; to lessen; to slacken (speed)

vermindering *n* rebate; decrease; reduction

vermink *vb* to mutilate; to maim

vermis *vb* to miss

vermoë *n* ability; power; capacity; riches; wealth

vermoed *vb* to suspect; to presume; to suppose

vermoede *n* suspicion; presumption; supposition

vermoedelik *adj* probable; *adv* probably; presumably

vermoei *vb* to fatigue; to tire; to exhaust

vermoeid *adj* tired; weary

vermoeiend *adj* tiring; tedious

vermoënd *adj* wealthy; rich

vermom *vb* to mask; to disguise; *adj* disguised; masked

vermoor *vb* to murder; to kill

vermors *vb* to squander; to waste

vermorsel *vb* to crush; to smash; to pulverize

vermuf *adj* mouldy; musty

vermurf (*or* **vermurwe**) *vb* to soften; to make soft; to mollify

vermy *vb* to shun; to avoid; to evade

vernaam *adj* important; distinguished; notable; *adv* especially

vernaamlik *adv* chiefly; especially; mainly

vernaamste *adj* staple

verneder *vb* to humble; to humiliate; to degrade

vernederend *adj* humiliating

verneem *vb* to understand; to learn; to ascertain; to enquire

verneuk *vb* to cheat; to swindle

verniel *vb* to destroy; to wreck

verniet *adv* in vain; unnecessarily; gratis

vernietig *vb* to destroy; to crush

vernietiging *n* destruction

vernis *n* varnish; *vb* to varnish

vernuf *n* intelligence; talent; ingenuity; expertise; genius; intellect

vernuftig *adj* ingenious; intelligent

vernuwe *vb* to renovate; to renew

vernuwing *n* renewal; renovation

veronagsaam (*or* **verontagsaam**) *vb* to neglect; to slight; to ignore

veronderstel *vb* to suppose; to assume

veronderstelling *n* supposition; assumption

verongeluk *vb* to fail; to miscarry (plan); to come to grief; to meet with disaster; to perish

verongelyk *vb* to wrong

verontagsaam *see* **veronagsaam**

verontheilig *vb* to desecrate

verontreinig *vb* to pollute; to defile

verontrus *vb* to alarm; to disturb; to agitate

verontskuldig *vb* to excuse; to apologize

verontwaardig *adj* indignant

verontwaardiging *n* indignation

veroordeel *vb* to condemn; to sentence

veroorloof *vb* to allow; to permit; *adj* allowed; permissible

veroorsaak *vb* to cause; to bring about

verootmoedig *vb* to humble; to humiliate

verorden *vb* to ordain; to decree

verordening *n* order; regulation; rule; bye-law

verouder *vb* to age; to grow old; to become obsolete

verower *vb* to conquer; to capture

verowering *n* conquest

verpag *vb* to lease

verpakking *n* packing
verpand *vb* to pawn; to pledge; to mortgage
verpersoonlik *vb* to personalize (stationery, etc.)
verpes *vb* to detest; to abhor; to infect; to contaminate
verplaas *vb* to shift; to move; to remove; to displace; to transfer
verplasing *n* transfer; removal; displacement
verplant *vb* to plant; to transplant
verpleeg *vb* to tend; to nurse
verpleegkunde *n* nursing
verpleegster *n* nurse
verpleër *n* male nurse
verpleging *n* nursing
verpletter *vb* to crush; to smash
verplig *vb* to oblige; to compel; *adj* obliged; bound
verpligtend *adj* compulsory
verpligting *n* obligation; liability
verraad *n* treachery; treason
verraai *vb* to betray; to disclose
verraaier *n* traitor; betrayer
verraderlik *adj* treacherous; traitorous
verras *vb* to surprise; to startle
verrassend *adj* surprising
verrassing *n* surprise; eye-opener
verregaande *adj* extraordinary; outrageous; scandalous
verreikend *adj* far-reaching
verrek *vb* to strain; to wrench; to strain
verreken *vb* to clear (cheques)
verreweg *adv* by far
verrig *vb* to do; to execute
verrigtinge *npl* proceedings
verroer *vb* to move; to stir
verroes *vb* to become rusty; to rust
verrot *vb* to decay; to decompose; *adj* rotten; decayed
verrotting *n* decay; putrefaction
verruil *vb* to exchange; to barter
verruim *vb* to widen; to broaden
verruk *vb* to delight; to enchant
verruklik *adj* enchanting; charming; enriching
verrukking *n* rapture; ecstasy
verryk *vb* to enrich
verryking *n* enrichment
vers[1] *n* verse; stanza

vers[2] *n* heifer
versaak *vb* to forsake; to renounce
versadig *vb* to satisfy; to appease
versag *vb* to soften; to mitigate
versagtend *adj* extenuating
versagting *n* alleviation; mitigation; relief
versaking *n* renouncement; neglect
versamel *vb* to collect; to gather; to compile
versameling *n* collection; compilation
versapper *n* liquidizer
verseël *vb* to seal
verseg *vb* to refuse
verseker *vb* to insure; to secure; to assure; to affirm; *adj* assured; *adv* surely; certainly
versekering *n* assurance; insurance
versekeringsmaatskappy *n* insurance company
versekeringspolis *n* insurance policy
versend *vb* to send off; to dispatch; to forward
versending *n* dispatch; consignment; shipment
verset *n* resistance; *vb* to resist
versien *vb* to service
versiening *n* service (car)
versiende *adj* far-sighted; long-sighted; far-seeing
versier *vb* to decorate; to adorn
versiering *n* decoration; ornament
versigtig *adj* careful; prudent
versigtigheid *n* care; prudence; caution
versilwer *adj* silver-plated
versin *vb* to invent; to concoct; to fabricate
versit *vb* to move; to shift
verskaf *vb* to furnish; to supply; to provide
verskafer *n* supplier
verskalf *n* heifer calf
verskans *vb* to fortify; to entrench
verskansing *n* rampart; earthwork; bulwark
verskeep *vb* to ship
verskeidenheid *n* variety; diversity
verskeie *adj* various; several; sundry; many
verskeping *n* shipment
verskerp *vb* to whet; to sharpen

verskeur *vb* to devour; to tear up

verskiet *n* distance; perspective; prospect

verskil *n* difference; disparity; discrepancy; *vb* to differ; to vary

verskillend *adj* different; various

verskimmel *vb* to get mouldy

verskoning *n* excuse; apology

verskoon *vb* to excuse; to pardon

verskoppeling *n* outcast

verskrik *vb* to frighten; to terrify; to horrify

verskrikking *n* horror; terror

verskriklik *adj* frightful; terrible; dreadful

verskroei *vb* to scorch; to singe; **—de aarde** *n* scorched earth

verskrompel *vb* to shrivel; to wrinkle

verskuif (*or* **verskuiwe**) *vb* to shift; to shove along; to postpone

verskuldig *adj* due; indebted; owing

verskyn *vb* to appear; to be published

verskyning *n* appearance; publication

verskynsel *n* phenomenon

verslaaf *vb* to enslave; *adj* enslaved; addicted; **— raak aan** *vb* to become addicted to

verslaafmiddel *n* habit-forming drug

verslaan *vb* to beat; to defeat; to conquer

verslae *adj* dismayed

verslag *n* report; account

verslaggewer *n* reporter

verslank *vb* to slim

verslanking *n* slimming

verslap *vb* to slacken; to relax; to flag

versleg *vb* to deteriorate

verslind *vb* to devour; to consume

verslons *vb* to ruin; to spoil; *adj* slovenly

versluk *vb* to choke

verslyt *vb* to wear out; to while away; *adj* threadbare; worn out

versmaad (*or* **versmaai**) *vb* to despise; to scorn

versmaat *n* metre (in poetry)

versmag *vb* to pine away; to languish

versmelt *vb* to melt; to melt down; to melt away away; to fuse

versmoor *vb* to stifle; to suffocate

versnapering *n* dainty; delicacy

versnel *vb* to accelerate

versnelling *n* acceleration; gear (motor)

versnelrenne *n* drag racing

versnipper *vb* to shred

versoek *n* request; petition; *vb* to request; to ask; to invite

versoeking *n* temptation

versoeksrif *n* petition

versoen *vb* to reconcile; to pacify; to placate

versoet *vb* to sweeten

versoeter *n* sweetener

versondig *vb* to annoy; to irritate

versool *vb* to resole; to retread

versorg *vb* to care for; to attend to

versorger *n* carer

versorging *n* care; maintenance

verspeel *vb* to squander; to gamble away

versper *vb* to barricade; to block

versperring *n* barricade; roadblock

verspied *vb* to spy; to reconnoitre

verspieder *n* spy; scout

verspil *vb* to waste; to squander

verspilling *n* waste; squandering

verspoel *vb* to wash away

verspot *adj* silly; ridiculous

versprei *vb* to scatter; to spread; to disperse

verspring *n* long jump; *vb* to long jump

verstaan *vb* to understand; to comprehend

verstaanbaar *adj* intelligible; comprehensible

verstand *n* sense; intellect; mind; intelligence; (*informal*) savvy

verstandelik *adj* intellectual; mental

verstandhouding *n* understanding

verstandig *adj* intelligent; sensible; wise

verstandtand *n* wisdom tooth

verstedelik *vb* to urbanize

verstedeliking *n* urbanization

versteen *vb* to petrify

verstekeling *n* stowaway

verstel *vb* to mend; to readjust; to change gears

verstelbaar *adj* adjustable

verstening *n* petrifaction; fossil

versterfreg *n* right of succession

versterk *vb* to invigorate; to strengthen; to reinforce; to fortify

versterking *n* support; reinforcement; fortification

versterkingsmiddel *n* tonic

versteur (*or* **verstoor**) *vb* to disturb; to upset

versteur(d) (*or* **verstoor[d]**) *adj* angry; annoyed

versteuring (*or* **verstoring**) *n* disturbance

verstik *vb* to stifle; to suffocate; to choke

verstok *adj* hardened; inveterate

verstoke *adj* hidden; concealed

verstom *vb* to dumbfound; to render speechless

verstommend *adj* amazing; breathtaking

verstoor *see* **versteur**

verstoor(d) *see* **versteur(d)**

verstoot *vb* to disown; to reject; to cast off

verstop *vb* to clog; to plug; to constipate; *adj* clogged up; plugged

verstopping *n* obstruction; constipation

verstoring *see* **versteuring**

verstoteling *n* outcast; pariah

verstrek *vb* to furnish; to provide; to supply

verstreke *adj* elapsed; expired

verstrekkend *adj* far-reaching

verstrooi *vb* to scatter; to disperse

verstrooi(d) *adj* distracted; absent-minded

verstrooidheid *n* absent-mindedness

verstrooiing *n* diversion; scattering

verstryk *vb* to elapse; to expire; to terminate

verstrykdatum *n* expiry date

verstuit *vb* to sprain (ankle); to dislocate

verstyf (*or* **verstywe**) *vb* to become numb; to stiffen

versuf *adj* dull; doting

versugting *n* sigh

versuim *n* neglect; default; *vb* to neglect; to omit

versuip *vb* to drown (animals); to flood (carburettor)

versuur *vb* to turn sour; to sour

verswaar *vb* to aggravate; to encumber

verswak *vb* to weaken; to grow weaker; to become weaker

versweer *vb* to ulcerate; to fester

verswelg *vb* to swallow up

verswering *n* ulceration; suppuration

verswik *vb* to sprain (ankle)

verswyg *vb* to keep silent; to suppress; to conceal

vertaal *vb* to translate

vertak *vb* to branch out; to ramify

vertakking *n* branching out; ramification

vertaler *n* translator

vertaling *n* translation; version

verte *n* distance

verteenwoordig *vb* to represent

verteenwoordiger *n* representative

verteer *vb* to digest; to spend; to use up

verteerbaar *adj* digestible

vertel *vb* to relate; to tell; to narrate

verteller *n* narrator; storyteller

vertelling *n* narrative; story; tale

vertikaal *adj* vertical

vertin *adj* tinned

vertolk *vb* to interpret; to explain

vertoning *n* show; performance

vertoon *n* show; sight; *vb* to show; to expose; to perform; to stage; to display

vertoonkas *n* display cabinet

vertoonrugby *n* professional rugby

vertraag *vb* to delay; to hold up; to retard; **—de aksie** *n* slow motion

vertraging *n* delay; retardation

vertrek[1] *n* departure; *vb* to leave; to depart

vertrek[2] *n* room; apartment

vertrek[3] *vb* to distort

vertroetel *vb* to spoil; to indulge

vertroos *vb* to console; to comfort

vertrou *vb* to trust; to rely on; to confide in

vertroubaar *adj* reliable

vertroud *adj* reliable; trustworthy; trusted; familiar with

vertroue *n* trust; confidence

vertroueling *n* confidant

vertrouensgaping *n* credibility gap

vertroueswendelaar *n* conman

vertroulik *adj* confidential; private; **streng —** *adj* strictly confidential

vertwyfeling *n* despair; desperation

vervaard *adj* frightened; alarmed

vervaardig *vb* to make; to manufacture

vervaardiger *n* manufacturer

verval *n* decline; decay; maturity; *vb* to decay; to decline; to fall due; to mature; to expire

vervaldag *n* due date; expiry date

vervalle *adj* dilapidated

vervals *vb* to adulterate; to falsify; to fake; to forge

vervalsing *n* fake; falsification

vervang *vb* to substitute; to replace

vervat *vb* to resume; to begin again; to continue

verveel *vb* to weary; to bore

verveer *vb* to moult

vervel *vb* to slough; to shed dead skin (snake)

vervelend *adj* boring; tiresome; tedious

vervelens: tot — toe *adv* ad nauseam

vervelig *adj* tedious; boring

verversing *n* refreshment

vervlieg *vb* to fly (time); to vanish; to evaporate

vervloek *vb* to curse

vervloeks! *interj* damn it!

vervoeg *vb* to conjugate

vervoeging *n* conjugation

vervoer *n* traffic; transport; transportation; conveyance; *vb* to convey; to carry; to transport

vervoering *n* ecstasy; rapture

vervolg *n* continuation; future; sequel; *vb* to continue; to pursue; to prosecute

vervolger *n* prosecutor

vervolging *n* pursuit; prosecution

vervreem *vb* to alienate; to estrange

vervuil *vb* to become dirty; to become choked with weeds

vervul *vb* to fulfil; to perform (a duty); to carry out

verwaai *vb* to blow away

verwaai(d) *adj* blown about; dishevelled; untidy

verwaand *adj* conceited; arrogant; stuck up

verwaandheid *n* conceit; conceitedness; arrogance

verwaarloos *vb* to neglect

verwaarloosde *adj* neglected

verwag *vb* to expect; to look forward to; to anticipate

verwagting *n* expectation; hope

verwant *n* relative; relation; *adj* related; allied

verwantskap *n* relationship; kinship

verwar *vb* to tangle; to intertwine; to confuse; to mix up; to muddle; *adj* tangled; tousled; muddled

verwarm *vb* to warm; to heat

verwarmer *n* heater

verwarming *n* heating

verwarring *n* confusion; perplexity

verwe *see* **verf**

verweer *n* defence; resistance; *vb* to defend; to resist

verweerder *n* defender

verwelf *n* vault

verwelk *vb* to wither; to fade

verwelkom *vb* to welcome; *n* welcome

verwen *vb* to spoil; to indulge

verwens *vb* to curse

verwer *n* painter (trade)

verwerf *vb* to acquire; to obtain

verwerk *vb* to work out; to process; to digest; to assimilate

verwerker *n* processor (data, words)

verwerklik *vb* to realize; to materialize

verwerp *vb* to reject; to decline; to refuse; to negate

verwerplik *adj* objectionable; unacceptable; untenable

verwesenlik *vb* to realize; to substantiate

verwikkeling *n* complication

verwilder *vb* to run wild; to scare away; to drive away

verwilder(d) *adj* wild; neglected

verwissel *vb* to exchange; to alternate; to commute

verwisseling *vb* change; exchange

verwittig *vb* to inform; to notify

verwoed *adj* furious; enraged; wild

verwoes *vb* to destroy; to ruin; to devastate

verwoeste(nd) *adj* destroyed; devastated

verwoesting *n* destruction; devastation; havoc

verwonder *vb* to surprise; to amaze; to astonish; *adj* astonished; surprised

verwondering *n* surprise; astonishment; wonder

verworpe *adj* depraved; unprincipled

verworpeling *n* reprobate; outcast
verwronge *adj* distorted; twisted
verwurg *vb* to strangle; to throttle
verwyder *vb* to withdraw; to move away; to alienate
verwyder(d) *adj* distant; remote
verwydering *n* estrangement; removal
verwyf *adj* effeminate
verwyl *vb* to linger; to stay
verwys *vb* to refer to
verwysing *n* reference
verwysnommer *n* reference number
verwyt *n* reproach; reproof; blame; *vb* to reproach; to blame; to rebuke
verydel *vb* to frustrate; to upset (plan); to foil
vesel *n* fibre; thread; filament
veselglas *n* fibreglass
vestig *vb* to establish; to found; to settle; to fix (upon)
vesting *n* settlement; establishment
vet *n* fat; suet; lard; dripping; bold face (printing); *adj* rich; fertile; fat; plump; bold (printing)
vete *n* feud; vendetta
veter *n* lace (shoe, boot, etc.)
veteraan *n* veteran
veteraanmotor *n* vintage car
veto *n* veto
vetplant *n* succulent
vetpuisie *n* acne
vetsug *n* obesity
vetterig *adj* fatty; greasy
viaduk *n* viaduct
videoband *n* video tape
vier[1] *n, determiner* four
vier[2] *vb* to celebrate; to observe; to keep
vierde *n, adj* fourth
vierdens *adv* in fourth place
vierduisend *n, adj* four thousand
vierhoek *n* quadrangle
vierkant *n* square
vierkantig *adj* square
vierkantswortel *n* square root
vierrigtingstop *n* fourway stop (street)
vierskaar *n* tribunal
vieruur *n, adj* four o'clock
vierwiel *n* quad bike
vierwieler *n* quad bike
vierwielfiets *n* quad bike
vierwielmotorfiets *n* quad bike

vies *adj* dirty; nasty; offensive; fed up; annoyed
vieslik *adj* dirty; filthy; loathsome
viets *adj* smart; spruce
vigs *n* AIDS
vigsverwantekompleks *n* AIDS-related complex (ARC)
viktimiseer *vb* to victimize
vilt *n* felt
vin *n* fin
vind *vb* to find; to come across; to meet up with
vindingryk *adj* clever; ingenious; resourceful
vinger *n* finger
vingerafdruk *n* fingerprint
vingerhoed *n* thimble
vingerwysing *n* indication; warning
vink *n* finch
vinkel *n* fennel
vinnig *adj* quick; sharp; eager
violet *adj,n* violet
violis *n* violinist
viool *n* violin; fiddle
viooltjie *n* violet
vir *prep* for; to
virtuele realiteit *n* virtual reality
vis *n* fish
visagtig *adj* fishy
visgereedskap *n* fishing tackle
visgerei *n* fishing tackle
visgraat *n* fishbone
vishoek *n* fish-hook
visier *n* visor; sight (gun)
visioen *n* vision; dream
vissmeer *n* fish paste
visolie *n* cod-liver oil; fish oil
visstok *n* fishing rod
visryk *adj* plenty of fish
visser *n* fisherman
visserman *n* fisherman; angler
visserskuit *n* fishing boat
vissery *n* fishery
visterman *n* fisherman; angler
visum *n* visa
visvang *vb* to catch fish; to nod
vit *vb* to find fault; to carp
vitamine *n* vitamin
vitrioel *n* vitriol
vla *n* custard
vlaag *n* gust; sudden squall

vlag *n* flag; standard
vlagdoek *n* bunting
vlagpaal *n* flagpole; flagstaff
vlak *adj* shallow; flat; level
vlakte *npl* plain; flatlands
vlakvark *n* warthog
vlam *n* flame; blaze; *vb* to blaze; to burn
vlambaar *adj* flammable
vlammend *adj, adv* ablaze
vlas *n* flax
vlees *n* flesh; meat
vleeslik *adj* carnal; sexual
vleeswording *n* incarnation
vleg *vb* to plait; to twist; to weave
vlegsel *n* string; braid; plait
vlei[1] *n* valley; dale; meadow
vlei[2] *vb* to flatter; to coax
vleis *n* meat; flesh
vleisbraai *n* braai; braaivleis; barbecue
vleisetend *adj* carnivorous
vleiskoekie *n* patty
vleiswond *n* flesh wound
vlek *n* stain; blot; spot; blemish; *vb* to soil; to blot; to stain
vlek(ke)loos *adj* spotless; pure
vlekvry *adj* stainless
vlekvrye staal *n* stainless steel
vlerk *n* wing
vlerksleep *vb* to impress; to court
vlerkswewer *n* hang-glider
vlermuis *n* bat
vleuel *n* wing; vane; grand piano; side aisle
vleuelklavier *n* grand piano
vlieënd *adj* flying
vlieënde piering *n* flying saucer
vlieënet *n* fly net
vlieënier *n* pilot; aviator; airman
vlieër *n* kite; pilot; aviator
vlieg[1] *n* fly (insect)
vlieg[2] *vb* to fly
vliegdekskip *n* aircraft carrier
vliegmasjien *n* aeroplane
vliegtuig *n* aircraft; plane; airliner
vliegveld *n* aerodrome
vlierboom *n* elder tree
vlies *n* fleece; membrane; film
vlinder *n* butterfly
vloed *n* flood
vloedgolf *n* tidal wave
vloedwater *n* floodwater; stormwater

vloei *vb* to flow; to stream
vloeibaar *adj* liquid; fluid
vloeiend *adj* fluent; easy; flowing
vloeihars *n* anime
vloeistof *n* liquid; fluid
vloek *n* oath; curse; swearword; *vb* to curse; to swear
vloerlys *n* floor
vlok *n* flake; tuft
vlooi *n* flea
vlooibyt *n* fleabite
vlooiespel *n* tiddlywinks
vlooimark *n* flea market
vloot *n* fleet; navy
vlootsoldaat *n* marine
vlossig *adj* flossy
vlot *n* raft; float (cash); *vb* to succeed; to move easily; to go smoothly; *adj* fluent; facile; *adv* afloat; fluently
vlug[1] *n* covey; bevy
vlug[2] *n* flight; escape; *vb* to flee
vlug[3] *adj* quick; nimble; agile
vlugbal *n* volleyball
vlughou *n* volley (tennis)
vlugopnemer *n* flight recorder; black box
vlugskrif *n* pamphlet
vlugsout *n* volatile salts
vlugteling *n* fugitive; refugee
vlugtig *adj* hasty; fleeting; cursory
vly *vb* to lay down; to nestle
vlym *n* lancet
vlymskerp *adj* very sharp
vlyt *n* diligence; industry
vlytig *adj* industrious; diligent
VN *see* **Verenigde Nasies**
voed *vb* to feed; to nourish
voeding *n* feeding; nourishment; nutrition
voedingsmiddels *npl* foodstuffs
voedsaam *adj* nourishing; nutritious
voedsel *n* food; nourishment
voedselvergiftiging *n* food poisoning
voeg *n* joint; seam; *vb* to join; to fit in; to seam; to weld
voegwoord *n* conjunction
voel *vb* to feel; to touch; to grope
voël *n* bird
voelbaar *adj* palpable; tangible
voëlent *n* mistletoe
voëlhok *n* aviary
voelhoring *n* antenna; feeler; tentacle
voeling *n* touch; feeling

voëlkyk *n* birdwatching
voëlkyker *n* birdwatcher
voëlverskrikker *n* scarecrow
voëlvlugblik *n* bird's-eye view
voëlvry *adj* outlawed; free as a bird
voer[1] *n* fodder; forage; *vb* to feed
voer[2] *n* to conduct; to transport; **oorlog —** *vb* to wage war
voerband *n* conveyor belt
voering *n* lining
voertaal *n* medium of instruction
voert! *interj* go away!;
voertsek! *interj* go away!; footsack!
voertuig *n* vehicle
voet *n* foot; footing
voetbal *n* football
voetbank *n* footstool
voetenent *n* foot (bed)
voetganger *n* pedestrian; hopper (wingless locust)
voetheelkundige *n* podiatrist; chiropodist
voetjie-voetjie (*or* **voetjie-vir-voetjie**) *adj* slowly; cautiously
voetpad *n* footpath
voetskimmel *n* athlete's foot
voetslaan *vb* to walk; to foot it; to footslog
voetslaanpad *n* hiking trail
voetspoor *n* footprint; footstep; track
voetstuk *n* pedestal
voetvolk *n* foot soldiers; infantry
vog *n* fluid; liquid; moisture
vogtig *adj* damp; moist
vokaal *n* vowel; *adj* vocal
vol *adj* full; filled
volbloed *adj* thoroughbred
volbring *n* fulfilment; accomplishment; *vb* to fulfil; to complete
voldaan *adj* paid; settled; satisfied
voldoen *vb* to satisfy; to pay; to comply with
voldoende *adj* sufficient; adequate
voldoening *n* satisfaction; payment
voleindig *vb* to finish; to complete
volg *vb* to follow; to succeed
volgeling *n* follower; supporter
volgende *adj* following; next
volgens *prep* as; per; according to
volgorde *n* order; sequence
volhard *vb* to persevere; to persist

volharding *n* perseverance; persistence
volhou *vb* to persevere; to maintain; to endure
volhoubaar *adj* sustainable
volhoubaarheid *n* sustainability
volk *n* people; nation
volkekunde *n* anthropology
volkereg *n* international law
volkereverhoudinge *npl* race relations
volkome *adj* perfect; complete; *adv* perfectly; absolutely
volkryk *adj* populous
volksdrag *n* national dress
volkskunde *n* folklore
volksleier *n* leader of the people
volkslied *n* national anthem
volkspele *npl* folk dancing
volksplanting *n* colony; settlement
volkstelling *n* census
volkswelsyn *n* social welfare
volledig *adj* complete; entire
volleerd *adj* skilled; accomplished
volmaak *vb* to fill; to complete; to perfect; *adj* perfect
volmaan *n* full moon
volmag *n* power of attorney; proxy
volmondig *adj* frank; candid
vol ontwikkelde vigs *n* full-blown AIDS
volop *adj* plenty
volslae *adj* complete; absolute; *adv* fully; totally
volstaan *vb* to suffice
volstrek *adv* absolutely; decidedly
volstruis *n* ostrich
volt *n* volt
voltallig *adj* full; complete; *adv* fully
voltooi *vb* to finish; to complete
voltreffer *n* direct hit
voltrek *vb* to execute; to solemnize; to perform (marriage ceremony)
voltyds *adv* full time
voluit *adv* in full
volvoer *vb* to accomplish; to perform
volwasse *adj* full-grown; adult
volwassene *n* adult
vomeer *vb* to vomit
vondeling *n* foundling
vonds *n* find; discovery
vonk *n* spark
vonkel *vb* to sparkle; to twinkle
vonkeling *adj* sparkling

vonkelwyn *n* champagne

vonkprop *n* spark plug

vonnis *n* sentence; judgment; *vb* to sentence; to condemn

voog *n* guardian; trustee

voogdy *n* guardianship

voor[1] *n* furrow

voor[2] *prep; adv; conj* before; in front of; previous to

vooraan *adj, adv* foremost; first in time; place; rank; in front

vooraand *n* eve; early evening

vooraf *adv* beforehand; previously

voorafgaande *adj* preceding; foregoing

voorarm *n* forearm; forehand; *adj* forehand

voorbaat: **by —** in anticipation; beforehand

voorbarig *adj* premature; rash; hasty

voorbedag *adj* premeditated

voorbeeld *n* example; pattern; instance; **by —** for example (e.g.)

voorbeeldig *adj* exemplary

voorbehoedmiddel *n* preventative; contraceptive; prophylactic

voorbehoedpil *n* contraceptive pill

voorbehou *vb* to reserve

voorbehoud *n* reservation; reserve

voorberei *vb* to prepare

voorbereiding *n* preparation

voorberig *n* preface; foreword

voorbeskikking *n* predestination

voorbidding *n* intercession

voorbode *n* forerunner; precursor; omen; foreboding

voorbok *n* ringleader

voorbrand *n* firebreak

voordat *prep; adv; conj* before

voordeel *n* advantage; gain; benefit

voordelig *adj* profitable; advantageous

voordeur *n* front door

voordra *vb* to recite; to give a recital; to deliver; to do a turn

voordrag *n* recitation; lecture; speech; recital

vooreergister *adv* three days ago

voorgaan *vb* to precede; to lead; to set an example

voorganger *n* predecessor

voorgee *vb* to pretend; to give odds; to handicap

voorgemelde *adj* above-mentioned

voorgenoemde *adj* above-mentioned

voorgenome *adj* intended; proposed

voorgereg *n* first course

voorgeskrewe *adj* prescribed; set

voorgestel *adj* proposed; introduced

voorgeslag *n* ancestors; forefathers

voorgeveg *n* preliminary bout; curtain raiser

voorgevoel *n* premonition; presentiment; foreboding

voorgrond *n* foreground

voorhamer *n* sledgehammer

voorhande *adv* in stock; on hand

voorhangsel *n* curtain; veil

voorheen *adv* formerly; in the past

voorhistories *adj* prehistoric

voorhoede *n* vanguard; advance guard; forward line

voorhof *n* forecourt

voorhoof *n* forehead

voorhou *vb* to present; to hold before

voorhuis *n* lounge; sitting room; drawing room

vooringenome *adj* prejudiced; bias(s)ed

voorjaar *n* spring

voorkamer *n* front room; sitting room; drawing room

voorkant *n* front; face

voorkeer *vb* to bar; to prevent; to block

voorkeur *n* preference

voorkom[1] *vb* to occur; to appear; to seem; to get ahead

voorkom[2] *vb* to prevent; to forestall

voorkome *npl* appearance; bearing; looks

voorkomend[1] *adj* obliging; affable

voorkomend[2] *adj* occurring

voorkomsveranderingsessie *n* makeover session

voorlaaste *adj* penultimate; last but one

voorland *n* fate; destiny

voorlê *vb* to submit; to lay before

voorlees *vb* to read aloud

voorletter *n* initial (letter)

voorliefde *n* preference; predisposition

voorlig *vb* to enlighten

voorloper *n* forerunner; leader

voorlopig *adj* provisional; preliminary

voormalig *adj* former
voorman *n* leader; foreman
voormiddag *n* forenoon; morning
voornaam *n* first name; christian name; forename
voornaamwoord *n* pronoun
voorneem *vb* to resolve; to determine
voorneme *n* intention; resolve
vooroordeel *n* prejudice
voorouers *n* ancestors
voorportaal *n* hall; lobby; foyer
voorpos *n* outpost
voorpraat *vb* to stick up for; to side with
voorpunt *adj* (*informal*) edgy
voorraad *n* stock; provision; stores
voorraadopname *n* stocktaking
voorrang *n* preference; precedence
voorrede *n* preface; foreword
voorreg *n* privilege; prerogative
voorruit *n* windscreen
voorsê *vb* to prompt
voorsetsel *n* preposition
voorsien *vb* to provide; to supply; to stock; to foresee; to anticipate
voorsit *vb to* preside; to take the chair
voorsitster *n* chairwoman
voorsitter *n* president; chairman
voorskiet *vb* to advance; to lend
voorskoot *n* apron; pinafore
voorskot *n* advance; loan
voorskrif *n* prescription; instruction
voorskryf (*or* **voorskrywe**) *vb* to prescribe (medicine, books)
voorslag *n* whiplash
voorsmaak *n* (fore)taste
voorsnybuffet *n* carvery
voorsnyery *n* carvery
voorsorg *n* precaution; care; provision
voorspel[1] *n* overture; prelude
voorspel[2] *vb* to predict; to prophesy; to foretell
voorspelling *n* prophecy; prediction
voorspoed *n* prosperity
voorspoedig *adj* prosperous; successful
voorspooksel *n* bad omen
voorspraak *n* mediation; intercession
voorsprong *n* advantage; start
voorstad *n* suburb
voorstander *n* promotor; champion; advocate

voorste *adj* first; foremost
voorstedelik *adj* suburban
voorstel *n* proposal; proposition; suggestion; *vb* to propose; to move; to introduce
voorsteller *n* proposer; mover
voorstelling *n* presentation
voortaan *adv* henceforth; from now on
voortbestaan *n* survival
voortbrengsel *n* product
voortbring *vb* to produce; to bring forth; to generate
voortdurend *adj* continuous; lasting; incessant; *adv* continually; incessantly
voorteken *n* omen; sign; symptom
voortgaan *vb* to continue; to proceed
voortgang *n* progress
voortou *n* lead
voortplant *vb* to propagate; to transmit
voortreflik *adj* excellent; first rate
voortrek *vb* to favour; to prefer
voorts *adv* further; besides
voortsit *vb* to continue; to carry on
voortspruit *vb* to arise; to spring from
voortvarend *adj* impulsive; impetuous
voortvloei *vb* to result; to arise
voortyds *adv* formerly
vooruit *adj, adv* beforehand; forward; ahead
vooruit betaal *vb* to pay in advance
vooruitbetaalbaar *adj* payable in advance
vooruitgaan *vb* to proceed; to get on; to make progress; to improve
vooruitgang *n* progress; advancement; improvement
vooruitkom *vb* to get on
vooruitloop *vb* to go first; to outdistance; to anticipate
vooruitsien *vb* to look ahead; to foresee
vooruitsig *n* prospect; outlook
vooruitskat *vb* to forecast
vooruitskatting *n* forecast
vooruitstrewend *adj* progressive
voorvader *n* ancestor; forefather
voorvaderlik *adj* ancestral
voorval *n* event; occurrence; incident; *vb* to take place; to occur
voorvegter *n* champion
voorvoegsel *n* prefix

voorwaar *adv* indeed; truly; in truth
voorwaarde *n* condition; stipulation
voorwaardelik *adj* conditional
voorwaarts *adj, adv* forward
voorwedstryd *n* curtain raiser
voorwendsel *n* pretext; pretence
voorwerp *n* object; article
voorwiel *n* front wheel
voorwielaandrywing *n* front-wheel drive
voorwoord *n* preface; foreword
voos *adj* spongy; pulpy; sickly
vorder *vb* to progress; to demand
vordering *n* progress; claim; demand
vorentoe *adj* forward; *adv* forward; in the front; to the fore
vorige *adj* former; past; last
vorm *n* form; shape; mould; *vb* to shape; to form; to mould
vorming *n* formation; moulding
vormlik *adj* formal; conventional
vors[1] *n* ridge (roof)
vors[2] *n* monarch; prince; ruler; sovereign
vors[3] *vb* to investigate; to search
vorstelik *adj* princely
vorstehuis *n* dynasty
vos *n* fox
vosperd *n* bay horse
vou *n* fold; crease; *vb* to fold; to pleat
voudeur *n* folding-door
voukatel *n* stretcher
voustoel *n* camp chair; folding chair
vra *vb* to ask; to question; to query; to interrogate
vraag *n* question; query; request; demand
vraagstuk *n* problem; question
vraagteken *n* question mark; query
vraat *n* glutton
vraeboek *n* catechism
vraelys *n* questionnaire
vraestel *n* exam paper
vrag *n* load; cargo; fare; rate
vragbrief *n* bill of lading; consignment note
vragmotor *n* lorry; truck
vragskip *n* cargo vessel; freighter
vragvry *adj* carriage paid; post free
vrank *adj* acrid; acid; tart; astringent
vrat *n* wart
vrede *n* peace; quiet; calm
vredeliewend *adj* peace-loving
vrederegter *n* justice of the peace

vredesproses *n* peace process
vredig *adj* peaceful; quiet
vreedsaam *adj* calm; peaceful
vreemd *adj* strange; unusual; foreign; alien; **in die —e** *adv* abroad
vreemdeling *n* stranger; foreigner
vrees *n* fear; apprehension; dread; scare; *vb* to fear; to dread; **— aanjaag** *vb* to frighten
vreeslik *adj* terrible; horrible; *adv* terribly; awfully
vreesagtig *adj* timid; afraid
vreeslik *adj* fearful; terrible; dreadful; *adv* terribly; awfully
vreet *vb* to eat (animals); to devour
vrek[1] *n* miser
vrek[2] *vb* to die (animals)
vrek[3] *adv* extremely
vreug(de) *n* joy; gladness
vriend *n* friend
vriendelik *adj* kind; friendly
vriendin *n* female friend
vriendskap *n* friendship; favour
vriendskaplik *adj* friendly; amicable
vries *vb* to freeze
vriesbrand *n* frostbite
vriespunt *n* freezing point
vroedvrou *n* midwife
vroeër *adj* former; late; *adv* formerly; previously; **— of later** *adv* sooner or later
vroeg *adj* early; timely; **— -vroeg** *adj* very early
vroegtydig *adv* in good time; early
vroetel *vb* to wallow; to root up (soil); to burrow
vroetelpappie *n* sugar daddy
vrolik *adj* merry; cheerful
vrolikheid *n* cheerfulness; merriment; hilarity; mirth
vroom *adj* pious; devout; saintly
vroomheid *n* piety; devoutness
vrot *vb* to rot; to decay; to putrefy; *adj* rotten; decayed; putrid
vrou *n* woman; wife
vrouearts *n* gynaecologist
vrouehater *n* misogynist; woman-hater
vroulik *adj* female; womanly; feminine
vroumens *n* woman; female
vrouevryheid *n* women's lib(eration)
vrug *n* result; effect
vrugafdrywing *n* abortion

vrugbaar *adj* fruitful; prolific; fertile
vrugreg *n* royalty (mining)
vrugte *n* fruit; results
vrugteboord *n* orchard
vrugteloos *adj* fruitless; *adv* fruitlessly; in vain
vrugtesap *n* fruit juice
vrugteslaai *n* fruit salad
vry[1] *vb* to woo; to court; to flirt
vry[2] *adj* free; bold; off duty
Vrydag *n* Friday
vrydenker *n* freethinker
vryer *n* suitor; lover
vryerasie *n* courting; flirtation
vryery *n* (*informal*) snog
vryf (*or* **vrywe**) *vb* to rub; to massage; to polish
vrygeestig *adj* freethinking
vrygeleide *n* safe conduct
vrygesel *n* bachelor
vrygewig *adj* generous; liberal
vryhandel *n* free trade
vryheid *n* freedom; liberty
vryheidvegter *n* freedom fighter
vryhoogte *n* clearance
vryhou *vb* to keep free
vrykamer *n* spare room
vrylaat *vb* to release; to liberate
vrylating *n* release; liberation
vryloop[1] *vb* to get off; to escape punishment
vryloop[2] *vb* to freewheel
vrymaak *vb* to liberate; to set free
vrymesselaar *n* freemason
vrymesselary *n* freemasonry
vrymoedig *adj* frank; candid
vrymoedigheid *n* frankness; candour
vrypag *n* freehold
vrypleit *vb* to exonerate
vrypos *n* free post
vrypostig *adj* bold; presumptuous
vrysinnig *adj* liberal
vryskut *n* freelance work
vryspreek *vb* to acquit; to discharge
vryspring *vb* to escape; to get off free
vrystel *vb* to exempt; to let off
vrystelling *n* exemption
vrywaar *vb* to protect; to guard
vrywe *see* **vryf**
vrywil *vb* to volunteer
vrywillig *adj* voluntary

vrywilliger *n* volunteer
vuil *adj* dirty; nasty; foul; obscene
vuilgoed *n* rubbish; dirt; weeds
vuis *n* fist
vuisgeveg *n* boxing match
vuisslag *n* punch
vul[1] *n* foal; filly; colt
vul[2] *vb* to fill; to stuff
vulkaan *n* volcano
vulkanies *adj* volcanic
vullis *n* rubbish; trash
vullishoop *n* rubbish dump
vullisblik *n* rubbish bin; trash can
vulpen *n* fountain pen
vurig *adj* fiery; passionate; fervent
vurk *n* fork
vurkhyswa *n* fork-lift truck
vuur *n* fire; flame; ardour
vuurherd *n* hearth; grate
vuurhoutjie *n* match
vuurmaakplek *n* fireplace; hearth
vuurpyl *n* rocket (firework, distress signal, etc.)
vuurpylrigter *n* rocket launcher
vuurslag *n* cigarette lighter
vuurspuwend *adj* volcanic; belching fire
vuurtoring *n* lighthouse
vuurvas *adj* fireproof
vuurvlieg *n* firefly
vuurvreter *n* fire-eater; hothead
vuurwapen *n* firearm
vuurwarm *adj* very hot
vuurwerk *n* firework
VV *see* **veldvoertuig**
VVK *see* **vigsverwantekompleks**
vy *n* fig
vyand *n* enemy
vyandelik *adj* hostile
vyandig *adj* hostile; antagonistic
vyf *n, determiner* five
vyfde *n, adj* fifth
vyfhoek *n* pentagon
vyftien *n, determiner* fifteen
vyftiende *n, adj* fifteenth
vyftig *n, determiner* fifty
vyftigste *n, adj* fiftieth
vyfuur *n, adj* five o'clock
vyl *n* file; *vb* to file
vysel *n* mortar
vyselstamper *n* pestle
vywer *n* pond; pool

W

wa *n* wagon; carriage; coach; truck
waad *vb* to wade; to ford
waag *vb* to risk; to venture; to stake
waagarties *n* stuntman
waaghals *n* daredevil; reckless person
waaghans *n* (*informal*) chancer
waagmoed *n* valour; pluck; daring
waagsport *n* extreme sports
waagstuk *n* risky undertaking
waai *vb* to blow; to fan
waaier *n* fan
waaierband *n* fan belt
waak *vb* to watch; to be awake
waakeenheid *n* intensive care unit
waaksaam *adj* watchful; vigilant
waan *n* delusion
waansin *n* insanity; madness
waansinnig *adj* insane; deranged; demented; distracted
waanwys *adj* conceited; presumptuous; opinionated
waar[1] *adj* true; real; genuine
waar[2] *adv* where
waar[3] *conj* whereas; since
waaraan *rel pron* on which; of whom
waaragter *inter pron* behind what
waaragtig *adv* truly
waarbo *rel pron* above which; over which; above whom; over whom; *inter pron* above what; over what
waarborg *n* warranty; guarantee; *vb* to guarantee; to warrant; to safeguard
waarby *rel pron* near which; near whom
waarde *n* value; worth
waardeer *vb* to value; to appraise; to assess; to appreciate
waardeerder *n* valuator; assessor; appraiser
waardering *n* regard; esteem
waardeur *inter pron* through what; *rel pron* through which
waardevol *adj* valuable; of great value
waardig *adj* worthy; dignified
waardigheid *n* dignity
waarheen *rel pron* where; to where
waarheid *n* truth; reality
waarin *inter pron* in what; in which

waarlangs *rel pron* along which
waarlik *adv* truly; really
waarmaak *vb* to confirm; to prove
waarmee *rel pron* with what; with which
waarmerk *n* stamp; seal; hallmark; *vb* to stamp; to hallmark; to certify
waarna *conj* after which
waarnaas *inter pron* beside what; next to what; *rel pron* beside which; next to which
waarnatoe *inter pron* where to; *rel pron* to which
waarneem *vb* to observe; to perform; to perceive
waarnemend *adj* acting; temporary
waarneming *n* observation; perception; substitution
waarom *inter pron* why; what for; *rel pron* round which
waaromtrent *inter pron* about what; *rel pron* about which
waaronder *inter pron* among what; under what; *rel pron* among whom; under which
waaroor *inter pron* about what; over what; *rel pron* about which; over which
waarop *inter pron* on what; *rel pron* on which
waarsê *vb* to tell fortunes; to foretell
waarsêer *n* fortune-teller; palmist; soothsayer
waarsku *vb* to warn; to caution
waarskuwing *n* warning; (text) alert
waarskynlik *adj* probable; likely
waarso *adv* where
waarsonder *inter pron* without what; *rel pron* without which
waarteen *inter pron* against what; *rel pron* against which
waartoe *inter pron* for what; *rel pron* to which
waartussen *inter pron* between which; among which; *rel pron* between which; among which
waaruit *inter pron* out of what; from

what; *rel pron* out of which; from which

waarvan *inter pron* of what; about what; *rel pron* whose; of which; about which

waarvoor *inter pron* why; for what; of what; *rel pron* for which; before which

waas *n* haze

waatlemoen (*or* **waterlemoen**) *n* watermelon

waenhuis *n* coach house; cart shed

wafel *n* waffle; wafer

wag *n* sentry; guard; watch; *vb* to wait; to expect; **— 'n bietjie** wait a bit; wait a moment

waggel *vb* to stagger; to totter; to reel

waghond *n* guard dog; watchdog

wagkamer *n* waiting room

waglys *n* waiting list

wagter *n* watchman; shepherd

wagwoord *n* password; parole

wakend *adj* vigilant; alert

waker *n* watcher

wakker *adj* awake; alive; vigilant

waks *n* shoe polish; boot polish

wal *n* bank; shore; embankment

walg *vb* to loathe; to disgust

walglik *adj* nauseating; disgusting

walm *n* thick smoke

walrus *n* walrus

wals *n* waltz; roller; *vb* to waltz; to dance; to roll

walvis *n* whale

wan *vb* to winnow

wanaangepas *adj* maladjusted

wanbegrip *n* misconception

wanbesteding *n* misappropriation; embezzlement

wanbestuur *n* mismanagement; misgovernment

wanbetaling *n* nonpayment; default

wand *n* wall

wandaad *n* misdeed; outrage

wandel *n* walk; conduct; behaviour; *vb* to walk; to take a walk

wandelaar *n* walker; pedestrian; hiker

wandeling *n* walk; stroll

wandellaan *n* mall (pedestrian, shopping)

wang *n* cheek

wangbeen *n* cheekbone

wangedrag *n* misbehaviour; misconduct

wanguns *n* envy

wanhoop *n* despair; *vb* to despair

wanhopig *adj* despairing; desperate

wankel *vb* to waver; to vacillate; to stagger; to totter

wankelmoedig *adj* undecided; wavering; irresolute

wanklank *n* discord; dissonance

wanneer *adv* when; if

wanorde *n* confusion; disorder

wanpraktyk *n* malpractice

wanskape *adj* misshapen; deformed

wanstaltig *adj* misshapen; deformed

want *conj* for; as for; because

wantrou *n* distrust; mistrust; suspicion; *vb* to distrust; to suspect; **mosie van —e** *n* motion of no confidence

wanvoeding *n* malnutrition

wapen *n* weapon; arm(s); coat of arms; crest; badge; *vb* to arm

wapenopslagplek *n* arms cache

wapenstilstand *n* truce; armistice

wapentuig *n* arms; weaponry

wapper *vb* to flutter; to float; to fly

warboel *n* muddle; confusion; mix-up

ware *npl* goods; wares; commodities

warm *vb* to warm; *adj* warm

warmte *n* warmth; heat; ardour

warrel *vb* to whirl; to swirl; to reel

warrelwind *see* **dwarrelwind**

wartaal *n* gibberish

was[1] *n* wax

was[2] *n* washing; *vb* to wash

was[3] *vb* to grow; to increase; **die —sende maan** *n* the waxing moon

was[4] *see* **wees**

wasbak *n* sink; wash-hand basin

wasem *n* steam; vapour; breath

wasgoed *n* washing

wasmasjien *n* washing machine

wasoutomaat *n* automatic washing machine

waspoeier *n* soap powder

wasser (*or* **waster**) *n* washer (ring, disc)

wasseret *n* launderette; laundromat

wassery *n* laundry

waster *see* **wasser**

wat *inter pron* what; *rel pron* who; that;

which; what; *indef pron* something; whatever

water *n* water; *vb* to water
wateragtig *adj* watery
waterbestand *adj* water-resistant
waterdig *adj* waterproof; watertight;
waterdraer *n* water carrier
waterhoof *n* hydrocephalus
waterhoos *n* waterspout
waterig *adj* watery; wishy-washy
waterlei *vb* to irrigate
waterlemoen *see* **waatlemoen**
waternat *adj* soaked (to the skin); wet through
waterpas *n* spirit level
waterpokkies *n* chickenpox
waterponie *n* jet ski
waterryk *adj* well-watered
waterski *n* water-ski
waterskilpad *n* turtle
waterstof *n* hydrogen
waterstofbom *n* hydrogen bomb
watersug *n* dropsy
waterval *n* waterfall
waterverf *n* watercolour
waterverfskildery *n* watercolour painting
waterwerend *n* water resistant
waterwyser *n* water diviner
watte *n* wadding; cotton wool
watter *determiner, pron* what; which
web *n* web
webdagboek *n* blog
webinskrywer *n* blogger
webjoernaal *n* blog
webtuiste *n* website
wed *vb* to bet; to wager
weddenskap *n* wager; bet
wedder *n* punter (horse racing); bookie (horse racing)
wedergeboorte *n* regeneration; rebirth
wederhelf *n* better half; spouse
wederkerig *adj* mutual; reciprocal
we(d)erkoms *n* return
wederliefde *n* mutual love
we(d)eropstanding *n* resurrection
wederparty *n* opponent; adversary
wederregtelik *adj* unlawful; illegal
we(d)erspannig *adj* rebellious; refractory
wedersyds *adj* mutual; reciprocal

wedervergelding *n* retaliation
wedloop *n* race (athletics)
wedren *n* race (cars, horses)
wedstryd *n* match; competition; contest
weduvrou (*or* **weduwee**) *n* widow
wedvaart *n* boat race
wedvlug *n* air race
wedywer *n* rivalry; competition; *vb* to vie; to rival; to compete
wee *n* woe; grief; pain
weef (*or* **wewe**) *vb* to weave
weefmasjien *n* loom
weefsel *n* tissue; texture; fabric
weefselkultuur *n* tissue culture
weeg *vb* to balance
weegskaal *n* scales; balance
week[1] *n* week
week[2] *vb* to soak; to steep in
week[3] *adj* soft; weak; tender
weekblad *n* weekly paper
weekdag *n* weekday
weekhartig *adj* tender; soft-hearted
weekliks *adj, adv* weekly
weekloon *n* weekly wages
weelde *n* luxury; abundance; wealth
weelderig *adj* luxuriant; luxurious
weeluis *n* bedbug
weemoed *n* melancholy; sadness
weemoedig *adj* sad; melancholy
ween *vb* to weep; to cry
weens *prep* on account of; concerning
weer[1] *n* weather
weer[2] *vb* to exert oneself; to defend
weer[3] *adv* again; once more; for a second time
weerbaar *adj* fit; able-bodied
weerbaarheid *n* preparedness
weerbarstig *adj* unruly; rebellious
weerberig *n* weather report
weerga *n* match; equal; peer
weergalm *vb* to echo; to reverberate
weergalming *n* echo; reverberation; *vb* to echo; to reverberate
weergaloos *adj* matchless; unequalled; unrivalled
weergawe *n* reproduction
weerglas *n* barometer
weerhaak *n* barb; barbed hook
weerhaan *n* weathercock
weerhou *vb* to restrain; to keep back; to hold back; to abstain

weerkaats *vb* to reflect; to resound
weerkaatsing *n* reflection
weerklank *n* echo; resonance
weerkunde *n* meteorology
weerlê *vb* to refute; to disprove
weerlig *n* lightning
weerloos *adj* defenceless
weermag *n* defence force; armed forces
weerman *n* private (army); serviceman
weersien *vb* to meet again
weersin *n* dislike; aversion
weerskante *adv* on both sides
weerskyn *n* reflection
weerspieël *vb* to reflect; to mirror
weerspreek *vb* to contradict
weerstaan *vb* to resist; to withstand
weerstand *n* resistance; opposition
weerstrewe *vb* to oppose; to thwart
weervas *adj* all-weather; **—te baan** *n* all-weather court
weervoorspelling *n* weather forecast
weerwil: in — van in spite of
weerwolf *n* werewolf
weerwraak *n* revenge
wees[1] *n* orphan
wees[2] *vb* to be
weeshuis *n* orphanage
weeskind *n* orphan
weet *vb* to know; to be aware of
weetal *n* know-all
weetgierig *adj* inquisitive; eager to learn
weg[1] *n* way; road; path
weg[2] *adj, adv* lost; gone; away
wegbly *vb* to stay away
wegbring *vb* to take away
wegdoen *vb* to dispose of
wegdoenbaar *adj* disposable
wegdraai *vb* to turn away; to branch off
weggaan *vb* to leave; to go away
weggooi *vb* to throw away; to lose
weghardloop *vb* to run away; to flee
wegjaag *vb* to chase away; to drive off; to expel
wegkruip *vb* to crawl away; to hide oneself
wegkruipertjie *n* hide-and-seek (game)
weglaat *vb* to omit
weglok *vb* to lure
wegloop *vb* to walk off; to run away; to desert

wegloper *n* deserter; runaway
wegneem *vb* to take away; to remove
wegneemete *n* take away (food)
wegraak *vb* to get lost
wegruim *vb* to clear away
wegskram *vb* to ricochet; to shy away; to evade
wegskuil *vb* to hide
wegsmyt *vb* to throw away
wegspoel *vb* to wash away
wegspring *vb* to jump away; to start off
wegstap *vb* to walk away
wegsteek *vb* to hide; to retain
wegsterf (*or* **wegsterwe**) *vb* to die away
wegtrek *vb* to pull away; to depart; to leave
wegvreet *vb* to corrode; to eat away
wegwyser *n* guide; signpost
wei *n* meadow; pasture; *vb* to feed; to graze (animals, people)
weiding *n* grazing; pasturage
weier *vb* to refuse; to decline
weiering *n* refusal
weifel *vb* to waver
weifeling *n* indecision; hesitation
weiland *n* pasturage; grazing
weinig *adj* little; few
wek *vb* to rouse; to wake; to stir
wekker *n* alarm clock
wekroep *n* clarion call; slogan
wel *adv* well; good
welbehaaglik *adj* comfortable; pleasant
welbehae *n* comfort; pleasure
welbekend *adj* well-known
weldaad *n* kindness
weldadig *adj* charitable; benevolent
weldadigheid *n* charity; beneficence
weldeurdag *adj* well-considered; well-thought-out
weldoen *vb* to do good
weldoener *n* benefactor
weldra *adv* soon; presently
weledel *adj* honourable
weleer *adv* formerly
weleerwaarde *adj* reverend
welf *n* arch; vault
welgeleë *adj* well-situated
welgeluksalig *adj* blessed

welgemanierd *adj* well-behaved
welgemoed *adj* cheerful; contented
welgeskape *adj* well-formed
welgesteld *adj* affluent; wealthy
welgevalle *n* pleasure; liking
welig *adj* lush; luxuriant
welke *inter pron* which; what
welkom *adj* welcome; acceptable
wellewend *adj* well-mannered; courteous
wellig *adv* perhaps
welluidend *adj* melodious
wellus *n* sensuality; lust; delight
wellustig *adj* voluptuous; sensual
welmenend *adj* well-meaning; sincere
welp *n* whelp; cub
welsand (*or* **wilsand**) *n* quicksand
welslae *n* success
welsprekend *adj* eloquent; articulate
welstand *n* wellbeing; health; welfare
welsyn *n* wellbeing; welfare
welvaart *n* welfare; prosperity; boom
welvarend *adj* prosperous; wealthy
welvoeglik *adj* proper; becoming; decent
welwillend *adj* favourable; friendly
welwillendheid *n* kindness; benevolence
wemel *vb* to swarm; to teem (with)
wen *vb* to win; to gain
wenakker *n* headland
wend *vb* to turn
wending *n* turn
wenk *n* hint; sign; tip
wenner *n* winner
wens *n* wish; desire; *vb* to wish; to desire
wenslik *adj* desirable
wentel *vb* to turn; to revolve; to orbit
wentelbaan *n* orbit
wenteltrap *n* spiral staircase
werd *n* worth
wêreld *n* world; earth; globe
wêreldberoemd *adj* world-famous
wêreldburger *n* cosmopolitan
wêrelddeel *n* continent
wêreldlik *adj* worldly; temporal; secular
wêrelds *adj* worldly; secular
wêreldstad *n* metropolis
wêreldtaal *n* universal language
wêreldwyd *adj* worldwide

wêreldwys *adj* worldly-wise
werf[1] *n* yard; farmyard; shipyard
werf[2] *vb* (*or* **werwe**) to enlist; to enrol; to recruit
werk *n* work; labour; employment; *vb* to work; to labour; to operate
werkbevrediging *n* job satisfaction
werk(s)dag *n* working day; weekday
werkloos *adj* unemployed; idle; inactive
werker *n* worker
werkesel *n* drudge
werkgewer *n* employer
werkgewersburo *n* employment agency
werk(s)groep *n* workshop (training)
werking *n* efficacy; action; working
werklik *adj* real; actual; *adv* really
werkloon *n* pay; wages
werkloos *adj* unemployed; idle; inactive
werkloosheid *n* unemployment
werk(s)man *n* workman; labourer
werknemer *n* employee
werkolis *n* workaholic
werksaam *adj* active; industrious; working; employed
werksessie *n* workshop (training)
werkslaaf *n* workaholic
werksoeker *n* job seeker
werkstaking *n* strike
werktuig *n* tool; implement
werktuigkunde *n* mechanics
werktuigkundig *adj* mechanical
werktuigkundige *n* mechanic
werktuiglik *adj* mechanical
werk(s)verrigting *n* job performance
werk(s)winkel *n* workshop
werkwoord *n* verb
werp *vb* to throw; to fling; to cast
werpsel *n* litter
werpskyf *n* discus; quoit
werpspies *n* javelin
werwe *see* **werf**[2]
werwel *n* vertebra
werwing *n* recruitment; canvassing
wes *adj, adv* west
wese *n* being; essence; nature
wesel *n* weasel; mink
wesen(t)lik *adj* essential; substantial; real

wesenloos *adj* vacant; blank; expressionless

wesp *n* wasp

wes(te) *n* west; the west; the occident

westelik *adj* westerly; western

westergrens *n* western frontier

westerkim *n* western horizon

Westerling *n* Westerner

wet[1] *n* law; act (law)

wet[2] *vb* to sharpen; to whet

wetboek *n* code (law); — **van strafreg** *n* penal code

wete *n* knowledge

wetenskap *n* scientific knowledge; science

wetenskaplik *adj* scientific

wetenskaplike *n* scientist

wetenskapfiksie *n* science fiction

wetenswaardig *adj* worth knowing; interesting

wet(s)geleerde *n* lawyer

wetgewend *adj* legislative; **—e liggaam** *n* legislature

wetgewing *n* legislation; legislature

wetlik *adj* legal; statutory

wetsartikel *n* article; clause of a law

wetsgehoorsaam *adj* law-abiding

wetsontwerp *n* bill; draft act

wetstoepassing *n* law enforcement

wetteloos *adj* lawless

wettig *vb* to legalize; to justify; *adj* legal; lawful; legitimate

wewenaar *n* widower

wewe *see* **weef**

wewer *n* weaver

wie *inter pron* who; whom; *indef pron* (he) who

wieg *n* cradle; cot; *vb* to rock; to lull

wiegelied *n* lullaby

wiegiedood *n* Sudden Infant Death Syndrome (SIDS); cot death

wiel *n* wheel

wieldop *n* hubcap

wielsporing *n* wheel alignment

wier *n* seaweed

wierook *n* incense

wig *vb* to wedge

wik *vb* to reflect; to weigh up

wikkel *vb* to envelop; to wrap; to engage; to totter

wil *n* will; desire; wish; *vb* to will; to desire; to want

wild *n* game; *adj* wild; savage; fierce

wilddief *n* poacher

wildebees (*or* **gnu**) *n* wildebeest; gnu

wildernis *n* wilderness

wildskut *n* hunter

wildstroper *n* poacher

wildvreemd *adj* quite strange

wildwagter *n* game ranger

wilg (*or* **wilger** *or* **wilge[r]boom**) *n* willow (tree)

willekeurig *adj* despotic; arbitrary

willig *adj* willing; ready

wilsand *see* **welsand**

wilskrag *n* willpower

wimpel *n* pennant; streamer

wimper *n* eyelash

wind *n* wind; breeze; flatulence

windbuks *n* airgun; pellet gun; boaster; windbag

winderig *adj* windy

windhoos *n* whirlwind; tornado

windmeul *n* windmill

windplaas *n* wind farm

windskeef *adj* skew; lopsided

windstilte *n* calm; doldrums

windtonnel *n* wind tunnel

windvlaag *n* squall; gust of wind

windwyster *n* weathercock

wingerd *n* vineyard

wingerdgriep *n* hangover

wingerdstok *n* vine

wink *n* wink; *vb* to wink; to beckon

winkbrou *n* eyebrow

winkel *n* shop; store

winkeldiefstal *n* shoplifting

winkelhaak *n* set square; try square

winkelier *n* shopkeeper; dealer

winkelprys *n* selling price

winkelsentrum *n* shopping centre

winkeltande *n* false teeth; dentures

wins *n* gain; profit

winsgewend *adj* profitable; lucrative

winsgrens *n* profit margin

winskoop *n* bargain

winter *n* winter

winterslaap *n* hibernation

wip *n* trap; snare; seesaw; *vb* to seesaw; to go up and down; to skip; to hop; to tilt; to tip

wipmat *n* trampoline

wipneus *n* turned-up nose

wipplank *n* seesaw

wipstert *n* wagtail

wiptuig *n* jolly jumper

wis[1] *vb* to wipe

wis[2] *adj* certain; sure

wiskunde *n* mathematics

wiskundig *adj* mathematical

wispelturig *adj* fickle; capricious

wissel *n* bill of exchange; draft; points; switch (railway); *vb* to exchange; to give change; to alter

wisselaar *n* money changer; interchange

wisselbou *n* crop rotation

wisselfonds *n* cash float

wisselkoers *n* exchange rate

wisselkruising *n* traffic interchange

wisselstroom *n* alternating current

wisselvallig *adj* uncertain; changeable; variable

wisser *n* wiper; eraser

wit *adj, n* white; *vb* to whitewash

witblits *n* grape brandy; mampoer

witbont *adj* white-spotted; piebald

witlood *n* white lead

witseerkeel *n* diphtheria

wittebroodsdae *n* honeymoon

witwortel *n* parsnip

woed *vb* to rage; to wreak havoc

woede *n* rage; fury

woedend *adj* infuriated; furious; violent

woefie *n* dog; doggie

woefietuiste *npl* kennels

woeker *n* usury; *vb* to practise usury

woekeraar *n* usurer

woekerplant *n* parasite

woel *vb* to fidget; to be restless; to work hard

woelwater *n* fidget

woelig *adj* fidgety; restless

Woensdag *n* Wednesday

woes *adj* waste; desolate; wild; savage; ferocious

woestaard *n* brute; ruffian

woesteny *n* wilderness; wasteland

woestyn *n* desert

wol *n* wool

wolagtig *adj* woolly

wolf *n* wolf

wolk *n* cloud

wolkekrabber *n* skyscraper

wolkbreuk *n* cloudburst

wolkombers *n* woollen blanket

wollerig *adj* woolly

wolwegif *n* strychnine

wond *n* wound; *vb* to wound; to hurt; to grieve

wonder *n* wonder; marvel; *vb* to wonder

wonderkind *n* child prodigy

wonderlik *adj* peculiar; strange; curious; wonderful; marvellous

wonderwerk *n* miracle

woning *n* residence; dwelling

woon *vb* to dwell; to reside; to live

woonbuurt *n* residential area

woongebied *n* township

woonhuis *n* residence; home

woonkamer *n* sitting room; living room

woonstel *n* flat

woonwa *n* caravan

woord *n* word; term

woordbreuk *n* breach of promise

woordeboek *n* dictionary

woordeboekmaker *n* lexicographer

woordelik *adj* literal; verbatim

woordeskat *n* vocabulary

woordewisseling *n* dispute; debate

woordskittery *n* verbal diarrhoea

woordspeling *n* pun; wordplay

woordverklaring *n* definition of a word; explanation of a word

woordverwerker *n* word processor

woordvoerder *n* spokesman; spokeswoman; spokesperson

word *vb* to take place; to become; to get (angry, etc.); to fall (silent, etc.)

wors *n* sausage

worsbroodjie *n* hot dog

worsrolletjie *n* sausage roll

worstel *vb* to wrestle; to struggle

worsteling *n* struggle; wrestle

wortel *n* root; origin; carrot; *vb* to take root

woud *n* wood; forest

wouterklouter *n* jungle gym

wraak *n* revenge; vengeance

wraakgierig *adj* vengeful; vindictive

wraaksugtig *adj* vindictive; vengeful

wrak *n* wreck; derelict

wrakwerf *n* scrap yard

wreed *adj* cruel; inhuman; barbarous

wreedaard *n* brute; cruel person
wreedheid *n* cruelty
wreek *vb* to revenge; to avenge
wrewel *n* resentment; annoyance; spite
wrewelig *adj* cross; resentful; spiteful
wriemel *vb* to wriggle; to swarm
wring *vb* to wring (hands, cloth); to twist
wrintie (*or* **wrintig**) *adv* indeed; actually; really
wroeging *n* remorse; compunction
wrok *n* grudge; rancour
wrywing *n* friction
wuif (*or* **wuiwe**) *vb* to wave; to beckon
wulps *adj* wanton; lascivious; sexy
wurg *vb* to strangle; to throttle; to choke
wurggreep *n* stranglehold
wurgketting *n* choke chain
wurgroof *vb* to mug
wurgsiekte *n* croup
wurm *n* worm; maggot; grub
wyd *adj* wide; spacious; large; broad
wydlopig *adj* verbose; wordy; long-winded
wydsbeen *adj* astride; astraddle
wydte *n* width; breadth
wyf *n* vixen; shrew; mean woman
wyfie *n* female (of animals)
wyk[1] *n* area; district
wyk[2] *vb* to withdraw; to yield; to give way
wyl[1] *n* instant; moment; short time
wyl[2] *conj* since; as; because
wyle *adj* late; deceased

wyn *n* wine
wynbou *n* wine growing; viticulture
wynkelder *n* wine cellar; winery
wynkelkie *n* wineglass
wynoes *n* vintage
wynstok *n* vine
wynvat *n* wine barrel; wine cask
wys[1] *n* manner; custom; way; mood (grammar)
wys[2] *vb* to show; to indicate; to demonstrate; to direct
wys[3] *adj* wise; prudent; impertinent; obstinate
wysbegeerte *n* philosophy
wyse *n* way; mood (grammar)
wyselik *see* **wyslik**
wyser *see* **wyster**
wysgeer *n* philosopher
wysheid *n* wisdom
wysie *n* melody; tune; air
wysig *vb* to amend; to modify; to alter
wysiging *n* amendment; modification; alteration
wyslik *adv* wisely
wysmaak *vb* to make believe; to impose on
wysneus *n* wiseacre; prig
wyster (*or* **wyser**) *n* pointer (on scales); hand (watch, clock)
wys(t)erplaat *n* dial
wysvinger *n* index finger; forefinger
wyt *vb* to impute; to accuse; to blame
wywater *n* holy water
wywepraatjie *n* idle gossip; silly talk

X

X-bene *npl* bow legs; bandy legs
xenofobie *n* xenophobia
Xhosa *n* Xhosa

xilofoon *n* xylophone
X-straal *n* X-ray

Y

yaleslot *n* yale lock
ydel *adj* vain; frivolous; useless; idle
ydelheid *n* vanity
yk *vb* to test; to adjust; to stamp
yl *adj* thin; rarefied
ylhoofdig *adj* light-headed; delirious
ys[1] *n* ice; *vb* to freeze
ys[2] *vb* to shudder; to shiver
ysbaan *n* ice rink; skating rink
ysbeer *n* polar bear
ysberg *n* iceberg
ysglas *n* frosted glass
ysig *adj* ice-cold
yskas *n* refrigerator; icebox
yskoud *adj* icy; ice-cold

yslik *adj* dreadful; horrible; huge
ysperiode *n* Ice Age; glacial period
ysreën *n* sleet
yssak *n* coolbag
ysskaats *n* ice skating
yster *n* iron
ystergietery *n* ironworks; iron foundry
ysterperd *n* motorcycle; train
ystersaag *n* hacksaw
ystervark *n* porcupine
ysterware *n* hardware; ironmongery
ywer *n* diligence; zeal
yweraar *n* zealot; fanatic
ywerig *adj* diligent; industrious; zealous

Z

zero *adj, n* zero
Zoeloe *n, adj* Zulu; **—-impie** Zulu regiment
Zoeloeland *n* Zululand

zoem *n* buzz(ing); drone; *vb* to buzz; to hum; to drone; to zoom; to whizz; **—in** to zoom in (camera)
zoemlens *n* zoom lens

English–Afrikaans Dictionary

English–Afrikaans

A

a *indefinite article* 'n
abacus *n* telraam
abandon *vb* prysgee; verlaat; afsien
abandoned *adj* verlate
abate *vb* bedaar; verflou
abattoir *n* slagplaas
abbess *n* abdis
abbey *n* abdy; klooster
abbot *n* ab
abbreviate *vb* afkort
abbreviation *n* afkorting; verkorting
abdicate *vb* afstand doen; neerlê
abdication *n* afstanddoening
abdomen *n* maag; buik
abduct *vb* ontvoer
abhor *vb* verafsku; verpes
ability *n* talent; vermoë
abjure *vb* afsweer
ablaze *adj, adv* brandend; vlammend; in ligtelaaie
able *adj* kapabel; knap; bekwaam; normaal; niegestremd; **be** — *vb* kan
able-bodied *adj* weerbaar; kragtig
ably *adv* knap
abnormal *adj* abnormaal
abode *n* verblyf
abolish *vb* afskaf; ophef
abomination *n* gruwel
abortion *n* miskraam; vrugafdrywing
about *adv* ongeveer; omstreeks; omtrent; plusminus; sowat; naastenby; *prep* oor; aangaande; betreffende; — **what** *inter pron* waarvan
above *prep* bo; bokant; — **what** *inter pron* waarbo; waaroor; — **which** *rel pron* waarbo; waaroor; — **whom** *rel pron* waarbo
above-mentioned *adj* voorgemelde; voorgenoemde; bogemelde; bogenoemde
abrasion *n* skaafplek
abridg(e)ment *n* verkorting
abridge *vb* verkort
abridged *adj* beknop; verkort

abroad *adv* anderland; buitelands
abrupt *adj* kortaf; plotseling
abscess *n* sweer; abses
abseil *vb* abseil
absent *adj* afwesig
absent-minded *adj* verstrooi(d); ingedagte; afgetrokke
absent-mindedness *n* verstrooidheid
absolute *adj* volslae; puur; totale
absolutely *adv* volkome; absoluut; opsluit; volstrek
absolution *n* absolusie
absorb *vb* opsuig; absorbeer; indrink
abstain *vb* onthou; weerhou
abstainer *n* afskaffer; onthouer
abstract *adj* abstrak; afgetrokke
absurd *adj* onsinnig; sinloos; absurd
abundance *n* oorvloed; weelde
abundant *adj* oorvloedig; ruim
abundantly *adv* ruim; ruimskoots; oorvloedig
abuse *n* misbruik; *vb* skel
abusive *adj* beledigend; — **language** *n* skel(d)woord
abyss *n* afgrond; kolk
acacia *n* (tree) doringboom; akasia
academy *n* akademie
accelerate *vb* bespoedig; versnel
acceleration *n* versnelling
accent *n* aksent; klem; klemtoon; tongval; *vb* beklemtoon
accept *vb* aanneem; neem; aanvaar
acceptable *adj* aanneemlik; welkom
acceptance *n* aanneming; aanvaarding
accepted *adj* aangenome
access *n* toegang
accessible *adj* toeganklik; genaakbaar
accessories *npl* bybehore; toebehore; benodigdhede
accident *n* ongeluk; ongeval; toeval
accidental *adj* toevallig
accidentally *adv* toevallig
acclaim *n* akklamasie
acclamation *n* akklamasie

acclimatize *vb* inburger; akklimatiseer

accommodate *vb* akkommodeer; herberg

accommodation *n* akkomodasie; huisvesting; tuisplek

accompany *vb* begelei; vergesel; saamgaan

accompanying *adj* meegaande; bygaande

accomplice *n* medepligtige

accomplish *vb* volvoer; volbring

accomplished *adj* volleerd; vaardig

accomplishment *n* totstandbrenging; vaardigheid; prestasie

according to *adv* volgens; na gelang van; ingevolge

accordingly *adv* dienooreenkomstig; ooreenkomstig

accordion *n* harmonika; trekklavier; pensklavier

accost *vb* aanspreek; bydam; toespreek

account *n* berig; verslag; rekenskap; rekening

account for *vb* verantwoord

accountable *adj* toerekenbaar; verantwoordelik

accountancy *n* rekeningkunde

accountant *n* rekeningkundige; rekenmeester

accounting *n* rekeningkunde

accrue *vb* oploop; toeval

accumulate *vb* opeenhoop; ophoop; oploop; opstapel

accurate *adj* akkuraat; noukeurig; strik

accusation *n* aanklag; beskuldiging

accuse *vb* aankla; beskuldig; betig; verkla

accused *n* aangeklaagde; beklaagde; beskuldigde

accuser *n* beskuldiger; aanklaer

accustomed to *adj* gewoond aan; **become — to** *vb* aanwen

ace *n* (playing cards) aas

achar *n* (pickle, relish) atjar

ache *n* pyn; seer

achieve *vb* bereik; presteer

achievement *n* prestasie; totstandbrenging

achiever *n* presteerder

acid *adj* vrank; suur; *n* suur

acid rain *n* suurreën

acknowledge *vb* erken; **— a debt** *vb* beken

acne *n* aknee; vetpuisie

acorn *n* akker

acoustics *n* akoestiek

acquaint *vb* bekend maak; in kennis stel; **be —ed with** *vb* ken

acquaintance *n* bekende; kennis

acquire *vb* aanleer; verkry; verwerf

acquired *adj* aangeleerd

acquisition *n* aanwins

acquit *vb* vryspreek

acquittal *n* ontslag

acre *n* akker

acrid *adj* vrank

acronym *n* letternaam; akroniem

across *adj* dwars; *prep* dwarsoor; oor

acrylic *adj* (fibre) akriel

act *n* daad; handeling; handel; bedryf; akte; (law) wet; *vb* handel; doen; **— as** *vb* fungeer; **— on** *vb* inwerk; **— towards** *vb* bejeën

acting *adj* waarnemend; plaasvervangend; *n* toneelspel

action *n* aksie; daad; handeling; inwerking; saak; werking

active *adj* aktief; bedrywig; werksaam; **to be very —** *vb* spook

actor *n* akteur; speler; toneelspeler

actress *n* aktrise; toneelspeelster

actual *adj* aktueel; werklik

actually *adv* wrintie

acute *adj* akuut; skerp

ad nauseam *adv* tot vervelens toe

adapt oneself *vb* aanpas

ADD *see* **attention deficit disorder**

add *vb* optel; bytel; byvoeg; aanvoeg; aanlas; **— on to** *vb* (by building) aanbou

add-on service *n* byvoegdiens

addendum *n* aanhangsel; addendum

adder *n* adder

addict *n* verslaafde

addicted *adj* verslaaf; **become — to** *vb* verslaaf raak aan

addition *n* aanvulling; toegif; aanvoeging; optelling

additional *adj* addisioneel; ekstra; bykomend

address *n* adres; toespraak; *vb* toespreek; aanspreek

adept *adj* ingewyde
adequate *adj* toereikend; voldoende
ADHD *see* **attention deficit hyperactivity syndrome**
adhere to *vb* vaskleef; aankleef; aanhang; trou bly aan
adherence *n* aanhanger
adherent *n* nakoming; ondersteuning; aanhanger; volgeling
adjacent *adj* aangrensend; nabygeleë
adjectival *adj* byvoeglik
adjective *n* byvoeglike naamwoord; adjektief
adjoin *vb* grens aan
adjoining *adj* aangrensend
adjourn *vb* verdaag; opskort
adjournment *n* verdaging
adjust *vb* aanpas; skik; vereffen
adjustable *adj* verstelbaar; — **spanner** *n* skroefsleutel
adjustment *n* aanpassing; aansuiwering; reëling
adjutant *n* adjudant
administer *vb* beheer; beredder; toedien; bedien
administrate *vb* administreer
administration *n* administrasie; bewind; beheer; (of an oath) eedafneming; (of justice) regspleging
administrator *n* administrateur; (estate) beredderaar
admiral *n* admiraal
admiration *n* bewondering
admire *vb* bewonder
admirer *n* bewonderaar; vereerder
admission *n* hekgeld; toegang; opname; toelating; **No —** (sign) Verbode toegang
admission fee *n* toegangsgeld; intreegeld
admission ticket *n* toegangskaartjie; toegangsbewys
admit *vb* toelaat; inlaat; aanneem
admittance *n* toelating
admonish *vb* teregwys; vermaan
admonition *n* teregwysing; vermaning
ado *n* gedoente
adolescent *n* adolessent; jeudige; *adj* opgeskote; adolessent; jeudig
adopt *vb* aanneem
adopted *adj* aangenome

adoption *n* aanneming
adore *vb* aanbid; vereer
adorn *vb* tooi; mooimaak; behang
adult *n* volwassene; grootmens; *adj* volwasse
adult education *n* onderwys vir volwassenes
adulterate *vb* vervals
adulterer *n* egbreker
adultery *n* egbreuk; owerspel
advance *n* aantog; voorskot; *vb* bevorder
advance guard *n* voorhoede
advance on *vb* aanruk
advanced *adj* gevorder
advancement *n* vooruitgang
advantage *n* voordeel; voorsprong
advantageous *adj* voordelig
adventure *n* avontuur; lotgeval
adventurer *n* avonturier; geluksoeker
adverb *n* bywoord
adverbial *adj* bywoordelik
adversary *n* teenparty; teenstander; wederparty
adverse *adj* ongunstig
adversity *n* teenspoed
advertise *vb* adverteer; aankondig
advertisement *n* advertensie; aankondiging
advertisement balloon *n* advertensieballon
advertising *n* reklame; — **firm** *n* reklamefirma; — **agency** *n* reklameagentskap
advice *n* advies; berig; raad; raadgewing
advisable *adj* raadsaam
advise *vb* aanraai; adviseer
adviser *n* adviseur
advisory *adj* raadgewend
advocate *n* advokaat; voorstander
aerial *n* antenne; lugdraad; — **view** *n* lugblik
aerobic *adj* aërobiese
aerobics *n* aërobiese oefening
aerodrome *n* vliegveld
aeronautics *n* lugvaart
aeroplane *n* vliegmasjien
aerosol *n* spuitkan; aërosolblik
aesthetic(al) *adj* esteties
affable *adj* minsaam; voorkomend

affair *n* affère; spul; spulletjie; geskiedenis; (love) verhouding

affect *vb* aantas; aandoen; ontroer

affectation *n* aanstellerigheid; gemaaktheid

affected *adj* aangedaan; bewoë; aanstellerig; gemaak; gekunsteld

affecting *adj* aandoenlik

affection *n* liefde

affectionate *adj* liefhebbend; toegeneë

affirm *vb* bevestig; verseker

affirmative *adj* toestemmend; — **action** *n* regstellende aksie

affix *n* agtervoegsel; *vb* aanheg

affliction *n* beproewing; besoeking; kruis

affluence *n* gegoedheid

affluent *adj* welgesteld

afford *vb* bekostig; bybring

affront *n* affront; belediging; afjak; *vb* affronteer

afloat *adv* drywend; vlot

afraid *adj* bang; beangs; bedug; benoud; huiwerig; vreesagtig; sku; bevrees

African *n* Afrikaan

African-American *n* Afrikaan-Amerikaan

Africans *npl* Afrikane

Afrikaans *n, adj* Afrikaans

Afrikaner *n* Afrikaner

after *adv* agterna; *conj* nadat; *prep* na; — **all** *conj* darem; — **death** *adj* nadoods; — **that** *adv* toe; dan; — **this** *adv* hierna; — **which** *conj* waarna

afterbirth *n* nageboorte

aftereffect *n* nawerking

afternoon *n* agtermiddag; namiddag

afternoon nap *n* middagdutjie; middagslapie

afterparty *n* napartytjie

aftertaste *n* nasmaak

afterwards *adv* agterna; daarna; later; naderhand

again *adv* al weer; nog; nogmaals; opnuut; weer; — **and** — *adv* oor en oor; herhaaldelik

against *prep* teen; teë; *prefix* anti; — **this** *adv* hierteen; — **what** *inter pron* waarteen; — **which** *inter pron* waarteen

age *n* leeftyd; ouderdom; eeu; *vb* verouder

aged *adj* bejaard; oud

agency *n* agentskap

agenda *n* sakelys

agent *n* agent

aggravate *vb* vererger; verswaar

aggregate *n* (soil and sand particles) aggregaat

aggressive *adj* aggressief; offensief

aghast *adj* ontsteld; geskok; ontsettend

agile *adj* vlug; vlugvoetig; buigbaar; (computing) soepel

agitate *vb* opstook; agiteer; verontrus

agitation *n* agitasie; opstoking; opgewondenheid; opskudding; aksie

agitator *n* oproermaker; opstoker; opsweper

AGM *see* **annual general meeting**

ago *prep* gelede

agony *n* angs; doodstryd

agony aunt *n* empatie-engel; troostante

agony column *n* hartseerhoekie; troosrubriek

agony uncle *n* troos-oom

agree *vb* rym; strook; akkordeer; ooreenkom; — **to** *vb* inwillig; — **upon** *vb* afspreek

agreeable *adj* aangenaam; aardig; genoeglik

agreement *n* afspraak; konsensus; ooreenkoms

agricultural *adj* landboukundig

agriculture *n* landbou

ah! *interj* ai; hè!

ahead *adj, adv* vooruit

aid *n* hulp; steun; behulp; *vb* help

aide-de-camp *n* adjudant

AIDS *n* vigs

AIDS-related complex *n* vigsverwantekompleks

ail *vb* haper; makeer; skeel; skort

ailing *adj* sieklik

ailment *n* kwaal

aim *n* doel; einddoel; mikpunt; oogmerk; *vb* aanlê; mik

aimless *adj* doelloos

air *n* lug; deuntjie; wysie; aria; *vb* uitsaai

air conditioning *n* lugversorging

air force *n* lugmag

air freshener *n* lugverfrisser

air hole *n* luggat

air miles *npl* lugmyle

air pocket *n* luggat
air race *n* wedvlug
air raid *n* lugbombardement
air travel *n* lugreis
air-raid shelter *n* skuifkelder
aircraft *n* vliegtuig
aircraft carrier *n* abbaskip; vlieg-dekskip
airgun *n* windbuks
airless *adj* lugledig
airline *n* lugredery; redery
airliner *n* vliegtuig
airmail *n* lugpos
airman *n* vlieënier
airport *n* lughawe
airs *npl* aanstellerigheid
airship *n* lugskip
airstrip *n* landingstrook
airtight *adj* hermeties; lugdig
airtime *n* lugtyd
airy *adj* lugtig
alarm *n* alarm; konsternasie; *vb* veront-rus
alarm bell *n* noodklok
alarm clock *n* wekker
alarmed *adj* ontstel(d); vervaard
alarming *adj* angswekkend; onrusba-rend; skrikwekkend; sorgwekkend
albino *n* albino
album *n* album
alchemy *n* alchemie
alcoholic *n* dranksugtige; alkoholis; *adj* alkoholies
alcohol *n* alkohol; spiritualieë; spiritus
alcove *n* alkoof
alder *n* (tree) els
alert *adj* wakend; *n* (SMS) boodskap
algebra *n* algebra
alias *n* alias
alien *adj* vreemd; *n* uitlander
alienate *vb* vervreem; verwyder
alight *vb* afklim; afstyg; uitstap
align *vb* (wheels) spoor
alive *adj* lewendig; wakker
all *adj* al; *pron* algar; — **alone** *adj* stoksielalleen; — **along** *adv* aldeur; — **and sundry** *pron* allerhande; — **at once** *adj* plotseling; *adv* me-teens; — **day** *adv* heeldag; — **kinds of** *adj* allerlei; — **of a sudden** *adv* eensklaps; — **powerful** *adj* almagtig;

— **round** *adv* rondom; — **the same** *conj* darem; — **the time** *adv* aldeur; almelewe; — **the while** *adv* almelewe
all-knowing *adj* alwetend
all-in wrestler *n* rofstoeier
all-in wrestling *n* rofstoei
all-risks policy *n* allerisikopolis
all-round *adj* alsydig; veelsydig
all-seeing *adj* alsiende
all-terrain vehicle *n* veldvoertuig
all-weather *adj* weervas; — **court** *n* weervaste baan
alleviate *vb* (pain) lenig
alleviation *n* verligting; versagting
alley *n* steeg; gang
alliance *n* alliansie; bond; verbintenis
allied *adj* aanverwant; verwant
alligator *n* kaaiman
allocate *vb* allokeer; toewys
allow *vb* toelaat; laat; permitteer; toe-staan; gun; vergun; veroorloof
allowance *n* toelaag; rantsoen; rabat
allowed *adj* geoorloof
alloy *n* allooi
allspice *n* piment
alluring *adj* aanloklik; verleidelik
allusion *n* toespeling
ally *n* bondgenoot
almanac *n* almanak; kalender
almighty *adj* almagtig
almond *n* amandel; — **cake** *n* makrol-letjie
almost *adv* amper; byna; omtrent; na-genoeg; haas; — **meaningless** *adj* nietig
alms *n* aalmoes
aloe *n* aalwyn; aalwee
alone *adj* alleen
along *prep* langs; — **here** *adv* hierlangs; — **the bottom part** *prep* onderlangs; — **the foot of** *prep* onderlangs; — **which** *rel pron* waarlangs
aloud *adv;* *adj* hardop
alphabet *n* alfabet
already *adv* al; alreeds; reeds
also *adv* ook; nog; alte
altar *n* altar
alter *vb* wissel; verander
alteration *n* verandering; wysiging
alternate *vb* afwissel; verwissel; *adj* af-wisselend

alternately *adv* beurtelings

alternating current *n* wisselstroom

alternative *adj* alternatief; (lifestyle) alternatiewe; n alternatief; keus(e)

although *conj* hoewel; alhoewel; al; ofskoon

altitude *n* hoogte

altogether *adv* altesame; heeltemal; opeen; geheel en al; totaal

always *adv* altyd; steeds; immer; aljimmers; almelewe

amalgamate *vb* saamsmelt

amalgamation *n* amalgamasie; samesmelting; ineensmelting

amateur *n* amateur

amaze *vb* verwonder; verbaas

amazed *adj* verbaas

amazement *n* verbasing

amazing *adj* verstommend

ambassador *n* ambassadeur; afgesant; gesant

amber *n* barnsteen

ambient *adj* omringend; omgewings

ambiguous *adj* dubbelsinnig; tweeledig

ambition *n* ambisie; eersug; heerssug

ambitious *adj* ambisieus; eersugtig; eergierig

ambulance *n* ambulans

ambush *n* hinderlaag; lokval

amend *vb* regstel; wysig

amendment *n* wysiging

amends *n* vergoeding

Amerasian *adj* Amerasies; *n* Amerasiër

American English *n* Amerikaanse Engels

American Indian *n, adj* Amerindiaan

Amerind *see* **Amerindian**

Amerindian (*or* **Amerind**) *n, adj* (linguistics) Amerindiaan

amethyst *n* ametis

amiable *adj* aanvallig; beminlik; lieftallig

amicable *adj* vriendskaplik

amiss *adj, adv* mis

ammonia *n* ammoniak

ammunition *n* ammunisie

amnesty *n* amnestie

among *prep* onder; tussen; uit; — **what** *inter pron* waaronder; — **which** *inter pron* waartussen; — **whom** *inter pron* waaronder

amorous *adj* verlief

amount *n* bedrag; som; hoeveelheid; *vb* bedra

amphetamine *n* amfetamine

amphibious *adj* tweeslagtig

ample *adj* uitvoerig; ruim

amply *adv* ruim

amputate *vb* afsit

amuse *vb* vermaak; amuseer

amusement *n* pret; vermaak

amusing *adj* amusant; grappenderwys; onderhoudend; vermaaklik

an *indefinite article* 'n

anaemia *n* bleeksug

anaesthesia *n* narkose

anaesthetic *n* narkose; verdowingsmiddel

anaesthetist *n* narkotiseur

analgesic *n* pynstiller

analyse *vb* analiseer; ontleed

analysis *n* analise; ontleding

anarchic(al) *adj* regeringloos

anarchy *n* anargie

ancestor *n* voorvader

ancestors *npl* voorgeslag; voorouers

ancestral *adj* voorvaderlik

anchor *n* anker

anchorage *n* ankerplaas

ancient *adj* oud

and *conj* en; sowel; — **also** *adv* asook; — **yet** *conj* maar

anecdote *n* anekdote

angel *n* engel; hemeling

angelic *adj* engelagtig

anger *n* woede; toorn; drif

angle *n* hoek

angler *n* hengelaar; visserman; visterman

anglicize *vb* verengels

angora goat *n* sybok

angry *adj* boos; grimmig; nydig; verergde; versteur(d); kwaad

angular *adj* hoekig

animal *n* dier; bees; *adj* dierlik

animal kingdom *n* diereryk

animate *vb* animeer; bemoedig; aanwakker

animated *adj* geanimeer

animation *n* animasie

anime *n* aniem; vloeihars

anise *n* anys

ankle *n* enkel
annals *npl* annale; jaarboeke
annex *n* aanbou; *vb* annekseer
anniversary *n* gedenkdag; jaarfees
announce *vb* aankondig; — **someone** *vb* aandien
announcement *n* aankondiging; bekendmaking; kennisgewing
announcer *n* radio-omroeper
annoy *vb* hinder; pla
annoyance *n* ergernis; wrewel
annoyed *adj* vies; versteur(d); **become** — *vb* vererg
annoying *adj* lastig; hinderlik; ergerlik
annual *n* jaarboek
annual general meeting *n* jaarvergadering
annual report *n* jaarverslag
annual sales *n* omset
annually *adv* jaarliks
annuity *n* annuïteit; jaargeld; rente
anode *n* positiewe pool
anonymous *adj* anoniem; naamloos; ongeteken(d)
anorak *n* jekker
anorexia *n* anoreksie
anorexic (*or* **anorectic**) *n* anoreksielyer; *adj* anoreksies
another *determiner* ander
answer *n* antwoord; *vb* beantwoord
answerable *adj* verantwoordelik
ant *n* mier
ant hill *n* miershoop
antagonistic *adj* vyandig
anteater *n* aardvark
antelope *n* antiloop; bok
antenna *n* antenne; voelhoring
antenuptial contract *n* huweliksvoorwaardekontrak
anthropology *n* antropologie; volkekunde
antiretroviral treatment *n* antiretrovirale behandeling (ARB)
antibiotic *n* antibiotikum
anticipate *vb* antisipeer; verwag; voorsien; vooruitloop
antics *npl* manewales
antidote *n* teenmiddel; teengif
antigen *n* antigeen
antipsychotic *adj* (drug) antipsigoties
antiquarian *adj* oudheidkundig

antique *adj* antiek
antique shop *n* antiekwinkel
antiquity *n* oudheid
antiseptic *adj* antisepties
antithesis *n* teenstelling
antiviral *adj* antiviraal
antivirus software *n* teenvirusprogram
anus *n* gat
anvil *n* aambeeld
anxiety *n* angs; kommer; kwelling; onrus; stres
anxious *adj* angstig; bekommerd; onrustig; ongerus; besorg
any *adj* enig
anyhow *adv* altans
anyone *pron* enigeen
anything *pron* enigiets; iets; — **but** *adv* allesbehalwe
apalled *adj* ontsettend
apart *adj* uiteen; *adj, adv* apart
apart from *prep* afgesien van
apartment *n* vertrek
ape *n* aap
aperture *n* gat
apologize *vb* verontskuldig
apology *n* apologie; ekskuus; verskoning
apoplectic fit *n* beroerte; toeval
apoplexy *n* beroerte
apostate *n* afvallige
apostle *n* apostel
apostrophe *n* afkappingsteken; apostroof
apparatus *n* apparaat; toestel
apparent *adj* blykbaar; klaarblyklik; oënskynlik; skynbaar
apparently *adv* blykbaar; klaarblyklik; oënskynlik; skynbaar
apparition *n* spook
appeal *n* appèl; beroep; *vb* appeleer
appear *vb* blyk; skyn; verskyn; optree
appearance *n* aansien; skyn; verskyning; voorkoms
appease *vb* paai; versadig
appendage *n* aanhangsel
appendicitis *n* appendisitis; blindedermontsteking
appendix *n* blindederm; bylae; byvoegsel; toevoegsel; (book) aanhangsel
appetite *n* aptyt; eetlus; honger; lus; trek

applaud *vb* toejuig; apploudisseer

applause *n* applous; handgeklap; toejuiging; byval

apple *n* appel; — **of discord** *n* twisappel

appliance *n* toestel

applicant *n* kandidaat; applikant

application *n* aansoek; applikasie; toepassing; aanvraag

applied *adj* toegepas

applied mathematics *n* toegepaste wiskunde

apply *vb* aanwend; geld; oplê; (bandage) aanlê; (brakes) rem

apply for *vb* aanvra

apply to *vb* toepas

appoint *vb* aanstel; benoem

appointment *n* aanstelling; benoeming; afspraak

apportion *vb* bestem

appraisal *n* taksasie

appraise *vb* takseer; waardeer

appraiser *n* taksateur; waardeerder

appreciate *vb* waardeer

apprehension *n* vrees

apprehensive *adj* bedug

apprentice *n* vakleerling; leerklerk

apprenticeship *n* leer; proeftyd; leerjare

approach *n* aantog; *vb* nader

approachable *adj* genaakbaar

approaching *adj* naderende

appropriate *adj* doelmatig; toepaslik; *vb* eien

approval *n* byval; sanksie

approve *vb* goedkeur; toejuig; toestem; — **of** *vb* beaam; billik; goedvind

approximate *vb* benader

approximately *adv* naaste(n)by

approximation *n* benadering

apricot *n* appelkoos

April *n* April

apron *n* voorskoot

aptitude *n* aanleg

aqualung *n* duiklong

aquarelle *n* akwarel

aquarobics *n* akwa-aërobiese oefeninge

arable land *n* kaalgrond

arbitrary *adj* willekeurig

arbitration *n* arbitrasie

arbitrator *n* skeidsregter

arbour *n* prieel; somerhuis

ARC *see* **AIDS-related complex**

arc lamp *n* booglamp

arcade *n* deurloop

arch *n* boog; welf

archaeological *adj* oudheidkundig

archaeologist *n* oudheidkundige

archaeology *n* oudheidkunde

archbishop *n* aartsbiskop

archery *n* boogskiet

archipelago *n* argipel

architect *n* argitek

architecture *n* boukuns

archive *n* argief

archivist *n* argivaris

ardent *adj* blakend

ardour *n* gloed; vuur; warmte

area *n* buurt; geweste; kontrei; oppervlakte; terrein; wyk

arena *n* kryt; arena

argue *vb* beredeneer; redeneer; stry

argument *n* betoog; redenering; pleidooi; bewysgrond

aria *n* aria

arid *adj* droog

arise *vb* ontspruit; ontstaan; voortspruit; voortvloei

aristocrat *n* aristokraat

arithmetic *n* rekene; rekenkunde

ark *n* ark

arm *n* arm; wapen; *vb* bewapen

arm-in-arm *adv* gearm

armchair *n* armstoel; leuningstoel

armed *adj* gewapen

armed forces *n* weermag

armistice *n* wapenstilstand

armour *n* harnas; pantser

armour plate *n* (ships, etc.) pantser

armoured *adj* gepantser

armoured train *n* pantsertrein

armpit *n* oksel

arms *npl* wapens; wapentuig

arms cache *n* wapenopslagplek

army *n* krygsmag; leër

army chaplain *n* veldprediker

around *adv* omheen; rond; *prep* om; rondom

arrange *vb* reël

arranged *adj* ingerig

arrangement *n* afspraak; inrigting; orde; reëling; skikking

arrest *n* arres; gevangeneming; inhegtenisneming; *vb* arresteer; aanhou
arresting *adj* pakkend
arrival *n* koms; oorkoms
arrive *vb* aankom; aanland; kom; opdaag
arrogance *n* verwaandheid
arrogant *adj* aanmatigend; arrogant; verwaand; oormoedig
arrow *n* pyl
arsenic oxide *n* rottekruid
arson *n* brandstigting
ART *see* **antiretroviral treatment**
art *n* kuns
art gallery *n* kunsgalery
artery *n* slagaar
artful *adj* listig
article *n* lidwoord; artikel; voorwerp; wetsartikel
articulate(d) *adj* welsprekend; geleed
artificial *adj* kunsmatig; nagemaak; vals
artificial eye *n* glasoog
artillery *n* artillerie; geskut
artisan *n* vakman; handwerkman
artist *n* arties; kunsskilder; kunstenaar; skilder
as *adv* daar; as; *conj* deurdat; omdat; toe; wyl; *prep* as; soos; — **for** *conj* want; — **if** *adv* kamma; *adv, conj, prep* as; asof
asbestos *n* asbes; garingklip
ascend *vb* klim; beklim; opklim; opstyg; styg
ascending *adj* opdraand(e)
ascent *n* opgang; opstyging
ascertain *vb* vasstel; verneem
ascribe *vb* toeskryf
ash[1] *n* as
ash[2] *n* (tree) es
ashamed *adj* bekaamd; skaam; **be —** *vb* skaam
ashen *adj* asvaal
ashtray *n* asbak
ask *vb* versoek; vra; — **out** *vb* uitvra
asparagus *n* aspersie
aspect *n* gesigspunt
asphalt *n* asfalt
aspire after *vb* ding
aspirin *n* aspirien
ass *n* esel
assassin *n* sluipmoordenaar

assassination *n* sluipmoord
assault *vb* aanrand
assegai *n* assegaai
assemble *vb* monteer; saamkom
assembly *n* samekoms; vergadering
assent *vb* beaam
assert *vb* beweer; — **oneself** handhaaf; laat jouself geld
assertion *n* bewering
assertiveness *n* selfgeldendheid; selfhandhawing
assess *vb* waardeer
assessment *n* (tax) aanslag
assessor *n* assessor; waardeerder
asset *n* aanwins; bate; besit
assign *vb* toewys
assignment *n* opgaaf
assimilate *vb* verwerk
assist *vb* help; assisteer; bystaan; ondersteun; aanhelp
assistance *n* bystand; hulp
assistant *n* adjunk; assistent; handlanger
assistant teacher *n* hulponderwyser
assisted suicide *n* bystandselfmoord
associate with *vb* omgaan
association *n* vereniging; omgang
assort *vb* sorteer
assortment *n* sortering
assume *vb* aanmatig; aanneem; veronderstel
assuming that *conj* aangenome
assumption *n* veronderstelling
assurance *n* assuransie; versekering
assure *vb* verseker
assured *adj* verseker
asterisk *n* sterretjie
asthma *n* asma
asthmatic *adj* aamborstig; asmaties
astonish *vb* verbaas; verwonder
astonishing *adj* verbasend
astonishment *n* verbasing; verwondering
astraddle *adj* wydsbeen
astray *adj, adv* byster
astride *adj* wydsbeen
astringent *adj* vrank
astrologer *n* sterrewiggelaar
astrology *n* astrologie; sterrewiggelary
astronaut *n* astronout; ruimteman; ruimtevaarder

astronomic(al) *adj* astronomies
astronomy *n* astronomie; sterrekunde
asunder *adv* uiteen
asylum *n* toevlug(soord)
at *prep* op; *adv* om; **— hand** *adv* byderhand
atheist *n* ateïs; godloënaar
athlete *n* atleet
athlete's foot *n* voetskimmel
athletic *adj* atleties
athwart *adv* dwarsoor
atlas *n* atlas
ATM *see* **automatic teller machine**
atmosphere *n* atmosfeer; dampkring
atom *n* atoom
atom(ic) bomb *n* A-bom; atoombom; kernbom
atomic *adj* atomies
atomic waste *n* kernafval
atone for *vb* boet
atrocious *adj* gruwelik; hemeltergend
atrocity *n* gruweldaad
attach *vb* heg; aanheg
attached *adv* hierby
attached to *adj* geheg aan; verkleef
attachment *n* geneentheid; inbeslagneming; verknogtheid
attack *vb* aanval; storm; aanpak; *n* aanval; bestorming
attain *vb* behaal; bereik; geraak
attempt *n* aanslag; *vb* beproef
attend *vb* bywoon; bedien; dien; vergesel; behandel
attend to *vb* versorg; omkyk
attendance *n* presensie; bediening
attendance register *n* presensielys
attendance roll *n* presensielys
attendant *n* bediende; oppasser; agterryer
attending physician *n* behandelende dokter
attention *n* aandag
attention deficit disorder *n* aandag(s)gebreksindroom
attention deficit hyperactivity syndrome *n* aandag(s)gebrekhiperaktiwiteitsindroom
attentive *adj* aandagtig; attent; oplettend
attestation *n* attestasie
attic *n* solderkamer(tjie)

attitude *n* houding
attorney *n* prokureur
attract *vb* aanlok; aantrek
attraction *n* attraksie
attractive *adj* aantreklik
attribute *vb* toeskryf
ATV *see* **all-terrain vehicle**
auction *n* vendusie; veiling; verkoping
auctioneer *n* afslaer; vendusieafslaer
audacious *adj* vermetel
audible *adj* hoorbaar
audience *n* gehoor; oudiënsie
audiovisual *adj* oudiovisueel
audiovisual aids *npl* oudiovisuele hulpmiddels
audit *n* oudit; *vb* ouditeer
auditor *n* ouditeur
auditorium *n* gehoorsaal
auger *n* boor
augmentation *n* vermeerdering
August *n* Augustus
aunt *n* tante
auntie *n* (*informal*) tannie
aurora borealis *n* noorderlig
authentic *adj* eg; outentiek
authenticity *n* egtheid
author *n* outeur; skrywer
authority *n* gesag; heerskappy; mag; outoriteit; owerheid; seggenskap
authorization *n* magtiging
authorize *vb* magtig
authorized *adj* bevoeg; geregtig
autobiography *n* outobiografie
autocrat *n* alleenheerser
autocratic *adj* outokraties
autograph *vb* outografeer
automated people mover *n* rolgang
automatic *adj* outomaties
automatic pilot *n* stuuroutomaat
automatic teller machine *n* kitsbank; outomatiese tellermasjien
automatic washing machine *n* wasoutomaat
autonomy *n* outonomie
autopsy *n* lykskouing; nadoodse ondersoek
autumn *n* herfs; najaar
autumnal *adj* herfsagtig
auxiliary verb *n* hulpwerkwoord
avail *vb* baat
available *adj* aanwesig; beskikbaar

avalanche *n* lawine
avarice *n* gierigheid
avaricious *adj* geldgierig
avatar *n* (computing) avatar
avenge *vb* wreek
avenue *n* laan; laning
average *adj* gemiddeld; middelbaar; *n* deursnee; **on** — *adv* in deursnee
averse to *adj* afkeurig van
aversion *n* afkeer; afsku; hekel; teensin; weersin
avert *vb* afkeer; afwend
aviary *n* voëlhok
aviation *n* lugvaart
aviator *n* vlieënier; vlieër
avoid *vb* ontduik; ontwyk; vermy
avowal *n* bekentenis
awake *adj* wakker; *vb* ontwaak; **be** — *vb* waak

awakening *n* ontwaking; opwekking
award *n* prys; toekenning; *vb* toeken; — **a prize** *vb* bekroon
awards ceremony *n* prysuitdeling
aware *adj* bewus; **be** — **of** *vb* weet
away *adj, adv* weg; *adv* heen
awe *n* ontsag
awful *adj* haglik; ontsaglik
awfully *adv* ontsaglik; vreeslik
awkward *adj* lomp; onbeholpe; onhandig
awl *n* els
awning *n* sonskerm
awry *adj* skeef
axe *n* byl
axiom *n* aksioma
axis *n* as; spil
axle *n* as
azure *n, adj* hemelsblou; asuur

B

babble *n* gebabbel; *vb* babbel
babbling *n* geruis
baboon *n* bobbejaan
baboon spider *n* bobbejaanspinnekop
baby *n* baba; kind
baby boom *n* babagolf
baby rabbit *n* hasie
baby-boomer *n* naoorlogse baba
babysitter *n* kroostrooster
Bach flower remedy *n* Bach-blommeraat
bachelor *n* jongkêrel; vrygesel
bacillus *n* basil
back *adv* agteruit; terug; *n* agterkant;
(chair) leuning; **at the —** *adv* agte-raan; *prep* agter; **— to front** *adv* ag-terstevoor
back door *n* agterdeur
back part *n* agterent
back rest *n* rugleuning
backup *n* rugsteun
backache *n* rugpyn
backbone *n* ruggraat
backfire *vb* terugplof
backlash *n* teenreaksie
backpacker *n* pakstapper
backside *n* agterkant; agterent
backstreet *n* agterbuurt
backward *adj* agterlik; *adv* agteraf
backwards *adv* agteroor; agteruit;
terug
bacon *n* spek; varkspek
bacterium *n* bakterie
bad *adj* sleg; verkeerd; lelik; olik; bedor-we; erg
bad friends *npl* kwaaivriende
bad omen *n* voorspooksel
bad smell *n* stank
bad weather *n* onweer
badge *n* kenteken; wapen
badly *adv* sleg; erg; lelik; deerlik
badminton *n* pluimbal
baffle *vb* teleurstel
bag *n* sak; tas
baggage *n* bagasie
bagpipe *n* doedelsak
bail *n* borg; borgtog

bailiff *n* balju; fiskaal
bait *n* aas; lokaas
bake *vb* bak; uitbak
baked *adj* gebak
baker *n* bakker
baking pan *n* koekpan
baking powder *n* bakpoeier
balance *n* balans; ewewig; skaal; weeg-skaal; (bank account) saldo; *vb* weeg;
balanseer; **— the books** *vb* afsluit
balcony *n* balkon
bald *adj* kaal
bald head *n* bles; kaalkop
bale *n* baal
ball *n* bal; dans; bal; bol
ballpark *n* benaderde bedrag; geskatte
bedrag
ballad *n* ballade
ballast *n* ballas
ballet *n* ballet
balloon *n* ballon
ballot box *n* stembus
ballot paper *n* stembriefie
ballpoint pen *n* bol(punt)pen
balm *n* balsem; salf
balsam *n* balsem
balsamic vinegar *n* balsemasyn
bamboo *n* bamboes
ban *n* verbod; *vb* inperk
banal *adj* banaal
banana *n* piesang
banana peel (*or* **skin**) *n* piesangskil
band *n* band; gord; strook; musiek-korps; orkes; bende; troep
bandage *n* verband; bindsel; *vb* verbind
bandaging *n* verbinding
bandleader *n* orkesleier
bandmaster *n* orkesmeester
bandoleer *n* bandelier
bandy legs *npl* X-bene
bandy-legged *adj* hoepelbeen
bang *n* bons
banish *vb* verban
banishment *n* ban
bank *n* bank; bank; wal; *vb* kas
bank overdraft *vb* oortrekking
bank teller *n* teller

banker *n* bankier; kassier
banknote *n* banknoot
bankrupt *adj* bankrot; insolvent
bankruptcy *n* bankrotskap
banner *n* banier; vaandel
banns *npl* huweliksgebooie
banquet *n* banket; feesmaal; gasmaal
bantam *n* (domestic fowl) kapokhoender
baobab *n* (tree) kremetartboom
baptism *n* doop
baptismal certificate *n* doopseël
baptismal font *n* doopvont
baptize *vb* doop
bar *n* balie; boom; grendel; hek; staaf;
stang; tralie; kroeg; kantien; buffet;
vb voorkeer
bar code *n* strepieskode
bar of soap *n* steen
barb *n* weerhaak
barbarian *adj* barbaars; *n* barbaar
barbarous *adj* barbaars; wreed
barbecue *n* braaivleis; vleisbraai
barbed hook *n* weerhaak
barbed wire *n* doringdraad
barber *n* barbier; haarsnyer
barbiturate *n* barbituraat
bare *adj* bloot; kaal; naak; nakend
bareback *adj* bloots
barefoot(ed) *adj, adv* kaalvoet; blootsvoet
bareheaded *adj* blootshoof
barely *adv* skraps
bargain *n* winskoop; kopie; *vb* kwansel
bark1 *n* geblaf; *vb* blaf
bark2 *n* bas
barking *n* geblaf
barley *n* gars; gort
barmaid *n* skinkjuffrou; skinkjuffie
barman *n* tapper
barn *n* skuur
barometer *n* barometer; weerglas
baron *n* baron
baroness *n* barones
barracks *n* barak; kaserne
barrel *n* vaatjie; vat; (gun) loop; tromp
barrel-organ *n* draaiorrel
barren *adj* dor; onherbergsaam; onvrugbaar; steriel
barricade *n* barrikade; versperring; *vb*
versper

barrier line *n* (solid white) sperstreep
barrister *n* advokaat; juris
barter *vb* inruil; ruil; verhandel; verruil
base *adj* laag; laaghartig; onedel;
snood; *n* basis; (baseball) bof
base metals *n* onedele metale
baseball *n* bofbal
bashful *adj* skaam
basil *n* (herb) basiel
basin *n* bak; kom; skottel; bekken
basis *n* basis; grondslag
basket *n* mandjie
bass *n* (voice) bas
bastard *n* baster
bat *n* vlermuis
bath *n* bad; — **shower** *n* stortbad
bathe *vb* baai
bathroom *n* badkamer
baton *n* staf
batsman *n* kolwer
battalion *n* bataljon
batter[1] *vb* slaan
batter[2] *n* (cricket, etc.) kolwer
batter[3] *n* deeg
battery *n* battery
battle *n* geveg; slag; veldslag
battlefield *n* slagveld
bay *n* bruin; baai; *adj* bruin
bay horse *n* vosperd
bayonet *n* bajonet
bazaar *n* basaar
be *vb* wees
be careful! *interj* pas op!
beach *n* strand; seestrand
beachcomber *n* strandjut
beacon *n* baken
bead *n* kraal; korrel
beadle *n* koster
beak *n* snawel; bek
beam *n* balk; boom; disselboom; straal
beam forth *vb* uitstraal
beam on *vb* bestraal
bean *n* boon
bean soup *n* boontjieso(e)p
bear *n* beer; *vb* baar
bear in mind *vb* onthou
bear out *vb* bewaarheid
bear witness *vb* getuig
bearable *adj* draaglik
beard *n* baard
bearer *n* toonder

bearing *n* voorkome
bearing no interest *adj* renteloos
beast *n* bees
beast of prey *n* roofdier
beat *n* klop; slag; *vb* bons; klop; afstof; (eggs) klits
beat down the price *vb* afding
beat off *vb* afslaan
beat out *vb* uitklop
beat the drum *n* trommel
beatbox *n* (music) blêrboks
beautician *n* skoonheidskundige
beautiful *adj* pragtig; skoon; kostelik
beauty *n* skoonheid
beauty spot *n* moesie
because *conj* omdat; oor; deurdat; — **of** *prep* oor; vanweë
beckon *vb* wink; wuif
become *vb* word; betaam
becoming *adj* behoorlik; betaamlik; gepas; welvoeglik
bed *n* bed; kooi
bed linen *n* beddegoed
bedbug *n* weeluis
bedding *n* beddegoed; kooigoed
bedlam *n* dolhuis
bedpost *n* styl
bedridden *adj* bedlêend
bedroom *n* slaapkamer
bedsheet *n* laken
bedside manner *n* doktersbenadering; dokterstakt
bedspread *n* sprei
bedstead *n* katel
bedtime *n* slaaptyd
bee *n* by
bee sting *n* angel
beech *n* (tree) eukeboom
beef *n* beesvleis
beefsteak *n* biefstuk
beehive *n* byekorf; korf
beer *n* bier
beer hall *n* tappery
beet *n* beet
beetle *n* kewer; tor
beetroot *n* beet
befall *vb* oorkom; toeval
before *adv* eerder; tevore; *conj* alvorens; *prep* voor; — **which** *inter pron* waarvoor
before long *adv* dalkies

beforehand *adj* vooruit; *adv* vooraf; vooruit
beg *vb* bedel; smeek; soebat; afsmeek
beggar *n* bedelaar
begging *n* gebedel
begin *vb* begin; aanvang; aanhef; aangaan; (conversation) aanknoop; — **again** *vb* hervat; vervat
beginner *n* aankomeling; nuweling
beginning *n* aanhef; aanvang; begin; beginsel; opkoms; staanspoor
begrudge *vb* misgun
behave *vb* aanstel; gedra
behaviour *n* gedrag; wandel
behead *vb* onthoof
behind *adv* agteraan; agterna; *prep* agter; — **what** *inter pron* waaragter; **be — others** *vb* agterstaan
behold *vb* aanskou
being *n* wese
belching fire *adj* vuurspuwend
belief *n* geloof; mening
believable *adj* geloofbaar
believe *vb* glo
believing *adj* gelowig
belittle *vb* verkleineer
bell *n* klok; bel
bellow *vb* brul; bulk
bellows *n* blaasbalk
bells and whistles *npl* foefies
belly *n* buik; pens; maag
belong to *vb* behoort aan
belong together *vb* saamhoort
belongings *n* toebehore
beloved *n* geliefde; *adj* bemind; gelief; lief
below *adv* neer; omlaag; *prep* benede
belt *n* lyfband; gordel; riem; gord
bench *n* bank; sitbank; regbank
benchmark *n* kriterium; maatstaf; norm
bend *n* draai; bog; *vb* buig
bendable *adj* buigbaar
beneath *prep* benede
benediction *n* seën
benefactor *n* weldoener
beneficence *n* weldadigheid
beneficial *adj* bevorderlik; heilsaam
benefit *n* baat; voordeel; nut; heil; *vb* bevoordeel; — **from** *vb* baat vind by
benevolence *n* welwillendheid

benevolent *adj* weldadig
bent *adj* krom
bequeath *vb* nalaat
bereavement *n* verlies
berry *n* bessie
berry juice *n* bessiesap
berth *n* baantjie
beseech *vb* smeek; besweer; afsmeek
beside *prep* langs; naas; newens; — **what** *inter pron* waarnaas; — **which** *inter pron* waarnaas
besides *adv* behalwe; boonop; bowendien; origens; tewens; verder; voorts; benewens; *conj* buitendien
besiege *vb* beleër
besmirch *vb* besmeer
best *adj* beswil; prima; *n* beste; **at —** *adv* hoogstens
best clothes *npl* kisklere
best man *n* strooijonker
bestial *adj* dierlik; beesagtig
bestseller *n* (book) trefferboek
bet *n* weddenskap; *vb* wed
betray *vb* verraai; verklap
betrayer *n* verraaier
betrothal *n* verlowing
betrothed *n* beminde; verloofde; **be —** *vb* verloof
better *adj* beter
better half *n* wederhelf
between *prep* tussen; — **that** *adv* daartussen; — **which** *inter pron* waartussen
between decks *n* tussendeks
beverage *n* drank
bevy *n* vlug
bewail *vb* bejammer
bewilder *vb* verbyster
bewitch *vb* paljas; betower
beyond *prep* oor; verby
beyond repair *adj* onherstelbaar
biased *adj* bevooroordeel(d); partydig
bib *n* borslap
Bible *n* Bybel
bibliography *n* bibliografie
bickering *n* gekibbel; harwar
bicycle *n* fiets
bid *n* bod; *vb* bied
bide one's time *vb* afwag
bier *n* draagbaar; baar
big bang *n* oerknal

bigamy *n* bigamie
bigness *n* grootte
bike *n* fiets
biker *n* fietsryer
bile *n* gal
bilingual *adj* tweetalig
bilious *adj* galagtig
bill *n* rekening; faktuur; bek; snawel; wetsontwerp; biljet; aanplakbiljet; gelag
bill of exchange *n* wissel
bill of fare *n* spyskaart; menu
bill of lading *n* vragbrief
billet *n* pos; *vb* inkwartier
billiard cue *n* biljartstok
billiards *n* biljart
billion *n* miljard
billow *n* golf
billy goat *n* bokram
bimbo *n* (*informal*) loskop; sekskat
binary *adj* tweeledig
bind *vb* bind; (books) inbind
binding *adj* geldig
binge drinking *n* drankvergryping
binoculars *n* verkyker
biodiesel *n* bio-diesel
bioethics *n* bio-ethiek
biodiversity *n* biodiversiteit
biography *n* biografie; lewensbeskrywing
biology *n* biologie
biometric *adj* biometries
bioscope *n* bioskoop; fliek
biosensor *n* biosensor
birch *n* roede; (tree) berkeboom
bird *n* voël
bird of passage *n* trekvoël
bird of prey *n* roofvoël
bird's-eye view *n* voëlvlugblik
birdwatcher *n* voëlkyker
birdwatching *n* voëlkyk
birth *n* geboorte; afkoms
birth certificate *n* geboortebewys
birth control *n* geboortebeperking
birthday *n* verjaar(s)dag; geboortedag
birthday party *n* verjaar(s)dagpartytjie
birthday present *n* verjaar(s)daggeskenk
birthmark *n* moedervlek
birthright *n* eersgeboortereg; geboortereg

bisect *vb* halveer
bisexual *adj* tweeslagtig
bishop *n* biskop
bishopbird *n* flap
bishopric *n* bisdom
bit *n* brokstuk; endjie; entjie; skerf; (horse's bridle) stang; gebit
bit by bit *adv* stuksgewys
bite *n* byt; hap; beet; knou; steek; *vb* byt; hap
bitter *adj* bitter
bitumen *n* asfalt
blab *vb* verklap
black *n, adj* swart
black and blue *adj* pimpel en pers; bont en blou
black box *n* vlugopnemer
black pudding *n* bloedwors
blackberry *n* braam
blacken *vb* (name) beskinder
blackjack *n* (plant) kakiebos
blacksmith *n* smid
bladder *n* blaas
blade *n* halm; (knife) lem; (grass) grashalm
blame *n* blaam; skuld; verwyt; *vb* blameer; aanreken
blameless *adj* onberispelik; onkreukbaar
blameworthy *adj* laakbaar
blank *adj* blanko; wesenloos
blanket *n* deken; kombers
blasphemy *n* godslastering
blast *n* ontploffing; *vb* (gun) skiet
blaze[1] *n* vlam
blaze[2] *n* (on a horse) kol
bleach *vb* bleik; uitbleik
bleak *adj* guur
bleat *n* geblêr; *vb* blêr
bleating *n* geblêr
bleed *vb* bloei
bleeding *n* bloeding
blemish *n* smet; vlek
blend *vb* meng; vermeng
blender *n* vermenger
bless *vb* seën
blessed *adj* geluksalig; geseën; salig; welgeluksalig
blessedness *n* geluksaligheid
blessing *n* seën; seënwens
blight *n* roes

blimp *n* blimp
blind *adj* blind; *vb* verblind; *n* blinding
blindfold *n* blinddoek; *vb* blinddoek
blindly *adv* blindelings
blindman's-buff *n* (game) blindemol
blindness *n* blindheid
blink *vb* knip
bliss *n* geluksaligheid
blissful *adj* salig
blister *n* blaar
block *n* blok; *vb* versper
block booking *n* blokbespreking
block up *vb* opdam
blockade *n* blokkade; *vb* blokkeer
blockbuster *n* (movie) blokbom
blog *n* webdagboek; webjoernaal
blogger *n* webinskrywer
bloke *n* (*informal*) kêrel; vent
blond *adj* blond
blood *n* bloed
blood clot *n* klont
blood money *n* bloedgeld
blood pressure *n* bloeddruk
blood sausage *n* bloedwors
blood transfusion *n* bloedoortapping; bloedtransfusie
blood relation *n* bloedverwant
blood-red *n, adj* bloedrooi
bloodbath *n* bloedbad
bloodhound *n* bloedhond; speurhond
bloodsucker *n* bloedsuier
bloodthirsty *adj* bloeddorstig
bloody *adj* bloederig
bloom *n* blom; blos; fleur; *vb* bloei
blossom *n* bloeisel; blom; *vb* bloei
blot *n* klad; vlek; *vb* beklad; vlek
blot out *vb* uitdelg; uitwis
blotting paper *n* kladpapier
blouse *n* bloes
blow[1] *n* hou; raps; slag
blow[2] *vb* aanblaas
blow away *vb* verwaai
blow one's nose *vb* snuit
blow out *vb* uitblaas
blow over *vb* afdryf; oorgaan
blow up *vb* opblaas
blown about *adj* verwaai(d)
blown-up *adj* opgeblaas
blubber *n* traan
blue *n, adj* blou
blue gum *n* (tree) bloekom

bluebottle *n* (fly) brommer
bluefish *n* pampelmoes
bluff *n* slenter; *vb* oorbluf
blunder *n* bok; flater; stommiteit; misgreep
blunt *adj* bot; kortaf; stoets; stomp
blurb *n* flapteks; omslagteks; prikkelteks
blurt out *vb* uitflap
blush *n* blos; *vb* bloos; kleur
BMI *see* **body mass index**
boa constrictor *n* luislang
boar *n* beer; burg
board *n* bord; kos; losies; plank; raad; *vb* inwoon; (ship, plane, etc.) inskeep
board and lodging *n* kos en blyplek
board of directors *n* direksie
boarder *n* kosganger
boarding house *n* koshuis
boarding school *n* kosskool
boardroom *n* raadskamer
boast *vb* beroem; praal
boaster *n* grootbek; windbuks
boasting *n* grootspraak; bluf
boat *n* boot; skip; skuit
boat race *n* roeiwedstryd; wedvaart
bob up and down *vb* dobber
bobbin *n* klos; tolletjie
bodily *adj* liggaamlik
body *n* liggaam; lyf; instansie
body double *n* (movie) lyfdubbel
body language *n* liggaamstaal; lyftaal
body mass index *n* liggaamsmassa-indeks
bodybuilder *n* spierbouer
bodyguard *n* lyfwag
Boer *n* Afrikaner
boffin *n* (*informal*) fundi; kundige; kenner
bogey *n* syfer
bogeyman *n* paaiboelie; skrikbeeld
boggy ground *n* deurslag
boil[1] *vb* kook; **— off** *vb* afkook; **— over** *vb* oorkook
boil[2] *n* bloedvint; buil
boiler *n* stoomketel; ketel
boiling water *n* kookwater
boisterous *adj* luidrugtig; uitgelate; onstuimig
bold *adj* kordaat; kranig; onbeskroom(d); onverskrokke; stout; vermetel; vry; vrypostig; (printing) vet

bold face *n* (printing) vet
bolster *n* peul
bolt *n* bout; grendel; knip; skuif; *vb* hol
bomb *n* bom
bombastic *adj* bombasties; geswolle
bond *n* obligasie; verband; samevoeging
bonds *npl* effekte
bone *n* been
bone of contention *n* twisappel
bones *npl* gebeente
bonnet *n* hoed; (car) kap; motorkap
bonus *n* bonus; premie; toegif; toelaag
bony *adj* benerig
boo *vb* uitjou
booby prize *n* fopprys; troosprys
book *n* boek
book a seat *vb* bespreek
book trade *n* boekhandel
book-keeper *n* boekhouer
bookbinder *n* boekbinder
bookcase *n* boekrak; kas
bookie *n* (*informal*) wedder
bookmark *n* bladwyser
bookseller *n* boekhandelaar
bookshelf *n* boekrak
bookworm *n* boekwurm
boom *n* donder; galm; gebulder; hek; valhek; welvaart; *vb* dreun; bulder
booming *n* gebulder
booster injection *n* skraaginspuiting
boot *n* skoen; stewel
boot polish *n* waks; skoenwaks; skoenpolitoer
boot sale *n* (car) bagasiebakvendusie
boot *n* veter
booted *adj* gestewel
booth *n* stalletjie; kraam
booty *n* buit; roof
booze *vb* (*informal*) suip
boozer *n* (*informal*) suiplap
boracic acid *n* boorsuur
border *n* boord; grens; rand; soom; **— on** *vb* grens
borderer *n* grensbewoner
bore[1] *vb* boor
bore[2] *vb* verveel
borehole *n* boorgat
boring *adj* vervelend; vervelig
born *adj* gebore; **be —** *vb* gebore; aankom
borrow *vb* leen; **— from** *vb* ontleen

borrow money *vb* opneem
bosom *n* boesem; bors; skoot
bosom friend *n* boesemvriend
boss *n* baas
botanical *adj* plantkundig
botanist *n* plantkundige
botany *n* botanie; plantkunde
botch *vb* knoei; konkel; verhaspel
both *determiner* beide; *pron, conj* albei
bother *n* beslommering; getob; *vb* foeter
botheration *n* gesukkel; gesanik
botox *n* botoks
bottle *n* bottel; fles; *vb* bottel
bottle up *vb* (feelings) opkrop
bottleneck *n* knelpunt
bottom *n* bodem; boom; fondament; grond; onderkant; onderste; **at the —** *adv* onderaan; **to the —** *adv* bodem; ondertoe
bottom layer *n* onderlaag
bottom lip *n* onderlip
bottom end *n* onderent
bough *n* tak
boulder *n* gesteente
bounce *n* bons; opslag; *vb* opspring
bouncer *n* uitsmyter
bound[1] *adj* gebonde; verplig
bound[2] *n* sprong
bound[3] *vb* begrens
boundary *n* grens; perk; (cricket) grenshou
boundless *adj* grensloos
bounty *n* gawe; premie
bouquet *n* ruiker
boutique *adj* (hotel, etc.) boutiek
bow[1] boog; knoop; lissie; strik
bow[2] *vb* buig
bow[3] *n* (ship) boeg
bow legs *npl* X-bene
bow tie *n* das; strikdas
bowel motion *n* stoelgang
bowels *npl* ingewande
bowl[1] *n* bak; kom
bowl[2] *n* rolbal; *vb* rol; (cricket) boul
bowler *n* (cricket) bouler
bowling *n* rolbal
bowls *n* rolbal
box[1] *n* bus; doos; kas; kis; koffer
box[2] *vb* boks
box office *n* loket
boxer *n* bokser

boxing match *n* vuisgeveg
boy *n* knaap; seun
boyfriend *n* ou
boys' school *n* seunskool
braai *n* vleisbraai
braaivleis *n* vleisbraai
brace *vb* span; aantrek
bracelet *n* armband
braces *n* kruisband
bracket *n* hakie
brackish *adj* brak
brag *vb* praal; beroem; bluf
bragging *n* geswets; grootspraak; bluf
braid *n* vlegsel
brain *n* brein; harsings
brain drain *n* kundigheidsverlies
brain teaser *n* breinknoop; denkprikkel
brainchild *n* geesteskind
brains *n* hoof; kop
brainstorm *n* dinkskrum
brainwave *n* blink idee; ingewing
braise *vb* stowe
brake *n* rem; briek; remskoen; *vb* rem; briek
brake pedal *n* rempedaal
brake shoe *n* remskoen
bramble *n* braam
bran *n* semels
branch *n* tak; **— off** *vb* wegdraai; **— out** *vb* vertak
branch office *n* takkantoor
branching out *n* vertakking
brand *n* brandmerk; fabrikaat; merk; *vb* (cattle) brand
brand new *adj* splinternuut; spiksplinternuut
brandy *n* brandewyn
brass *n* geelkoper
bravado *n* grootspraak
brave *adj* dapper; heldhaftig; kordaat; manhaftig; manmoedig; moedig; ridderlik; stout; stoutmoedig; *vb* braveer
brawl *n* rusie; twis; *vb* rusie maak; twis
brawn *n* sult
brazier *n* konka
breach *n* breuk
breach of promise *n* woordbreuk
bread *n* brood
bread knife *n* broodmes
bread roll *n* broodrolletjie

breadth *n* breedte; wydte
breadwinner *n* broodwinner
break *n* pouse; *vb* aanbreek; (habit) afwen; **— in** *vb* (horse) dresseer; tem; **— into** *vb* inbreek; indring; **— loose** *vb* losbars; losbreek; **— off** *vb* afbreek; uitmaak; **— out** *vb* uitbreek; **— up** *vb* kleinmaak; opbreek; uiteengaan
break-dancing *n* break-dans; toldans
breakdown *n* oponthoud; teenspoed; instorting
breakdown service *n* insleepdiens
breakdown van *n* teenspoedwa
breakers *n* (sea) branding
breakfast *n* ontbyt; brekfis; oggendete
breaking news *n* breeknuus; vars nuus
breakwater *n* golfbreker; seebreker
breast *n* bors; boesem
breastbone *n* borsbeen
breath *n* asem; adem; wasem
breathe *vb* asem; adem; blaas
breathing *n* asemhaling
breathless *adj* asemloos; ademloos
breathtaking *adj* verstommend
breed *n* ras; *vb* aanteel; teel
breeding *n* teelt
breeze *n* bries; wind
brew *vb* brou
brewery *n* bierbrouery
bribe *vb* omkoop; *n* omkoopgeld
bribery *n* omkopery
brick *n* baksteen; steen
bricklayer *n* messelaar
bride *n* bruid
bridegroom *n* bruidegom
bridesmaid *n* bruidsmeisie; strooimeisie
bridge *n* brug; oorbrug; (card game) brug
bridle *n* teuel; toom; *vb* beteuel
bridle path *n* rypad
bridleway *n* rypad
brief *n* opdrag; opgaaf; *adj* kort
briefly *adv* kortliks
brigade *n* brigade
bright *adj* helder; klaar; opgeruimd; opgewek; blink; lig
brighten *vb* opklaar
brightness *n* helderheid
brilliancy *n* glans

brilliant *adj* geniaal; glansryk; luisterryk; skitterend; briljant
brim *n* rand
brimful *adj* tjokvol
brimstone *n* swa(w)el
brine *n* pekel
bring *vb* bring; aandra; aanvoer; aanbring; saambring; **— about** *vb* bewerkstellig; daarstel; teweegbring; veroorsaak; **— along** *vb* aanhaal; saambring; meebring; **— back** *vb* terugbring; **— down** *vb* afbring; plant; **— forth** *vb* voortbring; (young) jong; **— forward** *vb* bybring; **— in** *vb* inneem; oplewer; **— out** *vb* uitbring; **— together** *vb* saambring; **— up** *vb* grootmaak; opbring; opvoed
brinjal *n* eiervrug
brink *n* kant
briny *adj* sout
Britain *n* Brittanje
brittle *adj* bros
broach *vb* opper
broad *adj* breed; wyd
broadband *n* breëband
broadcast *vb* uitsaai
broadcasting *n* uitsaaiwese; radio
broadcasting station *n* uitsaaistasie; draadloosstasie
broaden *vb* verruim
broadminded *adj* liberaal
broil *vb* braai
broiled *adj* gebraai
broke *adj* platsak
broken *adj* gebreek; gebroke; kapot; stukkend
broker *n* makelaar
bronchitis *n* brongitis
bronze *n* brons
brooch *n* borsspeld
brood *n* broeisel; *vb* broei
broody *adj* broeis
brook *n* spruit
broom *n* besem
broth *n* sop
brothel *n* bordeel
brother *n* broer; boet; broeder
brother-in-law *n* swaer
brotherly *adj* broederlik
brown *n, adj* bruin
brown hyena *n* strandjut

browse *vb* afwei
bruise *n* kneus; *vb* kneus
brunette *n, adj* brunet
brush *n* borsel; kwas; skermutseling; (artist) penseel; *vb* langes stryk; borsel; — **off** *vb* afborsel
brutal *adj* beesagtig; dierlik
brutally *adv* beesagtig
brute *n* bees; dier; monster; ondier; onmens; woestaard; wreedaard
brute force *n* spierkrag
bubble *n* blaas; borrel
bubble gum *n* kougom
bubble up *vb* opborrel; opwel
bubonic plague *n* builepes
bucket *n* emmer
bucket list *n* kluitklaplys
buckle *n* gespe; *vb* toegespe
buckle up *vb* vasgespe; *interj* gordel vas!
buckshot *n* loper
bud *n* knop; uitloop; uitspruitsel; *vb* bot
budding *adj* (author, etc.) ontluikend
buddy system *n* (safety) makkerstelsel
budget *n* begroting; staatsbegroting; *vb* begroot
buffalo *n* buffel
buffet meal *n* buffetete
buffoon *n* hanswors; harlekyn
bugbear *n* paaiboelie
bugging device *n* meeluisterapparaat
buggy *n* bokkie
bugle *n* horing
build *n* bou; liggaamsbou; statuur; *vb* aanlê; bou; — **a nest** *vb* nesskop; — **again** *vb* herbou; — **on to**; *vb* aanbou; — **up** *vb* opbou
builder *n* aannemer; bouer
building *n* aanbou; gebou
building site *n* terrein
building society *n* bouvereniging
building material *n* boustof
buildings *npl* opstal
built-in cupboard *n* muurkas
bulb *n* bol; gloeilamp
bulge out *vb* uitpeul; uitsak
bulimia *n* bulimia
bulk *n* massa
bulk posting *n* massaversending
bulky *adj* lywig; omvangryk
bull *n* bul; stier

bull's eye *n* kol; kolskoot
bulldozer *n* stootskraper
bullet *n* koeël
bulletin *n* bulletin
bulletin board *n* bulletinbord
bulletproof *adj* koeëlvry
bulletproof vest *n* koeëlvaste
bullfrog *n* brulpadda
bullion *n* staafgoud
bully *n* boelie; bullebak; rusiesoeker; *vb* baasspeel
bullying *adj* geniepsig
bulrush *n* palmiet; papkuil
bulwark *n* bolwerk; verskansing
bumblebee *n* hommel
bump *n* bons; knobbel; plof; stamp; *vb* stamp
bumpy *adj* hobbelagtig
bun *n* bolletjie; broodrolletjie
bunch *n* bos; tros
bundle *n* bondel; bundel; pak
bung *n* tap
bungle *vb* knoei; verknoei
bungler *n* sukkelaar
bungling *n* geknoei; gemors
bungy jumping *n* rekspring
bungy jumper *n* rekspringer
bunker *n* (golf) kuil
bunting *n* vlagdoek
buoy *n* baken; dobber
burden *n* las; drag; *vb* belaai; belas
burdened *adj* beswaar
burdock *n* klits
bureau *n* buro
bureaucracy *n* burokrasie
burgher *n* burger
burglar *n* dief
burglar alarm *n* diefalarm
burglary *n* huisbraak; inbraak
burgle *vb* inbreek
burial *n* begrafnis
burn *vb* brand; aanbrand; *n* brandplek; brandwond
burn down *vb* afbrand
burning *adj* heet; *n* verbranding; — **fiercely** *adj* ligtelaaie
burnt *adj* gebrand
burrow *vb* grawe; vroetel
bursary *n* studiebeurs
burst *vb* bars; verbreek; — **out** *vb* losbars; uitbars; uitbreek

burst into flames *vb* ontbrand; ont-vlam
burst into laughter *vb* uitskater
burweed *n* boetebossie
bury *vb* begrawe; begraaf
bus *n* bus
bus driver *n* busdrywer
bus service *n* busdiens
bus ticket *n* buskaartjie
bush *n* struik; (of a wheel) bus
bush shrike *n* kokkewiet
bush tea *n* bossiestee
bushbaby *n* nagaap
bushel *n* boesel
Bushman *n* Boesman
bushy *adj* ruig
business *n* besigheid; ambag; bedryf; beroep; saak; handelsaak; handel; spulletjie; affère
business knowledge *n* sakekennis
business-like *adj* saaklik
businessmen *npl* sakelui
bust *n* borsbeeld
bustard *n* korhaan
bustle *n* drukte; gedoe; gewerskaf; gewoel; opskudding
busy *adj* bedrywig; besig; druk
but *adv* slegs; *conj* dog
butcher *n* slagter
butcher bird *n* janfiskaal; laksman
butchered *adj* geslagte
butchery *n* slaghuis

butt *n* stoot
butter *n* botter; *vb* smeer
buttercup *n* botterblom
butterfly *n* skoenlapper; vlinder
buttermilk *n* karringmelk
buttock *n* boud
button *n* knoop
buttonhole *n* knoopsgat; (flower) ruikertjie ; *vb* bydam
buy *vb* inkoop; koop; aankoop; — **into** *vb* inkoop; — **off** *vb* uitkoop; — **out** *vb* uitkoop
buyer *n* koper
buying power *n* koopkrag
buzz *n* zoem; *vb* gons; zoem
buzzing *n* zoem; gesuis; suising
by *prep* by; aan; deur; met; per; uit; van; — **and** — *adv* strakkies; — **chance** *adv* toevallig; — **day** *adv* oordag; — **far** *adv* verreweg; — **itself** *adv* vanself; — **marriage** *adj* aangetroude; — **myself** *adv* in my enigheid; — **no means** *adv* gans; geensins; — **the way** *adv* terloops; — **virtue of** *prep* kragtens
by-election *n* tussenverkiesing
bye-law *n* verordening; **bye——s** *npl* reglement
by-product *n* neweproduk
bypass *n* (road) verbypad; (heart surgery) omleiding
bystander *n* omstander

C

cabaret *n* kabaret
cabbage *n* kopkool; kool
cabin *n* hut; kajuit
cabin staff *n* kajuitpersoneel
cabinet *n* kabinet; ministerie
cabinet maker *n* skrynwerker; meubelmaker
cabinet making *n* skrynwerk
cable *n* kabel
cablegram *n* kabelgram
cackle *vb* kekkel
cackling *n* gekekkel
cactus *n* kaktus
caddie *n* (golf) joggie
cadet *n* kadet; kwekeling
Caesarian operation *n* keisersnee
café *n* kafee
cafeteria *n* kafeteria
caffeine *n* kaffeïene
cage *n* kou; koutjie; kooi
cajole *vb* pamperlang
cake *n* gebak; koek; tert
calabash *n* kalbas
calamitous *adj* rampspoedig
calamity *n* onheil; ramp
calcified *vb* verkalk
calcify *vb* verkalk
calculate *vb* bereken; nareken; raam; reken; uitreken
calculation *n* raming
calculator *n* rekenaar; sakrekenaar
calendar *n* almanak; kalender
calf *n* kalf; (leg) kuit
calf love *n* kalwerliefde
calico *n* katoen
caliph *n* kalief
caliphate *n* kalifaat
call *n* beroep; *vb* aanroep; (phone) opbel; (at a house) aangaan; — **for** *vb* afhaal; — **in** *vb* inroep; opvra; inloop; — **in passing** *vb* aanloop; — **on** *vb* kuier; besoek; — **on a person** *vb* aangaan; —**out** *vb* uitroep; aflees; — **up** *vb* oproep
called *adj* genaamd; genoem; **be — after** *vb* heet
calling *n* geroep; roeping

callous *adj* gevoelloos; vereelt
callus *n* eelt
calm *adj* bedaard; besadig; kalm; ongeërg; rustig; vreedsaam; *n* vrede; *vb* kalmeer
calm down *vb* bedaar; afkoel
calmness *n* stilte
calorie *n* kalorie
calve *n* kalf
Calvinist *n* Calvinis
calyx *n* blomkelk; kelk
camel *n* kameel
camera *n* kamera
camisole *n* onderlyfie
camomile *n* kamille
camp *n* kamp; laer; *vb* kampeer
camp bed *n* veldbed
camp chair *n* voustoel
camp out *vb* uitkamp
campaign *n* kampanje; veldtog
camphor *n* kanfer
campus *n* kampus
can *n* kan; *vb* inlê
canal *n* grag; kanaal
canapé *n* kanapee
canary *n* kanarie
cancel *vb* afskryf; uitmaak; afsê; (leave) intrek
cancer *n* kanker
candid *adj* oop; ope; openhartig; reguit; rondborstig; volmondig; vrymoedig
candidate *n* kandidaat
candied peel *n* sukade
candle *n* kers
candlestick *n* blaker; kandelaar
candour *n* rondborstigheid; vrymoedigheid
candyfloss *n* spookasem
cane *n* lat; riet; rottang; stok
cane spirits *n* rietblits
canine *n* (tooth) hoektand
canister *n* trommel
canned *adj* ingelê
cannibal *n* kannibaal; mensvreter
cannon *n* kanon
cannonball *n* kanonkoeël
canoe *n* kano

canon *n* kanon
canonical *adj* kanoniek
canonization *n* heiligverklaring
canonize *vb* kanoniseer
canopy *n* hemel
cantaloupe melon *n* spanspek
cantata *n* kantate
canteen *n* kantien; tappery
canter *n* galopdraf
canvas *n* seil; seildoek
canvassing *n* werwing
cap *n* keps; mus
capable *adj* fluks; geskik; kapabel; bekwaam; — **of** *adj* vatbaar
capable of life *adj* lewensvatbaar
capacity *n* funksie; hoedanigheid; inhoud; vermoë
cape *n* mantel; kaap
Cape gooseberry *n* appelliefie; pampelmoesie
Cape robin *n* janfrederik
Cape wren *n* tinktinkie
caper *vb* bokspring
capital *n* hoofstad; kapitaal
capital letter *n* hoofletter
capital punishment *n* doodstraf
capitalist *n* kapitalis
capitulate *vb* kapituleer
capped leave *n* beperkte verlof
caprice *n* nuk
capricious *adj* wispelturig
capsize *vb* kantel
captain *n* kaptein; skipper; skeepskaptein
caption *n* onderskrif
captivate *vb* boei
captivating *adj* innemend
captive *adj* gevange
captivity *n* gevange(n)skap
capture *n* gevangeneming; inneming;
  vb inneem
car *n* motor
car bomb *n* motorbom
car boot sale *n* bagasiebakvendusie
car exhaust *n* uitlaat
car hijacking *n* motorkaping
car horn *n* toeter; horing
car jack *n* domkrag
caracal wild cat *n* rooikat
carat *n* karaat
caravan *n* karavaan; woonwa

carbide *n* karbied
carbolic *adj* karbol
carbolic acid *n* karbolsuur
carbon *n* koolstof
carbon copy *n* deurslag
carbon footprint *n* koolstofspoor
carbon paper *n* deurslagpapier
carbon tax *n* koolstofbelasting
carburettor *n* vergasser
card *n* kaart; kaartjie; *vb* (wool) kam
card-swipe machine *n* kaartveemasjien
cardboard *n* karton; bordpapier
cardiac arrest *n* hartversaking
cardinal *n* kardinaal
cardiogram *n* kardiogram
cardiograph *n* kardiograaf
care *n* ag; beslommering; hoede; omsigtigheid; toesig; versigtigheid; versorging; voorsorg; *vb* omgee; **I don't**
  — dit traak my nie
care for *vb* sorg; versorg
career *n* loopbaan; lewensloop
career along *vb* jakker
careful *adj* behoedsaam; sorgsaam;
  sorgvuldig; versigtig; **be —** *vb* oppas
careless *adj* agteloos; agte(r)losig; onbekommerd; ongerekend; onversigtig;
  slordig; sorgeloos
carelessness *n* nalatigheid
carer *n* oppasser; versorger
caress *vb* liefkoos; streel; troetel
caretaker *n* oppasser; opsigter; bewaker
cargo *n* lading; skeepslading; vrag
cargo vessel *n* vragskip
caricature *n* karikatuur; spotprent
carjacking *n* motorkaping
carnal *adj* sinlik; vleeslik
carnation *n* angelier
carnivorous *adj* vleisetend
carp *vb* vit; **— at** *vb* pik
carpenter *n* timmerman
carpenter's bench *n* skaafbank
carpet *n* tapyt
carport *n* motorskuiling
carriage *n* koets; rytuig; wa
carriage paid *adj* vragvry
carrier *n* draer; karweier; (on a car)
  draagrak
carrion *n* aas
carrot *n* wortel
carry *vb* aandra; vervoer; **— down** *vb*

afdra; — **forward** *vb* oorbring; — **off** *vb* skaak; — **on** *vb* voortsit; — **on a business** *vb* handel; — **out** *vb* uitrig; vervul; — **through** *vb* deursit; — **up** *vb* opdra; — **with difficulty** *vb* piekel

cart *n* kar

cart shed *n* waenhuis

carthorse *n* karperd

cartilage *n* kraakbeen

carton *n* karton

cartoon *n* spotprent

cartridge *n* patroon

carve *vb* kerf

carvery *n* voorsnybuffet; voorsnyery

carving *n* snywerk

case *n* kas; kabinet; kis; kis; doos; naamval; geval; saak; spul

cash *n* geld; kontant

cash box *n* geldtrommel

cash float *n* wisselfonds

cash flow *n* kontantvloei

cash on delivery *n* kontant by aflewering

cash register *n* kasregister

cash-and-carry *n* haal-en-betaal; koop-en-loop

cashback *n* kontant terug

cash-book *n* kasboek

cashbox *n* kas

cashier *n* kassier

casing *n* mantel

cask *n* ton; vaatjie; vat

casserole *n* kastrol

cast *n* (play, etc.) rolverdeling; rolbesetting; *vb* werp

cast iron *n* gietyster; gegote; *vb* giet

cast off *vb* verstoot

castle *n* burg; kasteel; slot

castor *n* (wheel) rolletjie

castor oil *n* kasterolie

castrate *vb* sny; ontman

casual *adj* ongerekend; terloops; toevallig

cat *n* kat

cat-o'-nine-tails *n* kats

cat's eye *n* (on a road) katoog

catalogue *n* katalogus; lys; pryslys

catamaran *n* tweeromper

catapult *n* rekker

catarrh *n* katar

catch *vb* haal; vat; betrap; (water)

opvang; — **hold of** *vb* aangryp; — **up** *vb* inhaal; opvang

catch a chill *vb* vat koue

catch a cold *vb* 'n verkoue kry; vat koue

catch fire *vb* ontbrand; ontvlam

catch fish *vb* visvang

catchment area *n* inloop; opvanggebied

catchment dam *n* vangdam

catechism *n* vraeboek

catechism class *n* katkisasie

category *n* kategorie

cater *vb* spysenier

caterer *n* spysenier

caterpillar *n* ruspe(r)

catharsis *n* katarsis; loutering

cathedral *n* katedraal

cathode *n* negatiewe pool

cattle *n* beeste

cattle auction *n* veeveiling

cattle farm *n* veeplaas

caucus *n* koukus

caught *adj* gevange

cauliflower *n* blomkool

cause *n* oorsaak; rede; *vb* aandoen; (illness) meebring; — **to conceive** *vb* bevrug; — **surprise** *vb* meeval

caustic soda *n* seepsoda

cauterize *vb* skroei

caution *n* omsigtigheid; versigtigheid; *vb* waarsku

cautious *adj* behoedsaam; omsigtig

cautiously *adv* voetjie-voetjie

cavalry *n* kavallerie; ruitery

cave *n* grot; spelonk; hol

cave in *vb* inkalwe; toeval

cavern *n* spelonk

caviar(e) *n* kaviaar

cavity *n* holte; duik

cayenne pepper *n* rissie

cayman *n* (crocodile) kaaiman

CCTV *see* **closed-circuit television**

CD *see* **compact disc**

CD player *n* kompakskyfspeler; laserskyfspeler

cease *vb* ophou; uitskei; — **work** *vb* staak

ceasefire *n* skietstaking; skietstilstand

cedar *n* seder

cede *vb* afstaan; oorgee

ceiling *n* plafon

celebrate *vb* feesvier; vier; (birthday) verjaar

celebrated *adj* vermaard

celebration *n* fuif

celery *n* selery

celestial *adj* hemels

celestial being *n* hemeling

celestial body *n* hemelliggaam

celibacy *n* selibaat

cell *n* sel

cell phone *n* selfoon

cellar *n* kelder

cellist *n* tjellis

cello *n* tjello

cellulose *n* sellulose

cement *n* sement

cemetery *n* begraafplaas; kerkhof

censor *n* sensor

censure *vb* bestraf; sensureer

census *n* sensus; telling; volkstelling

cent *n* sent

centenary *adj* honderdjarig; *n* eeufees

centennial *adj* honderdjarig

centimetre *n* sentimeter

centipede *n* duisendpoot

central *adj* middelste; sentraal

centralization *n* sentralisasie

centre *n* middel; middelpunt; sentrum

centre of gravity *n* swaartepunt

centrifugal *adj* middelpuntvliedend

century *n* eeu

ceramist *n* pottebakker

cerebral *adj* serebraal

cerebral palsy *n* serebraalverlamming

ceremony *n* plegtigheid; seremonie

certain *adj* gewis; seker; stellig; vas; wis; a — *pron* ene

certainly *adv* gewis; seker; sekerlik; verseker

certainty *n* sekerheid; vastheid; vastigheid

certificate *n* diploma; seël; sertifikaat

certificates *npl* papiere

certification *n* attestasie

certified *adj* gewaarmerkte

certify *vb* waarmerk; sertifiseer

cessation *n* staking; stilstand

cession *n* sessie

cesspit *n* put

cesspool *n* put

chafe *vb* skaaf; afskaaf

chaff *n* kaf

chain *n* band; ketting; kluister; *vb* boei

chain reaction *n* kettingreaksie

chair *n* setel; stoel; gestoelte

chair back *n* rugleuning

chairman *n* voorsitter

chairwoman *n* voorsitster

chalice *n* kelk

chalk *n* kryt

challenge *vb* tart; uitdaag

challenged *adj* (physically, etc.) gestrem(d)

chamber *n* kamer

chamber music *n* kamermusiek

chameleon *n* trapsoetjies; verkleurmannetjie

chamois leather *n* seemsleer

champagne *n* sjampanje; vonkelwyn

champion *n* kampioen; voorstander; voorvegter; bobaas

chance *n* kans; toeval

chancer *n* (*informal*) waaghals

chandelier *n* kroon

change *n* kleingeld; verandering; kentering; omkeer; oorgang; *vb* afwissel; — clothes *vb* verklee; — colour *vb* verkleur; — gears *vb* verstel

changeable *adj* onbestendig; veranderlik; wisselvallig

channel *n* kanaal

chaos *n* chaos; baaierd; (physics) chaos

chaotic *adj* chaoties

chap *n* kêrel; ou

chapel *n* kapel; kerk

chaplain *n* kapelaan

chapped *adj* skurf

chapter *n* hoofstuk; kapittel

character *n* karakter; inbors; gesteldheid; tipe

characteristic *adj* kenmerkend; *n* karakteristiek

characteristic feature *n* kenmerk

characterize *n* kenmerk

characterless *adj* karakterloos

charcoal *n* houtskool

charge *n* aanklag; beskuldiging; las; *vb* aanval; belas; — with *vb* aankla; beskuldig; verkla

charge office *n* polisiekantoor

charitable *adj* liefdadig; mededeelsaam; milddadig; weldadig

charity *n* aalmoes; genadebrood; liefdadigheid; weldadigheid

charm *n* doepa; paljas; toorgoed; *vb* aanlok

charming *adj* aanvallig; bekoorlik; bevallig; innemend; lieflik; sjarmant; verruklik

chart *n* kaart

charter *n* oktrooi

chase *n* jag; *vb* jaag; — **away** *vb* wegjaag

chasm *n* kloof

chassis *n* onderstel

chaste *adj* kuis; rein

chastise *vb* kasty; tugtig

chastisement *n* kastyding

chastity *n* reinheid

chat *vb* gesels; praat

chatline *n* geselslyn

chatroom *n* geselskamer

chatter *vb* snater; babbel; (teeth) klapper

chatterbox *n* babbelkous; kekkelbek

chatty *adj* spraaksaam

chauvinism *n* chauvinisme

chauvinist *n* chauvinis

cheap *adj* goedkoop

cheat *n* afsetter; boereverneuker; pypkan; *vb* bedrieg

check *n* kontrole; skaak; *vb* bedwing

check in *vb* inklaar

check-up *n* (medical) roetine-ondersoek

checked *adj* (material) geruit

checkered *adj* geruit

checkmate *n* skaakmat

cheek *n* kies; wang

cheekbone *n* wangbeen; jukbeen

cheeky *adj* parmantig; astrant; brutaal; domastrant

cheekily *adv* hans

cheer *vb* jubel; toejuig

cheer up *vb* opbeur; opkikker; opvrolik

cheerful *adj* blymoedig; lustig; onbesorg; opgeruimd; opgewek; plesierig; verblydend; vrolik; welgemoed

cheerfully *adv* goedsmoeds

cheerfulness *n* vrolikheid

cheering *n* gejuig; toejuiging

cheerleader *n* rasieleier

cheese *n* kaas

cheeseburger *n* kaasburger

chef *n* sjef

chemical *adj* chemies; skeikundig

chemical peel *n* chemiese afskilfering

chemist *n* apteker; skeikundige

chemist's shop *n* apteek

chemistry *n* chemie; skeikunde

cheque *n* tjek

cheque book *n* tjekboek

chequered *adj* geskakeer

cherish *vb* koester

cherry *n* kersie; sjerrie

chess *n* skaak

chess player *n* skaker

chess tournament *n* skaaktoernooi

chessboard *n* skaakbord

chessmen *n* skaakstukke

chest *n* bors; kas; kis; koffer

chest of drawers *n* laaikas

chestnut *n* kastaiing

chevalier *n* ridder

chew *vb* kou; (tobacco) pruim; — **the cud** *vb* herkou

chewing gum *n* kougom

chic *adj* sjiek

chicken *n* (bird) hoender; (meat) hoendervleis

chickenpox *n* waterpokkies

chicory *n* tjiekorie

chide *vb* beknor

chief *n* hoof; kaptein; opperhoof; owerste; sjef; *adj* kardinaal

chief executive *n* hoofbestuurder

chief mate *n* stuurman

chiefly *adv* grotendeels; veral; vernaamlik

chieftain *n* opperhoof

child *n* kind

child abuse *n* kindermolestering

child molester *n* pedofiel

child prodigy *n* wonderkind

child restraint *n* kindkeerder

childbirth *n* bevalling; kraam

childhood *n* kinderjare

childish *adj* kinderagtig; kinds

childlike *adj* kinderlik

childproof cap *n* kindveilige prop

children *n* kleingoed; kinders

children's home *n* kinderhawe

chill *n* kou; koue; rilling; verkoue; *vb* afkoel

chilli *n* rissie

chilly *adj* koud
chimney *n* skoorsteen
chimney sweep *n* skoorsteenveër
chimpanzee *n* sjimpansee
chin *n* ken
china *n* porselein
chink *n* spleet; *vb* (money) rammel
chintz *n* sis
chip *n* spaander
chipboard *n* spaanderbord; spaanderhout
chiropodist *n* voetheelkundige
chiropractor *n* chiropraktisyn
chirp *vb* piep; tjilp
chisel *n* beitel
chivalrous *adj* ridderlik
chlorine *n* chloor
CFC *see* chlorofluorocarbon
chlorofluorocarbon *n* chlorofluoorkoolstof
chloroform *n* chloroform
chock full *adj* (*informal*) stampvol; tjokvol
chocoholic *n* sjokoladevraat
chocolate *n* sjokolade
choice *adj* puik; uitgelese; *n* keur
choir *n* koor
choke *vb* stik; versluk; verstik; wurg; become —d with weeds *vb* vervuil
choke chain *n* wurgketting
cholera *n* cholera
choose *vb* kies; uitkies; uitsoek; verkies
chop *vb* kap; hak; — off *vb* afkap
choral singing *n* koorsang
choral society *n* sangvereniging
choral song *n* koorsang
chorale *n* koraal
chord *n* akkoord
chore *n* roetinetaak
chorus *n* koor; refrein
Christ *n* Christus
christen *vb* doop
christening *n* doop
Christian *adj* Christelik; *n* Christen
Christian name *n* doopnaam; voornaam
Christianity *n* Christendom
Christmas *n* Kersfees
Christmas carol *n* Kerslied
Christmas Day *n* Kersdag
Christmas Eve *n* Kersaand; Oukersaand

Christmas tree *n* Kersboom
chronic *adj* chronies
chronic illness *n* chroniese siekte
chronicle *n* kroniek
chronological *adj* chronologies; kronologies
chronological order *n* tydsorde
chronology *n* tydrekening
chrysalis *n* papie
chubby *adj* mollig
chuck out *vb* uitsmyt
chum *n* tjom
church *n* kerk
church pew *n* kerkbank
church steeple *n* kerktoring
churchwarden *n* koster
churchyard *n* kerkhof
churlish *adj* buffelagtig; honds; iesegrimmig
churn *n* karring
chutney *n* atjar; blatjang
ciabatta *n* ciabatta
cicada *n* sonbesie; boomsingertjie
cider *n* appelwyn
cigar *n* sigaar
cigarette *n* sigaret
cigarette end *n* stompie
cigarette lighter *n* vuurslag
cigarette stub *n* stompie
cinema *n* bioskoop; fliek; skouburg
cinnamon *n* kaneel
circle *n* kring; sirkel; ring; rondte; *vb* omsluit; omtrek; rond gaan
circuit *n* kringloop; sirkelgang; rondreis
circuit court *n* rondgaande hof
circular *n* omsendbrief; sirkulêre
circular letter *n* rondskrywe
circular saw *n* rolsaag; sirkelsaag
circulate *vb* sirkuleer; uitstrooi
circulation *n* omloop; sirkulasie; (periodical) oplaag
circumcision *n* besnydenis
circumference *n* omtrek; omvang; rondte
circumflex *n* sirkumfleks
circumspect *adj* omsigtig
circumstance *n* omstandigheid
circumstances *npl* toestand
circus *n* sirkus
cistern *n* spoelbak; reënbak

cite *vb* aanhaal
citizen *n* burger; staatsburger
citizenship *n* burgerreg
citrus *n* sitrus
city *n* stad
city dweller *n* stedeling
city hall *n* stadhuis; stadsaal
civic theatre *n* stadskouburg
civil *adj* siviel
civil rights *n* burgerreg
civil servant *n* amptenaar; staatsamptenaar
civil service *n* staatsdiens
civil war *n* burgeroorlog
civilian *n* burger
civilian clothes *n* burgerklere
civilization *n* beskawing; kultuur
civilized *adj* beskaaf
claim *n* eis; aanspraak; reg; vordering; *vb* opeis
claimant *n* eiser
clairvoyant *n* heldersiende
clamber *vb* klouter
clamorous *adj* luidrugtig
clamour *n* rumoer
clamp *n* klamp; kram; *vb* klamp; kram
clan *n* stam
clandestine *adj* heimlik
clang *vb* kletter
clap *n* klap; knal; (thunder) slag; *vb* apploudisseer
claptrap *n* slimpraatjies
clarify *vb* uitklaar; verduidelik
clarion call *n* wekroep
clarionet *n* klarinet
clash *n* uitval; *vb* aandruis
clasp *n* gespe; haak; klem; knip; slot
clasps *npl* beslag
class *n* klas; rang
class teacher *n* klasonderwyser
classic(al) *adj* klassiek
classification *n* klassifikasie
classify *vb* groepeer; indeel; klassifiseer; rangskik
classroom *n* klaskamer
clatter *n* ratel; *vb* kletter
clause *n* artikel; klousule; (law) wetsartikel
claustrophobia *n* noutevrees
claw *n* klou
clay *n* klei; erd

clean *adj* net; rein; sindelik; skoon; *vb* reinig; skoonmaak; — **out** *vb* uitskud
cleaner *n* skoonmaker
cleaning *n* reiniging
cleanse *vb* reinig
clear *adj* aanskoulik; begryplik; blykbaar; deurslaande; duidelik; helder; klaar; *vb* ontruim; baan; (forest) ontgin; (table) afdek; afneem; — **a cheque** *vb* verreken; — **customs** *vb* inklaar; — **away** *vb* opruim; wegruim; — **off** *vb* trap; — **out** *vb* uitskud; — **up** *vb* oorgaan; ophelder; opklaar; uitklaar
clear-headed *adj* nugter
clearance *n* vryhoogte
clearance sale *n* uitverkoop
clearly *adv* blykbaar
cleave *vb* klowe; kloof
clef *n* (music) sleutel
cleft *n* kloof
cleg *n* (insect) perdevlieg
clemency *n* genade
clench *vb* klem
clenched *adj* gebal
clergyman *n* dominee; geestelike; predikant
clerical *adj* klerklik
clerk *n* klerk; pennelekker
clever *adj* slim; handig; knap; kranig; kunstig; oorlams; skrander; gevat; vaardig; vindingryk
click *n* klik; *vb* (with the tongue) klik
client *n* kliënt
clientele *n* klandisie
cliff *n* krans; rots
cliffhanger *n* (TV series, movies) naelkouer
climate *n* klimaat; lugstreek
climax *n* klimaks; toppunt
climb *vb* beklim; bestyg; klim; klouter; opklim; styg; — **down** *vb* afklim; — **into** *vb* inklim; — **up** *vb* opklouter
clinch *vb* klink
cling *vb* kleef; klewe; vasklou
clingstone peach *n* taaipitperske
clinic *n* kliniek
clinical *adj* klinies
clinical thermometer *n* koorspen(netjie)
clip *n* knip; *vb* snoei

clipping *n* uitknipsel
clique *n* kliek
cloak *n* dekmantel; mantel; *vb* bemantel
cloakroom *n* kleedkamer
clock *n* horlosie; klok; uurwerk
clockwise *adv* haarom
clockwork *n* uurwerk
clod *n* kluit; pol; klont
clog *n* klomp; *vb* verstop
clogged up *adj* verstop
close[1] *adj* dig; trompop; agterhoudend; terughoudend; bedompig; swoel
close[2] *n* end; *vb* snoer; afsluit; — in *vb* aanbreek
close by *adv* naby; digby; ophande
close friend *n* boesemvriend
close to *prep* naby
close-fitting *adj* knap
closed *adj* geslote; toe; —d to others *adj* beslote
closed-circuit television *n* toe-kring-TV
closely *adv* na; — related *adj* naverwant
closing date *n* sluitdatum
closure *n* afsluiting; genesing
clot *n* swaap; *vb* klonter
cloth *n* doek; laken; lap
clothes *npl* kleding; klerasie; klere
clothes brush *n* klereborsel
clothing *n* kleding; klerasie; klere
cloud *n* wolk
cloud over *vb* betrek
cloudburst *n* wolkbreuk
cloudless *adj* onbewolk
cloudy *adj* betrokke; bewolk
clover *n* klawer
cloves *npl* naeltjies
clown *n* hanswors
club *n* klub; knopkierie
clubs *npl* (playing cards) klawers
cluck *vb* kloek
clue *n* leidraad
clumsy *adj* lomp; onbeholpe; onhandig; houterig
cluster *n* groep; tros
clutch *n* greep; *vb* gryp
cooperate *vb* meewerk; saamwerk
cooperation *n* koöperasie; medewerking; meewerking
coordination *n* koördinasie

coach *n* koets; rytuig; wa; *vb* afrig
coach house *n* waenhuis
coach-builder *n* rytuigmaker
coagulate *vb* stol
coal *n* kool; steenkool
coalition *n* koalisie
coarse *adj* grof; onguur; ru; — brown bread *n* grofbrood
coarseness *n* ruheid
coast *n* kus; seekus
coat *n* baadjie; bobaadjie; jas
coat of arms *n* wapen
coat of mail *n* pantserhemp
coat-tail *n* pant
coating *n* laag
coax *vb* flikflooi; paai; pamperlang; vlei
coaxing *n* gesmeek
cob *n* kop; (mealie) stronk
cobbler *n* skoenmaker
cobra *n* geelslang; kapel
cobweb *n* spinnerak
cocaine *n* kokaïen
coccyx *n* stuitjie
cock *n* haan
cockatiel *n* kokketiel
cockatoo *n* kaketoe
cockroach *n* kakkerlak
cocktail *n* skemerkelkie
cocktail party *n* skemerparty
cocky *adj* eiewys
cocoa *n* kakao
coconut *n* klapper; kokosneut
coconut shell *n* klapperdop
coconut tree *n* kokosboom
cod *n* kabeljou
cod-liver oil *n* lewertraan; visolie
code *n* kode; (law) wetboek; *vb* kodeer
coffee *n* koffie
coffee house *n* koffiehuis
coffee pot *n* koffiekan
coffer *n* kas
coffin *n* dood(s)kis; kis
cog *n* tand; kam; rat; tandrat
cohabit *vb* saamleef
coil *vb* kronkel
coil *n* (electricity) klos
coin *n* geldstuk; munt; muntstuk
coincidence *n* toeval
colander *n* vergiet
cold *adj* guur; huiwerig; koel; koud; *n* kou
cold war *n* koue oorlog

cold-blooded adj koelbloedig
colic n koliek
collaborate vb meewerk
collaboration n medewerking; samewerking
collaborator n meeloper
collagen n kollageen
collapse n inval; vb instort
collar n boordjie; kraag; halsband
collarbone n sleutelbeen
colleague n ampgenoot; kollega
collect vb insamel; kollekteer; opgaar; versamel; (debts) in; (taxes) invorder; — **together** vb (as in a shoal) skool
collectable adj invorderbaar
collected adj kalm
collectible adj inbaar
collection n bundel; versameling; (church, street) kollekte
collectively adj gesamentlik
college n kollege
collide vb bots; aanbots
collude vb heul
colon n dubbelpunt (:)
colonel n kolonel
colonial adj koloniaal
colonize vb koloniseer
colony n kolonie; nedersetting; volksplanting
colossal adj kolossaal; reusagtig
colostomy n kolostomie
colour n kleur; vb kleur
colour-blind adj kleurblind
colour-coded adj kleurgekodeer
coloured adj gekleurd
colouring n koloriet
colt n vul
column n kolom; pilaar; suil; (newspaper) rubriek
comb n kam
combat vehicle n vegtuig
combatant n vegter
combination n kombinasie
combine vb kombineer
combine harvester n stroper
combustible adj brandbaar
combustion n verbranding
come vb kom; — **into the possession of** vb toeval; — **across** vb aantref; tref; vind; — **along** vb aankom; — **to an end** vb eindig; — **back** vb

terugkom; — **down** vb afdaal; afkom; neerdaal; neerkom; — **to grief** vb verongeluk; — **in** vb binnekom; inkom; — **nearer** vb nader; — **off second best** vb die onderspit delf; — **off worst** vb die onderspit delf; — **out** vb uitkom; (as a homosexual) bekend maak; — **round** vb omkom; — **through** vb deurkom; — **to** vb bedra; — **to a stop** vb stilhou; — **together** vb saamkom; — **true** vb uitkom; — **up** vb opkom; — **up with** vb bykom
comedian n komediant
comedy n blyspel; komedie
comet n komeet
comfort n gemak; gerief; troos; welbehae; vb vertroos
comfortable adj gemaklik; grieflik; welbehaaglik
comforting adj verkwikkend
comic adj koddig; luimig
comic strip n prentverhaal; strokiesprent; strokiesverhaal
comic(al) adj komies
coming adj aankomend; n koms; —**of-age movie** grootwordfliek
comma n komma
command n order; vb aanvoer; order; — **respect** vb afdwing
commandant n kommandant
commandeer n oproep; vb kommandeer
commander n aanvoerder; gesaghebber; gesagvoerder; kommandant
commanding adj gebiedend
commandment n gebod
commando n kommando
commemorate vb herdenk
commemorative medal n gedenkpenning
commence vb aanvang; begin; aanhef
commencement n begin
commencing adj aanvanklik
commendable adj aanbevelenswaardig
commensurate adj eweredig
comment n glos
commentary n kommentaar
commerce n handel; koophandel
commercial adj kommersieel
commercial bank n handelsbank
commercial business n handelsaak**

commercial goods n koopwaar
commercial law n handelsreg
commercial venture n handelsonderneming
commiserate vb ontferm
commiseration n ontferming
commissariat n kommissariaat
commission n kommissie; opdrag
commissioner n kommissaris; opsiener
commit vb aanrig; pleeg; verbind; **— a crime** vb begaan; **— a sin** vb sondig; **— an offence** n vergryp
committee n komitee
commodities npl ware
commodity n artikel
common adj alledaags; banaal; gemeen; gemeenskaplik; gewoon; ordinêr
common sense n gesonde verstand
common waxbill n rooibekkie
commonly adv deurgaans; algemeen
commonplace adj gemeenplaas
commotion n kabaal; omhaal; omslag; opskudding
communicate vb mededeel; meedeel; **— pleasure** (or **praise**) gelukwens
communication n kommunikasie; mededeling; meedeling; verkeer
communicative adj mededeelsaam; meedeelsaam
communist n kommunis
community n gemeenskap; samelewing
commute vb pendel; verwissel
commuter n pendelaar
compact adj dig
compact disk n kompakskyf; laserskyf
companion n gesèl; kameraad; metgesel
companionship n kameraadskap
company n genootskap; geselskap; maatskappy; (business) kompanjie
company car n firmamotor
comparative adj vergelykend
compare vb monster; vergelyk met; meet
compared with prep teenoor
comparison n vergelyk; vergelyking
compartment n afdeling; kompartement; vak(kie)
compass n kompas

compasses n (pair of) passer
compassion n deernis; erbarming; medelye; mededoë; meedoë
compassionate adj barmhartig; jammerhartig
compatriot n landgenoot
compel vb noodsaak; dwing
compelling adj gebiedend
compensate vb kompenseer; tegemoetkom
compensation n kompensasie; skadevergoeding; vergoeding
compete vb wedywer; kompeteer; **— for** vb ding
competent adj kundig; bevoeg
competition n kompetisie; wedstryd; wedywer; konkurrensie
competitor n konkurrent; mededinger
compilation n samestelling; versameling
compile vb saamstel; versamel
complain vb kla
complainant n klaer
complaint n beklag; klagte; kwaal
complementary adj komplementêr
complete adj gesamentlik; kompleet; volkome; volledig; volslae; voltallig; geheel vb aanvul; **— a form** vb 'n vorm invul; **— disorder** n chaos
completely adv enemale: halsoorkop; spoorloos; geheel; **— dark** adj pikdonker
complex adj kompleks; saamgesteld
complexion n gelaatskleur; kleur
compliance n inskiklikheid
complicated adj gekompliseer; ingewikkel(d)
complication n verwikkeling
compliment n kompliment; pluimpie
comply with vb inwillig; naleef; voldoen
complying adj inskiklik
compose vb opstel; komponeer
composed adj bedaard; besadig; kalm
composer n komponis
composition n komposisie; opstel; samestelling
compositor n setter
compost n kompos
compound adj saamgesteld
comprehend vb begryp; verstaan

comprehensible *adj* verstaanbaar
comprehension *n* vuurmaakplek
comprehensive *adj* veelomvattend; —
  insurance *n* omvattende versekering
compress *vb* saamdruk
comprise *vb* behels; bevat
compromise *n* kompromis; vergelyk;
  vb kompromitteer
compulsory *adj* gedwonge; verpligtend
compunction *n* wroeging
compute *vb* reken
computer *n* rekenaar
computer science *n* rekenaarwetenskap
computer virus *n* rekenaarvirus
computer-aided *adj* rekenaargesteunde
computer-assisted *adj* rekenaargesteunde
computerize *vb* rekenariseer
comrade *n* kameraad; maat
comradeship *n* kameraadskap
concave *adj* hol
conceal *vb* bedek; bêre; ontveins; opkrop; verberg; verswyg
concealed *adj* verborge; verstoke
concealment *n* geheimhouding
concede *vb* inwillig
conceit *n* verwaandheid
conceited *adj* eiewys; pedanties; verwaand; waanwys
conceitedness *n* aanstellerigheid; verwaandheid
conceivable *adj* begryplik
conceive *vb* ontvang
concensus *adj* konsensus
concentration *n* konsentrasie
concept *n* konsep
conception *n* konsepsie; ontvangenis
concern *n* belang; saak; traak; *vb* aangaan
concerned *adj* gemoeid; **be — about**
  vb aanbetref; **be — with** *vb* betrokke
  wees by
concerning *prep* aangaande; betreffende; weens
concert *n* konsert
concertina *n* konsertina
concession *n* konsessie; toegewing
concise *adj* beknop; bondig
conclude *vb* afloop; besluit; afhandel

conclusion *n* end; gevolgtrekking; konklusie; slot
conclusive *adj* afdoende; beslis;
  (proof) deurslaande
concoct *vb* versin
concord *n* eendrag; ooreenstemming
concordance *n* samestemming
concourse *n* sameloop
concrete *n* beton
concur *vb* instem; ooreenstem; saamstem
concussion *n* harsingskudding
condemn *vb* vonnis; afkeur
condensation *n* kondensasie
condense *vb* kondenseer
condition *n* gesteldheid; kondisie; staat;
  toestand; voorwaarde; **— of great**
  distress *n* beproewing
conditional *adj* voorwaardelik
condom *n* kondoom
conducive *adj* bevorderlik
conduct *n* gedrag; houding; lewenswyse; voer; wandel; *vb* lei; (orchestra)
  dirigeer
conducted tour *n* rondleiding
conductor *n* dirigent; orkesmeester
cone *n* keël
confectioner *n* koekbakker
confectionery *n* banket; lekkergoed
confederation *n* bond; konfederasie
confer *vb* konfereer
conference *n* konferensie; samespreking
conference call *n* deeloproep
conference delegate *n* konferensieganger
confess *vb* bely; bieg; (sin) beken
confession *n* belydenis; bekentenis;
  konfessie
confidant *n* vertroueling
confide *vb* toevertrou; vertrou
confidence *n* vertroue
confidential *adj* vertroulik; konfidensieel
confine *vb* beperk; opsluit
confined *adj* bekrompe; **— to bed** *adj*
  bedlêend
confinement *n* bevalling
confirm *vb* bestendig; bevestig; goedkeur; onderskrywe; staaf; bekragtig;
  waarmaak; (religion) aanneem

confirmation *n* (religion) aanneming
confiscate *vb* verbeurd verklaar; konfiskeer; (property) beslag lê op
confiscated *adj* verbeurd
confiscation *n* konfiskasie
conflict *n* konflik; stryd
conflicting *adj* teenstrydig
confluence *n* sameloop; samevloeiing
conformity *n* ooreenkoms
confrontation *n* konfrontasie
confuse *vb* verwar
confused *adj* bedremmeld; beteuterd; onderstebo; verbouereerd
confusion *n* herrie; verleentheid; verwarring; wanorde; warboel
congeal *vb* bevries; stol
congenital *adj* aangebore
congestion *n* kongestie
congratulate *vb* felisiteer
congratulations *n* gelukwens
congregation *n* gemeente; kerk
conical *adj* keëlvormig; kegelvormig
conjecture *n* gis; gissing
conjugal *adj* egtelik
conjugate *vb* vervoeg
conjugation *n* vervoeging
conjunction *n* konjunksie; voegwoord
conjure *vb* besweer; goël; toor
conjuring *n* goëlery
conjuror *n* goëlaar
conman *n* boereverneuker; vertroueswendelaar
connect *vb* skakel; aansluit
connection *n* aansluiting; konneksie; verband; verbinding
connive *vb* heul
connoisseur *n* fynproewer; kenner
conquer *vb* oorwin; seëvier; verower; verslaan; inneem; kleinkry
conquerer *n* oorwinnaar
conquest *n* verowering
conscience *n* gewete; konsensie
conscientious *adj* konsensieus; nougeset
conscious *adj* bewus; **be — of** *vb* besef
consciousness *n* bewussyn; kennis
conscription *n* konskripsie
consecrate *vb* heilig; inseën; inwy; toewy
consecrated *adj* gewyde
consecutive *adj* opeenvolgend; gereeld

consecutively *adv* aaneengeslote; aanmekaar; agtereen
consent *n* jawoord; toestemming; *vb* toestem
consequence *n* gevolg; nasleep
consequently *adv* derhalwe; gevolglik
conservative *adj* konserwatief
conservatoire *n* konservatorium
conservatory *n* konservatorium
consider *vb* aansien; oorleg; aanmerk
considerable *adj* aanmerklik; aansienlik; beduidend; geruime
considerate *adj* attent; bedagsaam
consideration *n* bedenking; konsiderasie; oorleg; oorweging
considered *adj* oorwoë; **— opinion** *n* oorwoë mening
consignment *n* besending; sending; versending
consignment note *n* vragbrief
consist of *vb* bestaan uit
consolation *n* troos
consolation prize *n* troosprys
console *vb* troos; vertroos
consonant *n* konsonant; medeklinker
consort *n* gemaal; gemalin
conspicuous *adj* opvallend
conspiracy *n* sameswering
conspirator *n* samesweerder
conspire *vb* saamspan; saamsweer
constable *n* konstabel; polisieman
constant *adj* gedurig; gestadig; onveranderlik; standvastig
constantly *adv* steeds
constellation *n* gesternte; konstellasie; sterrebeeld
consternation *n* konsternasie; ontsetting
constipate *vb* verstop
constipated *adj* hardlywig
constipation *n* verstopping
constituency *n* kiesafdeling; kiesdistrik
constitute *vb* uitmaak
constitution *n* konstitusie; gestel
constrain *vb* dwing
construct *vb* aanbring; timmer
construction *n* aanbou; konstruksie; samestelling
constructive *adj* opbouend
consul *n* konsul
consulate *n* konsulaat

consult *vb* beraadslaag; konfereer; konsulteer; naslaan; raadpleeg
consultation *n* konsultasie
consulting *adj* raadgewend
consulting room *n* spreekkamer
consume *vb* verbruik; teer
consumer *n* verbruiker
consumption *n* longtering; tering; verbruik; konsumpsie
contact *n* kontak
contact lens *n* kontaklens
contagious *adj* besmetlik
contain *vb* behels; bevat; hou; inhou; insluit
container *n* drom; houer
container ship *n* houerskip
contaminate *vb* besmet; verpes
contemplate *vb* aanskou; beskou
contemplated *adj* oorwoë
contemplation *n* bespiegeling
contemporary *adj* tydgenoot; toenmalig
contempt *n* minagting; veragting
contemptible *adj* veragtelik
contend *vb* beweer
content *adj* tevrede; *n* inhoud
contented *adj* vergenoeg; welgemoed
contention *n* bewering
contentious *adj* twissiek; omstrede
contentment *n* tevredenheid
contents *npl* inhoud
contest *n* wedstryd; *vb* bestry
context *n* teks; verband
continent *n* kontinent; vasteland; wêrelddeel
continual *adj* aanhoudend; gedurig
continually *adv* gedurig; voortdurend
continuation *n* vervolg
continue *vb* duur; vervolg; aanbly
continuity *n* kontinuïteit
continuous *adj* deurlopend; onafgebroke; onophoudelik; voortdurend
contour *n* kontoer
contraceptive *n* voorbehoedmiddel
contraceptive pill *n* voorbehoedpil
contract *n* kontrak; ooreenkoms; verbintenis; *vb* inkrimp
contraction *n* ineenkrimping; inkrimping
contractor *n* aannemer; kontrakteur
contradict *vb* stry; teenpraat; teenspreek; weerspreek
contradiction *n* teenspraak
contradictory *adj* teenstrydig
contrary *adj* dwars; strydig; teendeel; teenoorgestel
contrast *n* kontras; teëhanger; teenhanger; teenstelling
contrast with *vb* afsteek by
contribute *vb* bydra
contribution *n* bydrae; insending; kontribusie
contributor *n* donateur; insender
contrive *vb* bedink; beraam
control *n* bedwang; beheer; kontrole; *vb* bedwing
controversial *adj* polemies; omstrede
controversy *n* dispuut
convene a meeting *vb* belê
convener *n* sameroeper
convenience *n* gerief
convenient *adj* geleë; gerieflik
convent *n* klooster; nonneklooster
convent school *n* kloosterskool
convention *n* konvensie
conventional *adj* konvensioneel; vormlik
conversation *n* gesprek; diskoers
converse *vb* spreek
convert *vb* bekeer; omskep
convex *adj* konveks; bol
convey *vb* vervoer; aanry
conveyance *n* vervoer
conveyor belt *n* voerband
convict *n* bandiet; *vb* skuld bewys; skuldig vind
conviction *n* gesindheid; oortuiging
convince *vb* oortuig
convincing *adj* oortuigend
conviviality *n* geselligheid
convoy *n* konvooi
convulsion *n* kramp; stuiptrekking
convulsions *npl* stuipe
convulsive *adj* krampagtig
coo *vb* kir
cook *n* kok; *vb* kook
cookery *n* kookkuns
cookery book *n* kookboek
cool *adj* kalm; koel; stuurs; *vb* afkoel; verkoel; **— down** *vb* (horse) koudlei
cool bag *n* koelsak; yssak
cool drink *n* koeldrank
coop *n* hok; kuip

cooperation *n* samewerking
copious *adj* uitvoerig
copper *n* koper
copper wire *n* koperdraad
copse *n* bossie
copy *n* afdruk; afskrif; eksemplaar; kopie; (newspaper) nommer; *vb* afskryf; **— out** *vb* oorskryf; uitskryf
copyright *n* kopiereg; outeursreg
coquettish *adj* koket
coral *n* koraal
coral reef *n* koraalrif
cord *n* tou; band; koord; lyn; snaar; snoer
cordial *adj* gul; hartlik; innig
cordon *n* kordon
cords *n* (trousers) ferweel
corduroy *n* ferweel
core *n* kern
coriander *n* koljander
cork *n* kurk; prop
corkscrew *n* kurktrekker; trekker
corn *n* graan; koring; liddoring
cornea *n* horingvlies
corner *n* hoek; *vb* vaskeer
cornerstone *n* hoeksteen
corona *n* ligkrans
coronary thrombosis *n* koronêre trombose
coronation *n* kroning
corporal[1] *n* korporaal
corporal[2] *adj* liggaamlik
corporal punishment *n* liggaamstraf; lyfstraf
corporation *n* korporasie
corps *n* korps
corpse *n* lyk
corpulent *adj* geset; swaarlywig
correct *adj* aangewese; juis; korrek; reg; *vb* korrigeer
correctly *adv* juis; goed
correction *n* korreksie; swaarlywig; verbetering
correctness *n* juistheid
correspond *vb* korrespondeer
correspondence *n* briefwisseling; korrespondensie
correspondent *n* korrespondent
corresponding *adj* ooreenkomstig
corridor *n* deurgang
corroborate *vb* bewaarheid

corrode *vb* invreet; uitvreet; wegvreet
corrosion *n* korrosie
corrugate *vb* riffel
corrugated *adj* geriffel
corrugated iron *n* sink
corrugation *n* riffel
corrupt *adj* bedorwe; korrup; verdorwe; *vb* bederf; omkoop
corruption *n* bederf; korrupsie; omkopery
corset *n* borsrok; korset
cosiness *n* geselligheid
cosmetic *adj* kosmeties
cosmetic surgery *n* plastiese chirurgie
cosmopolitan *n* kosmopoliet; wêreldburger; *adj* kosmopolities
cost *n* uitgawe; *vb* kos
cost price *n* fabrieksprys; inkoopprys
costs *npl* koste; onkoste
costume *n* drag; kostuum
cosy *adj* gesellig
cot *n* wieg
cot death *n* wiegiedood
cottage *n* hut; kothuis
cottage cheese *n* maaskaas
cotton *n* gare; katoen
cotton wool *n* watte
couch *n* kanapee
couch grass *n* kweek
couch potato *n* TV-slaaf
cough *n* hoes
cough up *vb* (phlegm) roggel
coughing fit *n* hoesbui
council *n* raad
council chamber *n* raadskamer; raadsaal
councillor *n* raadslid
counsel *n* oorleg; raad; raadgewing
count[1] *n* tel; *vb* optel; **— again** *vb* oortel; **— off** *vb* aftel
count[2] *n* graaf
countenance *n* aangesig; gelaat
counter[1] *n* teller
counter[2] *n* toonbank
counter-insurgence *n* teeninsurgensie
counter-order *n* teenbevel
counterattack *n* teenaanval
counterbalance *vb* opweeg
counterfeit *adj* nagemaak; *n* namaaksel
countermand *vb* afsê
counteroffensive *n* teenoffensief

counterpart *n* teëhanger; teenhanger
counterproductive *adj* teenproduktief
counterproposal *n* teenvoorstel
countess *n* gravin
counting *n* telling
countless *adj* onnoemlik; ontelbaar
country *n* land; platteland
coup d'état *n* staatsgreep
couple *n* paar; *vb* koppel
couplet *n* koeplet
coupon *n* koepon
courage *n* durf; moed
courageous *adj* manmoedig; moedig
course *n* beloop; gereg; koers; kursus; loopbaan; verloop; (river) loop
course of action *n* handelwyse
course of life *n* lewensloop
court *n* hof; *vb* vlerksleep; — **disaster** *vb* uitlok
court case *n* saak; hofsaak
court jester *n* hofnar
court martial *n* krygsraad
court of justice *n* gereg; geregshof; regbank
courteous *adj* beleef; galant; hoflik; manierlik; wellewend
courtesy *n* beleefdheid; galanterie
courting *n* vryerasie
courtyard *n* binneplaas
cousin *n* (female) nig; (male) neef
covenant *n* verbond
cover *n* dek; deksel; (book) omslag; *vb* bedek; (area) beslaan; (distance) aflê; — **up** *vb* inwikkel
covering letter *n* begeleidende brief
covet *vb* begeer
covetous *adj* geldgierig
covey *n* vlug
cow *n* koei; bees
coward *n* bangbroek; lafaard; papbroek
cowardly *adj* laf; lafhartig
coy *adj* preuts; sedig
crab *n* krap
crack *n* knak; kraak; skeur; (noise) knal *vb* bars
crack a whip *n* klap
cracker *n* klapper
crackle *vb* knetter
cradle *n* wieg
crafty *adj* arglistig; deurtrap; oorlams; slim

cram *vb* blok
crammed *adj* propvol
cramp *n* kramp
cramped *adj* benepe
crane *n* hyskraan; kraan; kraanvoël
crane one's neck *vb* uitrek
cranium *n* skedel
crank *n* kruk
crash *n* knal; smak
crash helmet *n* valhelm
crate *n* krat
crater *n* krater
crawl *vb* kruip; — **away** *vb* wegkruip
crayfish *n* kreef
crayon *n* kryt
craze *n* passie
crazy *adj* beduiweld; dol
creak *vb* kraak; knars; *n* gekraak; geknars
cream *n* room
cream of tartar *n* kremetart
crease *n* kreukel; plooi; rimpel; vou; *vb* frommel
crease resistant *adj* kreukeltraag
create *vb* skep; baar
creation *n* skepping
creator *n* maker; skepper
creature *n* skepsel
creatures *npl* gedierte
crèche *n* crèche
credentials *n* geloofsbriewe
credibility *n* geloofbaarheid; geloofwaardigheid
credibility gap *n* vertrouensgaping
credible *adj* aanneemlik; geloofbaar
credit *n* bate; krediet; *vb* krediteer
credit card *n* kredietkaart
credit note *n* kredietnota
creditor *n* krediteur; skuldeiser
credo *n* geloofsbelydenis
credulous *adj* goedgelowig; liggelowig
creed *n* geloof; geloofsbelydenis
creep *vb* kruip; — **into** *vb* inkruip
creeper *n* klimop
creepy *adj* grieselig; grillerig; rillerig
cremate *vb* veras; verbrand
cremation *n* lyksverbranding; verassing; verbranding
crematorium *n* krematorium
crepe *n* floers; lanfer
crescent *n* halfmaan; singel

crest *n* kam; kuif; wapen
crestfallen *adj* bekaf
crevice *n* spleet
crew *n* manskap; skeepsbemanning
crib *n* krip
cricket[1] *n* (insect) kriek
cricket[2] *n* (sport) krieket
cricket ball *n* krieketbal
cricket bat *n* krieketkolf
cries *npl* geroep; geskree(u)
crime *n* misdaad; gruweldaad; misdryf; vergryp; gruwel
criminal *adj* krimineel; *n* booswig
criminal law *n* strafreg
crimson *n, adj* karmosyn
cripple *vb* verlam
crippled *adj* kreupel; kruppel
crisis *n* keerpunt; krisis
crisp *adj* bros
criterion *n* maatstaf; kriterium
critic *n* kritikus; resensent
critical *adj* bedenklik; haglik; krities
criticism *n* aanmerking; kritiek; resensie
criticize *vb* hekel; kritiseer; resenseer; — **severely** *vb* roskam
crìtique *n* kritiek
croak *vb* kwaak
crochet *vb* hekel
crochet hook *n* hekelpen
crocheting *n* hekelwerk
crockery *n* breekgoed; erdewerk; skottelgoed
crocodile *n* krokodil
crook *n* skelm
crooked *adj* krom; skeef
croon *vb* neurie
crop *n* gesaaide; gewas; krop; oes; opbrings
crop rotation *n* wisselbou
crop up *vb* opkom
crops *npl* gesaaides
cross *adj* balhorig; dwars; nors; nydig; wrewelig; *n* kruis; *vb* deurkruis; — **over** *vb* oorgaan
cross a street *vb* oorsteek
cross-examination *n* kruisverhoor
cross-examine *vb* kruisvra; ondervra
cross-trainer *n* oefenskoen
crossbreeding *n* kruising
crossing *n* kruising; oortog; oorvaart

crossroad *n* kruispad; tweesprong
crossroads *n* dwarsstraat; oorweg
crosswise *adv* oorkruis
crossword puzzle *n* blokkiesraaisel
crouching *adj* gebukkend
croup *n* kroep; wurgsiekte
crow *n* kraai
crowbar *n* koevoet
crowd *n* gedrang; gewoel; hoop; klomp; lot; massa; menigte; skare; toeloop; toevloed; *vb* dring
crowd sourcing *n* groepkontraktering
crowd together *vb* dam
crown *n* kroon; diadeem; kruin; *vb* bekroon
crown of a hat *n* bol
crown jewels *npl* kroonjuwele
crown prince *n* kroonprins
crozier *n* staf
crucifix *n* kruisbeeld
crucify *vb* kruisig
cruel *adj* moorddadig; ongenadig; onmenslik; wreed
cruel person *n* wreedaard
cruelty *n* wreedheid
cruise *n* vaart; rondvaart; kruis; *vb* rondvaar
cruiser *n* kruiser
cruising speed *n* togsnelheid
crumb *n* krummel
crumble *vb* verbrokkel; verkrummel; — **away** *vb* afbrokkel; verbrokkel
crumple *vb* frommel; verfrommel
crusade *n* kruistog
crush *n* gedrang; *vb* platdruk
crust *n* kors; roof; (bread) korsie
crutch *n* kruk
cry *n* skree(u); uitroep; *vb* grens; — **out** *vb* uitroep
crybaby *n* grensbalie; skree(u)balie; tjankbalie
crying *n* geskree(u); skree(u)ery
crypt *n* grafkelder
crystal *n* kristal
crystallize *vb* kristalliseer
crystallized sugar *n* sandsuiker
cub *n* welp
cubbyhole *n* paneelkassie
cube *n* dobbelsteen; kubus
cubic *adj* kubiek
cubic measure *n* inhoudsmaat

cubicle *n* hokkie
cuckoo *n* koekoek
cucumber *n* komkommer
cud *n* koutjie
cuddle *vb* karnuffel
cuff *n* mansjet; omslag
cufflink *n* mansjetknoop
cul-de-sac *n* keerweer
cull *vb* uitdun
culpable homicide *n* strafbare manslag
culprit *n* skuldige
cultivate *vb* aankweek; teel
cultivate land *vb* bearbei; ontgin
cultivated land *n* saailand
cultivation *n* teelt
cultural *adj* kultureel
culture *n* kultuur
cultured pearl *n* kweekpêrel
cunning *adj* arglistig; geslepe; listig; onderduims; oorlams; slinks; slu; uitgeslape; *n* jakkalsstreek
cup *n* koppie; kommetjie; kelk; beker; drinkbeker
cupboard *n* kas
cupola *n* koepel
curate *n* hulpprediker
curator *n* kurator
curb *vb* intoom; matig
curdle *vb* skif; strem; klonter
cure *n* genesing; *vb* genees; sout; (skins) brei; — of *vb* afleer
cured *adj* gesout
curfew *n* klokreël
curio *n* kuriositeit; rariteit
curiosity *n* nuuskierigheid; rariteit; kuriositeit
curious *adj* nuuskierig; wonderlik
curl *n* krul; lok; *vb* friseer
currant *n* korent
currency *n* koers
current *adj* gangbaar; lopend; *n* stroming
current account *n* lopende rekening
current of air *n* tog
curriculum *n* kurrikulum; leerplan
curried mincemeat *n* bobotie
curry *n* kerrie
currycomb *n* roskam; *vb* roskam
curse *n* knoop; vloek; *vb* vervloek; verdoem

cursing *n* gevloek
cursory *adj* vlugtig
curtail *vb* besnoei; inkort
curtain *n* gordyn; voorhangsel; (theatre) skerm
curtain raiser *n* voorgeveg; voorwedstryd
curve *n* boog
curved *adj* krom
cushion *n* kussing; peul
custard *n* roomvla; vla
custodian *n* kurator
custody *n* arres; bewaring
custom *n* gebruik; gewoonte; reël; sede; tol; wys
custom(s) house *n* doeane
custom made *adj* doelgemaak
customary *adj* gebruiklik
customer *n* klant; kliënt
customers *npl* klandisie
cut *n* fatsoen; hou; kerf; raps; snit; sny; *vb* afsny; kap; knip; saag; sny; (diamonds) slyp; — down *vb* afkap; — into *vb* insny; — loose *vb* lossny; — off *vb* afkap; — out *vb* uitknip; uitsny; — short *vb* afsny; — up *vb* opsny
cut diamond *n* briljant
cut glass *n* kristal
cute *adj* oulik
cuticle *n* opperhuid
cutlet *n* kotelet
cutter *n* snyer
cutting *n* steggie; uitgrawing; uitknipsel
cuttlefish *n* inkvis; seekat
cyber *prefix* kuber
cyberbullying *n* kuberteistering
cyberharassment *n* kuberteistering
cyberspace *n* kuberruimte
cyberstalking *n* kuberagtervolging
cycad *n* sikadee
cycle *n* fiets; kringloop; siklus
cyclist *n* fietsryer
cyclone *n* sikloon
cylinder *n* silinder
cymbal *n* simbaal
cynic *n* sinikus
cynical *adj* sinies
cypress *n* sipres

D

DAB *see* **digital audio broadcasting**
dad *n* pa
daft *adj* beduiweld
dagger *n* dolk
dahlia *n* dahlia
daily *adj* daagliks; *adv* aldag
daily paper *n* dagblad
daily task *n* dagtaak
dainty *adj* kies; lekker; *n* versnapering
dairy *n* melkery
dairy products *npl* suiwel
daisy *n* madeliefie
dale *n* dal; kom; laagte; vallei; vlei
dam *n* dam; dyk; kuil
dam up *vb* dam; afdam; opdam
dam wall *n* damwal
damage *n* skade; letsel; afbreuk; *vb* beskadig
damaged *adj* defek
damages *npl* skadevergoeding
damask *n* damas
damn *vb* verdoem
damn it! *interj* vervloeks!
damnation *n* verdoemenis
damp *adj* bedompig; klam; natterig; vogtig
dampness *n* natheid; natterigheid
dance *n* bal; dans; wals; skoffel
dancer *n* danser
dancing pumps *n* dansskoene
dandruff *n* skilfers
danger *n* gevaar; nood; onraad
dangerous *adj* gevaarlik; verderflik; —y ill *adj* doodsiek
dare *vb* durf; aandurf
daredevil *n* waaghals
daring *adj* vermetel; *n* durf
dark *n* donker; duister; *adj* donker; duister; (complexion) blas
dark blue *n, adj* donkerblou
dark side *n* skadusy
darken *vb* verduister
darkness *n* donker; duister; duisternis
darling *n* hartlam; liefie; liefling; liefste; oogappel; skat; hartjie
darn *vb* stop
dart *n* pyl; werpspies; *vb* skiet

darts *n* (game) veerpyltjie
dash *n* haal; streep
dassie *n* klipdassie
data *n* gegewens
date *n* dadel; datum; jaartal; *vb* dateer
date rape *n* afspraakverkragting
daughter *n* dogter
daughter-in-law *n* skoondogter
dawdle *vb* talm; sloer
dawn *n* dagbreek; aanbreek; *vb* aanbreek; lig word
dawning *adj* ontluikend
day *n* dag; **the whole —** *n, adv* heeldag; **all —** *adv* heeldag
day shift *n* dagploeg
daybreak *n* dagbreek; aanbreek; **at —** *adv* by die aanbreek van die dag; **before —** *adv* douvoordag
dazzle *vb* verblind
deacon *n* diaken
dead *adj* afgestorwe; dooi; dooierig; dood; **the —** *n* dooie
dead beat *adj* doodmoeg
dead body *n* lyk
dead drunk *adj* smoordronk
deaden *vb* verdoof
deadline *n* spertyd
deadly *adj* dodelik; **— pale** *adj* bestorwe
deaf *adj* doof
deaf and dumb *adj* doofstom
deaf to *adj* onvatbaar
deafening *adj* oorverdowend
deal *n* handel; transaksie
deal *vb* (playing cards) gee
deal with *vb* behandel
dealer *n* handelaar; koopman; winkelier
dear *adj* dierbaar; gelief; kosbaar; lief; duur; *n* liefie
dearest *adj* liefste; *n* skat
dearest wish *n* hartewens
dearness *n* duurte
death *n* dood; sterfgeval; uiteinde; uiterste
death blow *n* genadeslag
death notice *n* dood(s)berig; roubrief
death rattle *n* geroggel
death sentence *n* doodvonnis

death toll *n* dodetol
deathbed *n* sterfbed
deathlike *adj* doods
deathly pale *adj* asvaal; doodsbleek
debase *vb* verlaag
debate *n* debat; woordewisseling; *vb* beraadslaag
debauched *adj* liederlik
debenture *n* obligasie
debility *n* swak; swakheid
debit *n* debet; *vb* debiteer
debris *n* opdrifsel; puin
debt *n* skuld
debtor *n* debiteur; skuldenaar
decade *n* tiental
decaf *adj* (*informal*) kafeïenvry
decaffeinated *adj* kafeïenvry
decamp *vb* verkas
decant *vb* afskink
decanter *n* kraffie
decapitate *vb* onthoof
decathlon *n* tienkamp
decay *n* agteruitgang; bederf; verderf; verrotting; verval; *vb* vergaan
decayed *adj* verrot; vrot
deceased *adj* afgestorwe; ontslape; oorlede; wyle; dooi; dood; **the — ** *n* dooie; oorledene; ontslapene
deceased estate *n* bestorwe boedel
deceit *n* bedrog
deceive *vb* bedrieg
deceived *adj* bedroë
deceiver *n* bedrieër
December *n* Desember
decent *adj* fatsoenlik; ordentlik; welvoeglik
decently *adv* behoorlik
deception *n* bedrog
deceptive *adj* misleidend
decide *vb* besluit; besleg; beslis
decided *adj* bepaald
decidedly *adv* sekerlik; beslis
decimal *adj* tiendelig
decimal place *n* desimaal
decipher *vb* ontsyfer
decision *n* besluit
decisive *adj* afdoende; deurtastend; beslis
decisive factor *n* deurslag
deck *n* dek
deck out *vb* uitdos

deckchair *n* dekstoel
declaim *vb* deklameer
declamation *n* deklamasie
declaration *n* afkondiging; betuiging; deklarasie; verklaring
declaration of intent *n* verklaring van voorneme
declaration of war *n* oorlogverklaring
declare *vb* afkondig; betuig; verklaar
declension *n* verbuiging
decline *n* afdraand(e); agteruitgang; insinking; verval; *vb* afslaan; (invitation) afwys
decoct *vb* afkook
decoction *n* aftreksel
decompose *vb* ontbind; verrot
decomposition *n* ontbinding
decor *n* toneelinkleding
decorate *vb* tooi; dekoreer
decoration *n* versiering
decoy *n* lokaas; lokvoël; *vb* lok
decrease *n* vermindering; *vb* afneem
decree *n* gebod; *vb* verorden
decrepit *adj* afgeleef; kaduks
dedicate *vb* opdra; toewy
dedicated bus lane *n* toegewese buslaan
dedication *n* inwyding
deduce *vb* aflei
deduct *vb* aftrek
deduction *n* aftrekking
deed *n* akte; bedryf; daad; oorkonde
deed of sale *n* koopbrief
deed of transfer *n* transportakte
deep *adj* diep; donker
deep-rooted *adj* ingewortel(d)
deepen *vb* uitdiep
deeply *adv* smoorlik
deface *vb* ontsier
default *n* versuim; wanbetaling
defeat *n* neerlaag; onderspit; verlies; *vb* uitklop
defect *n* defek; gebrek; leemte; oorloop
defective *adj* gebrekkig; onklaar; defek
defence *n* pleidooi; verdediging; verweer
defence force *n* verdedigingsmag; weermag
defenceless *adj* weerloos
defend *vb* verweer; beskerm; **— someone** *vb* in die bres tree

defendant *n* aangeklaagde; beklaagde; beskuldigde; gedaagde
defender *n* verweerder
defensive *adj* defensief
deficit *n* tekort
defile *vb* besoedel; verontreinig
define *vb* bepaal; definieer; omskrywe
defining *adj* bepalend
definite *adj* stellig
definition *n* bepaling; definisie; omskrywing
definition of a word *n* woordverklaring
deflated *adj* pap
deflated tyre *n* pap band
deform *vb* mismaak
deformed *adj* wanskape; wanstaltig
defraud *vb* bedrieg
defray *vb* bekostig; vergoed
defray expenses *vb* bestry
defuse a crisis *vb* ontlont
defy *vb* tart; trotseer; uitdaag; uittart
degeneracy *n* ontaarding
degenerate *vb* degenereer; ontaard
degeneration *n* ontaarding
degradation *n* verlaging
degrade *vb* verneder
degree *n* graad; rang; trap
dehydrate *vb* ontwater
deity *n* godheid
dejected *adj* bedruk; mismoedig; moedeloos; neerslagtig; droef
delay *n* getalm; oponthoud; uitstel; vertraging; *vb* draal
delay sentence *vb* opskort
delegate *n* afgevaardigde; gedelegeerde; *vb* afvaardig
delegation *n* delegasie
delete *vb* deurhaal
deliberate *vb* oorleg; beraadslaag; *adj* opsetlik
deliberately *adv* goedsmoeds
deliberation *n* oorleg; oorweging
delicacy *n* versnapering
delicate *adj* fyn; fyngevoelig; kies; kleinserig; teer; tingerig; swak
delicious *adj* lekker; heerlik
delight *n* behae; genoeë; glorie; skik; vermaak; wellus; *vb* verbly
delighted *adj* opgetoë
delightful *adj* heerlik

delineate *vb* uitbeeld; uitteken
delirious *adj* ylhoofdig
deliver *vb* afgee; aflewer; besorg; bestel; inlewer; lewer; oorbring; oorhandig; oorlewer; oplewer; uitlewer; verlos; voordra; — **from** *vb* bevry
deliver a speech *vb* afsteek
deliverance *n* uitredding
delivery *n* oorhandiging; uitlewering; aflewering; bestelling
delude *vb* verblind
deluge *n* sondvloed
delusion *n* waan
demand *n* aanvraag; eis; vordering; vraag; *vb* opeis; — **back** *vb* opvra; terugeis
demand payment *vb* invorder; aanskryf
demeanour *n* gedrag
demented *adj* waansinnig
demise *n* dood; sterfgeval
democracy *n* demokrasie
democrat *n* demokraat
democratic *adj* demokraties
demolish *vb* afbreek; sloop
demonstrate *vb* aantoon
demonstration *n* betoog; bewys; demonstrasie
demonstrative *adj* (pronoun) aanwysend
demure *adj* sedig
den *n* bof; hol
denial *n* ontkenning
denominator *n* noemer
denote *vb* aandui
denounce *vb* uitmaak
dense *adj* dig; dom; ruig; stomp; suf
dent *n* duik
dental floss *n* tandevlos
dentist *n* tandarts
dentures *n* kunsgebit; winkeltande
deny *vb* ontken; verloën
deodorant *n* reukweerde
deoxyribonucleic acid *n* deoksiribonukleïensuur
depart *vb* vertrek; heengaan; **the —ed** *n* (dead) oorledene; (dead) ontslapene
department *n* departement; gebied
departure *n* afreis; afskeid; vertrek; uittog
depend on *vb* afhang; reken op

dependence *n* afhanklikheid
dependent *adj* afhanklik; onderhorig
depict *vb* afskilder; beskryf
depiction *n* afbeelding
deplete *vb* uitput
deplore *vb* bejammer; betreur
deploy troops *vb* ontplooi
deportment *n* houding
deposit *n* bank; deposito; kas; *vb* deponeer
depraved *adj* verdorwe; verworpe
depreciate *vb* devalueer
depressed *adj* melancholies; neerslagtig; swaarmoedig; swartgallig
depression *n* depressie
deprivation *n* ontbinding
deprive *vb* beneem; beroof; ontbloot; ontneem
deprived *adj* ontbloot
depth *n* diepte
deputation *n* deputasie
deputize *vb* afvaardig
deputy *n* adjunk; afgevaardigde; plaasvervanger
derail *vb* ontspoor
derailment *n* ontsporing
deranged *adj* waansinnig
derelict *n* wrak
deride *vb* hoon; spot; smaad
derision *n* hoon; smaadheid; spot
derisive *adj* smadelik
derivation *n* afleiding; herkoms
derive *vb* aflei; **be —d from** *vb* afstam
descend *vb* afdaal; afgaan; daal; neerdaal; **— from** *vb* stam; **be —ed from** *vb* afstam
descendant *n* afstammeling; nakomeling; nasaat
descendants *npl* kroos
descending *adv* afdraand
descent *n* afkoms; herkoms
describe *vb* beskryf; omskrywe; aandui; kenskets; afskilder
description *n* omskrywing
desecrate *vb* ontheilig; verontheilig; skend
desert[1] *n* woestyn; sandwoestyn
desert[2] *vb* dros
deserter *n* afvallige; droster; oorloper; wegloper
deserve *vb* verdien

desiccate *vb* uitdroog
design *n* ontwerp; bestek; aanleg
designer *adj* (clothes, furniture, etc.) ontwerpers
desirable *adj* begeerlik; gewens; wenslik
desire *n* begeerte; lus; trek; sin; wens; sug; verlange; wil; *vb* begeer; wil; verlang
desired *adj* gewens; gewild
desist *vb* aflaat
desk *n* bank; buro; lessenaar; skryftafel
desktop publishing *n* lessenaarpublikasie
desolate *adj* woes; doods
despair *n* wanhoop; vertwyfeling
despairing *adj* wanhopig
desperate *adj* radeloos; wanhopig
desperation *n* vertwyfeling
despicable *adj* veragtelik
despise *vb* minag; verag; versmaad
despot *n* despoot
despotic *adj* willekeurig
dessert *n* nagereg; dessert
destination *n* bestemming
destiny *n* bestemming; lot; voorland
destitute *adj* behoeftig; hulpeloos; noodlydend
destitution *n* gemis
destroy *vb* verderf; breek
destroyed *adj* verwoeste(nd); **be —** *vb* ondergaan
destruction *n* ondergang; verdelging; verderf; vernietiging; verwoesting
detachment *n* afdeling
detailed *adj* breedvoerig; uitvoerig
detain *vb* ophou; vashou; (goods) aanhou; **— in conversation** *vb* bydam
detect *vb* betrap
detective *n* speurder
detention *n* hegtenis; **take into —** *vb* in hegtenis neem
deteriorate *vb* ontaard; versleg
deterioration *n* agteruitgang
determine *vb* bepaal; vasstel; voorneem
determined *adj* beslote; resoluut; vasberade; vasbeslote
deterrent *n* afskrik
detest *vb* haat; verafsku
detestable *adj* haatlik; verfoeilik
dethrone *vb* onttroon; (king) afsit

detonator *n* knaldop
detour *n* ompad; verlegging
detox *n* detoksifikasie
detract from *vb* afdoen
devastate *vb* teister; verwoes
devastated *adj* verwoeste(nd)
devastation *n* verwoesting
develop *vb* ontwikkel; uitwerk
developed *adj* ontwikkeld
developer *n* ontwikkelaar
development *n* ontwikkeling
deviate *vb* afwyk
deviation *n* verlegging
device *n* toestel; uitvindsel
devil *n* duiwel; bose; drommel
devise *vb* smee; uitdink
devoid of *adj* ontbloot van
devoted to *adj* verkleef
devotion *n* gehegtheid; verknogtheid;
  godsvrug
devour *vb* verslind; vreet; verskeur; inswelg; (animals) opvreet
devout *adj* vroom; godsdienstig; fyn
devoutness *n* vroomheid
dew *n* dou
dexterity *n* vaardigheid
dexterous *adj* behendig; knaphandig;
  vaardig
diabetes *n* suikersiekte
diabolical *adj* satanies
diadem *n* diadeem
diagnosis *n* diagnose
diagonal *adj* oorhoeks
diagonally *adv* oorhoeks
dial *n* wys(t)erplaat; *vb* skakel
dialect *n* dialek; streekspraak; tongval
dialogue *n* dialoog; samespraak
diameter *n* deursnee; middellyn
diamond *n* diamant
diamonds *npl* (playing cards) ruitens
diarrhoea *n* diarree
diary *n* dagboek
dictate *vb* dikteer
dictation *n* diktaat; diktee
dictator *n* diktator
dictatorship *n* diktatuur
dictionary *n* leksikon; woordeboek
die[1] *n* (dice) dobbelsteen; stempel
die[2] *vb* sterf; afklop; omkom; (animals)
  vrek; **— away** *vb* wegsterf; **— out** *vb*
  uitsterf

diehard *n* kanniedood
diet *n* dieet; *vb* op dieet stel; dieet hou
differ *vb* verskil; afwyk
difference *n* onderskeid; verskil
difference of opinion *n* meningverskil
different *adj* verskillend; onderskeie;
  uiteenlopend
differently *adv* anders
difficult *adj* moeilik; swaar; lastig; beswaarlik; moeitevol; netelig; ongemaklik; onhandelbaar
difficult job *n* heksewerk
difficulty *n* haakplek; knel; moeilikheid; moeite; swarigheid; verknorsing
diffident *adj* halfslagtig
dig *vb* spit; delf; **— out** *vb* skep; **— up**
  vb omspit; omwoel; opgrawe
dig a trench *vb* dolf
digest *vb* opneem; verteer; verwerk
digestible *adj* verteerbaar
digestion *n* digestie; spysvertering
digger *n* delwer; grawer
digging spade *n* spitgraaf
digital *adj* digitaal
digital audio broadcasting *n* digitale
  oudio-uitsending
dignified *adj* afgemete; waardig
dignity *n* waardigheid
digress *vb* uitwei
dilapidated *adj* bouvallig; vervalle; kaduks; kapot
dilate *vb* uitsit
dilemma *n* dilemma
diligence *n* vlyt; ywer
diligent *adj* naarstig; oppassend; vlytig;
  ywerig
dilute *vb* verdun
dim *adj* flou; dof; *vb* verdof; (light)
  demp
dimension *n* afmeting; dimensie; maat
diminish *vb* afneem; verklein
diminutive *adj* diminutief; *n* verkleinwoord
din *n* geraas
dine *vb* dineer
dining room *n* eetkamer
dinner *n* middagete; dinee
dinner time *n* etenstyd
diocese *n* bisdom
dip *n* dip; *vb* dip; **— in** *vb* indompel; **—
  into** *vb* indoop

diphtheria *n* witseerkeel
diphthong *n* tweeklank
diploma *n* diploma; akte
diplomat *n* diplomaat
diplomatic *adj* diplomaties
direct *adj* direk; oombliklik; regstreeks; *vb* stuur; adresseer
direct hit *n* voltreffer
direction *n* bestuur; direksie; koers; leiding; rigting
directly *adv* onmiddellik; oombliklik; regstreeks; aanstons
director *n* bestuurder; direkteur
directory *n* gids
dirge *n* klaaglied
dirt *n* drek; slyk; vuilgoed
dirt-cheap *adj* spotkoop
dirty *adj* vuil; goor; liederlik; morsig; onsindelik; smerig; vies; vieslik; *vb* bemors; bevuil; **become —** *vb* vervuil
disabled *adj* gebreklik
disadvantage *n* nadeel
disadvantageous *adj* nadelig
disagree *vb* afwyk
disagreeable *adj* onaangenaam; aardig
disagreement *n* onenigheid
disappear *vb* verdwyn
disappearance *n* verdwyning
disappoint *vb* teleurstel
disappointed *adj* teleurgestel
disapprove *vb* afkeur
disarm *vb* ontwapen
disarmament *n* ontwapening
disarrange *vb* omkrap
disaster *n* ramp; onheil
disastrous *adj* rampspoedig
disavow *vb* verloën
disband *vb* ontbind
disc *n* skyf
disc jockey *n* platejoggie
discard *vb* afdank
discern *vb* onderskei
discernible *adj* kenbaar
discerning *adj* oordeelkundig; skerpsinnig
discharge *n* ontslag; ontlasting; rehabilitasie; *vb* afdank; (gun) afskiet
disciplinary *adj* dissiplinêr
discipline *n* dissipline; tug
disclose *vb* openbaar; oopgaan; uitbring; verklik; verraai; ontsluier

discolour *vb* verkleur
discomfort *n* ongemak; ongerief
disconcert *vb* ontstel
disconnect *vb* (electricity) uitskakel
disconnected *adj* onsamehangend
disconsolate *adj* ontroosbaar
discontent *n* misnoeë
discontented *adj* ontevrede; onvergenoeg
discontinue *vb* staak
discord *n* wanklank; onenigheid; onvrede; tweedrag; tweespalk; verdeeldheid; dissonant
discordant *adj* onenig; onwelluidend
discount *n* afslag; korting; diskonto; rabat; *vb* verdiskonteer
discourage *vb* ontmoedig; afskrik
discouragement *n* ontmoediging
discourse *n* diskoers
discover *vb* agterkom; ontdek
discovery *n* ontdekking; vonds
discredit *vb* uitbak
discreet *adj* beskeie
discrepancy *n* verskil
discretion *n* beskeidenheid; diskresie
discus *n* werpskyf
discuss *vb* bespreek; beredeneer; bepraat; debatteer; verhandel
discussion *n* debat; diskussie; samespreking
disdain *n* minagting
disease *n* kwaal; siekte
diseased *adj* siek
disembark *vb* land; ontskeep
disentangle *vb* ontwar
disfavour *n* onguns
disfigure *vb* mismaak; ontsier
disgrace *n* oneer; onguns; skandaal; skande; skandvlek
disgraceful *adj* skandalig; skandelik
disgruntled *adj* misnoeg
disguise *n* masker; *vb* bemantel
disguised *adj* vermom
disgust *vb* walg
disgusting *adj* mislik; walglik
dish *n* gereg; skottel
dish up *vb* opskep; inskep; opdien; opsit
dishcloth *n* vadoek; potdoek
dishearten *vb* ontmoedig; afskrik
disheartened *adj* moedeloos

dishes *npl* skottelgoed
dishevelled *adj* verwaai(d)
dishonest *adj* oneerlik
dishonesty *n* oneerlikheid
dishonour *n* oneer
disillusion *n* ontnugtering; *vb* ontnugter
disillusionment *n* ontnugtering
disinclined *adj* ongeneë; ongeneig
disinfect *vb* ontsmet
disinfectant *n* ontsmettingsmiddel
disinherit *vb* onterf
disinterested *adj* belangeloos; onbaatsugtig
dislike *n* afkeer; hekel; onlus; weersin
dislocate *vb* ontwrig; verstuit
disloyal *adj* ontrou
disloyalty *n* ontrou
dismayed *adj* verslae
dismiss *vb* afdank; afsit; bedank; ontslaan; ontslag gee; opsê
dismount *vb* afklim; afstyg
disobedience *n* ongehoorsaamheid
disobedient *adj* ongehoorsaam
disorder *n* wanorde
disorderly *adj* ongereeld; onordelik
disown *vb* verstoot
disparage *vb* geringskat; verkleineer
disparity *n* verskil
dispatch *n* versending; *vb* versend
dispensable *adj* misbaar
disperse *vb* uiteengaan; versprei; verstrooi
displace *vb* verplaas
displacement *n* verplasing
display *n* uitstalling; *vb* vertoon; pronk
display cabinet *n* vertoonkas; toonkas
display case *n* toonkas
displease *vb* mishaag
displeased *adj* misnoeg
displeasure *n* misnoeë; ongenoeë
disposable *adj* wegdoenbaar
disposal *n* beskikking
dispose of *vb* beskik; wegdoen
disposed *adj* geneë; gesind; gestem
disposition *n* aard; geaardheid; gemoedstoestand; geneentheid; gesindheid
disproportional *adj* oneweredig
disprove *vb* weerlê
dispute *n* dispuut; geskil; onvrede; rusie; woordewisseling; *vb* twis; bestry

disqualification *n* diskwalifikasie
disrespectful *adj* oneerbiedig
disrupt *vb* ontwrig
dissatisfied *adj* ontevrede; onvergenoeg; onvoldaan
dissect *vb* ontleed
dissection *n* ontleding
dissemble *vb* huigel
disseminate *vb* verbrei
dissension *n* verdeeldheid
dissenter *n* afgeskeidene
dissenting *adj* andersdenkend
dissertation *n* verhandeling; dissertasie
dissipated *adj* losbandig
dissolute *adj* losbandig
dissolution *n* ontbinding
dissolve *vb* oplos; smelt; ontbind
dissonance *n* wanklank
dissuade *vb* afraai; ompraat
distance *n* afstand; distansie; verskiet; verte
distant *adj* afgeleë; ver; verwyder(d)
distiguished *adj* aansienlik
distil *vb* distilleer; stook
distiller *n* stoker
distinct *adj* duidelik
distinction *n* onderskeid; onderskeiding
distinctive *adj* kenmerkend
distinctive mark *n* kenteken
distinguish *vb* onderskei
distinguished *adj* vernaam
distinguishing mark *n* kenmerk
distort *vb* verdraai; vertrek
distorted *adj* verwronge
distracted *adj* verstrooi(d); waansinnig
distress *n* nood; kommer; lyding; druk
distress signal *n* noodsein
distressed *adj* benard
distressing *adj* pynlik
distribute *vb* verdeel; uitdeel; uitgee; uitreik; strooi
distribution *n* verdeling; uitdeling; distribusie
district *n* distrik; kontrei; landstreek; streek; wyk
distrust *vb* verdink; wantrou
disturb *vb* verontrus; hinder; stoor
disturbance *n* onluste; onrus; steurnis; versteuring
disuse *n* onbruik

ditch *n* sloot; grag; grip
ditty *n* deuntjie
dive *vb* duik
diver *n* duiker
diverge *vb* uiteenloop; afwyk
divergent *adj* uiteenlopend
diversion *n* afleiding; verstrooiing
diversity *n* verskeidenheid
divert *vb* aflei; aftrek; afwend; (road) verlê
diverted website *n* herleide webwerf
divide *vb* deel; skif
divided *adj* verdeeld; onenig
dividend *n* dividend; deeltal
divider *n* deler
dividing wall *n* skeidsmuur; tussenmuur
divine *adj* goddelik
divine service *n* godsdiensoefening
divine worship *n* godsdiens
divinity *n* godheid
divisible *adj* deelbaar
division *n* afdeling; divisie; skeuring; verdeling
divisor *n* deler
divorce *n* egskeiding; skeiding; *vb* skei
divorced *adj* geskeide
divot *n* (golf) sooimerk
dizziness *n* duiseligheid
dizzy *adj* duiselig lighoofdig
DNA *see* **deoxyribonucleic acid**
DNA profiling *n* DNS-profilering
do *vb* maak; aanrig; **— a turn** *vb* voordra; **— carelessly** *vb* opdons; **— good** *vb* weldoen; **— homage** *vb* huldig; **— over again** *vb* oormaak; **— well** *vb* dy
do! *interj* toe!
docile *adj* gedwee; geseglik; handelbaar; mak
dock[1] *n* dok
dock[2] *vb* (horse's tail) afsny
docker *n* stuwadoor
dockyard *n* skeepswerf
doctor *n* dokter; algemene praktisyn; arts; geneesheer; medikus; praktisyn; (literature, etc.) doktor
doctor's degree *n* doktorsgraad
doctrine *n* leer; leerstuk; stelling
document *n* dokument; bewysstuk; geskrif; oorkonde; stuk

documents *npl* papiere
dodge *n* laai; *vb* koes
dodgeball *n* trefbal
doer *n* dader
dog *n* hond; woefie
doggie *n* (*informal*) woefie
dogma *n* dogma; leerstuk
dogmatic *adj* dogmaties
doldrums *n* windstilte
doll *n* pop
dolphin *n* dolfyn
domain *n* domein
dome *n* koepel; gewelf; dom
domestic *adj* huishoudelik; huislik
domestic servant *n* huishulp; diensbode
domestic animal *n* huisdier
domestic science *n* huishoudkunde
dominate *vb* domineer; oorheers
domination *n* oorheersing
domineer *vb* domineer
dominion *n* heerskappy
don't! *contraction* moenie!
donation *n* skenking
done *adj* klaar; gedaan; gereed; gaar
donga *n* donga; ravyn
dongle *n* (computing) dongel; geheuestafie
donkey *n* donkie; esel
donor *n* donateur; skenker; gewer
doom *n* verdoemenis
doomsday *n* oordeelsdag
door *n* deur
door handle *n* knop
doorjamb *n* styl
doorkeeper *n* deurwagter
door knob *n* deurknop
doormat *n* mat
doorpost *n* styl
doorstep *n* drumpel
doorway *n* ingang; poort
doppelganger *n* dubbelganger
dormitory *n* slaapsaal
dose *n* dosis; *vb* (animals) doseer
dot *n* dotjie; punt; stip; stippel; tittel
dote *vb* suf
doting *adj* versuf
dotted line *n* stippellyn
double *adv* dubbel; *n* dubbelganger; *vb* verdubbel
double chin *n* onderken

double-barrelled *adj* tweeloop
doubt *n* onsekerheid; twyfel; *vb* betwyfel
doubter *n* twyfelaar
doubtful *adj* twyfelagtig
dough *n* deeg
dove *n* duif
dowdy *adj* slordig
down[1] *adv* neer; omlaag; *prep* af; — **there** *adv* daaronder
down[2] *n* dons
down quilt *n* veerkombers
downfall *n* ondergang; val
downhearted *adj* bekaf
downhill *adj* bergaf; *adv* afdraand; bergaf
download *vb* (internet) aflaai
downpour *n* stortreën; slagreën
downright *adv* platweg
downside *n* nadeel
downsizing *n* afskaling; verkleining
downstairs *adv* benede
downstream *adv* stroomaf
downwards *adv* neer; ondertoe; benede
downy *adj* donserig
dowry *n* bruidskat
doze *vb* sluimer; — **off** *vb* indommel; inslaap; insluimer
dozen *n* dosyn
draft *n* konsep; ontwerp; opstel; skets; wissel
draft act *n* wetsontwerp
draft legislation *n* konsepwetgewing
drag *vb* rem; sleep; sleur; trek; aanpiekel; — **along** *vb* piekel; aansleep; — **behind** *vb* nasleep
drag racer *n* rensteljaer
drag racing *n* sleepren; versnelrenne
dragon *n* draak
dragonfly *n* naaldekoker
dragster *n* renstel
drain *n* riool; geut; *vb* aftap; drooglê
drainage *n* riolering; afwatering
dram *n* snapsie; sopie
drama *n* drama
drama queen *n* dramakoningin
dramatist *n* toneelskrywer
dramatize *vb* dramatiseer
drape *vb* drapeer
drastic *adj* drasties; ingrypend; kras
draught *n* sluk; slukkie; tog; trek

draughtboard *n* dambord
draughts *n* (game) dambord
draughtsman *n* tekenaar
draw *n* loting; *vb* tap; haal; teken; afteken; trek; (water) put; — **lots** *vb* loot; — **off** *vb* aftap; — **out** *vb* uithaal; — **roughly** *vb* skets; — **up** *vb* ophaal; optrek; stel; (report, etc.) opmaak
drawer *n* laai
drawing *n* tekening
drawing of lots *n* loting
drawing room *n* voorkamer; voorhuis
drawing pin *n* duimspyker
drawl *vb* teem
dread *n* vrees; *vb* dug; vrees
dreadful *adj* vreeslik; verskriklik; afgryslik; yslik
dream *n* droom; visioen; *vb* droom
dreamer *n* dromer
dreary *adj* triestig; naar; saai
dredge *vb* uitbagger
dregs *n* boomskraapsel; droesem; uitvaagsel
dress *n* rok; tabberd; drag; *vb* aantrek; — **a wound** *vb* verbind; — **up** *vb* uitdos
dress shirt *n* borshemp
dressed *adj* geklee
dressing gown *n* kamerjas
dressing room *n* kleedkamer
dressing table *n* spieëltafel
dressmaker *n* modiste
dribble *vb* (saliva) kwyl
drift *n* strekking; stroming; *vb* afdryf; trek; — **away** *vb* afdryf; — **ashore** *vb* aanspoel
drift ice *n* dryfys
drift-sand *n* stuifsand
driftwood *n* opdrifsel
drill *n* boor; boortjie; *vb* dril
drilled *adj* geoefen(d)
drink *n* dop; sopie; *vb* drink; — **in** *vb* indrink
drinkable *adj* drinkbaar
drip *n* druppel; *vb* druip
dripping *n* vet
drive *n* rit; *vb* dryf; stuur; — **along** *vb* aanjaag; — **around** *vb* omry; — **away** *vb* verwilder; verdryf; — **back** *vb* terugdryf; — **down** *vb* omry; — **in** *vb* inry; inslaan; — **off** *vb* wegjaag; — **on** *vb* aandryf; aanry

drive-by shooting *n* verbyry-skietery
driver *n* (golf) dryfstok
driveway *n* oprylaan
driving force *n* stukrag
driving range *n* (golf) dryfbaan
drizzle *n* motreën; stofreën; *vb* stofreën; stuif
drizzling rain *n* stofreën
droll *adj* koddig; komies; snaaks
dromedary *n* dromedaris
drone *n* zoem; *vb* zoem
droop *vb* afhang
drop *n* druppel; snapsie; *vb* drup; val; — **off** *vb* indommel; — **in** *vb* inloop
drop anchor *vb* anker
drop kick *n* (rugby) skepskop
drop of perspiration *n* sweetdruppel
dropout *n* uitsakker
dropsy *n* watersug
drought *n* droogte
drove *n* (livestock) trop
drown *vb* verdrink; (animals) versuip
drowned person *n* drenkeling
drowsy *adj* loom
drudge *n* sukkelaar; werkesel; *vb* swoeg
drug *vb* bedwelm; *n* dwelm; dwelmmiddel
drug addict *n* dwelmslaaf
drug addiction *n* dwelmafhanklikheid; dwelmverslawing
drum *n* drom; konka; tamboer; trommel; *vb* trommel
drum majorette *n* trompoppie
drummer *n* tamboer
drunk *adj* dronk; besope; beskonke; hoenderkop; *n* dronkaard
drunk driving *n* dronkbestuur
drunkard *n* dronkaard; dronklap; suiplap
dry *adj* droog; dor; *vb* droë; droog; afdroog; — **up** *vb* opdroë; uitdroog; verdroog; — **land** *n* droë
DTP *see* **desktop publishing**
dual carriageway *n* dubbelpad
dub *vb* oorklank
dubious *adj* twyfelagtig
duchess *n* hertogin
duchy *n* hertogdom
duck *n* eend
duck down *vb* koe(t)s; koets
duct *n* buis

due *adj* verskuldig
due date *n* (pregnancy) vervaldag
duel *n* duel; tweegeveg
duet *n* duet
dugout *n* uitgrawing
duiker *n* (antelope) duiker
duke *n* hertog
dull *adj* dom; bot; lusteloos; mat; saai; slap; traag; versuf; geesdodend; aaklig; dof; stomp; suf
dullness *n* botheid; domheid
dumb *adj* sprakeloos; stom; toe
dumbfound *vb* verstom
dumbfounded *adj* verbluf
dummy *n* (baby) fopspeen
dump *vb* (*informal*) afsê
dumpling *n* kluitjie
dumpster *n* stortbak
dunce *n* esel
dung *n* mis; drek
dung beetle *n* miskruier
dungeon *n* kerker
dupe *n* dupe
duplicate *n* afskrif; duplikaat
durable *adj* duursaam
duration *n* duur
during *prep* gedurende; onder; tydens; — **the day** *adv* bedags; — **the night** *adv* snags
dusk *n* skemer
dusky *adj* donker
dust *n* stof; *vb* afklop
duster *n* stoffer; stofdoek
dusty *adj* stowwerig
dutiable *adj* belasbaar
duty *n* plig; taak; diens; belasting; (import, etc.) tol
duty free *adj* tolvry
duvet *n* duvet
dwarf *n* dwerg
dweeb *n* (*informal*) bleeksiel
dwelling *n* huis; woning
dye *n* verf; *vb* (clothes) verf
dying *adj* sterwend
dyke *n* dyk
dynamic *adj* dinamies
dynamite *n* dinamiet
dynasty *n* dinastie; vorstehuis
dyslexia *n* disleksie; leesgebrek
dyspepsia *n* slegte spysvertering

E

E number *n* E-nommer
e-book *n* e-boek
e-business *n* e-besigheid
e-commerce *n* e-handel
e-reader *n* e-leser
each *adj* al; *pron* elk
each other *pron* mekaar
eager *adj* gretig; vinnig; — **to learn** *adj* weetgierig
eagerly *adv* graag
eagerness *n* graagte
eagle *n* arend; adelaar
ear¹ *n* oor
ear² *n* (cereal plant) aar; (mealie) kop
earache *n* oorpyn
eardrum *n* trommel
earl *n* graaf
earlobe *n* oorlel
early *adj* vroeg; *adv* vroegtydig; — **evening** *n* vooraand
earn *vb* verdien
earnest *adj* innig
earnestness *n* erns
earnings *n* inkomste
earplug *n* oorprop
earring *n* oorbel; oorkrabbetjie; oorring
earshot *n* gehoorafstand
earth *n* aarde; wêreld; grond; erd; **the** — *n* aardryk; **the** —**'s surface** *n* aardbol
earth tremor *n* aardskudding; aardskok
earthenware *n* erdewerk; — **pot** *n* erdepot
earthly *adj* ondermaans
earthquake *n* aardbewing
earthwork *n* bolwerk; verskansing
earthworm *n* erdwurm
earwig *n* (insect) oorkruiper; oorwurm
ease *n* gemak
easel *n* esel
easily frightened *adj* skrikkerig
easily offended *adj* puntenerig
east *adj, adv* oos; *n* ooste
east side *n* oostekant
east wind *n* oostewind
Easter *n* Paasfees; Pase
Easter Monday *n* Paasmaandag

easterly *adj* oostelike
eastern *adj* oostelike
eastern border *n* oostergrens
eastern frontier *n* oostergrens
eastward(s) *adv* ooswaarts
easy *adj* maklik; lig; gemaklik; vloeiend
easy chair *n* armstoel
eat *vb* eet; (animals) vreet; — **away** *vb* uitvreet; wegvreet; — **on the sly** *vb* snoep; — **up** *vb* opeet
eatable *adj* eetbaar
eater *n* eter
eating disorder *n* eetafwyking; eetversteuring
eavesdropper *n* luistervink
ebb tide *n* eb
ebony *n* ebbehout
eccentric *adj* eksentriek; sonderling
echo *n* eggo; naklank; weergalming; weerklank; *vb* weergalm; terugkaats
eclipse *n* eklips; verduistering; *vb* verduister; — **of the moon** *n* maansverduistering; — **of the sun** *n* sonsverduistering
ecology *n* ekologie; omgewingsleer
economical *adj* ekonomies; spaarsaam; suinig
economize *vb* spaar; besuinig; bespaar
economy *n* ekonomie
ecstasy *n* ekstase; geesvervoering; roes; verrukking; vervoering
eczema *n* roos
edge *n* boord; kant; omboor; rand; soom
edgy *adj* (*informal*) ultramodern; voorpunt
edible *adj* eetbaar
edict *n* edik
edify *vb* stig
edifying *adj* opbouend; stigtelik
edit *vb* redigeer
edition *n* uitgawe; druk; oplaag
editor *n* redakteur
editorial staff *n* redaksie
educate *vb* onderrig; oplei; onderwys
educated *adj* ontwikkeld
education *n* onderwys; opleiding; opvoeding

educational adj opvoedkundig
educator n opvoeder
edutainment n opvoedkundige vermaak
eel n paling; aal
efface vb uitwis
effect n effek; uitwerking; vrug; vb bewerk
effective adj doeltreffend; effektief; kragdadig
effectively adv raak
effeminate adj verwyf
efficacy n werking
efficient adj doeltreffend
effort n poging
e.g. see **for example**
egg n eier; (of a louse) neet
egg cup n eierkelkie
egg timer n eierkokertjie
eggbeater n eierklitser
eggplant n eiervrug
eggshell n eierdop
ego n ego
egoism n eiebaat
egotist n egoïs
egotistic adj selfsugtig
eiderdown n veerkombers
eight n, determiner ag(t)
eight o'clock n, adj ag(t)uur
eighteen n, determiner ag(t)tien
eighteenth n, adj ag(t)tiende
eighth n, adj ag(t)ste
eightieth n, adj tagtigste
eighty n, determiner tagtig
either determiner beide; conj of
eject vb uitsmyt
ejection seat n uitskietstoel
eland n eland
elapse vb verloop; verstryk
elapsed adj verstreke
elastic adj elasties; rekbaar; n gomlastiek
elasticity n elastisiteit; rek; veerkrag
elated adj opgetoë
elbow n elmboog
elder n ouderling; adj ouer
elder n (tree) vlierboom
elderly adj bejaard
eldest adj oudste
eldest brother n ouboet
elect vb kies; verkies; uitverkore
election n verkiesing; stemming; eleksie
elector n kieser
electoral division n kiesafdeling

electoral register n kieserslys
electric adj elektries
electrical adj elektries
electrically adv elektries
electrician n elektrisiën
electricity n elektrisiteit
electrification n elektrifikasie
electrify vb elektrifiseer
electronic adj elektronies
electronic bug n luistervlooi
elegance n swier
elegant adj elegant; sierlik; smaakvol
elegy n roudig
element n grondstof
elementary adj aanvanklik; elementêr
elephant n olifant
elephant tusk n olifantstand
elevate vb verhoog; veredel
elevating adj verheffend
elevation n veredeling
elevator n hyser
eleven n, determiner elf
eleven o'clock n, adj elfuur
elf n elf
elicit vb uitlok
eligible adj kiesbaar; verkiesbaar
eliminate vb elimineer; uitskakel
elixir n elikser
elliptical adj ellipties
elm n (tree) olm
elope vb skaak
eloquent adj welsprekend
elsewhere adv elders
elucidate vb ophelder; toelig
emaciated adj vermaerd; **become —** vb vermaer
email n e-pos
emanate vb uitstraal
embalm vb balsem
embankment n wal; dyk
embargo n verbod; inbeslagneming
embark vb inskeep
embarrassed adj verleë; verbouereerd; beteuterd
embarrassment n verleentheid
embassy n ambassade
embezzle vb verduister; ontvreem
embezzlement n wanbesteding
emblem n embleem; sinnebeeld
emblematic adj emblematies
embody vb beliggaam

embrace n omhelsing; vb aanneem; omhels
embroider vb borduur
embryo n embrio; kiem
emerald n smarag
emerald green n, adj smaraggroen
emergency call n noodoproep
emergency door n nooddeur
emergency measure n noodmaatreël
emergency message n noodberig
emergency shaft n (mining) noodskag
emery paper n skuurpapier
emetic n braakmiddel
emigrant n emigrant
emigrate vb trek; emigreer
emigration n emigrasie
emission n uitstraling
emit rays vb uitstraal
emoticon n emosikoon
emotion n aandoening; gemoedsaandoening; ontroering
emperor n keiser
emphasis n klemtoon; nadruk
emphasize vb aandik
emphatic adj uitdruklik; nadruklik
emphatically adv nadruklik; uitdruklik
empire n keiserryk; ryk
employ vb gebruik; huur; aanwend
employed adj werksaam
employee n werknemer; beampte
employer n werkgewer; indiensnemer; patroon
employment n werk; amp; baantjie; indiensneming
employment agency n werkgewersburo
empower vb bemagtig; magtig
empowered adj magtig
empress n keiserin
emptiness n ledigheid
empty adj leeg; hol; boomskraap; onbewoon(d); vakant; vb ledig
empty petrol tin n konka
enact vb uitvaardig
enamel n emalje; verglaassel; (teeth) glasuur
encamp vb kamp; leër; kampeer
encampment n kamp
enchant vb bekoor; betower; tower; verruk
enchanting adj verruklik
encircle vb omring; omsingel

enclose vb inkamp; insluit; omhein; omsingel
enclosed adj bygaande; ingesluit; adv hierby
enclosure n omheining
encounter n ontmoeting; vb ontmoet
encourage vb aanmoedig; aanspoor; aanwakker; bemoedig; besiel; sterk
encumber vb verswaar
encyclopedia n ensiklopedie
end n einde; ent; eindpunt; slot; uiteinde; afloop; vb uitraak; afloop; — **in** vb uitloop; uitgaan
endeavour n poging; vb streef
ended adj afgelope
endgame n eindpaal
ending n uitgang
endless adj eindeloos; onbegrens; oneindig
endorse vb endosseer; onderskrywe
endow vb begiftig
endowment n skenking
endurance n uithouvermoë
endure vb verdra; verduur; duld; uithou; ly; deurstaan; uitstaan; veel; dra; volhou
enemy n vyand
energetic adj deurtastend; fiks; flink; kragdadig
energetically adv flink
energy n energie; geeskrag; lewenslus
engage vb beset; inskakel; wikkel
engaged adj besig
engagement n verlowing
engine n enjin; lokomotief; masjien; motor
engine driver n masjinis
engineer n ingenieur; masjinis
English-speaking adj Engelssprekend
Englishman n (informal) rooinek
engrave vb graveer; insny
engraver n graveerder; graveur
engraving n gravure
enigma n raaisel
enjoy vb geniet; vermaak
enjoyable adj vermaaklik
enjoyment n genot; plesier; vermaak
enlarge vb uitbrei; vergroot; vermeerder
enlargement n uitsetting; vergroting; vermeerdering
enlighten vb verlig; voorlig
enlightened adj verligte

enlightenment *n* verligting
enlist *vb* werf; aanwerf
enliven *vb* besiel
ennobling *adj* verheffend
enormous *adj* enorm; geweldig
enough *adj, adv* genoeg; —! *interj* genoeg!
enquiry *n* navraag
enraged *adj* verwoed
enrich *vb* verryk
enrichment *n* verryking
enrol *vb* werf; inskryf; aansluit; aanwerf
enslave *vb* verslaaf
enslaved *adj* verslaaf
enter *vb* inloop; binnegaan; pos; boek
enteric fever *n* ingewandskoors
enterovirus *n* enterovirus; ingewandsvirus
enterprise *n* onderneming
enterprising *adj* ondernemend
entertain *vb* onthaal; trakteer
entertaining *adj* onderhoudend; vermaaklik
enthusiasm *n* geesdrif
enthusiastic *adj* entoesiasties; geesdriftig
entice *vb* lok; uitlok; verlok; aanlok; — **away from** *vb* afrokkel
enticing *adj* verleidelik
entire *adj* gans; volledig; gcheel; — **range** *n* toonladder
entirely *adv* gans; enemale; geheel
entirety *n* geheel
entitled *adj* geregtig; gewettig
entomology *n* insektekunde
entrails *n* binnegoed
entrance *n* ingang; intog; toegang; entrée
entrance fee *n* intreegeld; toegangsprys
entreaty *n* gesmeek
entrench *vb* verskans
entrust *vb* oorlaat; opdra; toevertrou
entry *n* entrée; intog; pos
enumerate *vb* opnoem
envelop *vb* wikkel
envelope *n* koevert; envelop
envious *adj* jaloers; nydig
environment *n* omgewing
environmental affairs *n* omgewingsake
environmental studies *n* omgewingsleer
envoy *n* gesant
envy *n* afguns; jaloesie; naywer; nyd; wanguns; *vb* beny

epicure *n* epikuris
epidemic *n* epidemie
epidermis *n* opperhuid
epilepsy *n* epilepsie; vallende siekte
epileptic *adj* epilepties
epileptic fit *n* toeval
epilogue *n* narede; oordenking
episcopal *adj* biskoplik
episode *n* episode
epistle *n* sendbrief
epitaph *n* grafskrif
equal *adj* ewe; gelyk; kiets; *n* eweknie; ewenaar
equal to *adj* opgewasse
equality *n* gelykheid
equalization *n* gelykstelling
equalize *vb* gelykmaak
equally *adv* ewe; gelyk
equation *n* vergelyking
equator *n* ekwator; ewenaar; middellyn
equestrian *n* perderuiter; ruiter
equilateral *adj* (triangle) gelyksydig
equilibrium *n* ewewig
equip *vb* toerus; uitrus
equipment *n* toerusting; uitrusting; mondering
equity *n* ekwiteit
equivalent *adj* ekwivalent
era *n* jaartelling; tydrekening
eradicate *vb* uitroei
erase *vb* skrap; uitvee
eraser *n* wisser
erect *adj* regop; orent; penorent; *vb* bou
erection *n* aanbou
erf *n* standplaas
ermine *n* hermelyn
erode *vb* uitkalf
err *vb* feil; dwaal
errand *n* boodskap
erratum *n* drukfout
erroneous *adj* onjuis
error *n* fout; misverstand; vergissing; dwaalbegrip; dwaling; abuis
erupt *vb* uitbars; uitbreek
eruption *n* uitbarsting; uitslag
escalator *n* roltrap
escape *n* vlug; ontkoming; ontsnapping; ontvlugting; uitredding; uitweg; heenkome; *vb* ontgaan; — **punishment** *vb* vryloop
escarpment *n* platorand

escort *n* eskort; geleide; metgesel; *vb* begelei

especially *adv* vernaam; insonderheid

espionage *n* spioenasie

essay *n* opstel; verhandeling

essence *n* wese

essential *adj* essensieel; onmisbaar; wesen(t)lik

establish *vb* instel; oprig; stig; vasstel; vestig; **— a friendship** *vb* aanknoop

established *adj* gevestig; uitgemaak

establishment *n* gestig; vesting

estate *n* boedel; eiendom

esteem *n* aansien; ag; agting; hoogagting; respek; skat; waardering

esteem highly *vb* hoogag; hoogskat

esteemed *adj* gesien

estimate *n* kwotasie; prysopgawe; raming; skat; skatting; begroting; *vb* begroot

estimation *n* skatting; gissing

estrange *vb* vervreem

estrangement *n* verwydering

etch *vb* ets

etching *n* ets

eternal *adj* ewig

eternity *n* ewigheid

ether *n* eter

ethical *adj* eties; sedelik

ethics *n* etiek; sedeleer

ethnic *adj* etnies

ethnic cleansing *n* etniese suiwering

etiquette *n* etiket

etymology *n* etimologie

EU *see* **European Union**

eucalyptus *n* (tree) bloekom

eucalyptus oil *n* bloekomolie

eulogy *n* lof; lofrede

euro *n* euro

eurosceptic *n* euro-skeptikus

European Union *n* Europese Unie

eurozone *n* eurosone

evacuate *vb* ontruim

evade *vb* vermy; ontgaan; ontwyk; uitdraai; wegskram

evangelic(al) *adj* evangelies

evangelist *n* evangelis

evaporate *vb* verdamp; uitwasem; vervlieg

evaporation *n* verdamping

evasive *adj* kopsku; ontwykend

eve *n* vooraand

even *adj* effe; ewe; gelyk; kiets; **— although** *conj* almiskie; **— if** *conj* al; **— though** *conj* al

evenly *adv* selfs

evening *n* aand

evening paper *n* aandblad

evening star *n* aandster

evenness *n* effenheid

event *n* gebeurtenis; voorval

ever *adv* aljimmers; ooit

evergreen *adj* groenblywend

everlasting *adj* ewig; onverganklik

every *adj* al; *pron* elk; **— day** *adv* aldag; **— time** *adv* telkens

everyone *pron* iedereen; elkeen

everybody *pron* elkeen; almal; iedereen; algar

everything *pron* alles

everywhere *adv* alom; oral(s)

evict *vb* uitsit

evidence *n* bewys; getuienis; teken

evident *adj* blykbaar; klaar; **be —** *vb* blyk

evidently *adv* glo; skynbaar

evil *adj* boos; sleg; snood; *n* euwel; kwaad

evoke *vb* uitlok

evolution *n* evolusie; ontwikkeling

evolve *vb* ontwikkel

ewe *n* ooi

ex-pupil *n* oudleerling

ex-serviceman *n* oudgediende

exact *adj* presies; noukeurig; juis; stip; net; gelykluidend

exacting *adj* veeleisend

exactitude *n* juistheid

exactly *adv* presies; juis; stip; kompleet; juistement; klokslag

exaggerate *vb* oordrywe

exaggerated *adj* oordrewe

exalted *adj* verhewe

exam paper *n* vraestel

examination *n* eksamen; ondersoek; verhoor

examine *vb* keur; ondersoek; verhoor; bekyk; **— with care** *vb* deurloop

examiner *n* eksaminator

example *n* rigsnoer; toonbeeld; voorbeeld

excavate *vb* grawe; opgrawe; uitdiep; uithol

excavation *n* uitgrawing

exceed *vb* oorskry

exceeding *adj* uitbundig
exceedingly *adv* hoogs; uitermate; uiters
excel *vb* oortref; uitblink; uitmunt; uitsteek
excellence *n* uitnemendheid
excellent *adj* kostelik; puik; uitmuntend; uitnemend; uitstekend; voortreflik
excellently *adv* meesterlik
except *prep* behalwe; buiten; uitgesonder
exception *n* uitsondering; eksepsie
excerpt *n* uittreksel; ekserp
excess *n* oordaad; oorskot; surplus
excessive *adj* buitensporig; onmatig; oorbodig; oordadig; uitbundig
excessively *adv* smoorlik; uitermate; ultra
exchange *vb* wissel; inruil; — **blows** *vb* handgemeen raak; — **control** *n* valutabeheer; — **rate** *n* wisselkoers
exchequer *n* skatkis
excise[1] *vb* uitsny
excise[2] *adj* (duty) aksyns
excite *vb* opwen; prikkel
excited *adj* opgewonde
excitement *n* gemoedsaandoening; opgewondenheid
exciting *adj* spannend
exclaim *vb* uitroep
exclamation *n* uitroep
exclude *vb* uitsluit
excluding *prep* uitgesonder
exclusive *adj* eksklusief; uitsluitend
exclusively *adv* eksklusief; uitsluitend; uitsluitlik
excommunication *n* ban
excrement *n* uitwerpsel
excrete *vb* uitskei
excursion *n* toer; uitstappie
excusable *adj* vergeeflik
excuse *n* ekskuus; verskoning; uitvlug; jakkalsdraai; dekmantel; *vb* ekskuseer
execute *vb* uitvoer; verrig; teregstel
execution *n* uitvoering; teregstelling
executioner *n* beul
executor *n* eksekuteur
exemplary *adj* voorbeeldig
exempt *vb* onthef; uitsonder; vrystel
exemption *n* uitsondering; vrystelling
exercise *n* oefening; *vb* dril

exercise book *n* oefenboek; skrifte; skryfboek
exert *vb* inspan; uitoefen; — **oneself** *vb* weer
exertion *n* inspanning
exhale *vb* uitwasem
exhaust *vb* afmat; uitput; vermoei
exhaust pipe *n* uitlaatpyp
exhausted *adj* afgemat; kapot; pootuit; tam; mat
exhaustion *n* uitputting
exhibit *n* bewysstuk; uitstalling; *vb* tentoonstel
exhibition *n* skou; tentoonstelling
exhibition centre *n* uitstalsentrum
exhumation *n* uitgrawing
exhume *vb* opgrawe
exile *n* balling; ballingskap; banneling; *vb* verban
exist *vb* bestaan; lewe; leef
existence *n* aansyn; bestaan; lewe; leef
exit *n* uitgang
exit fare *n* uitgangreisgeld
exodus *n* uittog
exonerate *vb* onthef; vrypleit
exorbitant *adj* peperduur
exotic *adj* uitheems
expand *vb* swel; uitdy; uitsit; oopgaan; ontluik
expansion *n* uitsetting
expat *n* (*informal*) uitgewekene
expatriate *adj* uitgeweke; *n* uitgewekene; *vb* ekspatrieer
expatriation *n* ekspatriasie; uitwyking
expect *vb* wag; verwag
expectation *n* verwagting
expectorate *vb* roggel
expedient *adj* raadsaam
expedition *n* ekspedisie; tog
expel *vb* ban; uitsit
expendable *adj* misbaar
expenditure *n* uitgawe
expense *n* uitgawe
expenses *npl* koste; onkoste
expensive *adj* duur; kosbaar
expensiveness *n* duurte
experience *n* ervaring; ondervinding; *vb* beleef
experienced *adj* ervare
experiment *n* eksperiment; proef; proefneming

experimental *adj* proefondervindelik
expert *adj* deskundig; *n* deskundige
expertise *n* kundigheid; vernuf; sake-vernuf
expire *vb* verval; verstryk
expired *adj* verstreke
expiry date *n* verstrykdatum; vervaldag
explain *vb* verduidelik; ekspliseer; op-helder; toelig; uiteensit; uitleg; beduie; verklaar; vertolk
explanation *n* uiteensetting; verklaring; oplossing; uitleg; toeligting; verduide-liking; (of a word) woordverklaring
explicit *adj* uitdruklik
explicitly *adv* uitdruklik
explode *vb* ontplof; uitbars; losbars
exploit *vb* uitbuit; eksploiteer
exploitation *n* eksploitasie; uitbuiting
explosion *n* ontploffing; uitbarsting
explosive *n* ontplofbaar; ontploffing-stof; plofstof; *adj* (situation) plofbaar
explosive sound *n* klapper
exponent *n* eksponent
export *n* uitvoer; *vb* uitvoer; eksporteer; (computing) eksporteer
exportation *n* eksport
expose *vb* vertoon; ontmasker; blootstel; — **to public contempt** aan die kaak stel
exposure *n* blootstelling
expound *vb* uitleg
express *vb* uit; uitdruk; uitlaat; — **great sorrow** *vb* betreur; — **in words** *vb* inklee; *adj* uitdruklik; ekspres; spoedig
express service *n* sneldiens
express train *n* eksprestrein; sneltrein
expression *n* bewoording; gesegde; trek; uiting; uitdrukking
expressionless *adj* wesenloos
expressive *adj* uitdruklik; expressie; veelseggend
expressiveness *n* seggingskrag
expressly *adv* uitdruklik; ekspres
expressway *n* snelweg
expulsion *n* uitsetting
exquisite *adj* keurig
extend *vb* rek; strek; — **to** *vb* reik

extension *n* uitbreiding
extension ladder *n* skuifleer
extensive *adj* omvangryk; uitgebrei; uitgestrek; veelomvattend
extent *n* grootte; omvang; **to an —** *adv* tot 'n mate
extenuating *adj* versagtend
exterior *n* buitenste; uiterlik
exterminate *vb* uitdelg; uitroei; verdelg
extermination *n* verdelging
external *adj* ekstern; uitwendig; uiterlik
externally *adv* uiterlik
extinct *adj* dood; uitgeblus; uitgesterf; (volcano) uitgewerk; **become —** *vb* uitsterf
extinguish *vb* blus; doodblaas; doof; uitblaas; (fire) demp
extol *vb* loof
extort *vb* afdwing; uitsuig; — **money** *vb* afpers
extra *adj* ekstra; los; *n* toegif; — **earnings** *n* byverdienste
extra virgin *adj* ekstra suiwer (olive oil, etc.)
extract *n* aftreksel; ekstrak; uittreksel; ekserp; *vb* afskei
extraction *n* trekking; herkoms
extradite *vb* uitlewer
extraordinary *adj* besonders; buitenge-woon; verregaande
extravagance *n* oordaad; verkwisting
extravagant *adj* buitensporig
extreme *adj* uiterste
extreme sports *n* waagsport
extremely *adv* ultra; erg; — **dark** *adj* pikdonker
extremity *n* uiterste; uiteinde
exuberant *adj* uitgelate
eye *n* oog; kyker
eye specialist *n* oogarts
eye-opener *n* verrassing
eyeball *n* oogappel
eyebrow *n* winkbrou
eyelash *n* ooghaar; wimper; oogwim-per
eyelid *n* ooglid
eyetooth *n* hoektand
eyewitness *n* ooggetuie

F

fable *n* fabel
fabric *n* fabrikaat; stof; weefsel
fabricate *vb* versin
face *n* gesig; gelaat; aangesig; voorkant; *vb* trotseer; **— the consequences** *vb* aanvaar
face-lift *n* verjonging(s)kuur
facet *n* faset
facile *adj* vlot
facilitate *vb* vergemaklik
fact *n* feit; **as a matter of — ** *adv* feitlik
faction *n* aanhang; party
faction fight *n* stamgeveg
factor *n* faktor
factory *n* fabriek
factory worker *n* fabriekswerker
faculty *n* fakulteit
fade *vb* verkleur; kwyn; verlep; verwelk; uitbleik; verbleek
faded *adj* vaal; flets; verbleek
faeces *npl* ontlasting
fail *vb* faal; misluk; mis; teenloop; verongeluk; **— an exam** *vb* dop; druip
failure *n* mislukking; fiasko
faint *adj* flou; bleek; dof; *n* beswyming; *vb* beswym; **become — ** *vb* verdof; verflou
faint-hearted *adj* flouhartig
fainting fit *n* floute; beswyming; toeval
fair[1] *adj* blond; middelmatig; taamlik; onpartydig; eerlik; regmatig; skiklik; redelik; billik
fair[2] *n* kermis
fairly *adv* eerlik; taamlik; nogal
fairway *n* (golf) skoonveld
fairy *n* elf; fee
fairy story *n* sprokie
fairy tale *n* sprokie; sage
faith *n* geloof
faithful *adj* gelowig; trou; getroue
fake *adj* oneg; *n* vervalsing; *vb* vervals
falcon *n* valk
fall *n* agteruitgang; val; *vb* afneem; **— asleep** *vb* insluimer; inslaap; **— down** *vb* neerslaan; omval; afval; **— due** *vb* verval; **— in battle** *vb* sneuwel; **— into the habit of** *vb* aanwen;

— off *vb* afval; **— open** *vb* oopval; **— out** *vb* uitval; **— over** *vb* omkantel; **— silent** *vb* word stil
fallacy *n* dwaalleer
fallible *adj* feilbaar
falling *adj* vallend
fallow *adj* braak
fallow land *n* braakland; ouland
false hem *n* stootkant
false start *n* ongelyke wegspring
false step *n* misstap
false teeth *n* kunsgebit; winkeltande
falsehood *n* leuen; leuentaal; onwaarheid
falsification *n* vervalsing
falsify *vb* vervals
falter *vb* haper
fame *n* faam; opgang; roem; vermaardheid; glorie
familiar *adj* eie; familiêr; gemeensaam; **— with** *adj* vertroud met
family *n* gesin; familie; geslag; huis; huisgesin; **— bible** *n* huisbybel; **— circle** *n* familiekring; **— credit** *n* gesinskrediet; **— friend** *n* huisvriend
family name *n* van
family tree *n* stamboom; geslag(s)boom
famine *n* hongersnood
famished *adj* uitgehonger; **be — ** *vb* uithonger
famous *adj* beroemd; befaamd; roemryk; vermaard
fan *n* waaier; *vb* aanblaas; waai
fan belt *n* waaierband
fanatic *n* dweper; fanatikus; drywer; yweraar
fanatic(al) *adj* fanatiek; dweepsiek; **be — about** *vb* dweep
fanaticism *n* dweepsug
fancy *n* gier; gril; hersenskim; verbeelding; *vb* fantaseer
fancy-dress ball *n* maskerbal
fang *n* slagtand
fantastic *adj* fantasties
far *adv* ver; **as — as** *conj, prep* tot
far and wide *adv* heinde en ver**

far away *adj, adv* veraf
far-off *adj, adv* veraf
far-reaching *adj* ingrypend; verreikend; verstrekkend
far-seeing *adj* versiende
far-sighted *adj* versiende
farce *n* klug; komedie
fare *n* reisgeld; vrag
farewell *n* vaarwel
farm *n* plaas; boerplaas; *vb* boer
farm stall *n* plaaskiosk
farmer *n* boer
farmyard *n* werf
farrier *n* hoefsmid
farther *adv* verder
farthing *n* duit
fascinate *vb* boei; betower
fascinating *adj* boeiend; bekoorlik
fashion *n* mode; kleredrag; manier; fatsoen; snit
fashionable *adj* modern; deftig
fast *vb* vas
fast train *n* sneltrein
fasten *vb* heg; aanheg
fastidious *adj* kieskeurig
fat *adj* dik; lywig; *n* vet
fata morgana *n* lugspieëling
fatal *adj* dodelik; fataal; noodlottig
fatalist *n* fatalis
fatality *n* fataliteit
fate *n* lot; noodlot; voorland
father *n* vader
Father Christmas *n* Kersvader
father-in-law *n* skoonvader
fatherhood *n* vaderskap
fatherland *n* vaderland
fatherless *adj* vaderloos
fatherly *adj* vaderlik
fathom *n* vadem; *vb* peil; deurgrond
fatigue *vb* vermoei
fatigued *adj* boeglam
fatty *adj* vetterig
fault *n* fout; gebrek; tekortkoming; euwel; skuld; feil
faultless *adj* feilloos; onberispelik
faulty *adj* foutief; gebrekkig; onvolmaak; defek
favour *n* guns; vriendskap; *vb* begunstig
favourable *adj* gunstig; welwillend
favourite *adj* gunsteling; *n* geliefkoosde
favourite pursuit *n* liefhebbery

fax *n* faks
fear *n* angs; vrees; *vb* bang wees; dug
fearful *adj* vreeslik
fearless *adj* onbevrees; onbeskroom(d)
feasible *adj* doenlik; uitvoerbaar
feast *n* fees; banket; gasmaal; smulparty; *vb* smul; feesvier
feast day *n* feesdag
feather *n* veer; pluim
feather-bed *n* bulsak
featherweight *adj* veergewig
feature *n* gelaatstrek
February *n* Februarie
fed *adj* (animals) gevoerde
fed up *adj* vies; buikvol
federation *n* federasie
fee *n* honorarium
feeble *adj* swak
feed *vb* voer; voed; wei; — **on** *vb* aas
feedback *n* terugvoer(ing)
feeder *n* borslap
feeding *n* voeding
feeding bottle *n* pypkan
feel *vb* gevoel; betas; (pulse) pols; — **like** *vb* lus
feeler *n* voelhoring
feeling *n* gevoel; gewaarwording; voeling
feelings *npl* gemoed; gevoelens
feign *vb* huigel; veins
feigned *adj* gewaande
fell *vb* (tree) kap; vel
fellow *n* kêrel; ou
fellow man *n* naaste; ewenaaste; ewemens; medemens
fellow worker *n* ampgenoot
fellow countryman *n* landgenoot
fellow prisoner *n* medegevangene
felt *n* vilt
female *adj* vroulik; *n* vroumens; (animals) wyfie; — **friend** *n* vriendin; — **leader** *n* leidster; — **pig** *n* sog; — **teacher** *n* juffrou
feminine *adj* vroulik
fence *n* heining; omheining; afskutting; *vb* skerm; — **in** *vb* inkamp; omhein; — **off** *vb* afsluit
fencing *n* (art of) skermkuns
fender *n* modderskerm
fennel *n* vinkel
ferment *vb* gis; rys
fermentation *n* gisting

fern *n* varing
ferocious *adj* woes
ferret out *vb* uitvis; uitvors
ferry *n* pont; veer
ferryboat *n* pont
fertile *adj* vrugbaar; geil; vet
fertilizer *n* misstof
ferule *n* plak
fervent *adj* vurig
fester *vb* sweer; versweer
festival *n* fees
festive *adj* feestelik
festivity *n* festiwiteit
fetch *vb* haal; afhaal
fête *n* kermis
fetter *vb* boei; kluister; *n* kluister
feud *n* vete; onvrede
fever *n* koors
fever blister *n* koorsblaar
fever tree *n* koorsboom
feverish *adj* koorsagtig; koorsig
few *determiner; adj* party; weinig; min; *n* bietjie
fiancé *n* aanstaande; verloofde
fiancée *n* aanstaande; verloofde
fiasco *n* fiasko
fibre *n* vesel; draad
fibreglass *n* veselglas
fickle *adj* wispelturig; veranderlik; onstandvastig
fiction *n* fiksie; verdigsel; fabel
fictitious *adj* fiktief; verdig
fiddle *n* viool; *vb* peuter
fiddlestick *n* (*informal*) strykstok
fiddling (*or* **fiddly**) *adj* gepeuter
fidelity *n* trou
fidget *n* woelwater; *vb* woel
fidgety *adj* ongedurig; woelig
field *n* veld; land; akker; — **of stubble** *n* stoppelland
field-marshal *n* veldmaarskalk
fierce *adj* hewig; fel; wild
fiery *adj* vurig
fifteen *n, determiner* vyftien
fifteenth *n, adj* vyftiende
fifth *n, adj* vyfde
fifty *n, determiner* vyftig
fiftieth *n, adj* vyftigste
fig *n* vy
fight *n* geveg; stryd; spook; (war) kryg; *vb* baklei

fighter *n* stry(d)er; vegter
fighter plane *n* vegvliegtuig
figurative *adj* figuurlik; figuratief; — **language** *n* beeldspraak
figuratively *adv* figuurlik
figure *n* figuur; gedaante; gestalte; beeld; lees; postuur; syfer
filament *n* vesel
file *n* vyl; (papers) lêer; *vb* vyl
file transfer protocol *n* lêeroordragprotokol (LOP)
fill *vb* vul; volmaak; — **up** *vb* opvul; opstop; invul; (ditch) demp
filled *adj* vol
fillet *n* (meat, fish) fillet
filling *n* (tooth) tandvulling; (tooth) stopsel
filly *n* vul
film *n* film; rolprent; vlies; *vb* verfilm; opneem
film noir *n* film noir
film star *n* filmster; rolprentster
filter *n* filter; *vb* filtreer
filth *n* drek
filthy *adj* vieslik; morsig; liederlik
fin *n* vin
final *adj* finaal; eindelik; beslis; *n* finale
finale *n* finale
finally *adv* eindelik; oplaas; uiteindelik
finance *n* finansiewese
financial *adj* finansieel; geldelik; — **year** *n* diensjaar
Financial Times Stock Exchange Index *n* Financial Timeseffektebeursindeks
financier *n* finansier
finch *n* vink
find *n* vonds; *vb* bevind; — **fault** *vb* vit; — **out** *vb* agterkom; ontdek; uitvind
fine[1] *adj* fyn; keurig; mooi; piekfyn; skoon; **as — as hair** *adj* haarfyn
fine[2] *n* boete; geldboete; *vb* beboet
fine comb *n* fynkam
finery *n* tooi; opskik
finger *n* vinger
fingerprint *n* vingerafdruk
fingertip *n* top
finish off *vb* afmaak
finished *adj* op; gedaan; klaar; boomskraap; afgelope
fir *n* (tree) den; denneboom

fir cone *n* dennebol
fir needle *n* dennenaald
fir wood *n* dennehout
fire *n* vuur; brand; *vb* (gun) afskiet; — **upon** *vb* beskiet
fire alarm *n* brandalarm
fire brigade *n* brandweer
fire engine *n* brandweerwa
fire escape *n* brandtrap; nooddeur
fire extinguisher *n* brandblusser
fire hose *n* brandslang
fire hydrant *n* brandspuit
fire-eater *n* vuurvreter
firearm *n* vuurwapen
firebreak *n* voorbrand
firefighter *n* brandweerman; brandslaner
firefly *n* vuurvlieg
fireman *n* stoker
fireplace *n* kaggel; vuurmaakplek; es; haard
fireproof *adj* vuurvas; onbrandbaar
fireside *n* haard
firewood *n* brandhout
firework *n* vuurwerk
firm[1] *adj* ferm; stewig; vas; vasberade; onwankelbaar; onwrikbaar; standvastig; stellig; pal
firm[2] *n* (business) firma
firmly *adv* vas
firmness *n* vastheid; vastigheid
first *n, adj* eerste; voorste; *adv* (in time, place, rank) vooraan; **at** — *adv* aanvanklik; — **coat** *n* (paint) grondverf; — **course** *n* (meal) voorgereg; — **layer** *n* grondslag; — **mentioned** *n* eersgenoemde; — **name** *n* voornaam
first aid *n* eerstehulp; noodhulp
first class *adj* eersteklas; beste
first-born *adj* eersgeborene
first-rate *adj* prima; uithaler
firstly *adv* eers; eerstens
fiscal *n* fiskaal
fiscal shrike *n* laksman; janfiskaal
fish *n* vis; *vb* vis; visvang; — **out** *vb* uitvis
fish-hook *n* vishoek
fish oil *n* visolie; traan
fish paste *n* vissmeer
fishbone *n* graat; visgraat
fisherman *n* visser; visserman; visterman

fishery *n* vissery
fishing boat *n* visserskuit
fishing rod *n* visstok
fishing tackle *n* hengelgerei; visgereedskap; visgerei
fishy *adj* visagtig
fissure *n* skeur; spleet
fist *n* vuis
fit1 *adj* gepas; geskik; weerbaar; *vb* aanpas; — **in** *vb* voeg; inpas; — **out** *vb* monteer; toerus; uitrus; **be — for purpose** *vb* deug
fit2 *n* toeval
fitter *n* monteur
fitter and turner *n* passer en draaier
fitting *adj* paslik
fittings *npl* beslag; benodigdhede; toebehore
five *n, determiner* vyf
five o'clock *n, adj* vyfuur
fix *n* verknorsing; *vb* bepaal; bestem; — **upon** *vb* vestig
fixed *adj* vas; gereeld; gevestig; bepaald; pal; bestem
flabbergasted *adj* verbouereerd
flag[1] *n* vlag; vaandel
flag[2] *vb* verslap
flagpole *n* vlagpaal
flagstaff *n* vlagpaal
flake *n* vlok
flame *n* gloed; vlam; vuur
flamingo *n* flamink
flammable *adj* vlambaar
flank *n* flank
flannel *n* flennie
flannelette *n* flenelet
flap *n* flap; klap; klep; *vb* flap; fladder
flare *n* fakkel; seinfakkel
flash *n* blits; flits; *vb* bliksem; flits
flashback *n* terugflits
flashlight *n* flitslig
flask *n* bottel; fles
flat[1] *adj* plat; horisontaal; vlak; effe; *n* (music) mol
flat[2] *n* woonstel
flatline *vb* (heart) sterf
flatlands *npl* vlakte
flatten *vb* platdruk
flatter *vb* mooipraat; streel; vlei; flikflooi
flattering *adj* strelend

flatulence *n* wind
flautist *n* fluitspeler
flavour *n* smaak
flaw *n* kraak
flax *n* vlas
flea *n* vlooi
flea market *n* vlooimark
fleabite *n* vlooibyt
flee *vb* vlug; ontvlug
fleece *n* vag; vlies; *vb* pluk
fleet *n* vloot
fleeting *adj* verganklik; vlugtig
flesh *n* vleis; vlees
flesh wound *n* vleiswond
flexible *adj* buigsaam; soepel; plooibaar
flexitime *n* skiktyd
flick *n* raps; *vb* raps; — **away** *vb* afklop
flicker *vb* flikker
flight *n* vlug; ontvlugting
flight recorder *n* stemopnemer; vlugopnemer
fling *vb* gooi; smyt; werp; — **away** *vb* afsmyt; — **down** *vb* afstort
flintlock *n* snaphaan
flippant *adj* ligsinnig
flirt *n* flerrie; *vb* vry
flirtation *n* vryerasie
float *n* dobber; (cash) vlot; *vb* dobber; dryf; — **along** *vb* aandryf
flock *n* trop; kudde; swerm; *vb* drom; — **together** *vb* skool
flog *vb* gésel; afransel
flood *n* vloed; *vb* oorstroom; (carburettor) versuip
floodlight *n* spreilig
floodwater *n* vloedwater
floor *n* vloer; verdieping; afdeling
flora *n* flora
florin *n* floryn
florist *n* bloemis; blomkweker
flossy *adj* vlossig
flounce *n* strook
flour *n* meel; meelblom
flourish *n* tierlantyntjie; *vb* bloei
flourishing *adj* florerend
flow *vb* loop; stroom; spoel; — **down** *n* afloop; — **out** *vb* uitvloei; — **together** *vb* saamvloei
flower *n* blom; *vb* bloei; blom
flowerbed *n* akkertjie; blombedding; beddinkie; perk

flower girl *n* strooimeisie
flowerpot *n* blompot; vaas
flowing *adj* vloeiend
flu *n* griep
fluctuate *vb* skommel
flue *n* (chimney) pyp
fluent *adj* vloeiend; vlot
fluently *adv* vlot
fluff *n* dons
fluffy *adj* donserig
fluid *adj* vloeibaar; *n* vloeistof
fluke *n* gelukslag
fluorescent lamp *n* fluoresseerlamp
fluorescent paint *n* fuoreseerverf; glimverf
flushed *adj* verhit
fluster *vb* oorbluf
flute *n* fluit
flute-player *n* fluitspeler
fluted *adj* geriffel
flutter *vb* fladder; wapper
fly[1] *n* (trousers) gulp; *vb* vlieg; wapper; (time) vervlieg; — **at** *vb* bevlieg; — **in** *vb* invlieg
fly[2] *n* (insect) vlieg
fly net *n* vlieënet
flying *adj* vlieënd
flying saucer *n* vlieënde piering
foal *n* vul
foam *n* skuim; *vb* bruis; skuim
foam rubber *n* sponsrubber
foaming *adj* briesend
fob off *vb* afskeep; aansmeer
focus *n* brandpunt; fokus
fodder *n* voer
fog *n* mis; newel
foggy *adj* mistig
foghorn *n* mishoring
foil *vb* verydel
foist off *vb* aansmeer
fold[1] *n* vou; plooi; rimpel; *vb* kreukel; plooi; — **in** *vb* invou; — **up** *vb* opvou
fold[2] *n* kraal; skoot
folding chair *n* voustoel
folding-door *n* voudeur
foliage *n* lof; lower
folio *n* folio
folk dancing *n* volkspele
folklore *n* volkskunde
follow *vb* aanhang; naloop; — **with the eye** *vb* nagaan

follower *n* volgeling; aanhanger
followers *npl* gevolg; aanhang
following *n* trein; *adj* onderstaande; volgende; eerskomende
folly *n* dwaasheid; gekheid
foment *vb* aanblaas
fond of *adj* geheg aan; verlief; *vb* mal oor; **be** — *vb* hou van
fondle *vb* liefkoos
fondness *n* gehegtheid
font *n* bekken
food *n* ete; kos; spys(e); voedsel; — **for a journey** *n* padkos
food poisoning *n* voedselvergiftiging
foodstuffs *npl* lewensmiddele; eetware; voedingsmiddels
fool *n* gek; dwaas; sot; stommeling; swaap; bog; nar; *vb* pypkan
fool's paradise *n* luilekkerland
foolish *adj* mal; gek; sot; onsinnig; onverstandig; onwys; dwaas
foolish talk *n* flouiteit
foolishness *n* malheid; sotterny
foolproof *adj* peutervry
foot *n* voet; poot; (of a bed) voetentent; — **it** *vb* voetslaan; — **rule** *n* duimstok
foot soldiers *npl* voetvolk
football *n* sokker; voetbal
footing *n* vastrapplek; voet
footman *n* lakei
footpath *n* paadjie; voetpad
footprint *n* spoor; voetspoor
footsack! *interj* voertsek!
footslog *vb* voetslaan
footstep *n* voetspoor
footstool *n* voetbank
footwear *n* skoen
for *adv* om; *conj* want; *prep* namens; — **a time** *adv* tydlank; — **ever** *adv* altyd; — **example (e.g.)** by voorbeeld; — **goodness' sake!** *interj* om hemelswil!; — **hours** *adv* urelank; — **no reason** *adv* sommer; — **shame!** *interj* sies!; — **the rest** *adv* origens; — **the sake of** *prep* ter wille van; — **this purpose** *adv* hiertoe; — **this reason** *adv* hierom; hieroor; — **what reason** *adv* hoekom; — **what** *inter pron* waarom; — **which** *inter pron* waarvoor
forage *n* voer
forbearance *n* geduld

forbearing *adj* verdraagsaam
forbid *vb* belet; verbied
forbidden *adj* ongeoorloof; verbode
force *n* geweld; krag; noodsaak; *vb* dwing
forced *adj* gedwonge
forceps *n* tang; trekker
forces *npl* troepe
ford *n* drif; *vb* waad
fore: **to the fore** *adv* vorentoe
forearm *n* voorarm; onderarm
foreboding *n* voorgevoel; voorbode
forecast *n* vooruitskatting; *vb* vooruitskat
forecourt *n* voorhof
forefather *n* voorvader; —**s** *npl* voorgeslag
forefinger *n* wysvinger
foregoing *adj* voorafgaande
foreground *n* voorgrond
forehand *n* voorarm; *adj* voorarm
forehead *n* voorhoof
foreign *adj* vreemd; uitheems
foreign country *n* buiteland
foreign currency *n* valuta
foreign trade *n* oorsese handel
foreigner *n* uitlander; vreemdeling
foreman *n* voorman
foremost *adj* voorste; vooraan; *adv* vooraan
forename *n* voornaam
forenoon *n* voormiddag
forensic medicine *n* regsgeneeskunde
forerunner *n* voorbode; voorloper
foresee *vb* voorsien; vooruitsien
forest *n* bos; woud
forestall *vb* voorkom
foretaste *n* voorsmaak
foretell *vb* voorspel; waarsê
forever *adv* altyd
foreword *n* voorwoord; voorberig; voorrede
forfeit *vb* verbeur
forfeited *adj* verbeurd
forge *vb* smee; vervals
forged *adj* nagemaak; vals
forget *vb* vergeet; verleer
forgetful *adj* vergeetagtig
forgive *vb* vergeef; vergewe
forgiveness *n* vergewing; vergifnis
fork *n* vurk; tweesprong; (in a branch) mik

fork-lift truck *n* vurkhyswa
form *n* vorm; gedaante; figuur; *vb* formeer; **— a queue** *vb* toustaan; **on —** *adv* op peil
formal *adj* formeel; gekunsteld; vormlik; afgemete; styf; **— statement of beliefs** *n* geloofsbelydenis
formality *n* formaliteit
format *n* formaat
formation *n* vorming
former *adj* gewese; voormalig; vorige; vroeër; **the —** *n* eersgenoemde
formerly *adv* vroeër; eertyds
formidable *adj* gedug
formula *n* formule
formulate *vb* formuleer
fornication *n* ontug
forsake *vb* versaak; begeef
fort *n* fort
forthcoming *adj* aanstaande
fortieth *adj, n* veertigste
fortification *n* versterking
fortify *vb* versterk; verskans
fortnightly *adv* veertiendaags
fortress *n* fort
fortunate *adj* gelukkig; geseën
fortune *n* fortuin; hawe; lot
fortune-teller *n* waarsêer
fortune's favourite *n* gelukskind
forty *n, determiner* veertig
forward *adj* vorentoe; vooruit; ouderwets; onbeskeie; *adv* vorentoe; vooruit; *vb* aanstuur; **— journey** *n* heenreis; **— line** *n* voorhoede
fossil *n* fossiel; verstening
foster *vb* kweek; aankweek
foster child *n* pleegkind
foster parents *npl* pleegouers
foul *adj* vuil
found *vb* grondves
foundation *n* fondament; grond; grondslag; stigting
foundation garment *n* korset
foundation stone *n* hoeksteen
founder[1] *n* grondlêer
founder[2] *vb* (ship) vergaan
foundling *n* vondeling
foundry *n* gietery
fountain *n* fontein; oog
fountain pen *n* vulpen
four *n, determiner* vier

four o'clock *n, adj* vieruur
four thousand *n, determiner* vierduisend
fourteen *n, determiner* veertien
fourteenth *n, adj* veertiende
fourth *n, adj* vierde
fourway stop *n* vierrigtingstop
fox *n* vos
foyer *n* voorportaal
fraction *n* breuk
fracture *n* breuk
fragile *adj* tingerig; bros
fragment *n* stuk
fragrance *n* geur; aroma
fragrant *adj* geurig
frail-care unit *n* sorgsentrum
frailty *n* swakte
frame *n* raam
frame of mind *n* gemoedstemming; stemming
frame saw *n* spansaag
franchise *n* stemreg
frank *adj* frank; onomwonde; openhartig; rondborstig; volmondig; vrymoedig; onbewimpeld; *vb* frankeer
frankly *adv* onomwonde; ronduit
frankness *n* rondborstigheid; vrymoedigheid
fraternal *adj* broederlik
fraternize *vb* verbroeder
fraud *n* swendel
fraudulent *adj* oneerlik
fray *vb* uitrafel
freckle *n* sproet
free *adj* vry; gratis; kosteloos; frank; ongebonde; oop; ope; *vb* bevry; **— as a bird** *adj* voëlvry
free kick *n* strafskop
freepost *n* vrypos
free trade *n* vryhandel
freedom *n* vryheid
freedom fighter *n* vryheidvegter
freedom of the press *n* persvryheid
freehold *n* vrypag
freelance work *n* vryskut
freemason *n* vrymesselaar
freemasonry *n* vrymesselary
freethinker *n* vrydenker
freethinking *adj* vrygeestig
freewheel *vb* vryloop
freeze *vb* ys; bevries

freezing point *n* vriespunt
freight *n* las
freighter *n* vragskip
French bean *n* snyboontjie
frenzied *adj* koorsagtig
frequent *adj* veel; veelvuldig
frequently *adv* veel; dikwels
fresh *adj* fris; koel; vars; groen; — **milk** *n* soetmelk
fresher *n* groentjie
freshman *n* groentjie
freshwater *n* soetwater
fret *vb* knies
fretful *adj* knieserig
Freudian *adj* Freudiaanse
friar *n* monnik
friction *n* wrywing
Friday *n* Vrydag
fried *adj* gebraai
friend *n* vriend; maat
friendly *adj* vriendelik; vriendskaplik; welwillend; bevriend; — **fire** *n* eievuur
friendship *n* vriendskap
frigate *n* fregat
fright *n* skrik; skok; ontsetting
frighten *vb* afskrik; ontstel; vrees aanjag
frightened *adj* bang; vervaard; **be** — *vb* skrik
frightful *adj* verskriklik
fringe *n* fraiing
frisky *adj* dartel
fritter *n* poffertjie
frivolous *adj* ligsinnig; ydel; futiel
frizz *vb* friseer
frog *n* padda
frolic *vb* baljaar
from *adv* vandaan; *prep* uit; — **now on** *adv* voortaan; — **time immemorial** *adv* van hoeka se tyd af; — **time to time** *adv* periodiek; — **which** *inter pron* waaruit
front *n* voorkant; gewel; — **but one** *n, adj* naasvoor; — **door** *n* voordeur; **in** — *adj, adv* vooraan; — **line** *n* frontlinie; — **room** *n* voorkamer; — **wheel** *n* voorwiel
front-door key *n* huissleutel
front-wheel drive *n* voorwielaandrywing
frost *n* ryp

frostbite *n* vriesbrand
frosted glass *n* ysglas
froth *n* skuim; *vb* bruis; skuim
frown *n* frons
fruit *n* vrugte
fruit juice *n* vrugtesap
fruit salad *n* vrugteslaai
fruitful *adj* vrugbaar
fruitless *adj* nutteloos; vergeefs; vrugteloos
fruitlessly *adv* vrugteloos
frustrate *vb* verydel
fry *vb* bak; (in a pan) braai
FTP *see* **file transfer protocol**
FTSE *see* **Financial Times Stock Exchange Index**
fuck! *interj* (*vulgar*) fok!
fuel *n* brandstof
fugitive *n* vlugteling
fulfil *vb* volbring; nakom
fulfilment *n* volbring
full *adj* vol; voltallig; breedvoerig; uitvoerig; — **of vitality** *adj* danig; — **up** *adj* sat; trommeldik
full moon *n* volmaan
full point *n* punt (.)
full stop *n* punt (.)
full-blown AIDS *n* vol ontwikkelde vigs
full-grown *adj* volwasse; groot
full-time *adj* heeltyds; *adv* voltyds; heeltyds
fully *adv* volslae; voltallig
fumbling *adj* gepeuter
fume(s) *n* damp
fun *n* pret; plesier; grap; skerts; speletjie
fun run *n* pretloop
function *n* funksie
fund *n* fonds
funeral *n* begrafnis
funeral procession *n* lykstoet
funeral service *n* lyksdiens
fungus *n* swam
funnel *n* tregter; skoorsteen
funny *adj* snaaks; koddig; potsierlik; raar; grappenderwys
fur *n* bont; pels
fur coat *n* pelsjas
furious *adj* woedend; rasend; grimmig; verwoed; dol
furlough *n* verlof
furnace *n* oond**

furnish *vb* meubileer; stoffeer; verskaf; verstrek

furnished *adj* gemeubileer

furniture *n* meubels; huisraad; beslag

furrow *n* ploegvoor; voor; grip

further *adv* verder; voorts

furtively *adv* steelsgewys

fury *n* raserny; woede

fuse[1] *vb* smelt; versmelt

fuse[2] *n* (electricity) sekering; lont

fuselage *n* romp

fusion *n* fusie; ineensmelting; samesmelting

fuss *n* bohaai; drukte; gedoe; gedoente; kaskenade; omhaal; omslag; ophef; opskudding; *vb* peuter

fussy *adj* puntenerig

futile *adj* futiel; tevergeefs; vergeefs

futility *n* futiliteit

future *adj* toekomend; toekomstig; *n* toekoms

future generations *npl* nageslag

G

G-spot *n* G-kol
gable *n* gewel
gadget *n* katoeter
gag[1] *n* prop
gag[2] *n* (*informal*) (joke) grap
gagging order *n* muilbandbevel
gain *n* aanwins; gewin; profyt; voordeel; wins; *vb* behaal
gainsay *vb* teenpraat; teenspreek
gait *n* gang; loop; pas
gale *n* storm; stormwind
gall *n* gal
gallantry *n* galanterie
galleon *n* (ship) galjoen
gallery *n* galery
galley *n* galei
gallop *n* galop; *vb* galop
gallows *n* galg
gallstone *n* galsteen
galvanic *adj* galvanies
galvanize *vb* galvaniseer
galvanized iron *n* sink
gamble *vb* dobbel; — **away** *vb* verspeel
gambol *vb* spartel
game *n* spel; speletjie; (tennis) pot; wild; — **of chess** *n* skaakspel; — **of draughts** *n* damspel
game ranger *n* boswagter; wildwagter
gamut *n* toonladder
gang *n* bende; troep
gang of robbers *n* rowerbende
gangrene *n* koudvuur
gangster *n* rampokker
gangway *n* (ship) loopplank
gaol *n* tronk; gevangenis
gaolbird *n* tronkvoël
gaolbreak *n* ontsnapping
gap *n* gat; hiaat; leemte; opening
gap year *n* oorslaanjaar
gape *vb* gaap
gaping *adj* gapend
garage *n* garage; (business) motorhawe; (home) motorhuis
garden *n* tuin; hof
garden hose *n* tuinslang
garden shears *n* snoeiskêr
gardener *n* tuinier

gardenia *n* katjiepiering
gargle *vb* gorrel
garlic *n* knoffel
garment *n* kledingstuk
garnet *n* granaat; granaatsteen
garnish *vb* garneer
garret *n* solder
garrison *n* garnisoen; *vb* beman
garter *n* rekker
gas *n* gas
gas mask *n* gasmasker
gash *n* sny
gasket *n* (car) pakstuk
gaslight *n* gaslig
gasp *n* snik; *vb* snik; snak; — **for breath** *vb* hyg
gastric fever *n* maagkoors
gasworks *n* gasfabriek
gate *n* deur; hek; poort
gate money *n* hekgeld
gate-crasher *n* hekstormer
gateway *n* poort
gather *vb* in; pluk; raap; vergader; versamel; — **in** *vb* insamel; — **flowers** *vb* afpluk
gathering *n* byeenkoms; saamtrek; vergadering
gaudy *adj* opsigtelik
gauge *n* meter; peil; *vb* meet
Gautrain Rapid Rail Link *n* Gautrein-snelspooraansluitpunt
gauze *n* gaas; sifdraad
gay icon *n* gay-ikoon
gay person *n* (*informal*) moffie
gaze *vb* staar; — **at** *vb* aangaap; aanstaar
gazelle *n* gasel
gear *n* rat; versnelling; gereedskap
gearbox *n* ratkas
gearwheel *n* tandrat
gecko *n* geitjie
geek *n* bleeksiel
gelatine *n* gelatien
geld *vb* (horse) sny
gelding *n* reun(perd)
gem *n* edelgesteente; juweel; kleinood
gemsbok antelope *n* gemsbok

gender *n* geslag
gender gap *n* geslagsgaping
genealogical table *n* geslag(s)register
genealogical tree *n* stamboom
genealogy *n* geslagkunde
general *adj* algemeen; globaal; universeel; *n* generaal
general practitioner *n* algemene praktisyn; huisarts
generally *adv* algemeen; globaal; gewoonlik
generate *vb* opwek; voortbring
generation *n* generasie; geslag
generation gap *n* generasiegaping; ouderdomsgaping
generous *adj* edelmoedig; gul; mild; rojaal; vrygewig; edel
genet *n* muskeljaatkat
genitals *n* geslagsdele; geslagsorgane
genius *n* genie; vernuf; genialiteit
genre *n* genre
gentle *adj* mak; sag; saggeaard; sagsinnig
gentleman *n* heer
gentleness *n* sagtheid
gently *adv* saggies; soetjies
genuine *adj* opreg; reël; waar; deugdelik
genuineness *n* egtheid
geography *n* aardrykskunde; geografie
geology *n* aardkunde; geologie
geometry *n* geometrie; meetkunde
geranium *n* malva
germ *n* kiem
German measles *n* Duitse masels
germinate *vb* ontkiem; kiem
germination *n* ontkieming
gesture *n* gebaar
get *vb* haal; aanskaf; (angry, etc.) word; **— at** *vb* bykom; **— ahead** *vb* voorkom; **— bedsores** *vb* deurlê; **— better** *vb* aansterk; **— burnt** *vb* aanbrand; **— change** *vb* (money) kleinmaak; **— engaged** *vb* verloof; **— food down** *vb* inkry; **— free** *vb* loskom; vryspring; **— gooseflesh** *vb* hoendervleis kry; **— in** *vb* inkry; instap; **— into difficulty** *vb* vasbrand; **— into one's stride** *vb* op dreef kom; **— loose** *vb* loskom; **— lost** *vb* verdwaal; wegraak; **— mouldy** *vb* verskimmel; **— off** *vb* afkom; vryloop;

— on *vb* vooruitgaan; vooruitkom; **— out** *vb* uitraak; uitstap; **— ready** *vb* gereed mak; klaarmaak; **— rid of** *vb* afkom; **— stuck** *vb* vassteek; **— the better of** *vb* uitoorlê; **— up** *vb* opstaan; **— well** *vb* aard; **— with** *vb* akkordeer
GGE *see* **greenhouse gas emissions**
ghee *n* ghi
gherkin *n* agurkie
GHG *see* **greenhouse gas**
ghost *n* spook; gees; skim
ghost story *n* spookstorie
giant *adj* tamaai; *n* reus
giant stride *n* reuse skrede
gibberish *n* gebrabbel; wartaal
gibe *n* skimp
giddiness *n* duiseligheid; naarheid; narigheid
giddy *adj* duiselig; naar; **become —** *vb* duisel
gift *n* gawe; geskenk; present; talent
gifted *adj* begaaf; geniaal; talentvol
giftedness *n* genialiteit
gigabyte *n* gigagreep
gigantic *adj* reusagtig
giggle *vb* giggel
giggling *n* gegiggel
gild *vb* verguld
gilding *n* verguldsel
gill *n* kieu
gilt *n* verguldsel
gimlet *n* boor; boortjie
gimmick *n* truuk
gin *n* jenewer
ginger *n* gemmer
ginormous *adj* (*informal*) reusagtig; kolossaal; enorm
gipsy *n* sigeuner
giraffe *n* kameelperd
gird *vb* gord
girdle *n* gordel; gord
girl *n* dogter; meisie; nooi
girls' school *n* meisieskool
gist *n* kern
give *vb* gee; skenk; toebring; verleen; **— a lift** *vb* oplaai; **— a recital** *vb* voordra; **— away** *vb* verklik; (wedding) verklap; **— back** *vb* teruggee; **— birth to** *vb* baar; beval; **— change** *vb* wissel; **— evidence** *vb* getuig; **— in**

vb ingee; — **notice** *vb* opsê; — **odds** *vb* voorgee; — **off** *vb* afgee; uitwasem; — **out** *vb* opraak; — **reasons for** *vb* motiveer; — **rein to** *vb* botvier; — **support** *vb* aanmoedig; — **up** *vb* afsien; opgee; prysgee; — **up luxuries** *vb* afskaf; — **way** *vb* swig; wyk

giving back *n* teruggawe

gizzard *n* krop

glacial period *n* ysperiode

glacier *n* gletser

glad *adj* bly

gladden *vb* verbly; verheug

gladiolus *n* swaardlelie; swaardblom

gladly *adv* graag

gladness *n* blydskap; vreug(de)

glance *n* aanblik; blik; oogopslag; *vb* aanblik; sydelings kyk; **at a —** *adv* sommer; — **over** *vb* insien

gland *n* klier

glaring *adj* skril

glasnost *n* deursigtigheid; openheid

glass *n* (for drinks and substance) glas

glass ceiling *n* glasplafon

glass-eye *n* glasoog

glassblower *n* glasblaser

glaze *n* (pottery) glasuur; verglaassel

gleam *vb* glans

glen *n* dal

glide *vb* sweef

glider *n* sweeftuig

glimmer *vb* skemer

glistening *adj* blink

glitter *vb* blink; flikker; glinster; skitter

glittering *adj* skitterend

global *adj* globale

global positioning system *n* globale-posisioneringstelsel

global warming *n* aardverwarming

globe *n* aardbol; wêreld; bol

gloomy *adj* somber; droefgeestig; droewig; mismoedig; swaarmoedig; swartgallig; treurig; triestig; betrokke; duister

glorious *adj* heerlik

glory *n* roem; luister; glorie

gloss[1] *n* glans

gloss[2] (*or* **glossary**) *n* glos(sarium); woordelys

glove *n* handskoen

glow *n* gloed; skynsel; *vb* gloei

glowing *adj* blakend; gloeiend

glow-worm *n* glimwurm

glue *n* gom; lym; *vb* plak; lym; — **together** *vb* vasplak

glutton *n* vraat; veelvraat

gluttonous *adj* gulsig; snoep

glyc(a)emic index *n* glisemiese indeks

glyc(a)emic load *n* glisemiese lading

glycerine *n* gliserien

gnat *n* muggie

gnaw *vb* knaag; kou; kluif

gnu *n* wildebees; gnu

go *vb* gaan; loop; tree; — **about** *vb* rondgaan; — **away** *vb* heengaan; trap; weggaan; *interj* voert!; voertsek!; — **back** *vb* teruggaan; — **by** *vb* verbygaan; — **first** *vb* vooruitloop; — **in** *vb* intrek; binnegaan; — **into exile** *vb* uitwyk; — **off** *vb* afgaan; — **out** *vb* uitgaan; (tide) verloop; — **over** *vb* oorgaan; oorkyk; — **past** *vb* passeer; — **pink** *vb* bloos; — **quickly** *vb* aanroer; — **round with** *vb* omgaan; — **shopping** *vb* inkopies doen; — **smoothly** *vb* vlot; — **straight** *vb* pyl; — **together** *vb* saamgaan; — **through** *vb* beleef; deurmaak; oorkyk; — **under** *vb* ondergaan; — **up** *vb* opgaan; — **up and down** *vb* wip; — **wrong** *vb* teenloop

go-between *n* tussenganger

go-cart *n* knortjor

goal *n* doel; einddoel; eindpaal

goal kick *n* doelskop

goal line *n* doellyn

goalpost *n* doelpaal

goalposts *npl* doelwitte

goat *n* bok

goat's milk *n* bokmelk

goatee beard *n* bokbaard

goats *n* bokke; kleinvee

goblet *n* drinkbeker

God *n* God; Heer; god

God-fearing *adj* godvresend

godchild *n* peetkind

goddess *n* godin

godless *adj* goddeloos

godly *adj* godsalig

godparent *n* peet

godparents *npl* peetouers

goggles *n* stofbril

gold *n* goud; *adj* goud-; goue
gold bar *n* staafgoud
gold dust *n* stofgoud
gold foil *n* goudblad
gold leaf *n* goudblad
gold mine *n* goudmyn
gold ore *n* gouderts
gold reef *n* goudrif
golden *adj* goue
golden handshake *n* tattatjek
goldsmith *n* goudsmid
golf *n* gholf
golf club *n* gholfstok
golf course *n* gholfbaan
golf links *n* gholfbaan
gone *adj* weg; skoonveld; *adv* weg
gong *n* ghong
good *n* goed; goedheid; *adj* goed; gaaf; gawerig; soet; braaf; *adv* wel; **be —** **for** *vb* deug; **a — many** *pron* heelwat; **— quality** *n* deug; **— wishes** *npl* seënwens
good afternoon! *sentence substitute* goeiemiddag!
good day! *sentence substitute* goeiedag!; dag!; totsiens!
good evening! *sentence substitute* goeienaand!; naand!
good luck! *sentence substitute* sterkte!
good morning! *sentence substitute* goeiemôre!; môre!
good night! *sentence substitute* goeienag!; nag!
goodbye! *sentence substitute* adieu!; totsiens!; tatta; vaarwel
good-for-nothing *n* niksnuts; deugniet
good-natured *adj* gemoedelik; goedaardig; goedig; goed
goodness *n* goed; goedheid
goodness knows! *interj* nugter weet!
goods *npl* goed; hawe; negosie; goedjies
goods train *n* goederetrein
goody-goody *adj* soetsappig
Google *n* Google; *vb* gegoogel
goose *n* gans
goosebumps *n* hoendervleis
gooseflesh *n* hoendervleis
gorge *n* ravyn
gorilla *n* gorilla
gospel *n* evangelie
gossip *n* gebabbel; kekkelbek; skinderpraatjies; (person) skinderbek; kekkelbek; *vb* kekkel
goth *adj* (music, fashion, etc.) goties
gourd *n* kalbas
gourmet *n* fynproewer
gout *n* jig
govern *vb* bestuur; beheers
governance *n* regering
governess *n* goewernante
government *n* regering; bewind; bestuur
government gazette *n* staatskoerant
governor *n* goewerneur
gown *n* toga
GPS *see* **global positioning system**
grab *vb* betakel
grace *n* genade; grasie
graceful *adj* grasieus
gracefulness *n* swier
gracious *adj* grasieus; genadig
grade *n* gehalte; graad; klas; rang
grader *n* (road) padskraper
gradient *n* steilte; val
gradual *adj* geleidelik
gradually *adv* geleidelik; allengs
graduate *n* gegradueerde; *vb* gradueer
graduation *n* gradering; promosie
graduation ceremony *n* gradeplegtigheid
graduation day *n* gradedag
graft *n* ent
grain *n* graan; greintjie; korrel; koring; (leather, wood) nerf; **— farmer** *n* koringboer; **— of sand** *n* sandkorrel
gram *n* gram
grammar *n* grammatika; taalkunde
grammatical *adj* grammatikale; taalkundig
granadilla *n* grenadella
granary *n* graanskuur; koringskuur
grand *adj* deftig; groots; grootskeeps; piekfyn; verhewe
grand piano *n* vleuel; vleuelklavier
grandchild *n* kleinkind
granddaughter *n* kleindogter
grandfather *n* grootvader; oupa
grandmother *n* grootmoeder; ouma
grandparents *npl* grootouers
grandson *n* kleinseun
granite *n* graniet
grant *n* skenking; subsidie; toekenning; toelaag; *vb* gun

grape *n* druif
grape brandy *n* witblits
grape jam *n* druiwekonfyt
grapefruit *n* pomelo
graph *n* grafiek
graphic *adj* grafies; aanskoulik
grasp *n* greep; *vb* pak; vat; begryp
grasping *adj* inhalig
grass *n* gras
grasshopper *n* sprinkaan
grassland *n* grasland
grassy plain *n* grasvlakte
grate[1] *n* rooster; vuurherd
grate[2] *vb* kners; rasper
grateful *adj* dankbaar; erkentlik
grater *vb* rasper
gratification *n* toelaag
gratify *vb* bevredig
gratifying *adj* bevredigend
gratis *adj* gratis; verniet; kosteloos; *adv* verniet
gratuity *n* fooi; gratifikasie
grave[1] *adj* ernstig; plegtig
grave[2] *n* graf
gravel *n* grint; gruis
graveyard *n* begraafplaas; godsakker
gravitation *n* aantrekkingskrag; swaartekrag
gravity *n* aantrekkingskrag; swaartekrag
gravy *n* sous
gravy boat *n* souskom
gravy train *vb* soustrein
graze *vb* afskaaf; (animals) wei; afwei
grazing *n* weiding; weiland
grease *n* ghries; teer; *vb* insmeer
greasy *adj* smerig; vetterig
great *adj* groot; to a — extent *adv* grootliks
great flood *n* sondvloed
great-grandchild *n* agterkleinkind
great-grandfather *n* oorgrootvader; oupagrootjie
great-grandmother *n* oorgrootmoeder; oumagrootjie
great-grandparent *n* grootjie
great-grandparents *npl* oorgrootouers
greater part *n* gros
greatly *adv* grootliks
greatness *n* grootheid; grootte
greed *n* hebsug; gierigheid

greedy *adj* gretig; gulsig; hebsugtig; inhalig; snoep
green *n* groen; grasperk; (golf) setperk; *adj* groen
green bean *n* snyboontjie
green beans *npl* groenboontjies
green pea *n* dopertjie
green technology *n* omgewingsvriendelike tegnologie
greenery *n* groen
greenhouse *n* kweekhuis
greenhouse gas *n* kweekhuisgas
greenhouse gas emissions *n* kweekhuisgasvrystelling (KGV)
greens *npl* groente
greet *vb* groet; begroet
greeting *n* groet; —s *npl* groete
grenade *n* granaat
grey *n, adj* grys; grou
greybeard *n* grysaard
gridiron *n* rooster
gridlock *n* verkeersknoop
grief *n* smart; droefheid; droef(e)nis; leed; hartseer; verdriet; wee
grievance *n* grief; beswaar
grieve for *vb* treur
grievous *adj* bitter
grill *n* rooster; *vb* braai
grilled *adj* gebraai
grimace *n* gryns; skewebek
grin *n* gryns; *vb* grinnik
grind *vb* maal; slyp; (teeth) kners
grindstone *n* slypsteen
grip *n* beet; vat; *vb* pak; vat; begryp
gripping *adj* aangrypend; pakkend
grit *n* grint; gruis
groan *n* kreun; *vb* kerm; kreun
groaning *n* gekerm
groats *npl* gort
grocer *n* kruidenier
groin *n* lies
groove *n* gleuf; groef
grope *vb* tas; voel; — about *vb* rondtas
gross *adj* bruto; *n* gros
gross weight *n* bruto gewig
grotto *n* grot
ground *n* aarde; grond; rede; terrein
ground-to-air missile *n* grond-tot-lugmissiel
group *n* groep; troep; *vb* groepeer
grow *vb* groei; aangroei; — angry

vb vererg; — **darker** *vb* skemer; —
mouldy *vb* beskimmel; — **numb
with cold** *vb* verkluim; — **old** *vb* verouder; — **thin** *vb* vermaer; — **up** *vb*
opgroei; — **weaker** *vb* verswak
growl *n* grou; knor; *vb* brom; knor
grown-up *n* grootmens; volwassene; *adj*
opgeskote
growth *n* gewas; geswel; groei; opgang
grub *n* wurm
grudge *n* nyd; wrok
gruff *adj* bars; stroef; stuurs
grumble *n* knor; *vb* brom; knor
grumbler *n* brompot
grumpy *adj* knorrig
grunge music *n* grungemusiek
grunt *n* knor
grunter *n* (fish) knorder
guarantee *n* borgtog; garansie; onderpand; waarborg; *vb* borgstaan
guard *n* brandwag; wag; eskort; geleide;
hoede; skut; *vb* behoed
guard dog *n* waghond
guard of honour *n* erewag
guardian *n* bewaker; voog
guardian angel *n* beskermengel
guardianship *n* voogdy
guava *n* koejawel
guerrilla warfare *n* guerillaoorlog
guess *n* raaiskoot; gis; gissing; *vb* raai;
gis
guestimate *n* raairaam
guest *n* besoeker; gas; kuiergas
guest speaker *n* gasspreker
guidance *n* leiding
guide *n* gids; leier; rigsnoer; wegwyser;
vb lei
guide dog *n* gidshond

guided reading *n* begeleide lees
guideline *n* leidraad; riglyn
guiding star *n* leidster
guild *n* gilde
guillotine *n* valbyl
guilt *n* skuld
guilty *adj* skuldig; — **person** *n* skuldige
guinea fowl *n* tarentaal
guitar *n* ghitaar; kitaar
gulf *n* afgrond; golf
gull *n* meeu
gullet *n* keelgat; slukderm
gullible *adj* goedgelowig
gully *n* donga
gulp *n* sluk; *vb* sluk
gum[1] *n* gom
gum[2] *n* (mouth) tandvleis
gum tree *n* gomboom
gun *n* geweer; kanon; roer
gunman *n* rampokker
gunner *n* kanonnier
gunpowder *n* buskruit; kruit
guns *npl* geskut
gunsmith *n* geweermaker
gurgling *n* geroggel
gush *vb* opwel
gust *n* rukwind; vlaag; — **of wind** *n*
windvlaag
gutter *n* geut
guy *n* (*informal*) kêrel; ou; vent
guzzle *vb* slurp; suip
gymnasium *n* gimnasium
gymnast *n* gimnas
gymnastics *n* gimnastiek
gynaecologist *n* ginekoloog; verloskundige; vrouearts
gypsum *n* gips

H

habit *n* aanwensel; gewoonte; gebruik; sede; sleur
habit-forming drug *n* verslaafmiddel
hacker *n* kuberkraker; stelselinbreker
hackneyed *adj* afgesaag
hacksaw *n* ystersaag
haddock *n* skelvis
haemorrhage *n* bloeding; *vb* bloei
haemorrhoids *npl* aambeie
haggle *vb* afding; knibbel; kwansel
hail[1] *n* hael
hail[2] *vb* aanroep
hail and ride *vb* roep en ry
hailstone *n* haelkorrel
hailstorm *n* haelbui; haelstorm
hair *n* haar
hair comb *n* haarkam
hairbrush *n* haarborsel
haircut *n* haarsny
hairdresser *n* haarsnyer; kapper
hairdryer *n* haardroër
hairpin *n* haarnaald
hairpin bend *n* s-draai
hairsplitting *n* haarklowery
hairstyle *n* kapsel
hairy *adj* harig
hake *n* stokvis
half *n* helfte; *prefix* half-
half-breed *n* baster
half-dead *adj* halfdood
half-done *adj* halfklaar
half-full *adj* halfvol
half-grown *adj* halfwas
half-hearted *adj* halfhartig
half-moon *n* halfmaan
half-time *n* rustyd
half-yearly *adj, adv* sesmaandeliks
halfway *adj, adv* halfpad; halfweg
hall *n* saal; voorportaal; lokaal
hall stand *n* hoederak; kapstok
hallmark *n* stempel; waarmerk
hallmarked *adj* gewaarmerkte
hallucination *n* hersenskim; sinsbedrog
halo *n* ligkrans
halt *vb* stop; —! *interj* halt!
halter *n* halter; strop
halve *vb* halveer

ham *n* ham
hamburger *n* frikkadelbroodjie; hamburger
hamlet *n* gehug
hammer *n* hamer; (gun) haan
hammerhead *n* (bird, shark) hamerkop
hammock *n* hangmat
hamper *n* mandjie
hand *n* hand; (watch, clock) wyster; **be in the —s of** *vb* berus; **— down** *vb* oorlewer; **— in** *vb* indien; inlewer; **— on** *vb* aangee; **— out** *vb* uitdeel; **— over** *vb* afgee; oorgee; oorhandig; opgee; uitlewer
hand-fed animal *n* hansdier
hand-fed calf *n* hanskalf
handbag *n* handsak
handbill *n* strooibiljet
handbook *n* handboek
handcuff *n* boei; *vb* boei; **—s** *npl* handboeie
handful *n* handvol
handicap *vb* voorgee; agterstel
handiwork *n* handewerk; handwerk
handkerchief *n* sakdoek
handle *n* handvatsel; hef; hingsel; slinger; steel; *vb* behandel
handling *n* handeling
handout *n* strooibiljet
hands-free *adj* loshand
handshake *n* handdruk
handsome *adj* aansienlik; fraai; knap; mooi
handwork *n* handewerk; handwerk
handwriting *n* handskrif; skrif
handy *adj* byderhand; handig
handyman *n* nutsman; handlanger
hang *vb* hang; ophang; **— down** *vb* afhang; **— onto** *vb* vashou
hang-glider *n* vlerksweeftuig; (person) vlerkswewer
hangman *n* laksman
hangover *n* babelas; wingerdgriep
hanker after *vb* hunker
hanky *see* **handkerchief**
haphazardly *adv* lukraak
happen *vb* gebeur; toeval

happen to *vb* oorkom
happiness *n* geluk
happy *adj* gelukkig; plesierig
harbour *n* hawe; seehawe
hard *adj* hard; hardvogtig; moeilik; stram; beswaarlik; (times) benard
hard labour *n* dwangarbeid; hardepad
hard of hearing *adj* hardhorig
hard up *adj* platsak
harden *vb* verhard
hardened *adj* gehard; vereelt; verstok
hardly *adv* skaars; kwalik
hardship *n* ongemak; ontbering
hardware *n* ysterware
hardworking *adj* fluks
hare *n* haas
harelip *n* gesplete lip
harem *n* harem
harm *n* moles; *vb* benadeel
harmful *adj* skadelik
harmless *adj* onskadelik; skadeloos
harmonica *n* harmonika
harmonious *adj* eendragtig
harmonium *n* harmonium
harmony *n* harmonie; ooreenstemming; samestemming
harness *n* tuig; *vb* optuig
harp *n* harp
harpoon *n* harpoen
harrow *vb* eg
harsh *adj* bars; bitsig; stroef
hartebeest *n* (antelope) hartbees
harvest *n* gewas; oes
harvest time *n* oestyd
has *vb* het
haste *n* haas; spoed
hasten *vb* spoed; verhaas
hasty *adj* haastig; driftig; vlugtig; voorbarig
hat *n* hoed
hat stand *n* kapstok
hat-trick *n* driekuns
hatbox *n* hoededoos
hatch[1] *n* broeisel; *vb* broei
hatch[2] *n* kap; luik
hatchback *n* (car) luikrug
hatchet *n* byl
hate *n* haat
hateful *adj* haatlik
hatpin *n* hoedespeld
hatred *n* haat

haughtiness *n* trots
haughty *adj* aanmatigend; hooghartig; hoogmoedig; hovaardig; trots
haulier *n* karweier
haunch *n* heup; **—s** *npl* hurke
haunt *vb* spook
haunted house *n* spookhuis
have *vb* om te hê; hê; **— a cold** *vb* verkoue het; **— a good time** *vb* fuif; geniet; **— hold of** *vb* beethê; **— intercourse** *vb* seks hê; omgang hê; **— on** *vb* aanhê; **— to** *vb* moet
havoc *n* verwoesting
hawk[1] *n* valk
hawk[2] *vb* vent
hawker *n* venter
hawser *n* kabel
hawthorn *n* haagdoring
hay *n* hooi
hay fever *n* hooikoors
haystack *n* hooimied
hazard *n* gevaar
hazardous *adj* gevaarlik; riskant; gewaag
haze *n* newel; waas
hazy *adj* dynserig
he *pers pron* hy; *pron* diegene
he-goat *n* bokram
head *n* kop; harspan; hoof; owerste; knop; kopstuk; (bed) koppenent; **— of a hammer** *n* hamerkop; **— over heels** *adv* halsoorkop; **go — over heels** *vb* bolmakiesie slaan; **— over heels in love** *adj* smoorverlief
head teacher *n* prinsipaal
headache *n* hoofpyn; kopseer
heading *n* hoof; kopstuk; opskrif; rubriek
headland *n* kaap; wenakker
headquarters *n* hoofkwartier
headstrong *adj* koppig; eiesinnig; halsstarrig; hardhoofdig; balhorig
headwind *n* teenwind
heal *vb* genees; heel
healer *n* heler
healing *n* heelkunde
healing-power *n* geneeskrag
health *n* gesondheid; welstand
healthy *adj* fiks; gesond
heap *n* hoop; mied; stapel; **— of sand** *n* sandhoop; **— up** *vb* stapel; ophoop

hear *vb* verhoor; hoor
hearing *n* verhoor; gehoor
hearing distance *n* gehoorafstand
hearse *n* lykswa; roukoets
heart *n* gemoed; hart
heart attack *n* hartaanval
heart bypass *n* hartomleiding
heart disease *n* hartkwaal
heart failure *n* hartversaking
heart transplant *n* hartoorplanting
heart-rending *adj* hartbrekend; hartroerend; hartverskeurend
heart-shaped *adj* hartvormig
heartbeat *n* hartklop
heartbreaking *adj* hartbrekend
heartburn *n* sooibrand
hearth *n* vuurherd; haard
heartless *adj* harteloos
hearts *npl* (playing cards) hartens
heartsore *adj* hartseer
hearty congratulations! *sentence substitute* veels geluk!
heat *n* hitte; warmte; *vb* verhit; stook
heated *n* verhit
heater *n* verwarmer
heath *n* heide
heather *n* heiblom
heating *n* verwarming
heatstroke *n* hittesteek
heatwave *n* hittegolf
heave *n* deining; *vb* dein
heaven *n* hemel
heavenly *adj* hemels
heavens *npl* uitspansel
heaviness *n* swaarte
heavy *adj* swaar; loom; **— rain** *n* slagreën; **— shower** *n* stortreën
heckle *vb* hekel
hectare *n* hektaar
hedge *n* heining; laning
heed *vb* let op; oplet
heel *n* hak
heifer *n* vers; **— calf** *n* verskalf
height *n* hoogte
heinous *adj* snood
heir *n* erfgenaam; **— to the throne** *n* troonopvolger
heirloom *n* erfstuk
helicopter *n* helikopter
helipad *n* heliblad
hell *n* hel

helm *n* helm; roer; stuur
helmet *n* helmet
helmsman *n* stuurman
help *n* hulp; bystand; steun; toevlug; *vb* assisteer; **with the — of** met behulp van; **— along** *vb* aanhelp; **— out** *vb* uithelp; tereghelp
helper *n* assistent
helpful *adj* behulpsaam; hulpvaardig
helping *n* skeppie
helpless *adj* hulpeloos; onbeholpe
hem *n* soom; *vb* soom; omsoom; omboor
hemisphere *n* halfrond; hemisfeer
hemp *n* hennep
hen *n* hen; hoender
hence *conj* vandaar
henceforth *adv* voortaan
hencoop *n* hoenderhok
henhouse *n* hoenderhok
her *poss pron* haar
herald *n* herout
heraldic *adj* heraldies
herb *n* kruid
herbage *n* opslag
herbivorous *adj* grasetend; plantetend
herculean strength *n* reusekrag
herculean task *n* reusetaak
herd *n* kudde
here *adv* hier; hierso; alhier
hereafter *adv* hierna; hiernamaals
hereditary *adj* aangebore; erflik; oor-erflik; **— law** *n* erfreg
heresy *n* kettery; dwaalleer
heretic *n* ketter
herewith *adv* hierby; hiermee
heritage *n* erfenis
hermaphrodite *n* hermafrodiet; transie
hermit *n* kluisenaar
hernia *n* breuk
hero *n* held
heroic *adj* heldhaftig; **— deed** *n* heldedaad
heroine *n* heldin
heroism *n* heldemoed
heron *n* reier
herring *n* harder; haring
hesitate *vb* (speech) stamel; aarsel
hesitation *n* weifeling
hexagonal *adj* seshoekig
hi! *interj* haai!

hiatus *n* hiaat
hibernate *vb* oorwinter
hibernation *n* winterslaap
hiccup *n* hik
hide[1] *vb* opkrop; **— oneself** *vb* wegkruip
hide[2] *n* vel; huid
hidden *adj* verborge; verstoke; geheim
hide-and-seek *n* wegkruipertjie
hideous *adj* afskuwelik; foeilelik
hiding place *n* skuilplek
high *adj* hoog; lank
high blood pressure *n* hoë bloeddruk
high priest *n* hoëpriester
high school *n* hoërskool
high tide *n* hoogwater
high treason *n* hoogverraad
high water *n* hoogwater
high-born *adj* hooggebore
high-pitched *adj* hoog
high-spirited *adj* fier
highest *adj* opperste
highly *adv* hoogs; **— necessary** *adj* hoognodig; **— priced** *adj* peperduur
Highness *title* Hoogheid
highwayman *n* struikrower
hijack *vb* kaap
hike *n* stap; stapper
hiker *n* wandelaar
hiking trail *n* voetslaanpad
hiking trip *n* staptoer
hilarious *adj* skree(u)snaaks
hilarity *n* vrolikheid
hill *n* heuwel; hoogte; rant; rug
hillock *n* bult
hilly *adj* heuwelagtig
hilt *n* handvatsel; hef
him *pers pron* hom
hind leg *n* agterpoot
hinder *vb* hinder; belemmer; belet
hindrance *n* beletsel; hinder; hinderpaal
hinge *n* hingsel; skarnier
hint *n* wenk
hip *n* heup
hip replacement *n* heupvervanging
hip-hop music *n* hip-hop-musiek
hippopotamus *n* seekoei
hire *n* huur; *vb* verhuur; **— out** *vb* pag
his *poss pron* sy; syne
hiss *vb* sis; **— at** *vb* uitjou

historian *n* historikus
historic *adj* histories
historical *adj* histories
history *n* geskiedenis; historie
hit *vb* stoot; raps; neuk; **— against** *vb* aanbots
hitch *n* defek
hitch on *vb* aanhaak
hitchhike *vb* duimgooi
hitchhiker *n* ryloper
hither *adv* hierheen; hiernatoe
hoarse *adj* hees; aamborstig; skor; rou
hoax *vb* fop; *n* foppery
hobby *n* stokperdjie; tydverdryf; liefhebbery
hock *n* hak
hockey *n* hokkie
hoe *n* skoffel
hog *n* swyn; vark; burg
hoist *vb* hys; ophaal
hold[1] *n* (ship) ruim; (ship) skeepsruim
hold[2] *vb* vat; hou; **— back** *vb* weerhou; terughou; **— before** *vb* voorhou; **— down** *vb* onderdruk; onderhou; **— fast** *vb* vashou; **— office** *vb* beklee pos; **— one's own** *vb* standhou; **— under** *vb* onderhou; **— up** *vb* vertraag
holder *n* toonder
holding a different opinion *adj* andersdenkend
hole *n* gat; kuil
hole in one *n* kolhou
holiday *n* rustyd; vakansie
holiday-maker *n* vakansieganger
holiness *n* heiligheid
hollow *n* holte; *adj* hol; **— out** *vb* uithol; uitkalf
hollyhock *n* stokroos
holy *adj* heilig
holy water *n* wywater
homage *n* eer; eerbetoon; hulde
home *n* huis; **at —** *adv* tuis
home economics *n* huishoudkunde
home medicine cupboard *n* huisapteek
home medicine chest *n* huisapteek
home page *n* (computing) tuisblad
home remedy *n* huismiddel
home rule *n* selfbestuur
home shopping *n* tuisinkope

home straight (*or* **stretch**) *n* pylvak
home visit *n* huisbesoek
homeless *adj* dakloos
homely *adj* gelykvloers; huislik
homemade leather shoe *n* velskoen
homeopath *n* homeopaat
homeopathic *adj* homeopaties
homeopathy *n* homeopatie
homesickness *n* heimwee
homeward *adv* huiswaarts
homework *n* huiswerk; tuiswerk
homicide *n* manslag
homing device *n* aanpeiltoestel
homogeneous *adj* gelyksoortig; homogeen
homologous *adj* gelykluidend
homophobia *n* homofobie
homosexual *n, adj* homoseksueel; *n* (*informal*) moffie
honest *adj* eerbaar; eerlik; reguit; regskape; braaf
honestly *adv* eerlik
honesty *n* eerlikheid
honey *n* heuning
honey badger *n* ratel
honey-bird *n* heuningvoël
honeymoon *n* wittebrood(sdae); huweliksreis
honeysuckle *n* kanferfoelie
honorarium *n* honorarium
honorary degree *n* eregraad
honorary member *n* erelid
honour *n* eer; ere; *vb* huldig
honourable *adj* agbaar; agtenswaardig; eerbaar; weledel
honours *npl* honneurs
hood *n* tent
hoodwink *vb* blinddoek
hoof *n* hoef
hook *n* haak; hoek; — **in** *vb* inhaak; — **on** *vb* aanhaak
hooker *n* (rugby) haker
hooliganism *n* straatboewery
hoop *n* hoepel
hooray! *interj* hoera!; hoerê!
hoot *vb* toeter
hooter *n* toeter
hop *n* sprong; (plant) hop; *vb* wip; huppel
hope *n* hoop; verwagting; *vb* hoop
hopeful *adj* hoopvol

hopeless *adj* hopeloos; reddeloos
hopper *n* (*informal*) (wingless locust) voetganger
horizon *n* horison; gesigseinder; kim
horizontal *adj* horisontaal
horn *n* toeter; (animal) horing
hornpipe *n* horrelpyp
horny *adj* eeltagtig
horrible *adj* afgryslik; afskuwelik; vreeslik; yslik; aaklig; — **weather** *n* hondeweer
horribly *adv* aaklig
horrify *vb* verskrik
horror *n* afskrik; afsku; gruwel; verskrikking
horse *n* perd; — **with a blaze** *n* bles; **led** — *n* handperd
horse racing *n* perde(wed)renne
horsefly *n* perdevlieg
horseman *n* perderuiter; ruiter
horsepower *n* perdekrag
horseradish *n* peperwortel
horseshoe *n* hoefyster
horticulture *n* tuinbou
hosepipe *n* tuinslang
hospitable *adj* gasvry; herbergsaam
hospital *n* hospitaal
host *n* gasheer
hostage *n* gyselaar
hostel *n* tehuis
hostess *n* gasvrou
hostile *adj* vyandelik; vyandig
hot *adj* warm; heet
hot-air balloon *n* lugballon
hot dog *n* worsbroodjie
hot pursuit *n* opvolgaanval
hot-headed *adj* heethoofdig
hot-tempered *adj* opvlieënd; kwaai
hotel *n* herberg; hotel
hothead *n* drifkop; vuurvreter
hothouse *n* broeikas; kweekhuis
hour *n* uur
hour hand *n* uurwyser
hourglass *n* eierkokertjie; sandlopertjie
house *n* huis; *vb* huisves
house magazine *n* firmablad
house-trained *adj* (pets) sindelik
house rent *n* huishuur
housebreaking *n* huisbraak; inbraak
household *n* gesin; huisgesin; huishouding; — **members** *npl* huisgenote

housemate n huisgenoot
housemother n huismoeder
housewife n huisvrou
housing n huisvesting
hovel n krot; pondok
hover vb sweef
hovercraft n kussingtuig
how adv hoe; hoedanig; hoekom; —
  long adv hoe lank; — **much** adv hoeveel; — **many** adv hoeveel
however conj egter; nogtans; ewe(n)
  wel; trouens; dog
howl vb huil; grens; tjank
howling adj gebrul
hub n naaf
hubbub n bohaai; lawaai
hubcap n naafdop; wieldop
hue n koloriet
hug vb aandruk; karnuffel
huge adj kolossaal; reusagtig; tamaai;
  yslik; — **task** n reusetaak
hull n (ship) romp
hum vb zoem; gons
human adj menslik
human being n mens; skepsel; aardbewoner
human race n menseras
human relations n menseverhoudinge
human resources npl mensebronne
human rights npl menseregte
human trafficking n mensehandel
humanitarian n mensevriend
humanity n mensdom; mensheid
humankind n mensheid
humble adj nederig; deemoedig; onderdanig; ootmoedig; vb verneder
humiliate vb verneder; verootmoedig
humiliating adj vernederend
humility n deemoed; ootmoed
humorist n humoris
humorous adj humoristies; luimig
humour n bui; geestigheid; humor; luim
hump n boggel
hunch n suspisie; boggel; bult
hundred n, determiner honderd
hundredth n, adj honderdste
hunger n honger
hunger strike n eetstaking
hungry adj hongerig
hunt n jag
hunt down vb agterhaal

hunter n jagter; wildskut
hunting n jag
hunting dog n jaghond
hunting spider n jagspinnekop
hunting trip n safari
hurl vb afsmyt
hurrah! interj hoera!
hurricane n orkaan; stormwind
hurried adj haastig; gejaag
hurriedly adv inderhaas
hurry n gejaag; haas; vb aanroer; —
  along vb aandruk; — **on** vb aanjaag
hurt n pyn; wond; knou; letsel; kneus;
  grief; vb beseer; seer maak; adj (feelings) gekrenk
husband n eggenoot; man
hush vb sus
husk n dop; peul
husky adj hees; skor
hut n hut; pondok
hyacinth n hiasint
hydraulic adj hidroulies
hydrocephalus n waterhoof
hydrochloric acid n soutsuur
hydrofoil n skeerboot
hydrogen n waterstof
hydrogen bomb n waterstofbom
hydrophobia n hondsdolheid
hyena n hiëna
hygiene n gesondheidsleer; higiëne
hymn n gesang; himne; lied; lofsang
hypercritical adj hiperkrities
hypermarket n hipermark; alleswinkel
hypertension n hipertensie; hoë bloeddruk
hyphen n koppelteken (-)
hyphenate vb afkap van woorde
hypnosis n hipnose
hypnotic n hipnoties
hypnotism n hipnotisme
hypnotize vb hipnotiseer
hypochondria n ipekonders
hypochondriac(al) adj hipokondries
hypocrisy n huigelary; skynheiligheid
hypocrite n huigelaar; skynheilige
hypocritical adj skynheilig; geveins;
  dubbelhartig
hypothesis n hipotese
hysterectomy n histerektomie
hysterical adj histeries
hysterics n histerie

I

I *pers pron* ek
I spy *n* (game) aspaai
ice *n* ys; glasuur
Ice Age *n* ysperiode
ice floe *n* dryfys
ice rink *n* skaatsbaan; ysbaan
ice skating *n* ysskaats
ice-cold *adj* yskoud; ysig
ice-cream *n* roomys
iceberg *n* ysberg
icebox *n* yskas
icicle *n* yskeël; ysnaald
icing *n* glasuur
icon *n* ikoon
icy *adj* yskoud
idea *n* idee; begrip; besef; denkbeeld;
    gedagte; nosie; opvatting
ideal *n* ideaal
idealist *n* idealis
identical *adj* identies; selfde
identify *vb* identifiseer; uitken; vereen-
    selwig
identity *n* identiteit
idiom *n* idioom; spraakgebruik
idiomatic *adj* idiomaties
idiot *n* idioot
idle *adj* lui; werkloos; ydel; ledig; *vb* (en-
    gine) luier
idle gossip *n* wywepraatjie
idleness *n* ledigheid
idol *n* afgod; god
idolatry *n* afgodediens; beeldediens
idolize *vb* verafgood
if *adv* wanneer; *conj* indien; — **need be**
    adv desnoods
ignite *vb* ontbrand
ignoble *adj* onedel
ignorance *n* onkunde; onbekendheid
ignorant *adj* onkundig; onwetend
ignore *vb* ignoreer; veronagsaam; dood-
    swyg; negeer
iguana *n* likkewaan
ill *adj* siek; sleg; erg
ill at ease *adj* ontuis
ill-fated *adj* noodlottig
ill-luck *n* teenspoed
ill-mannered *adj* ongemanierd; ongepoets

ill-treat *vb* mishandel; om sleg te behan-
    del; moor
ill-use *vb* mishandel
illegal *adj* onwettig; onregmatig; weder-
    regtelik
illegible *adj* onleesbaar; onduidelik
illicit *adj* ongeoorloof
illiterate *adj* ongeleer(d); ongeletter(d);
    onontwikkeld
illiterate person *n* analfabeet
illness *n* siekte
illogical *adj* onlogies
illuminate *vb* verlig
illumination *n* illuminasie; verligting
illusion *n* illusie; droombeeld; sinsbe-
    drog
illustrate *vb* illustreer
illustrated *adj* geïllustreer
illustration *n* illustrasie; prent
image *n* beeld; beeltenis; ewebeeld
imaginable *adj* denkbaar
imaginary *adj* denkbeeldig; fiktief; —
    ailments *npl* ipekonders
imagination *n* verbeelding; fantasie
imagine *vb* dink; fantaseer; verbeel
imbecile *n* idioot
imitate *vb* naboots; namaak; navolg
imitation *n* imitasie; namaaksel
immaculate *adj* piekfyn
immature *adj* onryp
immeasurable *adj* onskatbaar; on-
    meetlik; onafsienbaar
immediate *adj* onmiddellik; oombliklik
immediately *adv* onmiddellik; oom-
    bliklik; dadelik
immemorial *adj* onheuglik
immense *adj* onmeetlik
immerse *vb* dompel; indompel
immigrant *n* immigrant
immigration *n* immigrasie
immoderate *adj* onmatig
immodest *adj* onbeskeie
immoral *adj* immoreel; onkuis; onsede-
    lik; sedeloos
immorality *n* onsedelikheid; ontug
immortal *adj* onsterflik
immortalize *vb* verewig

immovable *adj* onbeweegbaar; onbeweeglik; onroerend; pal
immune to *adj* onvatbaar
impact *n* uitwerking
impala *n* (antelope) rooibok
impartial *adj* onpartydig; onsydig; onbevange
impassable *adj* onbegaanbaar
impassive *adj* onaandoenlik
impatience *n* ongeduld
impatient *adj* ongeduldig
impeccable *adj* onberispelik
impecunious *adj* onvermoënd
impede *vb* belemmer; hinder; teenhou; **be —ed** *vb* haper
impel *vb* dryf
impenetrable *adj* ondeurdringbaar
imperative *adj* imperatief; noodsaaklik
imperceptible *adj* onmerkbaar
imperfect *adj* imperfek; onvolkome; onvolmaak; onvoltooi
imperialism *n* imperialisme
imperishable *adj* onverderflik; onverganklik
impersonal *adj* onpersoonlik
impertinence *n* onbeskaamdheid
impertinent *adj* onbeskaamd; parmantig; wys
imperturbable *adj* ongeërg
impervious to *adj* onvatbaar
impetuous *adj* voortvarend
impetus *n* aandrif
impi *n* impi
implant *n* inplanting; *vb* inplant
implement *n* instrument; werktuig
implore *vb* smeek; soebat
impolite *adj* onbeleef
impoliteness *n* onbeleefdheid
import *n* invoer; *vb* invoer; (computing) importeer
import duty *n* invoerreg
importance *n* belangrikheid; betekenis; gewig
important *adj* belangrik; groot; ingrypend; noemenswaardig; vernaam; hoof
importation *n* invoer
importer *n* invoerder
impose *vb* imponeer; oplê; **— on** *vb* wysmaak
impossible *adj* onbegonne; onbestaanbaar; onmoontlik

impostor *n* bedrieër
impotence *n* onmag; onvermoë
impound *vb* skut
impoverish *vb* verarm
impracticable *adj* onuitvoerbaar
impress *vb* indruk; imponeer; inprent
impression *n* impressie; indruk; (book) oplaag
impressive *adj* indrukwekkend
imprint *vb* inprent; **— page** *n* (book) kolofonblad
imprisoned *adj* gevange
imprisonment *n* gevange(n)skap; tronkstraf
improbable *adj* onwaarskynlik
improper *adj* onbehoorlik; onbetaamlik; onfatsoenlik; ongepas
improve *vb* verbeter; veredel; vooruitgaan
improvement *n* beterskap; verbetering; veredeling; vooruitgang
improvisation *n* improvisasie
imprudent *adj* onversigtig
impudence *n* onbeskaamdheid
impudent *adj* astrant; brutaal; domastrant; onbeskaamd; onbeskof; parmantig
impulse *n* aandrif
impulsive *adj* voortvarend
impure *adj* onrein
impute *vb* betig; wyt
in *adj* op; *prep* aan; **— a circle** *adv* rondomtalie; **— a hurry** *adv* inderhaas; **— a jiffy** *adv* tjop-tjop; gou-gou; **— a moment** *adv* flussies; nou-nou; **— a similar way** *adv* insgelyks; **— a way** *adv* sommerso; **— a whisper** *adv* fluisterend; **— addition** *adv* boonop; *prep* daarby; **— another country** *adv* anderland; **— anticipation** *adv* by voorbaat; **— arrears** *adv* agterstallig; **— between** *adv* daartussen; tussendeur; **— broad daylight** *adv* helder oordag; **— case** *conj* indien; **— custody** *adv* in hegtenis; **— daytime** *adv* bedags; **— fighting trim** *adv* strydvaardig; **— flames** *adv* in ligtelaaie; **— fourth place** *adv* vierdens; **— front** *adj, adv* vooraan; **— front of** *prep, adv, conj* voor; **— full** *adv* voluit; **— good shape** *adj* op peil;

— **good time** *adv* betyds; vroegtydig; — **half** *adj* middeldeur; — **duplicate** *adv* in duplo; — **in italics** *adj* kursief; — **love** *adj* verlief; — **no time** *adv* tjop-tjop; gou-gou; — **order** *adj* agtermekaar; *adv* agtereen; — **order of time** *adj* chronologies; — **order that** *adv* sodat; *conj* dat; — **order to** *adv* om; — **pairs** *adv* gepaard; — **pieces** *adv* aan flenters; — **poor health** *adj* kaduks ;— **proportion to** *adj* na gelang van; — **question** *adj* onderhawig; — **rags** *adv* aan flenters; — **respect of** *prep* ingevolge ;— **short** *adv* kortliks; kortom; — **spite of** *prep* ondanks; trots; in weerwil van; nieteenstaande; — **stock** *adv* voorhande; — **tatters** *adv* aan flenters; — **terms of** *prep* ingevolge; kragtens; — **that** *conj* darem; *adv* daarin; — **that manner** *adv* sodoende; — **the afternoon** *adv* middae; smiddags; — **the course of time** *adv* mettertyd; — **the daytime** *adv* oordag; — **the evening** *adv* saans; — **the first place** *adv* eerstens; — **the front** *adv* vorentoe; — **the loop** *adv* lus; — **the meantime** *adv* ondertussen; — **the morning** *adv* smorens; soggens; — **the name of** *prep* namens; — **the neighbourhood of** *adv* omstreeks; — **the olden days** *adv* vanmelewe; — **the past** *adv* voorheen; — **the rear** *adv* agteraan; — **second place** *adv* tweedens; — **those days** *adv* toe; — **transit** *adv* onderweg; — **truth** *adv* voorwaar; — **turn** *adv* beurtelings; — **two** *adv* middeldeur; — **vain** *adj* vergeefs; vrugteloos; *adv* verniet; — **what** *inter pron* waarin; — **which** *inter pron* waarin
in-crowd *n* in-kring
in-service training *n* indiensopleiding
In(n)uit *n, adj* In(n)uïet
inability *n* onvermoë; onmag
inaccessible *adj* onbereikbaar; ongenaakbaar; ontoeganklik
inaccurate *adj* onnoukeurig
inactive *adj* werkloos
inadequate *adj* ontoereikend; onvoldoende
inalienable *adj* onvervreembaar

inattentive *adj* onoplettend
inaudible *adj* onhoorbaar; onverstaanbaar
inaugurate *vb* inwy
inauguration *n* inwyding
inborn *adj* ingebore
incalculable *adj* onberekenbaar
incapable *adj* onbekwaam; onvermoënd
incarnation *n* vleeswording
incautious *adj* onbedagsaam
incense *n* wierook
incentive *n* spoorslag
incessant *adj* aanhoudend; onophoudelik; voortdurend
incessantly *adv* voortdurend
inch *n* duim
incident *n* voorval
incidental *adj* terloops
incidentally *adv* terloops
incision *n* kerf
incisor *n* snytand
incite *vb* aanhits; ophits; oprui; opsteek; opstook; opsweep; stook; aanvuur
inciter *n* opstoker
inclination *n* lus; neiging; sinnigheid; geneentheid; geneigdheid
incline *n* skuinste; *vb* helling
inclined *adj* geneë; geneig; gesind; hellend
include *vb* insluit; opneem; saamvat; omvat
included *adj* inkluis
inclusion *n* inbegrip
inclusive *adj* ingesluit; inklusief
inclusivity *n* inklusiwiteit
incognito *adv; adj* incognito
incoherent *adj* onsamehangend
incombustible *adj* onbrandbaar
income *n* inkomste
income support *n* inkomstesteun
income tax *n* inkomstebelasting
income tax return *n* opgaaf
incomparable *adj* onvergelyklik
incompetent *adj* onbevoeg
incomplete *adj* onvolledig; onvoltooi; onvolkome
incomprehensible *adj* onbegryplik; onbevatlik; onverstaanbaar; raaiselagtig
inconceivable *adj* onbegryplik; ondenkbaar

inconsiderate *adj* onnadenkend
inconsistent *adj* inkonsekwent; strydig
inconsolable *adj* ontroosbaar
inconstant *adj* onstandvastig
inconvenience *n* ongemak; ongerief
inconvenient *adj* hinderlik; ongeleë; ongerieflik; onvanpas
incorporate *vb* inkorporeer; inlyf
incorrect *adj* foutief; onjuis
increase *n* groei; styging; vergroting; verhoging; vermeerdering; *vb* aangroei
incredible *adj* ongelooflik
incredulous *adj* ongelowig
incubator *n* broeimasjien
incurable *adj* ongeneeslik
indebted *adj* verskuldig
indecency *n* onbetaamlikheid
indecent *adj* onbehoorlik; onbetaamlik; onfatsoenlik; onkuis
indecision *n* tweestryd; weifeling
indeed *adv* mos; voorwaar; wrintie; inderdaad; *conj; interj* inderdaad
indefinite *adj* onbepaald; onbestemd
indelible *adj* onuitwisbaar
indemnification *n* vergoeding
indemnify *vb* vergoed
indent *vb* (paragraph) inkeep
indenture *vb* inboek
independence *n* selfstandigheid
independent *adj* onafhanklik; selfstandig
indescribable *adj* onbeskryflik
indestructible *adj* onverwoesbaar
index *n* indeks; register; tabel
index finger *n* wysvinger
indicate *vb* aandui; aanwys; toon; wys
indication *n* vingerwysing
indifferent *adj* onverskillig
indigent *adj* arm; hulpbehoewend; nooddruftig; noodlydend
indigestible *adj* onverteerbaar
indigestion *n* indigestie; slegte spysvertering
indignant *adj* verontwaardig
indignation *n* verontwaardiging
indigo blue *n, adj* blousel
indirect *adj* indirek
indiscreet *adj* onbeskeie
indispensable *adj* broodnodig; onmisbaar; onontbeerlik

indisposed *adj* ongesteld
indisputable *adj* onbetwisbaar
indistinct *adj* onduidelik
individual *n* individu; persoon
indivisible *adj* ondeelbaar
indolent *adj* laks
indoor work *n* binnewerk
indoors *adv* binnenshuis
induce *vb* noop; oorhaal
induct *vb* inseën
induction *n* ontgroening; oriëntering; — sermon *n* intreepreek
indulge *vb* bevredig; vertroetel; verwen
indulgence *n* aflaat
indulgent *adj* toegeeflik; toegewend
industrial *adj* industrieel
industrialist *n* nyweraar
industrious *adj* arbeidsaam; vlytig; werksaam; ywerig
industry *n* bedryf; industrie; nywerheid; vlyt
inedible *adj* oneetbaar
inert *adj* lui
inevitable *adj* onvermydelik
inexact *adj* onnoukeurig
inexcusable *adj* onverantwoordelik
inexhaustible *adj* onuitputlik
inexorable *adj* onverbiddelik
inexperienced *adj* onervare; onbedrewe; ongeoefen
inexplicable *adj* onverklaarbaar
inextinguishable *adj* onuitbluslik
infallible *adj* onfeilbaar
infamous *adj* eerloos
infantry *n* infanterie; voetvolk
infatuation *n* roes
infect *vb* aansteek; besmet; verpes
infection *n* infeksie; aansteking
infectious *adj* aansteeklik; besmetlik; — disease *n* aansteeklike siekte
inferior *adj* gering; minder; laer; minderwaardig; ondergeskik; sleg; *n* (person) mindere
inferiority *n* minderheid
infertile *adj* onvrugbaar
infidelity *n* ontrou
infiltrate *vb* insypel
infinite *adj* oneindig
infirm *adj* gebreklik
inflame *vb* ontsteek; ontvlam; beroer
inflamed *adj* ontstoke**

inflammation *n* inflammasie; ontsteking; brand
inflate *vb* opblaas; opswel
inflated *adj* opgeblaas
inflection *n* fleksie
inflexible *adj* onbuigbaar
inflict *vb* oplê; toebring
influence *n* invloed; inwerking; *vb* beïnvloed
influential *adj* invloedryk
influenza *n* griep; influensa
influx *n* toevloed
infomercial *n* adverteerprogram; inligtingadvertensie
inform *vb* berig; aansê; onderlê; — against *vb* aandra
informal dance *n* boere-disko; dansparty; sokkiejol
informant *n* beriggewer
information *n* gegewens; informasie; inligting; — superhighway *n* infosupersnelweg
informative *adj* leersaam
informer *n* referent
infringe *vb* verkrag
infringement *n* inbreuk
infuriated *adj* woedend
infusion *n* aftreksel
ingenious *adj* vernuftig; vindingryk; kunstig
ingenuity *n* vernuf
ingot *n* staaf
ingratitude *n* ondankbaarheid
ingredient *n* bestanddeel
inhabit *vb* bewoon
inhabitant *n* inwoner; bewoner; ingesetene
inhale *vb* intrek; inasem
inharmonious *adj* onwelluidend
inherit *vb* beërf; erf; oorerf
inheritance *n* boedel; erfenis; nalatenskap
inhospitable *adj* ongasvry; onherbergsaam
inhuman *adj* onmenslik; wreed
initial *adj* aanvanklik; *vb* parafeer; *n* voorletter
initiate *vb* inisieer; inwy
initiation *n* ontgroening
initiative *n* inisiatief
initiator *n* inleier

inject *vb* spuit; inspuit
injection *n* inspuiting
injure *vb* knou; beseer; benadeel
injurious *adj* nadelig
injury *n* skade; nadeel; knak; knou; letsel; afbreuk
injustice *n* onreg; onregverdigheid
ink *n* ink
ink stain *n* inkvlek
inkblot *n* inkvlek
inlaid *adj* ingelê
inland *adv* binneland
inlay *vb* inlê
inlet *n* inham
inmate *n* huisgenoot
inn *n* herberg
innate *adj* aangebore; eie; ingebore
inner *adj* innerlik; inwendig
inner circle *n* binnekring
innermost *adj* binneste
innocence *n* onskuld
innocent *adj* kinderlik; onbedorwe; onnosel; onskuldig
innumerable *adj* ontelbaar
inoculate *vb* ent; inent
inoculation *n* ent; inenting
inorganic *adj* anorganies
inquire *vb* ondersoek
inquiry *n* ondersoek
inquisitive *adj* nuuskierig; weetgierig; — person *n* agie
inquisitiveness *n* nuuskierigheid
inroad *n* inval
insane *adj* waansinnig; kranksinnig; mal; sinneloos; deurmekaar
insanity *n* waansin
insatiable *adj* onversadiglik
inscribe *vb* inskryf
inscription *n* onderskrif; opskrif
inscrutable *adj* ondeurgrondelik
insect *n* gogga; insek
insecticide *n* insekdoder
insects *npl* insekte; gediertes
insensible *adj* gevoelloos; ongevoelig
insensitive *adj* ongevoelig
inseparable *adj* onafskei(d)baar; onafskeidelik; onskei(d)baar
insert *vb* inlas
inside *adv* binne-in; binnekant; *prep* binne
insight *n* deursig; insig

insignificant *adj* nietig; onaansienlik; onbeduidend

insincere *adj* onopreg

insinuate *vb* insinueer

insinuation *n* insinuasie; toespeling; verdagmaking

insipid *adj* laf; smaakloos

insist *vb* aanhou; — **upon** *vb* aandring

insolence *n* onbeskoftheid

insolent *adj* onbeskaamd; onbeskof

insoluble *adj* onoplosbaar

insolvency *n* insolvensie

insolvent *adj* bankrot; insolvent; **be —** *vb* bankrot speel

insomnia *n* slapeloosheid

inspan *vb* inspan

inspect *vb* inspekteer; besien

inspection *n* inspeksie

inspector *n* inspekteur

inspiration *n* inspirasie; ingewing

inspire *vb* besiel; inboesem; aanvuur

install *vb* aanbring; aanlê

instalment *n* paaiement

instance *n* geval; instansie; voorbeeld

instant *adj* oombliklik; kits

instant coffee *n* kitskoffie

instantaneous *adj* oombliklik

instantly *adv* oombliklik; kits

instead of *prep* pleks; in stede van

instigate *vb* aanhits; aanstig; ophits; oprui; opstook; aansit

instigated *adj* opgemaak

instigation *n* aandrang

instigator *n* opstoker

instil *vb* bybring

instinct *n* instink

instinctive *adj* instinkmatig; onwillekeurig

instinctively *adv* instinkmatig

institute *n* instituut; *vb* instel

institution *n* gestig; inrigting; stigting

instruct *vb* onderrig; gelas

instruction *n* instruksie; opdrag; lering; onderrig; voorskrif

instructive *adj* leersaam

instructor *n* instrukteur

instrument *n* instrument; middel

instruments *npl* gereedskap

insufficient *adj* ontoereikend; onvoldoende

insulate *vb* isoleer

insulation *n* isolering; — **tape** *n* isoleerband

insult *n* belediging; afjak; *vb* affronteer; afjak

insurance *n* assuransie; versekering

insurance company *n* versekeringsmaatskappy

insurance policy *n* polis; versekeringspolis

insure *vb* verassureer; verseker

insurgent *adj* opstandig; *n* oproermaker

insurmountable *adj* onoorkoomlik

insurpassable *adj* onoortrefbaar

insurrection *n* oproer; opstand

intact *adj* onaangeroer; ongeskonde

intake *n* inlaat

integration *n* integrasie

intellect *n* intellek, vernuf; verstand; brein

intellectual *adj* geestelik; verstandelik; — **power** *n* geesvermoëns

intelligence *n* verstand; vernuf; berig; tyding

intelligent *adj* intelligent; skerpsinnig; skrander; slim; vernuftig; verstandig

intelligible *adj* verstaanbaar

intend *vb* bedoel; meen; voorhê

intended *n* aanstaande; *adj* voorgenome; bestem

intense *adj* intens

intensive *adj* intensief

intensive care unit *n* sorgeenheid; waakeenheid

intention *n* bedoeling; intensie; oogmerk; voorneme; plan

intercede *vb* pleit

intercept *vb* onderskep; opvang

intercession *n* voorbidding; voorspraak

interchange *n* wisselaar

intercity bus *n* tussenstedelike bus

intercourse *n* seks; omgang

interest *n* belang; rente; — **free** *adj* renteloos; — **rate** *n* rentekoers

interested *adj* belanghebbend

interesting *adj* interessant; boeiend; wetenswaardig

interface *vb* (computing) koppel

interfere *vb* bemoei; inmeng

interim *n* tussentyd

interior *adj* inwendig; *adv* binneland; *n* interieur

interjection *n* tussenwerpsel
intermediary *n* tussenpersoon
intermediate *adj* intermediêr
intern *n* intern *vb* interneer
internal *adj* innerlik; intern; inwendig
internal exam *n* interne eksamen
international *adj* internasionaal
international law *n* volkereg
internment *n* internering
internship *n* internskap
interplanetary *adj* interplanetêr
interpret *vb* tolk; vertolk
interpretation *n* tolking; interpretasie
interpreter *n* tolk
interrogate *vb* verhoor; interrogeer
interrogation *n* ondervraging
interrupt *vb* onderbreek; versteur; afbreek
intersect *vb* kruis
intersection *n* kruising
intersperse *vb* invleg
interstice *n* tussenruimte
intertwine *vb* invleg; verwar
interval *n* pouse; rustyd; speeltyd; tussenpoos; tussentyd; afstand
intervene *vb* ingryp
intervention *n* tussenkoms
interview *n* onderhoud; samespreking
intestine *n* derm
intestines *npl* binnegoed; ingewande
intimacy *n* intimiteit
intimate *adj* intiem; familiêr; bevriend
into *prep* in
intolerable *adj* ondraaglik; onduldbaar; onuitstaanbaar
intolerant *adj* onverdraagsaam
intonation *n* stembuiging
intoxicate *vb* bedwelm
intoxicated *adj* dronk; beskonke; besope
intoxicating *adj* bedwelmend
intoxication *n* roes
intranet *n* (computing) intranet
intransitive *adj* onoorganklik
intrepid *adj* onverskrokke
intricate *adj* ingewikkel(d)
intrigue *n* intrige; komplot; *vb* konkel
introduce *vb* voorstel; inlei
introduced *adj* voorgestel
introduction *n* aanbeveling; inleiding
introspection *n* selfondersoek
intrude *vb* indring

intruder *n* indringer
intrusive *adj* opdringerig
inundate *vb* oorstroom
invade *vb* inval
invalid[1] *n* invalide; sieke
invalid[2] *adj* ongeldig
invaluable *adj* onskatbaar; onwaardeerbaar
invasion *n* inval; strooptog
invective *n* skel(d)woord
invent *vb* uitdink; uitvind; bedink; versin
invention *n* uitvinding; uitvindsel; verdigsel
inventory *n* inventaris
invertebrate *adj* ongewerwel(d)
inverted commas *npl* aanhalingstekens (' ')
invest *vb* beklee(d); inlê; uitsit; (money) belê
investigate *vb* ondersoek; navors
investigation *n* ondersoek
investment *n* geldbelegging
inveterate *adj* ingewortel(d); verstok
invigilator *n* opsiener; toesighouer
invigorate *vb* versterk
invincible *adj* onoorwinlik
invisible *adj* onsigbaar
invitation *n* uitnodiging
invite *vb* versoek; nooi; **— tenders** *vb* aanbestee
inviting *adj* aanloklik
invoice *n* faktuur
invoke *vb* aanroep; inroep
involuntarily *adv* onwillekeurig
involuntary *adj* onwillekeurig
involve *vb* betrek; (danger) meebring
invulnerable *adj* onkwesbaar
iodine *n* jodium
iota *n* jota
irascible *adj* oplopend
iris *n* (eye) iris; (flower) flap
iron *n* yster; *vb* stryk; **— out** *vb* uitstryk
iron foundry *n* ystergietery
iron-clad *adj* pantserskip
ironical *adj* ironies
ironing board *n* strykplank
ironmongery *n* ysterware
ironworks *n* ystergietery
irony *n* ironie
irrational *adj* redeloos

irreconcilable *adj* onversoenlik
irrefutable *adj* onweerlegbaar
irregular *adj* ongereeld; onreëlmatig; ongelyk
irreparable *adj* onherstelbaar
irreproachable *adj* onbesproke
irresistible *adj* onweerstaanbaar
irresolute *adj* besluiteloos; wankelmoedig
irrespective of *prep* ongeag
irresponsible *adj* onverantwoordelik
irretrievable *adj* reddeloos
irreverent *adj* oneerbiedig
irrevocable *adj* onherroeplik
irrigate *vb* besproei; waterlei; bewater; sproei
irritable *adj* prikkelbaar
irritate *vb* prikkel; irriteer
irritated *adj* geprikkel

irritation *n* irritasie; prikkeling
isn't it? *question tag* né?
island *n* eiland
isle *n* eiland
isolate *vb* afsonder; isoleer
isolated *adj* afgesonder; geïsoleer(d)
isolation *n* isolasie; afsondering
isosceles *adj* (triangle) gelykbenig
issue *n* uitgawe; serie; uitslag; afloop; *vb* uitgee
isthmus *n* landengte
it *pers pron* hom; hy; *pron* dit
italics *n* kursief
itch *n* jeuk; skurfte; *vb* jeuk; kriewel
itching *n* jeukte; gekriewel
itinerary *n* reisplan
ivory *n* ivoor; olifantstand
ivy *n* klimop

J

jab *n* inspuiting; *vb* steek; aanpor
jabber *vb* snater
jack *n* (playing cards) boer; (car, etc.) domkrag
jack up *vb* opdomkrag
jack-in-the-box *n* kaartmannetjie
jackal *n* jakkals
jacket *n* baadjie; bobaadjie; jekker; (book) omslag
jagged *adj* hoekig
jail *n* tronk; gevangenis
jailbreak *n* ontsnapping
jam¹ *vb* klem; knel; **traffic —** *n* verkeersknoop
jam² *n* konfyt
janitor *n* deurwagter
January *n* Januarie
japonica *n* japonika
jar *n* pot; kruik
jasmine *n* jasmyn
jasper *n* jaspis
jaundice *n* geelsug
javelin *n* werpspies
jaw *n* kaak; kakebeen
jawbone *n* kakebeen
jealous *adj* jaloers; **be — of** *vb* beny
jealousy *n* jaloesie; afguns; naywer
jeans *n* jeans; jannas
jeer *n* hoon; skimp; spot; spotlag; *vb* hoon; spot
jelly *n* jellie
jerk *n* ruk; *vb* ruk
jersey *n* trui
jest *n* grap; korswel; skerts *vb* gekskeer; korswel
jester *n* nar
jet¹ *n* (plane, etc.) straal
jet² *n* (jewellery) git
jet of water *n* sproeier
jet-black *n, adj* gitswart; pikswart
jet engine *n* straler
jet fighter *n* straalvegter
jet lag *n* straaldraal
jet plane *n* straalvliegtuig; straler
jet set *n* stralerkliek
jet-setter *n* stralerjakker
jet-ski *n* waterponie

jetliner *n* straler
jetty *n* hawehoof; pier
jewel *n* juweel; kleinood
jeweller *n* juwelier
jigsaw puzzle *n* legkaart
jingle *vb* rinkink
job *n* baantjie; pos
job description *n* posbeskrywing
job performance *n* werk(s)verrigting
job satisfaction *n* werkbevrediging
job seeker *n* werksoeker
jockey *n* jokkie
jog *vb* draf
jogger *n* drawwer
jogging *n* drafsport; pretdraf
join *vb* las; voeg; aanlas
join hands *vb* saamwerk
joined *adj* gelas
joiner *n* meubelmaker; skrynwerker
joinery *n* skrynwerk
joining *n* aansluiting
joining together *n* samevoeging
joint *adj* gemeenskaplik; gesamentlik; *n* (in the body) gewrig
joint consultation *n* inspraak
joint owner *n* mede-eienaar
jointly *adv* gesamentlik; saam
joke *n* gek(skeerdery); grap; klug; korswel; spot; skerts; *vb* gekskeer
joker *n* grapmaker
jolly jumper *n* wiptuig
jolt *vb* hobbel; skud
jostle *vb* verdring
jot down *vb* aanstip
journal *n* dagboek; joernaal
journalist *n* joernalis
journey *n* tog; trek; reis; **— about** *vb* rondtrek; **— through** *vb* deurreis
joy *n* blydskap; geluk; vreug(de)
joyful *adj* bly; blymoedig; verblydend; heuglik
jubilee *n* jubileum
judge *n* regter; rigter; *vb* oordeel; beoordeel
judg(e)ment *n* oordeel; diskresie; uitspraak; vonnis
judicial *adj* juridies

judicious *adj* oordeelkundig
jug *n* beker; kan
juggle *vb* goël
juggler *n* goëlaar
juggling *n* goëlery
juice *n* sap
juicy *adj* sappig; mals
jukebox *n* blêrkas
July *n* Julie
jumble sale *n* rommelverkoping
jumbo jet *n* makrostraler
jump *n* sprong; *vb* spring; — **around** *vb* omspring; — **away** *vb* wegspring; — **off** *vb* afspring
jump the queue *vb* indruk
jumping castle *n* springkasteel
junction *n* aansluiting; sameloop; samevloeiing; verbinding
June *n* Junie
Jungian *adj* Jungiaans
jungle *n* oerwoud; ruigte
jungle gym *n* wouterklouter
junior *n, adj* junior

junk[1] *n* rommel
junk[2] *n* (boat) jonk
junk food *n* prulkos
jurisdiction *n* gebied
jurisprudence *n* regsgeleerdheid; regswetenskap
jurist *n* regsgeleerde
juror *n* juris
jury *n* jurie
just *adj* reg; kompleet; billik; *adv* net; *conj* maar; — **a little** *adv* effens; — **as** *adv* ewe; nes; — **as much** *adv* eweveel; — **like** *adv* nes; — **now** *adv* netnou; nou-nou; strakkies; vaneffe; (future) flussies; (past) flus
justice *n* geregtigheid; regverdigheid; justisie; reg; regter
justice of the peace *n* vrederegter
justify *vb* regverdig; verantwoord; wettig
justly *adv* tereg
juvenile *n* jeugdige

K

(k)nick-(k)nack *n* snuistery; tierlantyntjie
kangaroo *n* kangaroe
kapok *n* kapok
keel *n* kiel
keen *adj* skerp; — perception *n* deursig
keep *vb* behou; hou; bewaar; nakom; onderhou; vier; — an eye on *vb* dophou; — back *vb* agterhou; weerhou; — behind *vb* agterhou; — company with *vb* verkeer; — free *vb* vryhou; — off *vb* afbly; afhou; — on *vb* ophou; — pace with *vb* bybly; byhou; — quiet *vb* stilbly; swyg; — silent *vb* verswyg; — up *vb* ophou
keepsake *n* aandenking; soewenier; gedagtenis; herinnering
kelim *n* kelim
kennel *n* hok; hondeherberg
kennels *npl* woefietuiste
kerb *n* randsteen
kerbstone *n* randsteen
kernel *n* kern; pit
kettle *n* ketel
key *n* sleutel; (music) toets
keyboard *n* klawerbord
keyhole *n* sleutelgat
keynote *n* grondtoon
khaki *n, adj* kakie
kick *n* skop; *vb* trap; — up a fuss *vb* opskop
kid *n* snuiter
kidnap *vb* ontvoer; skaak
kidnapper *n* ontvoerder; skaker
kidney *n* nier
kids *npl* (*informal*) kleingoed
kill *vb* doodmak; afmaak; van kant maak
killjoy *n* pretbederwer; spelbreker
kilogram *n* kilogram
kilometre *n* kilometer
kind[1] *adj* minsaam; vriendelik; goedgunstig; goedig
kind[2] *n* aard
kind-hearted *adj* gemoedelik; goedhartig
kindergarten *n* kindertuin

kindle *vb* aanstook; ontsteek; opsteek
kindling *n* aansteking; ontsteking
kindness *n* goedheid; guns; weldaad; welwillendheid
kindred *adj* aanverwant; — spirit *n* geesverwant
kinesiology *n* kinesiologie
king *n* koning
kingdom *n* koninkryk; ryk
kink *n* kink
kinship *n* verwantskap
kiosk *n* kiosk
kippered herring *n* bokkom
kiss *n* soen; kus; *vb* soen; kus; — away *vb* afsoen
kitchen *n* kombuis
kitchenalia *n* kombuisgoed
kite *n* vlieër
kloof *n* ravyn
knack *n* kuns
knapsack *n* knapsak
knave *n* (playing cards) boer
knead *vb* knie
knee *n* knie
knee-cap *n* knieskyf
knee-deep *adj* kniediep
kneel *vb* kniel
knickers *n* kniebroek
knife *n* mes
knight *n* ridder
knighthood *n* ridderskap
knit *vb* brei
knitted things *n* breigoed
knitting *n* breiwerk; breigoed
knitting needle *n* breinaald
knob *n* knop; knobbel
knobkerrie *n* knopkierie
knock *n* klop; slag; stamp; *vb* klop; — about *vb* swier; opdons; — at the door *vb* aanklop; — down *vb* omry; neerslaan; — off *vb* (*informal*) (work) tjaila; — over *vb* omvergooi
knockout blow *n* genadeslag
knot *n* knoop; kink; strik; (in wood) kwas; knoes; *vb* strik
know *vb* ken; weet
know-all *n* weetal

know-how *n* sakevernuf
knowing *adj* uitgeslape
knowledge *n* kennis; kunde; medewete;
  meewete; wete
known *adj* bekend

knuckle *n* kneukel
kosher *adj* kosjer
kraal *n* kraal
krans *n* krans
kudu *n* koedoe

L

label *n* etiket
laboratory *n* laboratorium
laborious *adj* arbeidsaam
labour *n* werk; arbeid; kraam; *vb* arbei
labour force *n* mannekrag
labourer *n* arbeider; werk(s)man
labyrinth *n* doolhof; labirint
lace *n* kant; (shoe) veter
lace work *n* kantwerk
lack *n* gebrek; gemis; *vb* makeer
lackey *n* lakei
lacklustre *adj* slap; mat
lacquer *n* lak; *vb* verlak
lactic acid *n* melksuur
lactose *n* melksuiker
lad *n* knaap
ladder *n* leer
ladle *n* lepel; potlepel; spaan; — into *vb* inskep
lady *n* dame
lady's man *n* hartebreker
lag behind *vb* agterbly; uitsak
lager *n* laer
lagoon *n* strandmeer
lair *n* leër
lake *n* meer
lamb *n* lam
lambada *n* lambada
lame *adj* kreupel; kruppel; lam; mank
lament *vb* jammer; bekla
lamentable *adj* beklaenswaardig
lamentation *n* jammerklag
lamenting *n* gekerm
lamp *n* lamp
lamp shade *n* lampkap
lance *n* spies; lans
lancet *n* vlym
land *n* land; *vb* land; aanland; undeveloped — *n* braakland
land tax *n* grondbelasting
landed property *n* vasgoed
landfill *n* grondopvulling
landing strip *n* landingstrook
landlord *n* huisbaas; verhuurder
landmine *n* landmyn
landowner *n* grondeienaar; grondbesitter
landscape *n* landskap

landscape gardener *n* tuinbeplanner
lane *n* laan; steeg
language *n* taal; spraak; native — *n* landstaal; — of a country *n* landstaal
languish *vb* kwyn; sukkel; versmag
languishing *adj* smagtend
lantern *n* lantern
lap[1] *n* rondte
lap[2] *n* skoot
lap[3] *vb* lek
lapdog *n* skoothondjie
laptop *n* skootrekenaar
lapwing *n* kiewiet
lard *n* varkvet; vet
larder *n* spens
large *adj* groot; wyd; be at — *vb* losloop; — banner *n* spandoek; — number *n* veelheid; — quantity *n* boel; — streamer *n* spandoek; — wave *n* brander
largely *adv* grotendeels
largeness *n* grootheid
larkspur *n* ridderspoor
larva *n* larwe
larynx *n* gorrel; strottehoof; larinks
lascivious *adj* wulps
laser *n* laser
lash *n* gésel
last[1] *n* laaste; *adj* eindelik; laas; laaslede; vergange; vorige; laaste; at — *adv* eindelik; oplaas; uiteindelik; — but one *n* naasagter; *adj* voorlaaste
last[2] *vb* duur; standhou
last[3] *n* (shoe) lees
last night *n, adv* gisteraand; vannag
last post *n* taptoe
lasting *adj* duursaam; permanent; voortdurend
lastly *adv* laas
latch *n* lat
late *adj* laat; gewese; vroeër; wyle; (dead) oorlede
lately *adv* vergange; onlangs; laat
later *adv* agterna; later; verder
latest *adj, adv* laaste; very — *adj, adv* allerlaas

lathe *n* draaibank
lather *vb* inseep
Latin *n, adj* Latyn
latitude *n* breedte
latter *n* laasgenoemde
lattice *n* tralie
laudable *adj* loflik
laugh *n* lag; *vb* lag; — **loudly** *vb* skater; — **out loud** *vb* uitlag; uitskater
laughing gas *n* laggas
laughter *n* gelag; lag
launch[1] *n* plesierbootjie
launch[2] *n* loods; *vb* bekendstel; loods; lanseer
launch pad *n* lanseerblad
launderette *n* wasseret
laundromat *n* wasseret
laundry *n* wassery
laurel *n* (tree) lourier
laurels *n* louere
lava *n* lawa
lavatory *n* privaat
lavender *n* laventel
lavish *adj* kwistig; rojaal; danig
law *n* reg; regswetenskap; regte; wet
law court *n* geregsaal
law enforcement *n* wetstoepassing
law of succession *n* erfreg
law-abiding *adj* wetsgehoorsaam
lawful *adj* geoorloof; regmatig; wettig
lawless *adj* bandeloos; wetteloos
lawn *n* grasperk; perk
lawsuit *n* geding; regsaak
lawyer *n* advokaat; juris; regsgeleerde; wet(s)geleerde
lax *adj* laks
laxative *n* lakseermiddel; purgeermiddel
lay *vb* lê; — **a charge** *vb* aanreken; — **bare** *vb* ontbloot; — **before** *vb* voorlê; — **bricks** *vb* messel; — **down** *vb* aflê; neerlê; vly; — **in** *vb* inlê
layer *n* laag; bedding; (hen) lêer
layman *n* leek
layout *n* uitleg
lazy *adj* lui; traag; **be** — *vb* luier
lazybones *n* luiaard; lamsak
lead[1] *n* lood
lead[2] *n* leiding; leidraad; leiriem; voortou; *vb* lei; — **away** *vb* aflei; — **off** *vb* afbring; — **up to** *vb* opvoer
leader *n* aanvoerder; hoof; leier; voorloper; voorman; inleidingsartikel; kopstuk; (newspaper) hoofartikel ; (of a people) volksleier
leadership *n* leierskap
leading article *n* (newspaper) hoofartikel; inleidingsartikel
leaf *n* (plant) blaar; blad; (book, etc.) blad
league *n* bond; verbond
leak *n* lek; *vb* lek; — **out** *vb* uitlek
leakage *n* lek
leaky *adj* ondig
lean[1] *adj* maer
lean[2] *vb* hel; — **on** *vb* leun
leap *n* sprong; *vb* spring; — **down** *vb* afspring
leap year *n* skrikkeljaar
learn *vb* leer; aanleer
learned *adj* geleer
learner *n* leerder; leerling
learning *n* kunde
lease *n* bruikhuur; bruikleen; huur; huurkontrak; pag; *vb* huur; pag; verpag
leash *n* leiriem
leasing *n* bruikhuur
least *adj* minste; **at** — *adv* altans; minstens
leather *n* leer
leather work *n* leerwerk
leave[1] *n* verlof; vergunning; *vb* laat
leave[2] *vb* vertrek; — **to others** *vb* oorlaat; — **alone** *vb* afbly
leave-taking *n* afskeid
leaves *n* (foliage) lof
lecture *n* lesing; referaat; voordrag; *vb* doseer
lecturer *n* dosent; lektor; referent
ledge *n* rand
ledger *n* grootboek
leech *n* bloedsuier
leek *n* prei
lees *n* (sediment) droesem
left[1] *n, adj* linker
left[2] *adv* oor
left over *vb* oorskiet
left side *n* linkerkant
left-handed *adj* links
left-handed person *n* hotklou
leftovers *npl* oorskietkos
leg *n* been; poot; boud; (trouser) pyp
leg of mutton *n* skaapboud

legal *adj* wetlik; wettig
legal advice *n* regsadvies
legal point *n* regspunt
legal practice *n* regspraktyk
legalize *vb* wettig
legend *n* legende; sage
legendary *adj* legendaries
legible *adj* leesbaar; duidelik
legion *n* legioen
legislation *n* wetgewing
legislative *adj* wetgewend
legislature *n* wetgewende liggaam; wetgewing
legitimate *adj* eg; gegrond; gewettig;
 wettig
leisure *n* gemak
leisurely *adv* tydsaam
lemon *n* suurlemoen
lemon juice *n* suurlemoensap
lemonade *n* limonade
lend *vb* leen; voorskiet; — **out** *vb* uitleen
length *n* lengte; duur; ent
lengthen *vb* verleng
lengthily *adv* uitvoerig
lengthy *adj* uitvoerig
lenient *adj* toegeeflik; toegewend
lens *n* lens
lentil *n* lensie
lentil soup *n* lensiesop
leopard *n* luiperd
leper *n* melaatse
leprosy *n* melaatsheid
less *adj* minder; *determiner*; *adj* min
lessee *n* huurder; pagter
lessen *vb* verklein; verminder
lesson *n* les
lessor *n* verhuurder
let *vb* laat; verhuur; — **fly** *vb* losbars;
 — **go** *vb* los; loslaat; — **in** *vb* inlaat;
 — **off** *vb* vrystel; aflaat; — **out** *vb* uitlaat; verklap; — **through** *vb* deurlaat
letter *n* brief; letter; sendbrief
letter box *n* briewebus; posbus
lettuce *n* kropslaai; slaai
level *adj* plat; horisontaal; vlak; effe; *vb*
 baan; effen
level crossing *n* oorweg
lever *n* hefboom
leviable *adj* invorderbaar
levy *n* heffing

lexicographer *n* woordeboekmaker
lexicon *n* leksikon
liability *n* verpligting
liable *adj* onderhewig; — **to** *adj* aanspreeklik; *prep* behep
liar *n* leuenaar
liberal *adj* gul; mild; milddadig;vryge-
 wig; vrysinnig; liberaal
liberate *vb* verlos; vrylaat; vrymaak
liberation *n* vrylating
liberty *n* vryheid
librarian *n* bibliotekaris
licence *n* lisensie; vergunning
lick *vb* lek
lid *n* deksel
lie[1] *n* leuen; kluitjie; *vb* jok
lie[2] *vb* rus; lê; — **fallow** *vb* braak lê; —
 in wait for *vb* loer
lieutenant *n* luitenant
life *n* lewe; aansyn
life buoy *n* reddingsboei
life insurance *n* lewensversekering
life raft *n* reddingsvlot
life-size *adj* lewensgroot
lifeboat *n* reddingsboot
lifeguard *n* strandwag
lifeless *adj* dooierig; sielloos
lifelong *adj* lewenslang
lifestyle *n* leefstyl; lewenswyse
lifetime *n* leeftyd; lewensloop
lift *n* hyser; *vb* optel; oplig; beur; — **up**
 vb ophef; oplig; (eyes) opslaan
lift-off *n* opstyging; lansering
light[1] *adj* lugtig; *vb* aansteek
light[2] *n* lig; *vb* lig; *adj* lig
light breeze *n* koelte
light bulb *n* gloeilamp
light-headed *adj* lighoofdig; ylhoofdig
light-hearted *adj* lighartig; lughartig;
 lugtig
lighten *vb* verlig
lightening *n* verligting
lighthouse *n* vuurtoring
lighting *n* verligting; aansteking
lightly *adv* lugtig
lightning *n* weerlig; blits; bliksem
lightning-conductor *n* weerligafleier;
 bliksemafleier
like[1] *adj* dergelik; *adv; conj* as; *prep*
 soos; as; — **this** *adv* so; **the** — *n* gelyke

like[2] *vb* hou van; lus
likely *adj, adv* waarskynlik
likeness *n* ewebeeld; gelykenis
likewise *adv* desgelyks; insgelyks; ook
liking *n* sinnigheid; skik; smaak; trek; welgevalle
lilac tree *n* seringboom
lily *n* lelie
limb *n* ledemaat; liggaamsdeel
lime[1] *n* kalk
lime[2] *n* lemmetjie
lime-kiln *n* kalkoond
limestone rock *n* kalkbank
limit *n* limiet; grens; perk; eindpaal; *vb* begrens
limitation *n* bepaling
limited *adj* bekrompe; *vb* beperk
limp *vb* hink
limping *adj* kreupel; kruppel; mank
linden tree *n* lindeboom
line *n* lyn; reël; ry; streep
line judge *n* lynregter
lined *adj* (clothes) gevoerde
linen *n* linne
linesman *n* lynregter
linger *vb* draal; sloer; talm; verwyl
linguist *n* linguis; taalkundige
linguistics *n* taalkunde; taalkundig
liniment *n* smeergoed
lining *n* (clothes) voering
link *n* skakel; *vb* aansluit; skakel
linking up *n* aansluiting
linoleum *n* linoleum
linseed *n* lynsaad
linseed oil *n* lynolie
lintel *n* latei
lion *n* leeu
lioness *n* leeuwyfie
lip *n* lip
lipstick *n* lipstiffie
liqueur *n* likeur
liquid *adj* likied; vloeibaar; *n* vloeistof
liquidate *vb* likwideer
liquidation *n* likwidasie
liquidizer *n* versapper
liquor *n* drank
liquorice *n* drop
lisp *vb* lispel
list *n* lys; rol; *vb* opskrywe
listen *vb* hoor; luister; toeluister; **— to** *vb* aanhoor; **— together** *vb* meeluister

listless *adj* lusteloos; dooierig
listlessness *n* onlus
lit up *adj* verligte
literal *adj* letterlik; woordelik
literally *adv* letterlik
literary *adj* literaries; literêr
literature *n* lektuur; lettere; letterkunde; literatuur
lithe *adj* lenig
litre *n* liter
litter *n* rommel; werpsel
litterbug *n* rommelstrooier
little *adj* klein; weinig; min; bietjie; **— bit** *n* bietjie; **— finger** *n* pinkie; **— goat** *n* bokkie; **— man** *n* mannetjie; **— ones** *npl* kleinspan; **— person** *n* buks(ie); **— sister** *n* sussie; **— star** *n* sterretjie; **— stick** *n* stokkie; **— stream** *n* lopie
liturgy *n* liturgie
live *vb* lewe; bly; woon; **— on** *vb* bestaan; teer; **— in** *vb* inwoon; bewoon; **— together** *vb* saamleef
livelihood *n* bestaan
lively *adj* flink; fluks; lewendig; opgewek; hups; druk
liver *n* lewer
liver sausage *n* lewerwors
livestock *n* (cattle, etc.) vee
livestock market *n* veemark
living expenses *npl* verblyfkoste
living room *n* woonkamer; huiskamer
lizard *n* akkedis; geitjie
load *n* drag; las; skeepslading; vrag; *vb* belaai; (cargo) inneem; **— up** *vb* oplaai
loaf[1] *n* brood
loaf[2] *vb* rondloop; swier
loan *n* lening; voorskot; bruikleen; *vb* uitleen
loathe *vb* walg
loathsome *adj* vieslik
lobby *n* portaal; voorportaal
lobotomy *n* lobotomie
lobster *n* kreef; seekreef
local *adj* plaaslik; lokaal
locally *adv* alhier
locate *vb* plaas; stasioneer
location *n* lokasie
lock[1] *n* slot; sluis; *vb* afsluit; **— up** *vb* opsluit; toesluit

lock[2] *n* (hair) lok
locker *n* sluitkas
locket *n* medaljon
lockjaw *n* klem
locksmith *n* slotmaker
locomotive *n* lokomotief
locust *n* sprinkaan
lode *n* aar
lodge *vb* indien; inwoon; loseer
lodger *n* loseerder; bewoner
lodging *n* losies
lodgings *npl* intrek
loft *n* solder
lofty *adj* hoog; verhewe
log *n* blok
logarithm *n* logaritme
logbook *n* logboek
logic *n* logika
logical *adj* logies
loin *n* lende
loiter *vb* draai; sleur; drentel
loitering *n* getalm
lollipop *n* stokkielekker
loneliness *n* enigheid
lonely *adj* alleen; eensaam; verlate; afgesonder
long[1] *adj* lang; langdurig
long[2] *vb* hunker; smag; uitsien; verlang; snak
long ago *adv* lankal
long jump *n* verspring
long-sighted *adj* versiende
long-suffering *adj* lankmoedig
long-winded *adj* langdradig; omslagtig; breedsprakig; wydlopig; gerek
longing *adj* smagtend; *n* verlange
longingly *adv* reikhalsend
longitude *n* lengte
longstanding *adj* langdurig
longsufferance *n* lankmoedigheid
loo *n* (*informal*) kleinhuisie
look *n* aanblik; blik; kyk; *vb* lyk; kyk; — **someone up** *vb* opsoek; — **about** *vb* rondkyk; — **after** *vb* oppas; behartig; — **ahead** *vb* vooruitsien; — **around** *vb* omsien; — **at** *vb* aansien; aankyk; — **awry** *vb* skeefkyk; — **back** *vb* omkyk; — **back on** *vb* terugblik; — **down on** *vb* neersien; — **for** *vb* opsoek; soek; — **forward to** *vb* uitsien; verwag; — **good** *vb* pryk;

— **into** *vb* insien; — **over** *vb* deurkyk; oorkyk; — **round** *vb* omkyk; — **up** *vb* naslaan; (a word) opsoek; — **up to** *vb* opsien
looker-on *n* kyker
lookout *n* uitkyk; uitkyker; *vb* uitsien
look out! *interj* pas op!
looks *npl* voorkome
loom *n* weefmasjien
loop *n* lis; lissie; lus
loophole *n* skietgat
loose *adj* slap
loosely *adv* los
loosen *vb* los; losmaak
loot *vb* plunder; uitplunder
lop *vb* top
lopsided *adj* windskeef
loquacious *adj* spraaksaam
loquat *n* lukwart
Lord *n* Heer
lord *n* heer
lorry *n* lorrie; vragmotor; wa
lose *vb* mis; verbeur; verloor; weggooi; — **colour** *vb* verkleur; — **flesh** *vb* vermaer; — **hair** *vb* verhaar; — **touch with** *vb* afsterf; — **weight** *vb* afval
loss *n* verlies; skade; slag; nadeel
lost *adj* verlore; weg; *adv* weg; — **baggage** *n* verlore bagasie
lot *n* klomp; lot; perseel; spul; (auction sale) lot
lots *npl* (*informal*) boel
lottery *n* lotery; poslotery
lottery ticket *n* lootjie
loud *adj* hard; luid; — **laughter** *n* geskater; skaterlag
loud noise *n* knal
loud-hailer *n* luidroeper
loudly *adv* luid
loudspeaker *n* luidspreker
lounge *n* sitkamer; voorhuis
louse *n* luis
lovable *adj* beminlik
love *n* liefde; min; (tennis score) stroop; *vb* bemin; liefhê; **fall in — with** *vb* verlief raak op
love letter *n* minnebrief
love potion *n* doepa
love song *n* minnelied
love story *n* liefdesverhaal

loved *adj* dierbaar; bemind
loveless *adj* liefdeloos
lovely *adj* lieflik
lover *n* beminde; minnaar; vryer
loving *adj* liefhebbend
low[1] *adj* laag; plat
low[2] *vb* (cattle) bulk
low country *n* laeveld
low veld *n* laeveld
low-fat *adj* laevet
lower *adj* laer; *vb* verlaag
lower down *adv* ondertoe; onderlangs
lower half *n* (door) onderdeur
lower jaw *n* onderkakebeen
lower part *n* (body) onderlyf
lower side *n* onderkant
lowering *n* verlaging
lowest *adj* onderste
loyal *adj* lojaal; trou
loyalty *n* lojaliteit; trou
loyalty card *n* lojaliteitskaart
lozenge *n* tablet
lubricate *vb* smeer
lucerne *n* lusern
lucid *adj* helder
luck *n* fortuin
lucky *adj* gelukkig

lucrative *adj* winsgewend
lugg along *vb* aansleep
luggage *n* bagasie; pakkasie
lukewarm *adj* lou
lull *vb* wieg
lullaby *n* slaapliedjie; wiegelied
lumbago *n* lendepyn; spit
luminous *adj* liggewend
lump *n* kluit; massa; klomp; — **of sugar** *n* klont
lunatic *adj* kranksinnig; *n* gek
lunatic asylum *n* dolhuis; malhuis
lunch *n* middagete
lung *n* long
lunge *vb* (horse) lons
lure *n* lokaas; *vb* aanlok; weglok
lush *adj* mals; welig
lust *n* wellus; — **for power** *n* heerssug
lustre *n* glans; luister
lute *n* luit
luxuriant *adj* geil; weelderig; welig
luxurious *adj* weelderig
luxury *n* luukse; weelde
lying *adj* leuenagtig
Lyme disease *n* Lymesiekte
lyre *n* lier
lyric poetry *n* liriek

M

ma *n* ma
macaroni *n* macaroni; — **cheese** *n* macaroni en kaas
macaroon *n* makrolletjie
mace *n* staf
machine *n* masjien
mackerel *n* makriel
mackintosh *n* reënjas
mad *adj* mal; dol; kranksinnig; beduiweld; rasend; sinneloos; gek
Madam *title* juffrou; mevrou
madcap *n* malkop; maltrap
made-up *adj* opgemaak
madhouse *n* dolhuis
madman *n* gek
madness *n* malheid; raserny; waansin
maggot *n* maaier; wurm
magic *n* toorkuns
magic spell *n* paljas
magic word *n* toorwoord
magic lantern *n* toorlantern
magician *n* goëlaar; kularties; toorkunstenaar; towenaar
magistrate *n* landdros; magistraat
magnanimous *adj* grootmoedig
magnate *n* magnaat
magnesium *n* magnesium
magnet *n* magneet
magnetic adj magneties
magnetism *n* magnetisme
magnificence *n* prag
magnificent *adj* pragtig
magnify *vb* vergroot
magnifying glass *n* vergrootglas
magnitude *n* grootheid; grootte
mahogany *n* mahoniehout
maid of honour *n* hofdame
maiden *n* maagd
maiden name *n* nooiensvan
mail[1] *n* pos
mail[2] *n* (armour) pantser
mailbag *n* briewesak
mailing list *n* poslys
maim *vb* skend; vermink
main *adj* hoof
main road *n* grootpad; hardepad; transportpad

main subject *n* hoofvak
mainly *adv* grotendeels; vernaamlik
mainstay *n* staatmaker
maintain *vb* bewaar; handhaaf;onderhou; standhou;volhou
maintenance *n* instandhouding; onderhoud; versorging
maize *n* mielie
majestic *adj* majestueus; statig
majesty *n* majesteit
major *adj* mondig; *n* majoor
majority *n* meerderheid; merendee
make *n* maak; fabrikaat; *vb* maak; daarstel; — **a list** *vb* aanlê; — **an agreement** *vb* aangaan; — **an appointment** *vb* bestel; — **an exception** *vb* uitsonder; — **a knot** *vb* strik; — **a mess of** *vb* verbrou; verknoei; — **a mistake** *vb* begaan; feil; — **a noise** *vb* rumoer; raas; — **a note of** *vb* noteer; — **a remark** *vb* aanmerking maak op; — **a row** *vb* raas; — **the bed** *vb* opmaak; — **clear** *vb* ekspliseer; — **dry** *vb* droog; — **enquiries** *vb* inwin; — **even** *vb* effen; — **good** *vb* aanvul; — **haste** *vb* haas; — **improvements** *vb* aanbring; — **mention of** *vb* gewag maak van; — **out** *vb* ontsyfer; — **permanent** *vb* bestendig; — **pleasant** *vb* veraangenaam; — **pregnant** *vb* bevrug; — **progress** *vb* vooruitgaan; — **public** *vb* openbaar; publiseer; — **room** *vb* ruim; inruim; — **smaller** *vb* verklein; — **sober** *vb* ontnugter; — **soft** *vb* vermurf; — **someone believe** *vb* wysmaak; — **up** *vb* (a quarrel) afmaak; — **up for** *vb* goedmaak; — **worse** *vb* vererger; — **young again** *vb* verjong
make-up *n* grimering
makeover session *n* herskepsessie; mooimaaksessie; oormaaksessie; voorkomsveranderingsessie
maker *n* fabrikant; maker
maladjusted *adj* wanaangepas
malaria *n* malaria
male *adj* manlik; *n* mannetjie

male nurse *n* verpleër
malevolent *adj* kwaadwillig
malicious *adj* boosaardig; haatlik; kwaadaardig
malignant *adj* kwaadaardig
mall *n* (pedestrian) wandellaan
malleable *adj* smeebaar
malnourished *adj* ondervoed
malnutrition *n* ondervoeding; wanvoeding
malpractice *n* wanpraktyk
malt *n* mout
mam(m)a *n* mama; ma; mum; mummy
mamba *n* (snake) mamba
mammal *n* soogdier
mampoer *n* witblits; home distilled brandy made from peaches, etc.
man *n* man; manskap; mens; *vb* beman
man-of-war *n* oorlogskip
manage *vb* beheer; bestuur; aanlê
manageable *adj* handelbaar
management *n* beheer; bestuur; direksie
manager *n* beheerder; bestuurder; direkteur
mandarin orange *n* naartjie
mandate *n* bevelskrif; mandaat
mandolin *n* mandolien
mane *n* maanhaar
manganese *n* mangaan
manger *n* krip
mango *n* mango
manhandle *vb* karnuffel
manhole *n* mangat; luik; skouput
mania *n* manie
maniac *n* maniak
manicure *n* manikuur
manifest *adj* kenbaar
manifesto *n* manifes
manifold *adj* veelsoortig; veelvuldig
mankind *n* mensdom
manly *adj* manlik; manhaftig
manna *n* manna
mannequin *n* mannekyn
manner *n* manier; styl; trant; wys; — **of speaking** *n* spreektrant
manners *n* sede
manoeuvre *n* maneuver
manpower *n* mannekrag
manservant *n* dienskneg; kneg
manslaughter *n* manslag; strafbare manslag

mantelpiece *n* skoorsteenmantel
mantle *n* mantel
manual *n* handleiding; handboek; leerboek
manual labour *n* handearbeid
manufacture *n* fabrikasie; maak; *vb* fabriseer
manufacturer *n* fabrikant; nyweraar; vervaardiger
manure *n* mis; misstof
manuscript *n* handskrif; manuskrip
many *adj* baie; veel; verskeie; *adv* menig; menige; — **a one** *determiner* menigeen
many-sided *adj* veelsydig
map *n* kaart; landkaart
marble *n* marmer
March *n* Maart
march *n* mars; tog; *vb* marsjeer; aanruk
marchioness *n* markiesin
mare *n* merrie
margin *n* kant
marginal *adj* marginaal; grens-
marginal seat *n* grenssetel; marginale setel
marginalize *vb* marginaliseer
marigold *n* gousblom
marijuana *n* dagga
marine *n* vlootsoldaat
marine insurance *n* seeversekering
maritime law *n* seereg; skeepsreg
mark *n* merk; kenmerk; merkteken; teken; *vb* afteken; tjap; — **of esteem** *n* huldeblyk; — **out** *vb* afsteek; — **with a date** *vb* dateer
market *n* mark; debiet
market price *n* markprys
market research *n* marknavorsing
market square *n* markplein
marmalade *n* marmelade
marmot *n* marmotjie
marquee *n* markeetent
marquis *n* markies
marriage *n* huwelik; eg; egverbintenis; trou
marriage ceremony *n* huweliksbevestiging
marriage counsellor *n* huweliksberader
married *adj* getroud; gehuud
married life *n* huwelikslewe
marrow *n* murg

marrowbone *n* murgbeen
marry *vb* trou; **— again** *vb* hertrou
marsh *n* moeras
marshall *n* maarskalk
marsupial animal *n* buideldier
martial law *n* krygswet
martingale *n* (harness) springteuel
martyr *n* martelaar
martyrdom *n* martelaarskap
marvel *n* wonder
marvellous *adj* wonderlik
masculine *adj* manlik
mask *n* masker; mombakkies; sluier; *vb* vermom
masked *adj* gemasker; vermom
mason *n* messelaar
mass *n* gros; massa; mis
mass media *n* massamedia
mass production *n* massaproduksie
massacre *n* bloedbad; slagting; *vb* uit-moor
massage *vb* masseer; vryf
massive *adj* massief
mast *n* mas
master *n* baas; meester; gebieder
master of ceremonies *n* tafelheer
masterly *adv* meesterlik
masterpiece *n* meesterstuk; kunsstuk
mastery *n* oorhand
masticate *vb* kou
mat *n* mat
match[1] *n* eweknie; gelyke; portuur; weerga; wedstryd; *vb* paar; **be a — for** *vb* ewenaar
match[2] *n* vuurhoutjie
matchless *adj* onvergelyklik; weerga-loos
mate *n* maat; *vb* paar
material *adj* stoflik; *n* materiaal
materialistic *adj* materialisties
materialize *vb* verwerklik
maternity *n* moederskap
mathematical *adj* wiskundig
mathematician *n* wiskundige
mathematics *n* wiskunde; matesis
Matric *n* Matriek
matriculate *vb* matrikuleer
matriculation *n* matrikulasie
matrimonial *adj* egtelik
matrimony *n* huwelik
matron *n* huismoeder; matrone

matter *n* saak; geval; kwessie; ding; stof; *vb* makeer; **— at issue** *n* geskil-punt; **— of form** *n* formaliteit
mattress *n* matras; bulsak
mature *adj* ryp; volwasse; *vb* ryp word; verval
maturity *n* rypheid; verval
mausoleum *n* praalgraf
maxim *n* spreuk
maximum *n* maksimum
May *n* Mei
may *vb* mag
maybe *adv* dalk
mayor *n* burgemeester
maze *n* doolhof
mazurka *n* masurka
me *pers pron* my
meadow *n* vlei; wei
meagre *adj* karig; maer; skraal
meal[1] *n* etenstyd; eetmaal; maal; maal-tyd
meal[2] *n* meel
meal time *n* etenstyd
mealie *n* mielie
mealie cob *n* mieliekop
mealie meal *n* mieliemeel
mealie porridge *n* mieliepap
mean[1] *n* gemiddelde; *adj* gemiddeld
mean[2] *adj* laag; **— woman** *n* wyf
mean[3] *vb* bedoel
meander *vb* kronkel
meaning *n* bedoeling; betekenis; sin
meaningful *adj* sinvol
meaningless *adj* sinloos
meanness *n* laagheid
means *n* medium; middel; raat
meanwhile *adv* intussen; ondertussen; onderwyl; middelerwyl; *conj* solank
measles *n* masels
measure *n* maatreël; mate; (music) maat; *vb* meet; peil; **— of capacity** *n* inhoudsmaat; **— off** *vb* afmeet
measurement *n* afmeting
measuring *n* meting; **— rod** *n* meetstok
meat *n* vleis; vlees
mechanic *n* meganikus; werktuigkun-dige
mechanical *adj* meganies; werktuiglik
mechanics *n* werktuigkunde
medal *n* medalje; penning
medallion *n* medaljon**

meddle *vb* bemoei; inmeng
meddlesome *adj* bemoeisiek; orig
meddlesomeness *n* bemoeisug
media *n* media
media centre *n* mediasentrum
median *n* mediaan
mediate *vb* bemiddel; tussenbei kom
mediation *n* tussenkoms; voorspraak
mediator *n* middelaar; tussenganger; tussenpersoon
medical *adj* medies; geneeskundig
medical examination *n* mediese keuring
medical practitioner *n* medikus
medical science *n* geneeskunde
medication *n* medikasie
medicinal *adj* geneeskragtig
medicine *n* medisyne; geneesmiddel
medieval *adj* middeleeus; — **tournament** *n* steekspel
mediocre *adj* derderangs; middelmatig
meditate *vb* oorpeins; peins
meditation *n* oordenking; nabetragting; oorpeinsing; gepeins
meditative *adj* nadenkend; peinsend
medium *n* medium; middel; *adj* gemiddeld; middelmatig; — **of instruction** *n* voertaal
meek *adj* deemoedig; gedwee; nederig; saggeaard
meekness *n* deemoed; lydsaamheid
meercat *n* meerkat
meet *vb* ontmoet; saamkom; vergader; teenkom; afhaal; tref; — **again** *vb* weersien; — **halfway** *vb* tegemoetkom; — **up with** *vb* vind; — **with** *vb* aantref; — **with disaster** *vb* verongeluk
meeting *n* byeenkoms; ontmoeting; samekoms; sitting; vergadering
meeting place *n* vergaderingplek
melancholic *adj* swaarmoedig
melancholy *n* weemoed; *adj* weemoedig
melodious *adj* melodieus; sangerig; welluidend
melody *n* melodie; wysie
melt *vb* smelt; versmelt; — **away** *vb* versmelt; — **down** *vb* versmelt
meltdown *n* ineenstorting
member *n* lid; (church) lidmaat; (band) musikant

member state *n* lidland
members of a household *npl* huisgenote
membrane *n* vlies
memento *n* gedagtenis
memoir *n* gedenkskrif
memorable *adj* onvergeetlik; gedenkwaardig; heuglik
memorial *n* gedenkteken
memorize *vb* memoriseer
memory *n* geheue; aandenking; gedagtenis; heugenis
menace *n* dreigement; *vb* bedreig
mend *vb* lap; herstel; oplap
meningitis *n* harsingvliesontsteking
menstruation *n* menstruasie; maandstonde; stonde
mental *adj* verstandelik
mental faculties *npl* geesvermoëns
mental hospital *n* sielsiekehospitaal
mental patient *n* sielsieke
mental struggle *n* gemoedstryd
mentality *n* mentaliteit
mentally deranged *adj* sielsiek
mentally handicapped *adj* swaksinnig
mention *n* melding; gewag; *vb* aanroer
menu *n* spyskaart; menu; (computing) kieskaart
merchandise *n* negosieware; koopwaar
merchant *n* handelaar; koopman
merciful *adj* genadig; barmhartig
merciless *adj* onbarmhartig
mercury *n* kwiksilwer
mercy *n* genade
mere *adj* bloot; alleen; simpel; louter
merely *adv* bloot; enkel; slegs; louter
merge *vb* saamsmelt; verenig
merging *n* ineensmelting
meridian *n* meridiaan
merino sheep *n* merino
merit *n* verdienste
mermaid *n* meermin
merriment *n* vrolikheid
merry *adj* vrolik; lustig
merry-go-round *n* mallemeule
mess *n* gemors; *vb* mors
message *n* boodskap
messenger *n* bode; afgesant; — **of the court** *n* geregsbode
metal *n* metaal
metal detector *n* (metaal)verklikker

metallic *adj* metaalagtig
metamorphosis *n* gedaanteverwisseling
metaphor *n* metafoor; beeld
metaphysical *adj* metafisies
meteor *n* meteoor
meteorology *n* weerkunde
meter *n* meter
method *n* metode; metodiek; handel-wyse; sisteem
methodical *adj* metodies
methylated spirits *n* brandspiritus
metre *n* metrum; meter; (poetry) vers-maat; digmaat
metric *adj* metries
metrical *adj* metries
metro *n* moltrein; ondergrondse spoor-weg; **— station** *n* moltreinstasie
metropolis *n* wêreldstad
mettle *n* fut
mew *vb* miaau
miaow (*or* **miaou**) *vb* miaau
mica *n* mika
microbe *n* mikrobe
microchip *n* mikroskyfie·
microcomputer *n* mikrorekenaar
microfilm *n* mikrofilm
microlight *n* mikrotuig
microphone *n* mikrofoon
microscope *n* mikroskoop
microwave *n* mikrogolf
microwaveable *adj* mikrogolfbaar
midday *n, adj* middag; twaalfuur; **at —** *adv* smiddags
middle *n* midde; *adj* middelste; middel-baar; **— course** *n* middeweg
middle-aged *adj* middeljarig
Middle Ages *n* Middeleeue
middle finger *n* middelvinger
middleman *n* tussenpersoon
middling *adj* middelmatig
midge *n* (insect) muggie
midnight *n* middernag
midst *n* midde
midstream *n* midstroom
midwife *n* verloskundige; vroedvrou
midwifery *n* verloskunde
might *n* mag
mighty *adj* magtig
migraine *n* migraine; skeelhoofpyn
migrant labour *n* trekarbeid
migration *n* verhuising

mild *adj* lig; sag
mile *n* myl
militant *adj* militant
military *adj* militêr
military campaign *n* krygstog
military force *n* troepmag
military man *n* militêr
military service *n* krygsdiens
military tattoo *n* taptoe
milk *n* melk
milk churn *n* karring
milk tart *n* melktert
milk thistle *n* suidissel
milk tooth *n* melktand; muistand
milkshake *n* bruismelk
Milky Way *n* Melkweg
mill *n* meul
miller *n* meulenaar
milligram *n* milligram
millimetre *n* millimeter
milliner *n* modiste
million *n* miljoen
millionaire *n* miljoener
millipede *n* duisendpoot
mimic *vb* naboots; napraat; koggel
mimicry *n* mimiek
mimosa *n* (tree) doringboom; kameel-doringboom
mince *n* maalvleis; gemaalde vleis; *vb* maal; hak
mince pie *n* Kerspastei
minced meatball *n* frikkadel
minced patty *n* frikkadel
mind *n* gees; gemoed; psige; siel; sin; verstand; *vb* bekreun
Mind Map *n* ideëkaart
mindful of *adj* gedagtig; bedag
mine[1] *n* myn; *vb* myn; delf
mine[2] *poss pron* myne
mine dump *n* sandhoop
miner *n* myner; mynwerker; delwer
mineral *n* delfstof; mineraal
mingle *vb* meng
minimize *vb* minimeer
minimum *n* minimum
mining industry *n* mynbou
miniskirt *n* miniromp
minister *n* minister; dominee; predi-kant; geestelike; gesant
ministerial *adj* ministerieel
ministration *n* bediening

ministry *n* kabinet; ministerie
mink *n* wesel
minor *adj* minder; kleiner; minderjarig; mineur; *n* minderjarige; (music) mineur
minority *n* minderheid
mint *n* kruisement; munt
minuet *n* menuet
minus *prep* min; minus; *adj* min; minus
minute[1] *adj* klein; haarfyn
minute[2] *n* (time) minuut; *vb* notuleer; **—s** *npl* (meeting) notule
miracle *n* wonderwerk
mirage *n* lugspieëling
mire *n* modder; slyk
mirror *n* spieël; *vb* weerspieël
mirth *n* vrolikheid
misanthrope *n* mensehater
misappropriation *n* wanbesteding
misbehaviour *n* wangedrag
miscarriage *n* miskraam; mislukking
miscarry *vb* misluk; (plan) verongeluk
miscellaneous *adj* allerlei
mischief *n* kattekwaad; kwaad
mischievous *adj* ondeund; onnutsig; baldadig; gruwelik
misconception *n* wanbegrip
misconduct *n* wangedrag
misdeed *n* misdaad; wandaad
misdemeanour *n* vergryp
misdirected *adj* misplaas
miser *n* gierigaard; vrek
miserable *adj* miserabel; ellendig; power; beroerd; armsalig; jammerlik; rampsalig; erbarmlik; deerlik
miserliness *n* gierigheid
miserly *adj* gierig
misery *n* ellende; jammer
misfortune *n* ongeluk
misgovernment *n* wanbestuur
mishap *n* ongeval
mislay *vb* verlê
mislead *vb* verlei
misleading *adj* misleidend
mismanagement *n* wanbestuur
misogynist *n* vrouehater
misplaced *adj* misplaas
misprint *n* drukfout
Miss *title* juffrou; mejuffrou
miss *vb* mis
miss out *vb* oorslaan

misshapen *adj* wanskape; wanstaltig
missile *n* missiel
mission *n* sending
missionary *n* sendeling
mist *n* mis; newel
mistake *n* fout; flater; vergissing; misgreep; dwaling; *vb* vergis; **by —** per ongeluk; per abuis; **be —n** *vb* misgis; misreken; vergis
mistletoe *n* voëlent
mistress *n* meesteres; minnares
mistrust *n* argwaan; verdenking; *vb* wantrou
misty *adj* mistig; dynserig
misunderstanding *n* misverstand
misuse *n* misbruik
mite *n* (insect) miet
mitigate *vb* versag
mitigation *n* versagting
mitre *n* myter
mitten *n* moffie
mix *vb* meng; vermeng; aanmaak; **— up** *vb* verwar; **— with** *vb* omgaan
mix-up *n* warboel
mixed *adj* gemeng; deurmekaar; bont
mixture *n* mengsel
moan *n* kreun; *vb* kreun; sug; kerm
moaning *n* gekerm
moat *n* grag; singel
mob *n* gepeupel; skare
mobile *adj* mobiel
mobile phone *n* selfoon
mobilization *n* mobilisasie
mobilize *vb* mobiliseer
mock *vb* spot; beskimp
mockery *n* gespot; spot; skimp
mode *n* metode; **— of dress** *n* kleredrag
model *n* model; patroon; toonbeeld; *vb* modelleer
moderate *adj* gematig; middelbaar; *vb* matig
moderation *n* matigheid; gematigdheid
modern *adj* modern; hedendaags; nuwerwets; huidige
modernism *n* modernisme
modest *adj* beskeie; ingetoë; sedig
modesty *n* beskeidenheid
modification *n* wysiging
modify *vb* wysig; temper
modulation *n* stembuiging

mohair *n* bokhaar
moist *adj* klam; nat; vogtig
moisten *vb* bevogtig
moisture *n* vog
molar *n* kiestand; maaltand
molasses *n* swartstroop
mole[1] *n* (skin) moesie
mole[2] *n* (animal) mol
molecule *n* molekule
molehill *n* molshoop
moleskin *n* molvel
molest *vb* molesteer
mollify *vb* vermurf
moment *n* oomblik; moment; bietjie; kits; wyl; **a — ago** *adv* flus; vaneffe
momentarily *adv* momenteel
momentary *adj* momenteel
monarch *n* monarg
monarchy *n* monargie
monastery *n* abdy; klooster
Monday *n* Maandag
monetary *adj* finansieel; geldelik
money *n* geld
money changer *n* wisselaar
moneylender *n* geldskieter
mongoose *n* muishond
mongrel *n* (*informal*) baster; *n* (dog) brak
monitor *vb* meeluister; *n* monitor
monk *n* monnik
monkey *n* aap
monologue *n* monoloog
monopoly *n* monopolie; alleenhandel
monorail *n* lugbus
monorail system *n* eenspoorstelsel
monosyllabic *adj* eenlettergrepig
monotonous *adj* eentonig; geesdodend
monotony *n* eentonigheid
monster *n* monster; gedrog; ondier; onmens
monstrous *adj* monsteragtig
month *n* maand
monthly *adj, adv* maandeliks
monthly magazine *n* maandblad
monument *n* monument; gedenkteken
mood[1] *n* bui; luim; gemoedstemming; stemming; humeur
mood[2] *n* (grammar) wyse; wys
moody *adj* humeurig; nukkerig
moon *n* maan
moon landing *n* maanlanding

moonlight *n* maanlig
moor[1] *n* heide
moor[2] *vb* meer
moral *adj* moreel; sedelik; *n* moraal
morale *n* moed; moreel
morality *n* moraliteit
morals *n* sede
moratorium *n* moratorium
more *adj* meer; **— or less** *adv* naaste(n) by; plusminus; **— than enough** oorgenoeg; **— than once** *adv* meermaal
moreover *conj* buitendien; *adv* bowendien
morgue *n* lykshuis
morning *n* oggend; voormiddag; môre
morning glory *n* purperwinde
morphine (*or* **morphia**) *n* morfien
morsel *n* brokstuk; hap; skerf
mortal *adj* sterfling; stoflik; *n* aardbewoner
mortal fear *n* doodsangs
mortality *n* sterfte
mortar *n* messelkalk; dagha; mortier; vysel
mortgage *n* verband; *vb* verpand
mortgagee *n* verbandgewer
mortgager *n* verbandhouer
mortuary *n* lykshuis
mosaic *n* mosaïek
mosque *n* moskee
mosquito *n* muskiet
moss *n* mos
most *adj* mees; **at —** *adv* hoogstens
mostly *adv* mees; meesal
motel *n* motel
moth *n* mot
mother *n* moeder; ma; mama
mother tongue *n* moedertaal
mother-in-law *n* skoonmoeder
mother-of-pearl *n* perlemoen
motherhood *n* moederskap
motion *n* beweging; mosie; ontlasting; **make a — of no confidence** *vb* wantrou
motionless *adj* botstil; onbeweeglik; roerloos
motivate *vb* motiveer
motive *n* motief; dryfveer; rede
motley *adj* bont
motorbike *n* motorfiets; ysterperd
motorcar *n* motor; kar

motto *n* leuse; slagspreuk; strydleuse
mould[1] *n* kim
mould[2] *n* vorm; *vb* knie
moulding *n* vorming
mouldy *adj* vermuf
moult *vb* verveer; verhaar
mount *n* berg; *vb* bestyg; *vb* (horse) op-klim
mountain *n* berg
mountain pass *n* nek
mountain range *n* bergketting; gebergte
mounted *adj* berede
mourn *vb* rou; treur
mournful *adj* treurig
mourning *n* rou
mouse *n* muis
mousetrap *n* muisval
moustache *n* snor; snorbaard
mouth *n* mond; bek; snater; muil
mouth-organ *n* mondfluitjie
mouthful *n* slukkie
mouthpiece *n* mondstuk
movable *adj* roerend; mobiel
movables *npl* roerende goedere
move *n* skuif; set; *vb* skuif; beweeg; voorstel; — **about** *vb* rondtrek; — **away** *vb* verwyder; — **easily** *vb* vlot; — **in** *vb* intrek; — **into** *vb* betrek; — on *vb* deurloop; — **out of** *vb* verhuis; — **stealthily** *vb* sluip; — **up** *vb* (at school) oorsit
moved *adj* (emotion) aangedaan; bewoë
movement *n* beweging
mover *n* voorsteller
movie *n* rolprent
moving *adj* aandoenlik; roerend
mow *vb* maai
mower *n* maaier
MP player *n* mp-speler
Mr *title* meneer
Mrs *title* mevrou
much *determiner; adv* baie; veel
muck *n* drek
mucous *adj* slymerig
mucous membrane *n* slymvlies
mucus *n* slym; snot
mud *n* modder; slyk
muddle *n* warboel; baaierd; *vb* verwar
muddled *adj* deurmekaar; verwar
muddy *adj* modderig; troebel

mudguard *n* modderskerm
muffler *n* serp
mug[1] *n* beker; kommetjie
mug[2] *vb* straatroof
mugger *n* straatrower
mulberry *n* moerbei
mule *n* muil; esel
multicoloured *adj* veelkleurig
multicultural *adj* multikultureel
multimedia *n* multimedia
multinational *adj* veelvolkig
multiple *n* veelvoud
multiple choice *n* veelkeusig; — **questions** *npl* veelkeusige vrae
multiplication *n* vermenigvuldiging
multiply *vb* vermenigvuldig
multiracial *adj* veelrassig; veelvolkig
multitude *n* veelheid; lot
mumble *vb* prewel
mummy[1] *n* ma; mamma
mummy[2] *n* (Egyptian) mummie
mumps *n* pampoentjies
mundane *adj* ondermaans
municipal *adj* stedelik
municipal complex *n* stadhuis
municipality *n* munisipaliteit; stads-raad
murder *n* moord; *vb* moor
murderer *n* moordenaar
murderous *adj* moorddadig
murmur *vb* murmel; lispel; ruis
murmur(ing) *n* geruis
muscadel *n* muskadel
muscle *n* spier
muscovy duck *n* makou
muscular *adj* gespier; — **force** *n* spierkrag
muse *n* muse; *vb* mymer
museum *n* museum
mushroom *n* sampioen
music *n* musiek; toonkuns
musical *adj* musikaal
musical box *n* speeldoos
musician *n* musikus
musk *n* muskus
muskmelon *n* spanspek
muslin *n* neteldoek
mussel *n* mossel
mustard *n* mosterd
muster *vb* monster
musty *adj* muf; vermuf

mute *adj* stom
mutilate *vb* vermink; ratbraak
mutilation *n* skending
mutiny *n* muitery; *vb* muit
mutter *vb* mompel; prewel; brom
mutton *n* skaapvleis
mutual *adj* onderling; wederkerig; wedersyds; — **love** *n* wederliefde
muzzle *n* snoet; muilband
my *pers pron* my

my word! *interj* mastig!
myrrh *n* mirre
myrtle *n* mirt
mysterious *adj* misterieus; geheimsinnig; diepsinnig
mystery *n* geheim; misterie
mystic(al) *adj* mistiek
myth *n* mite; sage
mythology *n* mitologie; fabelleer; godeleer

N

nag *vb* pik; lol
nagging *n* gesanik
nail *n* spyker; nael; *vb* nael; — **down** *vb* vasspyker
naive *adj* naïef
naivety *n* naïwiteit
naked *adj* kaal; naak; nakend; ontbloot
nakedness *n* naaktheid
name *n* benaming; naam; *vb* noem; naam gee; heet
name tag *n* naamplaatjie
named *adj* genaamd; genoem
nameless *adj* naamloos
namely *adv* naamlik
nameplate *n* naambord
namesake *n* naamgenoot; genant
nanotechnology *n* nanotegnologie
nap *n* dutjie
napkin *n* servet
nappy *n* luier; doek
narcissus *n* narsing
narcosis *n* narkose
narcotic *n* verdowingsmiddel; slaapdrank
narrate *vb* verhaal; vertel
narrative *n* verhaal; vertelling
narrator *n* verteller
narrow *adj* eng; benepe; nou; smal; — **pass** *n* noute
narrow-minded *adj* bekrompe; kleingeestig; kleinsielig; enghartig
narrowly *adv* skraps
narrowness *n* noute; engte
NASA *see* **National Aeronautics and Space Administration**
nasal *adj* nasaal
nastily *adj* lelik
nasty *adj* goor; grieselig; lelik; onaardig; vies; vuil; aaklig
NATO *see* **North Atlantic Treaty Organisation**
nation *n* nasie; volk
national *adj* nasionaal
National Aeronautics and Space Administration *n* Amerikaanse Nasionale Lugvaart en Ruimteadministrasie

national anthem *n* volkslied
national dress *n* volksdrag
national road *n* nasionale pad
nationalism *n* nasionalisme
nationality *n* nasionaliteit
nationalize *vb* nasionaliseer
nationwide *adj* landswyd
native forest *n* oerwoud
native land *n* geboorteland
native language *n* landstaal
native soil *n* geboortegrond
natural *adj* natuurlik; ongekunsteld; eie
natural resources *n* natuurbronne
natural science *n* natuurwetenskap
naturalization *n* naturalisasie
naturalize *vb* naturaliseer
naturally *adv* natuurlik; uiteraard
nature *n* aard; geaardheid; eienskap; gesteldheid; inbors; wese; natuur
nature conservation *n* natuurbewaring
naught *n* nul
naughty *adj* stout; ondeund; onnutsig; baldadig; gruwelik; onbruikbaar; onwettig
nauseating *adj* walglik
nauseous *adj* mislik
nautical *adj* seevaartkundig
nautical mile *n* seemyl
naval battle *n* seeslag
naval force *n* seemag
nave *n* naaf
navel *n* nael; nawel
navigable *adj* bevaarbaar
navigate *vb* bevaar; vaar
navigation *n* seevaart; skeepvaart
navigator *n* seevaarder
navy *n* vloot; seemag
navy blue *n*, *adj* marineblou
near *adv*, *adj* naby; dig; (foreleg) linker; *adv* na; *prep* naby; aan; — **which** *rel pron* waarby; — **whom** *rel pron* waarby
near-sighted *adj* kortsigting
nearby *adj* naby; *adv* naby; digby; ophande
nearer *adv*, *adj* nader

nearest *adv,adj* naaste
nearly *adv* amper; byna; haas; nagenoeg; omtrent
neat *adj* net; netjies; sindelik; agtermekaar
neatness *n* netheid
necessary *adj* benodig(de); nodig;
noodsaaklik
necessity *n* noodsaak; noodsaaklikheid
neck *n* hals; nek
necktie *n* das
necklace *n* halsband
nectar *n* nektar; godedrank
nectarine *n* nektarien; kaalperske
need *n* behoefte; nood; *vb* behoef
neediness *n* gemis
needle *n* naald
needle case *n* naaldekoker
needlecraft *n* naaldwerk
needlework *n* handwerk; naaiwerk;
naaldwerk
needy *adj* arm; behoeftig; hulpbehoewend; nooddruftig
negate *vb* verwerp
negative *adj* negatief; ontkennend
negatively *adv* ontkennend
neglect *n* versuim; versaking; *vb* afskeep
neglected *adj* verwaarloosde; verwil-
der(d); **be —** *vb* agterstaan
neglectful *adj* nalatig
negligence *n* nalatigheid
negligent *adj* nalatig; agteloos; agte(r)
losig
negotiate *vb* onderhandel; verhandel
negotiation *n* onderhandeling
negotiator *n* onderhandelaar
neigh *vb* runnik; hinnik
neighbour *n* buurman; ewenaaste;
naaste
neighbourhood *n* buurt; omtrek; omstreke
neighbouring *adj* naburig; nabygeleë;
omliggend
neither . . . nor *conj* nog; nog . . . nog
nephew *n* susterskind; broerskind;
neef; nefie
nerd *n* (*informal*) bleeksiel
nerve *n* senuwee; moed
nervous *adj* senuweeagtig; skrikkerig

nervous attack *n* senuaanval
nervous system *n* senustelsel
nest *n* nes
nest egg *n* neseier
nestle *vb* vly
net[i] *n* net
net(t)[2] *n* (profits) netto
netting *n* gaas
network *n* (computing) netwerk
neuralgia *n* neuralgie; senupyn; sinkings
neurosis *n* senusiekte
neurotic *n* senulyer; *adj* senusiek
neuter *adj* onsydig; *vb* (male animals)
sny; ontman; (female animals) spei
neutral *adj* neutraal; onsydig
neutrality *n* neutraliteit
neutralize *vb* neutraliseer
never *adv* nimmer; nooit; **—!** *interj*
nooit!
nevertheless *adv* tog; *conj* almiskie
new *adj* nuut; nuwerwets
new edition *n* herdruk
New Year *n* Nuwejaar
New Year's Eve *n* Oujaarsdagaand
New Year's resolution *n* Nuwejaars
voorneme
new-laid *adj* vars
newcomer *n* aankomeling
news *n* nuus; berig; tyding
news broadcast *n* nuusuitsending
news item *n* nuusberig
newspaper *n* koerant; nuusblad; blad
next *adj* volgende; eerskomende; toekomend; aankomend; aanstaande;
— door to *prep* naasaan; **— to this**
adv hiernaas; **— to** *prep* langs; naas;
naasaan; newens; **— to what** *inter*
pron waarnaas; **— to which** *inter*
pron waarnaas
next door *adv* hiernaas
next of kin *n* naasbestaande
nib *n* pen(punt)
nibble *vb* knabbel; peusel
nice *adj* mooi; fraai; oulik; fyn; gaaf;
gawerig; lekker; netjies; aardig
nicely *adv* lief
niche *n* nis
niche market *n* nismark
nick *vb* inkeep
nickel *n* nikkel**

nickname *n* bynaam; skel(d)naam
nicotine *n* nikotien
niece *n* susterskind; broerskind; nig; niggie
night *n* aand; nag; **at —** *adv* saans
night shift *n* nagskof
night watchman *n* nagwag
night school *n* aandskool
night session *n* aandsitting
nightingale *n* nagtegaal
nightly *adj, adv* nagtelik
nightmare *n* nagmerrie
nil *n* nul
nimble *adj* rats; vlug
nine *n, determiner* nege
nine o'clock *n, adj* nege-uur
ninefold *adj* negevoud
nineteen *n, determiner* negentien
nineteenth *n, adj* negentiende
ninetieth *n, adj* negentigste
ninety *n, determiner* negentig
ninth *n, adj* negende
nipple *n* nippel; speen; tepel; tiet
nit *n* (louse egg) neet
nitrate *n* nitraat
nitric acid *n* salpetersuur
nitrogen *n* stikstof
no *adj, pron* geen; *determiner* geen; *adv* nee; *sentence substitute* nee
no one *n* niemand; *pron* geeneen
nobility *n* adel
noble *adj* adellik; edel
nobleman *n* edelman
nobody *n* niemand
nocturnal *adj* nagtelik
nod *n* knik; *vb* knik; visvang
noise *n* geraas; lawaai; rumoer; geluid; gedruis; herrie; kabaal; spektakel; gedoe; gedoente
noise abatement *n* geraasbestryding
noiselessly *adv* soetjies
noisy *adj* luidrugtig
nomad *n* nomade
nomadic *adj* nomadies
nomenclature *n* naamwoord
nominal *adj* nominaal
nominate *vb* nomineer; benoem
nomination *n* nominasie; benoeming
non *prefix* nie
non-commissioned officer *n* onder-offisier

nonfiction *n* niefiksie
nonpayment *n* wanbetaling
nonplussed *adj* verbluf
nonracial *adj* nierassig
nonrigid airship *n* blimp
nonconformist *n* afgeskeidene
none *adj, pron* geen (*or* g'n); *determiner* geen
nonsense *n* nonsens; kaf; kafpraatjies; malheid; malligheid; onsin; gekheid; sotterny; **sheer —** *n* puur onsin
nonsensical *adj* absurd
noon *n* middag; twaalfuur; *adj* twaalf-uur; **at —** *adv* smiddags
noose *n* lis
norm *n* standaard
normal *adj* normaal; niegestremd
north *n* die noorde; *adj* noord(e)-; *adv* noord
north side *n* noordekant
North Atlantic Treaty Organisation *n* Noord-Atlantiese Verdragsorganisasie
north wind *n* noordewind
north-east *adj, adv* noordoos; *n* noord-ooste
north-west *adj, adv* noordwes; *n* noor-weste
northerly *adj* noordelik
northern *adj* noordelik
northern hemisphere *n* noorderhalf-rond
northern lights *n* noorderlig
nose *n* neus; snuit
nosegay *n* ruiker
nostril *n* neusgat
not *adv* nie; **— at all** *adv* allesbehalwe; geensins; *interj* gans en gaar nie!; **— clear** *adj* onduidelik; **— less than** *determiner* minstens; **— one** *adj, pron* geen (*or* g'n); *determiner* geen; *pron* geeneen; **— selected** *adj* ongekeur; **— touch upon** *vb* daarlaat; **— watertight** *adj* ondig; **— wealthy** *adj* onbemiddeld
notable *adj* vernaam
notch *n* keep; kerf; *vb* inkeep
note *n* aantekening; biljet; glos; notisie; (music) noot; *vb* aanteken; **— down** *vb* opteken
notebook *n* aantekeningboek

noted *adj* aangeteken; beroemd
notepaper *n* skryfpapier
noteworthy *adj* merkwaardig
nothing *n* niks; niet
nothingness *n* niet
notice *n* kennisgewing; aanmaning; bekendmaking; berig; bulletin; merk; notisie; *vb* bemerk
noticeable *adj* merkbaar
notifiable *adj* aanmeldbaar; — **disease** *n* aanmeldbare siekte
notify *vb* aankondig; aanmeld
notion *n* idee; begrip; benul; besef; denkbeeld; nosie
notorious *adj* befaamd; berug; oorbekend
notwithstanding *prep* ongeag; nieteenstaande
noun *n* naamwoord
nourish *vb* voed
nourishing *adj* voedsaam
nourishment *n* voeding; voedsel
novel *n* roman
novelist *n* romanskrywer
novelty *n* nuwigheid
November *n* November
novice *n* groentjie; leek; nuweling
now *adv* nou; tans; — **and then** *adv* af en toe
nowadays *adv* hedendaags; teenwoordig
nowhere *adv* nêrens
nozzle *n* tuit
nuance *n* skakering
nuclear bomb *n* atoombom; kernbom; A-bom

nuclear fallout *n* kernas
nuclear power *n* kernkrag
nuclear powered *adj* kernaangedrewe
nuclear war *n* kernoorlog
nuclear weapons *npl* kernwapens
nucleus *n* kern
nude *adj* naak; nakend
nudism *n* nudisme
nudist *n* nudis; kaalbas
nudity *n* naaktheid
nuisance *n* las; laspos; oorlas; plaag; steurnis
null and void *adj* ongeldig
numb *adj* dof; **become** — *vb* verstyf
number *n* nommer; getal; syfer; aantal; klomp; tal; tel
numberplate *n* nommerplaat
numbness *n* verdowing
numbskull (*informal*) *n* klapperdop
numeral *n* telwoord
numerical *adj* numeries
numerous *adj* talryk; sterk
nun *n* non
nurse *n* verpleegster; *vb* verpleeg; soog; behandel
nursery *n* blomkwekery; kwekery
nursery school *n* kindertuin; kleuterskool; peuterskool
nurseryman *n* blomkweker
nursing *n* verpleegkunde; verpleging
nut *n* neut; (with bolt) moer
nutcracker(s) *n* neutkraker
nutmeg *n* muskaatneut; neut
nutrition *n* voeding
nutritious *adj* voedsaam
nymph *n* nimf

O

oak tree *n* akkerboom; eikeboom
oar *n* roeispaan; riem
oasis *n* oase
oat sheaf *n* hawergerf
oath *n* eed; vloek
oats *npl* hawer
ob-gyn *n* (*informal*) ginekoloog
obedience *n* gehoorsaamheid
obedient *adj* onderdanig; dienswillig; geseglik; **be —** *vb* gehoorsaam
obelisk *n* naald; suil
obese *adj* swaarlywig
obesity *n* vetsug
obey *vb* gehoorsaam; luister; nakom
obituary *n* dood(s)berig
object[1] *n* ding; voorwerp; doel; oogmerk
object[2] *vb* objekteer
objection *n* beswaar; objeksie; bedenking; teenwerping
objectionable *adj* verwerplik; stuitig
objective *n* mikpunt
obligation *n* verpligting
oblige *vb* gerief; noodsaak; verplig
obliged *adj* verplig; **be — to** *vb* moet
obliging *adj* inskiklik; diensvaardig; voorkomend
oblique *adj* skuins
oblivion *n* vergetelheid
oblong *adj* langwerpig
obscene *adj* vuil
obscure *adj* duister
obscurity *n* duister
observance *n* inagneming
observation *n* observasie; waarneming; opmerking; aanmerking
observatory *n* observatorium; sterrewag
observe *vb* observeer; waarneem; opmerk; aanmerk; bemerk; bespeur; naleef; oplet; sien; vier
obsession *n* obsessie
obsolete *adj* verouder(d); **become —** *vb* verouder
obstacle *n* hinder; hindernis; hinderpaal; struikelblok; swarigheid; beletsel
obstetrician *n* ginekoloog

obstetrics *n* verloskunde
obstinate *adj* koppig; hardkoppig; halsstarrig; hardnekkig; steeks; obstinaat; onversetlik; wys; balsturig; **— person** *n* dikkop
obstruct *vb* belemmer; bemoeilik
obstruction *n* obstruksie; haakplek; verstopping
obtain *vb* kry; bekom; opdoen; verkry; verwerf; (information) inwin
obtainable *adj* verkrygbaar
obtrusive *adj* opdringerig
obtuse *adj* stoets; stomp
obvious *adj* ooglopend; vanselfsprekend; klaarblyklik; blykbaar; deursigtig; aangewese; **be —** *vb* blyk
obviously *adv* blykbaar
occasion *n* geleentheid; okkasie
occupant *n* bewoner
occupation *n* nering; okkupasie; besigheid
occupational therapy *n* arbeidsterapie
occupied *adj* besig; beset
occupier *n* inwoner
occupy *vb* bewoon; okkupeer; (a place) beset
occur *vb* inval; gebeur
occurrence *n* gebeurtenis; voorval
occurring *adj* voorkomend
ocean *n* oseaan; see
ocean current *n* seestroming
ochre *n* oker
octagon *n* ag(t)hoek
octave *n* oktaaf
October *n* Oktober
odd *adj* onpaar; potsierlik; raar; sonderling; eksentriek; los
odd number *n* onewe getal
ode *n* lofsang; ode
odour *n* geur; reuk
oesophagus *n* slukderm
of *prep* van; uit; **— age** *adj* mondig; **— course** *adj* natuurlik; **— great value** *adj* waardevol; **— its own accord** *adv* vanself; **— old** *adv* van hoeka se tyd af; **— one accord** *adv* eens; **— that** *adv* daarvan; **— this**

onion

adv hiervan; — **what** *inter pron* waarvan; — **which** *inter pron* waarvan; — **whom** *rel pron* waaraan

off *prep* af; uit; — **and on** (*or* **on and —**) *adv* af en toe

off duty *adj* vry

off-colour *adj* oes

off-peak traffic *n* slapverkeer

off-road racing *n* veldrenne

off-white *n, adj* naaswit

offal *n* afval

offence *n* misdryf; vergryp; aanstoot; belediging; ergernis

offend *vb* beledig; krenk; kwes

offended *adj* geraak

offender *n* oortreder

offensive *adj* offensief; ergerlik; stuitend; vies

offer *n* aanbod; bod; tender; *vb* aanbied; offer

offering *n* offer; offerande

office *n* kantoor; amp; buro; departement

officer *n* amptenaar; offisier

official *adj* offisieel; *n* amptenaar

officially *adj* offisieel

officiate *vb* fungeer

officious *adj* gedienstig

offline *adv* (computing) vanlyn

offshoot *n* spruit; suier

offside *adj* (sport) onkant

offspring *n* kroos; nageslag; nakomelingskap; saad; spruit; loot

often *adj* veel; vaak; *adv* dikwels

oh! *interj* ag; ai; o!

oh dear! *interj* gits!

oh no! *interj* ag nee!

oil *n* olie; *vb* smeer

oil of cloves *n* naeltjieolie

oil painting *n* olieverfskildery

oil pipeline *n* oliepypleiding

oil rig *n* olieboortoring

oilcan *n* oliekan

ointment *n* salf; smeergoed

old *adj* oud; — **bachelor** *n* oujongkêrel; — **man** *n* oukêrel; grysaard; — **motorcar** *n* tjor(rie)

old age *n* ouderdom; oudag

old crock *n* knol

old maid *n* oujongnooi

old-age home *n* ouetehuis

old-fashioned *adj* outyds; ouderwets

oldest *adj* oudste

oleander *n* oleander; selonsroos

olfactory organ *n* reukorgaan

oligarchy *n* oligargie

olive *n* olyf

olive oil *n* olyfolie

olympiad *n* (maths, chess, etc.) olimpiade

omelette *n* omelet

omen *n* voorbode; voorteken

ominous *adj* onheilspellend

omission *n* uitlating

omit *vb* uitlaat; versuim; nalaat

omnipotence *n* almag

on *adj* op; *adv* om; *prep* aan; — **a large scale** *adv* grootskeeps; grootskaals; — **account of** *prep* kragtens; vanweë; weens; oor; — **all fours** *adv* handeviervoet; — **behalf of** *prep* ten behoewe van; — **board** *adv* (ship, plane, etc.) aan boord; — **both sides** *adv* weerskante; — **form** *adv* op peil; — **hand** *adv* voorhande; — **heat** *adv* (animals) bronstig; op hitte; — **high** *adv* opwaarts; — **one's back** *adv* agteroor; — **purpose** *adv* opsetlik; ekspres; — **that** *adv* daarop; — **the contrary** *adv* inteendeel; — **the ground floor** *adv* gelykvloers; — **the left** *adv* links; — **the same floor** *adv* gelykvloers; — **the sly** *adv* stilletjies; — **the subject of** *prep* aangaande; — **the way** *adv* onderweg; — **this side** *adv* duskant; — **what** *inter pron* waarop; — **which** *inter pron* waarop; *rel pron* waaraan

on-ramp *n* oprit

once *adv* eenkeer; eenmaal; eens; **at —** *adv* dadelik; direk

once more *adv* nogmaals; opnuut; al weer; weer

one *n* een; *pron* 'n mens; een; *adj* een; — **after the other** *adv* agtereen; beurtelings; — **another** *pron* mekaar; — **of these days** *adv* eersdaags

one day *adv* eendag; eenmaal

one o'clock *n, adj* eenuur

one-sided *adj* eensydig

one-way street *n* eenrigtingstraat

onion *n* ui

online *adj, adv* (computing) aanlyn
onlooker *n* toeskouer
only *adj* alleen; bloot; enig; enigste;enkel; *adv* net; *conj* maar;
only just *adv* pas
onomatopoeia *n* onomatopee
onwards *adv* aan
onyx *n* oniks
ooze *vb* syfer
opal *n* opaal
opaque *adj* ondeurskynend
open *adj* oop; ope; *vb* inwy
open air *n* buitelug
open day *n* opedag
opener *n* (debate, etc.) inleier
open-road tolling *n* ooppadtolinvordering
opening *adj* ontluikend; *n* inwyding
openly *adv* openlik; ronduit
opera *n* opera
operate *vb* sny; werk; hanteer; — **on** *vb* opereer
operation *n* operasie
operator *n* operateur
ophthalmologist *n* oogarts
opinion *n* opinie; mening; opvatting; sienswyse; denkwyse; dunk; gedagte; gesindheid; insig; oordeel
opinion poll *n* opiniepeiling
opinionated *adj* waanwys
opium *n* opium
opponent *n* opponent; teenparty; teenstander; wederparty
opportunity *n* geleentheid; kans
oppose *vb* opponeer; teenwerk; weerstrewe; dwarsdrywe
opposite *adj* teenoorgestel; teendeel; daarteenoor; *prep* oor
opposite number *n* teëhanger
opposite side *n* oorkant
opposition *n* opposisie; teenkanting; teenstand; weerstand
oppress *vb* onderdruk; verdruk; beklem
oppressed *adj* bedruk; beklemd
oppression *n* onderdrukking
oppressive *adj* benoud
optic(al) *adj* opties
optical illusion *n* gesigsbedrog
optician *n* brilmaker; gesigskundige
optimism *n* optimisme
optimist *n* optimis

option *n* opsie
optional *adj* fakultatief
optometrist *n* oogkundige
or *conj* of; — **else** *adv* anders
oracle *n* orakel
oral *adj* mondeling
orang-outang *n* orang-oetang
orange *n* soetlemoen; lemoen; (colour) oranje; *adj* oranje
orange juice *n* lemoensap
oration *n* rede
orator *n* redenaar
orb *n* kring
orbit *n* baan; wentelbaan; *vb* wentel; — **of the earth** *n* aardbaan
orchard *n* boord; vrugteboord
orchestra *n* orkes
orchid *n* orgidee
ordain *vb* verorden
order *n* volgorde; orde; opdrag; verordening; las; bestelling; *vb* bestel; — **someone around** *vb* baasspeel; **out of** — *adj, adv* onklaar
orderly *adj* ordelik; reëlmatig; gereeld; ordonnans
ordinal number *n* rangtelwoord
ordinary *adj* alledaags; ordinêr; gewoon; gemeen
ordination *n* inwyding
ore *n* erts
organ *n* orgaan; orrel
organism *n* organisme
organist *n* orrelis
organize *vb* organiseer
organized *adj* ingerig
oriental *adj* oostelike
orientation *n* oriëntering
origin *n* afkoms; herkoms; oorsprong; wortel
original *adj* origineel; oorspronklik; aanvanklik
originality *n* oorspronklikheid
originally *adv* oorspronklik
originate *vb* ontstaan
ornament *n* ornament; sieraad; versiering; tooi; tooisel
ornamental *adj* sierlik
orphan *n* wees; weeskind; — **animal** *n* hansdier; — **calf** *n* hanskalf; — **lamb** *n* hanslam
orphanage *n* weeshuis

orthodontist *n* ortodontist
orthodox *adj* ortodoks; regsinnig
orthography *n* spelling
orthopaedic *adj* ortopedies
orthopaedist *n* ortopeed
oscillate *n* slinger
ostensible *adj* oënskynlik
ostensibly *adv* sogenaamd
ostrich *n* volstruis
other *n, adj* ander; **— side** *n* oorkant
otherwise *adv* anders; andersins
otter *n* otter
ouch! *interj* ai!
ought to *vb* behoort
ounce *n* ons
our *pers pron* ons
out *adv* om; *prep* uit; **— of that** *adv*
daaruit; **— of what** *inter pron* waaruit; **— of which** *rel pron* waaruit
out of breath *adj, adv* uitasem
out of doors (*or* **outdoors**) *adv* buitenshuis; buite
out of order *adj, adv* onklaar
out of sight *adv* skoonveld
out of sorts *adj* oes; olik
out of the way *adv* agteraf
out-of-the-way place *n* uithoek
outbuilding *n* buitegebou
outburst *n* uitval
outcast *n* balling; banneling; verstoteling; verworpeling; verskoppeling; paria
outcome *n* uitkoms(te); resultaat; uitvloeisel
outdistance *vb* vooruitloop
outer skin *n* nerf
outer world *n* buitewêreld
outermost *adj* buitenste
outfit *n* toerusting; uitrusting
outhouse *n* buitegebou
outing *n* uitstappie; kuier; ekskursie
outlawed *adj* voëlvry
outlet *n* uitgang; uitlaat; uitloop; uitweg
outline *n* skema; omtrek; geraamte; *vb* omlyn
outlive *vb* oorlewe
outlook *n* vooruitsig
outlying district *n* uithoek
outmanoeuvre *vb* uitoorlê
outpatient *n* buitepasiënt
outpost *n* voorpos

output *n* uitset; opbrings; produksie
outrage *n* wandaad
outrageous *adj* verregaande; skandalig; skandelik
outshine *vb* oorskadu
outside *adj* buitekant; *adv* buite; buitekant
outside world *n* buitewêreld
outsider *n* buitestaander
outsource *vb* uitkontrakteer
outspan *n* uitspanning; *vb* uitspan
outspoken *adj* reguit
outstanding *adj* uitstaande; (payment) agterstallig; **be —** *vb* uitstaan
outward *adj* uitwaarts; uitwendig; uiterlik
outward appearance *n* uiterlik
outward journey *n* heenreis; uitreis
outwardly *adv* uiterlik
outwards *adv* uitwaarts
outwit *vb* uitoorlê
oval *adj* ovaal; ellipties
ovary *n* eierstok
ovation *n* ovasie
oven *n* bakoond; oond; stoof
over *adv* om; omver; *prep* bo; **— there** *adv* gunter; **— what** *inter pron* waarbo; waaroor; **— which** *rel pron* waarbo; waaroor; **— whom** *rel pron* waarbo
over-friendly *adj* danig
overall *adj, adv* oorpak
overboard *adv* oorboord
overburden *vb* oorlaai
overcast *adj* bewolk; betrokke; **become —** *vb* toetrek
overcharge *vb* oorlaai; oorvra
overcoat *n* jas; oorjas
overcome *adj* bevange; *vb* kafloop
overconfident *adj* oorgerus
overdo *vb* oordrywe
overdone *adj* oordrewe
overdraw *vb* (banking) oortrek
overdrive *n* snelrat
overeat *vb* ooreet
overestimate *vb* oorskat
overexertion *n* oorspanning
overflow *n* oorloop; uitloop; *vb* oorstrom; oorloop
overhaul *vb* opdoen
overhead line *n* oorhoofse lyn
overhead projector *n* truprojektor**

overhear *vb* afluister
overload *vb* oorlaai
overlook *vb* oorsien
overpower *vb* oorweldig; oormeester
overproduction *n* oorproduksie
overripe *adj* oorryp
overseas *adv* oorsee
oversee *vb* oorsien
overseer *n* opsigter; opsiener
oversensitive *adj* liggeraak
overshadow *vb* oorskadu
overstatement *n* oorbeklemtoning
overstimulate *vb* oorprikkel
overtake *vb* inloop; agterhaal
overtime *n* oortyd; oorwerk
overture *n* ouverture; voorspel
overwhelm *vb* oorweldig; oorrompel; oorstelp; oormeester

overwork *n* oorwerk; oorspanning
ow! (*or* **ouch!**) *interj* eina!
owe *vb* skuld
owing *adj* verskuldig
owl *n* uil
own *adj* eie
own up *vb* erken
owner *n* eienaar; eienares
ox *n* bees; os
ox-wagon *n* ossewa
oxhide *n* osvel
oxidize *vb* oksideer
oxygen *n* suurstof
oyster *n* oester
ozone *n* osoon
ozone friendly *adj* osoonvriendelik
ozone layer *n* osoonlaag

P

pa *n* pa

pace *n* pas; tempo; stryk; stap; skrede; tred; tree

pacemaker *n* gangmaker

pacify *vb* sus; versoen; ontwapen

pack *vb* inpak; — up *vb* pak

package *n* pakket

package deal *n* pakketakkoord

packed *adj* propvol; stampvol

packet *n* pakket

packing *n* verpakking

pact *n* verdrag

pad *n* (cricket) skut

paddle *vb* plas

paddle wheel *n* skeprat

paddling pool *n* plaspoel

padlock *n* hangslot

paediatrician *n* kinderarts

paedophile *n* pedofiel

pagan *adj* heiden

page[1] *n* (book) bladsy; pagina; *vb* pagineer

page[2] *n* (boy) page

paginate *vb* pagineer

paid *adj* voldaan

pail *n* emmer

pain *n* pyn; leed; smart; wee

painful *adj* pynlik; smartlik; eina; seer

painfully *adv* eina

painkiller *n* pynstiller; pyndoder

painless *adj* pynloos

paint *n* verf; *vb* skilder; verf

painter *n* (artist) skilder; kunsskilder; (trade) verwer

painting *n* skildery; skilderstuk

pair *n* paar; — of tackies *n* tekkie; — of tongs *n* tang

pair off *vb* paar

palace *n* paleis

palaeontology *n* paleontologie

palatable *adj* smaaklik

palate *n* verhemelte

pale *adj* bleek; vaal; flets; verbleek; turn — *vb* verbleek

pale blue *n*, *adj* ligblou

palette *n* palet

pallbearer *n* draer

pallid *adj* bleek

palm[1] *n* (hand) palm

palm[2] *n* (tree) palm; palmboom; — branch *n* palm; — leaf *n* palmblad

palm off *vb* aansmeer

palm oil *n* palmolie

palmist *n* waarsêer

palpable *adj* voelbaar; tasbaar

pamper *vb* troetel; koester

pamphlet *n* pamflet; vlugskrif

pan *n* (cooking) pan

pancake *n* pannekoek

panel *n* paneel

panel beater *n* paneelklopper

panel van *n* paneelwa

panic *n* paniek

panic-stricken *adj* paniekbevange; paniekerig

panicky *adj* paniekbevange; paniekerig

panorama *n* panorama

pant *vb* hyg; puff

pantheism *n* panteïsme

panther *n* panter

pantihose *n* broekiekouse

pantomime *n* gebarespel

pantry *n* spens

pants *n* (pair of) broek

papacy *n* pousdom

papal *adj* pouslik

papal bull *n* bul

paparazzi *npl* joernaliste

papaw *n* papaja

paper *n* opstel; referaat; papier; *vb* behang; (a wall) plak; uitplak

paper mill *n* papierfabriek

paper-hanger *n* plakker; behanger

papers *npl* papiere

par *n* (golf) syfer; pari; below — *adj* onder pari

parable *n* gelykenis

parabola *n* parabool

parachute *n* valskerm

parachutist *n* valskermspringer

parade *n* parade; praal

parade float *n* sierwaens

paradise *n* paradys

paradox *n* paradoks
paradoxical *adj* paradoksaal
paraffin oil *n* lampolie; paraffien
paragraph *n* paragraaf
parallel *adj* ewewydig; parallel
parallel bars *npl* brug
paralyse *vb* verlam
paralysed *adj* lam
paralysis *n* verlamming; lamheid
paramedic *n* paramedikus
paramedical *adj* paramedies
parapet *n* borswering
paraplegic *n* parapleeg
parasite *n* parasiet; woekerplant
parcel *n* pakkie; pakket; pak
parcel post *n* pakketpos
parched *adj* droog
parchment *n* perkament
pardon *n* amnestie; grasie; vergewing; vergifnis; *vb* ekskuseer; — me! *interj* eksuus!
pardonable *adj* vergeeflik
pare *vb* skil
parent *n* ouer
parental *adj* ouerlik
parenthesis *n* parentese
parents-in-law *npl* skoonouers
pariah *n* paria; verstoteling
parish *n* gemeente
park *n* park; *vb* parkeer
park and ride *n* parkeer-en-ry
parkade *n* parkade
parking meter *n* parkeermeter
parking place *n* parkeerplek
parking space *n* parkeerplek
parliament *n* parlement
parliamentary *adj* parlementêr
parody *n* parodie
parole *n* parool; wagwoord
parricide *n* vadermoord
parrot *n* papegaai
parry *vb* afwend
parse *vb* ontleed
parsnip *n* witwortel
parsonage *n* pastorie
part *n* aandeel; bestanddeel; deel; gedeelte; part; rol; *vb* skei; — of a journey *n* skof; — of the body *n* liggaamsdeel
part of speech *n* rededeel
partake *vb* (food, etc.) nuttig

partial *adj* eensydig; gedeeltelik; partydig
partially *adv* gedeeltelik
participate *vb* deel; — in *vb* deelneem
participation *n* inspraak
participle *n* deelwoord
particle *n* krieseltjie; partikel
particular *adj* besonder; kieskeurig
particularly *adv* besonder
parting *n* skeiding
partition *n* afskorting; afskutting; beskot; skeidsmuur; tussenmuur
partition off *vb* afskort
partly *adv* deels; gedeeltelik; — worn *adj* halfslyt
partner *n* vennoot; deelgenoot
partnership *n* vennootskap; maatskappy
partridge *n* patrys
party *n* party; fuif; geselskap; troep; *vb* fuif
pass *n* pas; permit; engte; (mountain) pas; poort; (football) aangee; *vb* aanreik; verloop; (a bill) aanneem; — away *vb* sterf; verbygaan; — faeces *vb* kak; — on *n* aangee; aanstuur; — one's time *vb* slyt; — over *vb* oorstap; — round *vb* rondgee; — sentence *vb* vel; — through *vb* deurtrek
passable *adj* gangbaar
passage *n* gang; deurgang; deurtog; oortog; oorvaart; pas; passasie; vaart
passenger *n* passasier
passer-by *n* verbyganger
passing *adj* verbygaand
passion *n* passie; hartstog; drif; toorn
passion fruit *n* grenadella
passionate *adj* driftig; hartstogtelik; vurig
passive *adj* lydelik; passief
Passover *n* Paasfees
passport *n* paspoort
password *n* wagwoord
past *n* verlede; *adj* vorige; vergange; verlede; *adv* gelede
pasta *n* pasta
paste *n* pasta; *vb* plak
pasteboard *n* karton
pastor *n* pastoor
pastoral *adj* herderlik
pastry *n* gebak; pastei

pasturage *n* weiding; weiland
pasture *n* wei
pat *n* tik
patch *n* lap; — **up** *vb* oplap
patella *n* knieskyf
patent *n* patent; oktrooi; *vb* patenteer
paternal *adj* vaderlik
paternity *n* vaderskap
path *n* pad; baan; weg
pathetic *adj* pateties; hartroerend
pathogen *n* patogeen
patience *n* geduld; lankmoedigheid; lydsaamheid; — **of Job** *n* jobsgeduld
patient *adj* geduldig; verdraagsaam; lankmoedig; *n* pasient; sieke; lyer
patio *n* stoep
patriarch *n* patriarg; aartsvader
patriot *n* vaderlander
patriotism *n* patriotisme; vaderlandsliefde
patrol *n* patrollie; *vb* patrolleer
patron *n* beskermheer; patroon
pattern *n* patroon; voorbeeld; model
patty *n* vleiskoekie
paunch *n* boepens; pens
pause *n* pouse; tussenpoos; poos
pave *vb* straat; bestraat
pavement *n* sypaadjie; plaveisel; bestrating
pavilion *n* paviljoen
paw *n* poot; klou
pawn[1] *n* pand; *vb* pand; verpand
pawn[2] *n* (chess) pion
pawnbroker *n* pandjiesbaas
pawnshop *n* pandjieswinkel
pay *n* salaris; besoldiging; werkloon; gasie; *vb* bekostig; loon; — **a visit** *vb* aflê; — **attention** *vb* oplet; — **attention to** *vb* ag slaan op; gee aandag aan; — **back** *vb* uitkeer; — **in advance** *vb* vooruit betaal; — **off** *vb* afbetaal; aansuiwer; — **out** *vb* uitbetaal; uitkeer
payable in advance *adj* vooruitbetaalbaar
payment *n* betaling; afbetaling; voldoening
PC *see* **political correctness**
pea *n* ertjie
pea pod *n* ertjiedop
peace *n* vrede

peace of mind *n* sielsrus
peace process *n* vredesproses
peace-loving *adj* vredeliewend
peaceful *adj* vreedsaam; vredig; stil
peach *n* perske
peach brandy *n* mampoer; perskesnaps
peach jam *n* perskekonfyt
peacock *n* pou
peak *n* spits; piek; top; toppunt
peak hour *n* spitsuur
peak period *n* spitstyd
peak traffic *n* spitsverkeer
peal *n* galm
peanut *n* grondboontjie
pear *n* peer
pear tree *n* peerboom
pearl *n* pêrel
peat *n* turf
pebble *n* klip
peck *n* pik
peculiar *adj* eienaardig; buitengewoon; besonder; sonderling; eie; wonderlik
peculiarly *adv* besonder
pecuniary *adj* geldelik
pedagogic *adj* opvoedkundig
pedagogics *n* pedagogiek
pedagogue *n* pedagoog
pedagogy *n* opvoedkunde; pedagogiek
pedal *n* pedaal; trap
pedantic *adj* pedanties
peddle *vb* vent
pedestal *n* voetstuk
pedestrian *n* voetganger; wandelaar
pedicure *n* pedikuur
pedigree *n* stamboom; geslag(s)boom
pedlar *n* venter
peel *n* skil; *vb* afskil; — **off** *vb* afskilfer
peep[1] *n* gepiep; *vb* piep
peep[2] *vb* gluur; loer — **in** *vb* inloer
peephole *n* kykgat
peer[1] *n* gelyke; weerga; edelman
peer[2] *vb* gluur; loer; — **at** *vb* tuur
peerless *adj* onvergelyklik
peevish *adj* knorrig; nors
peewit *n* (bird) kiewiet
peg *n* bout; *vb* vaspen; — **out** *vb* (*informal*) afklop
pelican *n* pelikaan
pellet *n* koeël
pellet gun *n* windbuks
pelvis *n* bekken

pen[1] *n* hok; kraal
pen[2] *n* pen
penal code *n* wetboek van strafreg
penalty *n* boete; straf
penalty kick *n* strafskop
pending *adj* onbeslis
pendulum *n* pendule; slinger
penetrate *vb* deurdring; indring
penguin *n* pikkewyn
peninsula *n* skiereiland
penitent *adj* boetvaardig
pennant *n* wimpel
penny *n* penning
penpusher *n* pennelekker
pension *n* pensioen
pension funds *n* pensioenfonds
pensioner *n* pensioenaris; pensioentrekker
pensive *adj* nadenkend; peinsend
pent up *adj* verkrop
pentagon *n* vyfhoek
pentameter *n* pentameter
penultimate *adj* voorlaaste
people *n* volk; mensevri(e)nd; *vb* bevolk
pepper *n* peper; *vb* inpeper
peppermint *n* peperment
per *prep* per; ten; volgens
per cent *adv;* *n* persent
perceive *vb* merk; bemerk
percentage *n* persentasie
perceptible *adj* merkbaar
perception *n* persepsie; waarneming; gewaarwording
percolate *vb* filtreer
percolator *n* filter
percussion band *n* slagorkes
percussion cap *n* doppie
perestroika *n* perestroika
perfect *adj* perfek; volkome; gaaf; *vb* volmaak; **in — health** *adj* blakend
perfection *n* perfeksie
perfectly *adv* volkome
perfidious *adj* troueloos
perforate *vb* perforeer
perform *vb* uitvoer; vertoon; betrag; **— a duty** *vb* vervul; **— a marriage ceremony** *vb* voltrek
performance *n* prestasie; uitvoering; vertoning; spel; (theatre) opvoering
perfume *n* parfuum; reukwater
pergola *n* prieel

perhaps *adv* altemit; dalk; dalkies; miskien; soms; wellig
peril *n* gevaar
perilous *adj* gevaarlik
period *n* periode; tydperk; termyn; tyd; tydvak
periodic(al) *adj* periodiek
periodical *n* tydskrif
periodically *adv* periodiek
periods *npl* maandstonde
periscope *n* periskoop
perish *vb* sneuwel; vergaan; verongeluk
peritoneum *n* buikvlies
periwinkle *n* alikreukel
perjury *n* meineed; eedbreuk
permanent *adj* permanent; vas
permeate *vb* deurdring
permissible *vb* veroorloof
permission *n* toestemming; permissie; vergunning; toelating; verlof; jawoord
permissiveness *n* permissiwiteit
permit *n* permit; geleibrief; pas; *vb* gedoog
pernicious *adj* verderflik
perpendicular *adj* penregop; regop; loodreg
perpetrate *vb* pleeg
perpetrator *n* dader
perplex *vb* verbyster
perplexed *adj* bedremmeld; verleë
perplexity *n* verwarring
persecute *vb* agtervolg
perseverance *n* volharding
persevere *vb* volhard; volhou; aanhou; vastrap
persist *vb* volhard; deurdryf
persistence *n* volharding
person *n* persoon; mens; **— from Africa** *n* Afrikaan; **— in love** *n* verliefde
personal *adj* persoonlik
personality *n* persoonlikheid
personalize *vb* (stationery, etc.) verpersoonlik
personnel *n* personeel
perspective *n* perspektief; sienswyse
perspiration *n* sweet; **a drop of —** *n* sweetdruppel
perspire *vb* sweet
perspiring *adj* besweet
persuade *vb* ompraat; oorhaal; oorreed; beweeg

pertinent *adj* ter sake
peruse *vb* nalees; oorlees
perverse *adj* pervers
perverted *adj* verdorwe
pessimism *n* pessimisme
pessimist *n* pessimis
pessimistic *adj* pessimisties
pest *n* pes; plaag
pest control *n* plaagbeheer
pester *vb* neul
pesticide *n* insekdoder; plaagdoder
pestilence *n* pestilensie
pestle *n* stamper; vyselstamper
pet *n* liefling; troeteldier; *vb* troetel; vertroetel; **— animal** *n* troeteldier
pet lamb *n* hanslam
pet shop *n* troeteldierwinkel
petition *n* petisie; versoeksrif; smeekskrif; versoek; beswaarskrif; bede; *vb* petisioneer
petrifaction *n* verstening
petrify *vb* versteen
petrol *n* petrol
petrol pump *n* petrolpomp
petrol tank *n* petroltenk
petting zoo *n* troeteldieretuin
petty *adj* beuselagtig
petulant *adj* moedswillig
pew *n* bank
pewter *n* tin
phantasy *n* fantasie
phantom *n* spook
pharmaceutical *adj* farmaseuties
pharmacist *n* apteker
pharmacy *n* apteek; farmasie
pharynx *n* keelholte
phase *n* fase; stadium
phase out *vb* uitfaseer
pheasant *n* fisant
phenomenon *n* verskynsel
philanthropic *adj* filantropies; mensliewend
philanthropist *n* filantroop; mensevriend
philanthropy *n* filantropie
philately *n* filatelie
philology *n* filologie
philosopher *n* filosoof; wysgeer
philosophize *vb* filosofeer
philosophy *n* filosofie; wysbegeerte
phishing *n* (internet fraud) uitvissing

phlegm *n* slym; roggel
phlegmatic *adj* flegmaties
phoenix *n* feniks
phone *n* foon; *vb* opbel
phone call *n* oproep
phonetics *n* fonetiek
phosphate *n* fosfaat
phosphorus *n* fosfor
photo(graph) *n* foto; portret; **take a —** *vb* fotografeeer
photocopy *vb* fotostateer
photogenic *adj* fotogenies
photograph album *n* fotoalbum
photographer *n* fotograaf; afnemer
phrase *n* frase; term
physalis *n* pampelmoesie
physical *adj* liggaamlik; fisiek
physical exercise *n* liggaamsoefening
physician *n* arts; dokter; geneesheer; internis; medikus
physics *n* fisika; natuurkunde
physiognomy *n* fisionomie
physiology *n* fisiologie
physiotherapy *n* fisioterapie
physique *n* fisiek
pianist *n* pianis
piano *n* klavier; **— accompaniment** *n* klavierbegeleiding
pick[1] *n* pik; *vb* pik
pick[2] *n* keus(e); *vb* kies
pick at one's food *vb* peusel
pick off *vb* afpluk
pick up *vb* optel; opraap; raap; lig; opneem
pick out *vb* uitkies
pick-me-up *n* regmakertjie; opknappertjie
pick-up truck *n* bakkie
pickaxe *n* pik
picked *adj* uitgelese
picket *n* staakwag
pickle *n* pekel; *vb* insout; inlê
pickled *adj* gesout; ingelê; **— meat** *n* sult
pickpocket *n* grypdief; sakkeroller; goudief
picnic *n* piekniek; veldparty
picture *n* beeld; prent; skilderstuk; skildery; tafereel
picture book *n* prenteboek
picture frame *n* lys
picture rail *n* lys

picturesque *adj* skilderagtig
pie *n* pastei
piebald *adj* witbont
piece *n* stuk; brokstuk; endjie; skerf; ent; entjie; — **of good luck** *n* gelukslag
piecemeal *adv* stuksgewys
piecework *n* stukwerk
pier *n* hawehoof; pier
pierce *vb* boor; deurboor
piercing *adj* snerpend
piet-my-vrou *n* piet-my-vrou; redchested cuckoo
piety *n* vroomheid; godsvrug
pig *n* vark; swyn
pigeon *n* duif
pigeonhole *n* hokkie; vak(kie)
pigsty *n* varkhok; swynehok
Pilates *n* Pilates
pilchard *n* pelser
pile[1] *n* hoop; mied; — **up** *vb* opeenhoop; ophoop; opstapel
pile[2] *n* stapel; brandstapel
piles *npl* aambeie
pilgrim *n* pelgrim
pilgrimage *n* bedevaart; pelgrimsreis
pill *n* pil
pillage *vb* stroop
pillar *n* pilaar; suil; — **of support** *n* steunpilaar
pillar box *n* briewebus
pillory *n* kaak
pillow *n* kussing
pillowcase *n* kussingsloop; sloop
pillowslip *n* kussingsloop
pilot *n* vlieënier; vlieër; loods; stuurman
pimple *n* puisie
pin *n* speld; bout; *vb* speld(e); — **together** *vb* vasspeld; — **on** *vb* aansteek
pinafore *n* voorskoot
pincers *n* knyptang
pinch *n* knyp; knel; (of salt) knippie; *vb* knel; knyp; vaslê
pincushion *n* speldekussing; naaldekussing
pine *vb* kwyn; — **away** *vb* uitteer; versmag; — **for** *vb* smag
pine cone *n* dennebol
pine needle *n* dennenaald
pine tree *n* denneboom

pine wood *n* dennehout
pineapple *n* pynappel
pink *n, adj* pienk
pinnacle *n* spits
pint *n* pint
pintail duck *n* pylstert
pioneer *n* pionier; baanbreker
pious *adj* godsalig; godvresend; vroom
pip *n* pit
pipe *n* buis; (tobacco) pyp
pipeline *n* pypleiding
piquant *adj* pikant
pirate *n* seerower; rower
pistol *n* pistool
piston *n* suier
pit *n* put; kuil; (motor racing) kuip; (stomach) holte
pitch[1] *n* pik
pitch[2] *n* hoogte; (music) toonhoogte; (cricket) kolfblad; *vb* slinger; (a tent) opslaan
pitch-black *n, adj* pikswart
pitch-dark *adj* pikdonker
pitcher *n* kruik
pitchfork *n* gaffel
pitfall *n* valstrik
pithy *adj* kernagtig
pitiable *adj* jammerlik
pitiful *adj* armsalig; beklaenswaardig; deerlik; erbarmlik
pitiless *adj* meedoënloos
pity *n* jammer; jammerte; medelye; mededoë; meedoë; ontferming; erbarming; deelneming; *vb* bekla
pivot *n* spil
placard *n* plakkaat
placate *vb* versoen
place *n* plek; plaas; instansie; *vb* plaas; neersit; lê; — **of honour** *n* ereplek; — **behind** *vb* agterstel
placenta *n* nageboorte
plagiarism *n* plagiaat
plagiarist *n* letterdief
plague *n* pes; plaag
plain *adj* eenvoudig; duidelik; gelykvloers; onaansienlik; onomwonde; *n* veld; vlakte
plainly *adv* onomwonde; platweg
plaintiff *n* eiser; beskuldiger; klaer; aanklaer
plait *n* vlegsel; *vb* vleg; — **in** *vb* invleg

plan *n* plan; aanleg; ontwerp; tekening; opstel; bestek; uitleg; *vb* beraam

plane[1] *n* vliegtuig

plane[2] *n* (tool) skaaf; *vb* afskaaf

plane[3] *n* plataanboom

planet *n* planeet

plank *n* plank

plant *n* plant; *vb* aanplant

plantation *n* plantasie

plaque *n* gedenkplaat; (teeth) plaak

plasma screen *n* plasmaskerm

plaster *n* pleister; — **of Paris** *n* gips

plastic *adj* plasties; *n* plastiek

plastic surgery *n* plastiese chirurgie

plate *n* plaat; bord

plate glass *n* spieëlglas

plateau *n* plato; plaat; hoogvlakte

platform *n* platform; verhoog

platonic *adj* platonies

platoon *n* peloton

play *n* drama; toneelstuk; stuk; speling; spel; speletjie; *vb* baljaar; (instrument) bespeel; — **a trick** *vb* 'n bak poets ; — **billiards** *vb* biljart; — **boisterously** *vb* rinkink; — **cards** *vb* kaartspeel; — **dice** *vb* dobbel; — **draughts** *vb* dam; — **the flute** *vb* fluit; — **truant** *vb* stokkiesdraai

playboy *n* losbol; swierbol

player *n* akteur; speler

playful *adj* dartel; speels; — **skips and leaps** *npl* flikkers

playground *n* speelplek

playmate *n* speelmaat

playschool *n* peuterskool

playtime *n* speeltyd

playwright *n* toneelskrywer

plea *n* pleidooi; pleit; verdediging

plead *vb* pleit; bepleit; — **for** *vb* verdedig

pleasant *adj* aangenaam; genoeglik; gesellig; plesierig; strelend; vermaaklik; welbehaaglik; soet

please *vb* aanstaan; behaag; beval; *adv* asseblief; geliewe; —**!** *interj* toe!

pleased *adj* bly; ingenome; tevrede — **to meet you** *vb* aangename kennis

pleasure *n* pret; plesier; genot; welbehae; behae; skik; vermaak

pleat *n* plooi; vou

pledge *n* borg; pand; *vb* verpand

plentiful *adj* oorvloedig

plenty *n* oorvloed; *adj* volop; — **of fish** *adj* visryk

pleurisy *n* borsvliesontsteking

pliable *adj* buigsaam; plooibaar

pliant *adj* soepel

pliers *n* tang; knyptang

plod *vb* blok; — **on** *vb* sukkel

plot[1] *n* erf; hoewe; perseel

plot[2] *n* sameswering; intrige; komplot; *vb* konkel; — **together** *vb* saamspan

plotting *n* geknoei

plough *n* ploeg; *vb* ploeg

ploy *n* slenter

pluck *n* durf; waagmoed; *vb* pluk

plug *n* prop; *vb* verstop

plugged *adj* verstop

plum *n* pruim

plumb line *n* lood

plumber *n* loodgieter

plume *n* pluim

plump *adj* mollig; vet

plunder *n* roof; buit; *vb* roof; buit; plunder

plunge *vb* dompel; duik

plural *n* meervoud; *adj* meervoudig

plus *prep; adj, adv* plus

plus fours *npl* pofbroek

pneumonia *n* longontsteking

poacher *n* wilddief; wildstroper; stroper

pocket *n* sak

pocket money *n* sakgeld

pocketknife *n* sakmes

pod *n* dop

podcast *n* potgooi; internetluisteropname

podiatrist *n* voetheelkundige

podiatry *n* podiatrie

poem *n* gedig

poet *n* digter; poëet

poet laureate *n* hofdigter

poetic(al) *adj* digterlik; poëties

poetry *n* digkuns; poësie

point *n* punt; dotjie; spits; tip; top; onderwerp; kwessie; — **of intersection** *n* snypunt; — **of law** *n* regspunt; — **of view** *n* gesigspunt; standpunt; — **out** *vb* aanwys; uitwys; beduie; **to the** — *adj* saaklik; ter sake

point-blank *adv* botweg; *adj* trompop

pointed *adj* spits

pointer *n* (dog) jaghond; (on scales, etc.) wyster
pointless *adj* sinloos
points *npl* (railway) wissel
poison *n* gif; venyn; *vb* vergif; vergewe
poisoning *n* vergiftiging
poisonous *adj* giftig
poke *n* stoot; por; *vb* stoot; por
polar bear *n* ysbeer
polar region *n* poolstreek
pole *n* mas; paal; pool
polecat *n* muishond
polemic *adj* polemies
police *n* polisie
police dog *n* polisiehond; speurhond
police station *n* polisiekantoor
policeman *n* polisieman; agent
policy *n* beleid; politiek
polish *vb* glans; afvryf
polite *adj* beleef; hoflik; galant; manierlik; beskaaf; hups
politeness *n* beleefdheid
politic *adj* politiek
political *adj* politiek
political correctness *n* polities korrek
political science *n* staatsleer
politician *n* politikus
politics *n* politiek; staatkunde
polka *n* polka
pollen *n* stuifmeel
polling *n* stemming; — **officer** *n* stemopnemer
pollute *vb* besoedel; besmet; bevlek; verontreinig
polygamist *n* veelwywer
polygamy *n* veelwywery; poligamie
polygon *n* veelhoek
polytechnic(al) *adj* politegnies
pomegranate *n* granaat
pomelo *n* pampelmoes; pomelo
pommel *n* knop; saalknop
pomp *n* praal; staatsie
pond *n* vywer; plas
ponder *vb* broei; mymer
pontoon *n* pont
pony *n* ponie
poodle *n* poedel
pool[1] *n* poel; kuil; vywer; plas
pool[2] *n* pot; syndikaat; ring
poop *n* agterskip
poop deck *n* agterdek

poor *adj* arm; armsalig; behoeftig; eina; onbemiddeld; power
poorly *adj* eina; sleg
popcorn *n* springmielies
pope *n* pous; paap
poplar *n* (tree) populier
poppy *n* papawer
popular *adj* populêr; gewild
popularity *n* populariteit
population *n* bevolking
populous *adj* volkryk
porcelain *n* porselein
porch *n* portaal
porcupine *n* ystervark
pore[1] *n* porie
pore[2] *vb* tuur
pork *n* varkvleis; spek
pornographic *adj* pornografies
porous *adj* poreus
porpoise *n* bruinvis; seevark
porridge *n* pap
port[1] *n* hawe
port[2] *n* (left side) bakboord
port[3] *n* portwyn
port[4] *n* (computing) poort
portable *adj* draagbaar
portcullis *n* valhek
porter *n* deurwagter; kruier; portier
portfolio *n* portefeulje
porthole *n* patryspoort
portion *n* aandeel; deel; gedeelte; part; porsie; afdeling
portrait *n* portret; afbeelding; beeltenis
portrayal *n* afbeelding
pose *vb* poseer
poser *n* (question) strikvraag
posh *adj* deftig
position *n* pos; posisie; ligging; plek; stand
positive *adj* positief; seker
positively *adv* bepaald; beslis
possess *vb* besit; hê
possession *n* besit; besitting
possessions *npl* eiendom
possessive *adj* besitlik
possible *adj* moontlik; gebeurlik; denklik; bestaanbaar
possibly *adv* miskien; altemit; soms
post[1] *n* paal
post[2] *n* amp; pos; standplaas

post³ *n* pos; *vb* pos; (on internet) adverteer; aankondig; publiseer
post office *n* poskantoor; pos
post-free *adj, adv* vragvry; posvry
post-modernism *n* post-modernisme
post-office box *n* posbus
postage *n* posgeld
postage stamp *n* posseël
postal guide *n* posgids
postal order *n* posorder
postbag *n* briewesak
postcard *n* poskaart; briefkaart
poster *n* plakkaat; aanplakbiljet
posterity *n* nageslag; nakomelingskap
posthumous *adj* nadoods
posthumously *adv* nadoods
postman *n* briewebesteller; posbesteller
postmark *n* posmerk; stempel; tjap
postmaster *n* posmeester
postmortem *n* nadoodse ondersoek; lykskouing
postpone *vb* uitstel; opskort
postponement *n* uitstel
postscript *n* naskrif
posture *n* postuur
posy *n* ruiker
pot *n* pot
potato peel (*or* skin) *n* aartappelskil
potash *n* kalium
potassium *n* kalium
potato *n* aartappel
potential *n* potensiaal; *adj* potensieel
pothole *n* slaggat
potjiekos *n* potjiekos
potter¹ *n* pottebakker
potter² *vb* peuter
pottery *n* erdewerk
pouch *n* sak; tas
poultice *n* pap; pleister
poultry *n* pluimvee
pound¹ *vb* stamp
pound² *n* (money) pond; (weight) pond
pound³ *n* (for animals) skut
pour *vb* stort; (liquids) giet; — in *vb* skink; inskink; — off *vb* afwater; afskink; — out *vb* uitskink; uitstort; inskink
poverty *n* armoede
powder *n* poeier; stof
power *n* mag; gesag; vermoë; heerskappy; krag; moondheid

power of attorney *n* volmag
power station *n* kragsentrale
powerful *adj* kragtig; kragdadig; geweldig; stoer; magtig
powerless *adj* kragteloos; magteloos
practicable *adj* doenlik; uitvoerbaar
practical *adj* prakties
practically *adv* prakties
practice *n* gebruik; oefening; praktyk
practise *vb* oefen; uitoefen; praktiseer; instudeer; betrag; — a profession *vb* beoefen; — piracy *vb* kaap; — usury *vb* woeker; — witchcraft *vb* toor
practitioner *n* praktisyn
prairie *n* grasvlakte
praise *n* lof; prys; roem; *vb* loof; roem
praiseworthy *adj* loflik; lofwaardig; prysenswaardig
pram *n* kinderwaentjie
prance *vb* steier
prank *n* poets; kaskenade; —s *npl* fratse
prawn *n* krewel
pray *vb* bid
prayer *n* gebed; bede
prayer meeting *n* bidstond
preach *vb* preek
preacher *n* prediker
preamble *n* aanhef
precarious *adj* bedenklik
precaution *n* voorsorg
precede *vb* voorgaan
precedence *n* voorrang
precedent *n* presedent
preceding *adj* voorafgaande
precept *n* gebod
precious *adj* dierbaar; kosbaar; kostelik; edel
precious stone *n* edelgesteente
precipice *n* afgrond
precipitate *vb* verhaas
precipitous *adj* steil
precise *adj* presies; saaklik; sekuur; stip; strik; angsvallig
precisely *adv* presies; stip; juistement
preciseness *n* stiptheid
precision *n* stiptheid; juistheid
precocious *adj* ouderwets; oulik
precursor *n* voorbode
predecessor *n* voorganger
predestination *n* uitverkiesing; voorbeskikking

predicament *n* verknorsing
predicate *n* (grammar) gesegde
predict *vb* voorspel
prediction *n* voorspelling
predisposition *n* voorliefde
prefabricated house *n* opslaanhuis
preface *n* voorwoord; inleiding; voorberig; voorrede; *vb* inlei
prefect *n* prefek
prefer *vb* voortrek
preferable *adj* verkieslik
preferably *adv* liefs
preference *n* voorkeur; voorliefde; voorrang
prefix *n* voorvoegsel
pregnancy *n* swangerskap
pregnant *adj* swanger; **make —** *vb* bevrug
prehistoric(al) *adj* voorhistories; prehistories
prejudice *n* vooroordeel
prejudiced *adj* bevooroordeel(d); partydig; vooringenome
preliminary *adj* voorlopig; preliminêr; **— bout** *n* voorgeveg
prelude *n* voorspel
premature *adj* ontydig; voorbarig
premeditated *adj* voorbedag; opsetlik
premier *n* premier
premise (*or* **premiss**) *n* premis
premises *n* erf; perseel; (farm) opstal
premium *n* premie
premonition *n* voorgevoel
prenup *n* (*informal*) huweliksvoorwaardekontrak
prenuptial agreement *n* huweliksvoorwaardekontrak
prenuptial contract *n* huweliksvoorwaardekontrak
preoccupied *adj* ingedagte
preparation *n* voorbereiding; **—s** *npl* aanstaltes
prepare *vb* voorberei; berei; gereed maak; klaarmaak; aanmaak; brou
prepared *adj* paraat; gereed; ingerig; bereid; **— for** *adj* bedag
preparedness *n* weerbaarheid
prepay postage *vb* frankeer
preposition *n* voorsetsel
prerogative *n* voorreg
prescribe *vb* (medicine) voorskryf

prescribed *adj* voorgeskrewe
prescription *n* voorskrif; resep
presence *n* aanwesigheid; presensie; teenwoordigheid
present[1] *n* hede; *adj* aanwesig; huidige; lopend; onderhawig; **at —** *adv* hedendaags; tans; hede; **be — at** *vb* bywoon; **— everywhere** *adj* alomteenwoordig
present[2] *n* geskenk; *vb* aanbied; **— arms** *vb* aanslaan
present-day *adj* hedendaags
presentable *adj* presentabel; respektabel; toonbaar
presentation *n* oorhandiging; presentasie; voorstelling
presenter *n* promotor
presentiment *n* voorgevoel
presently *adv* aanstons; dalkies; strakkies; tans; weldra
preservation *n* behoud; preservasie
preserve *n* konfyt;*vb* bewaar
preserved *adj* ingelê
preside *vb* voorsit
president *n* president; voorsitter
press *vb* druk; pers; dring; (grapes) trap; **— against** *vb* aandruk; **— out** *vb* uitpers
pressing *adj* dringend
pressure *n* druk; aandrang; drang
pressure group *n* drukgroep
presumably *adv* vermoedelik
presume *vb* veronderste; vermoed; aanmatig
presumption *n* vermoede
presumptuous *adj* arrogant; vrypostig; waanwys
pretence *n* skyn; voorwendsel
pretend *vb* voorgee; veins; aanmatig; aanstel; huigel; simuleer
pretended *adj* geveins; gewaande; kamma
pretext *n* voorwendsel; uitvlug; jakkalsdraai
pretty *adj* mooi; fraai; net
prevail *vb* heers; geld
prevent *vb* keer; afweer
preventative *n* voorbehoedmiddel
previous *prep, adv, conj* voor
previously *adv* vroeër; tevore
prey *n* prooi; aas; *vb* aas

price *n* prys
price control *n* prysbeheer
price list *n* pryslys
priceless *adj* onwaardeerbaar
prick *n* prik; prikkel; steek
prickle *n* doring
prickly pear *n* turksvy
pride *n* hoogmoed; trots; (lions) trop
priest *n* pastoor; priester
priestess *n* priesteres
prig *n* wysneus
priggish *adj* pedanties
prim and proper *adj* preuts
primarily *adv* eers
primary *adj* oorspronklik; primêr; —
   education *n* primêre onderwys; —
   school *n* laerskool
prime *n* bloeityd; fleur; *adj* vernaamste;
   belangrikste; (minister) eerste
prime minister *n* premier
primeval *adj* oeroud
primitive *adj* primitief; — **man** *n* oermens
prince *n* prins; vors
princely *adj* vorstelik; grootskeeps
princess *n* prinses
principal *n* hoof; prinsipaal; hoofonderwyser; kapitaal
principal sentence *n* hoofsin
principle *n* beginsel; grondbeginsel;
   prinsipe
print *n* prent; drukskrif; druk; *vb* afdruk; druk
printed matter *n* drukwerk
printer *n* boekdrukker; drukker
printer's error *n* drukfout
printing *n* drukwerk; drukkuns
printing press *n* drukpers; pers
printing works *n* drukkery
priority *n* prioriteit
prism *n* prisma
prison *n* tronk; gevangenis
prison warder *n* tronkbewaarder
prisoner *n* gevangene; prisonier; tronkvoël
prisoner of war *n* krygsgevangene
privacy *n* afsondering
private *adj* privaat; vertroulik; onderhands; partikulier; geheim; *n* (rank)
   weerman
private school *n* privaatskool

private sector *n* privaatsektor
privatization *n* privatisering
privatize *vb* privatiseer
privilege *n* voorreg; bevoorreg
privileged *adj* bevoorreg
prize *n* prys; toekenning; buit
prize money *n* prysgeld
prize-giving *n* prysuitdeling
pro-choice *adj* (pressure group)
   pro-keuse
pro-life *adj* (pressure group) pro-lewe
proactive *adj* proaktief
probable *adj* vermoedelik; waarskynlik
probably *adv* vermoedelik
probation *n* proeftyd
probation officer *n* proefbeampte
probe *n* ondersoek
problem *n* probleem; vraagstuk; —
   area *n* knelpunt
procedure *n* prosedure
proceed *vb* aangaan; voortgaan; vooruitgaan; — **to** *vb* begeef
proceeding *n* prosedure
proceedings *npl* verrigtinge
proceeds *n* opbrings
process *n* proses; *vb* verwerk
procession *n* optog; prosessie; stoet
proclaim *vb* afkondig; proklameer; uitvaardig; verkondig
proclamation *n* afkondiging; proklamasie
procure *vb* besorg; kry
produce *n* maak; opbrings; produk; *vb*
   gee
producer *n* produsent
product *n* produk; voortbrengsel; —
   launch *n* promosie
production *n* produksie
productive *adj* produktief
productivity *n* produktiwiteit
profession *n* ambag; beroep; professie
professional *adj* professioneel; —
   rugby *n* vertoonrugby
professor *n* professor; hoogleraar
profile *n* profiel
profiling *n* profilering
profit *n* wins; profyt; baat; nut; — **by**
   vb profiteer
profit margin *n* winsgrens
profitable *adj* winsgewend; nuttig;
   voordelig

profound *adj* diep; diepsinnig
profoundly *adv* deerlik
progeny *n* nakomelingskap
program *n* (computing) program
programme *n* (radio, TV, etc.) program
programmer *n* (computing) programmeerder
progress *n* vordering; verloop; voortgang; vooruitgang; *vb* toeneem; vooruitgaan; — slowly *vb* sukkel
progressive *adj* progressief; vooruitstrewend
prohibit *vb* verbied
prohibited *adj* verbode
prohibition *n* verbod
project *n* projek; plan; ontwerp; *vb* projekteer
projectile *n* projektiel
projecting *adj* uitstaande
projection *n* projeksie
prolific *adj* vrugbaar
prologue *n* proloog
prolong *vb* uitrek; verleng
prominent *adj* uitstaande
promise *n* belofte; verbintenis; gelofte; *vb* beloof
promising *adj* hoopvol
promote *vb* verhoog; bevorder
promoter *n* promotor
promotion *n* promosie; verhoging
promotor *n* voorstander
prompt *adj* direk; pront; skielik; *vb* voorsê
prompter *n* souffleur
promptly *adv* direk; pront; skielik; stiptelik
prone to *adj* geneig
prong *n* tand
pronoun *n* voornaamwoord
pronunciation *n* uitspraak
proof *n* bewys; proef
prop *n* skraag; stut
propaganda *n* propaganda
propagate *vb* voortplant
propel *vb* stu
propeller *n* skroef
propensity *n* geneigdheid
proper *adj* behoorlik; betaamlik; gepas; geskik; paslik; passend; welvoeglik; eintlik
proper name *n* eienaam

properly *adv* behoorlik; goed
property *n* besitting; boedel; effekte; eiendom; eienskap; goed; hawe
prophecy *n* profesie; voorspelling; godspraak
prophesy *vb* profeteer; voorspel
prophet *n* profeet; siener
prophetess *n* profetes
prophylactic *n* voorbehoedmiddel
proportion *n* proporsie; verhouding
proportional *adj* proporsioneel
proportionate *adj* eweredig
proposal *n* aanbod; aansoek; voorstel
propose *vb* voorstel; opper
proposed *adj* voorgenome; voorgestel
proposer *n* voorsteller
proposition *n* voorstel
proprietor *n* eienaar; grondbesitter; grondeienaar
proprietress *n* eienares
prosaic *adj* prosaïes
prosaically *adv* prosaïes
prose *n* prosa
prosecute *vb* vervolg
prosecution *n* vervolging
prosecutor *n* aanklaer; vervolger
prospect *n* vooruitsig; verskiet; *vb* prospekteer
prospective *adj* aankomend
prospector *n* prospekteerder
prospectus *n* prospektus
prosper *vb* geluk; dy
prosperity *n* voorspoed; welvaart; geluk
prosperous *adj* florerend; voorspoedig; welvarend
prostitute *n* prostituut; straatvrou; straatvlinder
prostitution *n* ontug
protea *n* suikerbos
protect *vb* skut; begunstig
protection *n* hoede; skut; skerm
protective clothing *n* skermdrag
protégé *n* beskermeling
protein *n* proteïen(e)
protest *n* protes; *vb* protesteer
protocol *n* protokol
prototype *n* prototipe
protract *vb* rek
protrude *vb* peul; uitpeul; uitsteek
proud *adj* hoogmoedig; hooghartig; hovaardig; fier; groots; trots

prove *vb* betoog; bewys; staaf; **— true** *vb* bewaarheid

proverb *n* spreekwoord; spreuk

provide *vb* voorsien; aanskaf; verskaf; verstrek

provided that *conj* mits

province *n* provinsie

provincial *adj* provinsiaal

provision *n* voorraad; voorsorg

provisional *adj* voorlopig

provisions *npl* lewensmiddele

provocation *n* tarting

provoke *vb* uittart

prow *n* (ship) boeg

proximity *n* nabyheid

proxy *n* volmag; gevolmagtigde

prudence *n* omsigtigheid; versigtigheid

prudent *adj* versigtig; wys

prudish *adj* preuts

prune[1] *n* pruimedant; pruim

prune[2] *vb* afsny; snoei

pruning shears *n* snoeiskêr

prussian blue *n, adj* pruisiesblou

prussic acid *n* blousuur; pruisiessuur

pry *vb* spioeneer; **— into** *vb* inloer

psalm *n* psalm

pseudo *adv* kamma

pseudonym *n* pseudoniem; skuilnaam

psyche *n* psige

psychiatrist *n* psigiater

psychological *adj* sielkundig

psychologist *n* sielkundige; psigoloog

psychology *n* sielkunde; psigologie

psychopath *n* sielsieke

psychopathic *adj* sielsiek

psychosis *n* psigose

pub *n* herberg; kantien; tappery

puberty *n* puberteit

public *n* publiek; *adj* openbaar; publiek; **make —** *vb* openbaar; **— demonstration** *n* protesoptog; **— sale** *n* veiling; **— worship** *n* erediens; **—-private partnership** *n* openbare-privaat vennootskap

public house *n* herberg; kroeg

public prosecutor *n* staatsaanklaer

public relations *n* openbare betrekkings

public sector *n* owerheidsektor

public speaking *n* redevoering

publican *n* tollenaar

publication *n* publikasie; verskyning

publicity *n* publisiteit

publicly *adv* openlik

publish *vb* publiseer; uitgee; (banns) afkondig; **be —ed** *vb* verskyn

publisher *n* uitgewer

pudding *n* poeding

puddle *n* plas; poel

puff *vb* blaas

puff adder *n* pofadder

pugnacious *adj* strydlustig; veglustig

pull *n* ruk; trek; haal; *vb* ruk; trek; haal; aantrek; **— about** *vb* rondtrek; **— away** *vb* wegtrek; **— down** *vb* omruk; **— loose** *vb* lostrek; **— out** *vb* uithaal; uittrek; **— through** *vb* deurtrek; (illness) deurstaan; **— tight** *vb* vastrek; **— up** *vb* stilhou; ophaal; intoom

puller *n* trekker

pulley *n* katrol

pulmonary tuberculosis *n* longtering

pulp *n* moes

pulpit *n* kansel; preekstoel

pulpy *adj* voos

pulse *n* pols

pulverize *vb* vergruis; vermorsel

pumice stone *n* puimsteen

pump *n* pomp

pumpkin *n* pampoen; **— fritter** *n* pampoenkoekie

pun *n* woordspeling

punch *n* vuisslag

punctual *adj* presies; pront; stip

punctuality *n* stiptheid

punctually *adv* presies; pront; stiptelik

punctuation *n* interpunksie; punktuasie

punctuation mark *n* leesteken

puncture *n* lek; prik

punctured *adj* (tyre) defek

pungent *adj* pikant

punish *vb* straf; bestraf

punishable *adj* strafbaar

punishment *n* straf; bestraffing; kastyding

punter *n* (horse racing) wedder

pupa *n* papie

pupil[1] *n* leerling; skolier; skoolkind

pupil[2] *n* (eye) pupil; kyker

puppet *n* marionet; pop

puppy *n* hondjie; **— love** *n* kalwerliefde

purchase *n* inkopie; inkoop; koop; *vb* inkoop; aankoop; koop
pure *adj* vlek(ke)loos; onvervals; ongerep; rein; kuis; puur; skoon; louter; — **bred** *adj* raseg
purely *adv* louter
purgative *n* purgeermiddel
purgatory *n* vagevuur
purge *vb* purgeer; suiwer
purification *n* reiniging
purify *vb* louter; reinig; suiwer
purity *n* reinheid
purple *n, adj* pers; purper
purpose *n* doel
purr *vb* spin
purse *n* beurs
pursue *vb* vervolg; agtervolg
pursuit *n* vervolging
pus *n* etter
push *vb* druk; skuif; stoot; dring; — **aside** *vb* verdring; — **in** *vb* indruk; — **on** *vb* opdring; — **off** *vb* afstoot; — **out** *vb* uitstoot; — **through** *vb* deurdryf
put *vb* plaas; lê; — **at a disadvantage** *vb* agterstel; — **in order** *vb* orden; verhelp; — **into** *vb* insteek; — **into**

practice *vb* toepas; — **to music** *vb* toonset; — **off** *vb* uitstel; — **on** *vb* aansmeer; oplê; aansteek; (one's clothes) aantrek; aankry; (a belt) gord; (airs) aanstel; (on oath) beëdig; — **out** *vb* doof; (fire) blus; — **over** *vb* oorsit; — **right** *vb* regmaak; — **round** *vb* omsit; — **to shame** *vb* beskaam; — **together** *vb* saamstel; — **up** *vb* opslaan; opsteek; (for sale) opveil; — **up with** *vb* verlief neem
put-up job *n* deurgestoke kaart
putrefaction *n* verrotting
putrefy *vb* vrot
putrid *adj* vrot
putt *n* set; *vb* set
putter *n* setter
putty *n* stopverf
puzzle *n* raaisel; probleem
puzzling *adj* raaiselagtig; — **question** *n* strikvraag
pygmy *n* pigmee; dwerg
pyjamas *npl* pajama; slaapklere
pylon *n* kragmas
pyramid *n* piramide
python *n* luislang

Q

quack *vb* kwaak
quad bike *n* vierwiel; vierwieler; vier-wielfiets; vierwielmotorfiets
quadrangle *n* vierhoek
quadrille *n* kadriel
quagga *n* kwagga
quail *n* kwartel
qualification *n* kwalifikasie
qualified *adj* bevoeg
qualify *vb* kwalifiseer; bekwaam
qualifying *adj* bepalend
quality *n* kwaliteit; gehalte; hoedanig-heid; eienskap; allooi
quandary *n* verknorsing
quantity *n* kwantiteit; hoeveelheid
quarantine *n* kwarantyn
quarrel *n* rusie; geskil; twis; geding; *vb* kibble; twis
quarrelling *n* gekibbel
quarrelsome *adj* strydlustig; twisgie-rig; veglustig; kyfagtig
quarry *n* steengroef
quart *n* kwart
quarter *n* kwart; kwartaal; buurt; (of an hour) kwartier; (of an orange) skyf; *vb* inkwartier
quarterly *adv* driemaandeliks
quarters *npl* (military) kwartiere
quartet *n* kwartet
quartz *n* kwarts
quasi *adv* kamma
quaver *vb* tril
quay *n* kaai
queen *n* koningin
quell *vb* onderdruk; (riot) blus
query *n* navraag; vraag; vraagteken; *vb* vra
question *n* vraag; vraagstuk; kwessie; *vb* vra; betwyfel

question mark *n* vraagteken
questionnaire *n* vraelys
queue *n* tou; *vb* tou; — jumper *n* in-drukker
quibbling *n* haarklowery
quick *adj* gou; vinnig; spoedig; haastig; skielik; rats; vlug; fiks; fluks; snel; — as lightning *adv* bliksemsnel
quick-tempered *adj* opvlieënd
quick-witted *adj* spitsvondig
quickly *adv* gou; skielik; spoedig; fluks; gou-gou
quicksand *n* dryfsand; kwiksand; welsand
quid pro quo *n* iets vir iets
quiet *adj* kalm; rustig; stemmig; vredig; gerus; *n* rus; stilte; *vb* gerusstel
quietly *adv* saggies; stilletjies
quill *n* pen
quilt *n* deken; sprei
quince *n* kweper
quinine *n* kinien
quit *vb* (smoking, etc.) opgee
quite *adv* heeltemal; — at ease *adj* doodgerus; — empty *adj* dolleeg; — ready *adv* kant en klaar; — sim-ple *adj* doodeenvoudig; — still *adj* botstil; — strange *adj* wildvreemd
quits *adj* kiets
quiver *n* (for arrows) pylkoker
quiz *n* vasvrawedstryd; *vb* vasvra
quoit *n* werpskyf
quorum *n* kworum
quota *n* kwota
quotation *n* kwotasie; prysopgawe; no-tering
quotation marks *npl* aanhalingstekens
quote *vb* kwoteer; noteer; siteer
quotient *n* kwosiënt

R

rabbi *n* rabbi
rabbit *n* konyn
rabble *n* gepeupel; gespuis; skorriemorrie; uitskot
rabies *n* hondsdolheid
race[1] *n* ras; geslag; — relations *npl* volkereverhoudinge
race[2] *n* ren; (athletics) wedloop; (cars, horses) wedren; *vb* hardloop; nael
racecourse *n* re(i)siesbaan; renbaan
racehorse *n* re(i)siesperd; renperd
races *npl* re(i)sies
racing *n* gejaag
racing car *n* renmotor
racing driver *n* renjaer
racism *n* rassehaat; rassisme
racist *adj* rassis; *n* rassehater
rack *n* rak
racket *n* raket
racketeer *n* rampokker
radar *n* radar
radiant *adj* glansryk
radiate *vb* straal; uitstraal
radiation *n* uitstraling
radiator *n* verkoeler; radiator
radical *adj* radikaal
radio *n* radio; — listener *n* luisteraar; — station *n* uitsaaistasie
radioactive *adj* radioaktief
radiologist *n* radioloog
radish *n* radys
radius *n* radius; straal
raffle *n* lotery; *vb* loot
raft *n* vlot
rafter *n* balk; hanebalk;spar
rag *n* flenter; lap; flard
rag doll *n* lappop
rag procession *n* (student) jooloptog
rage *n* woede; *vb* bulder
rags *npl* toiings
raid *n* inval; strooptog
rail *n* leuning; spoor
rail car *n* (passenger) passasierswa
railing *n* reling; hek
railroad *n* spoorweg
railway *n* spoor; spoorweg
railway bridge *n* spoorbrug

railway carriage *n* (passenger) passasierswa
railway line *n* spoorlyn; treinspoor
railway sleeper *n* lêer; dwarslêer
railway timetable *n* spoorboek
railway track *n* treinspoor
rain *n* reën; natterigheid
rainwater *n* reënwater
rainbow *n* reënboog
rainy *adj* reënerig
rainy season *n* reëntyd
raise *vb* hef; ophef; teel; verhoog; aankweek; — objections *vb* aanvoer; — dust *vb* stuif
raisin *n* rosyn(tjie)
rake *n* hark; swierbol; *vb* hark; ophark
rally *n* saamtrek; tydren
ram *n* (sheep) ram; (battering) stormram; *vb* stamp; — down *vb* vasstamp
ramble *vb* swerf; rondswerf
rambler *n* omswerwer; (botanical) klimplant
rambling *adj* omswerwend; (speech) onsamehangend
ramification *n* vertakking
ramify *vb* vertak
rampart *n* verskansing
rancid *adj* galsterig
rancour *n* wrok
rand *n* rand
random *adj* toevallig; at — *adv* lukraak
random sample *n* steekproef
range *n* afstand; speling
rank *n* rang; — and file *n* die laer rangs
ransack *vb* plunder; deursnuffel
ransom *n* losprys; losgeld; *vb* loskoop
ranunculus *n* ranonkel
rap *n* klop; tik
rape *n* verkragting; *vb* verkrag
rapeseed oil *n* raapolie
rapid *adj* gou; snel; — fire *n* snelvuur
rapprochement *n* toenadering
rapture *n* verrukking; vervoering
rare *adj* seldsaam
rarefied *adj* yl
rarely *adv* selde
rarity *n* rariteit

rascal *n* karnallie; rakker; skelm; skurk; deugniet; swernoot; bokker
rash[1] *adj* ondeurdag; onverskillig; roekeloos; voorbarig; ligvaardig; onbedagsaam; onbekook
rash[2] *n* (skin) huiduitslag; uitslag
rashness *n* oormoed
rasp *n* rasper; *vb* rasper
raspberry *n* framboos
rat *n* rot
rat poison *n* rottekruid
rate *n* koers; tarief; vrag; *vb* taks; — **of exchange** *n* wisselkoers; — **of interest** *n* rentekoers
rates *npl* belasting
rather *adv* taamlik; eer; bietjie
ratio *n* verhouding
ration *n* rantsoen
rational *adj* rasioneel
ratsbane *n* rottekruid
rattan *n* rottang
rattle *n* klap; ratel; *vb* rammel; ratel
rattlesnake *n* ratelslang
rattling *n* geroggel
rave *n* raasparty; — **about** *vb* dweep
raven *n* raaf
ravine *n* kloof; ravyn
raving *adj* rasend; — **mad** *adj* stapelgek
raw *adj* rou; guur
raw material *n* grondstof
rawhide shield *n* skildvel
ray *n* straal; — **of light** *n* ligstraal
raze to the ground *vb* gelykmaak
razor *n* skeermes
re-echo *vb* naklink
re-elect *vb* herkies
re-make *vb* oormaak
recommend *vb* aanprys
reach *vb* bereik; reik; bykom; strek; — **high** *vb* (rugby) rank; — **out** *vb* uitstrek
react *vb* reageer
reaction *n* reaksie
read *vb* lees; aflees; — **aloud** *vb* voorlees; — **over** *vb* nalees; oorkyk; — **through** *vb* oorlees
readable *adj* leesbaar
reader *n* (book) leesboek
readily *adv* geredelik
reading *n* lesing; — **matter** *n* lektuur

reading book *n* leesboek
readjust *vb* verstel
ready *adj* paraat; gereed; bereid; klaar; gewillig; willig; — **for battle** *adj* strydvaardig; — **money** *n* kontant
ready-made *adj* pasklaar; gemaak
real *adj* eg; waar; regtig; eintlik; reël; werklik; wesen(t)lik; effektief
realistic *adj* realisties
reality *n* waarheid
reality TV *n* realisteit-TV
realize *vb* besef; realiseer
really *adv* regtig; werklik; eintlik; bra; feitlik; inderdaad
realm *n* ryk
ream *n* (paper) riem
reap *vb* oes; maai
reaper *n* maaier
rear *n* agterent; stert; *vb* grootmaak; teel; (a child) opbring
rearguard *n* agterhoede
rearview mirror *n* truspieël
reason *n* rede; oorsaak; grond; aanleiding
reasonable *adj* redelik; skiklik; ordentlik; bestaanbaar; billik
reasoning *n* redenering
rebate *n* vermindering; rabat
rebel *n* rebel; oproermaker; *vb* rebelleer
rebellion *n* opstand; rebellie
rebellious *adj* oproerig; opstandig; we(d)erspannig; weerbarstig
rebirth *n* wedergeboorte
reboot *vb* (computing) herlaai
reborn *adj* herbore; herskape
rebound *vb* terugkaats
rebuild *vb* herbou; verbou
rebuilding *n* herbou
rebuke *n* bestraffing; *vb* berispe; verwyt; roskam
recall *vb* herroep; onthou
receipt *n* kwitansie; ontvangs
receive *vb* ontvang; aanneem
receiver *n* ontvanger; — **of revenue** *n* ontvanger van inkomste
recent *adj* onlangs; laas; nuut
recently *adv* onlangs; laas
reception *n* onthaal; ontvangs; resepsie
receptionist *n* ontvangsdame
receptive *adj* ontvanklik
recess *n* reses; speeltyd

recipe *n* resep
reciprocal *adj* wederkerig; wedersyds
recital *n* voordrag
recitation *n* deklamasie; resitasie; voordrag
recite *vb* deklameer; opsê; resiteer; voordra
reckless *adj* ligvaardig; onverskillig; roekeloos; oormoedig; — **person** *n* waaghals
reckon *vb* reken
reckoner *n* rekenaar
reclaim *vb* aanwen; terugeis
recluse *n* kluisenaar
recognizable *adj* kenbaar
recognize *vb* eien; herken; ken; uitken
recoil *n* skop; terugslag; *vb* terugskrik; skop; — **from** *vb* deins
recollect *vb* bedink; herinner
recommend *vb* aanbeveel; aanraai
recommendation *n* aanbeveling
recompense *n* beloning; *vb* beloon
reconcile *vb* verenig; versoen
reconciliation *n* rekonsiliasie; toenadering
recondition *vb* opdoen
reconnoitre *vb* verken; verspied
reconquer *vb* herower
reconsider *vb* hersien
reconstruct *vb* rekonstrueer
reconstruction *n* herbou; rekonstruksie
record *n* aantekening; register; rekord; *vb* aanteken
recorder *n* griffier
recount *vb* oortel
recover *vb* herstel; aansterk; (debt) verhaal; (debt) invorder
recoverable *adj* invorderbaar
recovery *n* beterskap; genesing; herstel
recreate *vb* herskep; omskep
recreation *n* ontspanning; uitspanning
recreational facilities *n* ontspanningsgeriewe
recruit *n* rekruut; *vb* aanwerf
recruitment *n* werwing
rectangle *n* reghoek
rectangular *adj* reghoekig
rectify *vb* regstel
rector *n* rektor
rectory *n* pastorie

recycle *vb* herwin
red *n, adj* rooi
red roman *n* (fish) roman
red tape *n* burokrasie; rompslomp
red-chested cuckoo *n* piet-my-vrou
red-hot *adj* gloeiend; **be** — *vb* gloei
redbush tea *n* rooibostee
redeem *vb* loskoop; (loan) aflos
redress *n* herstel; verhaal
reduce *vb* verklein; reduseer; herlei; verlaag; afbring; — **expenses** *vb* besuinig
reduction *n* verlaging; vermindering; reduksie; afslag
redundant *adj* oorbodig; oortollig
reed *n* biesie; riet
reef *n* rant; rif
reel[1] *n ;* tolletjie; (cotton) rolletjie
reel[2] *vb* duisel; slinger
refer *vb* refereer; — **to** *vb* verwys
referee *n* skeidsregter; (testimonial) referent
reference *n* aanbeveling; getuigskrif; referensie; verwysing
reference book *n* naslaanwerk
reference number *n* verwysnommer; verwysingsnommer
reference work *n* naslaanwerk
referendum *n* referendum
refine *vb* louter; suiwer; veredel; verfyn; (oil, sugar) raffineer
refinery *n* (oil, sugar) raffinadery
reflect *vb* afspieël; bedink; besin; dink; nadink; terugkaats; weerkaats; weerspieël; wik
reflection *n* gepeins; nabetragting; oordenking; weerkaatsing; weerskyn
reflector *n* kaatser; trukaatser
reform *vb* hervorm; *n* hervorming
reformation *n* hervorming
Reformation *n* Kerkhervorming
reformed *adj* gereformeer
refractory *adj* we(d)erspannig
refrain *n* refrein
refresh *vb* lawe; opfris; verfris; verkwik
refreshing *adj* verfrissend; verkwikkend
refreshment *n* laafnis; lafenis; verfrissing; verversing
refrigerate *vb* verkoel
refrigerator *n* koelkas; yskas; — **truck** *n* koeltrok

refuge *n* heenkome; toevlug; toevlug(soord)
refugee *n* uitgewekene; vlugteling
refusal *n* weiering
refuse[1] *n* afval; uitskot
refuse[2] *vb* afslaan; — **admittance** *vb* afwys
refute *vb* weerlê; teenwerp; ontsenu
regain *vb* herwin
regal *adj* koninklik
regale *vb* vergas
regard *n* agting; eerbied; respek; waardering; *vb* beskou
regarding *prep* betreffende; insake
regardless *adv* ongeag; — **of** *adj* ongeag
regards *n* groete
regatta *n* roeiwedstryd
regenerate *vb* herskep
regeneration *n* regenerasie; wedergeboorte
regent *n* regent
regiment *n* regiment
region *n* streek; landstreek; geweste; kontrei; oord
register *n* register; sleutel; *vb* aanteken
registered *adj* aangeteken; — **voter** *n* stemgeregtigde
registrar *n* registrateur; griffier
registration *n* registrasie
regret *n* spyt; leedwese; *vb* betreur; berou; spyt
regular *adj* gereeld; reëlmatig; pront; gelykmatig; gelykvloeiend; gelykvormig; gestadig
regularly *adv* pront
regulate *vb* reël; reguleer
regulation *n* regulasie; bepaling; verordening; reëling
regulations *npl* reglement
rehabilitate *vb* rehabiliteer
rehabilitation *n* rehabilitasie
rehearsal *n* repetisie
rehearse *vb* instudeer; repeteer
reign *n* regering; *vb* regeer; troon
reiki *n* reiki
reimburse *vb* vergoed
rein *n* toom; leisel; teuel; teuelriem; — **in** *vb* intoom
reincarnation *n* reïnkarnasie
reindeer *n* rendier

reinforce *vb* versterk
reinforced concrete *n* gewapende beton
reinforcement *n* versterking
reject *vb* afkeur; afwys; verwerp; afstem; verdoem; verstoot
rejoice *vb* jubel; juig
rejoicing *n* gejuig
rejuvenate *vb* verjong
relapse *n* insinking; *vb* insink
relate *vb* verhaal; vertel; — **to** *vb* verbind aan
related *adj* aanverwant; verwant
relation *n* verwant; betrekking
relations *npl* familie
relationship *n* verwantskap
relative *n* bloedverwant; *adj* betreklik
relatively *adv* betreklik
relativity *n* relatiwiteit
relax *vb* ontspan; verslap
relaxation *n* ontspanning
release *n* ontslag; vrylating; *vb* los
relegate *vb* relegeer
relentless *adj* onverbiddelik
relevant *adj* ter sake
reliability *n* geloofwaardigheid
reliable *adj* betroubaar; vertroubaar; vertroud; getroue; geloofwaardig; deugdelik; — **person** *n* staatmaker
relic *n* kuriositeit
relief *n* verligting; uitkoms(te); laafnis; lafenis; ontlasting; ontsetting; reliëf; versagting
relieve *vb* verlig; aflos; lenig; ontlas
religion *n* geloof; godsdiens
religious *adj* godsdienstig
relinquish *vb* afsien
relish *n* smaak
reluctance *n* onwilligheid
reluctant *adj* onwillig
reluctantly *adv* skoorvoetend
rely on *vb* steun; vertrou
remain *vb* oorskiet; aanbly; — **behind** *vb* agterbly
remainder *n* oorskiet; oorblyfsel; oorskot; res; restant
remains *npl* oorskiet; oorskot
remark *n* aanmerking; opmerking; uitlating; *vb* opmerk
remarkable *adj* merkwaardig; opmerklik
remarry *vb* hertrou

remedial *adj* remediërend

remedy *n* middel; geneesmiddel; teenmiddel; verhaal; *vb* remedieer

remember *vb* herinner; onthou; gedenk

remembrance *n* herinnering; aandenking; nagedagtenis; gedagtenis; geheue; heugenis

reminder *n* aanmaning

reminiscence *n* herinnering

remnant *n* oorblyfsel

remodel *vb* hervorm

remorse *n* berou; gewetenswroeging; wroeging

remote *adj* afgeleë; ver; verwyder(d)

removal *n* oorplasing; verhuising; verplasing; verwydering; — **van** *n* verhuiswa

remove *vb* trek; oorplaas; — **scum** *vb* afskuim

render speechless *vb* verstom

renegade *n* afvallige; renegaat

renew *vb* vernuwe; hernuwe

renewal *n* vernuwing; hernuwing

rennet *n* kaasstremsel

renounce *vb* versaak

renouncement *n* versaking

renovate *vb* opknap; vernuwe; hernuwe

renovation *n* opknapping; vernuwing; hernuwing

renown *n* roem; vermaardheid

renowned *adj* roemryk; vermaard

rent *n* huur; huurprys; pag; *vb* pag

rent money *n* huurgeld

rental *n* huurgeld

renunciation *n* afstanddoening

reopen *vb* heropen

reorganize *vb* reorganiseer

repair *n* herstel; reparasie; *vb* regmaak; herstel

repatriate *n* repatrieer

repay *vb* vergeld

repeal *vb* ophef; afskaf; (act) intrek

repeat *vb* herhaal; napraat; nasê; oorsê; repeteer

repeatedly *adv* herhaaldelik; oor-en-oor; telkens

repel *vb* afslaan; afstoot; terugdryf

repent *vb* berou

repentance *n* berou; inkeer

repetition *n* herhaling; repetisie

replace *vb* vervang

replay *n* (TV) trubeeld

replenish *vb* aanvul

reply *n* antwoord; *vb* beantwoord; antwoord

report *n* gerug; rapport; verslag; skoot; *vb* berig; meld; aangee

reporter *n* rapporteur; referent; verslaggewer; (news) beriggewer

repose *n* rus; *vb* rus; uitrus

reprehensible *adj* laakbaar

represent *vb* verteenwoordig; verbeel

representative *n* verteenwoordiger

reprimand *n* opbrander; *vb* invlieg

reprint *n* herdruk; *vb* herdruk

reproach *n* verwyt; *vb* smaad; verwyt

reprobate *n* verworpeling; *adj* verworpe

reproduce *n* afdruk

reproduction *n* afdruk; reproduksie; weergawe

reproof *n* teregwysing; verwyt

reprove *vb* berispe; teregwys

reptile *n* reptiel

republic *n* republiek

reputation *n* eer; faam; reputasie

reputed *adj* vermeende

request *n* aansoek; aanvraag; versoek; vraag; *vb* aanvra; versoek

require *vb* behoef; vereis; verg

required *adj* benodig

requirement *n* vereiste

requirements *npl* benodigdhede

requisite *n* vereiste; *adj* nodig; vereis

requisition *n* rekwissie; *vb* opkommandeer

requite *vb* vergeld

rescue *n* redding; uitredding; *vb* bevry

rescuer *n* redder

research *n* ondersoek; *vb* navors

resemblance *n* gelykenis; ooreenkoms

resemble *vb* lyk

resentful *adj* haatdraend; wrewelig

resentment *n* wrewel

reservation *n* reservering; resessie; voorbehoud

reserve *n* reserwe; voorbehoud; *vb* reserveer

reserved *adj* agterhoudend; ingetoë; terughoudend

reserved *adj* eenselwig

reservist *n* reservis

reservoir *n* dam
reside *vb* bewoon
residence *n* woning; woonhuis; residensie; standplaas; verblyf; (government) setel
residency *n* residensie
resident *n* inwoner; bewoner; ingesetene
residential area *n* woonbuurt
residue *n* afsaksel; oorskot; besinksel
resign *vb* bedank; ontslagneem; neerlê; aftree; **— oneself** *vb* berus
resignation *n* ontslag
resigned *adj* gelate; onderworpe
resin *n* harpuis
resist *n* verset; verweer; *vb* teenstaan; verset; verweer
resistance *n* teenstand; verset; verweer; weerstand
resole *vb* versool
resolute *adj* ferm; resoluut; vasberade
resolution *n* resolusie; besluit
resolve *n* voorneme; *vb* voorneem; besluit
resonance *n* weerklank
resort to *vb* begeef
resound *vb* naklink; weerkaats
resource *n* hulpbron
resourceful *adj* vindingryk
respect *n* eerbied; aansien; opsig; *vb* hoogag; eerbiedig; **in — of** *prep* ten opsigte van
respectable *adj* respektabel; eerbaar; fatsoenlik; agtenswaardig
respectful *adj* eerbiedig
respective *adj* onderskeie
respectively *adv* onderskeidelik
respiration *n* asemhaling
respirator *n* respirator; gasmasker
respite *n* uitstel
respondent *n* gedaagde
responsible *adj* toerekenbaar; verantwoordelik; **— for** *adj* aanspreeklik
rest[1] *n* rus; stilstand; (music) rus; *vb* uitrus
rest[2] *n* oorskiet; res
rest camp *n* ruskamp
restaurant *n* restourant
restful *adj* rustig
restitute *vb* restitueer
restitution *n* restitusie; teruggawe

restless *adj* rusteloos; onrustig; ongedurig; woelig; **be —** *vb* woel
restlessness *n* onrus
restoration *n* restitusie; restorasie
restore *vb* restitueer
restrain *vb* inhou; beteuel; bedwing; intoom; matig; opkrop; temper; weerhou
restrained *adj* matig
restraint *n* bedwang; matigheid; selfbedwang
restrict *vb* inperk
restriction *n* beperking; inperking; **— password** *n* (iPhone, etc.) beperkingskode
result *n* uitslag; resultaat; uitkoms(te); gevolg; nasleep; effek; slotsom; uitvloeisel; uitwerking; vrug; *vb* ontspruit
results *npl* vrugte
resume *vb* hervat; vervat
resurrection *n* opstanding; we(d)eropstanding; herrysenis
retail price *n* kleinhandelprys
retail trade *n* kleinhandel
retain *vb* behou; wegsteek
retaliation *n* vergelding; wedervergelding
retard *vb* vertraag
retardation *n* vertraging
retention *n* behoud
retina *n* netvlies
retinue *n* stoet; trein; sleep
retire *vb* aftree; uittree
retired *adj* gewese; gepensioeneer; rustend
retirement *n* aftrede
retrace *vb* teruggaan
retract *vb* herroep; terugtrek
retread *vb* versool
retreat *n* aftog; skuilplek; terugtog; *vb* retireer; terugtrek
retrench *vb* besnoei
retrenchment *n* inkrimping
retribution *n* vergelding
retrieve *vb* herwin
retrospect *n* terugblik
retrospection *n* terugblik
retrovirus *n* retrovirus
return *n* terugkoms; terugkeer; we(d)erkoms; retoer; berig; staat; *vb*

terugkom; terugkeer; terugbring; (love) beantwoord; **— fire** *vb* terugskiet

return journey *n* retoereis; terugreis; heen-en-weertjie

return ticket *n* retoerkaartjie

returning officer *n* stemopnemer

returns *npl* ontvangs

reunion *n* reünie; hereniging

reunite *vb* herenig

revamp *vb* opknap

reveal *vb* openbaar; onthul; ontsluier; uitbring

revelation *n* ontdekking

revenge *n* weerwraak; wraak; *vb* wreek

revenue *n* inkomste

reverberate *vb* weergalm

reverberation *n* weergalming

revere *vb* eerbiedig; vereer

reverend *adj* eerwaarde; weleerwaarde

reverent *adj* eerbiedig

reversal *n* omkeer

reverse *vb* omkeer; *n* teenslag; terugslag; **— a car** *vb* omdraai; agteruit ry

reverse gear *n* trurat

reversed *adj* omgekeerd

review *n* hersiening; resensie; parade; *vb* beoordeel; resenseer

reviewer *n* resensent

revise *vb* hersien; nakyk; nasien

revised *adj* hersiene

revision *n* hersiening; revisie

revisit *vb* besoek weer

revival *n* herlewing; oplewing

revive *vb* bykom; herleef; opfris; opleef; oplewe

revoke *vb* herroep

revolt *n* oproer; opstand; rebellie; *vb* muit

revolting *adj* stuitend

revolution *n* omwenteling; revolusie

revolutionary *n* revolusionêr; *adj* revolusionêr; opstandig

revolve *vb* draai; wentel

revolver *n* rewolwer

reward *n* beloning; loon; vergelding; *vb* beloon; vergeld

rewrite *vb* oorskryf

rhapsody *n* rapsodie

rhebok *n* reebok

rhetorical *adj* retories

rheumatic *adj* rumaties; **— pains** *n* sinkings

rheumatic fever *n* sinkingskoors; rumatiekkoors

rheumatism *n* rumatiek

rhinoceros *n* renoster

rhombic skaapsteker *n* (snake) skaapsteker

rhubarb *n* rabarber

rhyme *n* rym; *vb* berym

rhythm *n* ritme

rhythmic(al) *adj* ritmies

rib *n* rib; ribbebeen

ribbon *n* band; lint

rice *n* rys

rich *adj* ryk; vermoënd; vet

riches *npl* rykdom; vermoë

rickety *adj* lendelam

rickshaw *n* riksja

ricochet *n* opslag; *vb* wegskram

riddle *n* raaisel

ride *n* rit; *vb* ry; **— in** *vb* inry

rider *n* ruiter

ridge *n* rand; rant; rug; (of a roof) vors

ridicule *vb* bespot

ridiculous *adj* belaglik; bespotlik; potsierlik; verspot

riding horse *n* ryperd

riding school *n* ryskool

riffraff *n* uitskot; uitvaagsel; gespuis; skorriemorrie

rifle *n* geweer; roer

rifle range *n* skietbaan

rigging *n* tuig

right *n* reg, aanspraak; *adj* korrek; reg; regter; haar; goed; *vb* regstel; **— over** *adv* dwarsoor; **— at the end** *adv* enduit; **— through** *adv* dwarsdeur; **to the —** *adv* regs; haarom

right hand *n* regterhand

right of succession *n* versterfreg

right of way *n* deurtog

right side *n* regterkant

right-angled *adj* haaks

right-handed *adj* regs

rightful *adj* regmatig

rightly *adv* reg; tereg

rights *n* regte

rigid *adj* onbuigbaar; stram; straf; styf

rim *n* kim

rind *n* bas; skil

ring[1] *n* ring; sindikaat; (boxing) kryt; **— finger** *n* ringvinger

ring[2] *n* bel; *vb* klink; **— up** *vb* opbel

ring-necked spitting cobra *n* rinkhals

ringleader *n* belhamel; voorbok

ringtone *n* luitoon

ringworm *n* omlope; douwurm

rinkhals *see* **ring-necked spitting cobra**

rinse *vb* afspoel; omspoel; spoel; uitspoel

riot *n* onluste; oproer

riot police *n* onluspolisie

riotous *adj* oproerig

rip *n* skeur; *vb* skeur; **— up** *vb* torring

ripe *adj* ryp

ripple *n* rimpel; riffel; *vb* rimpel; kabbel

rise *n* opdraand(e); opgang; opkoms; opslag; steilte; styging; *vb* opkom; opgaan; (yeast) gis

rising *n* opstyging; (sun) opkoms; **— ground** *n* opdraand(e); bult

risk *n* risiko; gevaar; kans; *vb* waag; durf

risky *adj* gevaarlik; riskant; gewaag; haglik; **— undertaking** *n* waagstuk

rissole *n* frikkadel

ritual *n* rituaal; ritueel; *adj* ritueel

rival *n* mededinger; konkurrent; *vb* meeding; wedywer; *adj* mededingend

rivalry *n* wedywer; konkurrensie

river *n* rivier

riverbed *n* bedding

riverbank *n* oewer; bank

rivet *n* nael; klinknael; *vb* klink

road *n* pad; baan; roete; weg

road deviation *n* padverlegging

road diversion *n* padverlegging

road rage *n* padwoede

road sign *n* padteken

roadblock *n* padblokkade; versperring; blokkade

roadhog *n* padvark

roadshow *n* bekendstellingstoer; inligtingstoer

roadworthy *adj* padwaardig

roam *vb* swerf; rondswerf; dool; dwaal

roar *vb* bries; brul

roaring *adj* gebrul; briesend

roast *vb* rooster; bak; (coffee) brand; **— meat** *n* braaivleis

roasted *adj* gebraai

rob *vb* buit; beroof; **— of** *vb* ontroof

robber *n* rower

robbery *n* diefstal; roof

robe *n* toga

robin redbreast *n* rooiborsie

robot *n* robot; (traffic light) verkeerslig

robust *adj* flink; fors

rock[1] *n* klip; rots

rock[2] *vb* hobbel; skommel

rock music *n* rock

rock rabbit *n* klipdassie; dassie

rockery *n* rotstuin

rocket *n* vuurpyl

rocket launcher *n* vuurpylrigter

rocking chair *n* rystoel

rocking horse *n* hobbelperd

rocky *adj* rotsagtig; steenagtig

rod *n* roede; staaf

rodent *n* knaagdier

rogue *n* skurk; skelm; kalant; karnallie; rakker; skobbejak; swernoot; vabond; bokker

role *n* rol

role play *n* rolvertolking

roll *n* bolletjie; rol; rolletjie; *vb* rol; wals; **— down** *vb* afrol; **— up** *vb* oprol

roller *n* rol; roller; wals

roller skates *npl* rolskaats

rolling *adj* golwend

romance *n* romanse

romantic *adj* romanties

romp *vb* baljaar; rinkink; stoei

rondavel *n* rondawel

roof *n* dak

roof garden *n* daktuin

roof of the mouth *n* verhemelte

roofless *adj* dakloos

rooibos tea *n* rooibostee

room *n* kamer; lokaal; plek; ruimte; vertrek

rooster *n* haan

root[1] *n* oorsprong; wortel

root[2]: **— out** *vb* uithaal; **— up** *vb* (soil) vroetel

root word *n* stamwoord

rope *n* koord; lyn; strop; tou; **— off** *vb* afsit

rosary *n* rosekrans

rose *n* roos

rose garden *n* roostuin

rose-coloured *n* rooskleurig
rosemary *n* roosmaryn
rosette *n* roset
roster *n* rooster
rot *vb* vrot
rotate *vb* ronddraai; roteer
rotation *n* omwenteling; rotasie
rotten *adj* vrot; verrot
rough *adj* skurf; ru; bars; hardhandig; onbehoue; onguur; globaal; stroef
roughly *adv* globaal; **— about** *adv* ongeveer
roughness *n* skurfte
round *adj* rond; *adv* om; *n* ronde; **— about** *adv* rondom; rondomtalie; **— off** *vb* afrond; **— which** *inter pron* waarom
round-about-way *n* ompad
round hut *n* rondawel
round robin *n* (sport) rondomtalie
rouse *vb* opwek; wek; aanwakker; **— up** *vb* beroer
rousing *adj* opwekkend
route *n* roete
routine *n* roetine; sleur; *adj* roetine
rove *vb* swerf
row[1] *n* twis; moles; spektakel; *vb* roei
row[2] *n* reeks; ry
rowdy *adj* baldadig
rower *n* roeier
rowing boat *n* roeibootjie
royal *adj* koninklik; rojaal
royalty *n* koningskap; (book, song, etc.) koninklikes; (mining) vrugreg
rub *vb* poets; skuur; vryf; **— in** *vb* insmeer; invryf; **— off** *vb* afvryf
rubber *n* rubber; gomlastiek
rubbish *n* rommel; vullis; vuilgoed; geklets; prul
rubbish bin *n* vullisblik
rubbish dump *n* ashoop; vullishoop
rubric *n* rubriek
ruby *n* robyn
rucksack *n* rugsak
rudder *n* roer; stuur
rude *adj* onbeskof; buffelagtig; grof; hardhandig; honds; onaardig; onbehoue; onbeleef; onbeskaaf(d); onfatsoenlik; ongemanierd; ongepoets; onopgevoed; ru; **— person** *n* buffel

rudeness *n* onbeskoftheid; ruheid; onbeleefdheid
ruffian *n* woestaard
rugby *n* rugby
rugby line-out *n* lynstaan
rugby match *n* rugbywedstryd
rugby player *n* rugbyspeler
rugged *adj* stroef
ruin *n* bouval; verderf; *vb* bederf; verslons; **be —ed** *vb* ondergaan
ruins *npl* murasie; puin; ruïne
rule *n* reël; maatstaf; norm; regering; rigsnoer; verordening; *vb* beheers; bestuur; (lines) linieer; **as a —** *adv* meesal
ruled *adj* (paper) geliniëer(d)
ruler *n* gebieder; regeerder; vors; (measuring) liniaal
rules *npl* reglement
rum *n* rum
rumble *vb* dreun; rommel; dawer; *n* gebulder
rumbling *n* gebulder; gedruis
ruminate *vb* herkou
rummage *vb* deursnuffel
rumour *n* gerug; riemtelegram; sprake
rump *n* boud
rumple *vb* kreukel; frommel
rumpus *n* moles
run *vb* loop; ren; hardloop; (a business) bedryf; *n* (cricket) lopie; (theatre) speelvak; **— after** *vb* najaag; naloop; **— along** *vb* aanloop; **— ashore** (*or* **aground**) *vb* strand; **— away** *vb* spaander; dros; **— down** *vb* afloop; afmaak; **— dry** *vb* vasbrand; **— free** *vb* losloop; **— out** *vb* uitloop; **— over** *vb* omry; **— short** *vb* kortkom; opraak; **— wild** *vb* verwilder
run-down *adj* pootuit
runaway *n* droster; wegloper
rundown *n* verduideliking
rung *n* sport
runner *n* loper
runner-up *n* naaswenner
running shorts *n* drafbroekie
runway *n* rolbaan; stygbaan
rupture *n* breuk
rural *adj* landelik; rustiek; **— districts** *n* platteland
ruse *n* lis

rush[1] *n* biesie
rush[2] *vb* storm; hol; **— in(to)** *vb* instorm
rush hour *n* spitsuur
rusk *n* beskuit; boer(e)beskuit
rust *n* roes; *vb* verroes; roes; **— stain**
  n roesvlek
rustic *adj* landelik; rustiek
rustle[1] *n* geritsel; ritseling; *vb* ritsel; suis
rustle[2] *vb* (cattle) stroop

rustling *n* geritsel; geruis; ritseling; suising
rustproof *adj* roesvry
rusty *adj* geroes; **become —** *vb* verroes
rut[1] *n* sleur; (in a road) knik
rut[2] *n* bronstyd; *vb* brons wees
rutting season *n* bronstyd
ruttish *adj* bronstig
rye *n* rog

S

sable antelope *n* sabel
sabotage *n* sabotasie; *vb* saboteer
saboteur *n* saboteur
sabre *n* sabel
sack *n* sak; *vb* (*informal*) afsê
sacrament *n* sakrament
sacred *adj* gewyde; heilig
sacrifice *n* offer; offerande; opoffering;
   vb opoffer
sacrilege *n* heiligskennis
sad *adj* droef; droefgeestig; droewig;
   melancholies; naar; pynlik; somber; treurig; verdrietig; weemoedig;
   hartseer; bedroef
saddle *n* saal; *vb* opsaal
saddle horse *n* ryperd
saddlecloth *n* saalkleedjie
sadism *n* sadisme
sadly *adv* ongelukkig
sadness *n* droefheid; weemoed
safari *n* safari
safe *adj* behoue; gerus; veilig; *n* brandkas; geldkas
safe conduct *n* vrygeleide
safe(ty) deposit box *n* bewaarkissie
safe haven *n* veilige hawe
safe sex *n* veilige seks
safeguard *vb* waarborg; beveilig
safekeeping *n* bewaring
safely *adv* gerus
safety *n* veiligheid
safety belt *n* veiligheidsgordel
safety catch *n* rus
safety clothing *n* glimdrag
safety glass *n* veiligheidsglas
safety pin *n* haakspeld; knipspeld
safety lamp *n* mynlamp
saffron *n* saffraan
sage *n* salie
sago *n* sago
sail *n* seil; *vb* seil; vaar
sailcloth *n* seildoek
sailing boat *n* seilboot
sailing vessel *n* seilskip
sailor *n* matroos; seeman
sailor's knot *n* maswerk
saint *n* heilige; sint

saintly *adj* vroom
sake *n*; for my — om my ontwil
salad *n* slaai
salad oil *n* soetolie
salamander *n* klipsalmander
salary *n* loon; salaris; besoldiging; —
   scale *n* salarisskaal
sale *n* verkoop; verkoping; omset; uitverkoop; vendisie; afset; debiet
sales manager *n* verkoop(s)bestuurder
sales person *n* verkoper
sales tax *n* verkoop(s)belasting
salient *adj* ooglopend
saliva *n* speeksel; spoeg
sallow *adj* vaal; blas
salmon *n* salm
salt *n* sout; *vb* pekel; inpekel; sout
salted *adj* gesout; — meat *n* soutvleis
saltpan *n* soutpan
saltpetre *n* salpeter
salutary *adj* heilsaam
salute *n* saluut; *vb* salueer; groet
salvage *vb* bêre
salver *n* skinkbord
salvia *n* salie
salvo *n* salvo
same *n* dieselfde; *adj* einste; selfde; homogeen; eenders
sample *n* proef; staaltjie; monster; eksemplaar; *vb* proe
sampling *n* monsterneming
sanatorium *n* sanatorium
sanctify *vb* heilig
sanction *n* sanksie; *vb* bekragtig
sanctity *n* heiligheid
sanctuary *n* heiligdom; toevlug(soord)
sand *n* sand
sand dune *n* duin
sandal *n* sandaal
sandalwood *n* sandelhout
sandbank *n* sandbank
sandbar *n* sandbank
Sandman *n* Klaasvakie
sandpaper *n* skuurpapier
sandwich *n* toebroodjie
sandy *adj* sanderig; — path *n* sandpad
sanitary *adj* sanitêr

Santa Claus *n* Kersvader
sap *n* sap
sapphire *n* saffier
sarcasm *n* sarkasme
sarcastic *adj* ironies; sarkasties
sarcophagus *n* sarkofaag
sardine *n* sardientjie
sash *n* serp
sash window *n* skuifraam
satanic(al) *adj* satanies
satchel *n* bladsak
satellite *n* satelliet; — **photo** *n* satellietfoto
satiated *adj* sat; trommeldik
satiety *n* bekoms
satin *n* satyn
satire *n* hekeldig; satire
satirical *adj* satiries
satisfaction *n* tevredenheid; ingenomenheid; voldoening; genoeë
satisfied *adj* tevrede; vergenoeg; voldaan
satisfy *vb* bevredig; stil; versadig; voldoen; — **one's thirst** *vb* les
satisfying *adj* bevredigend
saturated *adj* deurtrokke
Saturday *n* Saterdag
sauce *n* sous; blatjang
saucepan *n* kastrol
saucer *n* piering
saunter *n* slentering; *vb* slenter; drentel
sausage *n* wors
sausage roll *n* worsrolletjie
savage *adj* beesagtig; woes; *n* barbaar
savagely *adj* beesagtig
save[1] *prep* behalwe; uitgesonder
save[2] *vb* behou; spaar; — **up** *vb* opspaar
savings account *n* spaarrekening
savings bank *n* spaarbank
savour *vb* smaak
savvy *n* begrip; verstand
saw *n* saag; *vb* saag; — **off** *vb* afsaag
sawdust *n* saagsel
sawmill *n* saagmeul(e)
saxophone *n* saxofoon
say *vb* sê; opsê; *n* segenskap; — **again** *vb* herhaal; oorsê
saying *n* gesegde; spreekwoord; uiting
scab *n* roof; rofie; kors; skurfte
scabby *adj* skurf

scaffold *n* skavot
scaffolding *n* steier; stellasie
scald *vb* brand
scale[1] *n* skaal; weegskaal; —**s** *npl* weegskaal
scale[2] *n* skubbe; skilfer
scale[3] *n* tarief; toonladder
scan *n* skandering; *vb* skandeer
scandal *n* skandaal; opspraak; agterklap
scandalous *adj* skandalig; verregaande
scanner *n* leser; taster
scansion *n* skandering
scanty *adj* maer
scapegoat *n* sondebok
scar *n* litteken; merk; *vb* merk
scarce *adj* seldsaam; skaars; skraps
scarcely *adv* skaars; skraps; kwalik
scarcity *n* skaarste
scare *vb* skrik maak; bang maak; afskrik; *n* vrees, skrik; — **away** *vb* verwilder
scarecrow *n* skrikbeeld; voëlverskrikker
scarf *n* serp
scarlatina *see* **scarlet fever**
scarlet *n, adj* skarlaken
scarlet fever *n* skarlakenkoors
scatter *vb* rondstrooi; versprei; saai; sprei; strooi; uitstrooi; verstrooi; omwoel
scattering *n* verstrooiing
scene *n* toneel; spektakel; tafereel; skouspel
scent *n* spoor; reuk; reukwater; geur; aroma
sceptic *n* twyfelaar
sceptical *adj* ongelowig; skepties
sceptre *n* septer
schedule *n* lys, opgaaf; rooster; **on —** *adv* op tyd
scheduled flight *n* roostervlug
scheme *n* plan; skema
schism *n* skeuring
schizophrenia *n* skisofrenie
scholar *n* geleerde; leerling; skolier; — **patrol** *n* skolierpatrollie
scholarly *adj* geleer
scholarship *n* beurs; studiebeurs
school *n* skool; — **board** *n* skoolraad; — **building** *n* skoolgebou; — **fees**

npl skoolgeld; **— principal** *n* skoolhoof

schoolbag *n* bladsak; boeksak

schoolbook *n* skoolboek

schoolchild *n* skoolkind

sciatica *n* heupjig

science *n* wetenskap; **— fiction** *n* wetenskapfiksie

scientific *adj* wetenskaplik; **— knowledge** *n* wetenskap

scientist *n* wetenskaplike

scissors *npl* skêr; **pair of —** *n* skêr

scoff *vb* skimp

scold *vb* skel; raas; beknor

scolding *n* opbrander

scone *n* skon

scoop *n* skep; skop; spaan; *vb* skep

scooper *n* skepper

scooter *n* ryplank

scope *n* speling; ruimte

scorch *vb* skroei; verskroei; **—ed earth** *n* verskroeide aarde

score *n* telling; puntetelling; gelag; (music) partituur; *vb* opskrywe; (a try) aanteken

scoreboard *n* telbord

scorer *n* teller

scorn *n* hoon; spot; smaadheid; veragting; *vb* hoon; smaad; skimp

scornful *adj* smadelik

scorpion *n* skerpioen

scot-free *adj* skotvry

scoundrel *n* skobbejak; kalant; bliksem

scour *vb* skuur

scout *n* verkenner; verspieder; *vb* verken

scowl *n* frons

scramble *vb* klouter; **— up** *vb* opklouter

scrambled eggs *npl* roereiers

scrambler motorbike *n* veldfiets

scrambling *n* veldrenne

scrap *n* greintjie; snipper; **— value** *n* oorskotwaarde

scrap yard *n* wrakwerf

scrapbook *n* album; plakboek

scrape *n* knel; *vb* skaaf; skraap; **— off** *vb* afskraap

scrapheap *n* ashoop; afvalhoop

scrapings *npl* afskraapsel

scratch *n* krap; skraap; (hens) skrop;

vb krabbel; krap; skraap; **— out** *vb* deurhaal; skrap

scrawl *vb* krabbel

scream *n* gil; skree(u); gier; (*informal*) klug; *vb* kreet; gil; skree(u); gier

screaming *n* geskree(u)

screams *npl* geskree(u)

screech *vb* kras

screensaver *n* skermbeskermer; skermskut

screw *n* skroef; *vb* skroef; vasdraai; **— down** *vb* vasdraai; **— on** *vb* aanskroef

screwdriver *n* skroewedraaier

scribbler *n* aantekeningboek

scribe *n* skrifgeleerde

scroll *n* tierlantyntjie; *vb* (computing) rol op; **— bar** *n* (computing) rolbalk

scrub *vb* skrop

scrubbing brush *n* skropborsel

scrum *n* (rugby) skrum; *vb* skrum

scruple *n* beswaar

scrupulous *adj* angsvallig; nougeset

scrutineer *n* stemopnemer

sculptor *n* beeldhouer

scum *n* gespuis; skuim; uitvaagsel

scurvy *n* skeurbuik

scythe *n* seis

sea *n* see

sea legs *npl* seebene

sea level *n* seespieël; seevlak

sea lion *n* seeleeu

sea trip *n* seereis

sea turtle *n* seeskilpad

seagull *n* meeu; seemeeu

seal[1] *n* stempel; waarmerk; lak; *vb* seël; verseël; lak

seal[2] *n* rob; seeleeu; seehond

sealing wax *n* lak; seëllak

seam *n* aar; las; naat; soom; voeg

seamless *adj* naatlos

seamstress *n* naaister

seaport *n* seehawe

search *vb* soek; snuffel; vors; **— thoroughly** *vb* fynkam

search engine *n* (internet) soekenjin

searchlight *n* soeklig

seashell *n* seeskulp

seashore *n* seekus; seestrand

seasick *adj* seesiek

seaside *n* strand

season *n* seisoen; jaargety; speelvak; tyd; **— ticket** *n* seisoenkaartjie
seasonable *adj* tydig
seasonal *adj* seisoenaal
seat *n* bank; stoel; sitplek; sitbank; gestoelte; setel
seat belt *n* sitplekgordel; sitgordel
seaweed *n* seegras; seewier; wier
secede *vb* afval
second[1] *n, adj* (time) sekonde; **— hand** *n* (watch, clock) sekondewyster
second[2] *n* tweede; sekondant; *adj* tweede; *vb* sekondeer; **— biggest** *n, adj* naasgrootste; **for the — time** *adv* weer
second[3] *vb* (to another job) sekondeer
second-hand *adj* tweedehands; halfslyt; gebruik
second-rate *adj* tweederangs
secondary *adj* middelbaar; **— matter** *n* bysaak
secondary school *n* hoërskool
seconder *n* sekondant
secondly *adv* tweedens
secrecy *n* geheimhouding
secret *adj* heimlik; geheim; agterbaks; verborge; agterhoudend; onderhands; *n* geheim
secretary *n* sekretaris
secretary bird *n* sekretarisvoël
secretly *adv* agteraf; stilletjies; bedektelik
sect *n* sekte
section *n* afdeling; deursnee; seksie
sector *n* sektor
secular *adj* wêreldlik; wêrelds; sekulêr
secure *adj* sekuur; veilig; *vb* verseker
security *n* sekuriteit; veiligheid; garansie
security guard *n* sekuriteitswag; veiligheidswag
security police *n* veiligheidspolisie
sedate *adj* stemmig
sedative *n* kalmeermiddel
sediment *n* sediment; besinksel
seduce *vb* verlei
seducer *n* skaker
seduction *n* verleiding
see *vb* kyk; sien; **— through** *vb* deursien; deurgrond; **— to** *vb* omkyk
see-through *adj* deurskynend

seed *n* saad; kiem
seed potato *n* aartappelmoer
seedeater *n* (bird) saadeter
seek *vb* soek
seem *vb* skyn; lyk
seemingly *adv* oënskynlik; glo
seemly *adj* betaamlik
seep *vb* sypel
seer *n* siener
seesaw *n* wip; wipplank; *vb* hobbel; wip
segregation *n* segregasie
seismograph *n* seismograaf
seismology *n* aardbewingsleer
seize *vb* vat; pak; **— goods** *vb* lê beslag op
seized *adj* gevat
seizure *n* inbeslagneming; (goods) beslag; (illness) aanval
seldom *adv* selde
select *adj* uitgelese; *vb* kies
selection *n* seleksie; keuse; keuring; sortering; keur
selection board *n* keurraad
self *n* self; eie
self-catering unit *n* (holiday) selfsorgeenheid
self-confidence *n* selfvertroue
self-conscious *adj* selfbewus
self-control *n* selfbeheersing
self-defence *n* noodweer; selfverdediging
self-esteem *n* selfrespek
self-evident *adj* vanselfsprekend
self-examination *n* selfondersoek
self-government *n* outonomie; selfbestuur
self-preservation *n* selfbehoud
self-respect *n* selfrespek
self-righteous *adj* eiegeregtig
self-service *n* selfbediening; **— shop** *n* selfdienwinkel
self-sufficient *adj* selfgenoegsaam
selfish *adj* selfsugtig; baatsugtig
selfishness *n* selfsug; eiebaat
sell *vb* verkoop; **— by auction** *vb* opveil; veil; **— out of** *n* uitverkoop
seller *n* verkoper
selling price *n* verkoop(s)prys; winkelprys
semblance *n* sweem

semester *n* semester
semi *prefix* half
semi-darkness *n, adj* halfdonker
semidetached house *n* skakelhuis
semicolon (;) *n* kommapunt
semifinal *n* semifinaal
seminary *n* kweekskool; seminarie
semiprecious *adj* halfedel; — **stones** *npl* halfedelstene
semolina *n* griesmeel
senate *n* senaat
senator *n* senator
send *vb* stuur; send; — **for** *vb* ontbied; — **off** *vb* versend; — **on** *vb* aanstuur; — **over** *vb* oorstuur; — **messages via SMS** *vb* stuur SMS; teks
sender *n* sender
senile *adj* kinds
senior *adj* senior; — **citizen** *n* senior burger
sensation *n* sensasie; opskudding; gewaarwording
sensational *adj* opsienbarend
sense *n* betekenis; verstand; besef; rede; sin; — **of duty** *n* pligsgevoel
sense organ *n* sintuig
senseless *adj* sinloos; sinneloos; katswink
senses *npl* positiewe
sensible *adj* verstandig
sensitive *adj* sensitief; gevoelig; fyngevoelig; kleinserig
sensual *adj* sensueel; sinlik; wellustig
sensuality *n* wellus
sentence *n* sin; uitspraak; vonnis; *vb* veroordeel; vonnis
sentiment *n* gevoel; sentiment
sentimental *adj* sentimenteel
sentiments *npl* gevoelens
sentry *n* brandwag; skildwag; wag
separate *adj* afsonderlik; apart; *vb* skei; afskei
separately *adv* apart
separated *adj* geskeide
separation *n* skeiding
September *n* September
sepulchre *n* graf
sequel *n* vervolg
sequence *n* reeks; volgorde
sequestrate *vb* sekwestreer
sequestration *n* sekwestrasie

serenade *n* serenade
serene *adj* helder
sergeant *n* sersant
serial killer *n* reeksmoodenaar
serial number *n* reeksnommer
series *n* reeks
serious *adj* ernstig; bedenklik
seriousness *n* erns
sermon *n* predikasie; preek
serum *n* entstof; serum
serval wild cat *n* tierboskat
servant *n* bediende; dienaar
serve *vb* bedien; dien; — **up** *vb* opdien; opskep; (meal) opbring
server *n* (computing) bediener
service *n* diens; bediening; huur; (car) versiening; (dinner) stel; (dinner) eetservies; *vb* (car) versien
service charge *n* tafelgeld
serviceable *adj* bruikbaar; gedienstig
serviceman *n* weerman
serviette *n* servet
servile *adj* slaafs
session *n* sitting
set[1] *adj* voorgeskrewe; strak; *vb* (broken limb) spalk; (sun) ondergaan; (text) instel; — **an example** *vb* voorgaan; — **free** *vb* vrymaak; — **right** *vb* tereghelp; — **up** *vb* opslaan; (printing) set
set[2] *n* kliek; sit; (tennis) stel; (of furniture) stel meubels; (of teeth) gebit
set square *n* winkelhaak
setback *n* terugslag
setter *n* (dog) jaghond
setting *n* komposisie; (sun) ondergang
settings *npl* instellings
settle *vb* reël; aansuiwer; — **down** *vb* besink; — **one's account** *vb* afreken
settled *adj* afgereken; uitgemaak; voldaan; beklonke
settlement *n* afbetaling; kolonie; nedersetting; vesting; volksplanting
settler *n* setlaar
setup *n* (computing) opstelling
seven *n, determiner* sewe
seven o'clock *n, adj* sewe-uur
seventeen *n, determiner* sewentien
seventeenth *n, adj* sewentiende
seventh *n, adj* sewende
seventieth *n, adj* sewentigste

seventy *n, determiner* sewentig
several *adj* etlike; verskeie; *determiner* menig; menige
severe *adj* gedug; hewig; skerp; straf; streng
severity *n* strengheid
sew *vb* naai; — **on** *vb* aanwerk; vaswerk
sewer *n* riool; geut
sewerage *n* riolering
sewing *n* naaiwerk
sewing box *n* naaikissie
sewing cotton *n* naaigare
sewing machine *n* naaimasjien
sex *n* geslag; seks
sex appeal *n* sekstrek
sextant *n* sekstant
sexton *n* koster
sexual *adj* seksueel; vleeslik
sexuality *n* seks
sexy *adj* wulps; seksie
shabby *adj* kaal
shackle *n* kluister; skakel; *vb* kluister
shade *n* koelte; koloriet; skaduwee; skakering; *vb* beskadu
shadow *n* skaduwee; skim
shadowy *adj* skaduryk
shady *adj* skaduryk; — **side** *n* skaduweekant
shaft *n* skag; disselboom
shake *vb* skommel; skud; beef; — **hands** *vb* groet; — **off** *vb* afskud; — **out** *vb* uitskud; **the —s** *n* bewerasie
shakedown *n* kermisbed
Shakespearian *adj* Shakesperiaans
shaky *adj* bewerig; lendelam; onvas
shall *vb* sal
shallot *n* salot
shallow *adj* vlak
shame *n* skande; sonde; *vb* beskaam; —! *interj* sies tog!
shameful *adj* hemeltergend
shammy *n* seemsleer
shampoo *n* sjampoe; haarwasmiddel
shamrock *n* klawer
shanty *n* pondok; krot
shape *n* vorm; fatsoen; figuur; formaat; gedaante; *vb* formeer; **in good —** *adv* op peil
share *vb* taks; *n* aandeel; deel; gedeelte; part; porsie; — **of inheritance** *n* erfporsie

share call *n* deeloproep; telekonverensie
shareholder *n* aandeelhouer
shares *n* effekte
shark *n* haai
sharp *adj* skerp; bitsig; fel; straf; vinnig; *adv* klokslag; *n* (music) kruis
sharply *adv* klokslag
sharp turn *n* es
sharp-witted *adj* skerpsinnig
sharpen *vb* skerpmaak; slyp
sharpshooter *n* skerpskutter
shatter *vb* verbrysel
shatterproof *adj* splintervry
shave *vb* skeer
shaving *n* skaafsel; (wood) krul; spaander; *modifier* (as in shaving soap) skeer
shaving gel *n* skeerjel
shaving soap *n* skeerseep
shaving brush *n* skeerkwas
shavings *npl* (wood, grated cheese, etc.) skaafsels
shawl *n* sjaal; tjalie
she *pers pron* sy
she-goat *n* bokooi
sheaf *n* gerf
shear *vb* skeer
shears *n* (pair of) skaapskêr
shebeen *n* sjebien; smokkelkroeg
shed[1] *n* hok; loods; skuur; afdak
shed[2] *vb* afwerp; — **dead skin** *vb* (snake) vervel; — **hair** *vb* verhaar
sheep *n* skaap; kleinvee
sheep farm *n* skaapplaas
sheep farmer *n* skaapboer
sheepskin *n* skaapvel
sheer *adj* steil; — **rock face** *n* krans
sheet *n* plaat; (paper) blad; vel; blaadjie; (corrugated iron) sinkplaat; (zinc) vel sink
shelf *n* rak
shelf life *n* rakleeftyd
shell *n* dop; doppie; peul; skil; bom; granaat; skulp; *vb* (peas, nuts, etc.) uitdop; beskiet
shelter *n* herberg; onderdak; skuilplek; *vb* beskut
shepherd *n* herder; skaapwagter; veewagter; wagter
shepherdess *n* herderin**

sheriff *n* balju

shield *n* skild; — **bearer** *n* skildknaap

shift *n* skof; (work) ploeg; *vb* verkas; verskuif; versit; verplaas

shifting *n* verlegging

shifting spanner *n* skroefsleutel

shin *n* skeen

shine *n* skyn; skynsel; *vb* blink; — **on** *vb* bestraal

shiny *adj* blink

ship *n* skip; vaartuig; *vb* verskeep

ship's captain *n* skeepskaptein

ship's hold *n* skeepsruim

shipbuilding *n* skeepsbou

shipment *n* versending; verskeping; lading

shipowner *n* reder

shipping firm *n* redery

shipping line *n* skeepsredery

shipwreck *n* skipbreuk; **to be —ed** *vb* vergaan

shipyard *n* werf

shirk *vb* ontduik

shirker *n* lamsak

shirt *n* hemp

shirtsleeve *n* hempsmou

shit *vb* (*vulgar*) kak; *n* (*vulgar*) kak

shiver *n* gril; rilling; *vb* gril; beef; **the —s** *n* kouekoors

shivering *n* bewerasie (*or* bibberasie)

shivering fit *n* kouekoors

shivery *adj* huiwerig; rillerig

shoal[1] *n* sandbank

shoal[2] *n* skool

shock *n* skok

shock absorber *n* skokdemper

shocked *adj* ontsettend

shocking *adj* skokkend

shoe *n* skoen; *vb* (horse) beslaan

shoelace *n* skoenveter; veter

shoe polish *n* waks; skoenwaks; skoenpolitoer

shoemaker *n* skoenmaker

shoot *n* jag; skoot; (tendrils) rank; (plant) loot; spruit; uitspruitsel; *vb* skiet; — **at a target** *vb* skyfskiet; — **back** *vb* terugskiet; — **down** *vb* platskiet; — **forth** *vb* ontspruit; — **up** *vb* uitspruit

shootout *n* skietgeveg

shop *n* winkel

shopkeeper *n* winkelier

shoplifting *n* winkeldiefstal

shopping centre *n* winkelsentrum

shoptalk *n* vakpraatjies

shore *n* kus; strand; wal

short *adj* kort; kortstondig

short call *n* (visit) besoek

short circuit *n* kortsluiting

short cut *n* kortpad

short distance *n* endjie; entjie

short novel *n* novelle

short of breath *adj* kortasem

short story *n* kortverhaal

short time *n* wyl

short-lived *adj* kortstondig

short-sighted *adj* bysiende; kortsigtig; stiksienig

short-tempered *adj* oplopend

shortage *n* tekort

shortcoming *n* tekortkoming

shorten *vb* kort; afkort; verkort; inkort

shortening *n* verkorting

shorthand *n* snelskrif; stenografie

shortly *adv* kort; binnekort

shot *n* skoot; (pellets) hael

shotgun *n* haelgeweer

shoulder *n* skouer; (cattle) skof

shoulder blade *n* blad

shout *n* skree(u); *vb* skree(u); roep; uitroep

shouting *n* geroep; geskree(u); skree(u)ery

shove *vb* skuif; — **along** *vb* verskuif; — **off** *vb* afstoot

shovel *n* skopgraaf

show *n* skou; tentoonstelling; vertoning; *vb* vertoon; bewys

show house *n* skouhuis

show off *vb* pronk; pryk; spog

showcase *n* uitstalkas

shower *n* stort; (rain) bui; (rain) reënbui; (hail) haelbui; *vb* stort

showery *adj* buierig

showjumping *n* perdesport; skouspring

showy *adj* opsigtelik; uithaler

shrapnel *n* skrapnel

shred *n* snipper; *vb* versnipper

shrew *n* feeks; wyf

shrewdness *n* jakkalsstreek

shriek *vb* gil

shrike *n* fiskaal
shrill *adj* skril
shrimp *n* garnaal
shrink *vb* inkrimp; krimp; — **from** *vb* deins; — **back from** *vb* terugdeins
shrivel *vb* verskrompel
shroud *n* doodskleed; lykskleed
shrub *n* bos; bossie; struik
shrubs *n* struikgewas
shrug *vb* ophaal
shudder *n* gril; rilling; *vb* huiwer; gril
shuffle *vb* skuifel; (playing cards) skud
shuffling *adj* sleepvoetend
shun *vb* ontwyk; sku; vermy
shunt *vb* rangeer
shut *adj* geslote; toe; *vb* afsluit; — **in** *vb* insluit
shutter *n* blinding; hortjie; luik; vensterluik
shuttle *n* spoel
shuttle service *n* pendeldiens
shuttlecock *n* pluimbal
shy *adj* skaam; inkennig; skugter; kopsku; skrikkerig; skroomvallig; bedees; beskroomd; verleë; skaam
shy away *vb* wegskram
sick *adj* siek; naar; mislik
sick fund *n* siekefonds
sick person *n* invalide
sickbay *n* siekeboeg
sickle *n* sekel
sickly *adj* sieklik; pieperig
side *n* flank; kant; sy
side aisle *n* vleuel
side door *n* sydeur
side entrance *n* sydeur
side with *vb* voorpraat
sideboard *n* buffet
sideline *n* byverdienste
sidelong *adj* sydelings
SIDS *see* **Sudden Infant Death Syndrome**
siege *n* beleëring
siesta *n* middagdutjie
sieve *n* sif; *vb* sif
sift *vb* sif; uitpluis
sigh *n* sug; versugting
sigh *vb* (wind) suis
sight *n* sig; gesig; skouspel; vertoon; aanblik; (gun) visier; korrel
sign *n* teken; voorteken; merk;

merkteken; bewys; wenk; uithangbord; *vb* onderskrywe; teken
sign language *n* gebaretaal
signal *n* sein; sein; sinjaal
signature *n* handtekening; naamtekening; ondertekening; onderskrif
signboard *n* naambord; uithangbord
signet ring *n* seëlring
significant *adj* veelseggend; veelbetekenend
signify *vb* beduie; beteken
signpost *n* wegwyser
signwriter *n* letterskilder
silence *n* stilte; snoer
silencer *n* (car) klankdemper
silent *adj* stil; **be** — *vb* swyg; — **as death** *adj* doodstill
silently *adv* stilletjies
silhouette *n* silhoeët; skadubeeld
silk *n* sy
silk cotton *n* kapok
silkworm *n* sywurm
silliness *n* malligheid
silly *adj* flou; kinderagtig; laf; mal; onnosel; simpel; verspot; dwaas
silly joke *n* flouiteit
silly season *n* buite seisoen
silly talk *n* wywepraatjie
silo *n* silo; graansuil
silver *n* silwer; *adj* silwer
silver screen *n* (movies) silwerdoek
silver wedding *n* silwerbruilof
silverplated *adj* versilwer
silversmith *n* silwersmid
silverware *n* silwergoed
similar *adj* eenders; homogeen; gelyk; gelyksoortig; dergelik; ooreenkomstig; soortgelyk
similarity *n* gelykheid
similarly *adv* gelyk; eweneens
simmer *vb* stowe
simple *adj* eenvoudig; elementêr; naïef; ongekunsteld; simpel; louter
simplicity *n* eenvoud; naïwiteit
simplification *n* vereenvoudiging
simplify *vb* vereenvoudig
simply *adv* louter
simulate *vb* simuleer; veins
simultaneous *adj* gelyktydig
simultaneously *adv* gelyktydig
sin *n* sonde; *vb* sondig

since *adv* daar; gelede; sedert; sedert-dien; *conj* aangesien

sincere *adj* opreg; ongeveins; hartlik; innig; welmenend

sinew *n* sening

sinful *adj* sondig

sing *vb* sing; **— the praises of** *vb* aan-prys; besing

singe *vb* skroei; verskroei

singer *n* sanger; sangeres

singing *n* sang; **— in the ears** *n* gesuis

single *adj* alleen; eenlopend; alleenlo-pend; enkel; ongetroud

single bed *n* enkelbed

singlet *n* borsrok

sink *n* wasbak; *vb* sink; afneem; **— in** *vb* insink

sinkhole *n* sinkgat

sinner *n* sondaar; sondares

sip *vb* slurp

Sir *title* meneer

siren *n* sirene; mishoring

sirocco wind *n* sirokko

siskin *n* sysie

sister *n* suster

sister-in-law *n* skoonsuster

sisterly *adj* susterlik

sit *vb* sit; **— at** *vb* aansit; **— round** *vb* omsit; **— through** *vb* deursit; **— up** *vb* opsit

sitcom *n* sitkom

site *n* ligging

sitting *n* sessie; sitting

sitting room *n* sitkamer; woonkamer; voorkamer; voorhuis

situated *adj* geleë

situation *n* situasie; ligging; betrekking

six *n, determiner* ses

six o'clock *n, adj* sesuur

six-sided *adj* seskantig

sixteen *n, determiner* sestien

sixteenth *n, adj* sestiende

sixth *n, adj* sesde

sixtieth *n, adj* sestigste

sixty *n, determiner* sestig

size *n* grootte; formaat; maat; nommer; omvang; statuur

sjambok *n* sambok

skate *n* skaats; *vb* skaats

skateboard *n* skaatsbord; skaatsplank

skating rink *n* skaatsbaan; ysbaan

skein *n* (of yarn) string

skeleton *n* geraamte; skelet

skeleton staff *n* skaduweepersoneel

sketch *n* skets; skema; ontwerp; teken; *vb* afteken

sketchbook *n* sketsboek

skew *adj* windskeef

skid *n* rem; *vb* uitgly; rem

skilful *adj* behendig; knaphandig; kundig

skill *n* kundigheid; vaardigheid; kennis; kuns

skilled *adj* bedrewe; ervare; geskool; vaardig; volleerd

skim *vb* afroom; afskuim; deurkyk

skimmer *n* spaan

skin *n* vel; pels; huid; skil; *vb* afskil

skin disease *n* huidsiekte; velsiekte

skinny *adj* brandmaer; (*informal*) (dairy food, milk) laevet

skip[1] *vb* uitlaat; wip; huppel

skip[2] *n* hysbak

skipper *n* skeepskaptein; skipper

skipping rope *n* springtou

skirmish *n* skermutseling

skirt *n* romp

skittish *adj* (horse) skrikkerig

skittle *n* keël

skull *n* skedel; doodshoof; harspan

skunk *n* muishond

sky *n* hemel; lug; uitspansel

sky blue *n, adj* asuur; hemelsblou

skylark *n* lewerik

skylight *n* daklig

skyscraper *n* wolkekrabber

slab *n* plaat; plak; **— of chocolate** *n* plak sjokolade

slack *adj* slap

slacken *vb* verslap; (speed) verminder

slacker *n* luiaard

slag *n* (dross) slak

slam *vb* verdoem

slam dunk *n* (basketball) dompelskoot

slander *n* skinderpraatjies; *vb* beklad

slanderer *n* skinderbek

slant *vb* hel; oorhel

slanting *adj* skeef; skuins

slap *n* klap; opstopper; slag

slate *n* lei

slate roof *n* leidak

slaughter *n* slagting; *vb* slag; **— ani-mals** *npl* slagvee

slaughtered *adj* geslagte
slave *n* slaaf; **— away at** *vb* afsloof
slave trade *n* slawehandel
slaver *vb* (dribble) kwyl
slavery *n* slawerny
slavish *adj* slaafs
sleaze *n* aanstootlikheid
sledge *n* slee
sledgehammer *n* voorhamer
sleek *adj* glad
sleep *n* slaap; *vb* slaap
sleeping bag *n* slaapsak
sleeping sickness *n* slaapsiekte
sleepless *adj* slapeloos
sleeplessness *n* slapeloosheid
sleepwalker *n* slaapwandelaar
sleepy *adj* lomerig; slaperig; vaak
sleepyhead *n* slaapkop
sleet *n* ysreën
sleeve *n* mou
sleigh *n* slee
slender *adj* slank; tingerig; rank; teer;
   karig
slice *n* skyf; skyfie; sny
slide *n* skuif; *vb* gly; skuif; **— down** *vb*
   afgly
sliding door *n* skuifdeur
sliding scale *n* glyskaal
slight *adj* gering; lig; dun; *vb* geringskat
slightly *adv* effens; enigsins; bietjie
slim *adj* slank; *vb* verslank
slime *n* slym
slimming *n* verslanking
slimy *adj* slymerig
sling *n* slinger; verband
slip¹ *vb* glip; **— from** *vb* ontglip; **— off**
   vb afgly
slip² *n* steggie
slip-slops *n* plakkies
slipped disc *n* skyfletsel
slipper *n* pantoffel
slippery *adj* glad; glibberig; glipperig
slit *n* gleuf; skrefie; split
sliver *n* splinter
slogan *n* leuse; slagspreuk; strydleuse;
   wekroep
sloop *n* sloep
slope *n* hang; skuinste; opdraand(e);
   afdraand(e); *vb* hel
sloping *adj* hellend; skuins
sloping roof *n* afdak

slough *vb* (dead skin) vervel
slovenly *adj* onversorg; verslons
slow *adj* stadig; langsaam; traag; dooierig; agter
slow motion *n* vertraagde aksie
slowly *adv* langsaam; voetjie-voetjie;
   tydsaam
slug *n* slak
sluice *n* sluis
slum *n* agterbuurt; krotbuurt
slumber *vb* sluimer
slump *n* insinking
slurp *vb* slurp
sly *adj* slu; listig; agterbaks; deurtrap;
   geslepe; slim; **— person** *n* jakkals
smack *n* opstopper; (lips) smak; *vb* klap
small *adj* gering; klein; **— bit** *n* krieseltjie; **— cash** *n* kleingeld; **— dog**
   n brakkie; hondjie; **— fry** *n* goeters;
   — hill *n* koppie; **— hook** *n* hakie; **—**
   lake *n* pan; **— mouthful** *n* mondjievol; **— opening** *n* skrefie; **— packet**
   n pakkie; **— paw** *n* pootjie; **— pellet**
   of shot *n* haelkorrel; **— rifle** *n* buks;
   — shed *n* hokkie; **— talk** *n* slimpraatjies; **— thing** *n* kleinigheid; **—**
   village *n* gehug
small of the back *n* kruis
smallest *adj* minste
smallholding *n* hoewe
smallpox *n* pokkies
smalls *npl* (*informal*) kniebroek
smart *adj* slim; oulik; gevat; geestig;
   kranig; sjiek; uithaler; viets; uithaler;
   viets
smart card *n* slimkaart
smarting *adj* snerpend
smartphone *n* slimfoon
smash *vb* vermorsel; verbrysel; verpletter; inslaan; **— to bits** *vb* vergruis
smear *vb* aansmeer; smeer
smear campaign *n* smeerveldtog
smell *vb* geur; ruik (*or* reuk); snuffel; *n*
   aroma; geur; **— a rat** *vb* lont ruik
smelling salts *n* reuksout
smile *n* glimlag; *vb* glimlag
smiley *n* gesiggie
smith *n* smid
smithy *n* smidswinkel
smoke *n* damp; rook
smoke detector *n* rookklikker

smoker *n* roker
smokescreen *n* rookskerm
smooth *adj* glad; egalig; sag; effe; *vb* afskaaf
smoothie *n* skommeldrankie
smoothly *adv* glad
smoothness *n* effenheid; gladheid
smother *vb* smoor
smoulder *vb* smeul
smuggle *vb* smokkel
smuggler *n* smokkelaar
smuggling *n* smokkel; smokkelary
snack *n* peuselhappie
snack bar *n* snoephoekie; peuselkroeg
snacks *npl* snoeperye
snail *n* slak; — **mail** *n* (*informal*) slak-kepos
snake *n* slang
snake's hood *n* bak; bakkop
snap *vb* hap; knak; afbreek; — **at** *vb* byt; afsnou
snapdragon *n* leeubekkie
snapshot *n* kiekie; foto
snare *n* strik; valstrik; wip
snarl *n* grou; *vb* snou; — **at** *vb* afsnou
snatch *vb* gryp
sneak *vb* sluip
sneak thief *n* goudief; grypdief
sneer *n* gryns; spotlag; *vb* gryns; grin-nik; bespot
sneering *adj* smalend
sneeze *n* nies; *vb* to sneeze; — **aloud** *vb* proes
sniff *vb* snuif; snuffel
sniffle *vb* snik
snigger *vb* giggel
snip *vb* knip
sniper *n* skerpskutter
snippet *n* snipper
snob *n* snob
snobbery *n* snobisme
snoek *n* (marine fish) snoek
snog *n* kafoefelry; vryery
snooze *n* dutjie
snore *vb* snork
snoring *n* snork
snort *n* snork; *vb* snork; snuif; bries; (horse) proes
snot *n* snot
snout *n* bek; snoet; snuit
snow *n* kapok; sneeu; *vb* sneeu

snow shower *n* sneeubui
snow-white *adj* sneeuwit; spierwit
snowdrop *n* sneeuklokkie
snowflake *n* sneeuvlokkie
snowstorm *n* sneeubui
snub *n* afjak; *vb* afsnou
snuff *n* snuif
snuffbox *n* snuifdos
snug *adj* gesellig
so *adv* so; *conj* dus; — **far** *adv* dusver; tot sover; — **long as** *conj* solank; — **many** *adv* soveel; — **much** *adv* soseer; soveel; — **that** *adv* sodat; — **there!** *interj* dê!
so-called *adj* sogenaamd
soak *vb* week; — **with** *vb* deurtrek
soaked *adj* deurtrokke; druipnat; — **to the skin** *adj* waternat
soaking wet *adj* papnat
soap *n* seep; *vb* inseep
soap bush *n* seepbossie
soap dish *n* seepbakkie
soap opera *n* sepie
soap powder *n* waspoeier
soapstone *n* seepklip
soapsuds *n* seepsop
soar *vb* sweef
sob *n* snik; *vb* snik
sober *adj* nugter; sober; matig
sobriety *n* soberheid
soccer *n* sokker
sociable *adj* gesellig
social *adj* maatskaplik; sosiaal
social climber *n* sosiale vlinder
social intercourse *n* omgang
social networking *n* sosiale netwer-king
social security *n* bestaansbeveiliging; maatskaplike beveiliging
social welfare *n* volkswelsyn
social worker *n* maatskaplike werker
socialism *n* sosialisme
socialist *n* sosialis
socialite *n* sosiale vlinder
society *n* maatskappy; samelewing; ge-nootskap; geselskap; vereniging
sock *n* kous; sokkie
socket *n* (eye) holte; (hip) potjie; mof
sod *n* pol; sooi
soda *n* soda
soda water *n* sodawater

sodium *n* natrium
sodium bicarbonate *n* koeksoda
sofa *n* sofa; kanapee
soft *adj* sag; pap; week; mals
soft drink *n* koeldrank
soft goods *npl* sagteware; tekstielgoedere
soft-hearted *adj* weekhartig; jammerhartig
softball *n* sagtebal
soften *vb* versag; temper; vermurf
softly *adv* saggies
softness *n* sagtheid
software *n* (computing) programmatuur; sagteware
softy *n* (*informal*) papbroek
soil *n* grond; aarde; bodem; *vb* bemors; vlek
soiled *adj* bevuil
solar eclipse *n* sonsverduistering
solar heating *n* sonverhitting
solar power *n* sonkrag
solder *vb* soldeer
soldering iron *n* soldeerbout
soldier *n* krygsman; manskap; soldaat; —'s pay *n* soldy; —'s shoulder-belt *n* bandelier
sole[1] *adj* enig; enigste; uitsluitend
sole[2] *n* sool
sole[3] *n* (fish) tongvis
solely *adv* enkel; uitsluitend; uitsluitlik
solemn *adj* plegtig
solemnity *n* plegtigheid
solemnize *vb* voltrek
solicitor *n* prokureur
solicitous *adj* besorg
solid *adj* deeglik; solied; stabiel; stewig
solidarity *n* saamhorigheid; solidariteit
solidity *n* vastheid
solidly *adj* deeglik
soliloquy *n* alleenspraak; monoloog
solitary *adj* eensaam; eenselwig
solo *n* solo
soloist *n* solis
solution *n* oplossing
solve *vb* oplos
sombre *adj* somber
some *adj* party; *n* bietjie; *pron* sommige
somebody *pron* iemand
someone *n*, *pron* een; iemand; — who preys on others *n* bloedsuier
somersault *n* bollemakiesie

something *inter pron* wat; *pron* iets; — that causes vomiting *n* braakmiddel; — that sells *n* verkoper; — else *pron* iets anders
sometimes *adv* partykeer; partymaal; soms; somtyds
somewhat *adv* enigsins
somewhere *adv* êrens; iewers
son *n* seun
son-in-law *n* skoonseun
sonata *n* sonate
song *n* sang; lied; liedjie; gesang
songbird *n* sangvoël
sonnet *n* sonnet
soon *adj* gou; spoedig; *adv* binnekort; as — as *adv* sodra
sooner *adv* eer; eerder; veeleer; veelmeer; — or later *adv* vroeër of later
soot *n* roet
soothe *vb* kalmeer; gerusstel; stilmaak; sus; bedaar
soothing *adj* pynstillend
soothsayer *n* waarsêer
sophism *n* sofisme
sophist *n* sofis
soprano *n* sopraan
sorcerer *n* towenaar
sorcery *n* toorkuns
sore *n* seer; sweer; *adj* seer
sore throat *n* keelpyn; keelseer
sorrel *n* suring
sorrow *n* hartseer; smart; verdriet; droef(e)nis; leed; leedwese; rou; jammerte; spyt
sorrowful *adj* verdrietig; bedroef
sorry! *interj* jammer!; be — *vb* spyt
sort *n* aard; soort; *vb* sorteer
sortie *n* uitval
sosatie *n* sosatie
soul *n* siel
soulless *adj* sielloos
sound[1] *n* geluid; klank; *vb* klink; galm
sound[2] *adj* deeglik; dugtig; gaaf; gegrond; gesond; grondig; heel
soundly *adv* flink; vas
soup *n* sop
sour *adj* suur; *vb* versuur
sour fig *n* suurvy
sour milk *n* maas; suurmelk
source *n* bron; herkoms; oorsprong; oog

south *n* suide; *adj, adv* suid
south side *n* suidekant
South Africa *n* Suid-Afrika
South African *n* Suid-Afrikaner; Afrikaner
south coast *n* suidkus
south-east *adj, adv* suidoos; *n* suidooste
south-east wind *n* suidoostewind
south-easter *n* suidooster
south-west *adj, adv* suidwes; *n* suidweste
southerly *adj, adv* suidelik
southern *adj* suidelik
southern hemisphere *n* suiderhalfrond
southpaw *n* (boxing) hotklou
south-westerly *adj, adv* suidwestelik
souvenir *n* soewenier; aandenking; herinnering
sovereign *adj* soewerein; *n* pond; vors
sow[1] *vb* saai
sow[2] *n* sog; varksog
soya bean *n* sojaboontjie
space *n* spasie; plek; ruimte; tussenruimte; bestek; *vb* spasieer
space debris *n* ruimterommel
space shuttle *n* pendeltuig
space travel *n* ruimtevaart
space traveller *n* ruimtereisiger
spacecraft *n* ruimtetuig
spaceman *n* ruimteman
spacing *n* spasiëring
spacious *adj* wyd; ruim
spade *n* skop; graaf
spadeful *n* skepvol; spitvol
spades *npl* (playing cards) skoppens
spam *n* (emails) gemorspos; (emails) rommelpos
span *n* span
span saw *n* spansaag
spanner *n* sleutel
spar[1] *n* spar
spar[2] *vb* skerm
spare *vb* spaar; *adj* los; **— feelings** *vb* ontsien
spare part *n* onderdeel
spare room *n* vrykamer
spare wheel *n* noodwiel
sparing *adj* suinig
spark *n* vonk
spark plug *n* vonkprop

sparkle *vb* skitter; vonkel; flikker; flonker; glinster; tintel
sparkling *adj* vonkeling; flonkering; *n* tinteling
sparkling wine *n* bruiswyn; vonkelwyn
sparring partner *n* skermmaat
sparrow *n* mossie
sparse *adj* dun
spasm *n* kramp
spasmodic *adj* krampagtig
spatter *n* spatsel; *vb* spat
spay *vb* (dogs, cats) regmaak
speak *vb* praat; sê; spreek; **— to** *vb* aanspreek
speaker *n* redenaar; spreker
spear *n* spies; lans; speer; assegaai
spearfishing *n* spieshengel
special *adj* besonders; besonder; spesiaal; afsonderlik
specialist *n* spesialis; vakman
speciality *n* spesialiteit
specially *adv* besonder; ekstra
specific *adj* spesifiek; soortlik
specification *n* spesifikasie
specified *adj* bepaald
specify *vb* spesifiseer; (details) opgee
specimen *n* monster; tipe; proef
speck *n* spikkel; stip; stippel; tittel
speckled *adj* gespikkel; gevlek
spectacle *n* skouspel
spectacle case *n* brilhuisie
spectacles *npl* bril
spectacular *adj* skouspelagtig
spectator *n* toeskouer; kyker; omstander
speculate *vb* spekuleer
speculation *n* bespiegeling; spekulasie
speculator *n* spekulant
speech *n* spraak; taal; toespraak; voordrag; aanspraak; rede; redevoering
speech impediment *n* spraakgebrek
speechless *adj* spraakloos; sprakeloos
speed *n* spoed; snelheid; haas; vaart
speed bump *n* spoedwal
speed hump *n* spoedhobbel
speed limit *n* snelperk
speed trap *n* jaagstrik; snelstrik
speed wobble *n* spoedwaggel
speedily *adv* spoedig
speedy *adj* spoedig
spell[1] *vb* spel

spell[2] *n* toorwoord
spellchecker *n* (computing) speltoetser
spelling *n* spelling
spelling mistake *n* spelfout
spend *vb* bestee; spandeer; uitgee; ver-
    teer; deurbring; opmaak; — **one's**
    time *vb* slyt
spendthrift *n* deurbringer; spandabel
sperm *n* saad
sphere *n* sfeer; kring; gebied
sphinx *n* sfinks
spice *n* kruiem; spesery
spick and span *adj* agtermekaar; piek-
    fyn
spicy *adj* pikant
spider *n* spinnekop
spigot *n* tap
spill *vb* spil; stort; — **out** *vb* uitstort
spin *n* draai; ritjie; *vb* spin; tol; draai
spin doctor *n* beeldpoetser
spin-dryer *n* toldroër
spinach *n* spinasie
spinal cord *n* rugstring
spindle *n* spil
spine *n* ruggraat
spineless *adj* slapgat
spinster *n* oujongnooi
spiral *n* spiraal
spiral staircase *n* wenteltrap
spire *n* spits; toring
spirit *n* siel; gees; fut
spirit level *n* waterpas
spirit world *n* geesteswêreld
spirit(s) *n(pl)* spiritus; spiritualieë
spirited *adj* flink
spiritual *adj* geestelik
spiritualism *n* spiritisme; spiritualisme
spiritualist *n* spiritis
spit[1] *n* spoeg (*or* spuug)
spit[2] *n* (roasting) spit
spite *n* wrewel
spiteful *adj* wrewelig
spitfire *n* drifkop
spittle *n* speeksel; spoeg
splash *n* plons; spatsel; *vb* klots; plas
spleen *n* milt
splendid *adj* luisterryk; pragtig; puik
splendour *n* luister; majesteit; praal;
    prag
splice *vb* splits
splint *n* spalk; *vb* spalk

splinter *n* spaander; splinter
split *n* skeuring; spleet; *vb* bars; kloof
spoil *vb* bederf; verbrou
spoiled *adj* bedorwe
spoilsport *n* pretbederwer; spelbreker
spoke *n* speek
spoken language *n* spreektaal
spokesman *n* woordvoerder; spreek-
    buis; segsman
spokesperson *n* woordvoerder;
    spreekbuis
spokeswoman *n* woordvoerder;
    spreekbuis
sponge *n* spons
sponge off *vb* teer
sponger *n* parasiet
spongy *adj* voos
sponsor *n* beskermheer; peet; *vb* on-
    dersteun
spontaneous *adj* ongedwonge; spontaan
spoof mail *n* foppos
spoof website *n* fopwebwerf
spoofing *n* swendelary
spool *n* klos; spoel
spoon *n* lepel
spoonful *n* skep; skeppie
sporadic(al) *adj* sporadies
sport *n* sport
sports club *n* sportklub
sportsmanship *n* sportmanskap
spot *n* kol; plek; smet; spikkel; stip;
    stippel; vlek; **at this** — *adv* alhier
spot check *n* steekproef
spotless *adj* vlek(ke)loos; smetloos;
    onbesoedel(d)
spotlight *n* kollig
spotted *adj* bont; gespikkel; gevlek
spouse *n* gade; eggenoot; eggenote; ge-
    maal; gemalin; wederhelf
spout *vb* spuit; spat; *n* tuit
sprain *vb* verstuit; verswik
sprawl *vb* spartel
spray *vb* spuit; sproei
spray can *n* spuitkan
spray paint *n* spuitverf
spread *n* uitbreiding; *vb* uitbrei; —
    abroad *vb* uitstrooi; verbrei; — **out**
    vb sprei; uitsprei; — **over** *vb* bestryk
spreadsheet *n* ontledingstaat;
    spreiblad
spree *n* fuif

sprightly *adj* springlewendig
spring *n* bron; fontein; lente; voorjaar; (watch) veer; *vb* nael; — **from** *vb* voortspruit; — **upon** *vb* bespring
springboard *n* aanloopplank; springplank
springbok *n* springbok
springiness *n* veerkrag
sprinkle *vb* sprinkel
sprinkler *n* (irrigation) sproeier; (irrigation) sprinkelbesproeling
sprint *vb* nael
sprinter *n* sneller; naelloper
sprout *n* rank; uitspruitsel; *vb* rank; bot
spruce *adj* viets
spur *n* prikkel; spoor; *vb* spoor
spurred *adj* gespoor
spurt *vb* spat
sputum *n* roggel
spy *n* spioen; verspieder; verkenner; *vb* afloer; — **on** *vb* bespied; speur
squabble *n* harwar; *vb* dwarstrek
squad *n* peloton
squadron *n* (naval, etc.) eskader
squalid *adj* smerig
squall *n* rukwind; windvlaag
squander *vb* verkwis; vermors; verspeel; verspil; (money) deurbring
squandering *n* verspilling
square *adj* haaks; vierkantig; kwadraat; *n* kwadraat; plein
square root *n* vierkantswortel
squash[1] *n* kwas; gedrag; *vb* kneus
squash[2] *n* (vegetable) skorsie
squat *vb* op die hurke sit; plak
squatter *n* plakker; bywoner
squatting *n* plakkery
squeak *vb* piep
squeaky *adj* pieperig
squeamish *adj* mislik
squeamishness *n* narigheid
squeeze *vb* pers; knyp; — **out** *vb* uitdruk; uitpers; — **tightly** *vb* knel; — **together** *vb* saamdruk
squid *n* inkvis
squinting *n* skeel
squirrel *n* eekhorinkie
squirt *n* spuit; *vb* spuit
stab *n* steek; prik; stoot; por; *vb* steek
stability *n* stabiliteit; vastigheid
stable[1] *adj* stabiel

stable[2] *n* stal
stack *n* stapel; mied; *vb* stapel
stadium *n* stadion
staff *n* balk; notebalk; personeel; staf
stag party *n* ramparty
stage *n* skof; stadium; toneel; *vb* vertoon
stage fright *n* plankekoors; plankevrees
stage management *n* regie
stage manager *n* regisseur
stagger *vb* steier; waggel; wankel
staggered hours *n* skiktyd
stain *n* vlek; klad; smet; brandmerk; *vb* beklad; kleur
stained glass *n* gekleurde glas
stainless *adj* vlekvry; roesvry
stainless steel *n* vlekvrye staal
stair *n* trap
stair carpet *n* (trap)loper
staircase *n* trap
stairs *npl* 'n trap
stake[1] *n* brandstapel; paal
stake[2] *n* pot; *vb* waag
stakeholders *npl* belanghebbers
stale *adj* afgesaag; alledaags
stalk[1] *n* halm; steel; stingel; stronk
stalk[2] *vb* kruip; sluip
stalker *n* bekruiper; sluipjagter
stall *n* stal; kraam; stalletjie; padstal; *vb* op stal hou; gaan staan; (car, etc.) staak; vassit
stallion *n* hings
stalwart *n* staatmaker
stamen *n* meeldraad
stammer *vb* stamel; hakkel
stamp *n* seël; stempel; tjap; waarmerk; *vb* afstempel; tjap; waarmerk
stamp duty *n* seëlbelasting; seëlreg
stance *n* stand
stand *n* erf; stalletjie; standplaas; stellasie; *vb* staan; — **firm** *vb* vastrap; — **over** *vb* oorstaan; — **still** *vb* stilstaan; — **up** *vb* opstaan
stand surety *vb* instaan
standard *n* allooi; (school class) standerd; *adj* normaal
standby mode *n* bystandmodus
standing *n* stand; *adj* staande
standpoint *n* standpunt
stanza *n* stansa; strofe; vers; koeplet
staple[1] *n* kram; krammetjie; *vb* kram

staple[2] *adj* vernaamste; stapel
staple food *n* stapelvoedsel
stapler *n* kramdrukker; krammer
star *n* ster
starboard *n, adj* stuurboord
starch *n* stysel; *vb* styf
stare *vb* fikseer; staar; tuur; — **at** *vb* aangaap; aanstaar; betrag
starfish *n* seester
stark-naked *adj* poedelnaak
starling *n* spreeu
stars *npl* sterre; gesternte
start *n* aanvang; begin; staanspoor; skrik; voorsprong; *vb* aanvang; begin; lanseer; skrik; — **a race** *vb* afsit; — **a car** *vb* aanslaan; — **off** *vb* wegspring
starter *n* (sport) afsetter
startle *vb* skrikmaak; opskrik; verras; ontstel
starve *vb* uithonger; verhonger
starving *adj* uitgehonger
state *n* toestand; kondisie; moondheid; staat; staatsie; *vb* (reasons) opgee
state coach *n* praalkoets
state of emergency *n* noodtoestand
state of mind *n* gemoedstoestand
stately *adj* statig; plegtig; deftig; afgemete
statement *n* staat; opgaaf; rekening; verklaring; rapport; relaas
statesmanship *n* staatkunde
static *adj* staties
station *n* stasie; standplaas; *vb* stasioneer
stationary *adj* vas
stationery *n* skryfbehoeftes; skryfgoed
statistics *n* statistiek
statue *n* beeld; standbeeld
stature *n* statuur; liggaamsbou; gestalte
statute *n* statuut
statutory *adj* wetlik
stave *n* staaf; (music) balk; —**s** *n* (music) notebalk
stay *vb* bly; boer; — **away** *vb* uitbly; wegbly; — **indoors** *vb* inbly; — **overnight** *vb* oornag; — **up** *vb* opsit
steadfast *adj* onwankelbaar; onwrikbaar; standvastig
steady *adj* egalig; solied; vas; gestadig; oppassend; bestendig
steak *n* steak

steal *vb* steel; ontvreem; kaap; vaslê; — **along** *vb* sluip; — **into** *vb* insluip
stealthily *adv* oogluikend; steelsgewys
steam *n* stoom; damp; wasem
steam engine *n* stoommasjien
steamer *n* stoomboot
steamship *n* stoomboot; stoomskip
steel *n* staal
steep *adj* steil
steep in *vb* indompel; week
steeple *n* toring
steepness *n* steilte
steer[2] *n* stier; bul
steer[1] *vb* (vehicle, vessel) stuur; bestuur; — **to** *vb* aanstuur
steerage *n* tussendeks
steering gear *n* stuur
steering wheel *n* stuurwiel
stem *n* stam; stamwoord; steel; stingel; — **from** *vb* stam
stench *n* stank
stenographer *n* stenograaf
stenography *n* stenografie
step[1] *n* stap; maatreël; pas; skrede; sport; trap; *vb* stap; tree; — **in** *vb* instap; — **round** *vb* omstap; — **out** *vb* aanstap; — **over** *vb* oorstap
step[2] *prefix* stief
stepbrother *n* stiefbroer
stepladder *n* trapleer
stepmother *n* stiefmoeder
steppe *n* steppe
stepping stone *n* vastrapplek
stereophonic *adj* stereofonies
stereotype *n* stereotipe
sterile *adj* onvrugbaar; steriel
sterilization *n* sterilisasie
sterilize *vb* steriliseer
stern[1] *adj* hard; straf
stern[2] *n* agterskip
sternum *n* borsbeen
stevedore *n* stuwadoor
stew *n* bredie; stowevleis; *vb* stowe; — **cooked in a cast-iron pot** *n* potjiekos
steward *n* kelner
stewed meat *n* stowevleis
stick[1] *n* stok; lat; knopkierie
stick[2] *vb* kleef; — **fast** *vb* vassit; — **on** *vb* aanplak; opplak; — **to** *vb* aankleef; — **together** *vb* vasplak; — **up for** *vb* voorpraat

sticking-plaster *n* hegpleister
sticky *adj* taai; klewerig
stiff *adj* strak; stram; **— as a poker** *adj* stokstyf
stiffen *vb* styf; verstyf
stifle *vb* versmoor; smoor; verstik
stigma *n* stigma; brandmerk; skandvlek
stigmatize *vb* stigmatiseer
stiletto *n* stilet
still[1] *adj* rustig; *adv* nog; *conj* dog
still[2] *n* stookketel
stillborn *adj* doodgebore
stilt *n* stelt(e)
stilt walker *n* steltloper
stilted *adj* geswolle
stimulant *n* stimulant; prikkel
stimulate *vb* stimuleer; prikkel; opwek
stimulating *adj* stimulerend; opwekkend
stimulation *n* stimulasie; opwekking
stimulus *n* prikkel
sting *n* steek
stingray *n* pylstert
stinging nettle *n* brandnetel
stingy *adj* gierig
stink *n* stank; *vb* stink
stipulate *vb* stipuleer
stipulation *n* voorwaarde
stir *n* opspraak; *vb* roer; beroer; **— up** *vb* aanblaas; ophits; opstook
stirrup *n* stiebeuel
stirrup leather *n* stiegriem
stitch *n* steek; *vb* stik
stock *n* voorraad; (cattle, etc.) vee; **— up on** *vb* opberg
stock car *n* stampmotor
stock exchange *n* beurs; effektebeurs
stock exchange listing *n* notering op die beurs
stock farm *n* veeboerdery
stockbreeding *n* veeteelt
stockbroker *n* effektehandelaar
stocking *n* kous
stockpile *vb* opberg
stocks *n* effekte
stocktaking *n* voorraadopname
stockyard *n* veekraal
stoep *n* stoep
stoic(al) *adj* stoïsyns
stoke *vb* stook
stoker *n* stoker

stomach *n* maag; buik; pens
stomach ache *n* maagpyn
stomach complaint *n* maagkwaal
stone *n* klip; pit; steen; gesteente
stone-dead *adj* morsdood
stone-deaf *adj* stokdoof; potdoof
stonemason *n* steenhouer
stony-broke *adj* doodarm
stony *adj* steenagtig
stool *n* stoelgang; ontlasting; (furniture) stoel
stoop *vb* buk; buig
stooping *adj* gebukkend
stop *vb* keer; eindig; **— suddenly** *vb* vassteek
stop! *interj* halt!; basta!; genoeg!
stopcock *n* kraan
stoppage *n* oponthoud
stopper *n* prop
stopwatch *n* stophorlosie
store *n* winkel; pakhuis; magasyn; *vb* bêre (*or* berg); **— away** *n* stoor; bêre (*or* berg); **— up** *vb* opgaar
storehouse *n* bewaarplaas
storeman *n* magasynmeester
storeroom *n* pakkamer; stoor; bewaarplaas
stores *npl* voorraad
storey *n* verdieping
stork *n* ooievaar
storm *n* storm; onweer; swaarweer; *vb* storm; bestorm
stormwater *n* vloedwater
stormy *adj* onstuimig; stormagtig
story *n* storie; verhaal; geskiedenis; historie; relaas; vertelling; **tell a —** *vb* vertel
storyteller *n* verteller
stout *adj* dik; fris; geset
stove *n* oond; stoof
stow *vb* stu
stowaway *n* verstekeling
straggle *vb* tou; agterbly
straight *adj* reguit; reg; regstreeks; **— across** *adv* dwarsdeur; **— down** *adv* regaf; **— on** *adv* padlangs; **— out** *adv* botweg; **— up** *adj* penregop; regop
strain *n* inspanning; *vb* syg
strained *adj* gespanne
strainer *n* vergiet
strait *n* engte; see-engte; straat

straitjacket *n* dwangbuis
strand *n* string
stranded *adj* gestrand; **be —** *vb* strand
strandwolf *n* strandjut
strange *adj* snaaks; vreemd; aardig; raar; wonderlik
strangeness *n* onbekendheid; vreemdheid
stranger *n* vreemdeling; onbekende
strangle *vb* verwurg; wurg
stranglehold *n* wurggreep
strap *n* platriem; riem; strop
strategem *n* krygslis
strategy *n* strategie
stratum *n* laag
straw *n* strooi
straw hat *n* strooihoed
strawberry *n* aarbei
strawberry jam *n* aarbeikonfyt
stray *vb* afdwaal; verdwaal; afgaan
stray dog *n* rondloperhond
streak *n* streep; *vb* kaalhol
streaker *n* kaalnaeler; kaalholler
stream *n* stroom; spruit; stroming; *vb* vloei
streamer *n* wimpel
streamlined *adj* vaartbelyn
street *n* straat
street jargon *n* straattaal
streetwalker *n* straatvlinder
strength *n* krag; sterkte; **— of a giant** *n* reusekrag
strength of mind *n* geeskrag
strengthen *vb* sterk; styf; versterk
stress *n* klem; nadruk; spanning; *vb* beklem
stretch *n* trajek; plaat; *vb* span; rek; reik; **— forth** *vb* uitsteek; **— out** *vb* uitrek
stretched *adj* gerek; gespanne
stretcher *n* baar; draagbaar; rekker; voukatel
strew about *vb* rondstrooi
strict *adj* streng; stip; strik; nou
strictly *adv* stip
strictly confidential *adj* vertroulik
strictness *n* strengheid
stride *n* tree; skrede; haal; stap; *vb* tree; stap; stryk
strife *n* stryd; twis; verdeeldheid; onvrede
strike *n* staking; werkstaking; *vb* moker;

klap; (lightning) slaan; (lightning) bliksem; **— a note** *vb* aanslaan; **— off** *vb* skrap
striker *n* staker
striking *adj* opvallend; treffend; *n* (of a clock) klokslag
string *n* lyn; tou; rits; seilgare; snaar; koord; snoer; string; vlegsel; **— of pearls** *n* snoer pêrels
string orchestra *n* strykorkes
stringent *adj* streng
strip¹ *vb* ontklee; ontbloot
strip² *n* strook; **—s of salted and dried meat** *n* biltong
stripe *n* streep
strive *vb* streef; trag
stroke *n* aanslag; beroerte; haal; hou; set; slag; streek; streep; stryk; *vb* streel
stroll *n* slentering; wandeling; *vb* slenter; flenter
strong *adj* fris; stewig; kragtig; kras; gedugtig; heg; sterk
strong drink *n* drank; tiermelk
stronghold *n* burg; sterkte
strongroom *n* kluis
strontium *n* stronsium
strop *n* skeerriem; strop
strophe *n* strofe
structure *n* struktuur; konstruksie
struggle *n* stryd; worsteling; *vb* beur; **— along** *vb* aanpiekel; aansukkel
struggle literature *n* struggle-literatuur
strum *vb* tokkel
strychnine *n* wolwegif
stub *n* stomp
stubble *n* (beard) stoppelbaard; (field) stoppel
stubbly *adj* stoppelrig
stubborn *adj* hardkoppig; onversetlik; hardhoofdig
stuck-up *adj* verwaand
stud *n* stoet
stud farm *n* stoetery
studbook *n* stamboek
studhorse *n* hings
student *n* student
students' council *n* studenteraad
studies *npl* leerwerk
studio *n* ateljee
studious *adj* leergierig

study *n* leer; studeerkamer; studie; *vb* beoefen

stuff *n* goed; stof; *vb* opstop

stuffer *n* opstopper

stuffy *adj* bedompig; muf

stumble *vb* struikel; swik; **— along** *vb* strompel

stumbling block *n* struikelblok

stump *n* stomp; (cricket) paaltjie

stumpy *adj* stomp

stun *vb* bedwelm; verdoof

stun gun *n* bedwelmer

stunner *n* (*informal*) knewel

stuntman *n* waagarties

stupid *adj* dom; onnosel; stom; toe; onbevatlik; uilagtig; suf; **— person** *n* dikkop

stupidity *n* dwaasheid; stommiteit

stupor *n* verdowing

sturdy *adj* stoer

stutter *vb* hakkel; stotter

sty *n* hok

stye (*or* **sty**) *n* karkatjie

style *n* snit; styl; trant

stylish *adj* deftig, aantreklik

stylist *n* stilis

sub-tropical *adj* subtropies

subcommittee *n* subkomitee; onderkomitee

subconsciousness *n* onderbewussyn

subdivision *n* onderafdeling; onderdeel

subdue *vb* onderwerp; kleinkry

subheading *n* ondertitel

subject *n* onderwerp; tema; vak(kie); (of a country) onderdaan; (school) leervak; *vb* onderwerp; **— to** *adj* onderhewig; onderworpe; *prep* behep; *vb* blootstel

subject to approval *adv* onderworpe aan goedkeuring

subjection *n* onderwerping; blootstelling

subjective *n, adj* subjektief

subjunctive *n, adj* subjunktief

submarine *adj* ondersees; *n* duikboot

submission *n* onderwerping

submissive *adj* onderworpe; gedwee; berustend; lydelik

submit *vb* inlewer; voorlê; getroos

subordinate *adj* ondergeskik; onderhorig; *n* ondergeskikte

subpoena *n* dagvaarding; *vb* dagvaar

subscribe *vb* teken; **— to** *vb* inteken

subscriber *n* intekenaar

subscription *n* subskripsie

subside *vb* besink; insink; sak

subsidence *n* insinking

subsidize *vb* subsidieer

subsidy *n* subsidie; toelaag

substantial *adj* wesen(t)lik

substantiate *vb* staaf; verwesenlik

substantive *n* substantief; (grammar) naamwoord; *adj* substantief

substitute *n* plaasvervanger; substituut; *vb* vervang

substitution *n* waarneming

substratum *n* onderlaag

subtenancy *n* onderhuur

subtenant *n* onderhuurder

subterranean *adj* onderaards

subtitle *n* ondertitel; subtitel

subtle *adj* subtiel; spitsvondig

subtract *vb* aftrek; aftel

subtraction *n* aftrekking

suburb *n* voorstad

suburban *adj* voorstedelik

succeed *vb* geluk; vlot; opvolg; **— beyond expectation** *vb* meeval

success *n* sukses; welslae; opgang

successful *adj* suksesvol; voorspoedig

successively *adv* agtereenvolgens

successor *n* opvolger

succulent *adj* sappig; *n* vetplant

succumb *vb* val; beswyk

such *adj* dergelik; *adj, pron* sulke; **to — an extent** *adv* tot so 'n mate; soseer

such as *adv; conj; prep* soos; as

suck *vb* suig; **— out** *vb* uitsuig

sucker *n* suier

sucking pig *n* speenvark

suckle *vb* drink; suig; soog

sudden *adj* skielik; plotseling; onvoorsien; **— squall** *n* vlaag

Sudden Infant Death Syndrome *n* wiegiedood

suddenly *adv* plotseling; skielik; eensklaps

suet *n* vet

suffer *vb* ly; ondergaan; verdra; dra

sufferer *n* lyer

suffering *n* lyding

suffice *vb* volstaan

sufficient *adj* genoegsaam; toereikend; voldoende; genoeg;
sufficiently cooked *adj* gaar
suffix *n* agtervoegsel
suffocate *vb* versmoor; smoor; stik; verstik
suffocating *adj* benoud
sugar *n* suiker
sugar bush *n* suikerbos
sugar cane *n* soetriet; suikerriet
sugar daddy *n* vroetelpappie
suggest *vb* suggereer; stel voor; opper
suggestion *n* suggestie; voorstel
suicide *n* selfmoord
suit *n* pak; *vb* aanstaan
suitable *adj* toepaslik; doelmatig; geskik; paslik; passend; dienlik
suite *n* (rooms) stel
suitor *n* vryer
sulk *vb* knies
sulky *adj* humeurig
sulphate *n* sulfaat
sulphur *n* sulfer; swa(w)el
sulphuric acid *n* swa(w)elsuur
sultan *n* sultan
sultry *adj* benoud; swoel
sum *n* som; **— up** *vb* opsom; deursien
summarily *adv* summier
summarize *vb* opsom; saamvat
summary *n* opsomming; oorsig
summer *n* somer
summer holidays *n* somervakansie
summerhouse *n* prieel; somerhuis
summit *n* kruin; top; toppunt; (talks) spitsberaad
summon *vb* dagvaar; aanskryf; ontbied; sommeer
summons *npl* dagvaarding; oproep
sun *n* son
sunbeam *n* sonstraal
sunbonnet *n* kappie
sunburnt *adj* songebrand; (son)gebruin
Sunday *n* Sondag
Sunday best *n* (clothes) kisklere
Sunday school *n* Sondagskool
sundial *n* sonnewyster; sonwyser
sundowner *n* skemerkelkie
sundry *adj* velerlei; verskeie
sunflower *n* sonneblom
sunlight *n* sonlig
sunny *adj* sonnig

sunrise *n* sonop; sonsopgang; **at —** *adv* sonop
sunscreen *n* (lotion) sonskerm
sunset *n* sononder; sonsondergang; **at — ** *adv* sononder
sunshade *n* sonskerm
sunshine *n* sonskyn
sunspot *n* sonvlek
sunstroke *n* sonsteek
suntan *n* sonbruin; *vb* sonbruin
suntan lotion *n* sonbrandolie
superannuation *n* verjaring
superbug *n* superkiem
superficial *adj* oppervlakkig; kosmeties
superfluous *adj* oorbodig; oordadig; oortollig; orig
superior *n* (person) meerdere
superlative *adj* superlatief; oortreffend; *n* superlatief
supermarket *n* supermark; selfdienwinkel; alleswinkel
supernatural *adj* bonatuurlik
supersonic *adj* supersonies
superstition *n* bygeloof
supervise *vb* toesig hou
supervision *n* toesig; opsig
supervisor *n* toesighouer; opsigter; opsiener
supper *n* aandete
supple *adj* lenig; soepel
supplement *n* byvoegsel; toevoegsel
supplication *n* gesmeek
supplier *n* leweransier; verskafer
supply *n* aanbod; toevoer; *vb* toevoer; aanvoer; verskaf
support *n* steun; leuning; onderhoud; rugsteun; stut; skraag; versterking; *vb* onderhou; rugsteun
supporter *n* aanhanger; volgeling
suppose *vb* geloof; glo
supposed *adj* vermeende
supposition *n* onderstelling; vermoede; veronderstelling
suppress *vb* verswyg; onderdruk
suppressed *adj* gesmoord
suppression *n* onderdrukking
suppurate *vb* etter
suppuration *n* verswering
supremacy *n* oppermag
supreme *adj* oppermagtig; hoogste; soewerein

Supreme Court *n* Hooggeregshof
supreme power *n* oppermag
suppress *vb* onderdruk
sure *adj* gewis; positief; seker; stellig; vas; wis; bestendig
surely *adv* gewis; seker; verseker
surety *n* borg; sekerheid; **become —** *vb* borgstaan
surf *n* branders; golwe
surface *n* oppervlak
surfboard *n* branderplank; ryplank
surge *vb* dein
surgeon *n* chirurg; snydokter
surgery *n* snykunde
surging *adj* golwend
surly *adj* stuurs; nors; stug; iesegrimmig; **— person** *n* bullebak
surmount *vb* oorwin
surname *n* agternaam; van
surpass *vb* oorskry; oortref; uitblink; uitmunt
surplus *n* surplus; oorskot; *adj* oortollig
surprise *n* verrassing; verwondering; *vb* verwonder; bevreem(d)
surprised *adj* verwonder; **be —** *vb* skeefkyk
surprising *adj* verbasend; verrassend
surrender *n* oorgawe; uitlewering; *vb* oorgee; oorlewer; uitlewer; afgee
surrogate mother *n* surrogaatmoeder
surround *vb* omgewe; omring; omsingel
surrounding *adj* omliggend
surroundings *n* omgewing
surtax *n* heffing
surveillance camera *n* loerkamera
survey *n* opmeting; opname; oorsig; *vb* opmeet
surveyor *n* opmeter
survival *n* oorlewing; voortbestaan
survivalist *n* oorlewingskundige
survive *vb* oorlewe; deurkom
survivor *n* langslewende
susceptible *adj* ontvanklik; vatbaar
sushi *n* sushi
suspect *vb* verdink; vermoed; wantrou
suspected *adj* verdag
suspecting nothing *adj* perdgerus; doodgerus
suspend *vb* hang; ophang; (from school) skors

suspense *n* spanning
suspension *n* skorsing
suspension bridge *n* hangbrug; kettingbrug
suspicion *n* suspisie; vermoede; verdenking; agterdog; argwaan; wantrou
suspicious *adj* suspisieus; verdag; kwaaddenkend
sustainability *n* volhoubaarheid
sustainable *adj* volhoubaar
sustenance *n* leeftog
suture *n* naat
swaddling-cloth *n* luier
swagger *n* swier
swallow[1] *n* sluk; *vb* insluk; **— up** *vb* verswelg; opsluk
swallow[2] *n* swa(w)el
swamp *n* moeras
swan *n* swaan
swan song *n* swanesang
swarm *n* swerm; *vb* swerm; krioel
sway *vb* slinger
swear *vb* knoop; vloek; beëdig
swearing *n* geswets; gevloek
swearword *n* vloek; knoop
sweat *n* sweet; *vb* sweet
sweater *n* trui
sweatshop *n* afslooffabriek
swede *n* raap
sweep *vb* vee; **— out** *vb* uitvee
sweepstake *n* poslotery
sweet *adj* soet; lekker; lief; lieftallig; aanvallig
sweet on *adj* verlief
sweet pea *n* pronk-ertjie
sweet potato *n* patat
sweeten *vb* suiker; versoet
sweetener *n* versoeter
sweetheart *n* geliefde; hartlam; liefste; nooi; soetlief; beminde
sweetly *adv* lief
sweetness *n* soetigheid
sweets *npl* lekkergoed; soetigheid; *npl* lekkers
swell *vb* dein; peul; swel; uitdy; *n* (sea) deining; **— up** *vb* opswel
swelling *n* geswel; knobbel; puisie; buil
swift *adj* gou; rats; snel
swiftly *adv* gou
swill *vb* suip
swim *vb* swem; dryf

swimmer *n* swemmer
swimming bath *n* swembad
swimming costume *n* swempak; baai-
kostuum
swimming pool *n* swembad
swindle *vb* swendel; kul
swindler *n* swendelaar; afsetter
swindling *n* swendel
swine *n* swyn; vark
swing *n* skoppelmaai; slinger; swaai;
skommel; *vb* slinger; swaai; skommel;
— **round** *vb* krink
swipe *vb* (card) trek
swirl *vb* druis; warrel
switch *n* skakelaar; (railway) wissel; —
off *vb* skakel; uitskakel; afskakel; —
on *vb* skakel; aanslaan; inskakel
switchboard *n* skakelbord
swollen *adj* (river) geswolle
swoon *n* beswyming; *vb* beswym
swop *vb* omruil; ruil
sword *n* swaard; sabel
sworn *adj* beëdigde; geswore
swot *vb* blok
syllable *n* lettergreep; sillabe
syllabus *n* sillabus; leergang
symbol *n* simbool; sinnebeeld

symbolic(al) *adj* simbolies
symmetrical *adj* simmetries
sympathetic *adj* meegaande; meewarig; simpatiek
sympathize *vb* simpatiseer
sympathizer *n* meeloper
sympathy *n* simpatie; deernis; medegevoel; meegevoel; deelneming
symphony *n* simfonie
symptom *n* simptoom; teken; voorteken
synagogue *n* sinagoge
syncopate *vb* sinkopeer
syndicate *n* sindikaat
syndrome *n* sindroom
synod *n* sinode
synonym *n* sinoniem
synonymous *adj* sinoniem
synoptic *adj* sinopties
syntax *n* sinsbou; sintaksis
synthetic *adj* sinteties
syringe *n* spuit
syrup *n* stroop
system *n* stelsel; sisteem; gestel
systematic *adj* sistematies; stelselmatig

T

T-junction *n* T-aansluiting
table *n* tabel; dis
table tennis *n* tafeltennis
tablecloth *n* tafellaken
tableland *n* hoogvlakte
tablespoon *n* eetlepel
tablet *n* tablet; steen; (computing) tablet; (computing) tabletrekenaar
tabloid newspaper *n* poniekoerant
taboo *n* taboe
tack[1] *n* spyker; *vb* (sailing) laveer
tack[2] *n* (horses) tuig
tackie *n* seilskoen
tackle *n* fishing, etc.) takel; tuig; *vb* lak; plant
tact *n* tak(t)
tactful *adj* tak(t)vol
tactic *n* taktiek
tactless *adj* tak(t)loos
taffeta *n* tafsy
tail *n* stert
tailor *n* kleremaker; snyer
taint *n* blaam
take *vb* vat; aangryp; — **medicine** *vb* inneem; — **an oath** *vb* aflê; insweer; — **a photograph** *vb* afneem; fotografeer; — **a shower** *vb* stort; — **a walk** *vb* wandel; — **the chair** *vb* voorsit; — **the trouble to** *vb* doen moeite; — **action** *vb* optree; — **advantage of** *vb* profiteer; uitbuit; — **aim** *vb* aanlê; — **an interest in** *vb* belangstel; — **away** *vb* ontneem; wegbring; wegneem; beneem; afneem; — **down** *vb* afneem; — **by surprise** *vb* oorrompel; — **care** *vb* sorg; oppas; — **care of** *vb* behartig; oppas; — **counsel with** *vb* raadpleeg; — **cuttings** *vb* steg; — **for** *vb* hou; — **from** *vb* oorneem; — **hold of** *vb* aanpak; beetneem; — **in** *vb* flous; huisves; (clothes) inneem; — **measures** *vb* maatreëls tref; — **notice** *vb* oplet; — **one's degree** *vb* promoveer; — **out** *vb* uithaal; — **over** *vb* oorneem; — **part in** *vb* deelneem; — **pity on** *vb* ontferm; — **place** *vb* plaasvind; word; — **root**

vb wortelskiet; — **shelter** *vb* skuil; — **snuff** *vb* snuif; — **someone's arm** *vb* inhaak; — **steps** *vb* maatreëls tref; — **turns** *vb* aflos; — **up** *vb* opneem; opraap; opvat; — **with** *vb* saamneem; saamvat; meeneem
taken on *adj* aangenome
takeaway *n* (food) wegneemete
takeover *n* oorname
taking *n* (castle, town, etc.) inneming
takings *npl* ontvangs
talc *n* talk
talcum powder *n* talkpoeier
tale *n* storie; vertelling
talent *n* talent; aanleg; gawe; vernuf
talented *adj* talentvol; begaaf
talisman *n* doepa; talisman; toorgoed
talk *n* gepraat; opspraak; gebabbel; *vb* praat; spreek; gesels; — **nicely about** *vb* mooipraat; — **nonsense** *vb* praat kaf; — **over** *vb* bespreek
talkative *adj* spraaksaam
talking *n* gepraat; gesprek
talking head *n* pratende kop
tall *adj* groot; hoog; lang
tally *n* rym
tam(e)able *adj* tembaar
tamarind *n* tamaryn
tame *adj* mak; *vb* tem
tamper with *vb* peuter
tamper-proof *adj* peutervry
tan *n* sonbruin; *vb* looi; sonbruin
tangent *n* tangens
tangible *adj* tasbaar; voelbaar
tangle *vb* verwar
tangled *adj* verwar
tango *n* tango
tank *n* reënbak; tenk
tanner *n* leerlooier
tannery *n* leerlooiery; looiery
tap[1] *n* klop; tik; *vb* klop; tik
tap[2] *n* kraan; (barrel) tap; *vb* aftap; (telephone) meeluister
tape *n* band; lint
tape measure *n* meetband; maatband
tapestry *n* tapisserie
tapeworm *n* lintwurm

tar *n* teer
tarantula *n* bobbejaanspinnekop
tare *n* tarra
target *n* mikpunt; teiken; skyf
target shooting *n* teikenskiet
tariff *n* tarief
tarnish *vb* verdof; vuilmaak
tarpaulin *n* bokseil; seil
tarred road *n* teerpad
tart[1] *n* tert
tart[2] *adj* suur; vrank
task *n* taak; opgaaf
tassel *n* kwas
taste *n* smaak; trant; *vb* proe; smaak
tasteful *adj* smaakvol
tasteless *adj* smaakloos
tasty *adj* smaaklik
tatter *n* flenter
tattered *adj* verflenter
tatters *npl* toiings
tattoo *vb* tatoeëer
taunt *vb* tart
taut *adj* strak
tavern *n* herberg
tawny *n* (colour) geelbruin; *adj* vaal; geelbruin
tax *n* belasting; skatting; *vb* belas; takseer
tax clearance form *n* belastingklaringsvorm
tax-collector *n* ontvanger
taxable *adj* belasbaar
taxation *n* belasting
taxi *n* taxi
taxi stand *n* taxistaanplek
taxidermist *n* opstopper
tea *n* tee
tea cosy *n* mus; teemus
tea service *n* teeservies
tea strainer *n* teesiffie
teach *vb* leer; onderrig; onderwys; bybring
teacher *n* onderwyser; dosent; meester; (female) onderwyseres
teaching *n* lering
teacup *n* teekoppie
teak *n* (wood) kiaathout
team *n* span
team spirit *n* spangees
tear[1] *n* skeur; *vb* skeur; torring; **— off** *vb* afruk; **— out** *vb* uitskeur; **— up** *vb* verskeur

tear[2] *n* traan
tears *npl* trane; **shed —** *vb* trane stort
tearful *adj* treurig; vol trane
tease *n* terggees; kwelgees; *vb* jil
teaser *n* (marketing) lokteks
teaspoon *n* teelepel
teat *n* speen; tepel; tiet
techie *n* (*informal*) tekkie; rekenaarfoendie
technical *adj* tegnies; **— education** *n* vakonderwys; **— skill** *n* tegniek
technician *n* tegnikus
technique *n* tegniek
techno *n* (music) tegnomusiek
technology *n* tegnologie
tedious *adj* vervelend; vervelig; saai; langdradig;vermoeiend; gerek
tee *n* (golf) bof
teem with *vb* wemel; krioel
teenager *n* tiener; tienderjarige
teetotaller *n* afskaffer; geheelonthouer; onthouer
telecommunication *n* telekommunikasie
telegram *n* telegram
telegraph *n* telegraaf; *vb* telegrafeer; sein
telemarketing *n* telebemarking
telephone *n* telefoon; *vb* bel; skakel; telefoneer
telephone call *n* telefoonoproep
telephone directory *n* telefoongids
telephone number *n* telefoonnommer
telephone operator *n* telefonis
telescope *n* teleskoop; verkyker
televise *vb* beeldsaai; beeldsend
television *n* televisie; beeldradio
telex *n* teleks; *vb* teleks
tell *vb* verhaal; sê; **— a fib** *vb* jok; **— fortunes** *vb* waarsê; **— lies** *vb* lieg; **— tales** *vb* klik; lieg
telling off *n* vermaning
temper *n* natuur; temperament
temperament *n* natuur; temperament
temperamental *adj* temperamenteel
temperate *adj* gematig; sober
temperateness *n* gematigdheld
temperature *n* temperatuur
tempestuous *adj* stormagtig
template *n* sjabloon; templaat; meester; patroon

temple[1] *n* tempel
temple[2] *n* (head) slaap
tempo *n* tempo
temporal *adj* wêreldlik
temporary *adj* tydelik; waarnemend
temporarily *adv* tydelik
tempt *vb* uitlok; verlei; verlok
temptation *n* temptasie; verleiding; versoeking
tempting *adj* aanloklik; verleidelik
ten *n, determiner* tien
ten o'clock *n, adj* tienuur
tenacious *adj* taai; vashoudend
tenant *n* huurder; pagter
tenant farmer *n* bywoner
tend *vb* verpleeg
tendency *n* neiging; strekking; stroming; tendens
tender[1] *adj* gevoelig; mals; sag; teer; week; weekhartig
tender[2] *n* tender; *vb* tender; indien; inskryf
tender-hearted *adj* teerhartig
tendon *n* sening
tendril *n* rank
tenfold *adj, adv* tienvoud
tennis *n* tennis
tennis ball *n* tennisbal
tennis court *n* tennisbaan; baan
tennis player *n* tennisspeler
tenor *n* strekking; (voice) tenoor
tenpin bowling alley *n* tienkegelbaan
tense[1] *n* (grammar) tyd
tense[2] *adj* strak; styf
tension *n* spanning; stres
tent *n* tent
tentacle *n* voelhoring
tenth *n, adj* tiende
tepid *adj* lou
term *n* kwartaal; term; woord; termyn
term of office *n* dienstyd
terminal *n* terminus; *adj* terminaal
terminate *vb* afloop; verstryk
termination *n* afloop; einde
terminology *n* terminologie
terminus *n* eindpunt; terminus
termite *n* rysmier; termiet
terms of reference *npl* opdrag
terrace *n* terras
terrible *adj* vreeslik; verskriklik; ontsaglik; hewig; naar

terribly *adv* vreeslik; ontsaglik
terrier *n* terriër
terrify *vb* verskrik
terrifying *adj* skrikwekkend
territory *n* gebied; grondgebied; domein; bodem
terror *n* angs; ontsetting; verskrikking; skrik
terrorism *n* terreur; terrorisme
terrorist *n* terroris; *adj* terroriste
terse *adj* bondig; kernagtig
tertiary *adj* tersiêr
tertiary education *n* tersiêre onderwys
test *n* toets; proef; *vb* toets; keur; beproef
test case *n* toetssaak
test flight *n* toetsvlug
test match *n* toetswedstryd
test-tube baby *n* proefbuisbaba
testament *n* testament
testator *n* testateur
testify *vb* betuig; getuig
testimonial *n* getuigskrif
testimony *n* getuienis
text *n* teks; onderwerp; *vb* teks
text alert *n* waarskuwing
textbook *n* handboek; handleiding; leerboek
textile *n* tekstiel; — **industry** *n* tekstielnywerheid
texture *n* weefsel
thank *vb* bedank; dank; —**s** *n* dank
thank God! *interj* God sy dank!
thank you! *sentence substitute* dankie!
thankful *adj* dankbaar; erkentlik
thanks! *sentence substitute* dankie!; **many** —! *sentence substitute* baie dankie!
that *dterminer* dié; *conj* dat; opdat; — **one** *pron* daardie; — **way** *adv* soheentoe; soontoe
thatch *n* dekgras; riet; *vb* dek
thatch roof *n* rietdak
thatched roof *n* strooidak
thatcher *n* dekker
thaw *vb* ontdooi; dooi
the *definite article* de; die
theatre *n* teater; toneel; skouburg
theatrical company *n* toneelgeselskap
theft *n* diefstal
their *pers pron* hulle; hul

them *pers pron* hulle; hul
theme *n* onderwerp; stof; tema
then *adj* toenmalig; *adv* daar
thence *adv* daaruit
theologian *n* teoloog
theology *n* teologie; godgeleerdheid
theorem *n* stelling
theoretical *adj* teoreties
theory *n* teorie; — **of education** *n* pedagogiek; — **of relativity** *n* relatiwiteitsteorie
therapist *n* terapeut
therapy *n* terapie
there *adv* daar; daarheen; daarnatoe; daarso
thereabout(s) *adv* daaromtrent
thereby *adv* daardeur
therefore *adv* derhalwe; *conj* daarom
therein *adv* daarin
thereof *adv* daarvan
thereupon *adv* daarop
therewith *adv* daarmee
thermometer *n* termometer
these *definite article* dié; *pron* hierdie
thesis *n* stelling; tesis
they *n* mens; *pers pron* hulle
thick *adj* dik; lywig; — **and sticky** *adj* klewerig
thick smoke *n* walm
thicken *vb* aandik
thickness *n* dikte
thief *n* dief
thievish *adj* diefagtig
thigh *n* dy
thimble *n* vingerhoed
thin *adj* dun; fyn; maer; rank; skraal; smal; yl; *vb* verdun; — **out** *vb* uitdun
thin as a rake *adj* rietskraal
thin pancake *n* flensie
thing *n* ding; saak; — **of beauty** *n* pragwerk
things *npl* goedjies, goeters
think *vb* dink; geloof; glo; prakseer; — **over** *n* oorleg
thinking *n* denke
third *n, adj* derde
third party cover *n* (insurance) derdepartydekking
third-rate *adj* derderangs
thirst *n* dors
thirsty *adj* dorstig; **be —** *vb* dors

thirteen *n, determiner* dertien
thirteenth *n, adj* dertiende
thirtieth *n, adj* dertigste
thirty *n, determiner* dertig
this *determiner* dié; *adj* onderhawig; *pron* dit; — **afternoon** *n, adv* vanmiddag; — **day** *n, adv* hede; — **evening** *n, adv* vanaand; — **month** *n, adv* vandeesmaand; — **morning** *n, adv* vanmôre; — **way** *adv* hierheen; hierlangs; hiernatoe; — **week** *n, adv* vandeesweek; — **year** *n, adv* vanjaar
thither *adv* daarheen; daarnatoe; soheentoe; soontoe
thong *n* riem
thorax *n* ribbekas
thorn *n* doring
thorn tree *n* doringboom
thorny *adj* netelig
thorough *adj* sorgvuldig; grondig; deurtastend; stewig; dugtig
thoroughfare *n* deurgang; **No —** (traffic sign) Geen Deurgang
thoroughbred *adj* raseg; volbloed
thoroughly *adv* deeglik; deur en deur
those *determiner* die; diegene
though *adv* mos; *conj* al
thought *n* denke; gedagte; inval
thoughtful *adj* bedagsaam
thoughtless *adj* onbedagsaam; onnadenkend; ondeurdag; onbesonne; onbekook; gedagteloos
thousand *n, determiner* duisend
thrash *vb* afransel; foeter
thrashing *n* loesing; pak
thread *n* draad; gare; naaigare; vasel; vesel; *vb* insteek
threadbare *adj* verslyt
threadworm *n* haarwurm
threat *n* dreigement
threaten *vb* bedreig; dreig
three *n, determiner* drie; — **days ago** *adv* vooreergister
three o'clock *n, adj* drie-uur
three times *adv* driemaal
thresh *vb* (grain crops) dors
threshing-machine *n* dorsmasjien
threshold *n* drumpel
thrice *adv* driemaal
thrift *n* spaarsaamheid
thrifty *adj* spaarsaam; suinig

thrilled *adj* opgewonde
thriller *n* (book) riller
thrive *vb* gedy; tier
throat *n* keel; strot; gorrel
throb *vb* klop
throne *n* troon
throng *n* drom; toeloop; toevloed
throttle *vb* verwurg; wurg
through *prep* deur; **— the top** *adv* bodeur; **— what** *inter pron* waardeur; **— which** *inter pron* waardeur
throw *vb* gooi; smyt; werp; *n* (cover) oorgooilap; sierlap; **— away** *vb* weggooi; wegsmyt; **— down** *vb* afstoot; omgooi; afgooi; **— into confusion** *vb* omkrap; **— off** *vb* afgooi; afwerp; **— open** *vb* oopstel; **— up** *vb* opgooi
thrust *n* stoot; *vb* stoot
thud *n* plof; bons
thug *n* skurk
thumb *n* duim
thunder *n* donder; *vb* bulder; donder
thunderclap *n* donderslag
thunderstorm *n* donderbui; onweer; swaarweer
Thursday *n* Donderdag
thus *adv* so; sodoende; *conj* dus; **— far** *adv* hiertoe
thwart *vb* dwarsdrywe; teenwerk; weerstrewe
thyme *n* tiemie
thyroid gland *n* skildklier
tick *n* bosluis
ticket *n* kaartjie; kaart; biljet
ticket vending machine *n* kaartjiesmasjien
ticket-office window *n* loket
tickle *vb* kielie; kriewel; *n* gekielie
tickling *n* gekriewel
ticklish *adj* kielierig; kriewelrig
tidal wave *n* getygolf; vloedgolf
tiddlywinks *n* vlooiespel
tide *n* gety
tidiness *n* netheid
tidings *n* nuus; tyding
tidy *adj* netjies; sindelik; *vb* opruim; **— up** *vb* maak netjies; maak aan die kant; opknap
tie *n* das; band; *vb* aanbind; knoop; snoer; strik; **— up** *vb* meer; toebind
tiger *n* tier

tight *adj* styf; knap; eng; nou; spannend; strak
tighten *vb* aandraai; aanhaal; (nut) vasdraai
tightfisted *adj* snoep
tights *n* broekiekouse; spanbroek
tigress *n* tierwyfie
tilapia *n* kurper
tile *n* pan; dakpan; teël; *vb* teël
tiled roof *n* pandak
till[1] *conj* tot; totdat; *prep* tot
till[2] *n* kasregister; geldlaai
till[3] *vb* (soil) bewerk; (soil) bebou
tilt *vb* wip; kantel
timber *n* hout; timmerhout
timber trade *n* houthandel
timber yard *n* houtwerf
time *n* tyd; tydperk; termyn; stonde; poos; skoot; maal; **at any —** *adv* ooit; **at that —** *adv* dan; destyds; toe; **at the same —** *adv* meteen; tegelyk; tewens; **at the —** *adv* indertyd; toentertyd
time bomb *n* tydbom
time of life *n* leeftyd
time-consuming *adj* tydrowend
time-honoured *adj* eerwaardig
timely *adj* betyds; vroeg; tydig
timepiece *n* uurwerk
timetable *n* rooster; tydtafel
timid *adj* beskroomd; inkennig; skroomvallig; bedees; kopsku; skugter; verleë; vreesagtig; bang; skaam
timorous *adj* skroomvallig
tin *n* blik; tin
tin can *n* kantien
tinfoil *n* foelie
tincture *n* aftreksel; tinktuur
tingle *vb* tuit
tinkle *vb* tingel; klingel
tinkling *n* getingel; geklinkel
tinned *adj* vertin; blik
tiny amount *n* mondjievol
tip[1] *n* fooi; gratifikasie; wenk; *vb* fooi
tip[2] *n* punt; spits; tip
tip[3] *vb* omkantel; wip
tipple *n* borrel; *vb* drink
tipsy *adj* lekker; lekkerlyf
tiramisu *n* tiramisu
tire *vb* afmat; vermoei
tired *adj* moeg; afgemat; mat; vermoeid; tam; **— out** *adj* doodmoeg; boeglam

tiredness *n* lamheid
tiresome *adj* moeisaam; vervelend
tiring *adj* moeisaam; vermoeiend
tissue *n* snesie; weefsel
tissue culture *n* weefselkultuur
title *n* titel; benaming; opskrif; reg; aanspraak
title deed *n* transportakte
title page *n* titelblad
title role *n* titelrol
titled *adj* adellik
to *adv* om; te; *prep* tot; aan; by; jeens; na; teen; ter; toe; vir
to the fore *adv* vorentoe
to wit *adv* naamlik
to-do *n* omhaal
toad *n* padda
toadstool *n* paddastoel
toast[1] *n* heildronk
toast[2] *n* roosterbrood; vb braai
tobacco *n* tabak
tobacco pouch *n* tabaksak
today *n, adv* hede; vandag
toddler *n* peuter; kleuter
toe *n* toon
toffee *n* toffie; tameletjie
toffee apple *n* toffie-appel
toga *n* toga
together *adv* aanmekaar; gesamentlik; aaneengeslote; byeen; — **with** *adv* benewens
toggle key *n* (computing) opsiesleutel; (computing) opsietoets
toil *n* arbeid; *vb* afsloof
toilet *n* toilet; kleinhuisie
toiling *n* getob
token *n* bewys; blyk; merk; merkteken; teken
tolerable *adj* draaglik; redelik; skiklik; taamlik
tolerably *adv* taamlik
tolerant *adj* meegaande; verdraagsaam
tolerate *vb* duld; gedoog; ly; tolereer
toleration *n* toleransie
toll[1] *n* tol; — **pass** *n* toldeurgang
toll[2] *vb* (bell) lui
toll free *adj* tolvry
tollgate *n* tolhek
tomato *n* tamatie
tomb *n* praalgraf
tomboy *n* rabbedoe; malkop; maltrap

tombstone *n* grafsteen
tomorrow *n, adv* môre; **the day after** — *n, adv* oormôre; — **evening** *n, adv* moreaand; — **morning** *n, adv* môre-oggend
ton *n* ton
tone *n* klank; toon
toneless *adj* toonloos
tongue *n* tong
tongue twister *n* tongknoper
tonic *n* opknapmiddel; versterkingsmiddel
tonight *n, adv* vanaand; vannag
tonnage *n* tonnemaat
tonsil *n* mangel
tonsillectomy *n* tonsilektomie
tonsillitis *n* tonsilitis
tonsure *n* tonsuur
too *adv* ook; te; tewens; alte
tool *n* instrument; werktuig
tools *npl* gereedskap
toot *vb* toet
tooth *n* tand
toothache *n* tandpyn
toothbrush *n* tandeborsel
toothpaste *n* tandepasta
top *n* kruin; punt; spits; tol; top; *vb* top; **at the** — *adv* bo-op
top dog *n* bobaas; (*informal*) baas
top end *n* bo-ent
top hat *n* keil
topside *n* bokant
top-heavy *adj* topswaar
topaz *n* topaas
topic *n* onderwerp
topical *adj* aktueel
topple over *vb* omkantel; omslaan; omval
topsy-turvy *adj* onderstebo
torch *n* flitslig; toorts; flambou; fakkel
torment *n* pyniging; *vb* kwel; pynig
tormentor *n* terggees; kwelgees
torn *adj* stukkend; verflenter
tornado *n* tornado; windhoos
torpedo *n* torpedo; *vb* torpedeer
torso *n* romp
tortoise *n* skilpad
torture *n* pyniging; *vb* folter; pynig
tot *n* sopie; borrel; doppie; (child) peuter
total *n* totaal; *adj* bruto; finaal

totally *adv* volslae; totaal
totter *vb* waggel; wankel; wikkel
touch *n* kontak; tik; voeling; *vb* voel; aanraak; aandoen; tik; **— on** *vb* aanroer; aanstip
touch of *n* aandoening
touching *adj* aandoenlik; aangrypend; hartroerend; roerend; treffend
touchstone *n* toetssteen
touchy *adj* liggeraak; puntenerig
tough *adj* swaar; taai;hard
tour *n* rondreis; toer
tourism *n* toerisme; toerismebedryf; toeristebedryf
tourist *n* reisiger; toeris
tourist industry *n* toerismebedryf; toeristebedryf
tournament *n* toernooi
tousled *adj* verwar
tow *vb* sleep
towards *adv* heen; *prep* jeens
towbar *n* trekstang
towel *n* handdoek
tower *n* kerktoring; toring
town *n* dorp; stad
town clerk *n* stadsklerk
town coat of arms *n* stadswapen
town council *n* stadsraad
town hall *n* stadhuis; stadsaal
townhouse *n* meenthuis
township *n* woongebied
townsman *n* stedeling
towrope *n* sleeptou
toxin *n* gifstof
toy boy *n* (*informal*) katelknaap
toys *npl* speelgoed
trace *n* sweem; string; *vb* nagaan
track *n* spoor; voetspoor; paadjie; *vb* opspoor
tracker *n* spoorsnyer
tracksuit *n* sweetpak
tract[1] *n* streek
tract[2] *n* traktaatjie
traction *n* traksie
tractor *n* trekker
trade *n* ambag; beroep; handel; koophandel; handwerk; nering
trade mark *n* handelsmerk
trade school *n* ambagskool
trade union *n* vakbond
trade wind *n* passaatwind

trademark *n* fabrieksmerk
trader *n* handelaar
tradition *n* tradisie; oorlewering
traditional *adj* tradisioneel
traditional remedy *n* raat
traffic *n* verkeer; vervoer; transport
traffic control *n* verkeerbeheer
traffic fine *n* verkeersboete
traffic interchange *n* wisselkruising
traffic jam *n* verkeersknoop
traffic lights *npl* verkeersligte; (set of) robot
traffic sign *n* verkeersteken
traffic lane *n* baan
tragedy *n* tragedie; treurspel
tragic *adj* tragies
trail *n* rank; spoor
trailer *n* treiler; (movie) lokfilm
train *n* trein; ysterperd; sleep; stoet; *vb* afrig; oefen; dril
train bearer *n* sleepdraer
train driver *n* treindrywer
train driver *n* drywer
train platform *n* platform
trained *adj* geoefen(d); geskool
trainee *n* kwekeling; opleideling
trainer *n* opleier
training *n* opleiding; opvoeding; oefening
training course *n* opleidingskursus
training school *n* kweekskool
trait *n* karaktertrek; trek
traitor *n* verraaier
traitorous *adj* verraderlik
trajectory *n* trajek
tram *n* trem
tramcar *n* trem
tramp *n* boemelaar
trample *vb* trap
trampoline *n* springmat; trampolien; wipmat
trance *n* trans; geesvervoering
tranquillizer *n* kalmeermiddel
transaction *n* transaksie; handeling; handeling
transcribe *vb* transkribeer; oorskryf
transfer *n* oordrag; oorgawe; oorplasing; transport; verplasing; *vb* oorbring; oordra; verplaas
transferable *adj* oordraagbaar
transform *vb* herskep; omskep

transformation *n* gedaanteverwisseling
transformed *adj* herskape
transient *adj* verganklik
transition *n* oorgang
transitive *adj* transitief
transitory *adj* verbygaand
translate *vb* vertaal; oorsit
translation *n* vertaling
translator *n* vertaler
translucent *adj* deurskynend
transmit *vb* voortplant
transmitter *n* sender
transparent *adj* deursigtig; deurskynend
transpire *vb* uitlek
transplant *vb* plant; oorplant
transport *n* transport; vervoer; voer; *vb* aanry; vervoer
transport firm *n* redery
transportation *n* vervoer
trap *n* lokval; strik; val; valstrik; wip; *vb* vang
trapdoor *n* luik; valluik
trapeze *n* sweefstok
trapeze artist *n* sweefarties
trapezium *n* trapesium
trappings *npl* opskik
trash *n* kafpraatjies; vullis; bog; prul; uitskot
trash can *n* vullisblik
trauma *n* trauma
travel *n* reis; *vb* reis; toer; trek; — **about** *n* rondreis; — **over** *vb* bereis; — **through** *vb* bereis
travel agency *n* reisagentskap
traveller *n* reisiger
travelling expenses *n* reiskoste
travelling rug *n* reisdeken
travels *npl* swerftog
travesty *n* parodie
trawl *vb* treil
trawler *n* treiler
tray *n* skinkbord
treacherous *adj* slinks; vals; verraderlik
treachery *n* verraad
treacle *n* swartstroop
tread *n* tred; *vb* tree; — **on** *vb* betree
treadmill *n* trapmeul
treason *n* verraad
treasure *n* skat

treasure hunt *n* skattejag
treasurer *n* tesourier; penningmeester
treasury *n* skatkis; tesourie
treat *n* onthaal; fees; *vb* behandel; onthaal; (material) bearbei
treatment *n* behandeling; **receive —** *vb* behandeling ondergaan
treatise *n* referaat; verhandeling
treaty *n* traktaat; verbond; verdrag
treble *adj* driedubbel; drievoudig
tree *n* boom
tree trunk *n* boomstam
trellis *n* tralie
tremble *vb* beef; huiwer; rittel; sidder; tril
tremendous *adj* ontsaglik
tremor *n* trilling
trench *n* loopgraaf; sloot
trend *n* rigting
trespasser *n* oortreder
trestle *n* bok
trial *n* proef; toets; verhoor; beproewing
trial run *n* toetsrit
triangle *n* driehoek; (music) triangel
triangular *adj* driehoekig
tribal village *n* kraal
tribal war *n* stamoorlog
tribe *n* stam
tribunal *n* gereg; regbank; vierskaar
tributary *n* skatpligtig
trick *n* slenter; streek; laai; lis; poets; set; kaskenade; toer; truuk; *vb* bedrieg; fop
trick question *n* strikvraag
trickle *vb* drup; druip; biggel; — **out** *vb* uitlek
tricks *npl* fratse
tricky *adj* bedrieglik; oulik
trifle *n* kleinigheid; prul; tierlantyntjie; *vb* beusel; draai; — **with** *vb* speel
trifling *adj* beuselagtig
trigger *n* sneller
trigonometry *n* driehoeksmeting; trigonometrie
trim *vb* besnoei; garneer; skeer; top
trimming *n* tooisel
trinket *n* snuistery; sieraad
trio *n* trio
trip *n* reis; uitstappie; *vb* struikel; pootjie; — **along** *vb* trippel
trip switch *n* uitskopskakelaar

triple *adj* driedubbel; drievoudig
tripod *n* drievoet
trite *adj* afgesaag
triumph *n* oorwinning; sege; triomf; *vb* seëvier; **— over** *vb* triomfeer
trivet *n* drievoet
trivial *adj* alledaags
Trojan horse *n* (computing) Trojaanse perd
trolley *n* trollie
trolleybus *n* trembus
trombone *n* skuiftrompet; basuin
troop *n* troep; bende; (monkeys) trop
troop carrier *n* troepdraer
troops *npl* troepe
trophy *n* trofee
tropic *n* (line of latitude) keerkring
tropical *adj* tropies
tropics *npl* trope
trot *vb* draf
trouble *n* moeilikheid; moeite; beslommering; gesukkel; hinder; kommer; kwelling; las; onluste; onraad; oorlas; stoor; verdriet; verleentheid; **take the — *vb* die moeite doen**
troubled *adj* beswaar; **be —** *vb* bekreun; **be — over** *vb* bekommer
troublemaker *n* skoorsoeker; rusiesoeker
troublesome *adj* hinderlik; moeitevol
trough *n* bak; trog
trousers *npl* broek
trousseau *n* uitset
trout *n* forel
trowel *n* skop; troffel
truant *n* stokkiesdraaier
truce *n* stilstand; wapenstilstand
truck *n* trok; vragmotor; wa
truly *adv* eintlik; regtig; feitlik
trump *n* (playing cards) troef; *vb* troef
trumpet *n* basuin; tromp; trompet
trumpeter *n* trompetblaser
trunk *n* trommel; koffer; kis; stam; romp; (elephant) tromp; (elephant) slurp
trust *n* vertroue; trust; *vb* vertrou; geloof; glo
trusted *adj* vertroud
trustee *n* trustee; voog; administrateur
trusting *adj* goedgelowig
trustworthy *adj* geloofwaardig; solied; vertroud

truth *n* waarheid
try *vb* probeer; poog; trag; beproef; **— do something** *vb* beywer; **— for** *vb* probeer; **— on** *vb* aanpas; pas; **— to reconcile** *vb* toenader
try square *n* winkelhaak
tsar (*or* **czar**) *n* tsaar
tub *n* balie; kuip; ton; vaatjie; vat
tube *n* buis; moltrein; ondergrondse spoorweg; pyp
tube station *n* moltreinstasie
tuber *n* knol
tuberculosis *n* tering; tuberkulose
tuck *n* opnaaisel; plooi; snoepgoed
tuck shop *n* snoepwinkel
Tuesday *n* Dinsdag
tuft *n* kuif; vlok; bos; **— of grass** *n* pol
tug *n* sleepboot; ruk; *vb* ruk
tug-of-war *n* toutrek
tuition *n* onderrig; onderwys
tulip *n* tulp
tulle *n* tulle
tumble *vb* tuimel; **— down** *vb* afstort
tumble drier *n* tuimeldroër
tumbler *n* glas
tumour *n* tumor; geswel
tumult *n* storm
tune *n* wysie; deuntjie; liedjie; sang; stem; aria
tuned *adj* gestem
tuneful *adj* sangerig
tuner *n* instemmer; stemmer
tuning-fork *n* stemvurk
tunnel *n* tonnel
turban *n* tulband
turbulent *adj* onstuimig
turf *n* turf; sooi
turf racing *n* perde(wed)renne
turf war *n* (gangs) gebiedsoorlog
turkey *n* kalkoen
Turkish carpet *n* kelim
turmeric *n* borrie
turn *n* beurt; draai; keer; kentering; skoot; wending; *vb* draai; keer; wend; kink; tol; **— aside** *vb* afwend; uitdraai; uitwyk; **— away** *vb* wegdraai; **— back** *vb* omdraai; **— bad** *n* bederf; **— down a road** *vb* inslaan; **— into a road** *vb* indraai; **— off** *vb* afsluit; **— on** *vb* aandraai; **— out** *vb* omkeer; uitkom; **— over** *vb* omslaan; **— over**

pages *vb* blaai; omblaai; — **round** *vb* omdraai; — **sour** *vb* versuur; — **up** *vb* ombuig; opdaag; — **upside down** *vb* omkeer
turncoat *n* manteldraaier
turned-up nose *n* wipneus
turning point *n* keerpunt
turnip *n* raap
turnover *n* omset; afset
turnpike *n* tol
turnstile *n* draaihek
turntable *n* draaitafel
turpentine *n* terpentyn
turquoise *n, adj* turkoois
turret *n* torinkie
turtle *n* waterskilpad
turtle dove *n* tortelduif
tusk *n* slagtand
TV drama *n* naelkouer
twaddle *n* geklets
twelfth *n, adj* twaalfde
twelve *n, determiner* twaalf
twentieth *n, adj* twintigste
twenty *n, determiner* twintig
twenty-four-hour service *n* etmaaldiens
twice *adv* dubbel; tweemaal

twilight *n* halfdonker; skemer
twin *n* tweeling
twine *n* seilgare; *vb* rank
twinkle *vb* flikker; glinster; tintel; vonkel
twinkling *n* flonkering; tinteling
twist *n* draai; kink; *vb* kronkel; kink
twisted *adj* verwronge
twitter *vb* tjilp
two *n, determiner* twee
two o'clock *n, adj* twee-uur
two-faced *adj* tweegesig; skynheilig; dubbelhartig
tycoon *n* geldmagnaat
type *n* tipe; soort; drukskrif; *vb* tik
typewriter *n* tikmasjien
typewriting *n* tikskrif
typhoid fever *n* ingewandskoors; tifus
typhoon *n* tifoon
typhus *n* tifus
typical *adj* tipies
typing *n* tikskrif
typographer *n* tipograaf
typographical *adj* tipografiese
typography *n* tipografie; drukkuns
tyrant *n* tiran; despoot; dwingeland

U

udder *n* uier
ugly *adj* lelik; foeilelik
ulcer *n* sweer
ulcerate *vb* sweer; versweer
ulceration *n* verswering
ultimatum *n* ultimatum
ultraconservative *adj* verkramp
umbilical cord *n* naelstring
umbrella *n* sambreel
umpire *n* skeidsregter
UN *see* **United Nations**
unabated *adj* onverflou(d)
unable *adj* onvermoënd
unabridged *adj* onverkort
unaccented *adj* toonloos
unacceptable *adj* onaanneemlik; verwerplik; onaanvaarbaar
unaccountable *adj* onverklaarbaar
unaccustomed *adj* ongewend
unadulterated *adj* onvervals
unaffected *adj* ongekunsteld
unafraid *adj* onbevrees
unaided *adj* selfstandig
unaltered *adj* onveranderd
unanimity *n* eenheid
unanimous *adj* eenparig; eensgesind; eenstemmig; onverdeel(d); algemeen
unanimously *adv* algemeen
unanswered *adj* onbeantwoord
unapproachable *adj* ontoeganklik; ongenaakbaar
unarmed *adj* ongewapen
unattainable *adj* onbereikbaar
unattractive *adj* onaansienlik; onooglik
unavoidable *adj* onvermydelik
unaware *adj* onbewus
unawares *adv* onverwags
unban *vb* ontperk
unbaptized *adj* ongedoop
unbearable *adj* ondraaglik; onuitstaanbaar; onverdraagbaar; onduldbaar
unbelievable *adj* ongelooflik
unbend *vb* ontdooi; ontspan
unbiased *adj* onbevooroordeeld; onpartydig; onbevange
unbleached *adj* ongebleik
unblemished *adj* onbevlekte

unblock *vb* (account) ontblok
unbounded *adj* grensloos
unbreakable *adj* onbreekbaar
unbridled *adj* teuelloos; toomloos
unbuckle *vb* losgord
unburden *vb* ontlas; — **oneself** *vb* uitstort
unbutton *vb* ontknoop
uncalled for *adj* ongevraag
uncared for *adj* onversorg
unceasing *adj* onverpoos
uncertain *adj* onseker; onbeslis; wisselvallig; **be** — *vb* hink
uncertainty *n* onsekerheid
unchain *vb* ontketen
unchangeable *adj* onveranderlik
unchanged *adj* onveranderd
unchristened *adj* ongedoop
unchristian *adj* onchristelik
uncivilized *adj* onbeskaaf(d)
uncle *n* oom
unclean *adj* onrein; onsindelik
uncomfortable *adj* ongemaklik; ongerieflik; onbehaaglik
uncommon *adj* ongewoon; ongemeen
unconcerned *adj* onbekommerd; onbesorg
unconditional *adj* onvoorwaardelik
unconquerable *adj* onoorwinlik
unconscious *adj* bewusteloos; katswink; onbewus
unconsciously *adv* onbewus
unconstitutional *adj* ongrondwetlik
unconverted *adj* onbekeerd
uncovered *adj* ontbloot
undamaged *adj* onbeskadig; gaaf
undaunted *adj* onbevrees; onverskrokke; stoutmoedig
undecided *adj* besluiteloos; onbeslis; twyfelmoedig; wankelmoedig
undefended *adj* onbeskerm(d)
undeliverable *adj* onbestelbaar
under *prep* benede; onder; onderdeur; — **here** *adv* hieronder; — **which** *inter pron* waaronder
under age *adj* minderjarig

under one's breath *adv* binnensmonds; fluisterend
underachiever *n* onderpresteerder
undercarriage *n* onderstel
undercut *vb* onderkruip
underestimate *vb* onderskat
underfed *adj* ondervoed
underfeeding *n* ondervoeding
undergo *vb* ondergaan; — **an operation** *n* 'n operasie ondergaan
underground *adj* onderaards; ondergronds; *n* (train system) moltrein
underground railway *n* ondergrondse spoorweg
underground station *n* moltreinstasie
undergrowth *n* ruigte; struikgewas
underhand *adj* agterbaks; onderduims; onderhands; geniepsig
underline *vb* onderstreep; aandik
underling *n* ondergeskikte
undermentioned *adj* onderstaande
undermine *vb* ondermyn
underneath *prep* daaronder
underpants *n* (pair of) onderbroek
undersea(s) *adj, adv* ondersees
undersell *vb* onderkruip
undersigned *n* ondergetekende
understand *vb* gevoel; vat; begryp
understandable *adj* begryplik
understanding *n* begrip; verstandhouding
understatement *n* onderbeklemtoning
undertake *vb* onderneem
undertaker *n* aannemer; lyksbesorger
undertaking *n* onderneming
undervalue *vb* geringskat; onderskat
underwear *n* ondergoed; onderklere
undeserved *adj* onverdien(d)
undesirable *adj* ongewens; onwenslik
undeveloped *adj* onontwikkeld
undiminished *adj* onverminder(d)
undisciplined *adj* bandeloos
undisguised *adj* onbewimpeld
undisputed *adj* onbestrede; onbetwis
undissolved *adj* onopgelos
undisturbed *adj* ongehinder; ongemoei
undivided *adj* onverdeel(d)
undo *vb* losmaak; losryg; ontbind; ontknoop
undone *adj* ongedaan
undoubtedly *adv* ongetwyfeld

undress *vb* ontklee; uittrek; uitklee
undrinkable *adj* ondrinkbaar
undulate *vb* golf
unearned *adj* onverdien(d)
uneasy *adj* angstig; beangs; bekommerd; onbehaaglik; ongerus; onrustig; beswaar
uneatable *adj* oneetbaar
uneducated *adj* ongeleer(d); onopgevoed
unemotional *adj* onaandoenlik
unemployable *adj* onbruikbaar
unemployed *adj* werkloos
unemployment *n* werkloosheid
unencumbered *adj* onbelas
unenlightened *adj* verkramp
unequal *adj* onewe; ongelyk
unequalled *adj* ongeëwenaard; weergaloos
uneven *adj* ongelyk; onewe; hobbelagtig
unexpected *adj* onverwag; onvoorsien; plotseling
unexpectedly *adv* onverwags; onverhoeds
unfair *adj* onbillik; oneerlik; onredelik; onregverdig
unfaithful *adj* ontrou
unfamiliar *adj* onbekend
unfathomable *adj* ondeurgrondbaar; peilloos
unfavourable *adj* ongunstig
unfeeling *adj* hardvogtig; liefdeloos
unfeigned *adj* ongeveins
unfettered *adj* ongebonde
unfinished *adj* onvoltooi
unfit *adj* onbekwaam; ongeskik
unflagging *adj* onverflou(d)
unfold *vb* ontplooi; uitsprei
unforced *adj* ongedwonge
unforgettable *adj* onvergeetlik
unfortunate *adj* ongelukkig
unfounded *adj* ongegrond
unfriendly *adj* onvriendelik; stuurs
unfulfilled *adj* onbevredig
unfurl *vb* ontplooi
unfurnished *adj* ongemeubileer(d)
ungrateful *adj* ondankbaar
unguarded *adj* onbewaak
unhappy *adj* ongelukkig
unharmed *adj* onbeskadig

unharness *vb* uitspan; aftuig
unhealthy *adj* ongesond
unheard of *adj* ongehoor(d)
unhindered *adj* ongehinder; onbelemmer
unhurt *adj* behoue; ongedeerd; ongeskonde
unicellular *adj* eensellig
unicorn *n* eenhoring
uniform *adj* eenvormig; egalig; gelykmatig; gelykvormig; *n* mondering
unimaginable *adj* ondenkbaar
unimpeachable *adj* onkreukbaar
unimpeded *adj* onbelemmer
unimportant *adj* onbelangrik
uninhabited *adj* onbewoon(d)
uninjured *adj* ongedeerd; ongeskonde
uninterrupted *adj* onafgebroke; onverpoos
uninvited *adj* ongenooi
union *n* unie; samesmelting; samevoeging; eendrag; verbinding; verbintenis; vereniging
unique *adj* enig; uniek
unit *n* eenheid
unite *vb* saamvoeg; verenig
united *adj* eendragtig; gesamentlik
United Nations *n* Verenigde Nasies
unity *n* eendrag; eenheid; saamhorigheid
universal *adj* algemeen; alsydig; universeel; **— language** *n* wêreldtaal
universe *n* heelal
university *n* universiteit
university chair *n* leerstoel
unjust *adj* onbillik; onregverdig
unkind *adj* onvriendelik; onwelwillend
unknown *adj* onbekend; ongekend
unlace *vb* losryg
unlawful *adj* onwettig; onregmatig; ongeoorloof; wederregtelik
unlearn *vb* afleer; afwen; verleer
unless *conj* tensy
unlimited *adj* grensloos; onbegrens; onbepaald; onbeperk
unload *vb* aflaai; afpak
unlock *vb* ontsluit
unlucky *adj* ongelukkig
unmanageable *adj* onhandelbaar
unmanly *adj* onmanlik
unmarried *adj* ongetroud; eenlopend

unmask *vb* ontmasker; uitbak
unmatched *adj* onpaar
unmerciful *adj* ongenadig
unmistakably *adv* bepaald
unmixed *adj* onvermengd
unmoved *adj* onbewoë
unnatural *adj* onnatuurlik; teennatuurlik
unnavigable *adj* onbevaarbaar
unnecessarily *adv* verniet
unnecessary *adj* nodeloos; onnodig
unnerve *vb* ontsenu
unnoticeable *adj* onmerkbaar
unnoticed *adj* ongeag; onopgemerk; *adv* soetjies
unobserved *adj* ongemerk
unoccupied *adj* onbeset; onbewoon(d)
unopposed *adj* onbestrede
unpack *vb* afpak
unpaid *adj* onbetaal(d); onvoldaan
unparalleled *adj* ongeëwenaard; ongekend
unpardonable *adj* onvergeeflik
unperceived *adj* ongemerk
unpick *vb* lostorring; torring
unpleasant *adj* onaangenaam; onaardig; onbehaaglik; onplesierig; onsmaaklik
unpleasantness *n* naarheid; narigheid
unpolluted *adj* onbesoedel(d)
unpopulated *adj* onbevolk
unpractical *adj* onprakties
unpractised *adj* ongeoefen
unprecedented *adj* ongehoor(d)
unprejudiced *adj* onbevooroordeeld
unprepared *adj* onvoorbereid
unprincipled *adj* beginselloos; verworpe
unprofitable *adj* onvoordelig
unprotected *adj* onbeskerm(d)
unprovided for *adj* onversorg
unpunished *adj* ongestraf
unqualified *adj* onbevoeg
unquenchable *adj* onlesbaar; onblusbaar
unquestionable *adj* onteenseglik
unravel *vb* ontknoop; ontwar; uitrafel
unravelling *n* ontknoping
unreadable *adj* onleesbaar
unreasonable *adj* onredelik; onbillik
unrecognizable *adj* onkenbaar; onherkenbaar

unreliable *adj* onbetroubaar
unrequited *adj* onbeantwoord
unrest *n* onrus
unrestrained *adj* ongedwonge; toomloos
unrig *vb* aftuig
unripe *adj* onryp; groen
unrivalled *adj* weergaloos
unroll *vb* afrol
unruffled *adj* ongeërg
unruly *adj* weerbarstig; balsturig
unsaddled *adj* bloots
unsafe *adj* onseker; onveilig
unsatisfactory *adj* onbevredigend
unsatisfied *adj* onbevredig; onversadig
unsavoury *adj* onsmaaklik
unscathed *adj* heelhuids; ongedeerd
unscrew *vb* losskroewe
unscrupulous *adj* gewete(n)loos
unseasonable *adj* ongeleë
unseeded *adj* (sport) ongekeur
unseemliness *n* onbetaamlikheid
unseemly *adj* ongepas
unselfish *adj* onbaatsugtig; onselfsugtig
unserviceable *adj* ondienlik
unsettled *adj* onbestendig; onvoldaan
unshak(e)able *adj* onwrikbaar
unshrinkable *adj* krimpvry
unsightly *adj* lelik; onooglik
unsigned *adj* ongeteken(d)
unskilled *adj* ongeskool; onbedrewe;
baar; — labour *n* ongeskoolde arbeid
unsociable *adj* ongesellig
unsolvable *adj* onoplosbaar
unsolved *adj* onopgelos
unspeakable *adj* (joy) onuitspreeklik
unspoiled *adj* onbedorwe
unstable *adj* onbestendig; onvas
unsteady *adj* onvas
unsuccessful *adj* onggelukkig; vergeefs; be — *vb* teenloop
unsuccessfully *adv* onverrigtersake
unsuitable *adj* ongeskik; onvanpas
unsympathetic *adj* onwelwillend
untam(e)able *adj* ontembaar
untenable *adj* onhoudbaar; verwerplik
untested *adj* onbeproef
untidy *adj* slordig; verwaai(d)
untie *vb* losknoop; losmaak; ontbind
until *conj* alvorens; totdat; tot; *prep* tot

untimely *adj* ontydig
untiring *adj* onvermoeid
untold *adj* onbeskryflik
untouched *adj* onaangeroer; ongerep
untrained *adj* baar; ongeoefen; ongeskool
untried *adj* onbeproef
untrue *adj* leuenagtig; onwaar
untrustworthy *adj* onbetroubaar
untruth *n* leuentaal; onwaarheid
unused *adj* ongebruik
unusual *adj* ongewoon; vreemd; ongemeen
unutterable *adj* (sorrow, etc.) onuitspreeklik
unvaried in form *adj* uniform
unveil *vb* onthul; ontsluier
unwelcome *adj* ongenooi
unwell *adj* olik; ongesteld
unwholesome *adj* ongesond
unwilling *adj* ongeneë; ongewillig; onwillig
unwillingness *n* onwilligheid
unwind *vb* afrol
unwise *adj* onverstandig; onwys
unwittingly *adv* onbewus
unworthy *adj* onwaardig
up *adv* boontoe; op; uit; — here *adv*
hierbo; — there *adv* daarbo; — to
the present *adv* tot dusver
up the ante (*informal*) *vb* opkikker
up-to-date *adj* agtermekaar
uphill *adj, adv* bergop; opdraand
uphold *vb* handhaaf; ophou
upholster *vb* beklee(d); stoffeer
upholstery *n* stoffering
upkeep *n* instandhouding; onderhoud
upload *vb* (computing) laai op
upon *prep* op; aan
upper *adj* bo; boonste; hoër
upper half *n* bo-ent
upper hand *n* oorhand
upper lip *n* bolip
upper side *n* bokant
uppermost *adj* opperste
upright *adj* orent; penorent; regop;
staande
uproar *n* alarm; rumoer; kaskenade
uproot *vb* uitroei
upset *adj* ontstel(d); *vb* omgooi; (plan)
verydel

upside down *adj* onderstebo; *adv* agterstevoor
upstairs *adv* bo
upstream *adv* stroomop
upward *adv* opwaarts
upwards *adv* boontoe
uranium *n* uraan
urban *adj* stedelik; steeds
urbanization *n* verstedeliking
urbanize *vb* verstedelik
urge *n* aandrang; spoorslag; *vb* aandring; por; **— on** *vb* aanspoor; opdruk
urgency *n* drang
urgent *adj* dringend
urinate *vb* pis; water
urine *n* pis
urn *n* urn
us *pers pron* ons
usage *n* gebruik; spraakgebruik
use *n* gebruik; nut; **be of —** *vb* baat;

— roughly *vb* karnuffel; **— up** *vb* verbruik; opmaak
used *adj* gebruik; **— to** *adj* gewoond aan; **— up** *adj* opgemaak
useful *adj* bruikbaar; nuttig; dienlik; behulpsaam; **be —** *vb* deug
useless *adj* onbruikbaar; ondienlik; onnut; nutteloos; tevergeefs; ydel
usual *adj* gebruiklik; gewoon; **as —** *adv* oudergewoonte
usually *adv* deurgaans; gewoonlik
usurer *n* woekeraar
usury *n* woeker
utensils *n* gereedskap
uterus *n* baarmoeder
utmost *adj* bes; uiterste
utopian *adj* utopies
utter *vb* uit (*or* uiter); uitspreek
utterance *n* uiting
utterly *adv* uiters
uvula *n* kleintongetjie

V

vacancy *n* vakature
vacant *adj* vakant; oop; ope; wesenloos; ledig; (post) monbeset; **become** — *vb* oopval
vacate *vb* ontruim
vacation *n* vakansie
vaccinate *vb* ent; inent
vaccination *n* ent; vaksinasie
vaccine *n* entstof; spuitstof; vaksien
vacillate *vb* wankel
vacuum cleaner *n* stofsuier
vagrant *n* landloper
vague *adj* vaag; onbestemd
vain *adj* ydel
valance *n* val
valet *n* dienaar; kneg
valid *adj* deugdelik; geldig
valley *n* vallei; dal; laagte; vlei
valour *n* waagmoed
valuable *adj* waardevol
valuation *n* valuasie; taksasie
valuator *n* taksateur; waardeerder
value *n* waarde; prys; *vb* takseer; ag; skat
valve *n* klep
vampire *n* vampier
vandalism *n* vandalisme
vane *n* (weather) vleuel
vanguard *n* voorhoede
vanilla *n* vanielje
vanish *vb* verdwyn; vervlieg
vanishing *n* verdwyning
vanity *n* ydelheid
vaporize *vb* vergas
vapour *n* wasem
variable *adj* wisselvallig
variation *n* variasie
variegated *adj* veelkleurig
variety *n* variëteit; verskeidenheid
various *adj* onderskeie; verskeie; velerlei; verskillend; veelsoortig
varnish *n* vernis; *vb* verlak; vernis
vary *vb* verskil; afwissel
vase *n* vaas
vasectomy *n* vasektomie
vast *adj* uitgestrek; uitgebrei
vat *n* vaatjie; vat

vault *n* gewelf; grafkelder; kluis; verwelf; welf
veal *n* kalfsvleis
vegan *n* veganis
vegetable *n* groente
vegetarian *n* vegetariër
vegetation *n* plantegroei
vehement *adj* heftig
vehicle *n* voertuig; rytuig
veil *n* sluier; voorhangsel
vein *n* (blood vessel) aar; stemming; gees
Velcro *n* Velcro
veld school *n* veldskool
veldt *n* veld
velocity *n* snelheid
velvet *n* ferweel; fluweel; *adj* ferweelagtig
vendetta *n* vete
vending machine *n* muntoutomaat
vendor *n* verkoper; venter
venerable *adj* agbaar; eerwaardig
veneration *n* verering
vengeance *n* wraak
vengeful *adj* wraakgierig; wraaksugtig
venom *n* gif; venyn; vergif
venomous *adj* venynig
vent *n* split
ventilate *vb* lug; ventileer
ventilation *n* ventilasie
ventriloquist *n* buikspreker
venture *n* onderneming; *vb* waag; durf
venue *n* vergaderingplek
verb *n* werkwoord
verbal *adj* verbaal; mondeling; — **diarrhoea** *n* woordskittery
verbatim *adj* woordelik
verbose *adj* wydlopig
verdict *n* oordeel; uitspraak
verge *n* rand
verify *vb* nareken
vermicelli *n* vermicelli
vermilion *n, adj* (colour) vermiljoen
vermin *npl* goggas; gedierte
vernacular *n* landstaal
versatile *adj* veelsydig
verse *n* vers; koeplet; strofe; digmaat

version *n* vertaling
versus *prep* teen
vertebra *n* werwel
vertebrate *n* gewerwelde; *adj* gewerwel
vertical *adj* vertikaal; loodreg
verve *n* fut
very *adv* baie; bra; erg; heel; regte; — **beautiful** *adj* beeldskoon; — **best** *adj* allerbeste; — **early** *adj, adv* vroeg-vroeg; — **fine** *adj* haarfyn; — **funny** *adj* skree(u)snaaks; — **hard** *adj, adv* kliphard; — **hot** *adj* vuurwarm; — **important** *adj* gewigtig; — **last** *adj, adv* allerlaas; — **old** *adj* stokoud; — **poor** *adj* brandarm; doodarm; — **promising** *adj* veelbelowend; — **quiet** *adj* doodstill; tjoepstil; — **rich** *adj* skatryk; — **sharp** *adj* vlymskerp; — **simple** *adj* doodgewoon; — **thin** *adj* rietskraal; — **ugly** *adj* skree(u)lelik; — **well** *adv* bes; — **young** *adj* bloedjong
very low price *n* spotprys
vessel *n* skip; vaartuig
vest *n* onderhemp; frokkie; borsrok
veteran *n* oudgediende; veteraan
veterinary clinic *n* dierekliniek
veterinary surgeon *n* veearts
veto *n* veto
vex *vb* kwel; pla; treiter; **be —ed** *vb* erg; erger
via *prep* oor; per
viable *adj* lewensvatbaar
viaduct *n* oorbrug; viaduk
vibrate *vb* tril
vibration *n* trilling
vice-chairman *n* ondervoorsitter
vice-principal *n* onderhoof
viceroy *n* onderkoning
vicinity *n* nabyheid; omgewing; ontrek; *npl* omstreke
vicious *adj* kwaai; venynig
victim *n* slagoffer; dupe
victimize *vb* viktimiseer
victor *n* oorwinnaar
victory *n* oorwinning; sege; triomf
victuals *npl* eetware; spys(e)
video tape *n* videoband
vie *vb* wedywer
view *n* uitsig; gesig; insig; uitkyk; mening; oorsig; opvatting; sienswyse; vergesig; *vb* besigtig

viewer *n* (TV) kyker
vigilant *adj* waaksaam; wakker; wakend
vigorously *adv* flink
vigour *n* groeikrag
vile *adj* afskuwelik; laaghartig
village *n* dorp
villager *n* dorpenaar
villain *n* booswig
vindictive *adj* haatdraend; wraakgierig; wraaksugtig
vine *n* druiwestok; wingerdstok; wynstok
vinegar *n* asyn
vineyard *n* wingerd
vintage *n* wynoes; wynjaar; *adj* oud
vintage car *n* veteraanmotor; noagkar; toekamotor
violate *vb* skend; verbreek; verkrag
violation *n* inbreuk; skending; verkragting
violence *n* geweld
violent *adj* woedend; fors; gewelddadig; geweldig; heftig; fel
violet *n* violet; (flower) viooltjie; *adj* violet
violin *n* viool
violin bow *n* strykstok
violinist *n* violis
viper *n* adder
virgin *n* maagd
virtual reality *n* skynwerklikeheid; virtuele realiteit
virtually *adv* prakties; feitlik
virtue *n* deug
virtuous *adj* deugsaam
visa *n* visum
viscount *n* burggraaf
visibility *n* sig; sigbaarheid
visible *adj* aanskoulik; sigbaar
vision *n* droombeeld; droomgesig; gesig; visioen
visit *n* besoek; kuier; oorkoms; *vb* opsoek; kuier; besoek
visitation *n* besoeking
visitor *n* besoeker; gas; kuiergas
visor *n* visier
vitality *n* groeikrag
vitamin *n* vitamine
viticulture *n* wynbou
vitriol *n* vitrioel
vixen *n* feeks; heks; wyf

viz. *adv* naamlik
vocabulary *n* woordeskat; taalskat
vocal *adj* vokaal
vocal chord *n* stembande
vocalist *n* sanger; (female) sangeres
vocation *n* roeping; vak(kie)
vocational education *n* vakonderwys
vogue *n* mode; in — *adv* in die mode;
  be in — *vb* heers
voice *n* stem
voice recording *n* stemopname
void *adj* leeg
volatile salts *n* vlugsout
volcanic *adj* vulkanies; vuurspuwend
volcano *n* vulkaan
volley *n* salvo; sarsie; (tennis) vlughou
volleyball *n* vlugbal
volt *n* volt
voluble *adj* breedsprakig

volume *n* volume; bundel; deel; (of a
  periodical) jaargang
voluntary *adj* vrywillig
volunteer *n* vrywilliger; *vb* aanbied
voluptuous *adj* wellustig
vomit *vb* braak; opbring; opgooi; vomeer
vote *n* stem; mosie; *vb* stem; **— against**
  vb teenstem
voter *n* kieser; stemmer
voters' roll *n* kieserslys
vow *n* gelofte; *vb* sweer
vowel *n* klinker; vokaal
voyage *n* reis; seereis; vaart
vulgar *adj* vulgêr; banaal; gemeen
vulgarity *n* laagheid
vulnerable *adj* kwesbaar
vulture *n* aasvoël**

W

wadding *n* watte
wade *vb* waad
wafer *n* wafel
waffle *n* wafel
wag *n* grapmaker
wage(s) *n* loon; werkloon; verdienste; gasie; huur
wage dispute *n* loongeskil
wage earner *n* loontrekker
wage increase *n* loonverhoging
wage war *n* oorlog voer
wager *n* weddenskap; *vb* wed
wagon *n* wa
wagtail *n* kwikstertjie; wipstert
wail *vb* jammer
wailing *n* geween
waist *n* middel; lees
waistband *n* lyfband
waistcoat *n* onderbaadjie
wait *vb* wag; — **for** *vb* afwag; opwag; — **up** *vb* opsit; — **a bit** *vb* wag 'n bietjie; — **a moment** *n* wag 'n bietjie
waiter *n* bediende; kelner
waiting list *n* waglys
waiting-room *n* wagkamer
waive *vb* ophef; (a right) afsien
wake *vb* wek; — **up** *vb* ontwaak; —**n up** *vb* opwek
walk *n* gang; loop; toer; wandel; wandeling; *vb* gaan; loop; stap; stryk;wandel; — **along** *vb* aanloop; — **along on** *vb* aanstryk; — **away** *vb* wegstap; — **off** *vb* wegloop; — **on** *vb* aanstap; bewandel; — **out** *vb* uitloop; — **round** *vb* omstap
walker *n* loper; stapper; wandelaar
walkie-talkie *n* loopgeselser
walking *n* loop
walking stick *n* kierie
wall *n* muur; wand
wall in *vb* ommuur
wallet *n* portefeulje; tas
wallow *vb* vroetel
wallpaper *n* muurpapier; plakpapier; behangsel
walnut *n* okkerneut
walrus *n* walrus

waltz *n* wals
wander *vb* afdwaal; dwaal; ronddool; swerf; verdwaal; — **about** *vb* flenter; rondswerf
wanderings *n* swerftog
wannabe *n* (*informal*) na-aper
want *n* behoefte; gebrek; gemis; skaarste; wil; armoede; *vb* behoef
wanted *adj* benodig
wanting: be — *vb* ontbreek
wanton *adj* wulps
war *n* oorlog
warble *vb* sing
ward off *vb* afkeer; afweer
wardrobe *n* hangkas; kas; klerekas
warehouse *n* magasyn; pakhuis
wares *npl* ware
warlike *adj* krygshaftig; oorlogsugtig
warm *vb* verwarm; warm; *adj* warm
warmth *n* warmte
warn *vb* aanmaan; vermaan; waarsku
warning *n* aanmaning; vermaning; vingerwysing; waarskuwing
warrant *n* bevelskrif; magtiging; waarborg; *vb* instaan; waarborg
warranty *n* waarborg
warrior *n* krygsman; stry(d)er
wart *n* vrat
warthog *n* vlakvark
was *see* **wees**
wash *vb* was; afspoel; — **away** *vb* verspoel; wegspoel; — **out** *vb* uitkalf; uitspoel; — **up** *vb* afwas; — **up on the shore** *vb* aanspoel
wash-hand basin *n* wasbak
washer ring *n* wasser
washing *n* wasgoed; was
washing machine *n* wasmasjien
washtub *n* spoelbak
wasp *n* perdeby; wesp
wastage *n* slytasie
waste *n* afval; *vb* afslyt; *adj* woes
wasteful *adj* kwistig
wasteland *n* woesteny
wastepaper *n* skeurpapier
wastepaper basket *n* snippermandjie
watch *n* horlosie; oorlosie; wag; *vb* afloer

watchdog *n* waghond
watcher *n* waker
watchful *adj* waaksaam
watchman *n* wagter
water *n* water; *vb* besproei; water
water bottle *n* kraffie
water carrier *n* **waterdraer**
water diviner *n* waterwyser
water-resistant *adj* waterbestand; waterwerend
water-ski *n* waterski
watercolour *n* waterverf; akwarel; — **painting** *n* waterverfskildery
waterfall *n* waterval
waterfowl *n* bleshoender
watering can *n* gieter
watermark *n* peil
watermelon *n* waatlemoen
waterproof *adj* waterdig
waterspout *n* waterhoos
watertight *adj* waterdig
watery *adj* wateragtig; waterig
wattle and daub hut *n* hartbeeshuisie
wave *n* golf; wuif (*or* wuiwe); (sea) baar; (hair) krul; *vb* golf; wuif (*or* wuiwe); swaai
waver *vb* aarsel; wankel; weifel
wavering *adj* twyfelmoedig; wankelmoedig
wavy *adj* golwend
wax *n* was
waxbill *n* (finch) sysie; vinkie
way *n* pad; weg; ent; gang; manier; baan; beloop; wys; wyse; **be in the** — **of** *vb* stoor; **the other** — **round** *adv* andersom
way out *n* uitweg
waybill *n* geleibrief
we *pers pron* ons
weak *adj* flou; pap; kragteloos; slap; pieperig; week; eina; swak; **become** —**er** *vb* verswak
weaken *vb* ondermyn; verswak
weakling *n* swakkeling
weakness *n* swak; swakheid; swakte
wealth *n* weelde; gegoedheid; rykdom; vermoë; fortuin
wealthy *adj* ryk; gegoed; vermoënd; welgesteld; welvarend; bemiddeld
wean *vb* speen
weapon *n* geweer; wapen

weaponry *n* wapentuig
wear *vb* aanhê; dra; — **down** *vb* afslyt; — **out** *vb* afloop; slyt; afslyt; (clothes) afdra; (clothes) opdra; (shoes) deurloop
wear and tear *n* slytasie
wearable *adj* draagbaar
weary *adj* lomerig; moeg; vermoeid; *vb* verveel
weasel *n* wesel
weather *n* weer; — **a storm** *vb* deurstaan
weather forecast *n* weervoorspelling
weather report *n* weerberig
weathercock *n* weerhaan; windwyster
weave *vb* vleg; weef
weaver *n* wewer
web *n* rak; web
website *n* webtuiste; webblad
wed *vb* trou
wedding *n* bruilof; huwelik; troue
wedding cake *n* bruidskoek
wedding day *n* troudag
wedding reception *n* huweliksonthaal
wedding ring *n* trouring
wedge *n* keil; *vb* wig
wedlock *n* eg; huwelik
Wednesday *n* Woensdag
Wee Willie Winkie *n* Klaasvakie
weed *n* onkruid
weedkiller *n* onkruiddoder
weeds *npl* onkruid; bossies; vuilgoed
week *n* week
weekday *n* weekdag; werk(s)dag
weekend *n* naweek
weekly *adj, adv* weekliks
weekly paper *n* weekblad
weekly wages *n* weekloon
weep *vb* huil; ween; grens
weeping *n* geween
weeping willow *n* treurwilg
weevil *n* kalander
weigh *vb* afweeg; (anchor) ophaal; — **up** *vb* opweeg
weight *n* gewig; swaarte
weighty *adj* gewigtig; swaar
weir *n* studam
welcome *adj* welkom; *vb* begroet
weld *vb* las; sweis; smee
welded *adj* gelas; gesweis
welfare *n* heil; welstand; welsyn; welvaart

well[1] *adj* gesond; lekker; fris; *adv* terdeë;
　as — ** *conj* sowel; **as — as *adv* asook
well[2] *n* bron
well-behaved *adj* welgemanierd
wellbeing *n* welstand; welsyn
well-considered *adj* weldeurdag
well-formed *adj* welgeskape
well-founded *adj* gegrond
well-known *adj* bekend; oorbekend;
　welbekend
well-mannered *adj* gemanier; welle-
　wend
well-meaning *adj* welmenend
well-read *adj* belese
well-situated *adj* welgeleë
well-thought-out *adj* weldeurdag
well-to-do *adj* bemiddeld; gegoed
well-versed *adj* bedrewe; geoefen(d)
well-watered *adj* waterryk
werewolf *n* weerwolf
west *adj, adv* wes; *n* wes(te)
westerly *adj* westelik
western *adj* westelik; **— frontier** *n*
　westergrens; **— horizon** *n* westerkim
Westerner *n* Westerling
wet *adj* nat; *vb* bevogtig
wet through *adj* deurnat; druipnat;
　waternat
wet wipe *n* afveelappie
wetness *n* natheid
wettish *adj* natterig
whack *n* raps
whale *n* walvis
whalebone *n* balein
wharf *n* kaai
what *adv* hoe; *determiner* watter; wat;
　pron watter; wat; hoe; *inter pron* wat;
　welke; **for —** *inter pron* waarvoor; **of**
　— *inter pron* waarvoor; **— for** *inter*
　pron waarom
whatever *pron* wat
wheat *n* koring
wheedle *vb* pamperlang; **— out of** *vb*
　afrokkel
wheel *n* wiel
wheel alignment *n* wielsporing
wheelbarrow *n* kruiwa
wheelchair *n* rolstoel; rystoel
whelp *vb* welp
when *adv* wanneer; *adv; conj; prep* as;
　conj nadat

whence *adv* vandaan; vanwaar
where *adv* waar; waarso; *rel pron* waar-
　heen
where to *inter pron* waarnatoe
whereas *conj* aangesien; terwyl; waar
whet *vb* skerpmaak; slyp
whether *conj* of
whetstone *n* slypsteen
which *determiner; pron* watter; *inter*
　pron waarnatoe; welke
while *adv* onderwyl; *conj* terwyl
while away *vb* verdryf; verslyt
whim *n* gier; gril; luim; nuk; bui
whimsical *adj* buierig; nukkerig
whine *vb* teem; tjank
whip *n* gésel; sweep; peits; *vb* gésel;
　(cream) klits; **— up** *vb* opsweep
whiplash *n* voorslag
whirl *vb* dwarrel; warrel
whirlpool *n* draaikolk; kolk; maal-
　stroom
whirlwind *n* dwarrelwind; tornado;
　windhoos
whiskers *npl* snorbaard
whisper *n* fluistering; *vb* fluister; **in a**
　— *adv* fluisterend
whispering *n* fluistering
whistle *n* fluit; *vb* fluit
white *n, adj* wit
white ant *n* rysmier
white lead *n* witlood
white lie *n* noodleuen; witleun
white person *n* blanke
white pinewood *n* greinhout
white-spotted *adj* witbont
whitewash *vb* wit; kalk
whitlow *n* fyt
whizz *n* zoem
who *inter pron* wat; wie
whole *n* geheel; *adj* gans; heel
whole sum *n* totaal
wholesale trade *n* groothandel
wholesome *adj* gesond; heilsaam
wholly *adv* gans
whom *inter pron* wie
whooping cough *n* kinkhoes
whopper *n* (*informal*) knewel
whore *n* hoer
whose *inter pron* waarvan
why *adv* hoekom; *inter pron* waarvoor;
　waarom

wick *n* (of a candle) pit
wicked *adj* boos; goddeloos
wide *adj* breed; wyd; ruim
widen *vb* verruim
widow *n* weduvrou
widowbird *n* flap
widower *n* wewenaar
width *n* wydte
wife *n* vrou; eggenote
wig *n* pruik
wild *adj* onstuimig; verwilder(d); verwoed; woes; wild; **— animals** *npl*
ongedierte; **— duck** *n* eendvoël;
— flower *n* veldblom; **— hemp** *n*
dagga; **— olive** *n* (wood) olienhout
wildebeest *n* wildebees
wilderness *n* wildernis; woesteny
wilful *adj* eiesinnig; moedswillig
wilfully *adv* moedswillig
will[1] *n* testament; wil
will[2] *vb* sal
will-o'-the-wisp *n* dwaallig
willing *adj* bereid; gewillig; willig
willing to help *adj* hulpvaardig
willingly *adv* goedskiks
willow *n* (tree) wilg
willpower *n* wilskrag
wily *adj* slu
win *vb* wen
wind[1] *n* wind
wind[2] *vb* kronkel; draai; **— up** *vb* opwen
wind farm *n* windplaas
wind tunnel *n* windtonnel
windbag *n* windbuks
windmill *n* windmeul
window *n* venster; raam; **— enve-**
lope *n* ruitkoevert; vensterkoevert;
— frame *n* kosyn; **— shopping** *n*
vensterkykery
windowpane *n* ruit; vensterglas; vensterruit
windowsill *n* kosyn; vensterbank
windpipe *n* lugpyp
windscreen *n* voorruit
windscreen wiper *n* ruitveër
windsurfing *n* seilplankry
windy *adj* winderig
wine *n* wyn
wine barrel *n* wynvat
wine cask *n* wynvat
wine cellar *n* wynkelder

wine growing *n* wynbou
wineglass *n* kelkie; wynkelkie
winery *n* wynkelder
wing *n* vlerk; vleuel
wink *n* wink; knip; oogknip; oogwink;
vb wink; knip
winner *n* wenner
winnow *vb* wan
winter *n* winter
wipe *vb* vee; wis; **— dry** *vb* afdroog; **—**
off *vb* afvee; **— out** *vb* uitwis
wiper *n* wisser
wire *n* draad; telegram; *vb* telegrafeer
wire netting *n* ogiesdraad; sifdraad
wire-cutters *n* draadknipper
wireless *n* draadloos; radio
wiry *adj* taai
wisdom *n* wysheid
wisdom tooth *n* verstandskies; verstandtand
wise *adj* verstandig; wys
wiseacre *n* wysneus
wisely *adv* wyslik
wish *n* begeerte; verlange; wens; wil; *vb*
toewens; wens; **— for** *vb* begeer; **—**
good luck *vb* gelukwens
wishy-washy *adj* waterig
wit *n* gees
witch *n* heks; towerheks
witch doctor *n* toordokter
witch-hunt *n* heksejag
witchcraft *n* heksewerk; toorkuns
with *prep* by; met; van; **— difficulty**
adv beswaarlik; **— impunity** *adv*
straf(fe)loos; **— no air** *adj* lugledig;
— regard to *prep* omtrent; ten opsigte van; **— that** *adv* daarmee; dan; **—**
what *rel pron* waarmee; **— which** *rel*
pron waarmee
withdraw *vb* onttrek; opvra; terugtrek;
verwyder; aftrek; wyk
withdrawal *n* (of money) opvraging
wither *vb* verlep; verwelk; verdor
withered *adj* dor
withers *n* (of a horse) skof
withhold *vb* agterhou; onttrek; snoep
within *adv* binne-in; *prep* binne
without *prep* buiten; sonder; **— a sad-**
dle *adj* bloots; **— employment** *adj*
ledig; **— formality** *adj* summier; **—**
principles *adj* karakterloos; **— that**

adv daarsonder; — **what** *inter pron* waarsonder; — **which** *inter pron* waarsonder

withstand *vb* teenstaan; uitstaan; weerstaan

witness *n* getuie; *vb* bywoon

wits *npl* positiewe

witty *adj* geestig

woe *n* wee

wolf *n* wolf

woman *n* vrou; vroumens; mens; (in labour) kraamvrou

woman-hater *n* vrouehater

womanly *adj* vroulik

womb *n* baarmoeder

women's lib(eration) *n* vrouevryheid

wonder *n* verwondering; wonder; *vb* wonder; bevreem(d)

wonderful *adj* wonderlik

woo *vb* vry

wood *n* hout; woud

wood pigeon *n* bosduif

woodcarving *n* houtsnywerk

woodcutter *n* houthakker

wooden *adj* houterig

wooden floor *n* plankvloer

wooden shoe *n* klomp

woodwork *n* houtwerk

wool *n* wol

woollen blanket *n* wolkombers

woolly *adj* wolagtig; wollerig

word *n* woord

word processor *n* teksverwerker; woordverwerker

wording *n* bewoording

wordplay *n* woordspeling

wordy *adj* langdradig; omslagtig; wydlopig

work *n* arbeid; drukte; taak; werk; *vb* arbei; werk; — **a mine** *vb* ontgin; — **on odd jobs** *vb* skrop; — **hard** *vb* woel; spook; — **more quickly** *vb* aanwerk; — **on** *vb* inwerk; — **out** *vb* oplos; uitkom; uitreken; uitwerk; verwerk

work of art *n* kunsstuk; kunswerk

workaholic *n* werkolis; werkslaaf

workbox *n* naaikissie

worker *n* werker; arbeider

working *n* werking; *adj* werksaam

working day *n* werk(s)dag

workman *n* arbeider; werk(s)man; werker

workmanship *n* vakmanskap; fatsoen

works *npl* fabriek

workshop *n* ateljee; werk(s)winkel; (training) werk(s)groep; (training) werksessie

world *n* wêreld

world-famous *adj* wêreldberoemd

worldly *adj* wêreldlik; wêrelds

worldly-wise *adj* wêreldwys

worldwide *adj* wêreldwyd

worm *n* wurm

worn out *adj* afgeleef; verslyt

worried *adj* bekommerd

worry *n* getob; *vb* bekommer

worrying *adj* gepeuter

worse *adj* erger; **become** — *vb* vererger

worship *n* verering; *vb* aanbid

worshipper *n* vereerder

worth *n* waarde; werd; — **knowing** *adj* wetenswaardig; — **mentioning** *adj* noemenswaardig

worthy *adj* waardig

would-be *adj* kamma; kammakastig

wound *n* seer; wond; *vb* kwes; wond

wrangle *vb* kibble

wrap *vb* wikkel; — **up** *vb* inpak; inwikkel; toedraai

wrapping paper *n* toedraaipapier

wrath *n* toorn

wrathful *adj* toornig

wreak havoc *vb* woed

wreath *n* krans

wreck *n* wrak; *vb* verniel

wrench *n* sleutel; *vb* verrek

wrestle *vb* stoei; (professionally) rofstoei

wrestler *n* stoeier

wrestling *n* worsteling

wretch *n* drommel

wretched *adj* ellendig; rampsalig

wriggle *vb* kriewel; wriemel

wring *vb* (hands) wring

wrinkle *n* riffel; rimpel; *vb* verskrompel; riffel; rimpel

wrinkled *adj* gerimpel

wrist *n* gewrig

wristwatch *n* polshorlosie

write *vb* skryf; — **down** *vb* opskrywe;

opteken; — **off** *vb* afskryf; — **on** *vb*
aanskryf; — **out** *vb* uitskryf; — **poetry** *vb* dig
writer *n* skrywer
writing *n* geskrif
writing pad *n* skryfblok; skryfboek
writing table *n* skryftafel

written *adj* skriftelik
wrong *adj* verkeerd; sleg; *n* kwaad; *vb*
benadeel; — **way round** *adv* agterstevoor; — **idea** *n* dwaalbegrip; — **way**
n dwaalspoor
wrought iron *n* smeeyster
wry face *n* skewebek

X

X-ray *n* X-straal
xenophobia *n* xenofobie

Xhosa *n* Xhosa
xylophone *n* xilofoon

Y

yacht *n* jag; seiljag
yale lock *n* yaleslot
yard *n* jaart; werf; hof
yarn *n* gare
yawn *n* gaap
yawning *n* gaap
yea *sentence substitute* ja
year *n* jaar; — **of service** *n* diensjaar
yearbook *n* jaarboek
yearly *adv* jaarliks
yeast *n* gis; suurdeeg
yell *n* gier; gil; *vb* gil; skree(u)
yellow *n, adj* geel
yellow weaverbird *n* geelvink
yelp *vb* kef; tjank
yes *sentence substitute* ja
yes man *n* jabroer
yesterday *n, adv* gister; **the day before** — *n, adv* eergister
yet *adv* al; nog; tog; *conj* dog
yield *n* opbrings; uitset; *vb* afstaan; toegee
yield sign *n* toegeeteken

yo-yo *n* klimtol
yoghurt *n* jogurt
yoke *n* juk
yolk of an egg *n* dooier
yonder *adv* gunter
you *pers pron* jou; jul; jy; u
young *adj* jeugdig; vars; jong; — **chicken** *n* kuiken; — **girl** *n* jongmeisie; — **grass** *n* opslag; — **lady** *n* juffrou; nooi; — **man** *n* jongeling; jongkêrel; — **of animals** *n* jong; — **people** *n* jongspan; — **pig** *n* otjie
youngster *n* snuiter; —**s** *npl* kleinspan
your *determiner* jou; jul; u
Your Worship/Honour *title* Edelagbare
yours *poss pron* joune; uwe
youth *n* jeug; jongeling; jonkheid; jeugdige
youth hostel *n* jeugherberg
youthful *adj* jeugdig
yuppie *n* jappie

382

Z

zeal *n* ywer
zealot *n* dweper; yweraar
zealous *adj* ywerig
zebra *n* kwagga; sebra
zebra crossing *n* sebraoorgang
zenith *n* toppunt
zero *n* zero; nul; *adj* zero; —fare public transport *n* gratis openbare vervoer
zigzag *n* sigsag
zinc *n* sink
zinc ointment *n* sinksalf
zinnia *n* (flower) jakob-regop
zip *n* rits

zip fastener *n* rits; ritssluiter; treksluiter
zircon *n* sirkoon
zither *n* siter
zodiac *n* diereriem
zone *n* sone; lugstreek; gordel
zoo *n* dieretuin
zoological garden *n* dieretuin
zoology *n* dierkunde; soölogie
zoom *n* zoem; *vb* zoem in
zoom lens *n* zoemlens
Zulu *n, adj* Zoeloe; Zulu
Zulu regiment *n* Zoeloe-impie; Zulu-impi
Zululand *n* Zoeloeland; Zululan